The International Dictionary of Business

Hano Johannsen is the Manager of Surveys and Publications at the British Institute of Management and is the author of several books on various aspects of management, including a "Management Glossary."

G. Terry Page is Communications Consultant to the City University, London, and is a free-lance journalist and consultant.

A SPECTRUM BOOK

Prentice-Hall, Inc., Englewood Cliffs, New Jersey 07632

The International Dictionary of Business

Hano Johannsen
G. Terry Page

Library of Congress Cataloging in Publication Data

Johannsen, Hano.
   The international dictionary of business.

   (A Spectrum Book)
   Previous ed. published in 1975 as: International dictionary of management.
   1. Management—Dictionaries. 2. Business—Dictionaries. I. Page, G. Terry. II. Title.
HD30.15.J64 1981   658'.003   81-5852
ISBN 0-13-470823-7   AACR2
ISBN 0-13-470815-6 (pbk.)

Editorial/production supervision by Louise M. Marcewicz
Manufacturing buyer: Barbara A. Frick

Previously published under the title *International Dictionary of Management*

© 1981 by Prentice-Hall, Inc., Englewood Cliffs, New Jersey 07632

A SPECTRUM BOOK

All rights reserved.
No part of this book may be reproduced
in any form or by any means
without permission in writing from the publisher.

10 9 8 7 6 5 4 3 2 1

Printed in the United States of America

This Spectrum Book can be made available
to businesses and organizations at a special discount
when ordered in large quantities. For more information,
contact Prentice-Hall, Inc., General Book Marketing,
Special Sales Division, Englewood Cliffs, New Jersey 07632.

Prentice-Hall International, Inc., *London*
Prentice-Hall of Australia Pty. Limited, *Sydney*
Prentice-Hall of Canada, Ltd., *Toronto*
Prentice-Hall of India Private Limited, *New Delhi*
Prentice-Hall of Japan, Inc., *Tokyo*
Prentice-Hall of Southeast Asia Pte. Ltd., *Singapore*
Whitehall Books Limited, *Wellington, New Zealand*

Preface

The success of the first edition, especially in the United Kingdom and the United States, has encouraged us to undertake the task of updating, revising and expanding the original dictionary first published in 1975. The first edition had approximately 5,000 entries and we have now added a further 800 or so. It has again been very difficult to establish the parameters of management but, as in the first edition, we have taken a broad and, we hope, catholic view and included a wide range of terms which managers may come across in their daily work. Not all, of course, will be applicable to all managers, but in casting our net wide we have tried to cover both commonplace and specialist areas. We have not only taken the opportunity of making some corrections to the original entries but have also added numerous further cross-references, added many new terms and, in particular, expanded the United States coverage, so that taken as a whole we hope the book will be a practical and comprehensive reference work for those interested in management terminology. In this edition we have omitted the addresses of various employer, trade union, professional and other bodies for which there are entries, since they are forever changing and would provide information which may be out of date by the time the text is published. We feel the user can readily use other reference works to establish addresses, etc.

Our thanks go to Neil Wenborn for his helpful editorial work behind the scenes.

Hano Johannsen
G. Terry Page

The International Dictionary of Business

a

aanvullende gemeentebelasting. An additional local tax. See *Belgian income tax*.

AATUF. *All African Trade Union Federation*.

AB. *Aktiebolaj*.

abandonment. Where goods covered by an insurance policy, or the remains of such goods, are acquired by the insurance company in return for settlement for the total loss of the goods. Thus the goods are abandoned to the insurance company. The term is used particularly in marine insurance.

ABC. *Audit Bureau of Circulations*.

ABC method or analysis (or usage-value analysis). Analysis of a range of items eg stock levels, customers, sales territories etc into three groups: A = very important; B = important; C = marginal significance. The object is to sort the total into categories which should be handled and controlled in different ways. In the case of customers, for example, the A customers might be the responsibility of the sales manager and warrant regular visits whilst the C customers whose turnover and potential is insignificant might not justify regular visits at all. The approach is closely allied to *Pareto's law* and *eighty-twenty rule*.

Aberdeen Stock Exchange. One of UK provincial stock exchanges. See also *Stock Exchange* (UK).

ability to follow instructions test. *Personnel selection* and *vocational guidance* test devised as part of the *engineering apprentice test-battery* of the former National Institute of Industrial Psychology in the UK. See also *psychological test(ing)* and *test battery*.

ability to pay. Pay theory which implies that wage and salary levels should be based on a company's profitability. Increased profits mean higher pay levels, but lower profits seldom mean pay reductions.

above-the-line promotion. Term used by marketing men of *sales promotion* in the form of expenditure on advertising in the press, on television or in other media. The term *below-the-line promotion*, on the other hand, is used for such forms of sales promotion as reduced price special offers, premiums, and point-of-sale displays.

absenteeism. Absence from work by an *employee* during working hours. 'Voluntary absence' is that which the employee could have avoided. 'Involuntary absence' is that which he could not have avoided for such reasons beyond his control as sickness or accident.

absorption costing. Procedure for controlling the assignment of *indirect* or *overhead costs* to specialized product costing. A variety of methods is used for assigning overheads including the rate of cost per unit system (obtained by dividing the total overheads for a given *cost centre (center)* by the number of units produced), the standard cost rate used in conjunction with *standard costing*, direct materials cost percentage rate, direct wages cost percentage rate, *labo(u)r hour rate* and *machine hour rate*.

abusive dismissal. Dismissal of an employee in a manner which is lawful in that correct notice of termination of *contract of employment* is given, but is nevertheless an action that is an abuse or unfair use of managerial power. Under many legal systems, abusive dismissals are in themselves illegal. See also *unfair dismissal* and *wrongful dismissal*.

Academy of Management. US association of teaching staff in universities and colleges concerned with management and business training.

ACC. *Annual capital charge*.

accelerated depreciation. Depreciation of

an *asset* at a faster rate than under the usual *straight-line depreciation*. This makes for a faster return on capital.

accelerated vocational training. Uses *activity learning/teaching* methods off-the-job but with a realistic working or industrial environment.

acceptable quality level (AQL). Maximum number or percentage of defective items allowable under, for example, *acceptance sampling*.

acceptance credit. A company with a significant volume of export business may be able to arrange an acceptance credit facility with a bank or an *acceptance house* to an agreed percentage of the value of shipments within specified periods. The acceptance house or bank undertakes to accept *bills of exchange* drawn on it up to the agreed maximum figure in a certain period, these bills then being readily discountable with a *discount house*. Where the exporter normally draws bills of exchange on his overseas buyers, similar credit facilities may be granted against the collection of bills which he duly assigns to the bank by way of security.

acceptance house. Or accepting house. Financial house, usually a *merchant bank*, specializing in lending money on the security of *bills of exchange* or adding its name as endorser to a bill drawn on another party. A particular service to exporters is the granting of *acceptance credit* facilities. The leading UK acceptance houses are the 17 merchant banks in membership of the *Accepting Houses Committee*.

acceptance sampling. Form of *statistical quality control* in which a sample of items is inspected and tested, the results enabling a decision to be made as to whether to accept or reject the total quantity of items. See also *acceptable quality level, average outgoing quality, average outgoing quality limit*.

acceptance test. Made early in the progress of a project, etc with the object of checking that the finished work will be fit for its purpose.

acceptance test, consumer. See *consumer acceptance test*.

accepting house. As *acceptance house*.

Accepting Houses Committee. Body which governs the conduct and safeguards the standards of the leading *acceptance houses* in the UK. Some 17 merchant banks are in membership of the Accepting Houses Committee. Because of the high standing and reputation of the Committee *bills of exchange* drawn on its members tend to be discountable with *discount houses* at rates particularly advantageous to the drawer.

acceptor. See *bill of exchange*.

accessions rate (of labo(u)r). Total number of permanent and temporary additions to the payroll over a given period of time. Also known as *hiring rate* (US).

access time. Time taken to locate data in the store of a *computer* and transfer it to the *arithmetic unit*. The time taken largely depends on the type of computer.

accident book. Record kept by an employer of personal injuries suffered by employees at work.

Acción Coordinadora de las Instituciones Empresarias Libres (ACIEL). Major Argentinian *employers' association* with some 1,200 member firms.

accommodation bill. *Bill of exchange* drawn up with the intention that it should be discounted.

accommodation note. Document in which one party acts as guarantor for another in terms of creditworthiness etc.

accommodation party. Guarantor of a *bill of exchange*.

accomplishment/cost procedure (ACP). Technique for accurately comparing and contrasting costs and results of large-scale projects developed by Stanford University Research Unit (US). It is essentially a management information and reporting system for effectively managing complex projects.

accord and satisfaction. Legal term for the making and completion of an agreed variation of a contract. 'Accord' means there must be agreement that the contract be varied. 'Satisfaction' means satisfactory completion of the replacement contract.

accountability. Answerability for action carried out and performance achieved to others, eg by a manager to his superior or by the board of directors to its shareholders. Also used more loosely to describe responsibility.

accountable management. Making individuals or units responsible for performance measured as objectively as practicable and, as far as possible, with the cooperation of those individuals or units. It has much in common with *management by objectives* and is likely to involve the establishment of *cost* and *profit centres (centers)*.

accountancy conventions. Basic practices (practises) and assumptions concerning the preparation of accounts. They include consistency (like compares with like), conservatism (eg realism and pessimism about asset and stock values), the accounting entity (eg company, division, *cost centre (center)* or *profit centre (center)* — whatever unit or organization is treated as separate for accounting purposes), etc. Conventions are giving way to agreed Accountancy Standards.

accountant's return. Alternative term for *return on capital* or *book rate of return*.

account day. Stock exchange term. See *account period*.

account dealing. Stock exchange transaction for completion on the following account day. See *account period*.

account executive. Advertising, public relations, etc agency executive responsible for relations with a particular client or account.

accounting. Principles and techniques used in establishing, maintaining, recording and analyzing financial transactions. Normally involves the design of systems and procedures, keeping records, ensuring that the recording and handling of cash is undertaken properly and providing management with accounting data and reports.

accounting code. Or accounts code. Numerical or mnemonic code numbers or letters assigned to expenditure and/or income to enable costs and revenue to be classified and allocated internally to budget or cost centres.

accounting, human asset. See *human asset accounting*.

accounting models. Forms of simulation of a business situation in financial terms. Other forms of model of business situations include *computer* models and *mathematical models*.

accounting period. Period of time (a week, a calendar month or a four-weekly period) at the close of which a summary of financial and costing information is prepared and new records started. Ideally, the period chosen should be sufficiently short to reveal significant variations so that management can take prompt remedial action and of a constant length so that comparisons are meaningful.

accounting rate of return. As *rate of return*.

accounting ratios. As *financial ratios* or *management ratios*. See also *balance sheet ratios*.

account period. The London *Stock Exchange* operates in 23 fortnightly and two three-week account periods each year, people buying and selling shares being expected to settle their accounts at the end of each period, on the 'account days', unless they have *contango* or similar facilities. An exception to the account period arrangement is in the buying and selling of *gilt-edged* securities, transactions in these being settled daily.

accounts code. As *accounting code*.

accounts payable. Or *creditors*. Accounts on which monies are owed for goods or services.

accounts receivable. Or *debtors*. Accounts on which monies are due from customers. Sometimes cash may be raised against accounts receivable by pledging them as *collateral* for a loan, or by selling them to a commercial factor who pays an agreed figure less than the sum owed but takes responsibility for collecting the debt.

accretion. Growth of funds (eg pension) resulting from new contributions and/or interest received on capital investments.

accrual method. In accounting, a method used to take income into the accounts during the period in which the sales are made yet recording expenses only when incurred. That is, transactions are recorded at the time when they generate income rather than when they incur costs.

accruals. Amounts calculated as being owing for goods and services prior to their appearance in the balance sheet.

accrued expense (or liability). Expenditure incurred but not yet paid.

accrued revenue (or asset). Income or money earned but due to be received at a future date.

accumulation factor. Measure of the difference between present cash value and *terminal value*.

ACEF. *Australian Council of Employers' Federations.*

ACER speed and accuracy test. *Clerical aptitude test* in which pairs of numbers and names are checked against each other within a time limit. The test takes 10 to 15 minutes. See also *psychological testing* and *aptitude tests*.

achievement analysis. Examination of stages in the progress of a project, perhaps at *project milestones*.

achievement test. Or *attainment test*. General term used in *psychological testing*, particularly in the USA, for a test that measures achievement in a particular occupation (eg *job knowledge test*) rather than potential or *aptitude* or *intelligence*.

acid test ratio. Ratio of total cash, debtors *(accounts receivable)* and market value of saleable investments to *current liabilities*. The ratio is used as a guide to credit worthiness and for *credit rating*. Also known as *quick* or *liquid ratio*.

ACIEL. *Acción Coordinadora de las Instituciones Empresarias Libres*, a major Argentinian *employers' association*.

ACME. *Association of Consulting Management Engineers* (US).

acoustic coupler. Instrument used to connect a computer terminal to a telephone and thence to the *computer*.

ACP. *Accomplishment/cost procedure.*

acquisition. Purchase of one company by another for *cash* and/or *equity*. See also *merger* and *take-over bid*.

acquisitive society. View of the nature of man that holds he is wholly competitive, egoistic and greedy, and that his wants are insatiable. In management terms, this theory implies that one can explain and predict how people behave in the marketplace.

across-the-board settlement. Agreed pay increase that gives all the employees concerned an equal proportional increase in pay. Thus, such a settlement maintains existing differentials, unlike a *tapered increase*, a *stepped increase* or a *pro-tanto increase*.

AC test of creative ability. *Psychological test* of US origin devised particularly for engineers and engineering workers. See also *Purdue creativity test*.

Act for International Development 1961 (US). Established the *Agency for International Development* to administer the USA's overseas economic aid programmes in succession to the Development Loan Fund and the International Cooperation Administration.

action centred leadership. Packaged course on leadership developed in the UK by The Industrial Society based on John Adair's concepts. Has some affinities with *T-group training*.

action limit. *Quality control and reliability* term for the point at which action must be taken to rectify or reject an item.

action research. Commissioned research which attempts to combine the investigation of a specific problem area within an organization, with making recommendations for a solution and monitoring and evaluating implementation of resulting policies and procedures. Typically, the researcher is associated with an academic institution and the aim is to provide the researcher with real-life problems, come up with solutions after detailed investigation and discussion with inter-disciplinary colleagues and maintain a close relationship with the client whilst the new policies are put into effect.

action skill. Ability to carry out skilfully the behaviour required by a situation — eg in some forms of *T-group training* or *sensitivity training*.

action training. Training with a strong reliance on *activity learning* and such participative techniques as *case studies*, *role playing*, *games* and *simulations*.

active learning. As *activity learning*.

active money. Money actually in circulation or being used in business transactions.

activities analysis. One of three techniques identified by *Drucker* to be used in deciding the organization structure appropriate for a company, the other techniques being *decision analysis* and *relations analysis*. Activities analysis is used to establish what are the key activities in the company, as distinct from generalized assumptions.

activity. 1. An operation or work activity in *critical path* planning or *network analysis* as in *activity on arrow* or *activity on node*. **2.** *Work measurement* term for the task or operation being studied, this operation being broken down into *elements* for timing and rating.

activity chart. Diagram showing the breakdown and composition of a series of operations or a process plotted against a time scale.

activity learning/teaching. Or active learning. Learning through active participation and involvement such as project work and group discussions rather than in passive situations such as lectures or films. See also *discovery method* and *heuristic method*.

activity network. Network used in *network analysis/planning*.

activity on arrow. Commonly used method of representing a series of associated *activities* in *critical path scheduling* or *network analysis*. Each activity is denoted by an arrow, as in the diagram. This method of representation, though simple in concept, is often more complicated to use than the *activity on node* system which is described on the next page.

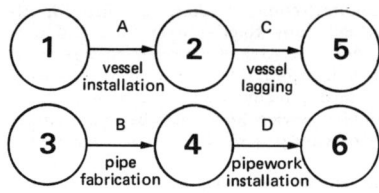

activity on arrow

activity on node. Method of representing a series of associated *activities* in *critical path scheduling* or *network analysis*. Each activity is denoted by a circle or 'node' instead of an arrow, which is conventionally used. The inter-relationships between each activity are shown by lines known as *dependancies*, as in the diagram, to form *precedence diagrams*.

activity rate (for working age population). Proportion of the population of a given age likely to be in employment or seeking employment.

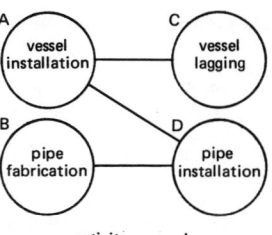

activity on node

activity ratio. Comparison showing actual against budgeted output during given hours (eg daily or weekly) of work. Expressed as:

$$\frac{\text{Standard hours of actual output}}{\text{Standard hours of budgeted output}} \times \frac{100}{1}$$

activity sampling. As *work sampling*.

activity vector analysis (AVA). *Psychological test* developed in the USA for use in *temperament and personality testing*. It has had mixed fortunes and reactions as a *personnel selection* test.

act of God. In law, an occurrence altogether beyond man's normal expectation or control — it is not necessarily synonymous with accident.

ACTU. *Australian Council of Trade Unions.*

actual market volume. Sum total of suppliers' sales made at a given *price* or in a given price range to a specific market segment. See also *market potential, market prospective, market segment capacity, market share*, and *overall market capacity*.

actuals. Goods or *commodities* that are physically available and which are bought and sold immediately (for example, at *spot markets*), as distinct from markets in *futures* where trading is in contracts for future delivery.

actuarial return. Or *internal rate of return*. The return on a project or enterprise as measured by *discounted cash flow* techniques.

actuary. Specialist in measuring risk in life assurance or insurance. See also *risk economist*.

adaptability test. *Mental ability* or *intel-*

ligence test used particularly in US industry for *personnel placement* purposes. It is used to predict performance in a wide range of occupations. See also *psychological testing*.

adaptable funding. See *controlled funding* (of pensions).

adaptive control. Method of *computer* control of industrial processes in which the computer makes calculations based on past experience to change the plant settings in order to improve its performance. Another method of control is *evolutionary operation* in which subtle changes are constantly made in operating settings in quest of improved performance.

adaptive program(me). Flexible form of *programmed instruction* in which sequencing of frames depends on responses of trainee/student. The sequence is made easier when a trainee has difficulty but kept hard enough to keep him at full stretch. Flexibility is sometimes so great as to require the use of a *computer*. See also *intrinsic branching, linear* and *skip program(me)*.

ADB. *Asian Development Bank.*

added hours. Notional extra hours of work when overtime rates apply. Eg where four hours are worked at time-and-a-half, the added hours are the two hours over and above basic *time-related payment scheme*.

added value. Value added to the cost of raw materials and bought out parts by the process of production and distribution.

addendum. 1. Addition or explanatory note at the end of a written report, survey, etc. **2.** Addition to a *motion* at a formal meeting. The procedure for handling an addendum is the same as that for an *amendment* though, unlike the latter, it does not seek to alter part or parts of the motion, but only to add to it.

add-on sales. Continuing sales made to a purchaser who is already a satisfied customer on the strength of earlier purchases. See also *multiple offer* and *solus offer*.

Adelaide Stock Exchange. One of six member stock exchanges of the *Australian Associated Stock Exchanges*.

adjournment, motion for. *Motion* at a formal meeting to the effect **a** that the meeting be adjourned either for a stated period or sine die (ie indefinitely), or **b** that discussion of a particular item of business be adjourned, usually until a stated future time. It is likely that a committee's *standing orders* will limit use of the former kind of motion for adjournment. The second kind, referring to a specific item of business, is often moved in an attempt at letting tempers cool down on contentious issues but the normal convention (or standing order) is that it may only be moved by someone who has not spoken earlier in the debate on the item. In addition, the normal rules for moving a motion apply to a motion for adjournment.

adjunctive program(me)s. Questions presented to trainees/students after they have studied instructional material such as a textbook to establish what learning has and what has not been achieved. Such questions sometimes known as *auto-elucidatory*.

adjusted earned income. Taxable income that is earned income.

adjuster. Insurance company employee specializing in evaluating claims and advising on policy liabilities and losses incurred. His role is to research into major claims and ensure settlements are fair and reasonable.

adjusting entry. An entry in accounts which indicates income earned or expenditure incurred but not yet due for settlement within the period of the accounts. This would apply to *accrued revenue* or *accrued expense*, for example.

administration. 1. Responsibility for efficient and effective operations and procedures. **2.** Area of management concerned with interpretation of policy and translating it into effective executive action. **3.** In public service area may be synonymous with management. **4.** Office management.

administration costs. *Indirect costs* charged to a department or factory, etc as its share of general administration costs for the organization as a whole over and above indirect costs attributable solely to the department or factory.

Administrative Management Society (AMS). US organization — formerly the National Office Management Association — concerned with office management. Holds conferences and meetings and conducts annual clerical salary surveys.

administrative management theory. *Organi-*

zation *structure*-oriented principles of general management developed by Henri *Fayol*.

ADMOS. Acronym of automatic device for mechanical order selection. A tape or card activated machine for checking stock availability, selecting quantities of goods required, recording stock balances and conveying items direct to the packing and despatch department.

ADR. *European Agreement on the International Carriage of Dangerous Goods.*

ad valorem. Description of a tax, duty or fee which varies in proportion to the value of the goods or services on which it is levied.

advance. Payment made in respect of work yet to be done or of goods yet to be received.

advance bill. Or *invoice*. See *pro forma.*

advance factory. Built by the UK Government in regions in need of development, the factory then being rented at attractive rates to an industrial firm setting up in the region. See also *Assisted Area, regional development grants.*

advertising. Presentation and/or publication of information or opinions on goods, services, institutions, etc with a view to attracting purchasers or to building up a *corporate image* or prestige among the public (advertising for the latter purpose is sometimes known as 'prestige advertising'). A distinction between advertising and *public relations* is that the latter is concerned with influencing points of view, but not with paid advertisements. See also *marketing mix.*

advertising agent (or agency). Specialist in the *advertising* aspects of *marketing* and in the planning and execution of advertising campaigns. Clients may be charged fees calculated on a percentage of the client's advertising budget or, alternatively, if the advertising agent is used by a client to design, prepare and place advertising in the media, the agent will be paid, not directly by the client firm, but by way of agency discount allowed by the media in which the advertisement is placed.

advertising contractor. Organization that sells advertising space for publishers, etc being paid a commission on sales.

advice note. Document sent by a supplier to a customer detailing goods despatched.

Advisory Council on Pensions and Welfare Benefits Programs. Advises the US Secretary of Labor on the operation and implementation of the Employee Retirement Income Security Act of 1974.

AE. *Anonymos Etairia*, a Greek form of *joint stock company*. See also *Greek companies.*

AEU. Former *Amalgamated Engineering Union* now the *Amalgamated Union of Engineering and Foundry Workers (AUEW).*

AfDB. *African Development Bank.*

affidavit. Sworn statement or declaration in writing.

affiliated company. One under the same ownership.

affiliated manager. Manager who places greater emphasis on being liked and staying on good terms with everybody than on exercising leadership and control.

affiliation needs. Psychologist's term for need for acceptance by one's peers.

affirmative action. US term for the hiring, employment and promotion of people previously discriminated against.

AFIA. Established in 1918 and originally known as the American Foreign Insurance Association.

AFL. *American Federation of Labor.*

AFL-CIO. *American Federation of Labor-Congress of Industrial Organizations.*

African Development Bank (AfDB). Established 1964 under the guidance of the United Nations *Economic Commission for Africa*. More than 30 African countries are members of the Bank.

African Trade Union Confederation (ATUC). Founded in 1962, the ATUC has some 40 member *trade unions* in 30 African countries. See also *All African Trade Union Federation (AATUF)* and *Pan-African Workers Congress (PAWC).*

AG. *Aktiengesellschaft.* See *Austrian companies, German companies* and *Swiss companies.*

Agency for International Development (AID). US government agency that handles

13

American overseas economic aid program(me)s. The AID was established in 1961 under the USA's *Act for International Development*, taking over and bringing together the work of the former Development Loan Fund and International Cooperation Administration. See also *Alliance for Progress* and *European Recovery Program(me)*.

agency shop agreement. Under the UK's *Industrial Relations Act 1971*, an agreement made between one or more employers and a *trade union*, or *joint negotiating panel of unions*, under which the individual worker belonged to a trade union or paid a regular contribution to it in lieu of *trade union dues*, unless he was a conscientious objector and made a contribution to charity instead. See also *post-entry closed shop*.

agent. Person or company authorized to act on behalf of another. The ownership of any goods handled does not pass, even though the agent may carry stock, and the entire profit, after deduction of such expenses as have been approved and a commission on the gross proceeds of sale, is accountable to the person appointing him (the 'principal'). See also *special agent*.

Agent de Change. *Stockbroker* on the *Brussels Stock Exchange* or the *Paris Stock Exchange* (or *Bourse*) or one of the *Swiss Stock Exchanges*. The former Exchange also has *Agents de Change Correspondants* who may only deal through an Agent de Change. Agents de Change on the Paris Stock Exchange are all members of the *Compagnie des Agents de Change* which elects the *Chambre Syndicale des Agents de Change* to implement the Bourse regulations and publish the Official List of *securities* in association with the *Commission des Operations de Bourse*.

Agent de Change Correspondant. *Stockbroker* who may deal on the *Brussels Stock Exchange*, but only through an *Agent de Change*.

Agente de Cambio y Bolsa. Spanish *stockbroker*. See *Spanish stock exchanges*.

Agenti di Cambio. Stockbrokers trading on the floors of the *Italian stock exchanges*. There are also authorized non-bidding dealers, or *remissiers*, who may buy and sell *securities* but not through trading floor biddings. Other people officially admitted to the exchanges are observers from banks and credit institutions with a paid up capital of at least L100 million.

age pattern analysis. Analysis of the age distribution among the different categories of employee in a firm. Can be a significant consideration in *manpower planning*.

aggregate manpower budgets (also plans). Broad budgets or plans not taking note of breakdowns between skills or between industries. See *manpower budgeting*.

aggregate supply (of labo(u)r). Total supply of labo(u)r without discerning between types of labo(u)r.

AGM. See *annual general meeting*.

agreed procedure. Negotiated between management and *trade union(s)* as the procedure to be followed in attempting to solve any grievances before resorting to *strike* action. Where a strike is called without first going through the agreed procedure, it is known as an *unconstitutional strike* or a *wildcat strike*. See also *disputes procedure, procedural agreement* and *engineering procedure*.

agribusiness. Production, processing, storage, transportation and distribution of farming supplies and produce.

Agricultural, Horticultural and Forestry Industry Training Board. Established August 1966 under the UK *Industrial Training Act 1964*.

Agricultural Wages Board for England and Wales. Under the Agricultural Wages Act 1948, the Board lays down a national minimum wage, holiday pay and holidays for agricultural workers somewhat in the manner of *wages councils*.

AH4 Test. Both a *verbal* and *non-verbal general intelligence test* (and also an element of *numerical aptitude test*), taking about an hour to conduct and used with different norms according to the level being tested. See *psychological testing, aptitude tests* and *test battery*.

AH5 Test. Higher level version of the *AH4 Test*.

Ahmadabad Share & Stockbrokers' Association. One of seven major stock exchanges in India.

AICPA. *American Institute of Certified Public Accountants*.

AID. *Agency for International Development* (US).

AIDA. Abbr for attention, interest, desire and action — four key requirements in successful selling. Used as a basis for many sales training programmes.

aided recall. *Market research* interview technique used to help interviewees remember events, products, etc by reminding them of associated events or things. It is a type of technique also used in psychological research.

AIIE. *American Institution of Industrial Engineers.*

AIMCO. *Association of Internal Management Consultants* (US).

aiming. Type of *psychomotor skill*. An individual's ability to perform swiftly and accurately a sequence of movements demanding eye-hand coordination. See also *motion study*.

Air Transport and Travel Industry Training Board. Established March 1967 under the UK *Industrial Training Act 1964*.

AIW. *Allied Industrial Workers of America.*

Aksjeselskap (A/S). Norwegian *joint stock company*.

Aktiebolaj (AB). Swedish *joint stock company*.

Aktiengesellschaft. *Joint stock company* under Austrian, German and Swiss company law, having the abbr *AG*. Also known in Switzerland as *Société Anonyme (SA)*. See also *Austrian companies, German companies* and *Swiss companies*.

Aktieselskab (A/S). A Danish public company or corporation. See also *Copenhagen Stock Exchange*.

Alexandria Stock Exchange. See *Bourse de valeurs d'Alexandria*.

ALGOL. Acronym of *Algorithmic Language*. A *computer language* used particularly for programming scientific problems.

algorithm. Logical sequence of deductions for problem solving. They are used to reduce problem solving tasks to a comparatively simple series of operations which at the same time indicate the order in which the operations should be carried out. Progress through an algorithm is determined by a 'yes' or 'no' answer at each stage. Sophisticated algorithms are used in, for example, complex computational processes. See also *decision tree* and *logical tree*.

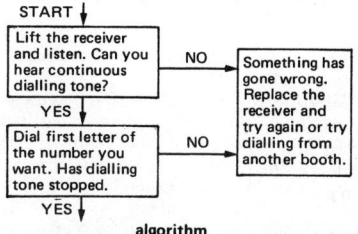

algorithm

Algorithmic Language. Source of the acronym, *ALGOL*. See also *computer language*.

All African Trade Union Federation (AATUF). One of the central organizations for African *trade unions*. See also *African Trade Union Confederation (ATUC)* and *Pan-African Workers Congress (PAWC)*.

all commodity volume. *Market research* and *retail audit* term for the turnover of all goods in a shop or shops. This information is used, for example, in evaluating the significance of the turnover in the product being market researched or audited.

all-fours. Lawyer's term for a direct legal precedent. Eg 'this matter is on all fours with the so-and-so case or judgment'.

Alliance for Progress. Agreement made in Uruguay in 1961 between the USA and most of the Latin American countries with the object of improving the economic life of South America. The Alliance is largely financed by the USA's *Agency for International Development*. See also the *Central American Common Market* and the *Latin American Free Trade Association*.

Allied Industrial Workers of America: international union. Milwaukee-based US labo(u)r union known as the *United Automobile Workers of America (UAW)* until 1956 and particularly active in the automobile industry though smaller than the *Automobile, Aerospace and Agricultural Implement Workers of America*.

all-in rate. Wage rate that incorporates various extras, such as bonus payments, in addition to the basic time-related payment scheme.

allocation. Use of mathematical techniques to allocate available men, machines and materials, to get optimum results. See also *operational research*.

allocation of overheads. Apportioning *indirect costs* and expenses (eg cleaning materials, lighting, heating and *depreciation*) which cannot be directly identified with particular cost centres (centers). The basis for apportioning will depend on the type of cost. Rent, for example, is typically charged to the cost centres (centers) on the basis of the number of square feet occupied. The aim is to ensure that all such costs together with the direct costs give a realistic picture of total costs.

allonge. Piece of paper attached to a *bill of exchange* to give space for extra endorsements when the back of the bill itself has been filled in.

all-or-none embargo. Where the employees of a company insist that privileges such as *payment-by-results* work or *overtime* should be granted equally to all or none of them without favo(u)ritism.

allowed time. As *standard time (1)* in *work study*.

all-union shop. As *closed shop*.

alongside-date. Date on which a ship is expected to be ready and in position to take on a particular cargo.

alphanumeric. Computer characters containing both letters and numbers.

alternate. Person empowered to deputize for the normal appointee – for example, on a works council, board of directors, etc.

alternate standard. *Work study* term for the alternative *standard time* when a specified different or alternative method of work is used.

alternating shift. Where *shift workers* change to a different shift periodically (often weekly).

alternative cost. Cost that will be incurred if management takes one of the particular alternative courses of action before it. The different alternative costs have to be taken into account in assessing *opportunity cost*.

alternative road. Method of learning through applications rather than by the more traditional method of learning from principles.

AMA. *American Management Association*.

Amalgamated Engineering Union. UK *trade union* founded in 1920, becoming the *Amalgamated Union of Engineering and Foundry Workers* in 1970.

Amalgamated Society of Railway Servants v Osborne (1910). UK lawsuit. The House of Lords gave an unexpected judgment that the Trade Union Act 1871 and the Trade Union Act Amendment Act 1876 did not permit *trade unions* to seek parliamentary representation or to make a compulsory *political levy* on their members. The *Trade Union Act 1913* later amended the House of Lords judgment to allow trade unions to have political objects but with *contracting-out* available to individual trade unionists.

Amalgamated Union of Engineering Workers (AUEW). Major UK *trade union* affiliated to the *Trades Union Congress*, and having an Engineering Section, a Construction Section, a Foundry Section, and a Technical and Supervisory Section (TASS). The total membership is more than one million. See also *Confederation of Shipbuilding and Engineering Unions*.

amalgamation. As *merger*. See also *take-over bid* and *acquisition*.

amendment. At a formal meeting, an amendment may be moved as what the mover of it believes to be an improvement in the action proposed in the *motion* before the meeting. An amendment should not be a *direct negative* or merely destructive in intent, and a chairman may also refuse to have it put to the meeting if he judges it to be either irrelevant or frivolous. Normal forms of amendment have the effect on an *original motion* of either **a** adding words, **b** deleting words, or **c** deleting words and substituting others. An amendment that merely adds words to the end of a motion is an *addendum*. If the mover of the motion and his seconder accept an amendment it is a common practice for it to be included in the motion without debate. Where they do not accept, the debate and vote on the amendment must be taken before those on the motion, the amendment being made to the motion when the vote on it is in the affirmative before the meeting proceeds to debate the motion. It is usual for each person present to have a right to speak on the amendment as well as on the motion, though the mover of the amendment does not usually have a *right of reply*. When an amendment has been voted, it is possible for further amendments to be moved to the motion, including to the part or parts affected by the earlier amendment. Where an amendment (or amendments) is carried, the resulting amended motion is known as a *substantive motion*.

American . See also entries under *US*.

American Bankers Association. Established in 1875, some 97 per cent of all banks in the USA now being members. The Association is the major national banking organization.

American Board of Examiners in Professional Psychology. Professional body providing examinations and certification for *occupational psychologists* and other psychologists in the USA.

American Federation of Labor (AFL). National organization of *trade unions* in the USA and Canada founded in 1881 and being particularly strong among *craft unions*. A rather more left-wing organization, the *Congress of Industrial Organizations*, was formed in 1935 but the two bodies settled their differences and merged in December 1955 to become the *American Federation of Labor and Congress of Industrial Organizations (AFL-CIO)*.

American Federation of Labor and Congress of Industrial Organizations (AFL-CIO). Formed in December 1955 from a merger in the USA and Canada between the *American Federation of Labor* and the more radical *Congress of Industrial Organizations*. The total membership of the trade unions forming the AFL-CIO is approximately 15 million (compared with, for example, approximately eleven million for the *Trades Union Congress* in the UK).

American Institute of Certified Public Accountants (AICPA). Professional association of accountants originally incorporated as American Institute of Accountants. Present name adopted in 1953.

American Institute for Free Labor Development. US organization which provides training for Latin American labo(u)r leaders.

American Institution of Industrial Engineers (AIIE). Professional body set up in 1948 for *work study* and similar engineers.

American Insurance Association. Established in 1866.

American International Underwriters Corporation. Established in 1926 as an association of US *insurance* underwriters.

American Management Association (AMA). Professional non-profit making body established in 1923 providing research, information, training and publications on a wide range of management subjects.

American Mining Congress. Major US *employers' association*, established in 1897.

American National Standards Institute Inc. Established in 1918, as the American Engineering Standards Committee, the Institute's members include 150 national *trade associations* and some 900 companies or corporations. The Institute represents the USA on the *International Organization for Standards*. It is concerned with establishing standards much in the manner of the *British Standards Institution*.

American Psychological Association. Professional body that includes in its activities the issuing of technical recommendations on *psychological testing* and for the guidance of *occupational psychologists*.

American selling price (ASP). US Customs valuation system whereby duty is levied not on the price of imported goods but on the price at which the comparable domestic product is freely offered for sale in the USA.

American Society of Association Executives. Established in 1920, has some 3,500 members who are executive officers of associations, societies, institutions, etc.

American Society of Mechanical Engineers. Professional organization with interests extending into such aspects of management as *industrial engineering* and *work study*. Established 1880.

American Stock Exchange. See *US stock exchanges*.

amortization. 1. As *depreciation*. 2. Ending of a debt by an agreed procedure such as arranging for all or part of it to be paid in instalments.

AMS. *Administrative Management Society.*

Amstel Club. Group of leading British and European banks and finance houses having reciprocal agreements for the financing of imports and exports between their countries.

Amsterdam Stock Exchange. Or *Vereeniging voor den Effectenhandel,* the principal and predominant stock exchange of the Netherlands, dating back to the early seventeenth century. Members of the Amsterdam Stock Exchange include both individual *stockbrokers* and corporate bodies such as banks. Specialist intermediaries on the Amsterdam Stock Exchange include the *Premie makelaars,* or options specialists; the *Hoeklieden,* a kind of stockjobber; and the *Commissionnairs in effecten* who act as intermediaries between the banks and the hoeklieden.

amtliche Kursmakler. Those German *stockbrokers* or *Makler* who are appointed by the government and have a role broadly similar to the *stockjobber* on the London *Stock Exchange.* Other German stockbrokers, not appointed by the Government are the *freie Makler.*

Amtlicher Markt. Official market for trading in *securities* on German Stock Exchanges. Other markets are the semi-official *Geregelter Freiverkehr* and the unofficial *Telefonverkehr.*

AMTORG. The state trading agency of the USSR.

amtskommunal indkomstskat. Local or county *income tax* in Denmark, as is *kommunal indkomstskat.* It is charged in addition to state income tax, church tax and net *wealth tax.* See *Danish income tax* for other taxes.

analog(ue) computer. *Computer* that processes data in the form of physical quantities, performing high speed and complex calculations, and being of value in simulating physical systems or in controlling industrial processes automatically. But an analog(ue) computer does not have the ability of a *digital computer* to store large quantities of data. See also *hybrid computer.*

analog(ue) models. Used in training, education and the management of enterprises to simulate industrial or business situations.

Analog(ue)s can be electrical, pneumatic, hydraulic, mathematical, etc.

analysis of variance (ANOVA). Statistical testing technique for determining whether variance between the mean on different sets of observations exceeds what may be expected by chance.

analytical estimating. Technique used particularly in production and works management to break down estimated times or costs for a job between identifiable component parts of the job so that it is possible to build up a reasonable estimate of the whole without going as far as using measurement techniques such as *work measurement* (if only during planning stages, because work cannot be measured until it exists).

analytic job evaluation. *Job evaluation* technique in which common features of jobs are compared in turn. Other job evaluation approaches include *dominant element job evaluation, integral job evaluation, job factor comparison, job grading, job ranking, points rating method, profiling systems* and *time span analysis.*

analytic method of selection. Detailed initial selection procedure in which the characteristics of each candidate are set out and compared under such heads as age, qualifications, experience, job stability and health. Cf the more cursory *overall impression method of selection.*

ANCOM. Andean Common Market covering Bolivia, Chile, Columbia, Ecuador, Peru and Venezuela.

angle of incidence. Angle at which the sales revenue line crosses the total cost line on a *break-even chart* (see illustration with that definition). Management strategy is normally to achieve as large an angle of incidence as possible since, broadly speaking, this gives a correspondingly high rate of profit once the break-even point has been passed. The area between the total cost line and the sales revenue line below the break-even point is known as the *losses wedge,* while the area between the sales revenue line and the total costs line above the break-even point is the *profits wedge.* The size of the latter is chiefly determined by the size of the angle of incidence. See also *margin of safety.*

annotated diagram. *Organization chart, flow chart,* etc.

annual capital charge. Method of projecting, testing and keeping under review the performance of an organization that has constant annual cash flows which can be compared with an annual capital charge. For less regular cash flow there are *discounted cash flow* techniques, etc.

annual general meeting (AGM). All UK companies are obliged under the *Companies Act* 1948 to hold a meeting every calendar year and not more than 15 months after the previous one. It provides an opportunity for *shareholders* to hear how the board has run the company, to raise questions, to declare *dividends*, to consider the accounts and auditor's report, to elect directors, to appoint auditors etc. The procedures are governed by Articles 47-74 of Table A of the Companies Act 1948.

annual premium costing (pensions). Where the cost of a total pension is expressed as a level annual premium payable each year until retirement. An alternative system, *single premium costing*, is to pay with each year's premium for the pension earned in that year. Annual premium costing is necessary, however, in such schemes as *final salary pension schemes* where pension is to be related to an unknown future salary. *Controlled funding methods* are used to forecast future salaries and establish reasonable present annual premium costings.

annual return. 1. Generally a document setting out certain information which has to be completed and filed annually to meet legal or quasi-legal regulations. In the UK, may refer specifically to the document required under the *Companies Act* 1948 which must be filed annually with the *Registrar of Companies* within 42 days of the *annual general meeting.* **2.** *Rate of return* on an *investment.* See also *return on assets managed, return on capital* and *return on investment.*

annual wage audit. System of regular, intensive reviews of the wage payment and *fringe benefits* structure of a company or organization with a view to alerting management to underlying trends that might have potential dangers for *industrial relations.* Factors highlighted by an annual wage audit might include differentials between shop floor and supervisory personnel; labo(u)r unit costs; amount or proportion of *overtime* worked; extra costs of *shift working; covered time* for which bonus is applicable but is not worked; the proportion of *bonus earnings* to total earnings; comparative earnings within and between departments; comparisons with earnings in neighbouring companies; major causes of *unproductive time;* and desirable salary levels.

annual usage value. *Stock control* term for the total value of an item used during a year.

annuity. Retirement pension purchased with a lump sum on reaching retirement age. It may be purchased by an individual *(purchased life annuity)* or it may be purchased from the maturing of an *endowment assurance policy* according to a formula prescribed by an *occupational pension scheme.* If an annuity is payable only for a limited number of years it may be known as an annuity certain.

annuity option rate. Or *guaranteed annuity option.* Where an insurance policy in respect of a *discretionary endowment pension scheme* guarantees that the endowment sum assured will be converted into pension at the intended rate, whatever the *immediate annuity rate* or going conversion rate at the time of maturity of the policy and retirement of the insured. See *'top hat' pension scheme.*

Anonymos Etairia (AE). A Greek *joint stock company* in which shareholders are liable only to the extent of the capital subscribed, in much the same way as in the UK and elsewhere. See *Greek companies* and *Athens Stock Exchange.*

ANOVA. See *analysis of variance.*

anticipation. Deduction made by a customer for paying before the due date, a practice and term more common in the USA than in the UK. A more usual arrangement in the UK is a *cash discount.*

anticipation stock. Raw materials, parts or finished goods purchased or manufactured in advance of expected demand or in anticipation of rising costs and prices.

Anti-Merger Act 1950. See *antitrust legislation* (US).

anti-pirating agreement. Or anti-poaching agreement. Convention observed by employers in a particular industry or locality that they will not recruit each other's employees.

antitrust legislation. Generic term for a number of US laws concerned with preserving a competitive and open market. The first was the Sherman Act of 1890 which prohibited monopolies and conspiracies and combinations in restraint of trade. Subsequent legislation, such as the Clayton Act, the Federal Trade Commission Act of 1914, the Robinson Patman Act of 1936, the Milletydings Act of 1937 and the Anti-Merger Act of 1950 enacted further laws for maintaining a free economy. As nearly all this legislation is predominantly of a general nature with few specific details of practices regarded as illegal, the interpretation and enforcement of antitrust legislation has proved very difficult.

Antwerp Stock Exchange. La Bourse de Fonds Publics d'Anvers (Fondsen en Wisselbeurs van Antwerpen). See *Belgian stock exchanges.*

AOQ. See *average outgoing quality.*

AOQL. See *average outgoing quality limit,*

aperture card. Punched card designed to store microfilmed documents, drawings, etc.

APEX. *Association of Professional, Executive, Clerical and Computer Staff* (UK).

apparent time. Local time by the sun and a strict interpretation of the world's *time zones* though political and economic considerations lead to some countries using a different local time for their own convenience. See Appendix: Time Zones.

application of funds. Normally part of an annual 'statement of source and application of funds' which accompanies the *balance sheet* and *profit and loss account.* It typically shows the origin of funds (eg profit before tax, *depreciation* and issue of *shares* or *debentures*) and what use was made of them during the period under review (usually for the financial year). It will, for example, show payments of dividends, taxation and purchase of plant and machinery, as well as changes in *working capital* and increases/decreases in *stocks.*

appraisal interview. Technique for assessing past performance and future potential in making a *salary review* or for management development.

appraisal method. 1. See *performance appraisal.* **2.** Method of calculating *depreciation* in which *asset* values are determined by making an appraisal at the start and finish of each accounting period. The depreciation is based on the difference between the two values. It is used in the USA particularly for small assets (eg small tools, etc).

appreciation training. Designed to give background or generalized understanding of a topic rather than working or detailed knowledge.

apprentice. Young person contracted or indentured, usually with an employer, to be trained for a *trade* or *occupation.* Traditions of craft apprenticeship date back to the Guilds of medieval times. In modern times there are also *commercial,* student, technician and graduate *apprentices.*

appropriation. Sometimes synonymous with *budget allocation* or when used as appropriation account describes that part of the *profit and loss account* which shows how the gross or more commonly net profit is appropriated to dividends or reserves, etc. Also used specifically in *advertising* as a budget for a campaign or period.

approved post-entry closed shop agreement. See *post-entry closed shop.*

approximation of laws (EEC). Among member states of the *Common Market,* the *Treaty of Rome 1957* intends, particularly in Articles 100-102, that the national laws of member states should be harmonised to the extent required to further the objectives of the Community. This provision might be invoked, for example, where variations between national industrial standards impede the Community's goal of free movement of goods within the total Common Market.

APT. *Programming language* used for controlling numerically controlled machines.

aptitude tests. Tests devised to help assess a person's ability to undertake particular types of work or to learn particular skills. Different types of aptitude test used in *personnel selection* include *verbal aptitude, numerical aptitude, spatial ability* or *aptitude, mechanical aptitude* and *clerical aptitude tests.* Other forms of *psychological testing* include *intelligence tests* and *temperament and personality tests.* See also *test-battery.*

APU occupational interest guide. *Interest test* or *inventory* used in *personnel selection,* career guidance, etc to build up a picture of the personal interests of a candidate or employee. The test consists of 112 choices between pairs of activities, resulting in a profile of eight interest categories, namely, outdoor; mechanical; computational and clerical; scientific; persuasive; artistic and musical; literary; and social service. See also *psychological testing*.

AQL. See *acceptable quality level*.

AR. *Account(s) receivable.*

Ar (test). *Arithmetic ability* test. See *test-battery*.

Arbeitsgemeinschaft der deutschen Wertpapierbörsen. *Federation of German Stock Exchanges.*

Arbeitsgerichte. Local labo(u)r court in Federal Germany, having jurisdiction to handle complaints by either employers or employees on industrial relations matters. Appeals from this court are made to a *Landesarbeitsgerichte*. The Federal Labo(u)r Court is the *Bundesarbeitsgerichte*.

Arbetsdomstolen. Sweden's national labo(u)r court.

arbitrage. Buying and selling of *stocks* and *shares*, currency, *bills of exchange*, etc in different markets at virtually the same time in order to take advantage profitably of different prices and rates.

arbitration. Procedure, either prescribed or customary, by which a dispute may be referred to an agreed third party for settlement or advice. Resort to arbitration does not normally carry the force of litigation or resort to law; the latter may in some circumstances be pursued by a party dissatisfied with arbitration. In some forms of contract, particularly in commerce and insurance, there may be an arbitration clause to which one of the parties may turn in the event of a dispute. In industrial relations, a *collective agreement* will normally provide for arbitration procedures as part of *disputes procedures* in the event of an *industrial dispute*.

Arbitration Act 1950 (UK). Provided for *trade dispute* or *industrial dispute* to be referred to an independent arbitrator where a written *arbitration agreement* existed between employer and employees.

arbitration agreement. Agreement that disputes may be referred to an independent arbitrator.

arbitration clause. Clause in an agreement which binds the parties to settle any dispute which may arise by arbitration (in UK see *Arbitration Acts* 1950 and 1975).

arbitration, commercial. See *commercial arbitration*.

Arbitration Committee of the Bradford Chamber of Commerce. One of three tribunals in the UK that may be used for private arbitration where commercial disputes arise between suppliers and customers, including between UK exporters and overseas buyers. The other two tribunals of the same kind are the *London Court of Arbitration of the London Chamber of Commerce and Industry* and the *City Corporation* and the *Tribunal of Arbitration of the Manchester Chamber of Commerce and Industry*.

archive. Back-up *computer* storage for files on magnetic tape.

area concentration. *Advertising* term for concentrating *marketing* effort on a particular geographical area.

area sampling. As *cluster sampling*.

Argentinian central bank. *Banco Central de la República Argentina.*

Argentinian Chamber of Commerce. *Cámara Argentina de Comercio.*

Argentinian employers' associations. See *Acción Coordinadora de las Instituciones Empresarias Libres (ACIEL)*.

Argentinian stock exchanges. Principal Argentinian *stock exchange* is the *Bolsa de Comercio*, Buenos Aires. There are also stock exchanges at Cordöba, Mar del Plata, Mendoza, Rosario and San Juan.

Argentinian trade unions. See *Confederación General del Trabajo (CGT)*.

argift på honorarer til utenlandske kunstnere. Norwegian tax on foreign artists' fees levied at a flat rate on gross fees instead of normal income taxes. See also *Norwegian income tax*.

arithmetic ability (Ar). *Personnel selection* and *vocational guidance* test devised as part of the *engineering apprentice test-battery* of the National Institute of Industrial Psychology in the UK. See also *psychological testing* and *test battery*.

arithmetic average. Statistical measure of central tendency obtained by dividing the sum of two or more quantities by the number of items

eg average of 5, 10, & 12 = $\frac{27}{3}$ = 9.

Also known as mean or arithmetic mean.

arithmetic mean. See *arithmetic average*.

arithmetic unit. Part of the *central processing unit* of a *digital computer*. Performs calculations at the command of the *program control unit* using data and program instructions provided by the *internal memory*. See *computer*.

arm's length market price. Stated price before any detailed negotiation.

arrangement. Debtor's plan for the settlement of unsecured debts or the extension of time over which repayments will be made.

array. Grouping of a number of values by magnitude, usually from the smallest to the largest, eg 5, 8, 12, 20, 30, 42.

arrow diagram. Diagram of events, each of which can only take place after an earlier event has been completed. Each arrow runs from a completed event to the next event to be commenced. Arrow diagrams are among the techniques used in *network analysis/planning*.

Article 87 of the International Labor Organization: Freedom of Association and Protection of the Right to Organize. An international agreement through the *International Labor Organization* that workers have the right to organize in *trade unions*.

Article 98 of the International Labor Organization: Right to Organize and to Bargain Collectively. States: 'Measures appropriate to national conditions shall be taken where necessary to encourage and promote the full development and utilization of machinery for voluntary negotiation between employers' organizations and workers' organizations with a view to the regulation of terms and conditions of employment by means of *collective agreements.*'

articles of association. Represent a contract between a company and its shareholders and set out the powers of the directors and the legal framework of the company. The articles of association are drawn up on the formation of a company together with the company *memorandum* which sets out the purpose for which the company has been formed and the amount and different classes of share capital.

Arusha Agreement (EEC). Associated four British Commonwealth countries, Kenya, Nigeria, Tanzania and Uganda, with the *Common Market* in advance of British entry. Under the Arusha Agreement these Commonwealth countries made reciprocal trading arrangements with the Community similar to those arranged under the Yaoundé Agreement, of July 1969, with ten African states that were formerly dependencies of member states of the Community.

A/S. *Aktieselskab*, a Danish public company or corporation. or *Aksjeselskap*, a Norwegian *joint stock company*.

asbestosis. Form of pneumoconiosis (dust disease of the lung) caused by the prolonged inhalation of asbestos fibres (fibers).

Asian Development Bank (ADB). Established in 1966 through the United Nations' *Economic Commission for Asia and the Far East*. There are some 35 member countries.

as is goods. Condition of sale that a buyer will accept delivery of goods ordered 'as they come' and without warranty.

ASLEF. *Associated Society of Locomotive Engineers and Firemen* (UK).

ASME. *American Society of Mechanical Engineers.*

ASP. See *American selling price*.

aspirational groups. Type of *reference group* brought together for the purpose of examining consumer buying motives. In an aspirational group, the individual is brought into contact with a group to which he aspires to belong, so that his buying behaviour is influenced by how he thinks the group behaves or purchases. Thus aspirational groups reveal snob motivations in buying. Other forms of reference group include *membership groups, dissociative groups, face-to-face groups,* and *family groups*.

Assembly. Official term for *European Parliament* (or *Parliamentary Assembly*) used in documents and pronouncements of the *Common Market* or *European Economic Community*, including the *Treaty of Rome 1957* which created the Community. The term 'European Parliament' began to emerge unofficially later.

assembly chart. As *Gozinto chart*.

assembly line balancing. Allocation of equal

workloads to work stations in order to attain an even work flow.

assembly line production. Type of *mass production* used for highly standardized items in which each worker carries out the same *task* on a succession of identical products as they are passed along to his or her position by a conveyor belt, each successive worker adding to the product. Normally, the conveyor belt keeps moving while the worker performs his task. Or the belt may be stopped for the operation to be carried out in the case of a production line where all the operations take approximately the same time. Assembly line production techniques have been particularly highly developed in the motor car industry where they have, however, highlighted the dangers of loss of *job satisfaction* in employees. Assembly line production is a form of *flow line production* though the latter term also covers forms of production in which the individual worker does not have to work precisely to the speed of a conveyor belt.

assessment. Tax levied on income, capital gains or profits. May also be used to describe a levy on shareholders or members of an organization for raising capital.

assessment centre. 1. Selection, appraisal and development of personnel with managerial ability normally undertaken internally by an assessor trained in certain basic techniques. **2.** An external organization providing advice and consultancy services in the selection and appraisal area.

assessment of trainees/students. *Continuous assessment* of student work has been developed in recent years as an alternative or complement to examinations.

assessment of training effectiveness. See *evaluation* and *validation*.

asset. Property, tangible or sometimes intangible, owned by a company. *Fixed assets* are capital equipment purchased for continued use in the company's manufacturing or other business activities, and gradually written off through *depreciation*. *Current assets* are of a less permanent and usually more easily realizable nature such as *cash, debtors, work-in-progress, stocks*, short-term *investments*, etc. *Liquid assets* consist of cash or items quickly convertible into cash. Fictitious assets and intangible assets have a book value rather than a real or realizable value.

assets managed. See *return on assets managed (ROAM)*.

asset stripping. *Acquisition* of a company, not in order to continue and develop its existing business and activities, but in order to sell off its more lucrative *assets* and activities with a view to making a quick profit irrespective of the effect of the break-up of the company on such considerations as employees' *job security* or customers' needs.

assign. To make over or transfer any property or right. The assignee is the person to whom the right or property is assigned. The assignor is the person who makes over or transfers the right or property.

assignment analysis. *Job evaluation* technique in which the tasks or assignments of which the job is composed are graded.

Assisted Area. Generic term used in the UK for the *Special Development Areas*, the *Development Areas* and the *Intermediate Areas* where regional development is particularly encouraged. See also *advance factory, regional development grants* and *industrial development certificates (IDCs)*.

Associaçao Comercial de Lisboa — Cámara de Comércio. Portuguese *chambers of commerce*, established in 1834.

associated company. In UK usage, a company of which less than 50 per cent of the share capital is owned. The assets are therefore not consolidated into the parent company accounts but are shown as a trade investment. In US terms, a corporation in which at least 50 per cent of the voting capital is owned by another.

associate director. Title sometimes given to senior managers, eg heads of major functions or divisions, which implies status and recognition. Such directors are neither members of the board nor have the duties and responsibilities of directors under the *Companies Act*.

Associated Society of Locomotive Engineers and Firemen (ASLEF). UK *trade union* affiliated to the *Trades Union Congress*.

associated states (EEC). Non-member states which have an *association agreement* or *preferential trade agreement* with the *Common Market* or *European Economic Community*.

association agreement (EEC). *Preferential*

23

trade agreement (between the *Common Market* and *associated states*).

association bargaining. As *multi-employer bargaining*.

l'Association Nationale pour la Formation Professionnelle des Adultes. Runs 120 French industrial training centres (centers), being controlled jointly by the Government, employers' associations and trade unions. See also *French industrial training* for other provision of training.

Association of British Chambers of Commerce. National body established in 1860 and able to advise on matters concerning *chambers of commerce*. Also noted for its group apprenticeship scheme in clerical work. About 100 *chambers of commerce* in the UK and some 16 in overseas countries are members of the Association. See also *London Chamber of Commerce*, the *National Chamber of Trade*, and *commercial arbitration*.

Association of Consulting Management Engineers (ACME). An American association founded in 1929 and representing management consultants.

Association of Management Consultants. US organization formed in 1959 to represent management consulting firms.

association of overseas countries and territories (EEC). Articles 131-136 of the *Treaty of Rome 1957* provide for arrangements to be made for the association with the *Common Market* of countries having special relationships with member states. Grants and loans to non-member states are made through the *European Development Fund* set up under the Yaoundé Convention of July 1969 agreed by the Community with ten African states. The Community also made the *Arusha Agreement* with three British Commonwealth countries, Kenya, Tanzania and Uganda, in advance of British entry.

Association of Professional, Executive, Clerical and Computer Staff (APEX). UK *trade union* for *white collar* workers affiliated to the *Trades Union Congress* and known until 1972 as the *Clerical and Administrative Workers' Union*.

Association of Scientific, Technical and Managerial Staffs (ASTMS). UK *trade union* for *white collar* staff affiliated to the *Trades Union Congress*.

Association of Teachers of Management (ATM). UK body set up in 1960 for teachers and training specialists in universities, polytechnics, colleges, etc interested in exchanging ideas and experience in management education. Publishes occasional papers on teaching developments and research findings.

Association of Teachers in Technical Institutions (ATTI). *Trade union* for technical college teachers in the UK.

Associazione in Partecipazione. 'Joint venture' under Italian Civil Law. See *Italian companies*.

assurance. Tends to be used interchangeably with *insurance* in practice but, technically, an assurance policy covers what is bound to happen but at an unknown time, while an insurance policy is taken out against what might happen.

ASTMS. *Association of Scientific, Technical and Managerial Staffs* (UK).

ASTRA. Abbr automatic scheduling with time integrated resource allocation. Form of *network analysis* for allocating resources and scheduling activities over time as a means of estimating completion dates.

ATA Carnet. International customs document, recognized by countries which are parties to the ATA Convention, and used by firms when sending or taking goods abroad temporarily, free of *customs duty*, as sales samples or as exhibits at an international exhibition.

at call. Term used of money lent in such a way that its repayment can be demanded virtually without notice.

Athens Stock Exchange. Founded in 1876, being modelled on the *Paris Stock Exchange*. The present-day Athens Stock Exchange is not very active and even nominally public companies in Greece have often remained in private hands. The only form of public company is the *Anonymos Etairia (AE)*. The Exchange is supervised by a small Stock Exchange Committee and there is an upper limit of 50 *stockbrokers*.

ATM. *Association of Teachers of Management* (UK).

ATP. Abbr for the *European Agreement on the International Carriage of Perishable Foodstuffs*.

at sight. Used of a *bill of exchange*, for example, means that it is payable immediately on presentation and does not first have to go through an acceptance procedure.

Attachment of Earnings Act 1971. UK legislation providing for certain debts to be collected from a debtor's earnings at source so that he is forced to pay up. The order is served on the debtor's employer who must comply within seven days. Orders may be made by the High Court, the County Court or a Magistrate's Court in respect of a debt of £5 or more or of regular payments such as alimony or maintenance payments for a wife or children.

attainment test. Or *achievement test.* Type of *psychological test* that measures knowledge in a particular area or attainment in a particular kind of skill rather than potential or *aptitude*.

attendance bonus (or money). Paid to an employee in recognition of regular attendance and/or good timekeeping.

attended time. Time or proportion of a period of time for which plant or machinery is used.

attestation. Witnessing of a signature to a document.

ATTI. *Association of Teachers in Technical Institutions* (UK), a *trade union* for college of further education teaching staff.

attitude(s). Predisposition to behave in a certain way and to take particular points of view. Cf *behavio(u)r* and *set*. An individual's *cognitions*, feeling and action tendencies with respect to the various objects in his world which as he develops become enduring systems, influencing his behavio(u)r or reactions to events.

attitude/knowledge/skill pattern. Parameters of a person's job performance in that attitude determines mental and physical approach, knowledge is necessary to know what to do, and skill is measure of ability to do it.

attitude scales. Questionnaire-based evaluation of an individual's basic attitude, how far it deviates from a central value, how tenaciously it is sustained, and its significance within the individual's total personality.

attitude survey. 1. Often used to determine attitudes of employees to their job and their employing organization. **2.** *Market research* technique based on interview or questionnaires to establish consumer views on new or existing products or services.

attorney. Lawyer (US). See also *barrister* and *solicitor*.

attorney, power of. See *power of attorney*.

attribute comparisons. *Market research* survey in which *respondents* are asked to choose which of a list of attributes is most appropriate to a particular brand or product. See also *product comparison, forced choice* and *free choice of products*.

attrition. The process by which average salary levels in an organization tend to decline over a period of time as staff are engaged at a lower salary than those they replace. Where an *incremental payment system* is in use this process may mean that an increase of say, three per cent to the salary bill because of *merit* increments at the beginning of the year may be eroded over the course of the year.

ATUC. *African Trade Union Confederation.*

Auckland Stock Exchange. One of four main stock exchanges in New Zealand.

audience measurement. Evaluation of the size of the readership, viewers and/or listeners for a communications medium and of its advertising effect.

audience research. As *media research.*

audiovisual aids. Used in learning, teaching and research. They include media and equipment, eg sound film and film strip projectors, television (both broadcast and closed circuit), and video tape recordings. See *audio aids.*

audit. 1. Process of verifying accounting records by an accountant or third party to ensure that the accounts truly represent the state of affairs. An independent auditor is normally appointed to audit companies' accounts annually — in the case of public companies in most countries he must be a qualified accountant. In addition to an annual audit some organizations — particularly larger ones — may have their own internal audit which checks on the accuracy and effectiveness of accounting procedures and systems, especially those concerned with the authorization and control of expenditure, and may also advise on improving internal methods. **2.** Systematic

checking or monitoring of management performance, as in *management audit*.
3. Systematic monitoring of product or service performance, as in *panel methods*.

Audit Bureau of Circulations (ABC). (UK). Independent organization which provides certificated evidence of the paid circulation of publications in the UK. This provides a valuable yardstick for advertisers.

Audit Bureau of Circulations (US). Independent organization providing certificated evidence of the paid circulation of publications in the USA. Established 1914. 4,200 members.

audit cycle. Period of time over which all sections of a company or organization are covered under *auditing by rotation*.

auditing by rotation. *Audit* system in which the major parts of the accounts of a company or organization are not all examined in depth each year, but receive special attention in turn in successive years. The span of time, usually about three years, over which all the major parts are covered is the *audit cycle*. Auditors usually avoid making their examinations too regular when operating auditing by rotation in order that their visits to sections of the organization should not become too predictable. See also *block check, financial ratios, test for depth,* and *volume checking*.

audit methods. As *panel methods* (market research).

auditor. Person or persons appointed to examine the accuracy of the accounts and records kept by a business or organization and to report on the financial aspects of the undertaking at a particular time. In the UK the auditor has to record his opinion whether the accounts represent a true and fair view of the company's transactions and financial structure. See also *audit*.

AUEW. *Amalgamated Union of Engineering Workers* (UK).

Aufsichtrat. See *Supervisory Board* (German industrial firms).

Aufsichtratsabgabe. Tax on fees receivable by directors of Austrian companies. See also *Einkommensteuer*, the Austrian income tax; and *Vermögensteuer*, a net *wealth tax* on the property of individuals.

Aufsichtratsteuer. Flat-rate directors' tax deducted at source from directors' fees receivable by non-resident supervisory directors of German companies. See also *Einkommensteuer*, the German income tax.

Australia, Associated Chambers of Commerce of. Established in 1901, its members include *chambers of commerce* in Adelaide, Brisbane, Darwin, Hobart, Ingham, Launceston, Melbourne, Newcastle, Perth, Sydney and Tamworth, together with State federations.

Australia, Institute of Directors in. Association for company directors.

Australian Associated Stock Exchanges. Established in 1937, has six member *stock exchanges*. The six member stock exchanges are **a** Brisbane Stock Exchange; **b** Adelaide Stock Exchange; **c** Hobart Stock Exchange; **d** Melbourne Stock Exchange; **e** Perth Stock Exchange; and **f** Sydney Stock Exchange.

Australian central bank. *Reserve Bank of Australia.*

Australian Council of Employers' Federations (ACEF). Established in 1905, the Council is the central organization for Australian *employers' associations*.

Australian Council of Trade Unions (ACTU). Established in 1927, the ACTU covers more than 150 *trade unions*.

Australian Institute of Management. Professional body for members of management and industrial and commercial organizations. Branches in Melbourne, Perth and Sydney.

Australian Victorian Employers' Federation. State organization for *employers' associations*.

Australian Workers' Union. Largest individual *trade union* in Australia, having about 170,000 members. It was first established in 1886 and affiliated to the *Australian Council of Trade Unions (ACTU)* in 1967.

Austrian Banks and Bankers, Association of. *Verband Österreichischer Banken und Bankiers.*

Austrian central bank. See *Österreichische Nationalbank.*

Austrian Chamber of Commerce. See *Bundeskammer der gewerblichen Wirtschaft.*

Austrian companies. Forms a company may legally take in Austria include: **a** one-man firm, or *Einzelfirma;* **b** partnerships, such as general partnership or *Offene Handelsgesellschaft (OHG)*, limited partnership or *Kommanditgesellschaft*, sleeping partnership or *Stille Gesellschaft;* **c** corporations, such as joint stock company or *Aktiengesellschaft*, limited liability company or *Gesellschaft mit beschränkter Haftung (GmbH)*, **d** cooperative or *Genossenschaft*. See also *Vienna Stock Exchange*.

Austrian Cooperative Central Bank. *Genossenschaftliche Zentralbank Aktiengesellschaft.*

Austrian employers' associations. See *Bundeskammer der gewerblichen Wirtschaft (Sektion Industrie)*.

Austrian Federation of Trade Unions. See *Österreichischer Gewerkschaftsbund.*

Austrian income tax. Or *Einkommensteuer.* A tax charged on total income and consisting of a wages tax on remuneration *(Lohnsteuer)* and a capital yields tax *(Kapitalertragsteuer)*. Austria also has the *Vermögensteuer*, a net *wealth tax* on the property of individuals; and the *Aufsichtratsabgabe*, a tax on fees paid to directors of Austrian companies.

Austrian Stock Exchange. See *Vienna Stock Exchange*.

autarky. National economic self-sufficiency without reliance on trade with outside world.

authoritarian theory. Assumes that human relations considerations are irrelevant in business, and that most people are naturally dependent, indolent, selfish and uncooperative. They therefore require strong direction and control to maintain discipline and achieve the appropriate goals. See also *economic man theory* and *Theory X* and *Theory Y.*

authority. Degree of power inherent in a specific job or function which enables the job holder to undertake and discharge his duties and responsibilities and make decisions. See also *span of control* and *management style.*

authorized capital. All the share capital which a company is able to issue according to its *articles of association.*

autocode. See *computer language.*

autocratic control. Tight personal control of a company or department by the chairman or a manager. Also known as *Caesar management*. See also *management style.*

auto-elucidatory and auto-instructional methods. Presentation of questions so that a trainee/student is passed to further material appropriate to the answers he/she gives. This happens, for example, when using *branching program(me)s* with *teaching machines* or *programmed texts.*

auto financing. Extent to which sales income provides a surplus (after allowing for payment of all expenses, taxes and dividend payments) to meet the cost of capital expenditure. Also known as self-financing.

automated programmed instruction. Term sometimes used of more sophisticated forms of *programmed instruction* — such as *intrinsic branching* or *computer assisted instruction* — when virtually all information is programmed and instructor or teacher has minimal role. Opposite approach, in effect, to *integrated programmed instruction.*

automatic cancellation. System under which any outstanding items at a particular point in time are deleted from an order and cancelled. Thus clerical systems are not impeded by balances and the purchaser is free to buy elsewhere or re-order at a later date. The term is sometimes used if the contract has a specified or implied completion date. After that date, no further deliveries will be accepted. An example of this may be when goods have been ordered specifically for a seasonal trade. See also *consignment note.*

automatic data processing (ADP). As *electronic data processing.*

automatic vending. Sale of goods, particularly foodstuffs, drinks, cigarettes, etc from coin-in-the-slot machines.

automation. 1. The execution of certain mental tasks by machine. 2. The use and application of complex mechanical, electronic, hydraulic and/or pneumatic, etc equipment in a manner that reduces or dispenses with human assistance or control.

automation engineering. Study of the principles and the devices of mechanized and automated sub-systems and the integration of these to provide automated systems.

automatization. Replacement and/or extension of human control by machine.

automistic competition. Economist's term for pure and direct competition, without government or any other form of intervention in the working of the market.

Automobile, Aerospace and Agricultural Implement Workers of America; international union, United (UAW). Major US labo(u)r union with headquarters in Detroit and a total membership of approximately 1,400,000. Its struggle for employer recognition included the so-called *'Battle of the Running Bulls'* in 1937 and the *'Battle of the Overpass'* in 1941. It made major strides in gaining further recognition from employers under the presidency of Walter Reuther from 1946.

autonomous bargaining. Where, in *workplace bargaining*, *trade unions* and *employers' associations* have very little control over proceedings. Autonomous bargaining is where local bargaining has been set up as a matter of policy rather than where it happens through erosion of the power of trade unions and/or employers' associations.

autonomous work groups. Form of *workers' participation* where each work group is responsible for organizing its work, for setting production targets and, sometimes, for organizing training. It is *task-based participation* rather than participation in policy making. Where there are autonomous work groups, the role of management is to provide supporting services rather than direct supervision, though management may retain control of such factors as the allocating of work and the timing of tea and meal breaks.

AUTOPERT. Use of special computer programs for rapidly developing and analyzing *PERT* and similar networks. By using programs which store basic *network analysis* components and modules all repetitive calculations are undertaken as a matter of routine.

AV. *Audiovisual.*

AVA. *Activity vector analysis.*

AVCO. See *average cost.*

average. 1. Normally synonymous with *arithmetic average* or mean — the most commonly used measure of central tendency. **2.** Used to describe other statistical measures of central tendency such as *median*, moving average or mode. **3.** Damage or loss to goods during sea transportation.

average adjuster. Insurance official skilled in assessing *average* — ie the value of damage or loss to goods at sea.

average cost (AVCO). *Stock control* technique for checking changing value of stock by multiplying the average unit cost of an item by the number of units in stock at the end of the period of time.

average cost of capital. See *capital cut-off point.*

average outgoing quality (AOQ). Average number of defective items, usually expressed as a percentage of the total items, identified under *acceptance sampling*.

average outgoing quality limit (AOQL). The maximum average number or percentage of defective items allowable under *acceptance sampling*.

average salary. Alternative term for *pensionable salary* in çalculations for an *average salary pension scheme*.

average salary pension scheme. Calculates pension in relation to the average or total income throughout working life, an agreed percentage of *pensionable salary* in each year being earned as the pension for that year's service. Thus such a scheme is more attractive than a *final salary pension scheme* to someone earning a high salary early in working life but less attractive to someone building up to a high salary from modest beginnings or to someone joining a scheme later in life. A variation on the average salary pension scheme is the *graded schedule pension scheme* under which salaries, and therefore pension earned, are grouped into *salary classes* instead of individual pensions being calculated on the basis of precise percentages of actual salaries. In the case of graded schedule schemes which are contributory pension schemes, employees' contributions are also stepped or graded in relation to the salary classes rather than individual salaries.

avoidable costs. Those that are incurred as a result of specific action or management decision rather than being an inherent and unavoidable part of the very existence of a business or organization (unavoidable costs of the latter kind might include factory buildings and basic equipment and labo(u)r costs). A management decision incurring avoidable costs might be one to develop a new product or go into a new market, the expected return justifying the avoidable cost or expenditure. Where management fails to make a choice or take an opportunity that would have produced a better net return than the choice it does in fact make, the lost revenue is an *opportunity cost*. See also *alternative cost*.

b

BACIE. *British Association for Commercial and Industrial Education.*

back orders. Items outstanding from previous deliveries. See also *automatic cancellation* and *consignment note.*

back pay. Wage/salary for work already done but for which proper payment has not been received. This differs from *retrospective payment,* which arises from an agreement to back date a new system or level of payment.

back-selling. Indirect form of *sales promotion* by stimulating the sales of a product or service further along the *sales chain.* Thus, in a sales chain consisting of, for example, manufacturer, wholesaler, retailer and *consumer,* back-selling by the manufacturer might consist of sales promotion among retailers to stimulate demand back along the chain through the wholesalers. A more common form of back-selling is where either the manufacturer or the wholesaler directs sales promotion at the consumer. Back-selling may also take the form of a component manufacturer indirectly promoting a component by promoting a product which incorporates it.

back-shift. Afternoon shift (2 pm to 10 pm) in a three-shift system. See *shift working.*

back to back credit. Type of credit allowed to an exporter by a *finance house* or bank acting as a go-between with a buyer in an export market.

backwardation. 1. Fee charged by a *stockbroker* for delaying a sale of shares. **2.** Where a *spot market* price is higher than the *forward market* price.

backward integration. Acquisition or take-over of a main supplier or manufacturer by a distributor or retailer of a product or service in order to be certain of supplies, or take-over of a raw materials supplier by a manufacturer for the same reason. The opposite process, usually intended to give control over markets, is *forward integration.*

backwash effect. Divergence in productivity between the developed countries' exports consisting mainly of manufactured goods, and those of the under-developed countries consisting largely of relatively low-productivity mining and agricultural commodities.

bad debts. Debts known to be irrecoverable and which are treated as losses and written off.

bail out (US). Methods of using corporate funds to provide payments to shareholders which are taxable at favourable *capital gains* rates.

balance of payments. Country's *balance sheet* of outgoings and receipts for a given period, this statement being divided between *current account* and capital account.
 Under current account, the basic payments are *visible imports* of goods and *invisible imports* of services, while the basic receipts are *visible exports* of goods and *invisible exports* of services (the latter including banking, insurance, tourism, shipping, and profits and interest payments from overseas).
 Under capital account, the basic payments include investment in, and long-term loans to, other countries and agencies; repayments of earlier loans from other countries and agencies; gifts to other countries; and short-term lending to other countries and agencies. Basic receipts under capital account include investment by, and long-term loans from, other countries and agencies; gifts by other countries; and short-term loans by other countries and agencies. Overall deficits or surpluses are brought into balance by movements in the *gold and foreign exchange reserves.* Also known as balance of trade or *merchandise balance.*

balance of trade. As *balance of payments.*

balance quantity. Output that must be

achieved by a particular intermediate stage in production if target final output is to be achieved.

balance sheet. Statement of a company's financial position at a particular point, normally at the end of a financial year, balancing *assets* against *liabilities* and showing the source and application of funds. Originally balance sheets were produced with liabilities shown on the left and assets on the right. Now they are often produced in vertical form showing fixed assets and net current assets (described together as capital, capital employed and then showing capital ownership). The complementary tool of *financial accounting* is the *profit and loss account* showing company performance over a particular period of time.

balance sheet ratios. Technique for measuring company and/or management performance by selecting appropriate ratios from the figures appearing in the *balance sheet*. Such ratios might include *profit* to *capital employed*, profit to sales, and current *assets* to *liabilities*, and might involve *stocks*, *working capital*, etc. Detailed balance sheet ratios include **a** liquidity and working capital ratios such as *current* ratio (or working capital ratio), *acid test ratio* (or liquid ratio or quick ratio), *gearing ratio*, and *debtors to sales ratio*, sales to fixed assets and sales to working capital or net current assets; **b** profitability ratios such as return on capital employed, and profit to sales; and **c** investment ratios such as dividend yield, ordinary *dividend cover, fixed interest cover, price/earnings ratio*, and *earnings* per share. See also *return on capital, return on assets managed, return on investments*, and *accounting ratios*.

balancing allowance. Deduction that may be made from taxable trading profits when the sale of an *asset* realizes a greater profit than the *written-down allowance* on it.

balancing charge. Sum that may be added to taxable trading profits if an *asset* is sold for a smaller profit than its *written-down allowance*.

balancing time. Changing working hours without changing the total hours worked. Limited and sometimes unofficial form of *flexible working hours*.

balloon note. Repayment of the major or a large part of a loan in a single payment, usually by *promissory note*, following smaller instalments.

Baltic Exchange (UK). More fully, the Baltic Mercantile and Shipping Exchange, which deals in shipping and air freight and chartering, and in grain.

banana republic. Name usually given to small tropical countries (eg Central American nations) which are dependent on their tropical fruit exports and typically on foreign capital as well. Term also used, often pejoratively, of any country similarly dependent on another.

Banca d'Italia. Italy's *central bank*, formed in 1893.

Banca Nationalà a Republicii Socialiste Romània. Romanian *central bank*, established originally in 1880.

Banco Central de Brasil. *Central bank* of Brazil, established in 1965.

Banco Central de la República Argentina. Argentinian *central bank*, established in 1935.

Banco de España. Bank of Spain, *central bank* established in 1829.

Banco de Portugal. Bank of Portugal, *central bank*, established in 1846.

band curve chart. Or cumulative band chart. Where the component parts of a whole are plotted on a graph, one above the other. The areas between the curves may then be shaded (see illustration) to show the composition of the whole. A band curve chart may be used to show the breakdown of production, sales, etc. See also *zone curve chart* and *surface chart*.

banded pack. Multiple package of products put together as a special sales offer or *sales promotion* measure.

banding. The rationalizing of pay structures and the substitution of a defined number of pay brackets or bands for a wide variety of separate rates. *Job evaluation* techniques are often used to establish which jobs should be placed within each band. The term 'broad banding' is sometimes used where a large range of jobs is placed within each band.

bandwidth. Term used in an application of *flexible working hours (fwh)* for the total working day of an establishment from earliest permitted starting time to the latest permitted finishing time. The bandwidth is composed of *core time* periods, when all

Bangladesh Bank

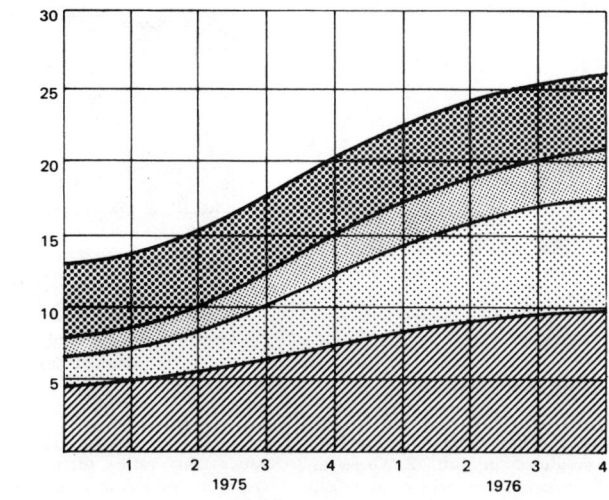

band curve chart

employees must be present, and *flexible time* periods, when employees choose their own working hours subject to completing their *daily contracted hours* (though there may be arrangements for carrying forward credit or debit balances of hours).

Bangladesh Bank. *Central bank*, established 1972.

bank draft. Or bank cheque (check) or demand draft. *Promissory note* issued by a bank.

banker's cheque (check). Cheque (check) drawn by a bank on another bank.

Bank for International Settlements (BIS) (Switzerland). Promotes cooperation between the *central banks* and provides back-up finance.

bank holiday. General term for a public holiday in the UK (literally, a day when the banks are not open for business). Cf *legal holiday* in the USA, etc.

Bank of Canada. Canadian *central bank* established in 1934.

Bank of China. See under *China, The People's Bank of* (central bank).

Bank of England. UK's *central bank*, acting as the government's banker and required to implement its financial and monetary policies, and to manage the national debt, the *Exchange Equalization Account* and transactions with other central banks and international agencies. The *Treasury* can give directives to the Bank of England which in turn can give directives to the *clearing banks*. The Bank of England was set up as a *joint stock company* by Act of Parliament in 1694. The Bank Charter Act 1844 divided the Bank between the issue department, issuing bank-notes and coins, and the banking department which handles bankers' *special deposits* and other deposits, the deposits of government departments and the Post Office Savings Bank, and some deposits from private customers. The Bank of England was nationalized in 1946.

Bank of Ghana. Ghanaian *central bank*, established in 1957.

Bank of Greece. Greek *central bank* formed in 1928.

bank rate. Rate of interest at which a country's *central bank* is prepared to lend to other banks. In the UK, bank rate had an immediate effect on short-term interest rates charged by *clearing banks*, etc until bank rate was officially ended as a UK institution in 1972 in favo(u)r of the less dramatic *minimum lending rate* system of the Bank of England. See also *Treasury Bills.*

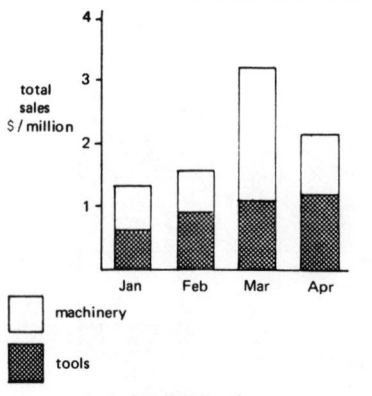

typical vertical bar chart

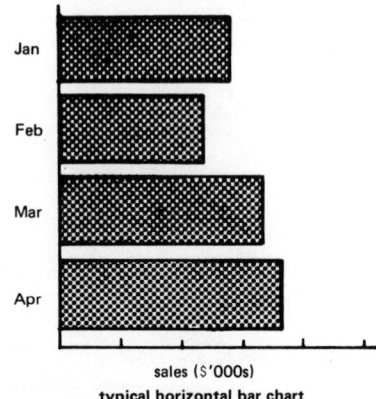

typical horizontal bar chart

bankruptcy. 1. Where a person is unable to pay his creditors in full. **2.** Where an individual or corporate debtor is judged legally insolvent. Any remaining property is thereafter administered for the creditors or distributed among them.

Banque de France. French *central bank*, established in 1800 and nationalized in 1946. It has some 260 branches in France.

Banque Nationale de Belgique. Belgian National Bank or *central bank*. Established in 1850.

Banque Nationale Suisse. National Bank of Switzerland, *central bank* established originally in 1905. Head Offices at Zürich and Berne plus various other offices. There are also some 30 cantonal banks.

bar. Generic term for lawyers practising as *attorneys* (US) or *barristers* (UK).

Barcelona Stock Exchange. Or *Bolsa de Barcelona*, one of the principal stock exchanges of Spain. See *Spanish stock exchanges*.

bar chart. Graphic representation of data (frequencies and magnitudes) by rectangles drawn to a scale proportional to the frequencies and magnitudes concerned. Developments of the bar chart are the *multiple bar chart* and the *component bar chart*. See *Gantt chart* and *histogram*.

bargain. 1. A contract or agreement based on negotiation. **2.** *Stock exchange* transaction between a *stockbroker* and a *stockjobber*.

bargaining creep. Edging forward of influence of *shop stewards* through piecemeal concessions, rather than through coherent *collective bargaining*. See also *workplace bargaining*.

bargaining range. Industrial relations term for the range within which a wage claim is likely to be settled, bearing in mind what the employees claim and the employers appear willing to offer.

bargaining scope. Range of items, *procedural* and/or *substantive*, to be covered by *collective bargaining* between management and *trade unions*; eg might extend beyond wages and hours of work to such matters as discipline, redundancy and scale of manning.

bargaining structure. Ground rules established in a company to facilitate bargaining between management and *trade unions*.

bargaining unit. Traditional term for unit of workers involved in *collective bargaining*.

barratry. 1. Legal term for a wilful misdemeanour by a ship's captain or crew against the interests of its owner or charterer. **2.** General legal term for stirring up quarrels or groundless lawsuits.

barrister. Qualified advocate who is a member of one of the UK Inns of Court and can plead in the higher courts. He does not deal directly with the client but through the client's *solicitor*. See also *attorney*.

Barth Premium Plan. *Payment-by-results* scheme developed in the USA by Carl G L Barth (1860-1939) based on relating *standard hours* produced to hours worked.

basal skin resistance (BSR)

See also *share of production plan*.

basal skin resistance (BSR). *Market research* term for the quality measured by a *psychogalvanometer (PSG)* in identifying people's reactions to products, *sales promotions*, etc. This equipment measures the electromagnetic change or basal resistance in a subject's skin on meeting the product or situation being tested, but its findings are not particularly sound scientifically in practical terms since it remains difficult to relate such electromagnetic change to particular emotions or feelings.

Basel Stock Exchange. Or *Börsenkammer des Basel-Stadt*, one of the principal stock exchanges of Switzerland. See *Swiss stock exchanges*.

base period. Reference point in time used for computation of index numbers or other measure of economic activity. For example, the level of a particular kind of activity might be taken to be 100 at a particular point in time, levels of activity at other times being given a number proportional to this figure. The base period is that for which the 100 figure applies.

BASIC. Acronym for *Beginners' All-purpose Symbolic Instruction Code*, an introductory *computer language* combining many of the facilities of more advanced languages such as *COBOL*, *ALGOL* and *FORTRAN*.

basic language. See *computer language*.

basic motion time (BMT). Akin to *predetermined motion time system*, BMT allows for such factors as distance, accuracy and force of movement. Established in Canada in the 1950s by P Presgrave and G B Bailey. See also *motion study*.

basic product. Or industrial product. Product marketed not to the public or consumer, but to industry as a component or constituent part in other products.

basic work data (BWD). *Work study* system akin to *predetermined motion time system* developed in the UK by British Rail, ICI and the Production Engineering Research Association.

BASIS. Booking and Sampling for Indirect Standards. See *clerical work evaluation*.

batch processing. Method of *computer* operation concentrating on one job at a time.

bear position

batch production. Manufacture of a quantity of a product but not in conditions of continuous or standardized production. Differs from the one-off production of *job production*, the standardized production of *mass production*, and the continuous production of *process production* or *assembly line* or *flow line production*.

'Battle of the Overpass'. Historic 1940 battle between *UAW* strikers and company police at the Ford Motor Company plant at River Rouge, USA. A year later, Henry Ford formally recognized the *UAW* under Walter Reuther.

'Battle of the Running Bulls'. Historic 1937 battle between police and strikers during a *UAW* sitdown strike at the General Motors plant at Flint, Michigan, USA.

battery. See *test battery*.

Bayesian statistics. Type of statistical analysis for decision making. Developed for translating subjective forecasts into mathematical probability curves. In many typical business situations there are no 'normal' statistical probabilities because alternatives are unknown or have not been tried before. Bayesian statistics use the best estimate of a given circumstance as if it were a firm probability.

BBA. Bachelor of Business Administration awarded by US universities.

BCTA. British-Canadian Trade Association.

BDA. *Bundesverband der deutschen Arbeitsgeberverbände* (the Confederation of German Employers' Federations).

B/E. *Bill of exchange.*

bear. Person who sells shares in the belief that their price is about to fall. He may then buy them back more cheaply. See also *bull*.

bearer bonds. Ones whose ownership can be transferred simply by handing over the bonds themselves. Attached to each bond is a sheet of coupons, one of which is removed on each *interest* date and presented for payment of the due interest. This operation is known as coupon clipping.

bear market. When the prices of shares generally are falling. Opposite to *bull market*.

bear position. Or short position. Where a

35

dealer in stocks, shares or commodities is committed to sell more of them than he has available for sale.

bed and breakfast deal. Type of *stock exchange* dealing in which investors establish tax losses to offset against *capital gains* by selling shares and then buying them back as a separate transaction.

Bedaux system. Early form of *payment-by-results* developed in the USA by C G Bedaux (1887-1944) and incurring considerable shopfloor disfavo(u)r, largely because it paid less than the *standard time* of later *work study*. See also *gain-sharing*.

Beginners' All-purpose Symbolic Instruction Code. *Computer language*, more commonly known as *BASIC*.

behavio(u)r. Response to stimulus from the internal or external environment. Influenced by perceptual ability in recognizing significance of the *stimulus*; by predetermining factors such as constitution, experience, interests and purposes — and by skill in responding appropriately. Cf *attitude* and *set*.

behavio(u)ral objectives. As *instructional objectives*.

behavio(u)ral science. Mainly psychological and sociological theories concerned with analyzing and explaining the behavio(u)r of the individual and the group in the working environment. Its applications cover such areas as communication, innovation, change, management styles, training and appraisal. The emphasis is on trying to establish an optimum working environment to which all can contribute effectively to realize both corporate and individual goals and aims.

behavio(u)r, interactive. See *interactive behavio(u)r*.

behavio(u)r, structural determinants of. See *structural determinants of behavio(u)r*.

behavio(u)r study. *Market research* statistical technique for assessing the behavio(u)r pattern and the opportunities existing in a particular market.

Belfast Stock Exchange. One of UK provincial stock exchanges. See also *Stock Exchange* (UK).

Belgian central bank. See *Banque Nationale de Belgique*.

Belgian chambers of commerce. See *Fédération Nationale des Chambres de Commerce et d'Industrie de Belgique*.

Belgian companies. There are seven legal forms of business organization under the Belgian Commercial Code, namely, **a** Partnership or *Société en Nom Collectif (SNC)* where all the partners are jointly and separately liable for the partnership liabilities; **b** Limited Partnership or *Société en Commandité Simple (SCS)*; **c** Partnership Limited by Shares or *Société en Commandité par Actions (SCA)* where certain partners are liable for the partnership debts while others are liable only up to the extent of their participation; **d** Joint Stock Company or *Société Anonyme (SA)* where shareholders are liable only to the extent of the capital subscribed (much the same as in the UK); **e** Private Limited Company or *Société de Personnes à Responsabilité Limitée (SPRL)* where shares are not negotiable and only individuals may hold shares; **f** Cooperative or *Société Coopérative*; **g** Credit Union or Union de Crédit.

Belgian employers' associations. See *Fédération des Industries Belges*.

Belgian General Federation of Trade Unions. See *Fédération Générale du Travail de Belgique* (FGTB).

Belgian income tax. Or *impôt des personnes physiques* or *personenbelasting*. There is also a *surcharge* on high incomes. There may also be additional local taxes — either **a** *centimes additionels* or *opeentiemen* or **b** *taxe communale additionelle* or *aanvullende gemeentebelasting*. Under these local taxes, a municipality of residence may levy a surcharge of not more than six per cent on an individual's income tax.

Belgian stock exchanges. Principal stock exchange of Belgium is the *Brussels Stock Exchange* or *la Bourse de Fonds Publics de Bruxelles*. The provincial stock exchanges are **a** Antwerp — Fondsen en Wisselbeurs van Antwerpen; **b** Ghent — Fondsen en Wisselbeurs van Gent; **c** Liège — Bourse de Fonds Publics de Liège.

Belgian trade unions. See *Fédération Générale du Travail de Belgique* (FGTB).

bell-horses. As *pacers*.

below-the-line promotion. Marketing term for *sales promotion* in such forms as reduced price special offers, premiums and point-of-sale displays. The term *above-the-*

belt and braces

line promotion, on the other hand, is used of sales promotion in the form of expenditure on *advertising* in the Press, on television or in other media.

belt and braces. Descriptive term for a policy involving initiating two separate courses of action either of which might be expected to achieve the desired objective if the other fails. Thus, if the belt does not keep the trousers up, the braces will — and vice versa.

benchmark jobs. Typical jobs in an organization used as examples or reference points against which other jobs can be compared by *ranking, job classification, points rating*.

benefit method of selling. Approach to selling that stresses the benefit to the *prospect* of buying the product or service.

Benelux. Link-up between Belgium, Luxembourg and the Netherlands that has passed through the stages of *customs union* (1947), a *Common External Tariff* (1948), a common trade and payments policy (1954), and *economic union* (1958-60).

Berliner Börse. Berlin Stock Exchange. See *German (Federal) stock exchanges*.

Bernreuter personality inventory. *Psychological inventory* developed in the USA for use in *temperament and personality tests*.

Besloten Vennootschap. Abb *BV*. A private or closed limited company under Netherlands law. Has become more common in recent years, particularly among family firms, as legislation has required more disclosure of information by the *Naamloze Vennootschap (NV)* or *joint stock company*.

Betriebsrat. *Works council* which is a legal requirement in Federal German industry under the *co-determination law*.

Better Business Bureaus. US voluntary consumer protection bodies concerned with maintaining ethical business standards. Grouped together since the 1970s in the Council of Better Business Bureaus Inc.

better conditions clause. Sometimes included in a *collective agreement* to the effect that any practices (practises) more favo(u)rable to employees than those spelt out in the agreement shall continue in force.

Beveridge Report (1942). UK report that presented proposals to the Government for a unified scheme of social insurance covering health, unemployment and industrial injuries. Lord Beveridge's proposal for a unified scheme of *flat-rate contributions* and *flat-rate benefits* was not implemented but it inspired the post-war 'welfare state'.

B/F. Brought forward.

Big Board. Governing body of the New York Stock Exchange. See *US stock exchanges*.

bill broker. Dealer in *bills of exchange*, etc.

billing. Gross turnover of an *advertising agency* over a given period.

bill of exchange (B/E). Defined in legal terms as a signed and unconditional order in writing addressed by one person to another requiring the person to whom it is addressed to pay on demand, or at a fixed or determinable future time, a sum certain in money to, or to the order of, a specified person or to bearer. A bill of exchange can be negotiated (that is, virtually used in lieu of cash or as evidence of ability to meet obligations elsewhere), or it can be discounted through a *discount house* (which purchases the bill of exchange immediately for an agreed sum less than the sum it will be worth when it matures), or it can be used as security for an advance made by a bank or an *acceptance house*. The personalities involved are the *drawer* who draws the bill; the *drawee* to whom the bill is addressed; the *payee* to whom it is payable; and, sometimes, an endorser who signs the back of the bill. This drawee is known as the acceptor once he accepts the bill. In the event of a bill being dishono(u)red after being discounted or used against an advance, the bank or discount house has a *right of recourse* against the drawer unless a bank has undertaken an obligation to pay the bill (that is, endorsed it) on behalf of the drawee. In this event the bank issues a *letter of credit* to the drawer who can then draw funds from the bank up to the sum stated in the bill of exchange. See also *eligible bills, irrevocable documentary acceptance credit,* and *time bill.*

bill of lading (B/L). Documentation relevant to a consignment of goods transported by ship, copies being sent ahead of the shipment to give proof of title to the consignor. Copies are also held by the exporter and sent with the goods.

bill of material. Document listing the materials and their quantities required for manufacturing or assembling a particular

37

product.

bill of sale (BS). Document transferring title to goods to another person or corporation though possession remains with the person making the transfer. It may be used to raise capital and on repayment of a loan the borrower retakes the title and ownership.

Bills Scheme. Operated by the *Export Credits Guarantee Department* in the UK. Under this Scheme an exporting firm can in certain circumstances be eligible for comprehensive guarantees of repayment against *bills of exchange* or *promissory notes* given directly by the ECGD to the firm's bank. Normally, the bank will then make advances against these guarantees. An extension of the Bills Scheme is the *Open Account Scheme* under which the ECGD makes guarantees to the exporting firm's bank in respect of short-term transactions on *open account terms*.

BIM. *British Institute of Management.*

binary notation. System used in *computers* in which all numbers are represented by combinations of the two digits, 0 and 1, the displacement of one digit to the left meaning multiplication by two instead of by ten as in the decimal system.

bin card. *Stock control* record card used by storekeepers, warehousemen, etc.

bio (US). Personal records or biographical details of a person. See also *curriculum vitae*.

biotechnology. As *ergonomics*.

BIS. 1. *Bank for International Settlements.* 2. *British Imperial System.*

bit. Contraction of binary digit. A single character in a binary number (see *binary notation*) or a unit of information within a *computer* storage device.

B/L. *Bill of lading.*

black capitalism. Term used to describe various policies (particularly in the USA in the late 1960s and early 70s) to increase the ownership and control of businesses by non-whites.

black-coated worker. As *white collar worker*.

black economy. Economic activities not recorded by official statistics, including transactions, such as wage payments, on which payment of tax is evaded illegally. This may happen, for example, in some cases of *moonlighting*.

blacking. Action of employees who during *industrial action* refuse to handle or work on goods or components that they consider are being processed or supplied by employers in a way which evades the industrial action. May take form of *sympathetic action* by workers in other organizations, or even industries, and may also continue after the end of the industrial action in which it began.

black-leg. Or *scab*. Worker who continues working during a *strike* or who takes a striker's place.

blanket agreement. *Collective agreement* resulting from *industry-wide bargaining* or *national bargaining*.

blanket coverage. Used particularly in *advertising* and *direct mail* to indicate promotions addressed to the public at large rather than to a specific target audience.

blanket market penetration. *Market penetration* over a wide range of the *market potential*.

blanket order. A standing order to supply certain products/services over time or against which specific quantities can be called for as required.

blind advertisement. Advertisement in which the advertiser does not reveal his name.

blind test. Test of consumer views of a product without revealing the identity of the product.

block. In data processing a group of words, digits or characters which are treated as forming a unit.

block check. Accounting/audit term for a detailed examination of a key part of the accounts of a company or organization. A block check may take the form of, for example, an examination of either **a** all account entries falling within a specified period; **b** all vouchers for amounts above a certain figure, or **c** all documents of a particular kind. See also *financial ratios*, *test in depth* and *volume checking*.

block design. 1. Form of *intelligence test* in

which the person being tested has to assemble coloured cubes to make up a given design. See also *psychological testing*. 2. *Market research* term for concentrating or clustering the sample used in a survey instead of using *random sampling*. The resulting *cluster sample* may be used as a *sampling point* and may be covered by, for example, a *canvass* or a *random walk*.

block diagram. Diagram presenting a macro view of a system, showing the overall relationships between its sub-systems.

blocked currency. Currency that may not be taken out of its country of origin, under the law of that country. A currency may be blocked for *balance of payments, exchange control* or political reasons.

block release. Releasing trainees from employment for blocks of time, usually of several weeks, for technical college studies. Something midway between *day release* and *sandwich courses*.

block vote. As *card vote*.

BLS Consumer Price Index. US cost-of-living index similar to UK *Retail Price Index*.

blue chip investment. One that is regarded as safe, though not actually *gilt-edged*. A blue chip investment is usually in *shares* in a well known and respected company.

blue collar trade union. Term sometimes used, particularly in the USA, for traditional manual worker *trade unions* to distinguish them from the growing *white collar trade unions* and *management trade unions*.

blue collar worker. As *manual worker*. See also *grey area occupations* and *white collar worker*.

blue-eyed boys. Employees regarded (particularly by other employees) as receiving favoured treatment from management.

blue laws. US laws which restrict the transaction of business on Sundays.

blue sky bargaining. Term used particularly in the USA of the making of totally unrealistic claims in *collective bargaining* etc.

blue sky laws. Federal or state legislation (US) governing the sale of stock and securities.

BMT. *Basic motion time.*

board of directors. Senior executives appointed by the shareholders to run a company. The activities and responsibilities of the board of directors are regulated by the company's *articles of association*. Directors may or may not themselves be shareholders.

Board of Education (Sweden). Runs over 300 basic industrial training courses, from operator to technologist level, at special training centres. The courses are used by the *Labour Market Board*.

body shop. US slang term for an *employment agency*.

bogey. US term from early days of *payment-by-results* schemes for the unofficial production target which a work group sets itself when it has loose *piece work* rates and restricts its effort and output, or indulges in *quota restriction*, for fear of management introducing *rate cutting*.

Bologna Stock Exchange. One of ten *Italian stock exchanges*.

Bolsa de Barcelona. Barcelona Stock Exchange, one of the principal stock exchanges of Spain. See *Spanish stock exchanges*.

Bolsa de Comercio Bogotá. Bogotá Stock Exchange, Colombia.

Bolsa de Comercio. See *Argentinian stock exchanges*.

Bolsa de Comercio (Buenos Aires). Buenos Aires Stock Exchange.

Bolsa de Comercio de Caracas. The principal stock exchange in Venezuela.

Bolsa de Comercio de Lima. Lima Stock Exchange.

Bolsa de Lisboa. Lisbon Stock Exchange. See *Portuguese stock exchanges*.

Bolsa de Madrid. Madrid Stock Exchange. See *Spanish stock exchanges*.

Bolsa de Porto. Oporto Stock Exchange. See *Portuguese stock exchanges*.

Bolton Report on Small Firms. *Report of the Committee of Inquiry on Small Firms Cmnd 4811* published Nov 1971 in UK. The report was concerned with the role, problems and needs of firms having fewer than 200 employees.

Bombay Stock Exchange. See *Indian stock exchanges*.

bond. 1. *Debenture* or *mortgage* (eg *bearer bonds*). **2.** Guarantees to pay a sum or perform a contract.

bonded goods. Goods held in a *bonded warehouse*.

bonded warehouse. Where goods intended for re-export are deposited in the custody of customs officers immediately on importation if the importer wishes to avoid payment of customs duty or other taxes such as purchase tax or value added tax. Before despatching goods from a bonded warehouse, an exporter has to complete a combined form of shipping bill and removal warrant and present it to the customs officers in time for them to make an official examination of the goods at the warehouse.

bond rating (US). Assessment of a *corporation's* ability to meet interest payments and redemption on a *bond*.

bonus earnings. Earnings over and above hourly paid rate or basic salary.

bonus schemes. Arrangements for relating *bonus earnings* to performance measured in terms of output, profits, sales or some individual target. The scheme will contain some formula for relating the reward to performance. An effective scheme should satisfy the following criteria: **a** there should be a clear relationship between effort and reward; **b** bonus should be high enough to provide adequate incentive; **c** bonus earning should not fluctuate too widely; **d** formula should not be changed arbitrarily.

bonus shares. Issue of additional free (scrip) *shares* to existing shareholders in proportion to their holdings when a company has built up considerable capital reserves in relation to the size of its *nominal capital* and its *board of directors* may decide to capitalize its reserves. See also *rights issue* for when a company is seeking new capital.

boodle. Counterfeit money or money obtained by corrupt or underhand dealings.

book debts. Amounts due from debtors.

Booking and Sampling for Indirect Standards. Abbr BASIS. See *clerical work evaluation*.

book inventory. Theoretical level of stocks or inventory based on records of existing stocks plus incoming goods less outgoing goods. As it is not based on a physical count of the stock items the book inventory figures will not reveal errors, pilfering, etc.

bookless accounting. As *slip system*.

book rate of return. Alternative term for *return on capital* or *accountant's return*.

book value. Value at which a company or asset(s) is shown in the accounting records. Book value is usually the written down value of the asset(s) taking into account original cost less accumulated *depreciation*. It should be distinguished from the *replacement* or *intrinsic market value*.

boom. Natural consequence in a *laissez-faire economy* of conditions of *inflation* in which prices rise faster than *real incomes*. The boom comes as firms reach a crescendo of competition for rare resources of *labour* and materials, pushing up costs, money, incomes, profits, and prices. The boom crashes when confidence and prices collapse before end-products can be sold, when a rush to sell shares brings on a falling or *bear market*, and when bottlenecks in supplies or a *balance of payments* crisis (competition for resources in boom conditions leads to increases in imports) leads to *lay-off* of workers.

Theoretically, the ending of a mild boom might have a cautionary effect on the community leading to a pegging of incomes and the holding down of price increases in what is called *disinflation*. In practice in a laissez-faire economy, however, when a boom crashes it is natural for businessmen to get shares and interests off their hands quickly before prices fall further, thus accelerating *deflation* and unemployment leading to a *slump* and *mass unemployment*. See also *trade cycle*.

booster training. Training to improve performance in current job, particularly the performance of the less productive workers in a unit. Sometimes known as *productivity training*. Cf *refresher training, updating training, upgraded training*.

bootstrap financing. Any method of generating cash flow without recourse to external sources. Includes converting fixed assets into cash, reducing overhead costs, and the prudent use of trade credit facilities.

Bordeaux Stock Exchange. See *Bourse de Bordeaux*.

borrowing allocation. Limit to which an organization is authorized to raise capital to meet its *capital expenditure* programme, this limit being fixed by its board of directors or other governing body or council.

borrowing time. Where under a *payment-by-results* scheme a worker uses time allocated for one task to push ahead with or complete another task.

Borsa Valori di Firenze. Florence Stock Exchange.

Borsa Valori de Genova. Genoa Stock Exchange.

Borsa Valori di Milano. Milan Stock Exchange, the principal one in Italy. See *Italian stock exchanges.*

Borsa Valori di Napoli. Naples Stock Exchange.

Borsa Valori di Palermo. Palermo Stock Exchange.

Borsa Valori di Turino. Turin Stock Exchange.

Börsenagent. Trader on one of the *Swiss stock exchanges.*

Börsenkammer des Basel-Stadt. *Basel Stock Exchange*, one of the principal *Swiss stock exchanges.*

Börsenkommissar. See *Börsenkommissariat.*

Börsenkommissariat. Body through which the canton of Zürich exercises its statutory control over the *Zürich Stock Exchange.* The executive responsible for implementing this control is the *Börsenkommissar.*

Börsenordnung. Stock Exchange Regulations applying in each of the Federal *German stock exchanges.*

Börsenvorstand. Stock Exchange Board responsible for running a Federal *German stock exchange.*

Börseräte. Members of the Council of the *Vienna Stock Exchange.*

Börse, Wiener. *Wiener Börse* or *Vienna Stock Exchange.*

börsombud. Members' agents approved by the *Stockholm Stock Exchange* Council as persons allowed to deal on the trading floor.

Boston Stock Exchange. One of about 20 major *US stock exchanges.* For address see

BOTB. *British Overseas Trade Board.*

BOTEX. *British Office for Training Exchange.*

bottom-up management. Term coined by William B Givern Jr in the USA for the responsibility and relationship down the *chain of command* as distinct from the more commonly recognized upward relationship.

bought in (or out) goods. Components purchased to be built into a company's products or *finished goods.* See also *stock control.*

Boulwarism. Form of *collective bargaining* named after a sometime vice-president of the General Electric Company in the USA. By this method the company makes its analysis of what it considers constitutes reasonable payment and refuses to bargain further unless further evidence is produced by the *trade unions* involved. Boulwarism has been severely criticized by the *National Labor Relations Board* as being against the spirit of the *Taft-Hartley Act.*

bourse. *Stock exchange* and/or *commodity market.* A word of French origin subsequently adopted or adapted in other lands and other tongues.

Bourse de Bordeaux. Bordeaux Stock Exchange.

Bourse de Fonds Publics de Bruxelles. *Brussels Stock Exchange.*

Bourse de Fonds Publics de Liège. Liège Stock Exchange.

Bourse de Lausanne. *Lausanne Stock Exchange.*

Bourse de Lille. Lille Stock Exchange.

Bourse de Luxembourg. Luxembourg Stock Exchange.

Bourse de Lyons. Lyons Stock Exchange. See *French stock exchanges.*

Bourse de Marseille. Marseille Stock Exchange. See *French stock exchanges.*

Bourse de Nancy. Nancy Stock Exchange. See *French stock exchanges.*

Bourse de Nantes. Nantes Stock Exchange.

See *French stock exchanges*.

Bourse de Paris. Principal French stock exchange. Established 1801. See also *French stock exchanges* and *Paris Stock Exchange*.

Bourse de Toulouse. Toulouse Stock Exchange. See *French stock exchanges*.

Bourse de Valeurs. See *Paris Stock Exchange* and *French stock exchanges*.

Bourse de Valeurs d'Alexandria. Alexandria Stock Exchange. One of two Egyptian stock exchanges.

Box-Jenkins techniques. Type of *exponential smoothing* techniques which, with computer aid, are used to improve forecasting and to take into account variations from earlier forecasts.

boycott. Refusal to take part in an activity or to use a product or service. See *primary boycott, secondary boycott* for meaning in industrial relations terms.

bracket tariff. See *forked tariff*.

Brad. *British Rate and Data*.

brain drain. Loss of skilled manpower from a country through emigration.

brainstorming. Or *buzz groups*. Bombardment of ideas between small groups of people uninhibitedly suggesting solutions, whether outlandish or well informed, to various problems. Good therapy for participants and can produce the occasional breakthrough idea that might otherwise never be touched on. Brainstorming may be used to help solve a wide range of management problems or for longer term purposes such as *technological forecasting*. Other techniques used for the latter purpose include the *Delphi approach, exploratory forecasting techniques, morphological research, normative forecasting techniques,* the *scenario writing approach*, and *technological trend extrapolation*.

branch and bound technique. Algorithmic decision-making technique originally devised in the early 1960s to identify optimum routes for salesmen.

branching network. Used in *network analysis* or *critical path* planning where the management of a project is left free to make a choice of *activities* at some points in the light of experience gained on the job. A branching network may provide for management to have discretion to attempt a particular method or activity but then switch to a different method if the first approach is unfruitful.

branching program(me). See *intrinsic branching program(me)*. Term used in *programmed instruction, teaching machines*, etc.

brand. Merchandise or service sold under proprietary or *trade mark* name.

brand awareness. Degree to which a *brand* or proprietary name is recognized by those in the market for such goods.

branded goods. Goods carrying the supplier's *brand* name.

brand leader. Product or brand that is an established leader in its field, or is marketed according to a strategy that assumes it is a leader. Such a strategy is likely to be quite different from that for a *market follower* introduced to compete with existing products, and different again from the strategy for a *pioneer product* of new design and/or function.

brand manager. Executive responsible for coodinating the marketing and related strategy for a particular product or range of products. Brand manager is sometimes synonymous with *product manager*, though the latter may be used of an executive concerned with a generic product rather than a particular brand or label.

Brazilian central bank. *Banco Central de Brasil.*

Brazilian stock exchanges. There are two stock exchanges a São Paulo; b Rio de Janeiro.

breakage. Allowance made for damaged or broken goods.

breakdown maintenance. Corrective operations carried out on machinery which has failed but for which advance provision has been made in the form of spares, materials etc.

break-even analysis. Determining of *break-even points* and the relationship between costs, volume of output, sales revenue and rate of profit. See *break-even chart*.

break-even chart. Management aid for identifying the relationship between *costs*, volume of output and *profit*, as shown in the examples (a) (b) (c) and (d) on pages 44-45.

It pinpoints the *break-even point*, the crossover point between making a *loss* and making a *profit*. A break-even chart also illustrates *fixed costs* and *variable costs*, the rate at which profit may be earned (the *angle of incidence*, the *profit wedge*, the *margin of safety* and the *losses wedge* become important here), and the *contribution*.

The vertical axis shows costs and revenue (or income) while the horizontal axis shows units or amount of sales or, sometimes, production. If amount of production, rather than sales, is indicated on the horizontal axis it becomes very important that management takes into account the effect of any goods produced but not yet sold (until they are sold they cannot produce profit). Indeed, more complex versions of the break-even chart may be used in analysis of the effect of such goods held in store or in process of distribution between being produced and being sold. The example of sales is illustrated here.

The class intervals or spacings marked out on the horizontal axis may be units of sales (eg x number of units) or value of sales (£y worth). In practice, it is usually preferable to use the latter unless a single product or size of product is being produced though, on the other hand, costs on the vertical axis are usually easier to attribute accurately to units of products than to value. Alternatively, the horizontal axis may be divided up in percentages of total production and/or sales capacity.

The break-even chart is a valuable management tool. However, management should be on guard against oversimplification. For example, fixed costs may in practice be *stepped costs*, perhaps giving an effect something like that illustrated in break-even chart (c). Many other variations are possible in the use of break-even charts, including the cash break-even chart (d). See also *contribution analysis*.

break-even point. 1. Point where a company or product's sales revenue equals its total cost (both *fixed costs* and *variable costs*) and there is neither *profit* nor *loss*. See *break-even chart*. **2.** Point where all the money invested in a project or enterprise (both initial or *start-up costs* and cumulative running costs) has been recovered and the cumulative value of *cash flow* is zero. The period until break-even is achieved is sometimes known as the *pay-out period*. The extent to which target and/or actual performance exceeds the break-even point is the *margin of safety*. See also *committed costs* and *managed costs*.

break-up value. Or liquidating value. Cash value of the assets of a company or corporation if it were to go out of business.

Bremen Wertpapierbörse. Bremen Stock Exchange. See *German (Federal) stock exchanges*.

Bretton Woods Conference. Conference of 44 countries held at Bretton Woods, USA, in July 1944 by the United Nations Monetary and Financial Conference. The Bretton Woods Conference did not accept the view of Lord Keynes (UK) and Harry Dexter White (USA) that it should create a strong central bank to combat far-reaching financial crises. Instead, the Conference gave birth to the *International Bank for Reconstruction and Development* (the *World Bank*) and the *International Monetary Fund* as independent organizations having a special relationship with the *United Nations Organization*. See also the work of *UNESCO*.

brick-by-brick forecasting. Used particularly in *marketing and sales forecasting* where it is an unsophisticated averaging out of views and opinions expressed by salesmen and customers.

brick areas. Sales territories broken down into areas having similar market potential based on population, outlets, etc.

Bridlington Principles 1939. Aimed at sorting out disagreements between UK trade unions over *recognition disputes* or allegations of 'poaching' of members or of *negotiating rights* by referring such allegations to the Disputes Committee of the *Trades Union Congress*. Principles further developed by the *Croydon Procedure* of 1969. See also *jurisdictional dispute, multi-unionism*.

Brisbane Stock Exchange. One of six members of the *Australian Associated Stock Exchanges*.

Brisch classification. Range of classification and coding systems developed to cover every facet of the activities of an engineering organization, including men, materials, operations, components, assemblies, products, tools, plant and scrap. The systems aim to give every item a meaningful and unique identity and provide a common language throughout an organization. There are two basic types of Brisch systems — monocode and polycode. See also *classification and coding systems*.

Bristol fashion. In good order, a term

43

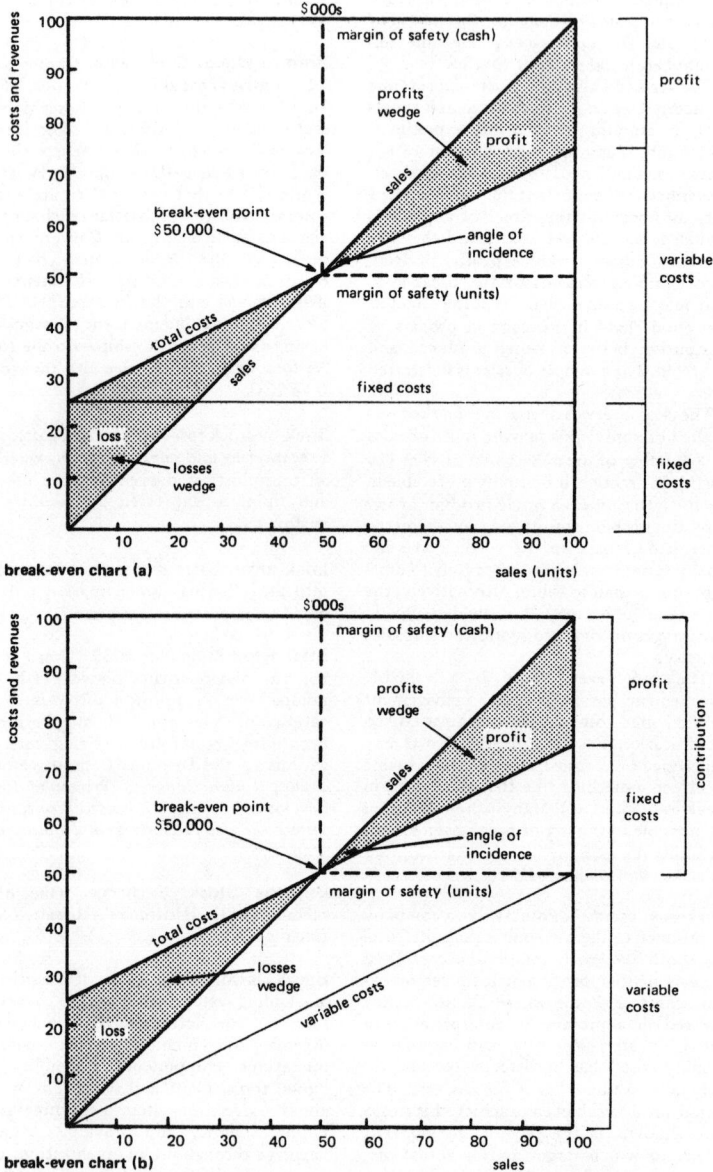

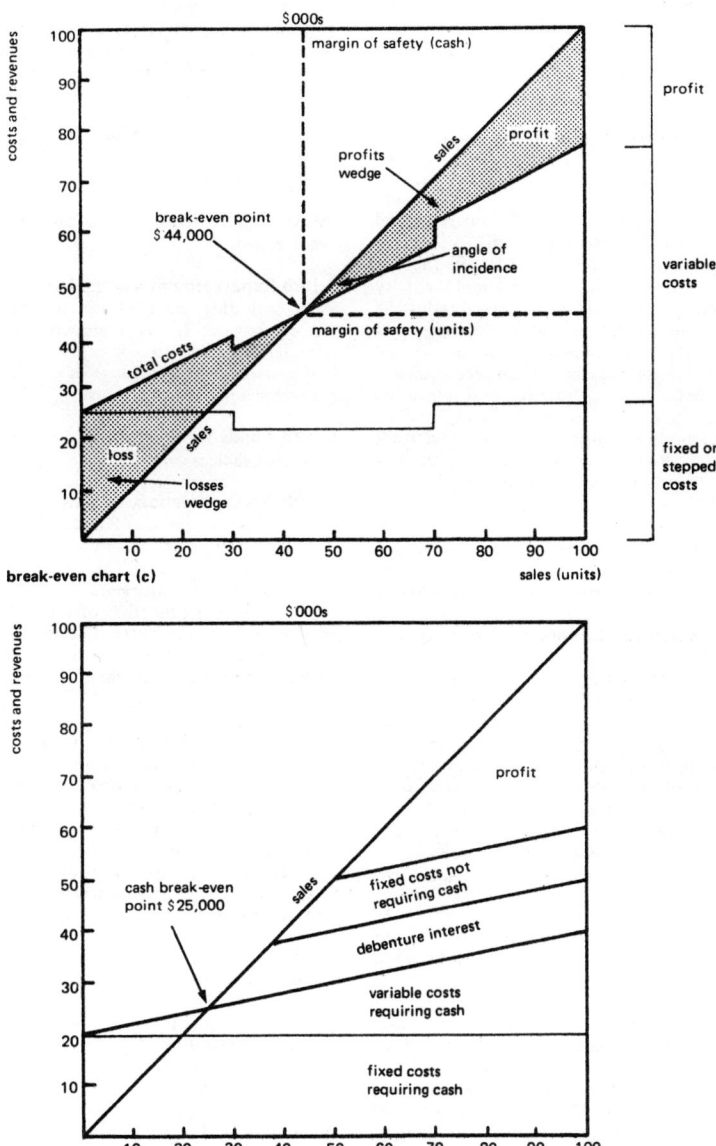

originating from the days when Bristol (UK) was a leading world port.

British. See also entries under *UK*.

British Airports Authority. UK Government agency responsible to the *Department of Trade* for promoting the civil air transport industry and airport facilities.

British-American Chamber of Commerce. Established 1920 to promote trade between the two countries.

British Association for Commercial and Industrial Education (BACIE). Voluntary organization, founded in 1919 in the UK and registered as an educational charity which specializes in all aspects of industrial and commercial education. Members of BACIE include individuals, industrial and commercial firms, government departments, industrial training boards, local education authorities, universities, colleges, professional bodies, trade associations and trade unions. BACIE is responsible for running the *British Office for Training Exchange (BOTEX)*.

British Business Graduates Society. UK organization formed in 1973 to promote the cause and status of business graduates.

British Business Schools. See *Franks Report*.

British Calibration Service. Provides UK Government-backed Certificates of Calibration and BCS badges for measuring instruments through laboratories specially approved by the Service. Laboratories approved in this way are in industrial organizations, Government and other research establishments, universities, etc. The advice of the BCS is available, not only to UK firms, but to prospective overseas buyers of British goods.

British-Canadian Trade Association. Operates from London to promote trade between the two countries.

British Commonwealth. See *Commonwealth (of Nations)*.

British Computer Society. Professional body founded in 1957. Grades of membership are Fellow (FBCS), Member (MBCS). Associate, Student and Applicant.

British Consultants Bureau. UK non-profit making body set up with Government backing in 1965 to promote the overseas work of UK consultants in agriculture, architecture, economics, education, engineering, industry, management, planning, surveying and other professions. The Bureau maintains liaison with international agencies, trade missions, finance houses and government departments, and assists in the formation of consortia. See also *Management Consultants Association* and *Overseas Finance and Projects Division (DTI)*.

British Employers' Confederation. Founder component, July 1965, of the *Confederation of British Industry*.

British Export Board. See *British Overseas Trade Board*.

British Export Houses Association. Organization including most of the leading UK export houses in its membership. The Association can advise UK exporters on the best choice of *export house* or *confirming house* for a particular purpose.

British Funds (or Stocks). UK *Government securities*, such as *consols*.

British Gas Corporation. Established 1 January 1973 under the *Gas Act 1972* to take over the running of the industry from the then Area Gas Boards. The Corporation's statutory responsibilities include that for the training and education of the 115,000 employees in the industry. Because of this, the *Secretary of State for Employment* decided to phase out the Gas Industry Training Board after July 1973.

British Imperial System (or Units) (BIS). System of units of measurement from which the *US Customary System* was derived, though the two systems vary at some points (for example, in liquid measurement). Both systems have the foot and the pound weight as basic units, and both are being superseded (particularly in scientific and technical work) by the *International System (SI)*.

British Institute of Management. Professional body founded in 1947 as independent, non-political and non-profit making organization. Provides information, publications and training services. Incorporates Management Research Groups, Centre for Physical Distribution Management, Centre for Farm Management and Asset Management Group.

British Insurance Association. Professional and advisory body.

British National Export Council. Forerunner of the *British Overseas Trade Board* (until the latter's formation on 1 January 1972).

British Office for Training Exchange (BOTEX). Secretariat operated by the *British Association for Commercial and Industrial Education* with government support to encourage British employers to second staff to overseas companies for specific training.

British Overseas Trade Board (BOTB). Established in May 1971 (being known until 1 March 1972 as the *British Export Board*) to make export promotion work relevant to the real needs of industry and commerce. Members of the BOTB are businessmen together with a representative of each of the three Government departments responsible for day-to-day export promotion work, namely, the Departments of Trade and Industry and the Foreign and Commonwealth Office.

British pavilions. Organized by the *Fairs and Promotions Branch* of the *Department of Trade* at certain international *trade fairs*. Exhibition space is made available in the pavilions to manufacturers and suppliers of UK goods and services at special rates. *British Weeks* are solely British trade fairs overseas.

British Productivity Council. Independent, self-financing UK body set up in 1952 (originally with government support) by both sides of industry to stimulate interest in methods of increasing productivity. The BPC is sponsored by the *Confederation of British Industry*, the *Department of Industry*, the *National Economic Development Office*, and the *Trades Union Congress*.

British Psychological Society. Professional and qualifying body for *occupational psychologists* (and clinical and educational psychologists).

British Rate and Data. Or, colloquially, 'Brad'. A monthly publication giving comprehensive current information on UK advertising media and rates. Media covered include newspapers, magazines and journals, yearbooks, television, radio, cinema, theatres, public transport and other outdoor advertising.

British Standards Institution. UK custodian of standards of measurement, nomenclature, safety, product performance, etc in virtually all areas of industrial, commercial

and professional activity. The Institution represents the UK on the *International Organization for Standards*. See also *American National Standards Institute Inc.*

British United Provident Association (BUPA). Provides its subscribers with private medical care in sickness or injury.

British Weeks. Major promotions or *trade fairs* organized by the *Fairs and Promotions Branch* of the *Department of Trade* to stimulate retail sales of British consumer goods — and to a lesser extent, capital goods — in selected overseas cities. A variation on a British Week is a British Shopping Week when the Branch, in cooperation with *Diplomatic Service Commercial Officers Overseas*, supports the local stores in an overseas town in promoting British goods.

broad-banded salary structure. Salary structure with a relatively small number of grades. A structure with a large number of grades is a *multi-grade salary structure*.

broad banding. See *banding*.

broker. Person who acts as an agent for others. For example, *insurance broker* and *stockbroker*.

brokerage. Payment made to a *broker* by his principal for the carrying out of buying or selling of goods, *shares*, etc.

brokerage house. Term used particularly in the USA for a partnership or company that acts as a broker for transactions in *stocks, shares, bills of exchange*, etc.

brokers' contract notes. Signed confirmation by *brokers* to their principals that their instructions have been carried out, whether buying or selling.

Brownlow Committee (US). Committee which reported to President Roosevelt in 1937 and is usually recognized as the first body to have advocated the use of management techniques in public administration. Its contribution is often compared with those in the UK of the 1961 *Plowden Report on the Control of Public Expenditure*, the *Fulton Report* and the 1967 *Redcliffe-Maud Report on the Management of Local Government*. The Brownlow Committee reported: 'Good management will promote in the fullest measure the conservation and utilization of our national resources and spell this out plainly in social justice, security, order, liberty, prosperity, in material benefit and in higher values of life'.

Brown-Spearman formula. Method of validating an *intelligence test*, particularly when its length has been increased and the validity of the extended test needs to be checked. See also *psychological testing*.

Brussels Stock Exchange. Or *Bourse de Fonds Publics de Bruxelles*. Founded originally in 1801, it lists a particularly high proportion of foreign companies at present but, on balance, is not a very active exchange. There are smaller *Belgian stock exchanges* at Antwerp, Ghent, and Liège. All public funds in Belgium are subject to control by the *Commission Bancaire*. The Brussels Stock Exchange is run by the Stock Exchange Committee, or *Commission de la Bourse*. Brokers authorized to operate are *Agents de Change*, and corresponding brokers, *Agents de Change Correspondants*, may also deal but only through the intermediary of an Agent de Change. A *Commission d'Appel* has jurisdiction over all four Belgian stock exchanges. See also *Belgian companies*.

Brussels Treaty Organization. Established by a defence, economic and cultural pact in March 1948 between Belgium, France, Luxembourg, the Netherlands and the UK. Expanded in May 1955 and became the *Western European Union*.

BS. 1. Balance sheet. **2.** Bill of sale.

BSI. *British Standards Institution*.

BSR. *Basal skin resistance*.

bucket shop. Old and informal term for a *brokers'* house of doubtful respectability.

budget. 1. Statement in quantitative and usually financial terms of the planned allocation and use of resources. **2.** An itemized list of expected income and expenditure for a specific future period. See *budgetary control*.

budget allocation. Amount of expenditure or income for a given financial or accounting period set down within a budget. See *capital appropriation*.

budgetary control. Means of controlling the activities of a business by forecasting future levels of activity and converting these into quantitative and ultimately monetary terms. Once the final budget is agreed it becomes a plan against which actual costs, revenue and performance are periodically reviewed and compared with the budget. This provides a systematic means of control enabling variances from budget to be monitored, corrective action — if necessary — taken or budgets to be revised. See also *fixed budget, flexible budget, master budget* and *standard costing*.

budget centre (center). Section of an organization that has its own *budget* for *budgetary control* purposes.

budget determination. Consideration and decision-making on the size of a budget.

Budget Treaty 1970. With full implementation of the *Treaty of Rome 1957*, the Budget Treaty 1970 regularized the *common budget* of the *Common Market* as controlled by the *European Commission*.

Buenos Aires Stock Exchange. Bolsa de Comercio (Buenos Aires). The principal Argentinian stock exchange.

buffer stock. Marginal quantity of materials or goods kept in store to safeguard against unpredictable shortages in further deliveries or to meet exceptional demand. Also known as reserve stock or safety stock.

bug. Fault or mistake in the design of a procedure, system or computer program. See also *debugging*.

building society. Financial institution (UK) in which the public invest money, these funds then being lent to house purchasers in the form of *mortgages* on freehold or leasehold property. The Building Societies Act 1962 legislates on the way in which building societies are run. The building societies' own professional organization is the Building Societies Institute.

build schedule. Statement and record of the modifications made to a project as it progresses, listing all drawings and other documentation. May be based on the original *product drawing list*.

built-in obsolescence. Inclusion in a product's design of factors which ensure that it will need to be replaced after a certain period of time. This obsolescence may be built in by use of materials of limited durability or by stylistic changes in later models that put a 'keeping-up-with-the-Joneses' type of pressure on the *consumer*. The application of built-in obsolescence is peculiar to certain *consumer durables*, such as cars. Built-in obsolescence is sometimes known as *planned obsolescence* though this latter term implies greater precision and control than is usually the case.

Bulawayo Stock Exchange. The Zimbabwean Stock Exchange. One of two *Zimbabwean stock exchanges*.

Bulgarian central bank. See *Bulgarska Narodna Banka*.

Bulgarian Chamber of Commerce. Responibilities include promoting export trade. Export/import trade is also handled by the Ministry of Foreign Trade.

Bulgarian Trade Unions, Central Council of. Covers 13 *trade unions* which have approximately 2,600,000 members.

Bulgarska Narodna Banka. Bulgarian National Bank, or *central bank*. Originally established in 1879.

bull. Person who buys *shares*, in the expectation that their price will rise in the short term so that a profit can be made. The opposite of a bull is a *bear*.

bull market. When the prices of *shares* generally are rising. Opposite of *bear market*.

bull position. Or long position. Situation of a dealer who is in the position of having more of a *commodity* or *securities* than he is able to sell.

bull weeks. When absenteeism is low in a factory and output high. In most industries, weeks just before holiday periods are seen as potential bull weeks when employees are particularly keen to earn high wages.

bumper strike. Now largely outdated type of *industrial action* in which strikers are directly supported financially by similar workers in other factories.

bumping. 1. Replacement of an employee by another who formerly held a more senior post particularly when current jobs become redundant. May extend as a chain reaction to other employees in lower grades. **2.** Demotion or dismissal of employees under pressure of contraction of business.

Bundesarbeitsgerichte. See *Arbeitsgerichte*.

Bundeskammer der gewerblichen Wirtschaft. Austrian Federal Economic Chamber, or *Chamber of Commerce*. It is linked with a chamber of commerce in each of the nine federal provinces, and has approximately 250,000 members

Bundeskammer der gewerblichen Wirtschaft (Sektion Industrie). Central *employers' association* in Austria. Established in 1896.

Bundesverband der Deutschen Industrie. Federation of German Industries.

Bundesvereinigung der Deutschen Arbeitsgeberverbände. Confederation of German *Employers' Associations* linked with 13 regional associations and 43 trade associations.

BUPA. *British United Provident Association.*

burden cost. As *indirect cost.*

bureaucratic organization. Term originated by Max Weber for describing typical government organization (though many large industrial and commercial concerns exhibit the same characteristics). The typical features of a bureaucratic organization include **a** vertical authority pattern; **b** maximum specialization; **c** close definitions as to duties, privileges and boundaries; **d** decisions based on expert judgment resting on technical knowledge and on disciplined compliance with the directives of superiors; **e** maximum use of rules; **f** impersonal administration of staff; **g** employment constituting a lifelong career for officials. See also *mechanistic organization*.

Bureau of Economic Analysis. *US Department of Commerce* agency responsible for providing and publishing statistical data on aggregate economic activity, manufacturing, and trade *inventories*, *gross national product*, income, industrial production, *balance of payments*, foreign investment, lending indicators, merchandise trade, *capital expenditure*, manufacturing capacity utilization, prices by type of expenditure, corporate *profits*, regional analysis, and personal and corporate savings and *investment.*

Bureau of Labor Statistics. Operating within the *US Department of Labor*, the Bureau provides statistical data on labo(u)r economics, labo(u)r-management relations, *productivity*, technological development, occupational safety and health, and the structure and growth of the economy. The Bureau publishes monthly, quarterly and annual reports on statistical trends, including the consumer price index.

Bureau of the Census. *US Department of Commerce* agency which conducts surveys and censuses. It collects, analyzes, publishes and distributes statistical data on social and economic activities for use by business, government and the public. See also *Bureau of Economic Analysis*.

Bureau of International Labor Affairs US. Division of the *US Department of Labor* concerned with protecting the interests of American employees in trade and tariff matters. Organizes skills retraining program(me)s to assist employees made redundant as a result of importing cheaper foreign goods.

Bureau of Standards. US Government agency attached to the *US Department of Commerce* and established in 1901. Concerned with all aspects of pure and applied measurement and establishment of standards of performance. See also *American National Standards Institute*.

Bureau of the Budget. US Government department with responsibility for integrating the plans of the different departments of government to produce national budgeting.

Bürolandschaft. As *open office planning*.

business agent. 1. As *agent*. **2.** US full time *trade union* official having negotiating and treasurer responsibilities at local level.

business criterion. As *commercial criterion* (management technique in public administration).

business game. Enactment by students or trainees of business situations based on presentation of skilfully selected information followed by progressive decision making leading to assessment of profitability and other crucial factors. Sometimes involves use of a computer. Often played competitively by teams, particularly in management training. Adjudication can be human or computerized. Sometimes known as management game.

Business Graduates Association. UK charitable association with corporate and individual members (approx 1,250 in 1974). Concerned with improving business education, assisting employers with advice on graduate employment.

business indicators. Statistical data on factors likely to have an effect on the level of business activity. Indicators with a forecasting value are known as leaders; those contemporaneous with the business activity are coincidents; while those that only become apparent after the activity are known as laggers.

business interruption insurance. Insurance against loss of business income following a break in production caused by such mishaps as explosion or fire.

business name. Name under which a person or organization trades and, under most legal systems, has to register. May be related to a trade mark.

business planning. Analysis of the objectives of all aspects of a company's business in order to determine research and development, manufacturing, marketing and acquisition programmes necessary to achieve the objectives and the financial and manpower resources required to carry out the programmes. See also *corporate planning*.

business purpose. Defined by *Drucker* as 'to create a customer'.

business ratios. As *management ratios*.

business unionism US. *Trade union* philosophy and practice (practise) of selling labo(u)r to the highest bidder.

'Business Week'. US journal established 1929.

busy-work. As *make-work*.

butty system. Early form of *labour-only subcontracting* in which the 'butty' was the gang leader who was paid by the employer/ contractor and who in turn paid wages to the members of the gang. The butty system was sometimes operated on a family basis with the head of the family as the butty. See also *gang system* and the *lump*.

buyer. Executive with responsibilities in the field of *purchasing* and *procurement*.

buyer credit. Credit allowed by a bank etc , to enable an individual or company to purchase goods or services. This is distinct from *supplier credit*.

buying. See *purchasing*.

buying behavio(u)r. Way in which a buyer behaves when deciding whether or not to buy a product or service and the factors that determine the behavio(u)r. These include rational and emotional factors, the life style of the purchaser and the particular *product life cycle*. See also *organismic theory*.

buzz groups. As *brainstorming*.

buzz-word. Pejorative way of describing the frequent use of fashionable management terms by those who do not necessarily understand their full meaning.

BV. Or *Besloten Vennootschap*, a private or closed limited company under Netherlands law. See also *Netherlands companies*.

bye-turnman. Person employed in *casual labo(u)r*.

by-product. Product which is not the main purpose or product for which a business or process is operated but is produced to optimize the total operation and/or take advantage of what would otherwise be waste material.

byssinosis. Lung disease allied to silicosis encountered amongst workers engaged in the manufacture of cotton products.

51

C

ca'canny. Type of *go-slow* or *goldbricking*. See also *irritation strike*.

CACM. *Central American Common Market*.

Caesar management. One-man or *autocratic control*. Management with power concentrated in one executive.

cafeteria system. Applied to remuneration implies a choice for the individual employee in the make up of his personal salary and *fringe benefits* package. A small but increasing number of employers give their more senior executives a degree of choice in straight salary or deferred benefits.

CAI (or CAL). *Computer aided instruction* (or learning).

Cairo Stock Exchange. (la) Bourse de Valeurs de Caire. One of the two principal *Egyptian stock exchanges*.

Calcutta Stock Exchange Association Limited. One of seven major *Indian stock exchanges*.

Calgary Stock Exchange. One of six major *Canadian stock exchanges*.

Calibration, certificates of. See *British Calibration Service*.

California psychological inventory (CPI). *Psychological inventory* developed in the USA for use in *temperament and personality tests*. The CPI is in part derived from the Minnesota multiphasic personality inventory, and covers 18 companies divided into four classes.

call. 1. As *call option*. **2.** Demand for payment of money. **3.** See *option dealing*.

callable bond. Or *redeemable bond*. Bond the redemption of which can be required at any time by the issuer.

call analysis. Examination of salesmen's visits or calls to customers and potential customers in order to gauge their effectiveness etc.

callback. *Market research* term for a visit to an interviewee or *informant* who has already been interviewed once or who was not available for interview at the time of the first visit. If the informant has already been interviewed once, a product may have been left for a *product placement test* between the two visits. See also *random sampling*.

call-back pay. Or call-in pay. Form of wage payment made for work undertaken when a worker on standby is called back to work.

called up capital. When the full price of a *share* is only partly paid for on issue — the remaining capital not called may be payable on allotment of the shares or in the future. In the event of winding up or *liquidation* the shareholder is liable for the outstanding capital.

calling cycle. Average period of time between salesmen's or maintenance engineer's calls on customers.

call-in pay. As *call-back pay*.

call off. To request delivery of part of an order as and when the goods are required.

call option. Right to complete a purchase at a specified price within a certain period of time. See *option dealing*.

call over. *Stock exchange* term for the practice (practise) in some smaller exchanges of *securities* being offered for sale, and in effect auctioned, at specific times. See also *trading post system*.

call premium. Payment which may have to be made by the issuer of a *callable bond* if he exercises his right to demand its redemption.

call rate. Number of contacts or visits made

53

call up. To call for the unpaid part of the price of *called up capital*.

Cámara Argentina de Comercio. Argentinian *Chamber of Commerce*, established in 1924.

Canadian central bank. *Bank of Canada*.

Canadian Chamber of Commerce Inc. Established in 1926, its members include more than 800 *chambers of commerce* and more than 2,700 companies and corporations.

Canadian Labor Congress (CLC). Established in 1965 by a merger of the Trades and Labor Congress of Canada and the Canadian Congress of Labor. About 60 per cent of its affiliated *trade unions* are based in the USA. About two million trade unionists are in the unions affiliated to the Congress.

Canadian Manufacturers' Association. National organization of *employers' associations*, etc, established in 1871.

Canadian stock exchange. The six major stock exchanges of Canada are: **a** Canadian Stock Exchange, Montreal; **b** Calgary Stock Exchange; **c** Montreal Stock Exchange; **d** Toronto Stock Exchange; **e** Vancouver Stock Exchange; **f** Winnipeg Stock Exchange.

c and f. *Cost and freight*.

canvass. Rather like a census, means obtaining views or information from people in a particular statistical or market research *universe* or *population*.

CAP. *Common Agricultural Policy* of the *European Economic Community (EEC)* or *Common Market*.

capacity. Ability to pay when a debt is due.

capacity cost. Cost of operating a plant or unit at full capacity.

capacity loading and schedule system (CLASS). *Computer software* package developed by IBM for factory shop floor control including measuring value of work in progress.

capital. Stock of money or goods used in a business enterprise. Such goods are either fixed capital, such as buildings, plant and machinery, or *working capital* or *circulating capital* consisting of raw materials, part-finished goods, components, finished goods in store, etc. See also *investment* and *consumption*. The sources of a company's capital may include *equity* capital, *retained earnings*, grants, overdrafts, and *loan capital*.

'Capital'. Federal German publication on business and economics.

capital account. Payments in a country's *balance of payments* other than those in its *current account*.

capital allowance. Allowances for writing down *assets* in lieu of depreciation.

capital appropriation. Sum of money set aside for future capital expenditure. See *budget allocation*.

capital budget. Budget listing capital or investment outlays and often also the sources of finances needed to sustain them.

capital commitments. Specifically capital expenditure contracted for but not yet paid. The Companies Act 1967 (UK) requires that such commitments should be noted in the annual accounts of UK companies.

capital consumption allowance. Charge against gross business product for the consumption of durable capital goods consisting of depreciation etc. It is deducted from the *gross national product* to reconcile it with national incomes.

capital cut-off point. Point to which a company or organization can acquire *capital* economically. Two ways of calculating the cost of acquiring capital up to this limit are the *marginal cost of capital* (the weighted average of the costs of new equity capital and of loan capital in the target *gearing* proportions) and the average cost of capital (the weighted average of the costs of funds in the gearing proportions in which they happen to be in use at any one time). The latter is not usually a useful formula because times and circumstances can change.

capital duty. UK tax paid by companies on formation or when increasing their *contributed capital*.

capital employed. 1. All fixed and current *assets* (gross capital employed). **2.** All fixed and current assets less current *liabilities* (net capital employed). **3.** The total shareholders' or proprietors' stake in the business. This normally means the total paid-up share capital plus reserves (as capital invested).

The net capital employed figure is of greater use to management, which is concerned with the profitable use of the sums available. The proprietors' net capital employed figure is of more use to the shareholders.

capital expenditure. Expenditure on *fixed assets*, or expenditure that has to be met by raising new capital rather than from current income.

capital expenditure budget. As *capital budget*.

capital, free movement of (EEC). See *free movement of capital (EEC)*.

capital gains tax. Tax on the profit accruing from the sale of capital interests and assets. Introduced in the UK in 1965, for example, as a tax on *profits* of more than £1,000 made by a company or an individual on the sale of *assets* or property. Types of gain excluded from UK tax include those on owner-occupied houses, private cars, National Savings Certificates, Premium Savings Bonds, Defence Bonds, National Development Bonds, *life assurance policies*, some types of *Government securities*, and certain windfalls.

capital goods. For use in production, investment, etc rather than for consumption. Eg buildings, plant, machinery. Usually synonymous with *fixed assets*.

capital intensive (industry or firm). Having high degree of capital investment and therefore mechanization (opposite of *labo(u)r intensive* in terms of numbers of employees.)

capital invested. See *capital employed*.

capitalism. Free market economy characterized by private ownership of industry and business.

capitalization issue. See *scrip issue*.

capitalization rate. Rate of return on an *investment*.

capitalize. 1. To issue a capitalization or *scrip issue*. **2.** to convert the *present value* of future income into *capital*.

capital market. Range of possible sources of supply of *capital*.

capital-output ratio. Relationship between *investment* and the flow of goods and services. Broadly, investment in industrial capital produces a relatively swift increase in the flow of goods and services and is therefore said to have a 'low capital-output ratio'. On the other hand, investment in the *infrastructure* of a national economy will tend to be less quickly productive and to have a 'high capital-output ratio'.

capital stock. 1. Total amount of *shares* or *stock* authorized for issue by a *corporation*. As *authorized capital*. **2.** *Par value* of permanently invested share capital in a corporation.

capital structure. Ratios in a *company* or *corporation* of loan and equity capital to total *capital*. See *gearing*.

capital surplus. Shareholder's *equity* arising, for example, from revaluation of assets (written up assets); amounts paid for shares in excess of par value.

capital transfer tax. As *gifts tax*.

CAPS. *Computer Assisted Placement Service* (UK universities and polytechnics).

card punch. Or key punch. Machine used in the preparation of *punched cards*.

card reader. Used to feed *punched cards* into a *computer*.

card-stacking method. *Merit rating* technique in which the names of each of a group of employees is written on a card for a manager or supervisor to stack in order of merit bearing in mind such factors as general productivity, quality of work, job knowledge, safety consciousness, cooperativeness, etc. Once stacked in order, the cards are usually divided between the poorest ten per cent; the next 20 per cent; the middle 40 per cent; the next 20 per cent; and the best ten per cent.

card steward. *Trade union* official or *shop steward* having responsibility for collecting trade union dues.

card vote. Or block vote. One taken by card at a *delegate meeting or conference*, each delegation leader (or delegate, where an organization has a single delegate) casting votes in proportion to the number of people he represents. He holds up a card on which is written the number of votes he is casting. What he votes for is likely to be according to a *mandate* from those he represents. Card votes are an unusual procedure only invoked when other forms of vote fail to produce a clear decision or when a major point has to be decided. See also *roll call vote*.

careers teacher. School teacher with special responsibility for advising on the complexity of career choices.

career structure. Pattern of career planning and succession within an employing organization taking into account *employer* needs, *employee* expectations, number of employers at all levels, *wastage* rates, age distributions, grade structure, changing needs for skills, potential promotion blockages, etc.

Caribbean Congress of Labo(u)r. Set up in 1960 to promote *trade union* recognition and activities.

Caribbean Employers' Confederation. Set up in 1960 with a special interest in industrial relations.

Caribbean Free Trade Association (CARIFTA). Set up in 1967 to work towards *customs union* and *free movement of labo(u)r* between Antigua, Barbados, Belize, Dominica, Grenada, Guyana, Jamaica, Montserrat, St Christopher-Nevis-Anguilla, St Lucia, St Vincent, and Trinidad and Tobago.

CARIFTA. *Caribbean Free Trade Association.*

carnet, ATA. See *ATA carnet.*

carnet, TIR. See *TIR carnet.*

Carpet Industry Training Board. Established in the UK in March 1966 under the *Industrial Training Act 1964.*

carry back. Tax reduction allowed to balance an earlier overpayment of tax.

carry forward (C/F). As *carry over.*

carrying charges. Interest charged on the balance owed when paying by instalments.

carrying costs. Cost of holding items in stock including interest on funds invested in stock, warehouse space, depreciation, obsolescence, insurance, etc.

carry over (CO). 1. Transferring an accounting entry to another column, page, book or account. Also known as carry forward. **2.** To postpone.

cartel. International agreement between several national monopoly or near monopoly companies which fix prices, market territories etc, to avoid competition.

cartogram. Or map-graph. Map shaded or marked to provide management with certain required information. For example, it might be shaded to indicate density of sales, etc, or it might be marked, possibly with flags, to indicate the positions of factories, distribution points, etc.

cascade network. Type of *critical path analysis* diagram which by incorporating *bar charts* indicates not only relationships between activities but also their relative scale and duration.

cascade tax. As *turnover tax.*

case history. True or realistic story of industrial or business situation used to illustrate training and promote discussion. See also *case study.*

case law. Law based on previous judicial decisions and precedent rather than statute and legislation. See also *common law.*

case method. Teaching or training virtually exclusively through the use of *case studies* to provide learning experiences that help the learner to develop habits and skills of analysis, clear reasoning, use of imagination and good judgment. Passive inputs, such as traditional lectures, are excluded in favo(u)r of active case study methods.

case study. Presentation, sometimes in conjunction with role playing, of ingredients of true or synthesized situations to develop judgement and know-how in trainees who, individually or as a group, evolve possible solutions. See also *case history* and *Harvard case method.*

cash. Money in hand or in the bank.

cash and carry. *Wholesale* outlet – or, sometimes, a *retail outlet* – at which customers pay cash, rather than buying on *credit,* and also provide transportation for their own purchases. In return, the customers pay reduced or *discount* prices.

cash before delivery (CBD). Stipulation that cash is paid for goods purchased before they are despatched.

cash book. Basic book of account for recording all receipts (debits) and payments (credits). Often each side has two columns (or more) indicating whether transactions were for cash or via the bank.

cash break-even chart. See *break-even chart*.

cash budget. Budget based on other budgets which indicates the timing of actual incoming and outgoing cash receipts and payments including taxation, interest, etc.

cash discount (cd). Allowable reduction in price provided payment is made in a stipulated period. See also *anticipation*.

cash flow. 1. Flow of cash required to finance operating expenses on the basis of a daily, weekly or other period. Where more cash is flowing into a project/enterprise than out of it there is said to be *positive cash flow*. In the opposite situation there is said to be *negative cash flow*. **2.** Statement showing the sources of all cash receipts, the items on which cash was spent and the overall effect of these transactions on liquid cash resources. See also *discounted cash flow*.

cash forecast. Schedule of the estimated cash flow through a business for a period of time. It takes account of money required for wages and salaries and the approximate dates for major items such as *capital expenditure*. It is usually unreliable beyond about three months' prediction but by comparing the actual performance with the forward estimate each month, variations are disclosed and can be adjusted in subsequent months.

cash on delivery (COD). Stipulation that goods will not be passed to their purchaser unless they are paid for on delivery.

cash ratio. Or *liquidity ratio*. **1.** Ratio of a bank's cash holdings and liquid assets to its total deposit liabilities. **2.** Ratio of a firm's liquid assets to its current liabilities.

cassette. Container with tape or film in manner making for quick loading and unloading of recorders and projectors. Also maintains tapes and slides in relatively clean and scratch-free condition.

cassette-loaded projector. Projects short films in loop form with easy starting and repeating facilities.

casting vote. May be made by the chairman of a meeting when there is a tie in voting. The chairman may use his casting vote irrespective of whether he has earlier used his ordinary, 'deliberative' vote.

casual labo(u)r. Workers not employed on a regular basis, but only as and when work is available. The casual labo(u)r system has been operated in certain industries where the availability and throughput of work have been uncertain. Casual labo(u)r thus makes for variations in wage payments from period to period, though these may be cushioned where a retainer is paid when there is no work. In general, the system has been unpopular with workers and *trade unions*, and has tended to be replaced by regular employment through the process of *de-casualization*.

catalog(ue) buying. Purchasing of goods from catalog(ue) by *direct mail*, by telephone or through salesmen rather than through *retail outlets*.

catalog(ue) store. Store where customers select goods from a catalog(ue) rather than from displays, usually at very competitive prices and with minimum of customer service.

category analysis. *Market research* technique for checking whether market conditions and opportunities are propitious for the development of a product.

Catt concept. Ivor Catt observed that employees will go to considerable lengths to ensure their own continuity of employment. The three key methods he describes are **a** 'Incomplete gambit' — not finishing work, or projects too quickly **b** 'Secretiveness' — keeping some tasks mysterious **c** 'Semi-blackmail' — keeping information on your boss for possible future use.

caveat emptor. Common law principle which implies that the customer should beware when buying goods or services. He should check price, suitability, etc before buying, for if he subsequently suffers loss the law may not support his claim.

caveat subscriptor. Common law principle meaning 'let the signer beware'. Applies particularly to signing of contracts and other legal documents for anyone signing these is held bound by the terms and conditions even though he may not have read them carefully or be aware of the legal implications.

CBA. *Cost-benefit analysis.*

CBD. *Cash before delivery.*

CBI. *Confederation of British Industry.*

CCT. *Common Customs Tariff* of the *Common Market.*

CCTV. *Closed circuit television.*

cd. *Cash discount.*

CEI. *Council of Engineering Institutions* in the UK.

cell(ular) organization. Organization of production plant and machinery as in *group technology* so that a range of components making up a product can be machined in one production 'cell' or area of the factory or by a small group of workers, rather than concentrating production of individual components in particular parts of the factory as in *flow line production.*

C Eng. *Chartered engineer* in the UK.

Census of Production. UK Government annual survey and statistics on firms' activity using the *Standard Industrial Classification.*

census survey. *Market research* or other kind of survey which involves an examination of the total prospective market, or, in statistician's terms, the universe or *total population.* A survey based on part of the market or population only is a *sample survey.*

centimes additionels. Additional local tax. See *Belgian income tax.*

Central American Common Market (CACM). Formed in 1960 when Costa Rica, Guatemala, Honduras, Nicaragua and Salvador signed the General Treaty on Central America Integration to establish a *free trade* area within a *common external tariff* and consultation on monetary policy. See also the *Latin American Free Trade Association (LAFTA).*

central bank. Bank which acts as the bank for a country's bankers and the government's means of controlling interest rates and the credit given by banks. Usually, it is also the government's own bank as in the case of, for example, the *Bank of England,* the *Banque de France,* the *Federal Reserve Bank* in the USA and the *Bank of Canada.* Central banks of the developed countries meet regularly to consider the desirability of collective action and are their countries' point of contact with international agencies such as the *International Monetary Fund.* (For individual central banks see under the names of the countries concerned.)

Central Conference. Final stage and last resort in the UK engineering industry's *disputes procedure.* Follows *Works Conference* and *Local Conference.* See *engineering procedure.*

Centrale Générale des Syndicats Libéraux de Belgique (CGSLB). *Central Organization of Belgian Liberal Unions,* one of the Belgian confederations of *trade unions.* Others are the *CSC* and the *FGTB.*

Centralna Rada Związków Zawadowych (CRZZ). Polish Central Council of *Trade Unions.*

Central Office of Information (COI). Publicity and information service used by UK Government Departments. Has special responsibilities for projecting national image overseas.

Central Organization of Belgian Liberal Unions. See *Centrale Générale des Syndicats Libéraux de Belgique (CGSLB).*

central processing unit (or processor) (CPU). *Arithmetic unit, program control unit* and *internal memory or store* of a *computer* which also has *peripheral equipment* consisting of the *input devices,* the *output devices* and the *external storage device.*

Central Services Unit for University Careers and Appointments Services (UK). National organization providing a vacant appointments notification system for member universities and polytechnics in the UK. See also *Computer Assisted Placement Service (CAPS).*

Central Standard Time (CST or CT). Local time at a point in the USA at the 90th meridian. See *standard time* and Appendix: Time Zones.

Centre for Educational Research and Innovation. Offspring of the *Organization for Economic Cooperation and Development,* with backing from the Ford Foundation and Shell.

Centre for Information Language Teaching. Source of information on foreign languages courses in UK colleges of further education. See also *Institute of Linguists.*

Centre for Interfirm Comparison (CIFC).
Set up in the UK originally in 1959 as an independent, autonomous, non-profit making organization by the *British Institute of Management* in association with the *British Productivity Council* to conduct *interfirm comparisons* of management ratios on a confidential basis. The comparisons are conducted by collecting key business figures and data on an anonymous, confidential and agreed uniform basis from a number of firms in an industry. The results are compared with other similar firms enabling their own performance to be evaluated and strengths and weaknesses to be highlighted.

CEO. Chief executive officer (US).

Ceramics, Glass and Mineral Products Industry Training Board (UK). Established July 1965 under the *Industrial Training Act 1964.*

CERN. *European Organization for Nuclear Research* based chiefly in Geneva, Grenoble and Paris.

Certificate in Supervisory Studies. See *National Examinations Board in Supervisory Studies.*

Certificate of Assurance. Received by an employee in the UK leaving a firm's *occupational pension scheme* that has *contracted-out* of the *state graduated pension scheme.* The Certificate of Assurance sets out the amount of pension to which the employee is entitled, a copy of it being sent to the *Department of Health and Social Security* for the pension earned to be incorporated in the employee's state pension. The amount of pension earned under the scheme must be at least equal — the *Equivalent Pension Benefit* — to the maximum the employee could have earned during the same period under the state scheme. See also the alternative *Payment in Lieu (PIL)* arrangement.

certificate of incorporation. Document confirming that a *company* or *corporation* has been legally incorporated. In the UK, for example, issued by the *Registrar of Companies* or in the USA by state officials.

Certificate of Non-Participation. Issued in the UK by the Registrar of Non-Participating Employment under the *National Insurance Acts* to *occupational pension schemes* that are *contracted-out* from the *state graduated pension scheme.*

certificate of origin. Sent with exported goods for the information of customs officers in order to establish any claim to preferential *tariff* rates by virtue of the goods' country of origin.

Certificate of Secondary Education. School examination taken in the UK at approximately same age as GCE O levels, but usually by less academic pupils. More open-ended examining approach than GCE. Grade 1 CSE usually equated with GCE.

certified accountant (UK). Member of professional Association of Certified and Corporate Accountants set up originally in UK in 1891. Members are recognized by the *Department of Trade* for the audit of public company accounts. Members may be fellows (FCCA) or associates (ACCA).

certified public accountant (CPA). US accountant who has received a certificate authorizing the practice of his profession because he meets the state's legal standards.

certionari. Higher court writ served on a lower court requesting a transcript of case proceedings so that the judgment and conduct of the case can be reviewed.

Československá obchodní komora. Czechoslovak *Chambers of Commerce*, established in 1949.

CET. *Common External Tariff* of the *Common Market.* Also known as its Common Customs Tariff (CCT).

Ceylon. Now *Sri Lanka.*

C/F. Carry forward.

CF. Cost and freight.

CFDT. Confédération Française Démocratique du Travail. See *French trade unions.*

cfi. Cost, freight and insurance. See *CIF*, the more usual usage.

CFTC. Confédération Francaise des Travailleurs Chrétiens. See *French trade unions.*

CGC. *Confédération Générale des Cadres*, a French confederation of *trade unions* for technical and management staff. See *French trade unions.*

CGIL. Confederazione Generale Italiana del Lavoro. See *Italian trade unions.*

CGSLB. *Centrale Générale des Syndicats Libéraux de Belgique*, one of the Belgian confederations of *trade unions*.

CGT. *Confederación General del Trabajo* (Argentine).

CGT. Confédération Générale du Travail. See *French trade unions*.

CGT-FO. *Confédération Générale du Travail-Force Ouvrière*, one of the smaller French confederations of *trade unions*.

chain, or chain store. Or multiple. Retail organization with a number of *retail outlets*.

chain discount. Series of trade discounts dependent on quantity or value of items purchased. Each discount in the chain is calculated separately after first deducting the previous discount.

chaining. As *syllogism*.

chain of command. Or line of command. Formal line of communication in a company or organization through which instructions and information are passed downwards and information passed upwards and laterally. See also *line management* and *staff management*. Adherence to the chain of command and its implied recognition of clear management authority is maintaining *unity of command*. The scale of direct authority relationships between levels of management is sometimes known as the scalar chain.

Chamber of Commerce of the United States. Organization which analyzes barriers to *productivity* and growth in the *private* and *public sectors of the economy*, seeking to improve labo(u)r—management relations, productivity, worker morale and product quality.

chamber of commerce (or trade). Local voluntary association of businessmen and tradesmen joining together for the purpose of promoting trade in general. Chambers of commerce exist in many countries, having originated in France in the sixteenth century. See also *ATA Carnet, certificate of origin, commercial arbitration*. (For the chamber of commerce organizations of different countries see under countries.)

Chambre de Commerce de Paris. Paris Chamber of Commerce, established in 1803. There are *chambers of commerce* in most large French towns and also nationally for some major industries.

Chambre de la Bourse de Genève. Geneva Stock Exchange, one of the principal stock exchanges of Switzerland. See *Swiss stock exchanges*.

Chambre Syndicale des Agents de Change. In collaboration with the *Commission des Operations de Bourse*, implements the rules and regulations of the *Paris Stock Exchange* (or *Bourse*) and publishes the Official list of securities. The Chambre is elected by the *Compagnie des Agents de Change*, the organization of *Agents de Change* or stockbrokers.

Chancellor of the Exchequer. UK Government cabinet minister with particular responsibility for national financial policy and performance, including the annual Budget and Finance Bill. His department of government is HM Treasury.

change agent. Third person, acting as a catalyst, who assists in the achievement of the smooth introduction and implementation of change. *Organization development* programmes involve the use of change agents who act by means of *interventions* in such areas as team work, the processes of interaction, problem solving and setting and maintaining objectives, meetings, interviewing techniques and *performance appraisal* schemes.

change of practice (practise) principle. Understanding between *trade unions* and employers that wage rates and *payment systems* will not be changed unless there is a change in working methods.

channel money. Interim payment made to seamen pending accurate calculation of wages due to them on being paid off at the end of a trip.

channel of distribution. As *sales chain*.

character. Expression used to summarize the willingness of a debtor to organize his affairs and pay his debts.

characteristics of easy movement. *Motion study* principles of easy human movement and working originated by *Gilbreth* and developed by Ralph M Barnes.

character recognition system. Sometimes used in the *input devices* of a *computer* to feed specific and prerecorded data into it more quickly and efficiently than with conventional *computer languages*. The main types of character recognition system are *optical character recognition* and *magnetic ink character recognition*.

charge account. A business arrangement providing credit so that goods or services can be obtained prior to payment.

chargehand. Worker who undertakes junior supervisory duties.

charm price. As *psychological price*.

charter. The hire of all or part of the cargo or passenger-carrying capacity of a ship, aircraft, etc for a particular purpose or a particular period of time.

chartered accountant. Member of the *Institute of Chartered Accountants* in England and Wales (or in Scotland or Ireland which have separate Institutes). Members are recognized by the *Department of Trade* to audit public company accounts. Members may be fellows (FCA) or associates (ACA).

chartered company. Type of UK company incorporated by the Crown, particularly in the 17th, 18th and 19th centuries. Examples include Hudson's Bay Company (1670), Bank of England (1694) and British South Africa Company (1889). Also used to describe companies set up under the Chartered Companies Act 1837 which enabled the monarchy to confer a charter by letters patent which did not provide for incorporation.

chartered engineer. Term used in the UK for corporate members of the 14 professional engineering institutions that constitute the *Council of Engineering Institutions*. A chartered engineer may put the letters *CEng* after his name.

Chartered Institute of Patent Agents. Professional organization whose members are patent agents in the UK and are able to advise on *patent* or design matters, to arrange UK registration with the *Patent Office*, and to advise on applications for protection in overseas countries, particularly in countries that subscribe to the *International Convention for the Protection of Industrial Property*. See also *Institute of Trade Mark Agents*.

check. US usage for UK *cheque*.

checking account. Or *current account*. Bank account from which withdrawals can be made without notice, but no *interest* (or sometimes a very small interest) is paid on money deposited in the account. Checking account is a US term while current account is a UK term. See also *deposit account* or *savings account*.

checking service. US term for *current account* facilities provided by banks including issue of cheque (check) books to customers and providing banking advice.

check-list. Series of carefully prepared inter-related questions designed to aid analysis or appraisal of a specific subject. It provides guidelines and acts as an aide mémoire.

check-off agreement. Where an employer agrees to deduct *trade union* dues from trade union members' wages, handing the dues over to the trade union. This helps the union in ensuring that dues are paid, and the employer in avoiding loss of working time for the dues to be collected.

check out. In self-service and supermarket stores the exit points where the value of goods purchased is checked, recorded and totalled and payment is made.

Chemical and Allied Products Industry Training Board. Established October 1967 under the UK *Industrial Training Act 1964*.

cheque. Written order to a bank to pay a specified sum from a deposit or current account there. Also known as *check* (US) or draft.

Chicago Stock Exchange. See *Midwest Stock Exchange*.

chief executive. Most senior executive in an organization, such as *managing director* in a UK *company*, or *president* of a US *corporation*.

Chief Registrar of Trade Unions and Employers' Associations. Office introduced in the UK by the *Industrial Relations Act 1971* and abolished by the *Trade Union and Labour Relations Act 1974*.

Chilean stock exchanges. There are two stock exchanges: **a** Santiago; **b** Valparaiso.

China, The People's Bank of. Chinese *central bank*, with more than 30,000 branches. Foreign exchange and settlements are handled by the Bank of China.

chip. Or *microchip*, or *silicon chip*. Very small-scale, integrated electronic micro-

chi-square. Statistical test to discover whether a difference between the findings of two surveys has any significance.

chose-in-action. Legal term for a right to the possession of a particular property or a sum of money in the event of a certain contingency, the right of possession being enforceable, if necessary, in a court of law. A *mortgage* is an example of a chose-in-action because the mortgagee retains qualified ownership of the property as a security.

Christchurch Stock Exchange. One of four major stock exchanges in New Zealand.

Christelijk Nationaal Vakverbond in Nederland (CNV). See *Netherlands trade unions*.

CIA. Cash in advance.

cif. Cost, insurance and freight. Implies that the seller of goods pays the freight and insurance charges to a named port or destination. See also *cost and freight*, *free on board* and *free on rail*.

CIFC. Centre for Interfirm Comparison.

CII. *Confederation of Irish Industry*.

Cincinnati Stock Exchange. One of 20 major *US stock exchanges*.

CIO. *Congress of Industrial Organizations*.

CIOS. Conseil International pour l'Organisation Scientifique.

circle chart. As *pie chart*.

circular flow of income. Process by which the *purchasing power* in an economy passes from hand to hand as purchases are made of goods and services. This circular flow tends to be expanded if the economy receives injections in the form of government expenditure, exports or industrial investment. On the other hand, income tends to be leaked from the circular flow if there are *withdrawals* in the shape of *savings*, taxation by central or local governments, or imports. Broadly, when the circular flow of income is not great enough to maintain *full employment*, a government tries to make injections greater than withdrawals. In a situation of *inflation*, the government will try to make withdrawals greater than injections. It can be said that all income is either passed on to others in the same economy through the purchase of home market-produced *consumer goods* or is leaked from the circular flow through withdrawals. The proportion of income which is passed on is known as the *propensity to consume*.

circulating assets. As *current* or *floating assets*.

circulating capital. As *working capital*. See also *capital*.

CISAL. Confederazione Italiana Sindicati Autonomi Lavoratori, one of the smaller Italian confederations of *trade unions*.

CISL. Confederazione Italiana Sindicati Lavatori. See *Italian trade unions*.

CISNAL. Confederazione Italiana Sindicati Nazionali Lavoratori, one of the smaller Italian confederations of *trade unions*.

City of London. Square mile of London in which national and international financial expertise and institutions are concentrated, including the *Bank of England*, the *Stock Exchange*, *Lloyds*, the *commodity markets*, the *Baltic Exchange*, etc. See also *Lombard Street*.

Civil Aeronautics Board (USA). US Government agency whose members are appointed by the President with Senate approval to regulate and promote domestic and international civil aviation. Established 1938. See also *Federal Aviation Administration*.

Civil Rights Act 1964. US Federal legislation establishing framework for reduction of racial discrimination. See also *Race Relations Act 1968* (UK).

CLASS. Capacity loading and schedule system.

classification and coding systems. Techniques for providing logical and meaningful systems of identification of information, data and components. The purpose is to arrange similar items into suitably selected categories or groups and allocate symbols or codes to aid retrieval. See *Brisch, Gildemeister, Nato, Niitmash, Opitz, PERA, Pittler, Vuoso* and *Zafo* classifications.

classification method. See *job classification method*.

Classification of Occupations and Directory of Occupational Titles (CODOT). Compiled in UK by the *Department of Employment* for use in the Department's employment and career guidance services, CODOT is also being used increasingly by industry, etc as an aid to the using and planning of manpower. CODOT is published in three volumes and is available from HMSO.

Classification of Training Information (UK). *Department of Employment* classification dividing training into ten major schedules or aspects: general; national considerations; the educational system; the working organization; training specialists; identification of training needs; the trainee; training administration; methods and aids; assessment of effectiveness. Each schedule is divided by ten and then by ten again. See *Universal Decimal Classification System (UDC)*.

classified advertisement. Published advertisement which appears in a particular category of advertisements presented in the same small-print format. See also *display advertisement*.

class market. One for exclusive and usually high-price *consumer goods*, as opposed to the 'mass market'.

class unionism. Concept of *trade union* structure based on the inclusion of workers of all kinds in a single multi-purpose union. The concept is regarded by some trade unionists as an answer to the power of *multi-national companies*. See also *industrial unionism*.

CLAT. See *Latin American Centre of Workers*.

Clayton Act 1914. See *antitrust legislation* (US).

CLC. *Canadian Labo(u)r Congress.*

Clean Air Acts 1956 and 1968. UK Acts inspired particularly by the 4,000 London smog deaths of 1952. Aimed at eventual elimination of industrial and domestic smoke. The Act's insistence on the use of smokeless fuels has greatly reduced urban atmospheric pollution.

clearing banks. Banks that are members of the *London Bankers' Clearing House* and each day clear cheques paid into them through this institution which sets off the amounts owing between banks so that the banks involved can settle the net totals of each day's transactions with single cheques drawn on the *Bank of England*. There is also the Committee of Scottish Clearing Bankers. The term 'clearing bank' is used loosely in the UK to mean any *commercial bank* or *joint stock bank*. The US equivalents are *member banks* while the Western European equivalents are *credit banks*.

clearing house. UK establishment set up by the *clearing banks* to offset daily banking transactions against each other by *cheques* (checks) etc, with settlements between banks being made with single payments.

clerical aptitude test. Used in *personnel selection*, etc, to test ability to check and classify words, figures, symbols, etc, quickly and accurately. These are qualities needed in some non-clerical as well as in clerical work. See also *psychological testing* and *aptitude tests*. Examples of clerical aptitude tests include the *ACER speed and accuracy test*; the *Morrisby speed test 1*; and the *NIIP group tests 20* and *61*.

clerical work evaluation (CWE). *Work study* technique developed in the UK by the P-E Consulting Group as a method of *work measurement* of *indirect labo(u)r* in offices. It uses the so-called Booking and Sampling for Indirect Standards (BASIS) method. See also *clerical work improvement program(me) (CWIP), clerical work measurement, group capacity assessment (GCA), variable factor programming (VFP)*, and *O & M*.

clerical work improvement program(me) (CWIP). *Work study*-type technique developed in the USA by W D Scott & Co as a method of *work measurement* in offices making use of *predetermined motion time systems*. See also *clerical work evaluation (CWE), clerical work measurement, group-capacity assessment (GCA), variable factor programming (VFP)*, and *O & M*.

clerical work measurement. Systematic analysis of clerical work in order to determine the amount of time it should take to perform the work assigned to an individual, a group of clerical staff or an office. Used as the basis for monitoring performance, ensuring the equitable distribution of work, determining staffing levels and providing the data for the budgeting of clerical costs.

clock card. Card used by employers when *clocking-in*.

clocking-in (or on). The recording by employees of the times at which they start and leave work, usually by punching a card in a *time clock*. The practice of clocking-in has been ended in some firms in recent years, particularly in those firms that have extended *staff status* to *blue collar workers*. See also *flexible working hours*.

close company. Company controlled by five or fewer shareholders and in which the public holds less than 35 per cent of the equity. Close companies must normally distribute all their investment income and a significant proportion of their trading profits.

close corporation. US term for *close company*.

closed circuit television (CCTV). Transmission of television signals by means of a cable or microwave link between transmitter and receiver. Can be in monochrome or colo(u)r and used in classroom or on shopfloor. Special usefulness in education and training, in dangerous environments, in confined spaces, and for security purposes. See also *open-circuit television*.

closed-loop. System or form of control in which there is automatic *feedback* of the output without interference from external factors, followed by automatic adjustment of the input to correct or modify the performance and output of the system. The system is thus self-balancing. Such sensitive control is likely to be achieved with the aid of a *computer*, particularly in the case of a complex application.

closed shop. Or *union shop*. System whereby it is a condition of employment that all workers must belong to a particular *trade union*. In the case of a *pre-entry closed shop* an employee must be a member of the relevant trade union prior to employment. In the case of a *post-entry closed shop* he must join the union after taking up employment if he is not already a member of it.

closure. Method of terminating discussion on an item at a meeting or conference, usually at the chairman's discretion or according to the rules of procedure or *standing orders* of the organization concerned. Formulae for a closure include **a** a motion from the floor *putting the question*, the vote being taken upon the passing of such a motion; or **b** the moving of *next business* or *previous question*, the passing of either kind of motion meaning that there shall be no further discussion. A closure may also be applied when a time limit has been reached, as when the *guillotine* is used in the UK House of Commons etc

cloth cap pension scheme. See *excepted provident fund (EPF)*.

Clothing and Allied Products Industry Training Board. Established October 1969 under the UK *Industrial Training Act 1964*.

CLU. Chartered Life Underwriter (US).

cluster analysis. Mathematical technique for sorting out a complexity of information on people, products, etc and separating them out into groups or clusters having broadly similar characteristics. Used particularly in *market research*.

cluster sampling. Used particularly in *market research* to select a sample so that the interviewees or *informants* tend to be grouped or clustered together geographically to reduce the travelling and costs of the interviewers. Care has to be taken that clustering for the benefit of interviewers is not taken so far that the sample becomes distorted. See also *random sampling, differential sampling, sampling, weighted sample* and *sampling point*.

C/N. Credit note.

CNAA. Council for National Academic Awards.

CNPF. *Conseil National du Patronat Français*, the French National Employers' Council.

CNV. *Christelijk Nationaal Vakverbond in Nederland*. See *Netherlands trade unions*.

CO. 1. Carry over. **2.** Company.

c/o. Care of.

coaching. Individual or small-group management training characterized by on-the-job training, continuous assessment and personal counselling and tuition.

coalition bargaining. Term used particularly in the USA for the situation where two or more *trade unions* join forces for the purposes of *collective bargaining*. Where employers join forces in this way it may be known as association bargaining or multi-plant bargaining.

COBOL. Acronym of *Common Business*

Oriented Language. See *computer language*.

cobweb theory. Supply and demand analysis where supply is a reflection of demand for a previous period and therefore does not reflect current demand; eg after a long industrial strike many customers will have found alternative supplies and existing suppliers will find it difficult to sell the same volume of goods as before the strike.

COD. *Cash* (or collect) *on delivery*.

Code du Commerce. French legal code on business relationships.

co-determination law. Federal German legislation which gives employees the right to be represented on the *supervisory board* of their employing company as well as on its *works council*, or *Betriebsrat*. The supervisory board (Aufsichtsrat) is the upper board in a two-tier board structure, the other being the management board (Vorstand), which is responsible for the day-to-day running of the firm. Co-determination is also used loosely to describe the variety of ways in which employees participate in the decision making and management process. See also *industrial democracy, participation, workers' participation*.

CODOT. *Classification of Occupations and Directory of Occupational Titles*.

coefficient of correlation. See *correlation*.

cognition. Person's individual view or image of the world which shapes his social behaviour. Cognition is the product of the following determinants in an individual: **a** his physical and social environment; **b** his physiological structure; **c** his wants and his goals; **d** his past experiences. See also *attitudes*.

cognitive dissonance. Condition where there is discord between a person's conscious attitudes and his/her behavio(u)r.

COI. *Central Office of Information* (UK).

coincidents. See *business indicators*.

coincident technique. Technique in *market research* interviewing in which a consumer or user is asked about something that is happening or something that he is doing at the time of the interview.

cold call. Unannounced approach by a sales representative leading, hopefully, to a sales interview.

Colegio de Agentes de Cambio y Bolsa. Stockbrokers' Association at one of the *Spanish stock exchanges*.

collateral. A guarantee given by a borrower as a safeguard for a loan, the safeguard usually being either a guarantee by a third party or deeds to property or an undertaking to transfer particular stocks and shares if necessary.

collateral units. As *staff management* units, serving *line management*.

collective agreement. As *collective bargain*.

collective bargain. Resulting from *collective bargaining*, a collective agreement between, on the one hand, an employees' organization, *trade union* or *bargaining unit* and, on the other hand, an employer or *employers' association* concerning the employment or non-employment of people and other factors such as *wages* and *conditions of employment*. Elements of a collective bargain may be a *procedural agreement* (on how the parties should conduct themselves towards each other, particularly in the event of dispute) and a *substantive agreement* (on matters of substance such as pay and discipline). The extent to which collective bargains are legally binding varies from country to country, and may be affected by government action such as *incomes policy*.

collective bargaining. Process or procedural rules for making agreement on *wages, conditions of employment*, etc between employers and employees collectively, the latter usually being represented by a *trade union* or *bargaining unit* of employees. The various levels of collective bargaining and agreements include *industry-wide bargaining* (ie nationally), *company agreement, factory agreement* or *plant agreement*, or *workplace bargaining*. The latter may be *autonomous bargaining* or a form of *fractional (or fragmented) bargaining*.
Legislation affecting collective bargaining has included the *National Labor Relations Act* in the USA and the *Industrial Relations Act 1971* and *Trade Union and Labour Relations Act 1974* in the UK. Article 98 of the International Labor Organization agreed the general case for collective bargaining.

collective contract. Type of *workers' control* stemming from *guild socialism* and based on the notion that a group of workers should be responsible for organizing and

65

supervising their own factory or shop in return for producing an agreed output. Has points of similarity with *autonomous bargaining*.

college. 1. University, school or technical institute normally offering degree courses. 2. Self-governing society for research, study and teaching forming part of a university. 3. Secondary education institution not supported by the state (particularly France).

college-based student. Student on a *sandwich course* etc who is not sponsored by an employer. A student having such a sponsor is an *industry-based student*.

college diplomas. Awarded by individual colleges, often in areas of learning for which there are no degrees or national qualifications though in some cases they are awarded as well as degrees or national qualifications.

college of advanced technology (CAT). CATs were ten designated colleges in the UK in the decade 1956-66 that developed particularly Diploma in Technology *sandwich courses*. Most became *technological universities* in the wake of the Robbins Report of 1963, though two were assimilated into existing universities.

College of Marketing. Run by the *Institute of Marketing* (UK) to provide a wide range of sales and marketing courses and conferences.

collision clause. Marine *insurance* clause indemnifying a shipowner against liability for damage caused to other ships in collisions.

Colombia Stock Exchange. *Bolsa de Comercio Bogotá*.

Colombo Brokers' Association. Sri Lanka's Stock Exchange.

Colombo Plan. Drawn up jointly in 1950 by a group of Commonwealth and other countries to promote economic cooperation and aid in south and south-east Asia. Member states include Afghanistan, Australia, Bhutan, Burma, Cambodia, Canada, Ceylon (now Sri Lanka), India, Indonesia, Japan, South Korea, Laos, Malaysia, Nepal, New Zealand, Pakistan, Persia (now Iran), Philippines, Thailand, Vietnam, the UK and the USA. The Commonwealth members of the Colombo Plan also set up the *Council for Technical Cooperation* to give help in public administration, agriculture and industry (including training), scientific research and development, public health, etc. Sources of funds have included member states, other Commonwealth countries, the USA and the *International Bank for Reconstruction and Development*. The *United Nations* Organization has also been a provider of know-how.

Colonial Development Corporation. Established in the UK under the Overseas Resources Development Act 1948, becoming the *Commonwealth Development Corporation* in 1963.

colo(u)r vision test. Test of degree of colo(u)r defectiveness or of colo(u)r blindness. In many types of work it is important that personnel should be able to distinguish between colo(u)rs (in electrical wiring, colo(u)r chemistry, for example) while in other types of work it is necessary to make judgements on how well colo(u)rs harmonize or combine (in some work in textiles, for example). Types of colo(u)r vision tests include the *CV (test)*, the *Edridge-Green tests*, the *Giles-Archer tests*, the *Holmgren wools test*, the *H-R-H pseudoisochromatic plates*, the *Ishihara tests*, and the *Stilling tests*. See also *visual abilities test, psychological testing* and *aptitude tests*.

column diagram. As *histogram*.

Combination of Workmen Act 1825. Laid down legal right of workers in the UK to combine and form *trade unions* for the purposes of *collective bargaining* to settle wages and hours. In effect, legalized combinations or trade unions thus reversing the Combinations Acts 1799-1800.

combine committee. *Joint shop stewards committee* formed in a *multi-plant company*, often without being formally recognized by the employer. A combine committee normally includes representatives from each plant in the company.

COMECON. *Council for Mutual Economic Assistance*. Established in 1949 for economic cooperation in Eastern Europe between Albania, Bulgaria, Czechoslovakia, East Germany, Hungary, Mongolia, Poland, Romania and the USSR. Albania withdrew in 1961.

Comité d'Entreprise. *Works council* which is a legal requirement in French industrial firms with more than 50 employees.

command. See *chain of command* and

principle of *unity of command*.

commanditaire. Type of partner in certain forms of partnership under Belgian or French company law who is liable only to the extent of his participation. See also *commandité*.

Commanditaire Vennootschap. Limited partnership under Netherlands law. See also *Netherlands companies*.

Commanditaire Vennootschap op Aandelen. Limited partnership with shares under Netherlands law. See also *Netherlands companies*.

commandité. Type of partner in certain forms of partnership under Belgian or French company law who is jointly and separately liable for the debts of the partnership while another type of partner, the *commanditaire*, is liable only to the extent of his participation. Forms of partnership having these two types of partner are the *Société en Commandité par Actions* in both Belgium and France, and the *Société en Commandité Simple* in France.

commando sales team. Sales force introduced over and above normal staffing for the purposes of a particular *sales promotion* campaign.

commerçant. Official designation for trader under French commercial law. See *French companies*, *Société en Nom Collectif*, *commandité* and *commanditaire*.

commercial agent. As *agent* or *mercantile agent*.

commercial apprentice. Young man or woman indentured or otherwise contracted to an employer to learn commercial skills, usually in conjunction with appropriate further education.

commercial arbitration (UK). Where commercial disputes arise between suppliers and customers, including between UK exporters and overseas customers, they are sometimes settled by private arbitration before one of the following tribunals: **a** *London Court of Arbitration of the London Chamber of Commerce and Industry and the City Corporation*. **b** *Tribunal of Arbitration of the Manchester Chamber of Commerce and Industry*. **c** *Arbitration Committee of the Bradford Chamber of Commerce*.

commercial bank. Or *joint stock bank*. A bank operating through a large number of local branches and largely in business to receive deposits and make short-term loans in dealing with private individuals, companies, organizations, etc. Commercial banks do not normally deal directly in the business of *investment banks* or *merchant banks*. In the UK commercial banks are sometimes loosely known as *clearing banks*. in the USA they are known as *member banks* and in Western Europe as *credit banks*.

commercial credit. As *mercantile credit*. See also *mercantile agent*.

commercial criterion. Or business criterion. Public administration management technique in which some of the criteria of a commercial organization or company are introduced. For example, all *inputs* into a department or unit are charged at a market rate whether they are purchased from outside or obtained from another part of the public service and, similarly, *outputs* are charged at a market rate. Thus set up in effect as a *cost centre*, the department or unit is then expected to make itself pay, in the sense of the value of outputs being greater than that of inputs. Where the public service requirement inherent in central or local government leads to an output being provided at a loss, this output is given a social benefit value for the purposes of applying the commercial criterion. See also *cross-charging*.

commercial insurance. Cover against business risks.

commercial paper. Type of negotiable *promissory note*.

commercial policy, common (EEC). See *common commercial policy (EEC)*.

Commercial Relations and Exports Division (DT). Divisions of the *Department of Trade* that advise UK businesses on the effect of another country's commercial law or regulations or trade restrictions; on UK relations with international bodies such as the *General Agreement on Tariffs and Trade*, the *Organization for Economic Cooperation and Development*, and the *United Nations Conference on Trade and Development*; on international commodity policy, international action on restrictive business practices, and diplomatic immunity and privileges; and on exporting to Communist countries.

Commission. Term for *European Commission* often used in documents and pronouncements of the *Common Market* or

European Economic Community, including the *Treaty of Rome 1957*.

commission. Payment made for obtaining sales, orders, etc, sometimes on a percentage basis.

commission agent. *Agent* paid on a *commission* basis for the business he obtains, the principal then dealing with the customer. The commission agent does not himself take a business risk in the manner of a *del credere agent*.

Commission on Civil Rights. US body which reports to the President and the Congress on the nature and extent of denial of equal protection of the laws on the basis of race, colo(u)r, religion, sex, national origin, age or handicap. The Commission is a clearinghouse and investigatory body for complaints on civil rights issues. It runs a library. See also *Equal Employment Opportunity Commission*.

commissionairs in effecten. Specialists on the *Amsterdam Stock Exchange* who act between banks and the *hoeklieden* or *stockjobbers*.

Commission Bancaire. Official body to whose control all public funds in Belgium are subject.

Commission d'Appel. Commission for Appeals with jurisdiction over the four *Belgian stock exchanges*.

Commission de la Bourse. Stock Exchange Committee that runs the *Brussels Stock Exchange*. The Committee for Listing, or Comité de la Cote, is responsible for admitting securities to the Official List. Commission de la Bourse is also the name of the committee of *Luxembourg Stock Exchange* members that advises Luxembourg's *Conseil d'Administration de la Bourse*, or Board of Directors of the Stock Exchange.

Commission des Opérations de Bourse. Responsible for running the *Paris Stock Exchange* (or *Bourse*), in association with the *Chambre Syndicale des Agents de Change*.

Commissione Interna. Works council which is a legal requirement in Italian industrial firms with more than 40 employees.

Commission on Industrial Relations (UK). Set up in its original form in 1969 on the recommendation of the *Donovan Royal Commission* and then adapted for the purposes of the *Industrial Relations Act 1971*. The original purpose of the CIR was to advise on *trade union* recognition etc. It was abolished by the *Trade Union and Labour Relations Act 1974*.

committed costs. Those to which the management of a project/enterprise are virtually irrevocably committed once the project/enterprise is under way. On the other hand, *managed costs* are those over which some degree of *management discretion* remains and which can be varied in the light of the progress of the project/enterprise (eg reduced to cut losses if things go badly). See also *break-even point, alternative costs*, and *costing system*.

Committee for Industrial Technologies. Set up in the UK in 1972 by the *Department of Trade and Industry*, to advise on the promotion of the economic benefits of multidisciplinary technologies such as *tribology, terotechnology*, corrosion technology and materials handling. Members drawn mainly from industrial, academic and professional organizations.

committee of inquiry (or investigation). *Conciliation Act 1896* (UK) empowered the *Minister of Labour* to set up committees of investigation in particular industries. Developed into Ministerial committees of inquiry such as, in the 1960s, the Devlin Committee of Inquiry into the Docks and the Motor Industry Joint Labour Council.

committee of inspection. May be set up in the UK under deeds of arrangement or *bankruptcy* proceedings when creditors are invited to nominate a small group of people to represent their interests. Meetings are held from time to time when the trustee has matters requiring approval. The committee is free to accept his recommendations or offer alternative proposals. The committee approves the distribution of funds to the creditors and in large or protracted cases it may approve more than one such 'dividend'.

Committee of Permanent Representatives. Consists of the ambassadors to the *European Economic Community* of each of the Community's member states. The Committee's principal role is to screen, from the point of view of consistency with individual national interests, proposals that are en route from the *Commission* to the *Council of Ministers*. The Committee is based in Brussels.

committee procedure. This varies with the type and degree of formality of a committee, but in general a committee meeting is conducted in the following way. The chair is taken by the committee chairman or vice-chairman or, if neither is present, a member elected to do so for that meeting only. Apologies for absence from those unable to be present is usually the first item on the agenda proper. Minutes of the previous meeting is normally the next item, the secretary either circulating the minutes in advance or reading them out. An *amendment* or amendments may be moved and seconded by members and, if agreed by a *majority*, the minutes are duly corrected. The chairman signs the agreed minutes as a correct record. The next item on the agenda is matters arising from the minutes, except for matters specifically included later in the agenda. After that, if appropriate, the secretary reports on any correspondence received and any action on it is decided by the committee.

Further typical items on an agenda include a financial report from the treasurer, reports from members delegated to other bodies, and motions proposed by members of the committee. The last two items on an agenda are usually 'any other business' and 'date of next meeting'. The chairman should not allow 'any other business' to be used by members to introduce motions of which the committee (both those present and those unable to be present) should have had due *notice of motion*. See *motion* for the handling of discussion and the processing of motions, amendments and *resolutions*. A committee will probably have a constitution and/or *standing orders*, including a procedure for any rescinding of resolutions.

commodity. Goods or produce being transferred to a manufacturer or consumer. The term is used particularly of certain foodstuffs and raw materials, such as grain, rice, tea, coffee, sugar, rubber, tobacco, tin, lead, zinc and copper. Different types of commodity trading are *actuals* and *futures*.

commodity exchanges. Markets for dealings in commodities nationally and internationally, the City of London being a particularly noted centre (center) though there are also major exchanges in the UK in Liverpool and Manchester. Dealings at commodity exchanges may be either in immediately available goods, known as *actuals*, or in *futures*, which are contracts for future delivery. For specialist commodity exchanges see *Corn Exchange, Fur Auctions, London Fruit and Wool Exchange, London Metal Exchange, Liverpool Cotton Exchange, Rubber Exchange, Tea Auctions, Wool Auctions.*

commodity volume, all. See *all commodity volume.*

Common Agricultural Policy (CAP). Policy of the *European Economic Community (EEC)* or *Common Market*. Fixes a common pricing policy among EEC member countries for agricultural products such as bread, butter, milk, meat, etc. CAP also provides for farmers to be subsidized and their farms modernized from the *common budget* to which all member states of the Common Market contribute. CAP and the common budget are controlled by the *European Commission*. CAP maintains the level of market prices broadly **a** by keeping the price of imports up to a minimum or *threshold price* by varying import levies, and **b** by supporting the home market at an *intervention price* slightly below the threshold price, and surplus being bought as *end price support* by the Community Agricultural Fund. (See also *target price, sluice-gate price, reserve [or fall-back] price* and *export subsidy [or restitution]*). CAP also prescribes a common policy for trade in agricultural products with non-member countries, including the subsidizing of exports. Articles 38 to 47 of the *Treaty of Rome* deal with agriculture.

common budget (EEC). Budget to which all member states of the *European Economic Community (EEC)* or *Common Market* contribute and from which such common policies as the *Common Agricultural Policy* are financed. All customs and other duties charged at the outer tariff 'wall' of the Common Market pass directly to the common budget which is controlled by the *Commission*. The full common budget arrangements were covered by the *Budget Treaty 1970*, and came into force on 1 January 1971, with a view to the Community becoming financially autonomous by 1978.

Common Business Oriented Language. Source of the acronym, *COBOL*. See *computer language.*

common carrier. Generally defined as 'one who undertakes to carry for hire from place to place the goods of anyone who employs him'. A common carrier cannot in law refuse to carry goods for people who deliver them to him and are prepared to pay a reasonable charge.

common commercial policy (EEC). In the

Common Market, Articles 110-116 of the *Treaty of Rome 1957* set out the common commercial policy to be adopted by member states in their relations with non-member states. Article 113 states, 'the common commercial policy shall be based on uniformly established principles, particularly in regard to tariff amendments to the conclusion of tariff and trade agreements, to the establishing of uniform practice as regards measures of liberalization, to export policy and to commercial protective measures including measures to be taken in cases of dumping or subsidies.'

The *Common Customs (or External) Tariff* became fully operational eighteen months ahead of schedule, in July 1968, including the system of import levies required under the *Common Agricultural Policy*. The *European Commission* has represented the Community within the *General Agreement on Tariffs and Trade (GATT)* and the *United Nations Conference on Trade and Development (UNCTAD)*. The Community has trade agreements with certain members of the European Free Trade Area (EFTA), it has negotiated *preferential trade agreements* with Greece, Israel, Malta, Morocco, Spain, Tunisia and Turkey, and it has agreed the *Yaoundé Convention* with ten African states and the *Arusha Agreement* with Kenya, Tanzania and Uganda. It has agreed, too, that there should be temporary safeguards for New Zealand products and that the UK should continue to honour the *Commonwealth Sugar Agreement* until the end of 1974. The Community also has a *Regulation* on anti-*dumping* procedures in line with GATT policy, and it has a common policy on export credit insurance.

common cost. Cost incurred generally and not readily attributable to particular activities or departments.

common currency (EEC). See *economic and monetary union (EEC)*.

Common Customs Tariff (CCT) or Common External Tariff (CET). Terms for the *Common External Tariff* around the *Common Market* member states.

common external tariff (CET). Customs duty or tariff charged in common by the member states of a common trading area and *customs union* on goods imported from non-member states. The *Common Market*, for example, has a common external tariff (though not so the *European Free Trade Area*). The Common Market's common external tariff (CET) is also known as its *Common Customs Tariff (CCT)*.

Common Farm System (EEC). See *Common Agricultural Policy (EEC)*.

Common Fisheries Policy (EEC). Of the *Common Market* or *European Economic Community* aims at establishing the right of each member state to fish in the territorial waters of all other members, with a so-called 'guide price' for fresh fish geared to market prices for the previous three years. Until January 1983 member states have control of waters up to six nautical miles from their coasts (a coast being treated as a base line drawn between headlands), with this limit extended to 12 nautical miles off some parts of the UK and Irish coasts.

Common Foreign Policy. See *Davignon Committee (Common Market)*.

Common Industrial Policy (EEC). Of the *Common Market* or *European Economic Community*. Following implementation of its *Common Customs (or External Tariff)*, and in step with its *rules of competition*, the Common Market aims at a common industrial policy in order that differing industrial standards between member states and related *restrictive trade practices* should not inhibit exploitation of the tariff-free market. Harmonization of technical standards and some pooling of know-how are part of this policy, together with legislation to aid the development of *multinational companies* and trans-national agreements between companies. In the long term, development of the Community's common industrial policy is expected to be related to its planned *economic and monetary union* and its *Common Technological Policy*.

Common Labo(u)r Market (EEC). *Free movement of labo(u)r* principles set out in Articles 48 and 49 of the *Treaty of Rome 1957* imply the establishing of a common labo(u)r market in the *Common Market* or *European Economic Community*. Only in the case of civil servants is a member state allowed to give priority to its own nationals.

common law. English system of law based on court decisions, the doctrines underlying them being custom and usage rather than statute or codified, written laws. See *case law*.

common legislation (EEC). See *approximation of laws (EEC)*.

common market. Where two or more

countries agree to form a *customs union* between themselves and a *common external tariff* against goods and commodities imported from other countries.

Common Market. Or *European Economic Community (EEC)* created by the *Treaty of Rome 1957* with, as founder members, France, West Germany, Italy, the Netherlands, Belgium and Luxembourg. The *Treaty of Accession 1972* expanded the Common Market from 1 January 1973 to include Denmark, the Irish Republic and the UK. The Common Market is a *customs union* with a *Common External Tariff* (all duties paid at the tariff wall being paid directly into the *common budget* controlled by the Commission) and is working towards fuller economic and *monetary union* and closer political union. The principal institutions of the Common Market are the *Council of Ministers*, the *European Commission*, the *European Court of Justice*, and the *Assembly (European Parliament)*.

The term 'Common Market' is usually used to embrace the *European Atomic Energy Community (Euratom)* and the *European Coal and Steel Community (ECSC)* as well as the EEC proper. The three communities were formally joined in the *Merger Treaty 1967*.

The official languages of the Common Market are Danish, English, French, German, Italian and Dutch, with official translations made available in Gaelic for the Irish.

For details of Common Market institutions, policies, etc see *approximation of laws; Arusha Agreement; association agreement; association of overseas countries and territories; associated states; Budget Treaty 1970; Committee of Permanent Representatives; Common Agricultural Policy; common budget; Common Commercial Policy; Common Customs Tariff or Common External Tariff; Common Fisheries Policy; Common Foreign Policy; Common Industrial Policy; Common Labour Market; Common Regional Policy; Common Social Policy; Common Taxation Policy; Common Technological Policy; Common Transport Policy; Commonwealth safeguards; Commonwealth Sugar Agreement; Community Agricultural Fund; community laws; community powers; Consultative Committee of Transport Experts; Council of Ministers; Davignon Committee; economic and monetary union; Economic and Social Committee; Euratom Treaty; Eurocrat; European Agricultural Guidance and Guarantee Fund; European Atomic Energy Community; European Coal and Steel Community; European Commission; European Communities Act 1972; European Confederation of Free Trade Unions; European Coordination Office; European Court of Justice; European Development Fund; European Economic Association (UNEUROP); European Investment Bank; European Parliament; European Social Fund; free movement of capital; free movement of labour; Luxembourg Declaration 1965; Merger Treaty 1967; Official Journal of the Communities; preferential trade agreement; primary legislation; rules of competition; secondary legislation; Trade and Industry; Treaty of Accession 1972; Treaty of Paris 1951; Treaty of Rome 1957;* and the *Yaounde Convention*. For examples of other forms of common market or free trade area see *Benelux; Brussels Treaty Organization; Central American Common Market; Colombo Plan; Comecon; European Free Trade Area; Latin American Free Trade Association; Caribbean Free Trade Association*. See also under *Commonwealth* entries.

Common Monetary Policies (EEC). See *economic and monetary union (EEC)*.

Common Regional Policy (EEC). Slowly emerging policy of the *Common Market* or *European Economic Community*, a slowness accentuated by the economic growth of the central areas formed by the Ruhr, southern West Germany, northern Italy, northern and eastern France, and the Low Countries.

Common Social Policy (EEC). In the *Common Market,* Articles 117-128 of the *Treaty of Rome 1957* provide for action on social policy by the community as a whole and for cooperation between member states to promote better living and working conditions and employment opportunities for workers. There has been early action to introduce a common policy for *vocational training*, and to set up the *European Social Fund* to meet part of the cost of vocational training and redeployment of workers. In the long term, the Common Market is working towards harmonization of social security schemes, a European system of industrial health and safety, and equal pay for men and women. One of the consultative committees of the Common Market, with representatives of both sides of industry, etc from all member states is the Economic and Social Committee established under Articles 193-198 of the Treaty of Rome.

common stock (US). *Corporation* stock whose holders have control and virtual ownership of the corporation, including appointment of directors and prior claims to dividends.

Common Taxation Policy (EEC). In the *Common Market*. Articles 95-99 of the *Treaty of Rome 1957*, dealing with taxation, set out to ensure that member states do not impose higher taxes on each other's goods than on their own. In the long term, all forms of taxation are to be harmonized between member states. The principal immediate requirement is that all member states operate a system of *value added tax*.

Common Technological Policy (EEC). Of the *Common Market* or *European Economic Community*. The Community was to develop a common technological policy. It is expected that with a *home market* of some 250 million people, the Common Market is in a position to embark upon advanced technologies in a manner comparable with the USA and the USSR. The common technological policy will have close contact with the *Common Industrial Policy* of the Common Market. Areas of cooperation under the Common Market are expected to include nuclear energy, computers, materials, transport technology and meteorological forecasting. There are also, of course, the bases provided by the *European Atomic Energy Community* and the *European Coal and Steel Community*.

Common Transport Policy (EEC). Of the *Common Market* or *European Economic Community*. Stated as a fundamental objective in Article 3 of the *Treaty of Rome*, and covered more fully in Articles 74 to 84, the common transport policy has been concerned chiefly with rail, road and waterways transport but must also embrace air and sea transport. The Treaty provides for a *Consultative Committee of Transport Experts* to advise the *European Commission*.

Common Vocational Training (EEC). See *common social policy (EEC)*.

Commonwealth (of Nations). Voluntary association of independent sovereign states, all of whom were formerly part of the British Empire. The Commonwealth was formally inaugurated, as the British Commonwealth, by the Statute of Westminster 1931. Member states of the Commonwealth come from all parts and continents of the world, and with a variety of races, languages and religions. They are also in a variety of stages of economic development. The present Commonwealth countries include some 11 that recognise HM Queen of England, some 14 that have opted for republican status and about five that are independent monarchies.

Commonwealth Chambers of Commerce, Federation of. Established in 1911, changing to present name and constitution in 1960. Exists to promote trade within the *Commonwealth* and with other countries. It has some 350 member *chambers of commerce*.

Commonwealth Development Corporation. Established in 1963 by a change of name from the *Colonial Development Corporation* which had been set up under the Overseas Resources Development Act 1948. It stimulates trade and industry in Commonwealth countries. The Corporation makes development loans, etc on a commercial basis and has borrowing powers up to £160 million.

Commonwealth Industries Association Ltd. Established in 1926, as the Empire Industries Association, taking present title in 1967 and aiming to strengthen *Commonwealth* relations through mutual preferential trade, investment, migration and scientific and technical cooperation.

Commonwealth Institute. Information and education centre about *Commonwealth* countries. Established in 1887 as the Imperial Institute, taking its present name in 1958.

Commonwealth Preference. System under which products and *commodities* from *Commonwealth* countries have been imported into the UK with import duties on them reduced or waived. On joining the *European Economic Community* on 1 January 1973, the UK sought to retain some elements of Commonwealth Preference in the cases of New Zealand dairy products and the *Commonwealth Sugar Agreement*. Some Commonwealth countries also sought recognition among the *associated states* of the EEC.

Commonwealth Producers' Organization. Promotes production and reciprocal trade in *Commonwealth* countries. Established in 1916.

Commonwealth safeguards (EEC). Included in the *Treaty of Accession 1972* under which the UK — and also Denmark and Ireland — entered the *Common Market* or *European Economic Community*, these safeguards were concerned particularly with

New Zealand exports of dairy produce to the UK and the position of the signatories to the *Commonwealth Sugar Agreement*.

Commonwealth Sugar Agreement (CSA). Arrangement for the UK to buy agreed quantities of sugar from Antigua, Barbados, Fiji, Guyana, India, Jamaica, Kenya, Mauritius, Swaziland, Trinidad and Tobago, Uganda, St Kitts-Nevis-Anguilla, and British Honduras. On Britain's entry into the Common Market, the Commonwealth Sugar Agreement was to continue until the end of 1974, suppliers under the CSA then having to supply the UK and other Common Market countries through either the Common Market's *association of overseas countries and territories* procedure or its provisions for *preferential trade agreements*.

communications mix. Combination of communications media and techniques considered appropriate for a particular purpose, such as a *promotional mix*.

(the) Community. Shortened version of *European Community*.

community action. Term used increasingly for a situation where the residents of a locality join together to take action to try to achieve a particular objective or to put right an injustice. See also *direct action*.

Community Agricultural Fund (EEC). Financed from the EEC's *common budget* to provide funds for the *Common Agricultural Policy*. Also known as the *European Agricultural Guidance and Guarantee Fund* or the FEOGA (its French initials).

Community Industry. Organization in the UK financed by the *Department of Employment* and run by the National Association of Youth Clubs to give employment to young people under 18 who would otherwise be unemployed.

community integration. Theory that workers are less *strike*-prone where they are more completely integrated with other workers in the community as a whole but more strike-prone where — as with coal miners and seamen, for example — their work leads them to live in their own isolated communities where they tend to develop and sharpen a *sub-culture* and industrial grievances peculiar to those communities.

community laws (EEC). Term for the *Regulations*, *Directives*, and *Decisions* of the *Council of Ministers* and *European Commission* of the *Common Market*. These edicts are normally in the fields of customs duties; agriculture; free movement of labour, services and capital; transport; monopolies and restrictive practices; state aid for industry; and policy in the coal, steel and nuclear energy industries. See also *Recommendations* and *Opinions* of the Council and the Commission.

community powers (EEC). Certain powers exercised jointly by the *Council of Ministers* and the *European Commission* of the *Common Market* countries at meetings in Brussels. Generally, a Minister can veto a proposal that 'affects his country's vital interests' but once a decision is taken in Brussels it is binding on all member states. Strictly speaking, however, the *Treaty of Rome 1957* provides for majority voting, and therefore does not recognize any right of veto, at meetings of the Council of Ministers. Informal recognition of the veto came about following France's *Luxembourg Declaration* of 1965 and was re-affirmed by a Heath-Pompidou communiqué in 1971. Edicts of the Council and the Commission are issued in the following forms. *Regulations* are binding in their entirety and apply directly in all member states. *Decisions* are also binding, but only on those towards whom they are specifically directed. *Directives* are binding on all member states, but the form and method of their implementation are at the discretion of the individual member states. *Recommendations* and *Opinions* do not have any binding force.

Community Relations Commission (CRC). Set up in the UK under the *Race Relations Act 1968* as a publicly financed body aiming to improve relations between people of different races. The Commission works partly through local community relations officers. See also *Race Relations Board* and *Civil Rights Act 1964* (US).

Compagnie des Agents de Change. Organization of *Agents de Change* or stockbrokers.

Compania colectiva. Partnership under Spanish law. See *Spanish companies*.

Companies Acts. UK statutes governing limited liability companies. The first 'Joint Stock Companies Acts' were passed in 1856. The acts mainly prescribing the legal requirements of company formation and operation are the Companies Acts of 1948 and 1967. The Companies Acts define an incorporated company as a separate legal entity consisting of an association of persons who contribute money and use it to earn profit in a trade or business.

Companies House. Repository for public inspection of records of UK companies registered with the *Registrar of Companies*.

company. As *corporation*. See also *articles of association, memorandum of association*, and under individual countries.

company agreement. Result of *collective bargaining* between management and *trade union(s)* at the level of a single company, possibly a multi-plant company. An agreement covering a single factory or plant is a *factory agreement* or *plant agreement*. Company agreements are often regarded as being more effective and responsible than the products of either of the two extremes of *industry-wide bargaining* and *workplace bargaining*. See also *autonomous bargaining* and *fractional (or fragmented) bargaining*.

company bargaining. *Collective bargaining* in quest of a *company agreement*.

company director. In the UK member of the *board of directors* appointed to run a company by its shareholders. A director may or may not be a shareholder himself. Broadly equivalent to *vice-president* in USA.

company memorandum. See *memorandum of association*.

company model. Computerized model of the overall operation and activities of a company or organization. Used in *corporate planning* and in forecasting what would be the effects of alternative decisions or of possible changes in market conditions. See also *marketing model*.

company secretary. Person in a British company responsible for ensuring that the legal obligations of the company are met, in particular the requirements of the *Companies Acts*. He is the official correspondent of the board of directors and may himself be a director. In many companies he may also be responsible for internal administration.

company union. As *staff association*.

comparative estimating. Form of *analytical estimating* based largely on the evidence of similar jobs in the past. See also *work study*.

comparative management. Research and study of management styles and practice internationally and cross-culturally.

comparative salary ratio. Or comp-ratio. Technique for measuring the effect of *salary increments* etc on the general level of pay within a salary grade. The ratio is expressed as the relationship of the actual average salary to the mid-point of the scale for the grade.

compensating rest. Or relaxation allowance. Time off granted to an employee to recover from particularly arduous work. It may be written into work study standards.

compensation. US term for all forms of remuneration. Includes not only pay but all types of employee *fringe benefits* such as pensions, insurance, stock options, bonus payments, etc. See also *total remuneration*.

competition, rules of (EEC). See *rules of competition*.

competitive strategy. Range of techniques including bidding, decision and operational gaming theories concerned with attempting to maximize the proportion of a limited 'prize' (eg market share) which one can gain in a competitive situation. See *operational research*.

component bar chart. Or, sometimes, compound bar chart. A *bar chart* on which the bars are divided into component parts, as in the illustration, to indicate how the totals represented by the bars are made up. See also *multiple bar chart* and illustration below.

composite conference. Combination of *Works Conference, Local Conference* and *Central Conference* to which a dispute was referred by the Central Conference under the *engineering procedure*, the *disputes procedure* for the UK engineering industry until it was ended in 1971.

composite motion. Combining a number of separate *motions* on a topic. The broad purpose of a composite motion at a meeting or conference is usually to concentrate discussion and save time. See also *omnibus motion* and *committee procedure*.

composition. When a receiving order is issued resulting in a debtor being declared *bankrupt*, he may offer a 'composition' whereby he undertakes to pay all creditors a certain sum. This must be approved by the Court and will not normally be accepted if less than 25 per cent of the total. It can be annulled by the Court if he fails to carry it out.

compound bar chart

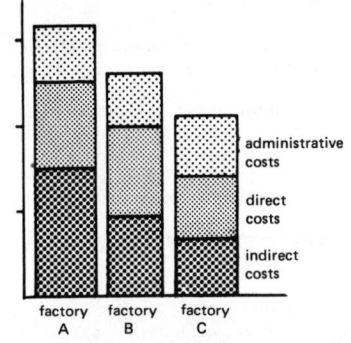

component or compound bar chart

compound bar chart. See *component bar chart*.

comp-ratio. See *comparative salary ratio*.

Comprehensive Employment and Training Act. US legislation of 1973 which seeks to provide the means of identifying and training for changing and future manpower needs. The Act is administered by the *Employment and Training Administration* of the *US Department of Labor*.

comptroller. See *controller*.

compulsory licence (license). Authorization to use a *patent* in spite of the objections of the patentee if a court rules that it is in the public interest for it to be so used.

compute (a bill). To calculate the date on which it falls due (pre-dates the modern term, 'computer').

computer. Machine or system that can handle and process data to instructions at very high speeds when these are provided in a prescribed form or *computer program* in *computer language*. The two basic types of computer are the *digital computer* and the *analog(ue) computer* with the main features of the two sometimes being combined in the *hybrid computer*. The high-speed work of a computer is done by its *central processing unit* with its *input device* translating the *input* data from human to computer language and the *output device* translating the computed data back into computer language. Basic types of personnel involved in computer work include *computer programmers* and *systems analysts*.

computer aided instruction/learning (CAI or CAL). Use of a *computer* to control presentation of teaching material to a trainee/student, several student terminals being linked to a central computer employing *multi-programming* and advanced teaching techniques such as *adaptive programming*.

computer language

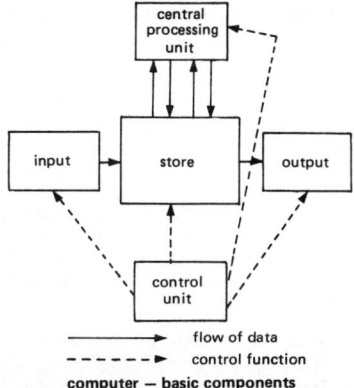

computer — basic components

Computer Assisted Placement Service (CAPS). UK non-profit making and confidential graduate recruitment service run jointly by the Standing Conference of University Appointments Services (SCUAS), the Standing Conference of Employers of Graduates (SCOEG) and the National Union of Students. It uses a tailor-made computerized matching system to provide a flexible and sensitive response to the needs and preferences of employers and final year undergraduates and postgraduates. See also *Central Services Unit for University Careers and Appointments Services*.

computer bureau. Agency hiring out computer time and/or know-how.

computer code. As *machine code*.

computer instruction code. As *machine code*.

computer language. Form of instructional medium or language comprehensible to a *computer* so that the computer can operate its own *machine code* (which activates its various mechanical operations) to process information in the way intended by the *programmer*. In its simplest form a computer language is known as a low-level (or basic) language or an autocode, and is a tool for dealing with the requirements of a particular computer and its machine code. More sophisticated languages, known as *high level languages*, are capable of being used to write *programs* for a wide range of types of computer and for highly complex problem-solving, *information storage and retrieval*, etc. The most popular high level language for commercial and industrial applications is *COBOL (Common Business Oriented Language)*, while the most common for scientific and mathematical applications are *ALGOL (Algorithmic Language)* and *FORTRAN* (acronym for *Formula Translation*). A high-level language specially developed in an attempt at combining the features and qualities of the commercial and scientific languages is *PL/1* (Programming Language 1). An introductory computer language combining many of the facilities of COBOL, ALGOL and FORTRAN is *BASIC*. A low-level but fairly complex language developed particularly for ICL 1900 series of digital computers is *PLAN* (Programming Language Nineteenhundred).

computer letter. Type of sales etc letter that is mass produced but using a computer programmed to type in individual details appropriate for particular recipients.

computer marked assessment. Term used by the *Open University* in the UK and others for an assessment of a student during a course arrived at by his/her answers to questions being marked by a *computer* and therefore being essentially quantitative and not providing the individual feedback and advice of, for example, a tutor marked assignment. See also *self assessment questions*.

computer memory. As *computer store*.

computer package. Or *software*. Group or package of facilities, services, programs, etc needed to handle a particular computer job or application. Packages for particular purposes are marketed by computer manufacturers, software specialists, data processing consultants, *computer bureaux*, etc.

computer program. Set of instructions to a *computer* to carry out a specific task, being written in the appropriate *computer language*.

computer programmer. Person responsible for writing a *computer program*, for translating a task or instructions from human language into *computer language*.

computer store. Part of a *computer* into which data can be fed, retained and retrieved. Also known as memory.

computer terminal. Input point or output point linked to a *computer* though possibly at some distance from it.

concealed surplus (of labo(u)r). Manpower surplus concealed by *labo(u)r hoarding*.

concentration analysis. Concentrating on those areas which are of major significance, eg major customers, key products, stock levels of expensive items, etc. A development of the *Pareto* concept.

concentration, theory of. See *theory of concentration*.

concentration ratio. Proportion of the total sales of an industry or industrial sector handled by a small number of large firms.

concession request form. Document used to record and authorize changes in drawing instructions for a product or project. See also *engineering query note*.

conciliation. Attempting to reconcile the positions and arguments of the two sides in a dispute. Also known as *mediation*.

Conciliation Act 1896 (UK). Following 1891 Royal Commission, provided for *conciliation* or *voluntary arbitration* in existing *trade disputes* or apprehended trade disputes. The *Conciliation Service* of the *Ministry of Labour* was developed to provide *conciliation* at the discretion of the Minister or at the request of either party to a dispute. The Conciliation Act was largely superseded by the *Industrial Courts Act 1919* which established the Industrial Court for voluntary arbitration.

Conciliation and Arbitration Service. Set up in UK in 1974 by *Secretary of State for Employment* as an independent agency to mediate in *industrial disputes*. Provided for in the *Protection of Employment Bill*.

Conciliation Officers. Members of *Conciliation and Arbitration Service* (UK).

Conciliation Service. Section of UK *Department of Employment* staffed by *Conciliation Officers* with powers originating under the *Conciliation Act 1896* and the *Industrial Courts Act 1919*. Succeeded by the *Conciliation and Arbitration Service* in 1974.

Conciliation (voluntary), Court of. Concerned not with making awards or judgements, but with offering a voluntary settlement to the parties to a dispute in UK.

conditions of employment. Points coming under such heads as health, safety, welfare, working conditions, length of working week, *job security*, etc that may be the subject of legislation or may be covered, in addition to wages, in *collective bargaining* between employers and *trade unions* or other employee representatives. Conditions of employment may also cover *fringe benefits*, particularly in *contracts of employment* for senior appointments.

Confederación General del Trabajo (CFT). Argentinian General Confederation of Labo(u)r, established in 1930 and covering *trade unions* with some 3,700,000 members.

Confederación Patronal Española. Spanish Employers Federation.

Confédération des Syndicats Chrétiens (CSC). Belgian Confederation of Christian Unions, a body particularly strongly supported in Flemish areas.

Confédération Française Démocratique du Travail (CFDT). See *French trade unions*.

Confédération Française des Travailleurs Chrétiens (CFTC). See *French trade unions*.

Confédération Générale des Cadres (CGC). General Confederation of Executives, a *trade union* organization concerned with technical and management staff. See also *French trade unions*.

Confédération Générale du Travail du Dependants. See *French trade unions*.

Confédération Générale du Travail. See *French trade unions*.

Confédération Générale du Travail du Luxembourg (CGT). Luxembourg General Confederation of Labo(u)r, formed in 1919 and covering *trade unions* which have approximately 32,000 members.

Confédération Générale du Travail — Force Ouvrière (CGT-FO). General Confederation of Labo(u)r — Workforce, one of the smaller French confederations of *trade unions* with a moderate Socialist political orientation. Other French confederations are the *CGT* (from which the CGT-FO originally broke away), the *CFDT*, the *CFTC*, and the *CGC*.

Confederation of British Industry (CBI). Formed in July 1965 from a merger of the then *British Employers' Confederation*, the *Federation of British Industries*, the *National Association of British Manu-*facturers and the *Industrial Association of Wales and Monmouthshire*. The CBI, in its own words, is the 'spokesman, advocate, top-level negotiator, adviser, forward-planner and general staff' of British business and industry. Its members include about 11,500 companies and some 220 *employers' associations* and *trade associations*.

Confederation of Irish Industry (CII). Founded in 1932, the CII seeks to promote the interests of business and industry in Ireland. Its membership consists of over 1500 firms and about 70 *trade associations*.

Confederation of Latin American Workers. Has member *trade unions* in some five countries.

Confederation of Shipbuilding and Engineering Unions. Federation of 24 *trade unions* in the UK shipbuilding and engineering industries. Has two main negotiating committees, for engineering and for shipbuilding.

Confederazione Generale dell'Industria Italiana (Confindustria). General Confederation of Italian Industry, the central organization for *employers' associations*. Originally formed in 1919.

Confederazione Generale Italiana del Lavoro. (CGIL). See *Italian trade unions*.

Confederazione Italiana Sindicati Autonomi Lavoratori (CISAL). See *Italian trade unions*.

Confederazione Italiana Sindicati Lavoratori (CISL). See *Italian trade unions*.

Conference Board. American independent non-profit research organization (formerly known as The National Industrial Conference Board) concerned with business economics, management, personnel administration. Established 1916 it now has over 4,000 corporate associates.

confidence level and limit. See *standard error*.

configuration. Combination of *hardware* and *software* forming a *computer* installation.

Confindustria. See *Confederazione Generale dell'Industria Italiana*.

confirming house. Type of *export house* of particular value to small and medium-sized firms in handling export sales. Its basic

77

function is to assist the overseas buyer by confirming, as principal, orders already placed so that the exporter may receive payment from the confirming house as and when the goods are shipped. Any credit period the buyer may require is arranged and carried by the confirming house which thus takes the credit risk over from the supplier. Information on confirming houses in the UK is available from the *British Export Houses Association*. See also *export club, export finance house* and *shipping and forwarding agent.*

conformer. Term used of a member of a *work group* working to a *fiddle* or restricted output informally agreed within the work group with the object of hiding loose *piece work* rates or of smoothing out piece work earnings. Thus the conformity is with the work group's policy, not with the employer's policy. A member of a work group who does not conform with the fiddle is known as a *job spoiler*.

conglomerate company (or group). Company or group with financial interests in a variety of industries.

conglomerate merger. Merger of companies from different industries to form a conglomerate.

Congress of Industrial Organizations (CIO). National organization of *trade unions* in the USA and Canada which was created in 1935 (for the first year it was known as the Committee for Industrial Organization) as a more radical and less craft union-based organization than the *American Federation of Labor (AF of L)* which had been established in 1881. The two organizations merged in December 1955 to form the *American Federation of Labor and Congress of Industrial Organizations.*

connected conversation interview. One in which the interviewee is encouraged to do most of the talking under the general prompting and guidance of the interviewer.

Connolly Occupational Interests Questionnaire. *Interest test or inventory* used in *personnel selection*, careers guidance, etc to build up a picture of the personal interests of a candidate or employee. The test consists of choices between 42 pairs of activities and 42 pairs of occupation titles, resulting in a profile of seven interest categories, namely, mechanical; computational and clerical; scientific; persuasive; artistic and musical; literary; and social service.

conscientious objector. Special meaning under the *Industrial Relations Act 1971* (UK) of a worker who conscientiously objected both to joining a *registered trade union* and to contributing to its funds under terms of an *agency shop agreement* or a *post-entry closed shop agreement*. Term still applies under *Trade Union and Labour Relations Act 1974.*

Conseil d'Administration de la Bourse. Board of Directors of *Luxembourg Stock Exchange*. It uses the advice of the *Commission de la Bourse*, a committee of stock exchange members.

Conseil d'Enterprise. *Works council* which is a legal requirement in Belgian firms with more than 150 employees.

Conseil de Gestion (Fr). *Management board.* See also *Conseil de Surveillance.*

Conseil de Gestion (Fr). *Management board. board.* See also *Conseil de Gestion.*

Conseil de Surveillance (Fr). *Supervisory Scientifique (CIOS).* The International Council for Scientific Management was founded in 1926 and includes in its membership the national management bodies from about 40 countries.

Conseil National du Patronat Français (CNPF). French National Employers' Council, the central employers' organization.

Conseils de Prud'Hommes. French labo(u)r courts which include lay judges from both sides of industry. They deal particularly with disputes arising out of *contracts of employment* and *collective bargains.*

Consejo Superior de Bolsas. Supreme Council of Stock Exchanges in Spain. See *Spanish stock exchanges.*

Consejo Superior de las Camaras Oficial de Comercio; Industria y Navegacion de España. Spanish Supreme Council of the Official Chamber of Commerce, Industry and Navigation, established in 1929.

consequences analysis. Project evaluation technique in which the effects of various alternative outcomes that might result from a major management decision are compared with the scale of company operations. The object is to assess the extent to which a shortfall or failure might affect the business. See also *alternative costs.*

consignment account. Special accounts must be kept by both a seller (or principal) and his *agent* to record the true ownership. When goods are distributed through agents, the ownership remaining vested in the seller, the transaction is said to be 'on consignment'. As the goods are no longer in the seller's possession, he cannot have them in 'stock'. As they have not been sold by the agent, they cannot be classed as 'sales'. They are therefore recorded as 'goods on consignment'. The agent, when accounting to his principal, will submit an 'account sales' so that the goods can then be recorded as sold.

consignment distributor. *Distributor* who pays for the goods he has bought only as he re-sells them.

consignment note. Document listing the goods that are supplied (by the consignor to the consignee) with a particular order. It is usually a copy taken from the *invoice* and is limited to quantity and description. If the supplier is out of stock with some items, they may be marked 'to follow'.

consignment stocks. Stock of goods being processed by *consignment accounts*.

consignor. See *consolidation*.

console typewriter. *Output device* on which a *computer* displays messages to its operator and through which the operator can input instructions to the computer.

consolidated accounts. Accounts of a parent or holding company which incorporate those of any subsidiaries.

Consolidated Fund. Or Account of Her Majesty's Exchequer. Account at the *Bank of England* into which government revenues are paid.

consolidation. Process by which goods can be accumulated until a consignment is large enough to merit a lower freight rate. The system is sometimes used to take advantage of return loads.

Consols. Irredeemable government consolidated stocks first issued with the launching of UK *National Debt* in 1694. See also *gilt-edged* and *government securities* and *blue chip investments*.

consortium. Association of corporations or companies formed to undertake projects or ventures, usually on a large scale requiring extensive expertise and/or financial resources.

consortium project. Where two or more companies undertake a project jointly, each taking agreed responsibilities. See also *project management*.

constant attendance allowance. Payable in the UK by the *Department of Health and Social Security* to persons so mentally or physically handicapped, including from industrial injuries, as to need constant care at home. See also *disablement benefit*.

constituent company. Subsidiary company which belongs to a parent or group of companies. The accounts are normally consolidated with the other organizations which make up the whole company.

Construction Industry Training Board (UK). Established July 1964 under the *Industrial Training Act 1964*.

constructive conflict. Theory attributed to *Mary Parker Follett* that conflict in industrial relations can have the merit of bringing out the issues really causing unrest. Virtually the same as *creative conflict*.

constructive dismissal. Legal term for situation where an employee leaves his employment on the face of it of his own accord, but in reality because the employer has made the employment intolerable. Under most legal systems this constitutes unfair dismissal.

consular invoice. *Invoice* for an *export* order which carries an endorsement by the importer's consul in the exporting country.

consultation. See *joint consultation*.

Consultative Committee of Transport Experts (EEC). Established under Article 83 of the *Treaty of Rome 1957* to advise the *European Commission* and through it the *Council of Ministers* on the development and implementation of the *common transport policy* of the *Common Market*.

consultative management. Style of management characterized by taking into account the views of the people being managed.

consume, propensity to. See *propensity to consume*.

consumer. Purchaser of *consumer goods* and services for immediate use and consumption. Marketing men also talk of the *progressive consumer* and the *retrogressive consumer*.

consumer acceptance test. *Market research* term for making a product or service available under controlled conditions in order to discover how far it is acceptable to consumers.

consumer action. Where customers or organizations representing their interests confront manufacturers, suppliers and/or government departments in direct action to seek improvement or changes in products and/or services. Consumer action has become common in most advanced societies, beginning in the 1960s in the USA and Sweden and being taken up equally strongly in the 1970s in the UK and other West European countries. One of the most notable pioneers of consumer action has been Ralph Nader in the USA. National organizations for consumers include the *Consumers' Union* in the USA (it actually dates back to the 1920s) and the *Consumer Association* in the UK. Action by consumer pressure groups has led to government action in the UK, USA and other countries.

Consumer Association. Established in UK in 1956 as an independent, non-profit making, consumer action body with the status of company limited by guarantee. The Consumer Association tests goods and services available to the public. Its publications include 'Which' and 'Motoring Which'.

Consumer Council. Set up in the UK in 1963 but disbanded in 1970. It could promote legislation, through the Board of Trade (the forerunner of the *Department of Trade*), but its influence was probably greatest through the mass media and by contact with national bodies and with local consumer groups, citizens' advice bureaux, retailers, manufacturers, *trade associations* and the public.

consumer credit. *Credit* facilities for *consumers*. Embraces special transactions such as *hire purchase, instalment purchase* and deferred payment.

Consumer Credit Protection Act. US law which lays down that credit terms for consumers must be clearly stated for charge and instalment accounts and contracts. Known as *truth in lending law*.

consumer disposable. Product sold to the public (the *consumer*) which is designed for once-only use or for disposal after a relatively short time. See also the longer lasting (usually) *consumer durable*.

consumer durable. Product sold to the public (the *consumer*) which is designed to last or be durable. The distinction between a consumer durable and a *consumer disposable* can sometimes seem to be a difference of degree rather than of kind, especially where a consumer durable has so-called *built-in obsolescence* or planned obsolescence.

consumer expendable. As *consumer disposable*.

consumer expenditure. Total expenditure in a national economy on goods and services for immediate consumption.

consumer goods. Goods purchased for use by the *consumer* or ultimate customer as distinct from capital equipment purchased by industry in the form of plant, machinery, etc, or industrial goods purchased by industry as components, raw materials, etc. Consumer goods may be divided between *consumer disposables* and *consumer durables*.

consumerism. Movement on behalf of *consumers* to improve *consumer goods* and services.

consumerisms. Characteristics of a *consumer society*.

consumer jury. Representative group of *consumers* whose views on products and proposed products are sought for *market research* purposes.

consumer panel. Or consumer purchase panel. Representative group of *consumers* who keep a record of their purchases of *consumer goods* for *market research*, etc, purposes. See also *dustbin check*.

Consumer Product Safety Commission. An independent US agency set up to protect the interests of the *consumer* in matters dealing with consumer products, eg safety standards. Under the direction of five commissioners appointed by the US President.

consumer promotions. *Sales promotion* aimed directly at the consumer or ultimate customer through cut-price offers, trading stamps, etc. Promotions aimed at distributors are known as *trade promotions*.

Consumer Protection Advisory Committee. Body of up to 15 Government-appointed

consumer purchase panel

members established in the UK under the *Fair Trading Act 1972*. It was intended that the Committee should investigate and report on particular consumer trade practices referred to it by the *Director-General of Fair Trading* or a Government Minister.

consumer purchase panel. As *consumer panel*.

consumer research. Branch of *market research* concerned particularly with markets for *consumer goods* and services intended for the individual's own use or consumption (eg anything from toothpaste to motor cars). The other major branch of market research is *industrial market research* which is concerned with the markets for goods and services sold to industry (eg anything from nuts and bolts to motor lorries).

consumer society. One whose economy and, to some extent, social values are based on the assumption that man is motivated by a desire for material goods and services. See also *free market agreement*.

consumer sovereignty. Concept that in a competitive society the consumer is 'king' and spends his money on the goods he prefers. To remain competitive and ensure a place in the market the producer must adjust to changes in consumer demand and taste.

Consumers' Union of the United States. *Consumer action* group established as long ago as the 1920s as a national focal point for defending the interests of consumers.

consumption. Economist's term for spending current income on present satisfaction. See also *investment*.

contact. *Market research* term for a person met in an interview though not necessarily providing enough information to be classified as an *informant*.

containerization. System and 'philosophy' of transportation and distribution of goods in standard size container loads to avoid the necessity for handling of individual goods or of a variety of types of container. Such a system is applicable to road, rail, air and sea travel, and its benefits in terms of labour and space economy are particularly evident at major transit points such as railheads, airports and docks.

contango facilities. Provisions by which, at the end of a *Stock Exchange* account period, a speculator does not settle his account but instead arranges to pay interest on the value of his share purchases until he sells them or until the end of the next account period. In recent years contango has largely been supplanted as a means of avoiding paying outright for share purchases by arranging with a *stockjobber* a simultaneous sale and purchase at a small profit to the stockjobber.

continental shift system. Form of *shift working* in which shift workers change shifts frequently, possibly two or three times a week.

contingency allowance. Work study term for an allowance built into *standard times* to take into account small tasks a worker has to undertake occasionally in addition to the work studied.

contingency planning. Plans prepared in advance laying down action to be taken if abnormal incidents should occur.

continuation option. Right of an insured person ceasing membership of a life assurance scheme and/or *widow's and orphans' pension scheme* during his/her working life to obtain *endowment assurance, whole life assurance,* or widow's pension cover up to the amounts for which he/she is covered under the scheme. See also *frozen pension* and *vested rights*.

continuity of employment. Under UK *Redundancy Payments Act 1965* and subsequent related legislation, continuity of employment is presumed for purposes of compensation, etc when an employee is re-engaged after *unfair dismissal*.

continuous assessment. Where the course or project work of a trainee/student is assessed continuously by the instructors/teachers during a course as a complement to or replacement for end-of-course tests or examinations.

continuous credit. Facilities to borrow up to a certain level, the borrower being able to repay all or part of the loan and then borrow it again as he/she wishes. The term is normally used of personal borrowing, *revolving facilities* being more often the term used of company borrowing.

continuous movements. *Motion study* or *work study* term for smooth and curved movements which avoid sharp changes of direction.

continuous production. As *flow line production*.

continuous shiftwork. Shift working designed to maintain a plant in continuous production, 24 hours a day, seven days a week.

continuous stocktaking. *Stock control* system that includes constant physical checks.

continuous timing. As *cumulative timing*.

contouring. Type of mathematical technique concerned with calculating the optimum solution to a management problem. It represents mathematical functions pictorially using contours, as on maps.

contract. Agreement between two or more parties which is enforceable by law.

contract for services. *Contract* by which a person undertakes to perform certain services for an employer, but not as an employee. A contract for services usually involves payment of a fee, rather than a salary, and does not carry the employment protection rights of, for example, a *contract of employment*.

contracting-in. Where a trade unionist's *trade union* dues include a *political levy* component only if he positively contracts to make such a payment. Introduced in the UK by the *Trade Disputes and Trade Union Act 1927* instead of the opposite process, *contracting-out*, which had been introduced by the *Trade Union Act 1913* and was later reinstated by the *Trade Disputes and Trade Union Act 1946*.

contracting-out (from trade union political levy). Introduced in UK by the *Trade Union Act 1913* in reversing the decision in the *Amalgamated Society of Railway Servants v. Osborne (1910)*. The 1913 Act laid down that a *trade union* could raise a *political levy* and have a *political fund*, in support of the Labour Party, but the provision for contracting-out ensured that individual trade unionists could exercise a political democratic right by opting not to pay a political levy. Contracting-out remained from 1913 Act until, in the wake of the *General Strike of 1926*, the *Trade Disputes and Trade Union Act 1927* introduced contracting-in. This remained in force until contracting-out was restored by the *Trade Disputes and Trade Union Act 1946*.

contracting-out (pensions). In UK where a firm's *occupational pension scheme* is contracted out of the *state graduated pension scheme* its members receive their occupational scheme benefits in addition to the flat-rate state pension, but will not receive any graduated pension for the period that they have been contracted out. In order to be contracted out, an occupational pension scheme must provide pension at least equivalent to the maximum state graduated pension scheme and it must also provide that an individual leaving the scheme has vested rights to the *Equivalent Pension Benefit* of the state. When an employee leaves a contracted-out occupational pension scheme, he/she must be given a *Certificate of Assurance* setting out the pension earned or the employer must make a *Payment in Lieu (PIL)* to the *Department of Health and Social Security* to be incorporated in the employee's state pension.

contract of employment. Individual contracts of employment became a legal requirement in UK with the *Contracts of Employment Acts 1963* and *1972*. The required minimum notice of termination of contract was extended by the *Industrial Relations Act 1971*, this latter Act also providing for the employee to be better informed by the employer on conditions of employment including *grievance procedure*. See also *contract for services*.

contract of service. Type of *contract of employment* usually applicable to a senior executive or a consultant. A contract of service often takes the form of *fixed-term contract*. In some situations, a contract of service on expiry may carry a *security of tenure* for the employed party similar to that of a contract of employment. See also *contract for services*.

contracts, illegal. See *illegal contracts*.

Contracts of Employment Act 1963. Introduced requirement in the UK for all employees to have formal contract specifying such points as minimum period of notice etc. Act modified by *Industrial Relations Act 1971* to provide an employee with minimum of six weeks' notice after ten years' employment or eight weeks' notice after 15 years; to give information on rights under any *agency shop agreement* or approved closed shop agreement; to specify holiday entitlement and sometimes, sickness or industrial injury benefit; to make provision for easier change of employer's name on a contract, after a takeover.

Contracts of Employment Act 1972. Consolidated and amended the *Contracts of Employment Act 1963* in the UK.

Contracts Preference Schemes. Under these schemes, firms in UK *Special Development Areas* and *Development Areas* have opportunities to tender for public contracts and where price, quality, delivery date and other considerations are equal, government purchasing departments, nationalized industries and other public bodies will place contracts with firms in these areas in preference to firms elsewhere.

contract research. Research undertaken for a commissioning organization which owns and benefits from the results.

contribución territorial rustica y pecuaria. Agricultural land tax in Spain. See *Spanish income tax*.

contribución territorial urbana. Urban land tax in Spain. See *Spanish income tax*.

contribuição industrial. Industrial tax on business income in Portugal. See *Portuguese income tax*.

contribuiçao predial. Property tax in Portugal. See *Portuguese income tax*.

contributed capital. Or paid-in capital. Money available to a company through the issue of its *shares*, as opposed to *debt capital* in the form of loans.

contributed value. Defined by *Drucker* as 'the difference between the gross revenue received by a company from the sale of its products or services, and the amount paid out by it for the purchase of raw materials and for services rendered by outside suppliers . . . It accounts for all the resources the business itself contributes to the final product and the appraisal of their efforts by the market.' See also *added value*.

contribution (analysis). Difference between the sales revenue from a product and the marginal cost or *variable costs* directly attributable to it. It is thus a combination of the contribution the product makes to the firm's profit and its contribution to *fixed costs*, as illustrated here in a simple form of *break-even chart*. Contribution analysis is a *management accounting* technique for establishing the contribution of each of a firm's products and showing how profits would be affected by changes in *product mix*.

contribution deduction schemes. As *check-off*.

contribution pricing. Setting price levels so

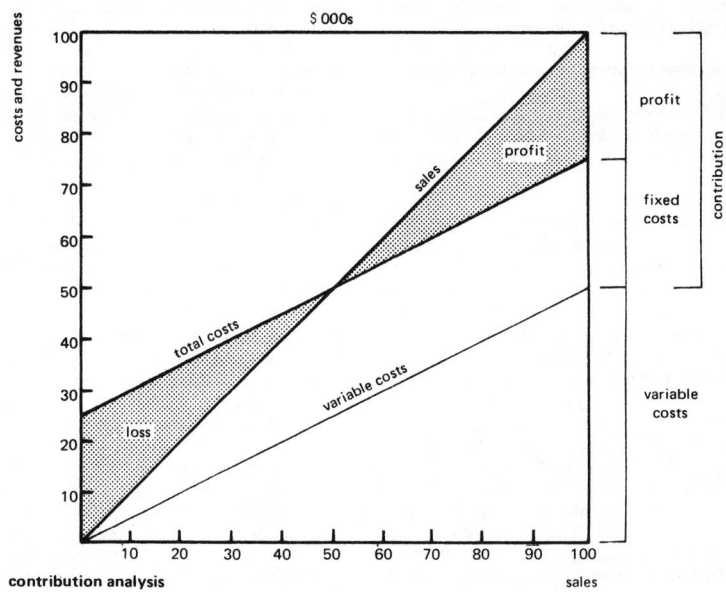

contribution analysis

that they at least cover *variable costs* and ideally go some way towards contributing to fixed costs and profits. See *contribution (analysis)*.

contributory negligence, employee's. See *employee's contributory negligence*.

contributory pension scheme. Where employees contribute to their *superannuation* or *pension* scheme, the contributions usually being either flat-rate or a percentage of salary.

control account. Or controlling account or total account. Account which totals and monitors a group of *ledger accounts*.

control console. Point where a person in charge of an automatic or semi-automatic system can exercise control, eg control desk from which instructor/teacher in *computer aided learning* or a *language laboratory* can monitor the performance of students.

controllable costs. Costs that vary with changes in production. Also used to describe any costs which are within the direct personal control of the manager of a department or unit.

controlled circulation journal. One that is financed entirely from advertising revenue, being sent free of charge to readers carefully selected as potential purchasers of the advertisers' products or services.

controlled company. See *holding company*.

controlled daywork. Term sometimes used for *measured daywork* when the daily production target is arrived at through *work measurement*.

controlled funding (pensions). Techniques used in the *annual premium costing* of pension schemes such as *final salary pension schemes* where the eventual pension will be related to an unknown future salary. Controlled funding techniques are used to forecast likely future salaries, and therefore realistic present premiums, the forecasts being made statistically safer by applying them to large groups of employees. Controlled funding techniques include adaptable funding, flexible funding and *planned funding*. Forecasting of future salaries and pensions is particularly critical in a *self-administered fund*. An alternative to annual premium costing is the *single premium costing* method where each year's premium pays for the pension earned in that year, a method feasible in such pension schemes as an *average salary pension scheme* or a *works pension scheme*.

controlled report. In *performance appraisal* procedures etc a type of report in which a senior manager works to a prescribed *checklist* in assessing the performance and ability of a more junior executive. Other management appraisal techniques include *free report, task-based appraisal, ranking, factor rating, forced choice approach* and *critical incident technique*.

controller. Senior financial executive, especially in US organizations, normally responsible for accounting records, reports and overall control of finances. May also be responsible for budgetary control and management accounting. Also known as comptroller.

controlling. Process of measuring and monitoring actual performance in comparison with pre-determined objectives, plans, standards and budgets and taking any corrective action required. Some control activities are automatic, as in automation.

control unit, program. See *program control unit* (of a computer).

convenience foods. Wholly or partly prepared or cooked when offered for sale and therefore ready for consumption with little or no further preparation.

convenience goods. *Consumer goods*, particularly *consumer disposables*, bought regularly or frequently by the general public (eg newspapers or perishable goods as distinct from *consumer durables* such as furniture).

convenience stores. Retail shops typically stocking a limited range of basic food and grocery products etc, and usually staying open for long hours and serving a local population.

convenor. Senior *shop steward* in a firm or plant, normally elected by the plant's *joint shop steward committee (JSSC)*, which is in most cases perforce a *multi-union* committee. See also *combine committee*.

convergent/divergent. One of the three spectra on which people are measured in *temperament and personality testing* (the other spectra being introversion/extroversion and stable/neurotic). At the convergent end of the convergent/divergent spectrum are types of personality that concentrate on the job in hand, while at the divergent end are types whose interests and quests for solutions to problems extend beyond their own fields. See also *psychological testing*.

conversational mode. Mode in which a *computer* can be given instructions and give an immediate response.

conversion cost. Cost of obtaining *added value* in selling: may refer to cost of converting potential into actual customers.

conversion training. Retraining for occupation that is slightly rather than radically different from previous occupation. Cf *booster training, refresher training, retraining, updating training, upgraded training.*

convertibility. Extent to which a currency is exchangeable for other currencies or for gold.

convertible debentures. See *debentures*.

convertible loan stock. Fixed interest stock whose holders have an option to convert the stock into *ordinary shares* at a later date.

convertible term assurance policy. Policy taken out on *term assurance* premiums and conditions with a clause permitting the insured to change to *endowment assurance* premiums and conditions at a later date, thus improving the long-term benefits of the policy in exchange for higher premiums.

cooling-off period. Postponement of a *strike* or other *industrial action* to give the parties to the dispute time in which to reconsider the position. An 80-day cooling-off period was introduced in the USA by the *Taft-Hartley Act 1948*.

Cooperatie. Cooperative under Netherlands law. See also *Netherlands companies*.

cooperative. Association of consumers or producers engaged in trade or business, sharing out the profits amongst members.

cooperative advertising. Where a manufacturer and a local agent or distributor share advertising effort and costs.

coordinating. Process of ensuring that the different parts of an organization and the people within it work smoothly together.

co-ownership. Shared ownership and usually control of an enterprise by employees.

copartnership scheme. Form of *profit sharing scheme* in which employees normally acquire shares in the employer's company in proportion to the net profits of the company and their own earnings.

Copenhagen Stock Exchange. Or *Københavns Fondsbørs*. Founded originally in the 1680s, it is the only Stock Exchange in Denmark.

copy. Text for an advertisement or for newspaper and other editorial material.

copy brief. Statement of the objectives and *copy strategy* of an advertising campaign.

copyright. Exclusive right to reproduce particular written material. It normally belongs originally to the author who may assign it to someone else such as a publisher, though the situation is a little more complex for some types of material. See also *patent* and *trade mark*.

copy strategy. Outline of the development of a product or brand and the information to be conveyed in *advertising* it. Part of the *copy brief*.

copy test. Test of advertising copy, either during its preparation or after its effect can be measured.

core course. Provides basic materials and ideas for the study of a topic while leaving teacher or instructor free to expand on it with his own ideas.

core time. Term used in an application of *flexible working hours (fwh)* for the periods during the day when all employees are required to be present at work. The rest of the day is *flexible time* in which each employee is free to choose his or her own working hours.

Cork Stock Exchange. One of two *Irish stock exchanges*.

Corn Exchange (UK). 200 years old specialist *commodity exchange* for dealings nationally in cereals between millers, merchants, brewers, manufacturers, etc.

corporate goals. As *corporate objectives*.

corporate identity program(me). Use of a standardized and immediately recognizable design theme by a company or organization to keep its name and 'image' before the

85

public, etc. This design theme is normally evident in such overtly promotional activities as *advertising* and *public relations*, but also in more functional areas such as packaging, product design, stationery and motor vehicle livery. A corporate identity program(me) may use aural images, such as slogans and signature tunes (eg in television advertising), as well as visual designs.

corporate image. Impression a company or other organization makes on the public, customers, even its own employees, perhaps as a positive result of a *corporate identity program(me)*. See also *house style*.

corporate management. Style and structure of management geared to considering problems and policies in the context of the total firm or organization and its resources, rather than a more departmentalized style in which the attitudes of individual managers are shaped by their sectional interests within the firm.

corporate objectives. Broad objectives and philosophy of a company, corporation or other organization, short and long term, covering the total range of the organization's activities. Corporate objectives may embrace *management style* and social attitudes as well as trading, financial, personnel, technical, public relations and *corporate planning* aims.

corporate planning. Or *'long-range' corporate planning*. Long-term planning involving all the departments of a company in the context of assumptions about developments in the market environment, etc, and, therefore, the desirable development of new products and new areas of business. Corporate planning quantifies as far as possible and often involves the use of *computers*. It involves the assessment of external threats and opportunities and internal strengths and weaknesses, and the evaluation of alternative strategies.

corporate secretary (US). Post broadly equivalent to *company secretary* in the UK.

corporate strategy. Can take in *corporate objectives* and *corporate planning* but is concerned particularly with the company or corporation in relation to its markets, its competitors and its environment generally.

corporation. 1. Association of people in a company constituted as an artificial 'legal person' quite separate and distinct from the people who may form its membership. It acts in its own name, has a common seal enabling it to identify its own acts and may sue or be sued. Normally endowed with perpetual succession. **2.** People combined into, or acting as, one body.

corporation tax. Flat rate tax on all company *profits* which replaced company income and profits tax in the UK in 1965 (though income tax remained payable, of course, on *dividends* distributed)

corpus. Principal or capital of a fund, estate investment, etc.

corrective advertising. Correction of a false or misleading claim in earlier advertising. May be required on the direction of the Federal Trade Commission in USA. Corrective advertising can be a major item in advertising budgets.

correlation. In statistics a measure of the relationship between two numerically valued random variables. When there is simultaneous increase or decrease in value of two sets of variables it is 'positive correlation'. When one set of variables increases and the other set decreases simultaneously it is 'negative correlation'. The degree of correlation is expressed by the coefficient of correlation in which a completely positive correlation between two variables is represented by the figure +1.0 while a completely negative correlation is represented by the figure −1.0. Figures between these two extremes will measure the degree of positive or negative correlation in accordance with the sign. A zero correlation shows that there is no relationship between the two variables.

correspondent banking. System by which banks, usually large ones, perform certain services for other banks in return for holding their credit balances.

corretores. Portuguese *stockbrokers*. See *Portuguese stock exchanges*.

COS. Cash on shipment.

CoSIRA. *Council for Small Industries in Rural Areas* (UK).

cost. Sum of money or equivalent expended in terms of labour, materials, use of equipment, rent, etc, to produce a product or service. To be distinguished from the *price* asked for the product or service and from the *value* of the product or service to the purchaser. See, for example, *committed costs, direct costs, fixed costs,* *imputed costs, indirect costs, managed costs, marginal costs, mixed costs, opportunity costs, semi-variable costs, stepped costs, uncontrollable costs, variable costs,* etc.

cost absorption. Accounting procedure for allotting *indirect costs* to a particular product.

cost accountant. One who concentrates on keeping, analyzing and advising on cost records and data.

cost accounting. Concerned primarily with the classification, recording, allocation and analysis of cost data to aid business planning and control.

cost and freight (c and f). Export sale terms under which the supplier of goods pays for their shipment to a port in the country of the purchaser, though the latter is normally responsible for their insurance on board ship. See also *cost, insurance, freight.*

cost approach to distribution, total. See technique of *total cost approach to distribution.*

cost-benefit analysis (CBA). Analytical technique involving a monetary assessment of total costs and revenues of a project, paying particular attention to social costs and benefits which do not normally feature in conventional costing exercises. The object is to identify and quantify as many tangible and intangible costs and benefits as possible. Leads into realms of *discounted cash flow.*

cost centre (center). Typically a department, unit or geographical location for which costs, eg direct materials, labo(u)r, expenses, etc can be ascertained and allocated to enable effective control of costs to be exercised. Normally a cost centre (center) attracts no revenue producing income. See *profit centre (center).*

cost-effectiveness. Analysis of benefits of particular expenditure to establish whether the same expenditure could be used more effectively or whether the same benefits are attainable with less expenditure. US Department of Defense introduced the technique.

cost estimate analysis. See *estimate analysis.*

cost hammock. Grouping together of the *costs* of a number of activities in *critical path analysis.*

cost inflation. See *cost-push inflation.*

costing. Process of identifying and apportioning costs. See also *absorption costing* and *marginal costing.*

costing system. System set up to monitor and control a company or organization's costs, keeping them as close as possible to budgeted costs and giving management a check on company operations and performance. Can be complemented by a continuous recording of *management ratios* that can give early warning of longer term trends. See also *management accounting.*

cost insurance and freight basis. Method of computing a nation's *balance of payments* taking into account the value of *invisible exports* and *imports* such as finance insurance and shipping services. The term is used particularly in the USA.

cost, insurance, freight. See *cif.*

cost-of-living index. Indicates the average cost of most, though not all, of the basic necessities of life for an average family. Typical indices are the *BLS Consumer Price Index* (US) and the *Retail Price Index* (UK).

cost-of-living sliding scale. As *threshold agreement.*

cost plus pricing. Calculation of prices by adding a percentage to the estimate of *cost.* Sometimes used in contract work involving large and difficult-to-anticipate costs. A cruder approach than that of techniques such as *product analysis pricing.*

cost-price squeeze. Pressure of increasing *costs* at a time when competition or other pressures make it difficult to put up *prices.*

cost-push inflation. Unstable economic conditions characterized by price increases caused primarily by increases in the costs of production rather than the pressure of increased demand for the product or service concerned. Inflation caused by the latter is *demand inflation.*

cost reduction plan. Type of incentive or *payment-by-results* scheme in which cost savings above an agreed level are shared between the employer and the employee in agreed proportions. The classic scheme of this kind was the Long Range Sharing Plan negotiated between Kaiser Steel and the *United Steelworkers of America* in the USA in 1962. See also *share of production plan.*

cost study. Critical examination of the component parts of the cost of a product or service.

cost variance. Where actual cost varies from standard cost arrived at by *standard costing*.

cost-volume-price relationship. See *break-even chart*.

Cotton and Allied Textiles Industry Training Board (UK). Established July 1966 under the *Industrial Training Act 1964*.

Council for Environmental Science and Engineering. Body composed of leading UK professional engineering and science institutions and concerned with the development of natural resources needed by highly industrialized economies and with the effects upon the environment of exploiting them.

Council for Mutual Economic Assistance. See *COMECON*.

Council for National Academic Awards. Autonomous body set up in the UK in September 1964 to award degrees comparable with university degrees to students in institutions, such as the *polytechnics*, which cannot confer their own degrees. CNAA degrees are BSc, BA, MSc, MA, MPhil, PhD.

Council for Small Industries in Rural Areas (CoSIRA). Operating in England, services include making loans in conjunction with private sources to manufacturing and servicing firms employing not more than 20 skilled workers, particularly those with export business. The Council also provides technical, commercial, financial and management advice. The Scottish equivalent is the *Small Business Division of the Scottish Development Agency*. The Welsh equivalent is the *Small Business Section of the Welsh Development Agency*. In Northern Ireland there is the *Local Enterprise Development Unit*.

Council for Technical Cooperation. Set up by Commonwealth members of the *Colombo Plan* to promote technical and scientific cooperation.

Council of Associated Stock Exchanges. UK organization administered from the Liverpool Stock Exchange. See also *Stock Exchange* (UK).

Council of Better Business Bureaus Inc (US). See *Better Business Bureaus*.

Council of Economic Advisors (US). Makes analyses of the US economy and advises the President.

Council of Engineering Institutions (CEI). Federation of 14 of the leading professional engineering institutions in the UK. Corporate members of these institutions are able, on the authority of the Royal Charter of the CEI, to call themselves *Chartered Engineers* and to use the abbreviation *CEng* after their names. The member institutions of the CEI are the *Institute of Marine Engineers;* the *Institution of Chemical Engineers;* the *Institution of Civil Engineers;* the *Institution of Electrical Engineers;* the *Institution of Electronic and Radio Engineers;* the *Institution of Gas Engineers;* the *Institution of Mechanical Engineers;* the *Institution of Mining Engineers;* the *Institution of Mining and Metallurgy;* the *Institution of Municipal Engineers;* the *Institution of Production Engineers;* the *Institution of Structural Engineers;* the *Royal Aeronautical Society;* and the *Royal Institution of Naval Architects*.

Council of Europe. Established in May 1949 by Belgium, Denmark, France, the Republic of Ireland, Italy, Luxembourg, the Netherlands, Norway, Sweden and the UK. These founder members were joined later by Austria, Cyprus, West Germany, Greece, Iceland, Malta, Switzerland and Turkey. The Council subscribes to the rule of law and to the principles of political freedom and individual liberty but it is a consultative body without real powers. The Council of Europe has a Committee of Foreign Ministers and a Consultative Assembly of member governments' representatives meeting in Strasbourg.

Council of Ministers (EEC). Supreme decision-making body of the *Common Market*, with responsibilities and *community powers* for the *European Economic Community (EEC)*, the *European Atomic Energy Community (Euratom)* and the *European Coal and Steel Community (ECSC)*. The Council of Ministers meets in Brussels or Luxembourg with the Foreign Ministers of the member states normally taking six-month turns as *President of the Council of Ministers*. The *Treaty of Rome 1957* provided for majority voting in the Council in the interests of faster decision making, but in practice (as a result of Gaullist pressure leading to the *Luxembourg Declaration*) the

Council has taken important decisions on unanimous votes so that, in effect, a Minister can veto a proposal that 'affects his country's vital interests'.

Policy proposals are tabled for the Council of Ministers by the *European Commission* which also has executive (and some judicial) responsibility for implementing Council decisions and policies. Proposals from the Commission to the Council may be routed through the *Committee of Permanent Representatives* (the member states' ambassadors to the EEC) who are concerned that proposals should not be damaging to national interests. Other major institutions of the Common Market are the *European Court of Justice* and the *European Parliament*, with the *European Social Fund* and the *European Investment Bank* having their special roles. The Council of Ministers may also consult the *Economic and Social Committee*.

Edicts of the Council of Ministers and/or the European Commission are issued in one of the following forms. *Regulations* are binding in their entirety and apply directly in all member states. *Decisions* are also binding, but only on those towards whom they are specifically directed. *Directives* are binding on all member states, but the form and method of their implementation are at the discretion of the individual member states. *Recommendations* and *Opinions* do not have any binding force. Articles 145-54 are the parts of the Treaty of Rome under which the Council of Ministers was established.

Council on Environmental Quality (US). Responsible for developing and coordinating environmental program(me)s.

Council on International Economic Policy (US). Advises the President on world economic questions.

counselling. *Personnel* function concerned with giving practical help to employees on personal problems both at work and in their private lives.

counter-purchasing. In international trading, the placement of an order by a purchaser with a supplier in another country on condition that goods to an equal or specified value are sold in the opposite direction between the two countries. Thus, for example, a buyer in an East European country might place an order for capital equipment with a company in the UK or USA on condition that either the same company or someone else in the UK or USA places an order with the East European country for, say, textiles or other *consumer goods*. It is not usually a bartering arrangement — two separate financial transactions are normally involved — but may be regarded as a form of *reciprocal trading*. *Chambers of Commerce* often assist in arranging such two-way transactions, government departments in the western world usually viewing them with considerable suspicion.

countervailing duty. Import duty introduced over and above any normal import duty on a product for the specific purpose of countering an *export subsidy* in — and therefore, in effect, *dumping* by — the *country of origin*. A notable recent example of a countervailing duty has been that introduced in 1962 by the *Common Market* or *European Economic Community* against certain US products such as carpets.

countervailing power. Economic theory, largely attributable to J K Galbraith, that a group holding excessive economic power may be countered and balanced by an opposing powerful group instead of being in a position to exploit others. The obvious and most quoted example of countervailing power in action is a powerful employer being opposed by a powerful *trade union* or combination of trade unions.

country of origin. That from which goods or *commodities* are being exported in a particular transaction. The goods or commodities may not have been produced there but may have been imported into that country, wholly or in part, under previous transactions. Exports of goods or commodities that have been produced within the country of origin are known as *domestic exports*.

coupling-up. Overlapping of *shift work* to ensure continuity of operation. *Hand-over pay* may be payable to employees with special coupling-up responsibilities.

coupon advertising. Incorporation in a newspaper or journal advertisement of a *reader reply form* for the reader to complete and send to the advertiser either placing an order for the goods/services advertised or requesting further information.

coupon clipping. See *bearer bonds*.

coupon pack. *Consumer goods* pack in which a *sales promotion* coupon is incorporated.

Court of Conciliation (UK). See *Conciliation (voluntary), Court of*.

cousins group. A group, in *group training methods*, which is composed of people of similar status in the same organization but who do not normally have close working contact.

covariance. Basic statistical concept abbreviated from the term 'common variance'. It is a measure of the extent to which two variables covary.

covenant. 1. Binding agreement *(contract)* between two parties. **2.** Clause in a contract.

covenants in restraint of trade. Provisions in a *contract of employment* to restrain an employee from making improper use of knowledge acquired in his work on leaving the employer to work in competition with him. Such provisions are illegal in common law unless the employer can show that they are necessary for the protection of his business. See also the *Patents Act 1949* in the UK.

cover. See *earnings/dividend ratio*.

coverage analysis. Mathematical technique for ascertaining the 'ideal' stock level which both minimizes the amount of capital tied up in stock and yet meets a given level of service. The principle employed is to relate the number of annual replenishment orders for a given item to the square root of the annual usage or sales. The method uses *random sampling* and provides the basis for establishing an optimum ordering policy together with an estimate of likely savings.

Coverdale training. Form of *sensitivity training* developed by Ralph Coverdale and Bernard Smith in the UK. It concentrates on setting real group tasks as distinct from *role playing*. Participants analyze their own task performance and the social processes which occurred. The object is to develop cognitive and social skills.

covered. 1. Term used particularly of dealings in foreign exchange in both *spot* and *forward markets* in such combination that no loss will be suffered, whatever happens to exchange rates during the period of the forward contract(s). **2.** General term for dealings in which loss will be avoided or restricted to a particular level, whatever happens.

covered time. Time spent on work for which a bonus or *piece work* scheme exists but where it is not used. Instead of *payment-by-results*, payment is on a daywork or other time-related payment scheme.

cowboy. As *rate-buster*.

CPA. 1. *Critical path analysis.* **2.** *Certified Public Accountant* (US).

CPI. *California Psychological Inventory.*

CPM. Critical path method. See *critical path analysis*.

CPP. Critical path planning.

CPU. *Central processing unit* (of a computer).

Cr. Credit or creditor.

craft control. Assertion of craft rights, customs and rules by *trade unions*.

craft guilds. Medieval custodians of the standards of craft training. Now, in the UK, have rather more ceremony-orientated existence as *Livery Companies* of the City of London.

craftsman. Skilled worker able to apply wide range of skills and know-how following apprenticeship/traineeship and appropriate technical education. Sometimes known, perhaps a little archaically nowadays, as a *journeyman*, an artificer or an artisan.

craft training. Training which, in conjunction with appropriate *further education*, and usually under terms of an *apprenticeship*, leads to status of *craftsman*, or, a little more archaically, *journeyman*.

Craft union. Or horizontal union. *Trade union* whose members are mainly skilled craftsmen who have served an apprenticeship (eg printing and engineering). This is in contrast to unions for general workers and white collar workers.

crash cost. Cost of a crash program(me) to complete a job or project compared with its normal cost.

Crawford small parts dexterity test. *Pegboard test* of *psychomotor skills*, originating in the US. The first part involves the use of tweezer-type instruments to place small pins in holes and then to place collars over the pins. The second part of the test involves screwing down small screws at speed. See also *psychological testing*.

crawling-peg (exchange rates). As *sliding-parity*.

creative conflict. Concept developed by

Mary Parker Follett that if opposing views can be integrated rather than simply resolved by compromise, conflict can be used as a means of achieving progress. Virtually as *constructive conflict*.

credit. 1. Time allowed for payment for goods and/or services or for the repayment of a loan. 2. Borrowing up to a certain limit allowed by a bank, etc, to an individual or a company (see also *buyer credit* and *supplier credit*). 3. Acknowledgement of payment by a debtor by entering the sum in an account (see also *ledger account*). 4. Right hand side of an account or an entry in it. 5. Total value of credit entries. 6. Positive balance remaining in an account. 7. Certification that a particular course of study has been completed.

credit agency. As *credit bureau*.

credit approval. Process by which customers' orders are examined and sanctioned for credit. In a small firm this may take the form of initialling or rubber stamping, but where a *computer* is used a special routine will list those customers who exceed their *credit rating*.

credit bank. Term in Western Europe for what is known in the UK as a *commercial bank* or a *clearing bank*, or in the USA as a *member bank*.

credit bureau. Organization providing business firms with credit information on prospective customers. As *credit agency*.

credit card. Tool of personal financial management of US origin, introduced into the UK in the late 1960s. Credit cards are sponsored by most of the leading *member banks (clearing banks)* and by retailers and wholesalers. The card carries the signature and code number of the holder who, on showing the card to a retailer etc, makes purchases on credit simply by signing the bill. He/she receives an account from the credit card company for all purchases made in a particular month after making the purchases, thus obtaining interest-free credit for that period. However, if payment is not made at this stage, interest is normally payable.

credit clubs, international. See *international credit clubs*.

credit control. 1. Procedures and policies aimed at checking and controlling the granting of credit facilities to customers. Includes obtaining references, setting credit limits and terms, and follow up procedures to obtain collection of debts outstanding. 2. Systems introduced by governments aimed at controlling bank and other forms of credit.

credit factoring. Range of financial services normally offering **a** ready cash for the face value of goods invoiced to customers, less a percentage; **b** operation of *sales ledger*; **c** *credit risk insurance*.

credit insurance. Provision of a guarantee or insurance that a supplier of goods or services will receive payment even if the customer does not himself make the payment. Such a service can be provided for exporters from the UK, for example, by the *Export Credits Guarantee Department*.

credit interchange. Exchange of information about a particular customer by firms mutually concerned, sometimes by personal contact, by letter or telephone. More often it is organized by a *credit club* or *trade association* or *credit bureau* or other special agency.

credit line. As *credit outstanding*.

credit manager. Executive responsible for determining customers' *credit ratings* as part of the *credit control* function.

credit note. Document issued to a customer to indicate that he is in credit for a certain sum of money. Issued to record faulty or returned goods or to adjust errors relating to previous invoiced charges.

creditor. One who is owed money by a company or individual, either as a result of making a loan or while awaiting payment for a product or service. The company or individual owing the money is the *debtor*. *Credit* allowed by a creditor may be either *buyer credit* or *supplier credit*.

credit outstanding. Or line of credit. Amount of money a company is prepared to allow a particular customer to owe at a particular point in time. It represents more than the unpaid *invoices* and will include goods in transit and part-finished work still to be supplied.

credit rating. Appraisal of credit worthiness of existing and potential customers/clients. Usually implies checking on financial standing and, if satisfactory, setting up credit limits.

credit-reporting agency. As *credit bureau*.

credit risk insurance. Cover against bad debts.

credit sale. Allowance by the vendor of credit to the purchaser to purchase particular goods or services. It may be arranged for the rest of the purchase price to be paid in instalments. In this event, the goods become the property of the purchaser at the time of purchase (which is one way in which credit sale differs from *hire purchase*), so that the vendor is, in effect, making a short-term loan. See also *lease (hire)*.

credit squeeze. Government measures to limit bank lending and *hire purchase* and other *credit sales* with the objective of damping down demand and inflation.

credit unions. US cooperative associations which attract deposits and make loans to members. They have some of the attributes of UK *building societies*.

criterion behavio(u)r. Term used particularly in *programmed learning*, but also in some other areas of training, for a detailed specification of what is expected of a trainee/student after training or a defined part of it. See also *behavio(u)ral objectives* and *terminal behavio(u)r*.

criterion group. Specially selected group of employees to whom *psychological tests* etc are administered, to assist in making an evaluation of the tests.

criterion test. Test to measure *terminal behavio(u)r* of a trainee/student after training and thus to establish extent to which he/she has achieved *criterion behavio(u)r* and objectives of training. Can also be a test before training to identify individual's training needs. See also *post-test*, *pre-test*, *skill testing*.

critical incident technique. 1. *Group training* method beginning with participants describing incidents in a given period which presented them with difficulties. **2.** Management technique devised by J C Flanagan which involves analyzing critical incidents of successful or unsuccessful job behavio(u)r which are used to produce a check-list for assessing performance.

critical path analysis (CPA). Or critical path method (CPM). Or critical path planning (CPP). Type of planning method or technique which shows the interrelationship in sequence of all the activities involved in undertaking a project. The network of activities highlights those operations or activities which are critical for the successful completion of the project within the scheduled or allocated time scale. CPA is distinguished from other network analysis techniques in two ways: **a** planning is separated from scheduling; **b** time and costs involved are directly related. See also *network analysis*, *PERT*, *activity on node*, *activity on arrow*, *cascade network*.

cross-booking. Where employees on *piece work*, or on a combination of piece work and day work, do not book the actual time taken on each job but, instead, book shorter than actual time on some jobs and complementary longer than actual time on other jobs in order to benefit or smooth out piece work earnings. Cross-booking may be associated with a *work group* informally restricting output under a *fiddle* or *quota restriction*. Cross-booking may also involve a worker in arranging *time up the cuff* — that is, booking longer than actual time on certain jobs in order to be able to book shorter than actual time on any later jobs that prove to have *tight rates*. Cross-booking may make use of *covered time* — that is, time not worked on bonus or piece work although a bonus scheme is applicable and available. Where time allocated for one task is actually used for another task, this is sometimes known as *borrowing time*.

cross-charging. Or *transfer pricing*. Where one service department within a company or organization charges for the use of its services by other parts of the organization either at cost or some agreed formula. See also *commercial criterion* (public administration).

cross-subsidization. Where the *profit* from one activity or enterprise is used to offset a loss on another activity. They may be quite different activities linked only by being in joint ownership.

crosswalk. Chart illustrating the relationship between different *budgets* in an organization.

Crown Agents for Overseas Governments and Administrations (UK). Non-profit making body which purchases goods on behalf of some 80 governments (particularly newly independent commonwealth countries) and more than 160 international and public authorities. The Crown Agents normally purchase by competitive tendering, buying directly from manufacturers for whom they can be an attractive channel for export sales.

Crown Proceedings Act 1947 (UK). Extended to the Government the vicarious liability responsibility of an employer for the wrongful acts of an employee in the course of his employment.

Croydon Procedure 1969 (UK). Aimed, in extension of the 1939 *Bridlington Principles*, at assisting the Disputes Committee of the *Trades Union Congress* in sorting out disputes between *trade unions*. The Croydon Procedure was evolved by a Special Congress of the TUC. See also *demarcation dispute, jurisdictional dispute, recognition dispute, multi-unionism.*

CRZZ. *Centralna Rada Związków Zawodowych*, the Polish Central Council of Trade Unions.

CSA. *Commonwealth Sugar Agreement.*

CSC. *Confédération des Syndicats Chrétiens*, one of the Belgian confederations of *trade unions* that is strongly supported in Flemish areas.

CST (or CT). *Central Standard Time.*

CSU. *Central Services Unit for University Careers and Appointments Services* (UK).

cumulative band chart. As *band curve chart*.

cumulative-part method. Training term where the operation to be learnt is divided into separate parts or elements and instruction and practice are given at the outset in the first part only, followed by the first and second parts together, and so on until the whole operation has been learned. The sequence may be represented as A, A + B, A + B + C, A + B + C + D. Cf *part method, progressive-part method, whole method.*

cumulative preference share. Type of *preference share* which is entitled to *dividend* in the following year if *profit* is not made to pay them in the current year.

cumulative timing. Or continuous timing. *Work measurement* timing method in which the times for the different *elements* of a job are recorded cumulatively on a continuously running watch instead of individually by the normal stop-watch *flyback timing* method.

currency bonds. Originally bonds issued by US railway companies and payable in US currency.

currency speculator. Person or organization calculatedly exchanging one currency for another in the expectation of making a profit from alterations in *exchange rates*. See also *hot money.*

current account. 1. That part of a country's *balance of payments* statement dealing with current imports and exports, visible and invisible (as opposed to the *capital account* part of the balance of payments statement). **2.** *Member bank, credit bank* or *clearing bank* account on which the bank does not pay interest but from which the customer can make immediate withdrawals. As *checking account.*

current assets. Or floating assets. Normally treated as all *stocks* (from *raw materials* to *finished goods*), *accounts receivable* (money owed by debtors), short term investments, and *cash*. Also known as circulating assets. See also *fixed assets.*

current liabilities. Liabilities or recognized claims which will be paid in the short term, normally within twelve months or the close of the financial year. Includes such items as payments due to creditors, including employees, bank overdrafts and interest, etc.

current ratio. Measures ratio of *current assets* to *current liabilities*. This gives a general indication of the adequacy of an organization's *working capital* and its ability to meet day-to-day payment obligations. The current ratio is widely held to be in order if its minimum value is 2 to 1. Though a useful yardstick this can in practice be misleading for the safety margin depends on the quality rather than the quantity of assets. See also *acid test ratio.*

current transaction. Transaction the payment for which appears in the *current account* of *balance of payments.*

current use value. As *existing use value* or user value.

current yield. Or running yield. Yield or return of stocks or shares obtained by dividing annual interest or dividend payment by the current market price and converting this to a percentage.

curriculum vitae (CV). Or resumé. Statement of the biographical details of a person used in personal records or in support of a job application, usually outlining educational and career or work experience. See also *bio*.

customary arrangement. Procedure normally followed in a particular industrial relations situation. May carry as much moral and legal right as an *agreed procedure*.

Customary System, US. See *US customary system*.

customer communication. Advertising and sales promotion to keep a customer, actual or potential, informed about a product or service.

customer segmentation. Dividing up of customers for *market segmentation*.

Customs and Excise (UK). See *Her Majesty's Customs and Excise*.

customs drawback. See *drawback*.

customs duty. As *tariff*.

Customs Tariff, Common (EEC). See *Common Customs Tariff*.

customs union. Situation in which a trading area embracing two or more member states has no trading or customs barriers between its members and may also have a common customs barrier or *common external tariff* against non-member states. See also *free trade area*.

cut-price industrial action (or sanctions). That in which workers take such action as *overtime bans*, working to rule, or *go-slows* rather than full *strike* action or complete withdrawal of labo(u)r. It is known as 'cut-price' because the employees taking the action do not lose all wages as they do in a strike.

CV. *Curriculum vitae*.

CV (test). *Colo(u)r vision test* in the *engineering apprentice test-battery* developed by the National Institute of Industrial Psychology in the UK. See also *psychological testing*, *visual abilities test*, and *aptitude tests*.

CWE. *Clerical work evaluation*.

CWIP. *Clerical work improvement program(me)*.

CWO. Cash with order.

cybernetics. Theory of communications and control mechanisms in living beings and machines; or the means of keeping a system or activity self-balancing and positively directed towards a prescribed goal by constant re-balancing of its sub-systems or sub-activities usually by *feedback concept*. In the training context there is, for example, a kind of cybernetic control implicit in *adaptive program(me)s*.

cycle billing. System of sending out statements to customers over a period of time instead of all at once. Under a cycle billing system the *sales ledger* is divided into sections — during the first week of the month statements would, for example, be sent out to all customers in the first section, during the second week to the customers in the next section and so on. Enables workload and remittances to be spread more evenly.

Czechoslovak central bank. See *Státni banka Céskoslovenská*.

d

DAF. *Dansk Arbeidsgivereforening*, the Danish Employers' Confederation.

daily contracted hours. Number of hours a day an employee has contracted to work, excluding *overtime*. Starting and finishing times may be specified or, in the case of an application of *flexible working hours (fwh)*, simply the number of hours to be worked daily. In an fwh application there is likely to be a procedure for carrying forward credit or debit balances of hours worked.

dangle. Arrow which lacks either a preceding or succeeding event in a network of the *activity-on-arrow* network

Danish central bank. See *Danmarks Nationalbank*.

Danish Employers' Confederation. *Dansk Arbeidsgivereforening (DAF)*.

Danish Federation of Trade Unions. See *Landsorganisationen i Danmark (LO)*.

Danish income tax. State income tax, or *indkomstskat til staten*, is a *progressive tax* charged on total income plus flat-rate dividend tax. A special flat-rate income tax, or *saerlig indkomstskat*, is also charged on certain *capital gains* and lump-sum payments in lieu of the ordinary progressive income tax. There are also local and county income taxes – *kommunal indkomstskat* and *amtskommunal indkomstskat* – and, in addition, the church tax, or *kirkeskat*, and a net wealth tax or *formueskat til staten*. An exceptional form of income tax is the seamen's tax, or *somandsskat*, which is deducted at source instead of the other taxes.

Danish National Bank. *Danmarks Nationalbank*.

Danish Stock Exchange. See *Copenhagen Stock Exchange*.

Danish Trade Unions, Federation of. See *Landsorganisationen i Danmark*.

Danmarks Nationalbank. Denmark's National Bank, or *central bank*, originally established in 1818.

Dansk Arbeidsgivereforening (DAF). Danish Employers' Confederation, established 1896 and having 23,500 members.

data base. Ordered and named collection of data particularly for use in computerized information systems.

data degradation. Loss of information or data as a result of a process not being reversible.

data logging. Use of a simple form of *computer* to record the performance of plant or equipment, though not to control it.

Datapost service. Provides next day delivery of commercial and business documents in some overseas countries.

data processing. Systematic processing of data by such methods as *computer* or the sorting of punched cards by hand or mechanically.

data transformation. Processing of raw data so that it can be compared with other data or used in statistical techniques.

Datel service. Transmits data to home and overseas addresses using conventional telecommunications facilities with the addition of special terminal equipment at the recipient's end.

Davignon Committee. Set up to investigate the possibility of the *Common Market* countries developing a *common foreign policy*.

dawn shift. Early morning shift.

day book. See *journal*.

day rate (or daywork). Basic *time-related payment scheme* (eg, and most commonly, 'so-much-an-hour'). May be used on its own or topped up with *payment-by-results*, an incentive payment scheme or some other form of *premium payment*. See also *measured daywork*, and *graded measured daywork*, *controlled daywork*, *stepped daywork* and *high day rate*.

day release. Release from employment, without loss of pay, for attendance on, usually, one day per week during term time at *further education* related to industrial employment and training. See also *block release*.

daywage. As *time-related payment*.

daywork. 1. As *timework*. **2.** As *casual labo(u)r*. See also *day rate*.

DCE. *Domestic credit expansion.*

DCF. *Discounted cash flow.*

dead hand. As *mortmain*.

dead horse work. Work for which workers have been paid in advance or which it is agreed must be repeated though it is not strictly necessary (the latter meaning originated in the US printing industry when it was agreed that standing type, though available, should not be used).

dead stocks, or stock. *Stocks (1)* for which there no longer appears to be a demand.

dead time. Waiting time for workers on *payment-by-results* schemes. In most schemes they are paid *daywage* or an agreed *fall-back pay* during dead time.

death duty. As *estate duty*.

debenture. Loan, or more commonly, a fixed-interest *prior charge* issued by a company in return for long-term loans. Normally, debentures are to be redeemed at a particular future date, with the stipulated interest on them being paid annually before dividends on both *preference shares* and *ordinary shares* and irrespective of whether the company makes a profit. Debenture holders also have first claim if the company goes into liquidation. Debentures may be of a particular kind such as mortgage debentures on specified assets (common among property companies, for example); or floating-charge debentures on a company's total assets where there are not appropriate particular assets; or convertible debentures which give their holders an option to convert them into ordinary shares at a fixed price at a fixed future date. See also *loan capital*.

debenture bond (US). Unsecured *bond*.

debenture capital. 1. Company capital obtained from the sale of *debentures*. **2.** As *debt capital*.

debit. 1. *Debt* recorded in an account. **2.** Left-hand side of an account. **3.** Entry on the left-hand side of an account. **4.** Negative balance on an account.

debt. 1. Obligation or liability to pay something. **2.** Money, goods or services that are owed.

debt capital. Loan on which a fixed annual *interest* is paid. Debt capital is repayable before *contributed capital* if a *company* goes into *liquidation*.

debtor. Person or organization which owes something to another.

debtors to sales ratio. Debtors expressed as a percentage of sales.

debt ratio. Ratio of *debt capital* to debt capital plus *contributed capital*.

debug. To seek or rectify faults in a plant or system.

decasualization. Process by which the workers in an industry are switched from a *casual labo(u)r* system to regular employment.

decelerating premium bonus. *Premium bonus sheme* in which the rate of bonus decreases as the time saved increases.

decision analysis. One of three techniques identified by *Drucker* to be used in deciding the organization structure appropriate for a company, the other techniques being *activities analysis* and *relations analysis*. Decision analysis is used to establish what are the key decisions in the company, as distinct from generalized assumptions.

decision band method. Single factor *job evaluation* technique, developed by Professor T T Paterson of Strathclyde University (UK), in which jobs at all levels in a company or organization are analyzed and graded in terms of decision levels. Broadly, the higher the level of decision called for, the greater the value of the job. Six basic levels of decision used in decision band method are, in descending order, policy-making decisions; programming decisions; interpretative decisions; routine decisions; automatic decisions; and vegetative decisions.

decision dynamics training. *Management development* technique developed by Strathclyde University (UK) using videotapes and simulation exercises with the emphasis on examining the overall operations of the decision making group rather than a detailed examination of self or others.

decision mapping via optimum networks (DEMON). Mathematical *network analysis* type technique for evaluating new product marketing plans. Takes into account payback period, *break-even point* and minimum level of profits required and chooses the best deployment of funds in terms of a marketing plan.

Decisions (EEC). Made by the *Council of Ministers* and/or the *European Commission* of the *Common Market* or *European Economic Community*. Decisions are binding but only on the member states or organizations etc towards which they are specifically directed. *Regulations*, Decisions, *Directives*, *Recommendations* and *Opinions* form the *secondary legislation* of the Common Market.

decision theory. Group of mathematical techniques for forecasting the unpredictable so that forecasting errors are kept to a minimum. The techniques include *game theory, risk analysis, sensitivity tests* and *utility theory.*

decision tree. Type of flow chart or visual aid which summarizes the various alternatives and options available in a complex (multi-shape) decision process. Normally drawn from left to right with lines or arrows representing possible choices linked by circles or nodes. The object is not to find optimum solutions but to represent visually a wide range of alternatives which can apply to specific procedures and decision making. Also known as logical tree.

Declaration of Philadelphia (US). Historic proclamation by an *International Labour Organization* conference in 1944 against poverty and for freedom of expression and association for workers.

declining balance method. As *reducing balance method.*

deductible. Allowable as a tax deduction.

deed. Sealed legal document by which conveyance, contract or bond is drawn up.

deed of arrangement. Document through which a person or company assigns or conveys his property to a trustee for the benefit of creditors. In the UK it must be registered under the Deeds of Arrangement Act and must satisfy the provisions of the Act. It normally constitutes an act of

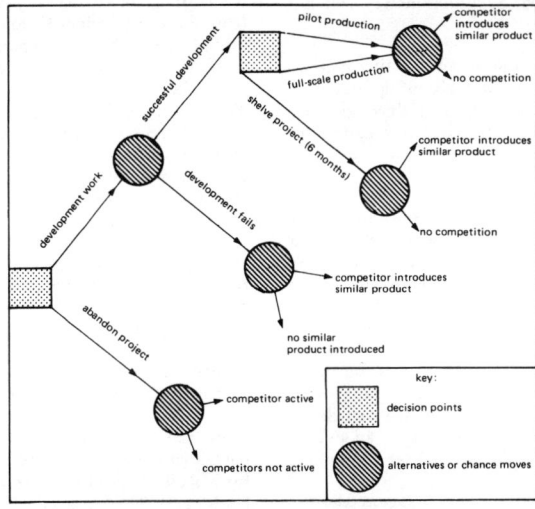

decision tree (for new product development)

bankruptcy but where the creditors are satisfied that no fraudulent intention exists, they will often accept a deed of arrangement, which enables them to realize the assets speedily and distribute the proceeds without incurring legal costs.

DEF 131A. Procedure published by UK Ministry of Defence laying down acceptance sampling standards for quality, tolerances, etc of goods.

deferred charges. Expenditure written off over a period of time, usually in annual instalments.

deferred compensation. Payments to be made by an organization to its employees at some future time, particularly after normal retirement age, eg pensions.

deferred shares or capital. Type of *share* or capital (fairly rare) which is entitled to a dividend only after a specified rate of dividend has been paid on the *ordinary shares*. A deferred share is more speculative than most, bringing in high dividends in good times but little or nothing in merely average times.

deferred tax accounting. Making adequate provision for anticipated future tax liabilities in the accounts of a company or organization.

deficit. Amount by which a sum of money falls short of the required amount.

deficit spending. Spending money which is borrowed.

define system. Simplified charting method used in *systems analysis* using only one symbol, an arrow. It was developed by Fisher-Price Toys Inc (US) to enable non-specialists to document and describe existing systems.

deflation. That part of the downward phase in a *trade cycle* where there is a downturn in economic activity, *purchasing power* and national incomes to an extent which introduces dangers of *mass unemployment* and *slump* conditions. A distinction should be made between deflation and *disinflation*, the latter being that part of the downward phase in a trade cycle where economic activity is damped down to combat *inflation* but not to an extent which would endanger *full employment*.

del credere agent. Type of agent or *distributor* who, like a *stocking agent*, does not purchase the goods he handles but, unusually, accepts responsibility for ultimate payment and pays his principal if the customer fails to do so. A del credere agent is normally paid a higher commission than that paid to a commission agent to compensate him for the risk he takes. See also *merchant, stockist, wholesaler*.

delegate. 1. To give authority to a person to act for others. **2.** Person authorized to act as a representative for another or others. See also *delegate meeting*.

delegate meeting (or conference). Where each of those present is a representative or *delegate* of others and is empowered to vote on their behalf. Each may have been given a *mandate* on what to vote for. The method of voting may be the *card vote* by which the delegates cast votes in proportion to the numbers of people they represent. An organization may send a single delegate or it may send a delegation of a number of representatives, the leader of whom votes in any card vote.

Delhi Stock Exchange Association Limited. One of seven major *Indian stock exchanges*.

deliberative vote. See *casting vote*.

delivery period. Period between the placing of an order and the delivery of goods.

Delphi approach. Technique akin to *brainstorming* sometimes used in *technological forecasting*, involving a panel of experts from a range of scientific and technological disciplines. Each expert separately makes his own intuitive forecast of the future of a particular area of technology or a problem. The different forecasts are analyzed and assembled in a combined report which is then sent to each of the panel of experts for them to make their separate assessments of the levels of probability of the different forecasts in the combined report. Similar techniques include *exploratory forecasting techniques, morphological research, normative forecasting techniques*, the *scenario writing approach* and *technological trend extrapolation*.

demand. Economist's term for a *want* for which the necessary purchasing power exists. Without the purchasing power, the want remains merely a want (eg in a particular household there may be a want for a Rolls Royce but a demand for a small family car). There is also a distinction to be

demand analysis. made between *final demand* by the user needing a product for its end function, complementary demand where two products are sold in conjunction and *indirect demand* for a product as a component to be incorporated in another product (also known as derived demand).

demand analysis. Identifying and measuring the factors at work in the market place affecting sales of a product or service.

demand deposit. Sum of money which can be withdrawn from a bank by a depositor without prior notice.

demand draft. As *bank draft*.

demand, elastic. See *elastic demand*.

demand elasticity. Responsiveness of sales or demand to relatively small changes in price. A product is said to be 'elastic' when a small change in price greatly affects demand. See also *price elasticity* and *price sensitive*.

demand, expansion. See *expansion demand*.

demand, income elasticity of. See *income elasticity of demand*.

demand, inelastic. See *inelastic demand*.

demand inflation. *Inflation* caused by an increase in demand that cannot be met, with the result that prices rise. *Cost push inflation* is caused by an increase in costs.

demand note. Invoice, bill or draft payable on presentation.

demand, price elasticity of. See *price elasticity of demand*.

demand pull. As *demand inflation*.

demand, replacement. See *replacement demand*.

demarcation dispute (or issue). *Industrial dispute* over question of which *trade union* should have the right to a particular job or task. See also *multi-unionism, jurisdictional dispute, recognition dispute*.

demise. As *lease*.

democratic leadership. Management style which encourages employee participation in planning, decision making, etc, and in which the manager plays a facilitating and permissive role.

democratic management. As *participative management*.

DEMON. *Decision mapping via optimum networks.*

demonstration stoppage (or strike). Strike arising, usually spontaneously, as a demonstration of workers' feelings on a particular issue rather than one mounted in the expectancy of a protracted struggle. A demonstration strike is also known as a *spontaneous strike*.

demotion payment. Made to an employee to compensate for being demoted.

Department of Education and Science. UK Government Department responsible for creating and implementing national educational policy. Has a complex relationship and sharing of powers with the Local Education Authorities. Senior Minister in Department is *Secretary of State for Education and Science*.

Department of Employment. UK Government Department responsible for labo(u)r relations, *conciliation services*, the *Factory Inspectorate*, employment and training, manpower planning, safety, health and welfare (though it is the *Department of Health and Social Security* that is responsible for National Insurance and *social security*). See also *Manpower Services Commission, Employment Service Agency* and *Training Services Agency*. The Department was known as the Department of Employment and Productivity from 1968 to 1970 and as the Ministry of Labour from 1916 to 1968. The senior Minister in the Department is the *Secretary of State for Employment*.

Department of Energy. UK Government Ministry formed in 1974 with responsibilities concerned with national demand and supply in all forms of energy, particularly the production of coal and of oil from the offshore fields. See also *Offshore Supplies Office*.

Department of the Environment. UK Government department whose responsibilities affecting industry and management include questions of building, planning permission and, through its Road Freight Division and International Transport Division, questions of road transportation (including advising on road transport in Europe). The DOE also carries out annual tests and roadside checks on commercial vehicles.

Department of Health and Social Security. UK Government department whose responsibilities include the operation of national insurance, the National Health Service and the assessing and paying of *social security benefits*.

Department of Industry. UK Government Ministry, until 1974 part of the Department of Trade and Industry, with responsibilities for regional and other industrial development. See also *Assisted Area*.

Department of Trade. UK Government ministry with responsibilities for commercial matters.

department store. Large retail shop having a number of departments or counters, each handling a different type of product.

dependancy. See *activity on node*.

depletion. *Cost* of the extent to which a *fixed asset* (eg natural resources) has physically diminished.

deposit. 1. To entrust money to a financial institution such as a bank or building society. **2.** Partial or initial payment of a debt or purchase price.

deposit account. *Clearing bank* account on which the bank pays interest to depositors who in return are normally required to give notice of withdrawals from the account. The equivalent in a US *member bank* is a *savings account*. Both differ from *checking account* (US) and *current account* (UK).

deposit administration fund (pensions). Or managed fund. An employers' pension scheme akin to a *self-administered fund* except that it is administered and its deposits invested by an *insurance company*, thus having some of the tax advantages of an assured fund.

deposit bank. Bank whose business includes handling *demand deposits*.

deposition. Testimony in a law case given under oath, particularly as a written statement by a witness for use in court. See also *affidavit*.

depreciation. Amount by which the value of *capital* equipment decreases over a period of time, as a result of business operations or technological innovation. It is the gradual exhaustion of capital assets employed in a business including wear and tear, obsolescence. Most common methods of depreciation are the *straight line* and *reducing balance* methods. As an accounting or paper transaction, depreciation is of taxation rather than *cash flow* significance. See also *displaced plant* and illustration opposite.

depression. Severe form of *recession*. Key characteristics include industrial stagnation, low prices, high unemployment and shortages of goods and cash. See *business cycle, unemployment*, etc.

depth interview. Or extended interview, in which the interviewee or *informant* is encouraged to relate opinions and information at length and in his own way. It is a technique and term used particularly in *market research* and has points of similarity with the *connected conversation interview* technique sometimes used in *personnel selection*.

derived demand. As *indirect demand*.

dermatitis. Unpleasant skin disease that can be caused by failure to observe accident prevention and cleanliness codes in dealing with alkaline solutions, acids, industrial oils, etc.

Design Centre (UK). Run by the Council for Industrial Design to publicize what it regards as well designed British products including, in recent years, designs that are effective and successful technologically. The Centre publishes the monthly journal 'Design', and maintains a register of industrial designers.

design factor. Term used particularly in *market research* to indicate the level of efficiency and reliability of a sample used for a survey. The datum point is that a completely *random sample* has a design factor of 1.0. If a sample is said to have a design factor of 1.2 this means that the *standard error* for the resulting survey findings is increased by a factor of 0.2 or 20 per cent.

de-skilling. Modifying methods of performing a job to reduce the level of skill or skills demanded.

desk research. Term used particularly in *market research* for the assembly, collation and analysis of information already published or in existence, as opposed to fieldwork to collect fresh information.

desk training. *On-the-job* commercial and clerical training. See also *in-company training*.

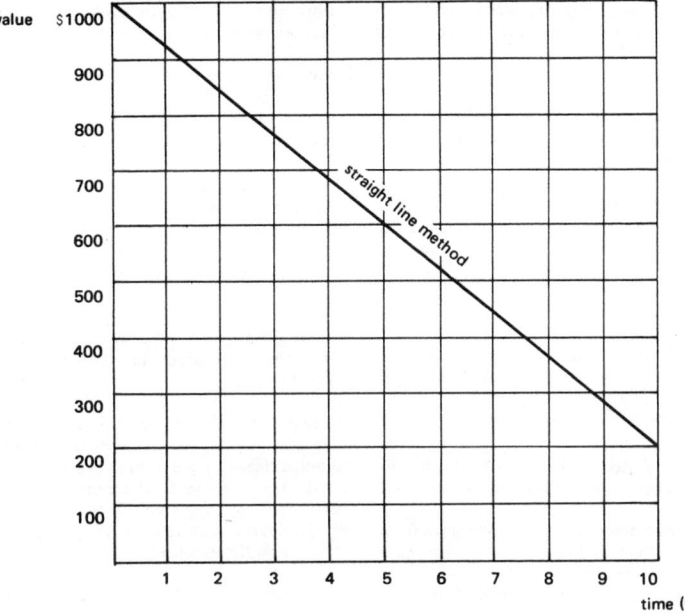

depreciation (straight line method)

detail man. Salesman whose principal task is providing information on products rather than obtaining orders.

Detroit Stock Exchange. One of the 20 major *US stock exchanges*.

Deutsche Bundesbank. *Central bank* of Federal Germany, formed in 1957 in a reorganization of the central banking system. There are also some 11 Land Central Banks.

Deutsche Mark. Basic unit of the Federal German currency.

Deutscher Gewerkschaftsbund (DGB). Central Federal German *trade union* organization, formed in 1949 and covering trade unions which have some 6,500,000 members.

Deutscher Industrie-und Handelstag. Association of Federal German Chambers of Industry and Commerce linked with *chambers of commerce* in most principal towns and with seven regional organizations.

devaluation. Reduction by a country of the official rate at which its currency is exchanged for other currencies. Devaluation may also be brought about in effect by introducing a *floating exchange rate*.

Development Area (UK). Type of *Assisted Area* under the regional development policies of the UK other types being *Special Development Areas* and *Intermediate Areas*. Firms providing employment in a Development Area are eligible for help from regional development grants, selective financial assistance, training assistance, special tax allowances, the *Contracts Preference Schemes* and the provision of *advance factories*. The Development Areas in the UK are, broadly speaking, Scotland, Wales, Cornwall and the North of England beginning at a point just north of Leeds. The Special Development Areas are certain areas within the Development Areas.

Development Corporation (UK). See *New Town*.

deviation. See *standard deviation*.

Dewey Decimal Classification (DC). See *Universal Decimal Classification*.

dexterity. Manipulative ability achieved through good coordination of *motor* and *perceptual skills*.

DGB. *Deutscher Gewerkschaftsbund.*

D-group. Type of *T-group* used in management training and development. The trainer attempts to relate group behavio(u)r to the participants' own work experience.

diadic product test. *Market research* term for a *product test* based on the *paired comparison* principle, *informants* being asked for comparative reactions to two products at a time (or the subjects of the test may be advertisements, types of packaging, etc). A ranking for a number of products, packs, etc can then be built up. See also *monadic product test* and *triadic product test*.

diagnostic ability. Ability to perceive accurately the relationships between people, ideas and situations.

diagnostic program. Or diagnostic routine. *Computer program* that finds faults in other programs and in the computer system.

dichotomous question. Marketing term for a survey question that is designed to produce one of two possible answers, the most common choice being between 'yes' and 'no'.

differential. Recognized difference in pay for different types and levels of employee.

differential costing. As *marginal costing*.

differential sampling. Or use of a weighted sample. Where the sample chosen for a survey or study is deliberately weighted or biased to give special attention to a particular element in the *population*. See also *random sampling* and *cluster sampling*.

diffusion index. Statistical device for summarizing the direction of movement of a large number of statistical series in one figure.

digital computer. *Computer* that handles data in digital or numerical form using *binary notation*. The digital computer can work at very high speeds on complex tasks, and has vast storage facilities. See also *analog(ue) computer* and *hybrid computer* (a combination of analog(ue) computer and digital computer).

dilutee. Term, often pejorative, for a worker who has undergone shortened training and often experiences difficulty in gaining *trade union* acceptance as a semi-skilled worker on the grounds that this would 'dilute' the level of skill in the workplace.

diminishing balance method. As *reducing balance method*.

diminishing return. Point beyond which the additional employment of resources (eg more labo(u)r or capital investment) yields less than proportionate increases in output.

diminishing returns industry. One where production becomes progressively more difficult and/or more expensive. This can happen in mining, for example, as tunnelling is extended or as mines become worked out.

dinar. Basic unit of currency in several countries as listed in Appendix: The World's Currencies.

Diploma in Management Studies (DMS). Awarded in the UK after either a full-time, block release or part-time course taken by graduates or students of similar standing. A national award approved by the *Department of Education & Science* or the *Scottish Education Department*.

Diplomatic Service Commercial Officers Overseas. Provide UK exporters with a world-wide trade promotion and information network in collaboration with the *Export Services Division* of the *Department of Trade*.

direct access storage. As *random access storage*.

direct action. Dealing directly with a problem or injustice instead of through established procedures of government and/or law. See also *community action*.

direct cost. Or *prime cost*. Costs directly attributable to the production of a particular product and which are usually allocated to cost centres. Direct cost is added to the manufacturing *indirect cost* (or factory *overhead*) to give *factory cost*.

direct costing. See *standard costing*.

direct debiting. System of regular but possibly variable payments through a bank under which the recipient instructs the bank on the amounts to be paid.

direct expense. *Direct cost* attributable to a particular expenditure.

directive interview. Used particularly in attitude surveys to record answers to a prepared list of questions.

Directives. 1. Executive orders of the US President or Government agencies. **2.** Made by the *Council of Ministers* and/or the *European Commission* of the *Common Market* or *European Economic Community*. Directives are binding on all member states, but the form and method of their implementation are at the discretion of the individual member states. *Regulations, Decisions,* Directives, *Recommendations* and *Opinions* form the *secondary legislation* of the *EEC*.

direct labo(u)r. 1. Workforce directly involved or identified in manfuacturing production or the provision of a service, as distinct from the ancillary or enabling part played by *indirect labo(u)r* such as maintenance workers. **2.** Use by a local authority or similar organization of its own employees or directly employed labo(u)r on construction or other work rather than using a contracting firm and its labo(u)r.

direct labo(u)r cost. *Cost* of *direct labo(u)r* (1).

direct mail selling. Sending specially prepared sales literature through the mail to specially selected prospective purchasers of a product or service, inviting them to place orders directly instead of through shops. Direct mail selling usually employs either *reader reply forms* or *reader reply cards* and they are usually reply paid (that is, postage is paid by the seller, not the *prospect)*.

direct mail shot. Batch of *direct mail selling* literature sent out to a number of addresses at the same time.

direct negative. *Amendment* to a *motion* proposing the direct opposite of the intention of the motion. The meeting or conference chairman should not accept a direct negative. The obvious course for anyone seeking to propose a direct negative is to vote against the motion itself.

director 1. Member of a *board of directors*. **2.** *Chief executive* of an institution.

director, company. See *company director*. See also *board of directors*.

Director-General of Fair Trading. UK official introduced under the *Fair Trading Act 1973*.

direct profit. *Sales revenue* minus *direct cost*.

direct response promotion. *Advertising* or other forms of *sales promotion* that aim to achieve a direct response from the reader or recipient, as with advertisements that incorporate a *reader reply card* or *form*. Another type of direct response promotion is *direct mail selling*. See also *direct selling*, *above-the-line* and *below-the-line promotion*.

direct review. Where work is checked or inspected regularly during production. *Indirect review* depends more on feedback from complaints and *returned work*.

direct selling. Actual selling and taking of orders for a company's goods and services by its sales force, etc. The term is usually used of selling to the public without use of a shop, as in *direct mail selling* or *direct response promotion*. See also *sales promotion* and *marketing mix*.

direct tax. Tax levied on some form of income or wealth.

direct wages. As *direct labo(u)r*.

direct worker. See *direct labo(u)r*.

Disabled Persons (Employment) Acts 1944 and 1958. Laid down in the UK, with the force of criminal sanctions, that all employers having not less than 20 employees should employ a quota of disabled workers. Exemptions granted to certain small firms. The Acts also required that appropriate training be given to disabled employees. Department of Employment is required to keep a *Disabled Persons Register* of people over school leaving age. The Acts empower the *Secretary of State for Employment* to reserve certain kinds of work for disabled people. The Acts also require the setting up of a *National Advisory Council on the Employment of the Disabled (NACED)* and local disablement advisory committees.

Disabled Persons Register. See *Disabled Persons (Employment) Acts 1944 and 1958*, which established the Register in the UK.

disablement benefit. Under the *National Insurance (Industrial Injuries) Acts*, disablement benefit may be payable in the UK to an employee if claimed within 156 days after an accident at work which leads to loss of physical or mental faculty irrespective of whether the employee is made incapable of work. An employee on *injury benefit* may transfer to sickness benefit within the 156-day period. Where the medical board judges a disablement to be less than 20 per cent a lump sum disablement pension is payable; for 20 per cent or more a disablement pension is payable, this pension not affecting other benefits such as *unemployment benefit* or *sickness benefit*. Disablement pension may be payable in the case of industrial diseases listed officially by the Department of Health and Social Security. A *constant attendance allowance* may be payable in cases of exceptionally severe disablement.

disbursement. 1. Expenditure incurred. 2. Cash paid out.

disc. Medium for external *computer* storage. An alternative medium is *magnetic tape*.

disclosure of information by employers. Legal or customary practice (practise) of disclosure of information about their undertakings by employers to *trade union* representatives for the purposes of *collective bargaining*.

discontinuous shiftwork. *Shift working* system that is not maintained around the clock.

discount. 1. Deduction of a specified amount or percentage from a price or cost. 2. Reduction in cost, value or quantity. 3. To purchase or sell a *bill of exchange* etc after deducting a sum equivalent to the amount of interest that will accumulate before it finally matures. 4. To advance money on a bill or similar document which is not due for immediate payment after deducting a sum for risk and interest.

discounted cash flow (DCF). Accounting/management technique for comparing the return on investment in projects of broadly similar risk but dissimilar *cash flow*. Because money in the hand is worth more than that in prospect, the technique is used to discount expected future cash flow at arbitrarily chosen rates to arrive at a *present value*. See also *equivalent mean investment period, actuarial return, internal rate of return,* and *net present value method*.

discounted payback. Forecasting technique. See *payback*.

discount house. 1. Cut-price retail store. 2. UK financial institution in business to purchase *promissory notes* etc at a discount and then either re-sell them or hold them until they mature.

discount market. Business conducted by UK *discount houses*.

discount store. As *discount house* (1).

discovery method. Method of teaching in which work is arranged and topics chosen so that trainee/pupil learns for himself rather than learning directly from the instructor/teacher. Sometimes known as heuristic method. See also *activity learning/teaching*.

discretion. Freedom of judgment and decision. See *time span of discretion*.

discretionary endowment pension scheme. As *'top hat' pension scheme*.

discrimination test. *Market research* term for a test in which people — the *informants* — are confronted with a number of products or packagings etc and asked to discern the difference between them. Such a test often takes the form of a *triadic product test*, which has the attraction of being statistically checkable.

disinflation. That part of the downward phase in a *trade cycle* where there is a downturn in economic activity, *purchasing power* and national incomes to an extent that combats *inflation* but does not endanger *full employment*. If the downturn continues to an extent introducing dangers of *mass unemployment*, disinflation is succeeded by *deflation*.

dispersion. Statistical values which measure the concentration or spread of items in a frequency distribution eg *standard deviation*.

displaced plant (or equipment). Plant made obsolete or taken out of commission earlier than had been expected at the time of its commissioning. This may happen, for example, when a newer, more technologically advanced process is introduced or when new materials or components are introduced requiring changes in the process. The unamortized residue of costs of such a displaced plant is normally taken to a displaced plant account and the amount outstanding after any proceeds from selling the plant is normally written off in annual instalments. See also *depreciation*.

display advertisement. Published advertisement designed to attract attention in its own right rather than being categorized as a *classified advertisement*.

disposable, consumer. See *consumer disposable*.

dispute. Traditionally, industrial relations disputes in general have been known as *trade disputes*, with the term *industrial dispute* becoming more common in modern times. Disputes involving inter-union rivalry may be *demarcation disputes*, *jurisdictional disputes* or *recognition disputes*.

dispute benefit. Or *strike pay*. Paid by *trade unions* to workers on *strike* to compensate for loss of their normal wages.

disputes procedure. Procedure agreed between employers, or *employers' associations*, and *trade unions* for resolving *industrial disputes*. It is also common for a *collective agreement* or an individual *contract of employment* to include an *agreed procedure* or *grievance procedure*. See also *engineering procedure*. The *Trades Union Congress* has the *Bridlington Principles* and the *Croydon Procedure* for dealing with disputes between *trade unions* in the UK.

dissatisfiers. Factors describing the relationship of the employee to the context or environment in which he does his work. These factors which may, for example, include company policy, salary, interpersonal relationships and poor working conditions, bring about job dissatisfaction known also as hygiene or maintenance factors. See *Herzberg's theory*.

dissociative groups. Type of *reference group* brought together for the purpose of examining consumer buying motives. Members of a dissociative group are an assortment of individuals of different kinds so that each tends to find unacceptable to himself the ideals, values and behaviour of the group as a whole. Thus this type of group brings out certain consumer dislikes. Other forms of reference group include *membership*, *aspirational*, *face-to-face*, and *family groups*.

distribution. Process or processes by which goods or services are transferred from the producer to the ultimate consumer. The term tends to be used particularly of retailing. See also *physical distribution management*.

distribution chain. As *sales chain*.

distribution channel. As *sales chain*.

distribution cost. 1. Cost of transportation (may also include warehousing, packing, etc). **2.** Cost of selling.

distribution mix. Combination of *sales chains* used by a *company* or other organization.

distribution planning. Determining the optimum methods of distribution and preparing and implementing program(me)s to put these methods into effect. This will involve **a** selecting the best channels of distribution; **b** evaluating the costs of alternative methods of distribution; **c** deciding on the best locations for warehouses and depots; **d** integrating transportation, storage and production flow aspects, to provide at least cost an increasingly direct product flow from the manufacturer or supplier to the customer with a minimum of product storage. Planned distribution often requires the use of *operational research* and *computers*. See also *physical distribution management*.

Distributive Industry Training Board. Established July 1968 under the *Industrial Training Act 1964*.

distributor. Type of *middleman* to whom a manufacturer has granted an exclusive or preferential right to buy and re-sell a specific range of products and/or services in particular markets or geographical areas. A consignment distributor is one who pays for goods only as he re-sells them. See also *del credere agent, merchant, stocking agent, stockist, wholesaler*.

District Inspector of Factories. See *Factory Inspectorate (UK)*.

divergent. See *convergent/divergent*.

diversification. Company policy to produce or market a wider range of products or services, usually in order to avoid overdependence on too few products or markets.

dividend. 1. Interest paid on *shares, stocks*, etc, normally expressed as a percentage per annum. The dividend or interest payable on stocks and shares is expressed as a percentage of nominal or *par value* stated on the share certificate and not the market value (which may be above, at or below par). See also *yield*. **2.** Pro rata payment to a *creditor* of a person adjudged *bankrupt*.

dividend cover. Extent to which a company ploughs back *earnings* as opposed to distributing them as dividend. If, for example, a company distributes half its earnings, the dividend is said to be covered twice.

dividend yield. *Dividend* on a share etc expressed as a percentage of the share price.

division of labo(u)r. Breaking tasks down into operations so that employees specialize in one area of activity.

DJI. *Dow Jones Index.*

DMS. *Diploma in Management Studies.*

Docks and Harbours Act 1966. Laid down new provisions in UK for employment of dock workers, provisions chiefly concerned with *decasualization* – ie a switch from casual labo(u)r to a guaranteed working week.

documentary bill. *Bill of exchange* to which the *payee* attaches documents showing that he has sent the goods involved in the contract or sale in order that the *drawee* will accept the bill.

documentary credit. See *irrevocable documentary acceptance credit.* Type of *credit* arrangement opened at a bank by an importer in favo(u)r of a person or company supplying goods from another country, the arrangement being that this supplier receives credit on presentation of specified documents.

dollar. Basic unit of the currencies of each of the USA, Canada, Australia, New Zealand, Mexico, Hong Kong, etc. See Appendix: World Currencies.

dollar area. Countries whose currency is linked with US dollar.

dollar diplomacy. Dealings motivated by financial interest.

dollar gap. Adverse balance of payments in a country with a *dollar* currency.

domestic bargaining. As *workplace bargaining.*

domestic credit expansion (DCE). Measure of the change in the *money supply*, normally expressed as a percentage (plus or minus) after adjustment to allow for the effects of changes in foreign exchange reserves and government borrowing overseas.

domestic exports. Exports of goods or commodities produced within the *country of origin.*

dominant element job evaluation. *Job evaluation* technique in which only the most important or dominant element in a job is used for a comparison with others. Other job evaluation techniques include *analytic job evaluation, integral job evaluation, job factor comparison, job grading, job ranking, points rating method,* and *profiling systems.*

dominoes test. Type of *non-verbal intelligence test* in which the testee has to complete a sequence of dominoes.

Donovan Royal Commission. UK Royal Commission on Trade Unions and Employers' Associations set up under Lord Donovan in 1965 and reporting in 1968 (Cmnd 3623). Donovan noted that 'Britain has two systems of industrial relations' and that informal *workplace bargaining* was becoming more powerful than the formal system of industry-wide *collective bargaining,* this situation carrying the dangers of indecision and anarchy (95 per cent of current stoppages in industry were for *unofficial strikes*).

doomsday strike. Type of *strike* likely to occur towards the end of the period covered by a wage agreement and when a fresh agreement has therefore to be negotiated by a certain imminent point in time in order to maintain continuity of operation. This kind of strike is obviously most common in companies or industries where fixed term wage agreements are negotiated.

dotting test. Sometimes used in *psychological testing* of fatigue and concentration. The person being tested has to mark with a dot the centres of circles passed in front of him or her at a regular rate but in irregular positions.

double bond. *Bond* (2) under which the recipient has to pay a penalty if he fails to pay the agreed sum or perform the agreed contract.

double call. Marketing term meaning that a member of management accompanies a salesman, agent or distributor on a visit to a customer.

double day shift. Two-shift system of *shift work*, the most usual shifts being from 6 am to 2 pm and from 2 pm to 10 pm. See also *coupling-up.*

double employment. Holding of two jobs by one person. This happens, for example, in *moonlighting.*

double entry. Normal method of bookkeeping or accounting in which transactions are entered both as a debit to one account and as a credit to another so that the totals of debits and credits are equal.

double pricing. Where a product carries two prices, either actually or by implication, offering to sell to *consumers* (the technique is used mostly with *consumer goods*) at the lower of the two prices. Examples of double pricing are **a** where a product carries one price billed as 'usual price' and another, lower price billed as 'our price', and **b** where a product is priced as so much off the 'recommended price' though usually, in the absence of legal enforcement, without actually indicating the so-called recommended price. Some countries have legislation to protect consumers against double pricing abuses.

double taxation. Where tax on the same income, profits, etc falls due in two or more countries according to the individual laws and regulations of those countries. There are double taxation agreements between most countries to arrive at a compromise so that the individual corporation etc involved does not have to pay the full taxes of both countries. See also *income tax.*

double taxation, export safeguard against. See *export safeguards against double taxation.*

double time. Payment of wages at twice *day rate* or *time rate*, most usually for certain *overtime* or working special hours.

Dow Jones Index (DJI). Index of share prices on the *Wall Street* Stock Exchange published by Dow Jones and Co Inc. The same company produces, either on its own or jointly, the 'Wall Street Journal', 'Barron's National Business and Financial Weekly', 'The National Observer', the 'AP-Dow Jones Economic Report', the 'AP-Dow Financial Wire', and the 'Dow Jones Broadcast Service'. See also *Financial Times Industrial Ordinary Index* in the UK.

downer. Short *strike* or stoppage intended to draw attention to a particular grievance. It usually involves workers in 'downing tools' but not leaving the factory premises. A 'downer' is a form of *demonstration strike.*

downgrading. Reducing the pay and/or job grade or level of a particular job.

downstairs merger (US). Merger in which the parent *corporation* becomes a subsidiary.

DP. Data processing.

downtime. Period when available plant is not being used productively. See also *idle time.*

draft. See *cheque.*

Dragsmar evaluation. Method of evaluating *computer* installation based on seven major areas — software, hardware, documentation, planning, testing, personnel and protection. The evaluation allows for positive and negative rating:
130 - 147 — superior
115 - 129 — satisfactory
 90 - 114 — average
 60 - 89 — poor
below 60 — take immediate corrective action.

drawback. Or customs drawback, is where an exporter is repaid or credited for customs duties paid on imported goods which are then re-exported either in their original form or as component parts of manufactured goods. In the case of goods imported specifically for re-export in the same form a simpler procedure for the importer/re-exporter is to deposit them in a *bonded warehouse.* See also *goods for process.*

drawee. Party, often a bank, that makes payments under a *bill of exchange* etc, on the instructions of a *drawer.*

drawer. Signator to a *bill of exchange*, etc, giving instructions for payment to the *payee* by the *drawee.*

drawing account. One used to record cash payments to a director, partner or employee to cover expenses or as advances for payments due.

drives, social. See *social drives.*

drive to maturity stage (or period). Term used by some economists for the stage of national *economic growth* following the *traditional society, pre-take-off* and *take-off stages.* In the drive to maturity stage, the nation or community uses industrialized production techniques to press forward with raising standards of living throughout the community. See also final stage of growth, namely, *maturity.*

droit. Legal right.

Drucker, Peter. US consultant, academic and writer on management topics who popularized the concept of *management by objectives* and has also made major contributions to the development of *corporate planning.* Born 1909.

dry goods. Or soft goods. Textiles, clothing, etc.

ds. Days after sight.

DT Statistics and Market Intelligence Library (UK). *Department of Trade* service providing information for firms, particularly on export markets and the *Common Market*.

dual membership agreement. Agreement between two *trade unions* for one of them to represent certain of the other's members in particular situations.

dual purpose trust. As *split-level investment trust*.

dual unionism. Where two or more *trade unions* represent similar types of workers in the same *bargaining unit*. The term is used particularly in the USA. Dual unionism is usually a situation in which the unions concerned are in a state of peaceful coexistence. Where they are more competitive the term *rival unionism* is more applicable.

Dublin Stock Exchange. One of two trading floors of the *Irish Stock Exchange*.

dues, trade union. See *trade union dues*.

dummy activity. Used in *critical path planning* and *network analysis* to indicate events not connected in the network by one activity but nevertheless having an essential relationship in time. A dummy activity is shown as a dotted arrow.

dump bin. Retail display container for goods.

dumping. When goods are sold in an export market at prices below those for the same goods in the exporter's home market (the exporter thus 'dumping' his excess production in a manner making for unfair competition with producers based in the export market itself). The *General Agreement on Tariffs and Trade (GATT)* has an anti-dumping code and the *European Economic Community (EEC)* has anti-dumping regulations. An export subsidy for a product in its country of origin can lead to dumping and sometimes produces the reaction of a *countervailing duty*, or special import duty, by the country importing the product. See also *unloading*.

Dundee Stock Exchange. One of UK provincial stock exchanges, part of *United Stock Exchange*. See also *Stock Exchange (UK)*.

Dunedin Stock Exchange. One of four main New Zealand stock exchanges.

durable, consumer. See *consumer durable*.

Düsseldorf Stock Exchange. Or *Rheinisch-Westfälische Börse zu Düsseldorf*, Rhenish-Westphalian Stock Exchange. One of two principal stock exchanges in Federal Germany, the other being Frankfurt.

dustbin check. *Market research* technique for checking the purchases of a test household over a given period of time by having the householder discard all empty packages in a specially provided dustbin. This gives a picture of the household's volume of consumption as well as its choice of products. In conjunction with a *pantry check* a dustbin check may be known as a *home audit*. See also *consumer panel* and *retail audit*.

Dutch. See under *Netherlands*.

dutch auction. 1. Where an article is put up for sale at a price which is gradually reduced until a sale is made. **2.** Where a vendor takes bids secretly from prospective buyers, the latter not knowing each other's identity and having to rely on the vendor's word for the amounts bid by the others.

duty. Government tax, especially on imports.

duty free. Description of goods exempt from customs *duty*.

dyad interaction. *Interaction behavio(u)r* between two people only.

dynamic programming. Techniques for dealing with a succession of *decision making*.

EAC. *East African Community.*

E and O E. 'Errors and omissions excepted'. Sometimes used on bills, invoices, statements, etc with the intention of absolving the person or organization issuing the document from errors contained in it. The practice (practise) is of doubtful legal value.

earned income. Income from wages, salary or fees.

earned surplus. As *retained earnings*.

earnings. 1. Wages or salary. **2.** Profits of a company available for distribution to shareholders after payment of tax and any *preference share* dividends.

earnings/dividend ratio. Ratio of company profits to dividends actually declared. Also expressed as 'cover' or 'times covered'. Thus, 'covered twice' would mean that the total profits amounted to twice the total dividends declared.

earnings drift. Extent to which wages or earnings rise above national rates through the influence of such factors as local rates, *overtime, workplace bargaining, payment-by-results* schemes, *bargaining creep*, etc. Also known as *wage drift*. Tends to be uneven in its incidence, as between industries and districts, but to happen most in conditions of *full employment* etc.

earnings-related supplement with injury benefit. Introduced in UK by the *National Insurance Act 1966* on top of the *flat-rate benefits and contributions* of the earlier National Insurance (Industrial Injuries) Acts.

earnings-related unemployment and sickness benefit. Where benefit paid is related to the normal earnings of the individual and, probably, to the insurance premium payments he has made in the past. Introduced in the UK by the *National Insurance Acts 1965* and *1966* on top of the *flat-rate benefits and contributions* that were the basis of the *Beveridge Report* and the original National Insurance Act. See also *graduated benefits and contributions* and *earnings-related supplement with injury benefit*.

earnings relationships. Relationships between the levels of earnings of the different *work groups* or *occupations* in a factory or plant.

earnings yield. Earnings per *ordinary share* after tax divided by market price of ordinary share x 100. See *price earnings ratio*.

East African Community (EAC). Form of *common market* set up in 1967 and involving Burundi, Ethiopia, Kenya, Somalia, Tanzania, Uganda and Zambia.

Eastern Standard Time (EST or ET). Local time at a point of the USA at the 75 meridian. See *standard time* and Appendix: Time Zones.

EBD. *Economic batch determination.*

ECA. *Economic Commission for Africa.*

ECAFE. *Economic Commission for Asia and the Far East.*

ECE. *Economic Commission for Europe.*

ECFTU. *European Confederation of Free Trade Unions.*

ECGD. *Export Credits Guarantee Department.*

ECLA. *Economic Commission for Latin America.*

ECMT. *European Conference of Ministers of Transport.*

econometrics. Branch of economics which is concerned with the application of mathematical and statistical methods to establish relationships (if any) between economic variables.

ships (if any) between economic variables.

economic and monetary union (EEC). After effecting full *customs union* between themselves, the member states of the *Common Market* planned to achieve the free flow of capital, goods, labour, services, traffic, etc of *economic union*, followed by the common currency and common financial institutions of *monetary union*. It was hoped that this process would be completed by 1980.

Economic and Social Committee (EEC). *Common Market* consultative Committee established under Articles 193-198 of the *Treaty of Rome*. The Committee includes representatives of employers, trade unions, producers, farmers, carriers, dealers, small craft industries, professional occupations and 'the general interest'. There is provision for the Committee to be consulted by either the *Council of Ministers* or the *European Commission*. The committee has 153 members. See also *common social policy* and the *European Social Fund* from which it is financed.

economic batch determination (EBD). *Production planning* and control term for an analysis of the economic batch size for a particular order or project. This involves taking into account such factors as the costs of planning, ordering, tooling, materials handling, making ready work and machines, and carrying unsold finished parts if more than immediate needs are produced. See also *break-even point*.

Economic Commission for Africa (ECA). One of four Regional Economic Commissions of the *United Nations*. Established in 1958.

Economic Commission for Asia and the Far East (ECAFE). One of four Regional Economic Commissions of the *United Nations*. It is concerned with developing the area economically, industrially and socially.

Economic Commission for Europe (ECE). Established by the Economic and Social Council of the United Nations with the object of stimulating economic activity and cooperation in and with Europe.

Economic Commission for Latin America (ECLA). One of the four Regional Economic Commissions of the *United Nations*.

economic depression. As *slump*.

economic development. See *economic growth*.

Economic Development Administration. Agency of the *US Department of Commerce* which administers special economic development adjustment program(me)s through grants, loans, loan guarantees and technical assistance. These program(me)s include public works program(me)s under the *Jobs/Public Works Employment Act* of 1977, and assistance to communities threatened by actual or potential loss of employment.

economic growth. Rate, usually measured annually, at which a nation or other community's *real income* or *national income*, or flow of goods and services, increases. See also *gross national product, investment, real income*. The rate of economic growth of a country is influenced particularly by its rate of *saving* and by its *capital-output ratio*. Five broad stages of national economic growth as countries develop can be defined as *traditional society, pre-take-off, take-off, drive to maturity*, and *maturity*.

economic indicators. As *business indicators*.

economic life. Length of time for which an investment yields a return.

economic lot size (ELS). Optimum ordering quantity for an item or component in *stock control* at lowest cost.

$$Q = \sqrt{\frac{2AS}{rv}}$$

Q = quantity to be ordered; A = ordering cost; S = annual sales; r = carrying cost; V = unit cost.

economic man theory. School of thought believing that employee motivation depends almost exclusively on financial incentives. This school of thought fell into disrepute during the Second World War as the existence of other kinds of motivation became more widely recognized. See also *authoritarian theory* and *management style*.

economic manufacturing quantity (EMQ). *Production planning* and control term for the optimum size of production run for a particular product in particular conditions arrived at by techniques such as *economic batch determination*. The minimum acceptable production run is the *minimum manufacturing quantity (MMQ)*. See also *break-even point*.

ECSC. *European Coal and Steel Community.*

Ecuador Stock Exchange. See *Quito Stock Exchange.*

EDF. *European Development Fund.*

EDP. *Electronic data processing.*

Edridge-Green lantern tests. Form of *colo(u)r vision test* in which the subject is presented with a number of lights of different colo(u)rs and different degrees of brightness.

Edsel. Ill-fated Ford car which was one of the most prominent new product failures in business history. Often used in case studies of new product development and *market research.*

educational technology. Organized design and implementation of learning systems taking advantage of modern visual aids and communications and teaching methods. A systems approach to the teacher-learning process.

ee. Errors excepted.

EEC. *European Economic Community* (or *Common Market*). May be used to mean 'European Economic Communities', embracing not only the European Economic Community proper but also *Euratom* and the *European Coal and Steel Community (ECSC).*

EEC/EFTA Information Unit (UK). Established by the *Department of Trade* as a central point for general enquiries about the *European Economic Community* and the *European Free Trade Association.*

Eenmanszaak. Proprietorship under Netherlands law. See also *Netherlands companies.*

Effektenbörsenverein Zürich. *Zürich Stock Exchange,* one of the principal stock exchanges of Switzerland. See *Swiss stock exchanges.*

efficiency ratio. As *activity ratio.*

effort bargain. Agreement between management and *trade unions* which lays down the amount of work to be done for the agreed wage, not just the hours to be worked. An effort bargain hinges not only on the level of pay but also on the *payment system* (eg *day rate, payment-by-results,* etc). See also *productivity bargaining* and *bargaining range.*

effort-reward probability. See *expectancy theory.*

EFTA. *European Free Trade Area.*

EFTA Information Unit (DT). See *EEC/EFTA Information Unit.*

ego-identity. Need to have others accept one's self-image as valid.

egoistic needs. Industrial psychologist's term for the personal sources of *job satisfaction* other than remuneration. These include self-respect, the respect of others, sense of achievement, status, prestige, etc. See also *dissatisfiers.*

Egyptian Stock Exchange. There are two stock exchanges: **a** Cairo; **b** Alexandria.

Eidgenössische Wehrsteuer. Or *impôt fédéral pour la défense nationale.* The federal national defence tax charged on total income from all sources in Switzerland. See *Swiss income tax.*

eighty-twenty rule. See *Pareto's law.*

Einfache Gesellschaft. Or *Société Simple.* A simple partnership under Swiss company law. See also *Swiss companies.*

Einkommensteuer. *Income tax* charged on personal incomes in Austria, Federal Germany and Luxembourg, consisting of a wages tax *(Lohnsteuer)* and a capital yields tax *(Kapitalertragsteuer)* on dividends and other distributions of company profits. There are also a net *wealth tax (Vermögensteuer)* and a tax on fees paid to company directors (a tax known as *Aufsichtratsabgabe* in Austria, and in Federal Germany as *Aufsichtsteuer*). In Federal Germany there is also a surcharge, or *Ergänzungsabgabe,* on income tax. In Luxembourg the Einkommensteuer is also known by the French term, *impôt sur le revenu.*

Einzelfirma. One-man firm under Austrian or German company law. See also *Austrian companies* and *German companies.*

elastic demand. Effect which a price change has on the demand for goods or services. Those which are very sensitive to price change are said to be elastic. The opposite is *inelastic demand.*

elastic demand curve

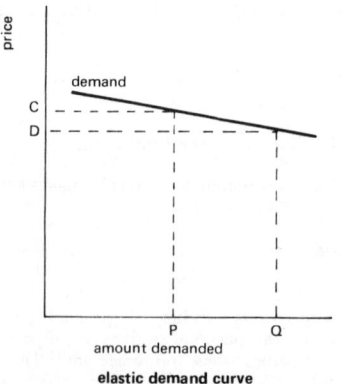

elastic demand curve

economic order quantity (EOQ). As *economic lot size*.

economic union. Where two or more countries unite their economies at least to the extent of permitting a free flow of capital, goods, labo(u)r, services and traffic between them. See *economic and monetary union (EEC)* for the particular plans and progress of the *Common Market*.

'(The) Economist'. UK weekly publication established in 1843. Coverage includes business and industry.

Electrical, Electronic, Telecommunications and Plumbing Union (UK). *Trade union* affiliated to the *Trades Union Congress*, and having approximately half a million members. See also *Confederation of Shipbuilding and Engineering Unions*.

Electrical Trades Union (ETU). Former name of the UK *Electrical, Electronic, Telecommunications and Plumbing Union*.

Electricity Supply Industry Training Board (UK). Established June 1965 under the *Industrial Training Act 1964*.

electronic data processing (EDP). Use of *computer* systems for data processing.

element (of work). Originated with *work study* practice of breaking work down into very small elements for *method study* and *work measurement*. Larger elements are appropriate in training except, for example, in *skills analysis training* of operatives.

eligible bills. Short-dated *bills of exchange* issued by *discount houses* etc for acceptance by banks. During times of strict *credit control* there may be a tendency for companies to issue 'eligible bills' rather than borrow on overdraft.

ELS. *Economic lot size.*

EMAS (UK). *Employment Medical Advisory Service.*

embargo. 1. Government directive prohibiting the entry of certain goods into a country for economic or political reasons. **2.** Restriction on the use or timing of a *press release*.

Emerson Efficiency Plan. Or Emerson Wage Payment Plan. An incentive scheme of the *gain sharing plan* or *share of production plan* kind originating in the USA.

EMF. *European Metalworkers Federation.*

EMIP. *Equivalent mean investment period.*

emolument. 1. Profit derived from office or employment. **2.** Payment for services rendered.

EMP. *Evaluated maintenance programming.*

employed person (or employee). One who works for an employer, as oppposed to a *self-employed person* working on his own account, or an *unemployed person* seeking employment, or a non-*employed person* neither in employment nor seeking it. See also *contract of employment* and *loaned employee*.

employee benefits. As *fringe benefits*.

employee handbook. Publication issued by an *employer* to each *employee* carrying information on the company, industrial relations procedures, welfare facilities, etc, and possibly to be referred to as an information source in each *contract of employment*.

employee, loaned. See *loaned employee*.

employee participation. See *participation*.

employee relations department. Usually synonymous with *personnel department*, though it may have a stronger *public relations* orientation.

employee relations index. Assessment of the quality of employee and personnel relations by noting trends in such factors as labo(u)r turnover, absenteeism, safety, medical needs, use made of suggestion schemes, grievances.

employee's contributory negligence. Contributory negligence on the part of an employee will reduce the damages awarded to him in an action against his employer for negligence under legal systems such as that in the UK. See also *employee's indemnity against liabilities and losses, safe working conditions, voluntary assumption of risk.*

employee's indemnity against liabilities and losses. An employee has indemnity under UK law against liabilities and losses properly incurred in the performance of his work. This is the case, for example, in claims against an employee for libel and slander unwittingly committed in carrying out his work, or when he is entrusted with an unlawful task without knowing its unlawful nature. There is more controversy where the negligence is the employee's own. See also *employee's contributory negligence, safe working conditions, vicarious liability, voluntary assumption of risk,* the *Law Reform (Contributory Negligence) Act 1945.*

employer reference. Where an employer seeks to use a *disputes procedure* or a *grievance procedure.* Such a step by the *trade union* side is known as a *union reference.*

employers' association. Association for employers that is concerned with questions of employment and industrial relations rather than the commercial and kindred matters that are the concern of a *trade association,* though some employers' associations also have a trade association function. In some countries employers are required by law to become members of the appropriate employers' association.

Employers' Liability (Compulsory Insurance) Act 1969. UK Act that came into force on 1 January 1972 with the object of ensuring that employers are always in a position to pay any industrial injuries damages payable to employees. The Act made it mandatory for employers to insure against liability for personal injury to their employees.

Employer's Liability (Defective Equipment) Act 1969. UK legislation making an employer liable for injury to workers caused by defective plant or equipment even if the employer had good reason to believe he had acquired safe equipment. This legislation made the *Employer's Liability (Compulsory Insurance) Act 1969* more necessary.

employers' organization. Term often used for *employers' association.*

employer strike insurance. US term for the operation by employers of a system of compensating each other for losses incurred as a result of *industrial action.* The system is similar to the *indemnity funds* operated by some employers' associations in the UK.

employment. Level of employment in a community ranging from *mass unemployment,* when *slump* conditions are experienced, to *full employment,* when the dangers of *inflation* are present particularly in a *laissez-faire economy.* See also *trade cycle.*

Employment Agencies Act 1973. UK legislation laying down that all *employment agencies* and *temporary staff contracting services* must obtain a licence from their local licensing authority. Previously in the UK, the question of registration and licensing of employment agencies had been decided at local authority level. The Act forbids agencies to charge job seekers a fee for finding or trying to find them jobs. The Act was the first UK legislation to distinguish between *temp(s)* and permanent job placing.

employment agency. Normally concerned with introducing office staff and unskilled or semi-skilled manual staff to prospective employers, the employer paying the agency a fee if he employs someone introduced in this way. Employment agencies do not normally attempt to apply *personnel selection* and testing techniques. An employment agency may also operate as a *temporary staff contracting service* hiring out *temps* or temporary staff. In many countries, employment agencies are required to register and to maintain certain standards of service. This happens in the UK, for example, under the *Employment Agencies Act 1973.*

'Employment and Productivity Gazette'. Monthly UK publication of the *Department of Employment* (HMSO).

Employment and Training Act 1973. Provided for the setting up as statutory bodies of the *Manpower Services Commission (MSC)* and, under it, the *Employment Service Agency (ESA)* and the *Training Services Agency (TSA).* The ESA had existed within the *Department of Employment* since early 1972, while the MSC had been set up in November 1972 with the blessing of both the *Confederation of British Industry* and the *Trades Union Congress.*

Employment and Training Act (Northern Ireland) 1950. Empowered the Ministry of

113

Health and Social Services, Northern Ireland, to operate training centres and give grants for training on employers' premises.

Employment and Training Administration. *US Department of Labor* agency which administers the Department's employment and training program(me)s including the *Comprehensive Employment and Training Act* of 1973 and the Federal-State Employment Security System; undertakes research, development and evaluation; administers national program(me)s for ethnic groups, migrant and seasonal farm workers, and the aged; and formulates and promotes apprenticeship program(me)s.

employment, continuity of. See *continuity of employment*.

employment costs. Wages or salary paid to an employee plus the related payments for insurance, pensions, etc that have to be met by the employer. *Overheads* related to the employee may also be included.

Employment, Department of (UK). See *Department of Employment*, formerly *Ministry of Labour*. The senior Minister is the *Secretary of State for Employment*.

employment exchanges. Former term for *Employment Offices* in UK.

employment, inventory of. Statement of the available and the required manpower in the different employee categories within a firm.

employment medical adviser (UK). Medical doctor working for the *Employment Medical Advisory Service (EMAS)*.

Employment Medical Advisory Service Act 1972. UK Act that became operational February 1973.

Employment Medical Advisory Service (EMAS). Launched in the UK in February 1973 by the *Department of Employment* under the *Employment Medical Advisory Service Act 1972*. Main priorities of the Service are **a** periodic medical examinations of workers engaged in hazardous trades, **b** help in advising young people starting work, and **c** occupational medicine and tackling industrial diseases.

Employment Offices. Operated by the *Employment Service Division* for the Department of Employment in the UK.

Employment Protection Bill. See *Protection of Employment Bill*.

Employment Service Division (ESD). Introduced in the UK by the *Employment and Training Act 1973* as a statutory body coming under the *Manpower Services Commission* and working alongside the *Training Services Division*. It had already been in existence within the *Department of Employment* since early 1972. As a statutory body, the ESD became responsible for employment offices, *jobcentres*, the *Occupational Guidance Scheme*, the *Professional and Executive Recruitment service (PER)*, the *Resettlement Transfer Scheme*, and the employment of disabled people under the *Disabled Persons (Employment) Acts 1944 and 1958*.

Employment Standards Administration. Unit of the *US Department of Labor* concerned with maintenance of standards in employment, industrial injuries, equal opportunities, etc.

employment test. *Aptitude test* or *achievement test* which a prospective *employee* is expected to pass as a condition of *employment*.

EMQ. *Economic manufacturing quantity*.

end-on-courses. 1. Where a college or university arranges six-months-in-industry/six-months-in-college *sandwich courses* so that there are two complete courses or entries of students each year. **2.** Courses arranged so that able students can progress to higher level courses.

endorsement. 1. Amendment to a contract permitting a change in the previous terms. **2.** Signature serving as evidence of legal transfer of ownership. **3.** Approval of a document or contract by signature. **4.** Acknowledgement of receipt of payment.

endowment assurance (or insurance) policy. Policy in which the sum assured is payable at the end of a fixed period if the insured is still alive then, or sometimes in part on an earlier death. This differs from a *whole life assurance policy* with which the sum assured is payable on death only. Strictly speaking, no element of life assurance is included in a so-called *pure endowment assurance policy* but the usual arrangement is for life assurance to be payable equivalent to the contributions to date plus profits (the latter only applying, of course, in the case of *with-profits endowment assurance*). See also *non-profit endowment assurance* or *without-profits endowment assurance*.

end price support. Principle of the *Common*

Agricultural Policy of the *European Community* that guarantees the prices of certain commodities, notably dairy products, at a level sufficient to provide a livelihood for Europe's poorest farmers (and, therefore, attractive profits for the larger and more efficient farmers). See also the *intervention price* and *threshold price* operated under the CAP.

ENEA. *European Nuclear Energy Agency.*

engineering apprentice test-battery. Range or battery of tests specially developed in the UK for or by the National Institute of Industrial Psychology for *personnel selection* and *vocational guidance* purposes. The battery tests for factors such as intelligence, educational attainment, trade aptitude and written English. Individual tests in the battery include: *ability to follow instructions test (Instr); arithmetic ability (Ar); colour vision test (CV); English vocabulary level (Voc); literacy test of written English (Comp): mechanical comprehension test (m); motor speed and accuracy mechanical test (Motor Spd Acc); non-verbal intelligence test (g); spatial ability test (k); verbal intelligence test (g(v)); Vernon Graded Arithmetic Test.* See also *test battery* and *psychological testing.*

Engineering Employers' Federation (UK). National *employers' association* or organization with more than 4,600 engineering firms.

Engineering Foundation (US). See *United Engineering Center (US).*

Engineering Industries Group Apprenticeship (EIGA) scheme. One of the pioneers in UK of group apprenticeship schemes, dating back to 1953.

Engineering Industry Training Board. Established July 1964 under UK *Industrial Training Act 1964.*

engineering procedure. Procedure under the national agreement (UK) between the *Engineering Employers' Federation* and the *Confederation of Shipbuilding and Engineering Unions* for settling *industrial disputes* in the engineering industry until the ending of the national agreement in 1971. The procedure for settling disputes began with a *Works Conference* called on the premises of the company involved at the request of the company or of the *trade union(s)* concerned, and arranged by the local Engineering Employers' Association.

The next stage was a *Local Conference* convened at the offices of the Employers' Association with a key part being taken by panels of employers and of union representatives not directly involved in the dispute and, if agreement was still not reached here, the next and final stage was the *Central Conference* involving senior employers and trade union officials who had no contact with the dispute. In the case of *white collar workers,* a regular *Staff Central Conference* was held in London. See also *composite conference.*

engineering query note. Document used in communication between manufacturing and design departments, particularly when dealing with production difficulties. See also *concession request form.*

English Tourist Board. UK organization responsible for promoting tourism. See also *Scottish Tourist Board, Wales Tourist Board.*

English vocabulary level (Voc). Personnel selection and vocational guidance test devised as part of the *engineering apprentice test-battery* of the National Institute of Industrial Psychology in the UK. See also *psychological testing* and *test battery.*

engross. To prepare a legal or official document by the prescribed process.

ENI. *Ente Nazionali Idrocarburi.*

Ente Nazionali Idrocarburi (ENI). Italian organization which coordinates state involvement in the petrochemical industry. See also *IRI.*

Environmental Quality, Council on (US). See *Council on Environmental Quality.*

Environmental Science and Engineering, Council for (UK). See *Council for Environmental Science and Engineering.*

environment-based learning. Where emphasis is not on the instructor/teacher teaching but on the trainee/student learning, in an environment where *educational technology* aids and the teacher are resources.

EOQ. *Economic ordering quantity.*

EPB. *Equivalent Pension Benefit.*

EPF. *Excepted provident fund* (pensions).

EPROM. *Computer store* which can be

erased by ultraviolet and is then ready for a new program.

Equal Employment Opportunity Commission. US commission which has enforcement responsibilities for federal government program(me)s aimed at ending discrimination based on race, colo(u)r, religion, sex or national origin in hiring, promotion, firing, wages and conditions of employment. The role of the Commission covers investigation of complaints, *conciliation,* bringing court actions, and publishing guidebooks on *affirmative action,* equal employment and federal anti-discrimination laws and regulations. See also *Commission on Civil Rights.*

Equal Pay Act 1970. UK Act to eliminate discrimination between men and women over pay and other terms and conditions of employment. The Act **a** establishes the right of an individual woman to equal treatment when in the same job as a man or in a job rated equal by *job evaluation* techniques; and **b** provides for an *Industrial Tribunal* to remove discrimination in *collective agreements,* employers' pay structures and statutory *wages regulation orders* which include provisions applying specifically to men only or to women only and which have been referred to the Tribunal.

equipment-type flow process chart. *Flow process chart* which shows the use made of plant and equipment.

equity. 1. The *ordinary shares* in a company or the value of its *assets* after allowance has been made for all *liabilities* other than those to shareholders themselves. Ordinary shares take precedence after *debentures* and *preference shares* in the distribution of profits. **2.** The term, equity capital, is sometimes used with the meaning of *risk capital* or venture capital. **3.** Branch of law providing legal remedies and justice for problems not covered by common or statute law. **4.** Something that is fair and impartial.

equity capital. *Capital* raised by a *company* or *corporation* by issuing *equity shares.* See also *equity.*

equity dilution. Dilution of the influence or control of the original *shareholders* as a result of the issue of new *shares.*

equity share. See *shares.*

equity share capital. *Nominal value* of all the *shares* of a *company* or *corporation.*

equivalent mean investment period (EMIP). Developed from the *discounted cash flow* technique, EMIP is a sophisticated method of assessing projects up to the *break-even point.*

Equivalent Pension Benefit. Where UK employee leaves a firm's *occupational pension scheme* that is *contracted-out* from the *state graduated pension scheme,* the employee has a vested right to the *Equivalent Pension Benefit* — that is, must be credited with at least as much pension entitlement as he would have earned in the state scheme. Either the employee is given a *Certificate of Assurance* setting out the pension earned or the employer makes a *Payment in Lieu (PIL)* to the *Department of Health and Social Security* to be incorporated in the employee's state pension.

Ergänzungsabgabe. *Surcharge* charged in Federal Germany on income tax or *Einkommensteuer.* See also *German (Federal) income tax, Kapitalertragsteuer, Aufsichtsratsteuer,* and *Lohnsteuer.*

ergonomics. Study of the relationship between man and his occupation, equipment and environment, and particularly the application of anatomical, physiological and psychological knowledge to the problems arising therefrom. Sometimes known vernacularly as fitting the job to the worker. A specialist involved in the study and application of ergonomics is the *occupational psychologist.* Ergonomics is known in the USA as *human engineering.*

error. *Market research/*statistics term for the difference between a computed or measured value and a correct value.

ESD (UK). *Employment Service Division.*

escalation clause. Clause in a commercial contract agreeing to an increase in *price* in the event of an increase in costs such as wages or raw materials.

escalator clause. 1. US term for a form of *threshold agreement* geared to the *BLS Consumer Price Index.* **2.** Provision for a cost of living increase as part of a *collective agreement.*

escrow agreement. 1. Arrangement sometimes made during *industrial action,* particularly in the USA, under which an employer makes available a certain sum of money to be used to pay a wage increase if an arbitrator rules that such an increase is

EST (or ET)

warranted. The arbitrator may actually hold the money pending his decision. **2.** General term for a written agreement not effective until certain conditions are fulfilled by the grantee.

EST (or ET). *Eastern Standard Time.* See also Appendix: Time Zones.

establishment expense. As *indirect cost.*

estate duty. Or death duty. Tax on the estate of a deceased person.

estimate analysis. Cost accounting procedure for estimating direct and indirect costs (including *administration costs*) and *profit* and selling *price.*

eta. Estimated time of arrival.

etd. Estimated time of departure.

ETU. UK *Electrical Trades Union,* the former name of the *Electrical, Electronic, Telecommunication and Plumbing Union.*

ETUC. *European Trade Union Confederation.*

Euratom. *European Atomic Energy Community.*

Euratom Treaty. Signed in Rome in 1957 to establish the *European Atomic Energy Community (Euratom)* at the same time that the *Treaty of Rome 1957* established the *European Economic Community (EEC).* The *Treaty of Paris 1951* had already established the *European Coal and Steel Community (ECSC).* These three Treaties are sometimes called the *primary legislation* of the *Common Market.* The three communities were then united under the *Council of Ministers* and the *European Commission* by the *Merger Treaty 1967.* With full implementation of the Treaty of Rome, the *common budget* was arranged through the *Budget Treaty 1970.* All three communities were covered by the *Treaty of Accession 1972* by which Denmark, the Irish Republic and the UK joined the *Common Market* on 1 January 1973.

Euro. Prefix normally indicating application throughout Europe, particularly in the member states of the *European Economic Community.*

Eurobonds. Bonds negotiable within the member states of the *European Economic Community.* See also *monetary union.*

European Association for Industrial Marketing

Eurocontrol. European Organization for the Safety of Air Navigation.

Eurocrat. Popular term for a person working for the *European Commission* or civil service of the *Common Market.* There are about 10,000 Eurocrats, working mainly in Brussels and Luxembourg but also elsewhere in the EEC countries.

Eurodollars. Dollar credits circulated in Europe and indeed anywhere outside the USA to facilitate business transactions. The Euro-dollar is a banking phenomenon that first appeared to a significant extent in the mid-1960s with the *City of London* as a major broking centre (center).

Eurofrancs. Francs traded and dealt in outside France but within the member states of the *European Economic Communities.* See also *monetary union.*

Euromarket. As *Common Market.*

Euromarks. Marks traded and dealt in outside Federal Germany but within the member states of the *European Economic Communities.* See also *monetary union.*

Euromart. As *Common Market.*

European Agreement on the International Carriage of Dangerous Goods (ADR). Lays down safeguards for the international transportation of dangerous goods such as explosives or inflammable or radioactive materials.

European Agreement on the International Carriage of Perishable Foodstuffs (ATP). Agreement on the safeguards necessary in the international transportation of perishable foodstuffs in insulated or refrigerated vans, etc.

European Agricultural Guidance and Guarantee Fund. Fund from which the support-buying, modernization, etc grants of the *Common Agricultural Policy* of the *Common Market* or *European Economic Community* are financed (with monies coming from the common budget). The Fund is sometimes known by its French initials, FEOGA. Also known as the *Community Agricultural Fund.*

European Association for Industrial Marketing Research (EVAF). Body set up in 1965 to build up contacts between marketing researchers in the European countries.

117

European Association for Personnel Management. Set up in 1962 to promote the cause of personnel management. Its members are the national associations of some 14 European countries.

European Association of Advertising Agencies. Set up in 1960 to maintain standards of service to advertisers. See also *International Advertising Association Inc.*

European Atomic Energy Community (Euratom). Running in parallel with the *European Economic Community (EEC)* and the *European Coal and Steel Community (ECSC)*, and established by the *Euratom Treaty 1957*, Euratom promotes the use of atomic energy for peaceful purposes among the Common Market member states. These states have a 'common market' in nuclear materials and equipment as they have in other goods through the EEC and the European Coal and Steel Community (ECSC). Euratom shares the main institutions of the EEC and the ECSC – namely, the *Council of Ministers*, the *European Commission*, the *European Court of Justice*, and the *Assembly (European Parliament)*.

European Coal and Steel Community (ECSC). Established by the *Treaty of Paris 1951* and operating from August 1952 among the *Common Market* founder member states – namely, France, Federal Germany, Italy, the Netherlands, Belgium and Luxembourg. The ECSC is financed by a levy on coal and steel production in the member states. Since the *Merger Treaty 1967* the ECSC has been run jointly with the *European Economic Community (EEC)* and the *European Atomic Energy Community (Euratom)* which were established by, respectively, the *Treaty of Rome 1957* and the *Euratom Treaty 1957*. The three organizations share the Common Market institutions, the *Council of Ministers*, the *European Commission*, the *European Parliament* and the *European Court of Justice*.

European Commission. Brussels and Luxembourg based civil service-type body which administers the *Common Market*, embracing the *European Economic Community (EEC)*, the *European Atomic Energy Community (Euratom)* and the *European Coal and Steel Community (ECSC)*. The European Commission formulates proposals for consideration by the *Council of Ministers* (the supreme decision-making body in the Common Market) and is responsible for implementing the Council's policies such as the *Common Agricultural Policy*. The European Commission also has its own so-called 'power of decision' and sometimes, in conjunction with the *European Court of Justice*, imposes fines on individuals, firms or even member states that break *Treaty of Rome* provisions or Community regulations on, for example, fair competition. The European Commission has charge of the *common budget* to which member states contribute and to which are passed all duties paid at the outer common tariff wall around the Common Market.

The European Commission has a staff of about 10,000 (sometimes known as *Eurocrats*) and is led by 14 Commissioners. All Commissioners are appointed by unanimous agreement of all the member states for a period of four years and, on appointment, swear before the European Court that they will not be influenced by national interests or considerations but will act as Europeans. Each Commissioner takes special responsibility for a particular area of the Commission's work.

Under Article 228 of the Treaty of Rome, the Commission is responsible for negotiating trade agreements with non-member countries on behalf of the Common Market. The Commission itself was established under Articles 155-163. Edicts of the Council of Ministers and/or the European Commission are issued in one of the following forms: *Regulations* are binding in their entirety and apply directly in all member states; *Decisions* are also binding, but only on those at whom they are specifically directed; *Directives* are binding on all member states, but the form and method of their implementation are at the discretion of the individual member states. *Recommendations* and *Opinions* do not have any binding force.

European Communities Act 1972. Legislation in the British Parliament that took the UK into the *European Economic Community* or *Common Market* on 1 January 1973 according to the *Treaty of Accession* which modified the *Treaty of Rome 1957* to include Denmark, the Irish Republic and the UK in the Common Market.

European Community. *European Economic Community (EEC)* or *Common Market*. The term may also embrace the *European Atomic Energy Community (Euratom)* and the *European Coal and Steel Community (ECSC)*. Sometimes the European Community is known simply as 'the Community'.

(the) European Company. Or *Societas*

Europea (SE). An idea mooted among member countries of the *European Economic Community (EEC)* for enabling a company to be established under Community law. It would stand outside the jurisdiction of national company law, providing a legal status for companies operating in a number of European countries.

European Components Service. *Department of Trade* service seeking out for UK components manufacturers enquiries for engineering components from European mass assembly manufacturers and wholesalers. The Service makes contact with potential UK suppliers through *chambers of commerce, trade associations*, etc.

European Confederation of Free Trade Unions (ECFTU). Organization, formed in 1969, representing and coordinating the *trade union* movements of the *member states* of the *Common Market* or *European Economic Community*. The European Confederation of Free Trade Unions is linked with the *International Confederation of Free Trade Unions (ICFTU)* and so does not include the Communist unions which have links with the *World Federation of Trade Unions*.

European Conference of Ministers of Transport (ECMT). Set up in 1953 to promote the rational development of inland transport in Europe. Some 18 European countries are members, with the USA as an observer and Japan as an associate member.

European Coordination Office. Receives from the employment services of the member states of the *Common Market* or *European Economic Community* monthly reports on people seeking work and job vacancies. The office then circulates this information to all member states to assist in implementation of the *free movement of labour* principles and provisions of the Common Market.

European Court of Justice. Court responsible for enforcing the *Treaty of Rome 1957* and the rules and regulations of the *European Economic Community (EEC)* or *Common Market*. The Court operates in Luxembourg and works with the cooperation of the *European Commission* and has a judge from each of the member states. The Court's procedure is broadly similar to that of the highest courts of the member states. In addition to the member states and institutions of the EEC, firms and individuals have the right to appeal to the European Court if they consider that the terms of the Treaty of Rome have not been properly applied in matters affecting them. Articles 164-188 of the Treaty established the European Court.

European Development Fund (EDF). *Common Market* institution, expected to be reorganized from February 1975 and set up by member states in the *Yaoundé Convention* of July 1969. The EDF will handle grants and loans to non-member states taking advantage of the provisions of the *Treaty of Rome 1957* for *association of overseas countries and territories*.

European Economic Association (UNEUROP). Set up in 1959 to provide advice and encouragement on economic cooperation between the member states of the *European Economic Communities* and the *European Free Trade Area*. It has offices in Brussels, Madrid, Milan, Munich, Paris and Rotterdam.

European Economic Community (EEC). Operates the *Common Market* under the *Treaty of Rome 1957*, which became operative on 1 January 1958, and the *Treaty of Accession, 1972*, which became operative on 1 January 1973. The founder members were France, West Germany, Italy, the Netherlands, Belgium and Luxembourg, these six being joined by Denmark, the Irish Republic and the UK under the Treaty of Accession. The Common Market/EEC operates a *customs union* or *Common Customs (or External) Tariff* and is working towards *economic and monetary union* by 1980, with *political union* possibly to follow later.

The principal institutions of the EEC are the *Council of Ministers*, the *European Commission*, the *European Court of Justice*, and the *Assembly* or *European Parliament*. The EEC has shared these institutions with the *European Atomic Energy Community (Euratom)* and the *European Coal and Steel Community (ECSC)* since the *Merger Treaty 1967*, and the abbreviation EEC is often used to mean European Economic Communities, taking in all three Common Market organizations.

Particular Community institutions, policies, etc are noted under *Common Market* together with a note of similar types of activity elsewhere in the world. See also *Decisions, Directives* and *Regulations*.

European Foundation for Management Development (EFMD). Body formed in 1971 with the aim of improving standards of *management development* in Europe. Members are both individuals and organizations.

European Free Trade Area (EFTA) European Nuclear Energy Agency (ENEA)

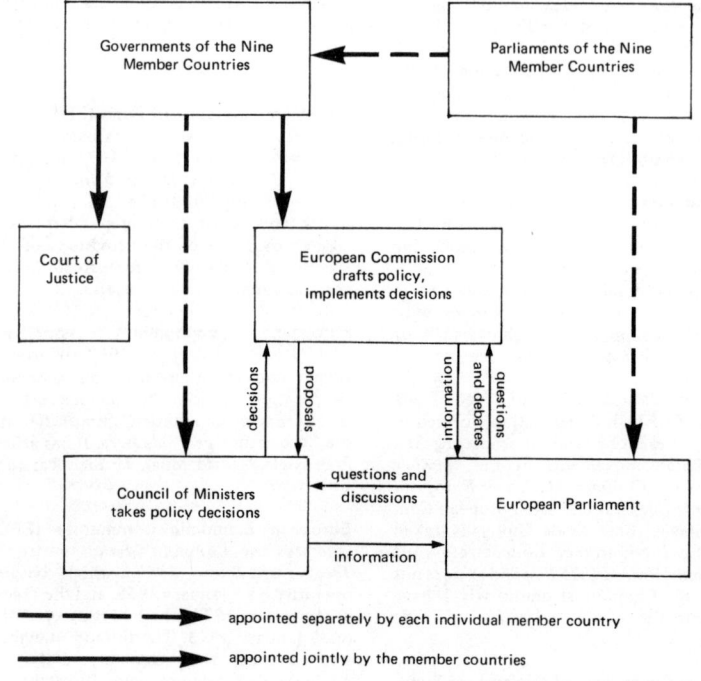

The European Community Institutions

European Free Trade Area (EFTA). Formed in November 1959 on the initiative of the UK as a counter to the *Common Market*. EFTA's nine founder members were Denmark, Sweden, Norway, Switzerland, Austria, Portugal, Finland, Iceland and the UK. Denmark and UK now belong to the EEC. There is no *tariff* wall between any two member states of EFTA, but, unlike the Common Market, EFTA is not a *customs union* and does not have a *common external tariff*.

European Human Rights Court. Established under the Human Rights Convention of the *Council of Europe* to safeguard individual rights by providing a means for individuals to bring actions against their national governments.

European Institute of Business Administration (INSEAD). International business school founded near Paris in 1958. Uses three official languages and has some 180 students from 25 countries.

European Investment Bank. Established by the *Common Market* under Articles 129 and 130 of the *Treaty of Rome 1957*, to make grants and loans for regional development, modernization schemes, and projects of common interest to member states. The Bank may also aid associate members and member states' dependencies. The Bank is managed by a Board of Governors provided by member states who subscribe to its capital in proportions laid down in its Statute as set out in a Protocol annexed to the Treaty of Rome.

European League for Economic Cooperation. Set up in 1946 to work for the economic integration of Europe.

European Metalworkers Federation (EMF). Confederation of *trade unions* that plays a powerful part in the *European Confederation of Free Trade Unions* and is also linked with the *International Metalworkers Federation*.

European Nuclear Energy Agency (ENEA). Run by the *Organization for Economic Cooperation and Development (OECD)* to promote the peaceful uses of nuclear energy. Some 18 European countries are members with, as associate members, Canada, Japan and the USA.

European Organization for Nuclear Research (CERN). Established in 1954 with the encouragement of *UNESCO* to engage in non-military research. Member states are Austria, Belgium, Denmark, France, West Germany, Greece, Italy, the Netherlands, Norway, Spain, Sweden, Switzerland and the UK. Observer states are Poland, Turkey and Yugoslavia. CERN has establishments in Geneva, Grenoble and Paris.

European Parliament (or Assembly). One of the major *Common Market* institutions, the Assembly or European Parliament (meeting in Strasbourg and Luxembourg) is composed of delegates from the parliaments of each of the member states. It is a consultative body, not a legislature, though it does technically have the power to dismiss the *European Commission* with a two-thirds majority, and has limited powers in relation to part of the *common budget*. Under the Treaty of Rome 1957 the European Parliament is known simply as the *Assembly*.

The supreme decision-making body in the Common Market is the *Council of Ministers*. Other major Common Market institutions, in addition to the European Commission, are the *European Court of Justice* and the *Committee of Permanent Representatives*. Articles 137-144 are the parts of the Treaty of Rome under which the European Parliament was established and now operates.

European plan. System of paying for hotel room and services separately from meal payments.

European Recovery Programme. Marshall Plan of 1947-51 under which American aid was made available to assist the economic recovery of Western Europe (such aid being refused in Eastern Europe). The *Organization for European Economic Cooperation (OEEC)* was set up under the European Recovery Programme.

European Social Fund. Established by the *Common Market*, under Articles 123 to 128 of the *Treaty of Rome 1957*, to help in the re-employment of workers rendered unemployed by technological and/or economic change, as part of the Community's *common social policy*. The Fund may repay a member state up to half its expenditure on vocational *retraining* and *redeployment* of workers. It may also aid both private and public undertakings and may also give aid to non-member states. The European Social Fund is financed from the Common Market's *common budget*.

European Trade Union Confederation (ETUC). Or Confédération européenne des syndicats (CES) or Europäischer Gewerkschaftsbund. Organization of European national federations of trade unions formed in 1973 with a particular concern to promote the interests of trade unionists in the *Economic Community*, though in fact the ETUC includes trade union federations from outside the Community.

European Units of Account. Devised in Luxembourg as an alternative to using national currencies for trading within the *Common Market*.

EVAF. *European Association for Industrial Marketing Research.*

evaluated maintenance programming (EMP). Planned preventive maintenance schedules for plant and machinery based on analysis of past performance and cost records.

evaluation (of training). Study of the financial and social effectiveness of a course (not its training effectiveness, which is *validation*). Takes into account *cost-benefit analysis* and *cost-effectiveness*.

event. 1. Identifiable stage completed in *network analysis*. **2.** In the context of transportation by ship, an event is any incident of which the insurer should be informed in case he wishes to modify the *insurance* cover.

evolutionary operation. Method of computer control of industrial processes in which subtle changes are constantly made in operating settings in quest of improved performance. As such improved performance is identified, the settings producing it are held and the process of searching for further improvement is continued. A similar technique to evolutionary operation is *adaptive control* in which the computer makes calculations based on past experience to improve the performance of plant.

EWS. *Experienced worker standard.*

excepted provident fund (EPF). Or retirement benefit scheme or cloth cap pension scheme. A type of pension scheme in which the whole of the benefit may be taken as a lump sum at normal retirement age instead of a pension proper. It is normally arranged in the form of *endowment assurance*, and may have the characteristics of an *average salary pension scheme* or a *final salary pension scheme* or a *money purchase pension scheme*. More often, however, an EPF scheme is a *non-contributory*, low flat-rate scheme intended particularly for hourly-paid manual workers (hence the term 'cloth cap pension') where a more generous type of pension scheme is not available to them. Where an EPF scheme is contributory, the insured person normally obtains tax relief in the same way as for *life assurance* in general.

exception principle. *Data processing* or management information system that reports only on those items where the actual results differ considerably from predetermined targets.

exception report. Report form used in *management by exception.*

excess. Amount of an insurance claim that must be deducted and met by the assured himself.

exchange control. Type of control introduced by a country over the ways in which its currency may be exchanged for other currencies. Exchange control is used where a country seeks to influence the internationally recognized value of its currency, as has been the case in the UK in post-war years because of its *balance of payments* problems. Exchange control, which obviously limits the *convertibility* of a currency, becomes the more necessary in a system of fixed *exchange rates* where currencies are not left to find their own competing levels.

Exchange Control Act 1947. UK legislation to give the Government control over the outflow of gold and currency from the *sterling area.*

Exchange Equalization Account. Managed by the *Bank of England* for the *Treasury* with the object of offsetting major fluctuations in the *exchange rate* of the pound. Set up under the Finance Act 1932, the Account has as its assets the UK's *gold and foreign exchange reserves* and sterling invested in *Treasury Bills.*

exchange losses. Financial losses suffered by individuals, companies, etc in investments, loans, transactions, etc as a result of changes in *exchange rates* between nations.

exchange rate. Rate at which a currency may be exchanged for other currencies.

exchange risk. Risk that future business will be affected by changes in the *exchange rate.*

Exchange Telegraph. UK publishers of *stock market intelligence* on a subscription basis.

excise duty. Tax levied on certain goods and services in their *country of origin* or manufacture. Notable examples in the UK are tobacco products and alcoholic drinks. Responsibility for the collection of excise duty in the UK lies with *Her Majesty's Customs and Excise.*

excise licence. Held by manufacturers and dealers in goods that are subject to *excise duty.*

excise tax. US federal and state tax levied on the manufacture and distribution of certain *consumer goods.* Goods on which federal excise tax is levied include tobacco, alcohol, gasoline and travel.

ex-dividend. Of shares or securities bought or sold without benefit of the latest dividend declared.

executive. 1. Person or group of people having managerial authority in an organization. **2.** The administration. **3.** Part of government responsible for implementing the decisions of the legislature.

executive director. Or inside director. *Company director* who is a full-time *employee* of the company.

executive search . See *head-hunter.*

exemption. Tax allowance deductible from gross annual income.

Eximbank. *Export-Import Bank of the United States.*

existing use value. As current use value or user value. *Price* that property, land, etc will fetch if it is to continue to be put to its existing use as opposed to the price it might fetch if put to a more profitable use. The best known illustration is probably the difference between the existing use value of agricultural land and its value if sold for development as building land.

exit interview. Interview with an employee who is in process of leaving the employing organization, the purpose of the interview being to gain an improved insight into employee perceptions.

'l'Expansion'. French monthly publication on economics and business.

expansion demand. Marketing term for demand related to completely new consumers or users entering the market for a particular type of product. *Replacement demand* is associated with *consumer durables* and *industrial capital goods*, while *repeat demand* is concerned with frequently purchased *consumer goods*, such as *consumer disposables*.

expectancy chart. Sometimes used following *psychological testing* to predict the performance in particular occupations of those being tested. An *individual expectancy chart* plots the predicted performance of an individual candidate or employee in a particular occupation. An *institutional expectancy chart* predicts the levels of efficiency within a work-force, note being made of such factors as the number of workers expected to be of above-average performance. Expectancy charts have been particularly highly developed in the USA.

expectancy theory. Theories about job performance and motivation developed by Georgopoulos, Mahoney, Jones, Vroom, Lawler and others. According to these theories an employee's motivation to perform effectively is determined by two variables: effort-reward probability and reward-value or valence. Effort-reward probability means an individual's subjective view that a given amount of effort in performing effectively will result in obtaining a given reward. Reward-value (or valence) refers to the individual's perception of the value of the reward or outcome that might be obtained by performing effectively.

expenditure. Conversion of cash into real *assets* by a company or organization. The opposite process, *revenue*, is the conversion of real assets into cash, and the difference between expenditure and revenue for a project/enterprise is its *profit* or *loss*.

expenditure tax. As *indirect tax*.

experience curve. As *learning curve* but also taking into account on-the-job improvement after the end of formal training.

experienced worker standard (EWS). Concept of the trained and experienced worker's output used by *Engineering Industry Training Board* et al in the UK in attempting to establish training standards.

expert witness. 1. Group method of instruction/learning whereby trainees/students cross-examine someone expert in a particular field. **2.** Expert called upon to give evidence in a court of law on a technical aspect of the matter in dispute.

exploratory forecasting techniques. Type of techniques, used for example in *technological forecasting*, in which projections are made based on present knowledge of a technology or product without trying to take into account likely developments in other fields. On the other hand, *normative forecasting techniques* begin with a consideration of the likely future structure and needs of society, and then consider the developments necessary to create that structure and meet those needs. Particular techniques of technological forecasting include *brainstorming*, the *Delphi approach*, *morphological research*, the *scenario writing approach*, and *technological trend extrapolation*.

exponential smoothing. Mathematical techniques for improving the accuracy of forecasting, particularly short-term, by weighting it to take the most recent trends into account. A very much simpler, but cruder, technique for weighting forecasts to take recent trends into account is the use of *moving averages*.

export agent. Person or company acting on behalf of an exporter in another country. Two types of *agent* are the *commission agent* and the *del credere agent*.

export club. Largely informal grouping of manufacturers, *shipping and forwarding agents*, banks, insurance companies, etc to cooperate or exchange experience on overseas markets and export procedures. Information on export clubs in the UK is available from the *Export Services Division (DT)*.

export controls, security. See *security export controls*.

Export Credits Guarantee Department (DT). Provides for UK firms an export *credit insurance* scheme and advice.

Export Data Branch (DT). Part of the *Export Services Branch* of the *Department of Trade* that provides UK firms with current information on tariff advantages overseas.

Exporters, Technical Help to (UK). See

Technical Help to Exporters service.

export finance house. Financial institution specializing in arranging *non-recourse* finance for exporters. Normally, it assists the exporter by giving credit directly to the overseas buyer without recourse to the exporter who receives payment from the export finance house against presentation of the relevant invoices, *bills of lading* and other shipping documents. It is the responsibility of the export finance house, in the UK, to arrange any cover with the *Export Credits Guarantee Department* and to check the credit worthiness of the overseas buyer, but the contract of sale remains between the exporter and the overseas buyer. Sometimes an export finance house takes responsibility for all formalities from collection of goods from the exporter to their delivery to the overseas buyer. Most bank managers are able to advise on choice of export finance house. See also *export house, export club,* and *confirming house.*

export house. Or export merchant house. Smooths the export of goods in, broadly, one or more of the following ways: **a** by acting as an export merchant, buying goods outright from a manufacturer and then selling or dealing in them in his own right; **b** by operating, in effect, as a manufacturer's export department or agent, the manufacturer remaining the principal but the export house taking responsibility for such matters as export sales promotion, credit risk on the overseas buyer, physical and clerical work, holding stocks of goods at home and overseas, progress chasing, export formalities, and after-sales service; **c** by acting for an overseas buyer, arranging shipment and insurance, progressing and despatching orders, and confirming (as a *confirming house*) and financing contracts on the buyer's behalf. See also *British Export Houses Association.*

Export-Import Bank of the United States (Eximbank). US Government agency founded in 1934 to provide financial and other assistance to exporters.

Export Intelligence Service (DT). *Department of Trade* service for UK firms run on a subscription basis providing items of information of the kinds provided by the *Export Services Division.*

export leasing. Where a potential overseas buyer cannot complete the purchase of plant or equipment for lack of funds or because of his own country's licensing regulations, it can sometimes be arranged for him to be supplied through a machinery-leasing company. The latter company purchases the equipment from the supplier (who receives immediate payment in full) and leases it to the overseas customer. Information on leasing companies is normally available from bank managers.

Export Licensing Branch (DT). Branch of the *Department of Trade* which advises on export regulations and formalities, prohibitions and restrictions, including *security export controls* on goods with strategic uses.

Export Office Procedure. Course devised by the *Department of Employment* to assist UK firms that export or seek to export. Has become part of *Training Within Industry* scheme.

Export Planning and Development Division (DT). Provides information for UK firms on finance for exports and export credits.

export safeguards against double taxation. If a firm is taxed in an overseas country on the profits it makes from selling there, it is usual for the foreign tax to be offset against its home tax liability on those same profits, perhaps under a specific double taxation agreement.

Export Services Division. Provides information for UK firms on export opportunities, market prospects, agencies, marketing, licensing, customs and tariff regulations, etc.

exports, temporary. See *temporary exports.*

export subsidy (or restitution)(EEC). Under the *Common Agricultural Policy* of the *Common Market* or *European Economic Community*, the *European Commission* pays an export subsidy or restitution to producers of cereals selling to non-member states, the subsidy bridging the gap between world prices and the EEC *intervention price.* See also *guide price, reserve (or fall-back) price, sluice-gate price, target price* and *threshold price.*

exposure. Special *public relations* and *marketing* meaning is the extent to which a product, person, etc is kept in the public eye through the press, television, etc and through public appearances.

ex-rights. Of shares or securities bought or sold without benefit or rights to subscribe to newly issued shares or stock usually at a discount from the market price.

ex ship. In a contract to supply goods by sea, this term means the buyer has to meet the cost of taking the goods from the ship.

extended interview. As *depth interview*.

external courses. Courses provided outside a firm or organization to which employees are sent for training considered appropriate to their needs.

external currency market. Market for transactions in a currency outside its country of origin and between foreigners. The practice (practise) began with the *Eurodollar* and has continued with other 'Euro' currencies.

external labo(u)r market. The *labo(u)r market* outside, but affecting, the individual employing organization.

external storage device. Part of the peripheral equipment of a computer that is available to the *central processing unit* as a standby data store.

External Tariff, Common (EEC). See *Common Customs Tariff* or *Common External Tariff*.

extrapolation. In statistics, normally implies estimating future trends based on an analysis of past figures and making wider deductions from a set of observable values.

extroversion. See *introversion/extroversion* (see also *temperament and personality testing*). Also 'extraversion'.

ex works (or warehouse). In a contract to supply goods, means that the buyer has to meet the cost of collection or carriage of the goods from the works or warehouse.

Eysenck personality inventory. Type of *personality test* used to measure an individual's position on the *introversion/extroversion* spectrum. It has been developed in the UK by Professor Eysenck. See also *psychological testing*.

f

face-to-face groups. Type of *reference group* brought together for the purpose of examining *consumer* buying motives. A face-to-face group is small enough to ensure that the individuals communicate with each other and that their tastes and values are brought out. Other forms of reference group include *membership groups, dissociative groups, aspirational groups,* and *family groups.*

face value. *Nominal value* of a share as opposed to its market value. Also known as *par value.*

facilities management. Sub-contracting of an organization's *computer* or *electronic data processing* activities to another organization.

facility visit. *Public relations* term for a press visit arranged for a party of journalists to gather material, photographs, etc and to interview people for a particular story.

FACT. *Factor analysis chart technique.*

FACT assembly test. Mechanical comprehension test of ability to visualize how mechanical parts fit together. The test was developed in the USA. See also *psychological testing.*

FACT coordination test. Test of *psychomotor skills* or, more specifically, of speed and accuracy in coordination of hand and eye. See also *psychological testing.*

factor. Or commission agent. *Agent* to whom goods are entrusted for the purpose of being resold for the owner. He is normally paid by way of commission. Factors usually sell in their own names and the buyer is often unaware of the owner's identity.

factor analysis. Mathematical technique for clarifying complex data and making meaningful correlations and deductions.

factor analysis chart technique (FACT). *Job evaluation* approach to determining the relative worth of management positions within a salary structure. Involves assigning points to the major elements of jobs.

factor comparison method. Analytical *job evaluation* technique for defining and assessing jobs in terms of certain common factors. Selected key jobs (having been factor-analyzed) and their wages are taken as datum points and cash values for the factors calculated. Factor comparison method is also known as *job factor comparison.*

factorial sample design. Term used particularly in *market research* for a survey designed to obtain data on a number of factors influencing a product's impact and to show which of these factors has the greatest influence. Factors tested for might include, for example, purchasers' preferences by age and by socio-economic grade, regional preferences, cultural influences, relative success in different types of retail outlet, volume of sales on different days of the week, etc. See also *Latin square design.*

Factories Act 1961 (UK). Consolidated factories legislation under the following heads; Part 1: Health (General Provisions). Part 2: Safety Provisions. Part 3: Welfare (General Provisions). Part 4: Health, Safety and Welfare. Part 5: Notification and Investigation of Accidents and Industrial Diseases. Part 6: Employment of Women and Young Persons. Part 7: Special Applications and Extensions. Part 8: The Domestic System. Part 9 covers wages. Part 10 deals with notices and returns. Part 11: Administration, gives powers to the *Factory Inspectorate.* Part 12 outlines the criminal sanctions. Parts 13 and 14 deal with the application and interpretation of the Act. There are also special provisions on factory lighting and on the docks and building industries.

See also *Offices, Shops and Railway Premises Act 1963.*

factoring. 1. Arrangement whereby book debts are handed over to a collection service which undertakes to guarantee payment on the date that it normally falls due. In addition, the factoring agents offer an extensive system of information on credit worthiness and debt collection service. **2.** Operating as a *factor*.

factoring company. 1. Firm that does not manufacture goods itself but acts either as a wholesaler or as an agent for a manufacturer. **2.** Type of finance house that buys invoice debts from firms, becoming responsible for all *credit control*, sales accounting and debt collection. Instead of buying debts at a discount, some factors undertake collection for their clients, at the same time ensuring them a constant flow of payments. Some factoring companies also help exporters in the selection of sales representatives and customers, handle export documentation, supervise and control goods on arrival and deal with customs and other transit arrangements.

factor rating. *Performance appraisal* and *job evaluation* technique in which managers are ranked in order for each of certain factors selected as indicating the extent to which they have qualities considered desirable. Other management appraisal techniques include *controlled report, free report, forced choice approach, ranking system,* and *task-based appraisal.*

factor rating and comparison, In *performance appraisal* procedures etc, a method of reporting on the performance of staff using multiple step scales or linear scales against a series of qualities or characteristics. Factor rating has sometimes been weakened by subjective judgments and has become less used as management appraisal systems have given way to *management by objectives.* Other management appraisal techniques include *free report, controlled report, critical incident, task-based appraisal,* ranking system and *forced choice report.* A form of factor rating, but of the job, not the man, is also used in establishing job factors in *job evaluation.*

factory. Defined under *Factories Act 1961* (UK) as any premises in which or in precincts of which persons are employed in manual labour in manufacturing or related processes by way of trade or for purposes of gain.

factory agreement. Product of *collective bargaining* on behalf of employees from the whole of a factory, as distinct from *workplace bargaining* on behalf of a smaller group or larger scale bargaining such as for *company agreements,* house agreements, or *industry-wide agreements.*

factory and office layout. Systematic analysis of factory and office facilities to bring about their optimum arrangement and to permit the most efficient work flow.

factory cost. *Direct cost* plus manufacturing *indirect cost.*

Factory Inspectorate (UK). Or, more properly, *HM Factory Inspectorate.* Some 500 factories inspectors cover about 250,000 factory premises in the UK. Operating under the *Department of Employment* the inspectors have extensive powers to enter, inspect and examine factories in order to ensure compliance with the *Factories Act 1961* and relevant public health regulations. A factory occupier must assist an inspector and it is an offence to obstruct him. Some warehouses employing young people also come under the Factory Inspectorate. Individual members of the Inspectorate are known as *HM Inspectors of Factories,* the inspector responsible for a particular area being the *District Inspector of Factories.* Employers or factory occupiers must keep a *General Register* for the District Inspector's information.

Fair Labor Standards Act 1938. US federal legislation regulating hours of work and pay in manufacturing or commercial organizations.

fair list. Type of *boycott* occasionally used by *trade unions* against firms not employing or not recognizing trade union labour. See also *union label.*

Fairs and Promotions Branch (DT). Part of the *Export Services Division* of the *Department of Trade* (UK), having responsibility connected with overseas trade promotions.

fair trade laws. US state laws which permit the laying down of *resale price maintenance.* Such US laws were especially aimed at eliminating the use of *loss leaders* to attract customers.

Fair Trading Act 1973. UK Act that covers monopolies, mergers and fair trading and aims to promote greater competition in industry and among retailers. The Act introduced a *Director-General of Fair Trading,* an *Office of Fair Trading,* and a *Consumer Protection Advisory Committee.* The Act was also designed to strengthen the

Monopolies Commission (re-naming it the *Monopolies and Mergers Commission)* and the Restrictive Practices Court. The Fair Trading Act was to abolish the post of *Registrar of Restrictive Trading Agreements* which had been operative under the *Restrictive Trade Practices Act 1956* and the *Resale Prices Act 1964*. See also *Unsolicited Foods and Services Act 1971*.

Fair Wages Clause. Included in UK Government, local authority and nationalized industry contracts for the supply of goods and services under the *Fair Wages Resolution 1946*. Also sometimes included in contracts of industries that receive financial or other assistance from the Government.

Fair Wages Resolution of the House of Commons 1946 (UK). Legislation which empowers the Government to use its economic bargaining power as a customer to ensure that contractors with the public service provide wages and conditions of employment comparable with those of local industry.

fall-back pay. Guaranteed minimum level of pay or, where appropriate, *pieceworkers' guarantee* or *minimum entitlement* written into a *payment-by-results scheme*, etc. See also *lieu payment*.

fall-back price (EEC). See *reserve price (EEC)*.

false market. *Market* in which prices are determined or influenced by unreliable information.

family groups. Type of *reference group* brought together for the purpose of examining *consumer* buying motives. It is a form of *membership group* in that the individuals concerned belong naturally to it and therefore tend to identify naturally with the group's ideals, values, tastes and behaviour. A family group is also a form of *face-to-face group* in that it is small enough to ensure that the individual's tastes and values are brought out. Other forms of reference group include *dissociative groups* and *aspirational groups*.

FAO. *Food and Agriculture Organization*.

Far East Exchange Limited. One of two *Hong Kong Stock Exchanges*.

Farmers Educational & Cooperative Union of America (National Farmers Union) (US). *Employers' association* in the USA. See also *National Grange*.

fas. *Free alongside ship.*

father of the chapel. *Shop steward* in the printing and publishing unions.

fat work. Work on which it is relatively easy to earn high bonus under a *payment-by-results* scheme. May also be known as *gravy jobs*. Work on which it is difficult to earn bonus may be known as *lean work* or *stinkers*. See also *goldbricking, job spoiler, loose rates* and *tight rates*.

Fawley Blue Book. Document on the management of construction work at the Esso Petroleum refinery at Fawley, UK, in the 1950s. Beginnings of *productivity bargaining* in the UK.

Fayol, Henri (1841-1925). First major thinker and writer on management — his 'General Principles of Management' (1916) examined the management process combining theory and the fruits of his personal experience with French industrial and mining business in the late 19th century.

FB. Freight bill.

FBI. *Fédération des Industries Belges,* the *Federation of Belgian Industry,* the central employers' organization.

FCI. *Finance Corporation for Industry Ltd* (UK).

FDG. *Freier Deutscher Gewerkschaftsbund.*

FDM. *Fundamental design method.*

feather bedding. 1. Term used particularly in the USA for *restrictive labo(u)r practices (practises)*. **2.** Where tax or trading regulations make it easy for a company to make a profit.

(the) Fed. Familiar term for the *Federal Reserve System* (USA).

Federal Aviation Administration. US Government agency set up in 1958 to promote air safety.

federal decentralization. One of two principles identified by *Drucker* as important in organization structure, the other being functional decentralization. Federal decentralization 'organizes activities into autonomous product businesses each with its own market and product and with its own profit and loss responsibility'.

Federal Deposit Insurance Corporation.

Body with which national banks in the US *Federal Reserve System* have to be insured.

Federal Energy Administration. US government agency (part of the *US Department of Energy* since 1977) responsible for encouraging energy conservation and ensuring that energy resources are efficiently and fairly distributed throughout the US.

Federal Energy Regulatory Commission. Independent commission operating within the *US Department of Energy* and having responsibility for establishing and enforcing rates and charges for oil pipelines, electric power transmission, and natural gas. The Commission issues licences (licenses) for hydroelectric projects, establishes *accounting* rules and procedures for regulated industries, and regulates mergers and security acquisitions of gas and power companies.

Federal German. See entries under *German*.

Federal Institute of Labo(u)r (Federal Germany). Autonomous public corporation responsible for the Federal German training scheme under the Vocational Training Act. The Institute's source of finance is from employers' and employees' contributions to the Social Insurance Fund.

Federal Mediation and Conciliation Service (US). Independent government agency mediating in *industrial relations* in the USA. See also *National Labor Relations Board*.

Federal Power Commission (US). Independent government agency in the USA.

Federal Reserve Bank. District bank of the US *Federal Reserve System*.

Federal Reserve System (or Board) (US). *Central bank* or central banking system in the USA, established in 1913 and consisting of the Federal Reserve Board (based in Washington) controlling twelve district or regional banks which in turn act as central banks to their members. The district banks are known as *Federal Reserve Banks* and their investing members as *national banks*. The larger commercial banks in the USA are required by law to be members of the Federal Banking System. In all, there are some 6,000 *member banks* which are national banks owning the capital of the reserve banks, receiving a fixed dividend in return. The surpluses earned by the Federal Banking System are paid into the US *Internal Revenue*. The governors of the Federal Reserve Board are appointed by the President of the USA with Senate approval. The Federal Reserve Banks are those of Boston, New York, Philadelphia, Cleveland, Richmond, Atlanta, Chicago, St Louis, Minneapolis, Kansas City, Dallas and San Francisco.

Federal Trade Commission (FTC)(US). Independent government agency in the USA.

Federal Trade Commission Act 1914. See *antitrust legislation* (US).

federated firm. One which is a member of an *employers' association* and for which the association acts in *collective bargaining* and *industrial relations* generally.

Fédération des Industries Belges (FIB). Belgian General Industrial Federation, or confederation of *employers' associations*. Established in 1946.

Fédération Générale du Travail de Belgique (FGTB). Belgian General Federation of Trade Unions, established in 1899. Has a socialist political orientation. Covers 15 *trade unions* which have approximately 800,000 members. See *Belgian trade unions*.

Fédération Internationale des Bourses de Valeurs. *International Federation of Stock Exchanges*.

Fédération Nationale des Chambres de Commerce et d'Industrie de Belgique. Federation of *Belgian chambers of commerce*, established in 1875.

Federation of Belgian Industry. *Fédération des Industries Belges (FIB)*, the central employers' organization.

Federation of British Industries. Founder component, July 1965, of the *Confederation of British Industry*.

Federation of German Federal Stock Exchanges. Or *Arbeitsgemeinschaft der deutschen Wertpapierbörsen*. See also *Germany (Federal) stock exchanges*.

Federation of International Civil Servants' Associations. Set up in 1952 to promote the concept of an international civil service, particularly among the staffs of *United Nations* organizations.

Federation of Netherlands Industry. *Verbond van Nederlandse Ondernemingen (VNO)*.

Federation of Protestant Christian Trade

Unions. See *Christelijk National Vakverbond (CNV) (Netherlands)*.

Federation of Stock Exchanges in Great Britain and Ireland. Set up in 1965 to coordinate the work of the London *Stock Exchange*, the UK provincial exchanges and the *Irish Stock Exchange*. Gave way in 1973 to the *United Stock Exchange* which united the trading floors of all the British and Irish exchanges.

FEDFA. French initials of the *European Agricultural Guidance and Guarantee Fund* operated by the *Common Market* or *European Economic Community*.

feedback concept. Term borrowed from electronics where it means the coupling of the output of a process to the input. Generally taken to mean arrangement to check performance of a system or process against certain standards and 'feeding back' any variations so that future performance can be adjusted and improved. See also *cybernetics*.

fellesskatt. Mutual tax in Norway. See *Norwegian income tax*.

FGTB. *Fédération Générale du Travail de Belgique*, one of the Belgian confederations of *trade unions*.

FHD. *First hand distribution.*

fiche. Short for *microfiche*.

fictitious assets. Items which must appear in the *balance sheet* for accounting reasons but which have no value and could not be realized. They include trading losses and formation expenses. See also *intangible assets*.

fiddle. Term of UK origin where a *work group* on loosely rated *piece work* records and holds production at informally agreed levels, somewhat in the manner of the US practices of *quota restriction* and aiming at *bogey* levels of production. A fiddle may involve *cross-booking* between jobs or the holding of *time up the cuff*. Members of the work group who work to the standards laid down by the fiddle are known as *conformers* while those who ignore the fiddle and work to the piece work rates without misrecording or holding back on effort are known as *job spoilers*. The general object of a fiddle or quota restriction is to hide *loose rates* (for fear of *rate cutting*) or to smooth out piece work earnings.

fidelity insurance. Type of insurance policy taken out by an employer against the possibility of a cashier, salesman or other employee embezzling funds.

fiduciary issue. Bank notes or paper money not backed by gold or silver.

fiduciary loan. One granted without security beyond the word and honour of the borrower.

field inspection. Or market visit. An inspection by a member of marketing management of selling performance in the field. Field inspections cover visits to branch offices and to agents and *distributors*, inspections of aspects of the marketing organization, visits to customers to assess their attitudes to the marketing and sales effort, double calls, *sales audits*, etc.

field research. Investigative research, in *market research* etc, consisting of visits, interviews, etc to collect fresh information as opposed to *desk research* on published or other existing information.

FIFO. First-in, first-out. Normally applied to method of costing or valuing stocks or inventories. Assumes that the first items purchased or produced are the first items sold. See also *LIFO*.

fifty-fifty sharing plan. As *Halsey Plan*. See also *payment-by-results*.

file. Data in the form of text — alphabetic, numeric or alphanumeric — in the *store* of a *computer*.

file interrogation program. *Computer program* written for the express purpose of examining the contents of computer storage files. May be used, for example, by an auditor where a company has a computer-based accounting system.

file posting. As *slip system*.

filter question. Or strip question. *Market research* term for a question which an interviewer only puts to an informant if it is made relevant by the answer given to the previous question. Thus the question, 'Do you eat cereals for breakfast?', might be followed by the filter question, 'What kind of cereals?', to be put only to informants answering 'Yes' to the first question.

final demand. *Demand* for a product for its end purpose or function (eg the motorist's demand for a car) as opposed to *indirect demand* for a component to be incorporated in another product (eg the demand for components to be incorporated in a car during manufacture).

final salary pension scheme. Calculates pension in relation to the final salary (or average of the last few years) being expressed as a fraction (most often one sixtieth or one eightieth) of final salary for each year of service with the employer. This scheme has many attractions for the individual employee, compared with the *average salary pension scheme*, since the final salary scheme is based on what is likely to be the career's highest salary and will certainly be that least eroded by *inflation*. In some cases a final salary pension scheme will also give a capital sum on retirement. It may also provide for increases in pension to compensate for any inflation after retirement. It is important to check, when assessing a final salary pension scheme, whether all the years of service count as pensionable *service* and whether the *pensionable salary* includes all normal earnings.

finance company (or house). Firm whose business is lending money.

Finance Corporation for Industry Ltd (UK). Established under the auspices of the *Bank of England* and leading *insurance companies, investment trusts* and *clearing banks* to provide finance for industrial developments which are in the national economic interest but for which funds are not obtainable from traditional sources. See also, for finance, for small and medium-sized firms, the *Industrial and Commercial Finance Corporation Ltd*.

Finance Houses Association. UK organization whose members include banks and finance houses.

financial accounting. Organizing and presenting of an organization's accounts for the internal information of management but particularly for reporting to shareholders. The two basic tools of financial accounting are the *balance sheet*, showing the company's financial position at a particular point in time, and the *profit and loss account*, showing the company's performance over the financial year. Another tool of financial accounting can be a *funds statement* detailing company investment and the source of funds for a particular period. See also *management accounting* and *stewardship accounting*.

financial leverage. As *gearing* or leverage.

financial ratios. See *accounting ratios* and *management ratios*.

financial statement. As *balance sheet*.

'Financial Times'. UK daily newspaper specializing in business and industry. Founded 1888.

Financial Times Industrial Ordinary Index. Indicator of the level of business on the UK stock market, based on the average prices of some 30 *blue chip* shares. The Index is published daily in the *'Financial Times'* and is available to subscribers to the Index telephone service. See also *Dow Jones/Index* in the USA.

financial year. Annual period chosen by a company as its accounting year.

fine control sensitivity. Type of *psychomotor skill*. An individual's ability to make delicately controlled muscular adjustments, particularly where larger muscle groups are involved. See also *motion study*.

fine paper. *Securities* on which the risk is so low as to be virtually nil.

finished goods. *Stocks* of completely manufactured products ready for sale to customers. Other forms of stocks include *raw materials stocks, bought-out goods* and *work-in-progress*. See also *stock control*.

fink. Derogatory term describing trade unionist who acts as an informer on union affairs to his employer. Used as a noun or a verb.

Finnish Central Bank. *Suomen Pankki*.

Finnish Central Chamber of Commerce.. *Suomen Keskuskauppakamari*. See also *Finnish Foreign Trade Association*.

Finnish Employers' Associations. See *Suomen Teollisuusliitto* (Federation of Finnish Industries) and *Suomen Puunjalostusteollisuuden Keskusliitto* (Central Association of Finnish Woodworking Industries).

Finnish Foreign Trade Association. Established in 1919. See also *Suomen Keskuskauppakamari* (Finnish Central Chamber of Commerce).

Finnish income tax. State income tax, or

valtion tulavero, is charged on total income from all sources. There is also a local income tax, or *kunnallisvero*, together with a church tax, or *kirkollisvero*, levied at a flat-rate on members of the Orthodox and Evangelical Lutheran churches. Finland also has a state net *wealth tax*. There is also a *seamen's tax*, or *merimiesvero*, deducted at source from seamen's income in lieu of income tax.

Finnish Stock Exchange. See *Helsinki Stock Exchange*.

Finnish Trade Unions, Confederation of. *Suomen Ammattiliittojen Keskusjärjestö (SAK)*.

firm. Loosely used to describe any business or, more specifically, a partnership.

firm's profile. Used in establishing the *payment system* appropriate to the firm. See *situation profile*.

first-day premium. Difference in price of *shares* between day of issue and the following day.

first hand distribution (FHD). Method of selling by wholesale distribution in very large consignments. The trading can be straightforward wholesaling or on *consignment account*.

first-in, first-out. *FIFO*.

first-line supervisor. Or front-line supervisor. *Supervisor* with direct and immediate responsibility for the management and work of *shopfloor* workers. Often synonymous with foreman, but also includes others immediately above the working chargehand level.

first-year allowance (UK). Form of *capital allowance* introduced in 1971.

fiscal drag. Time taken for governmental fiscal policy to take effect and achieve the desired impact.

fiscal measures. Government action to counteract *deflation* or *inflation* by tax changes. A budgetary surplus, where the government collects more than it spends, should have a deflationary effect — and vice versa. See also *monetary measures*.

fiscal year. *Financial year* used for the purposes of a government's fiscal or tax policy. This varies from country to country. In the UK, for example, the fiscal year runs from 6 April to 5 April, while in the USA it is from 1 July to 30 June. As tax year.

fisheries policy, common (EEC). See *common fisheries policy (EEC)*.

five fold grading scheme. *Personnel selection* interview procedure devised by John Munro Fraser under heads of first impression, qualifications, abilities, motivation, adjustment. See also *seven point plan*.

five-year guarantee (pensions). Provision in a *superannuation* or *pension* scheme that the pension will be paid for at least five years after retirement even if the pensioner dies earlier in the retirement period. In this event, the pension or a lump sum equivalent is paid to the pensioner's dependants or family for the remainder of the five-year period. See also *widows' and orphans' pension scheme*.

fixed assets. Capital equipment, such as plant, machinery, etc purchased for continued use in a company's manufacturing or other business activities, and gradually written off through *depreciation*. See also *current assets*.

fixed budget. *Budget* which is based on a forecast of ideal or normal capacity. It does not take account of possible variations in the level of activity as would a *flexible budget*.

fixed capital. See *capital*.

fixed charge (or expense). *Liability* involving a fixed payment irrespective of volume of business or level of activity.

fixed cost. Also known as standing cost. One that remains constant whatever the level of business activity (*rent*, for example, is likely to be in this category). A cost that remains constant until a particular new level of activity is reached and then changes to a new constant cost is known as a *stepped cost* (for example, if production is increased to the point where more factory space has to be rented). A *variable cost*, however, is one that varies virtually with the level of activity and may be constant per unit of volume. A cost that varies only indirectly with changes in the level of activity is known as a *semi-variable cost* (power is likely to be in this category, for example). A cost that has both fixed and variable elements is known as a *mixed cost* (an everyday example being the telephone bill with its combination of fixed rent and variable cost according to the number, type and length of calls made). See *break-even chart* and *point*.

133

fixed exchange rate. Where a country lays down an official *exchange rate* for its currency with other currencies instead of having a *floating exchange rate*.

fixed expenses. Those that remain constant regardless of the level of business activity. Expenses that vary with output or activity are *variable expenses*. See also *fixed cost*.

fixed interest cover. Ratio of net profit (before fixed interest) to the fixed interest and dividends payable. Indicates the cover available to holders of preference shares, debentures or other loan stock.

fixed-price contract. One in which the contractor or supplier undertakes to carry out specified work or services for a specified *price* that cannot be increased later for any reason including inflation.

fixed term contract (UK). Under the *Redundancy Payments Act 1965*, persons on a fixed-term contract for two years or more may claim a redundancy payment if the contract is not renewed, unless the employee has agreed to waive his right before the contract expires. Employees with fixed-term contracts of less than two years may add together successive contracts for calculation of continuity.

flag of convenience. Flag of a country where ships are registered with little government control over their standards of operation.

flash pack. Consumer pack advertising a consumer deal or special offer.

flat rate benefits and contributions. Basis of the 1942 *Beveridge Report* (UK) recommendation that a unified social security system be introduced. The original *National Insurance Act* and *National Insurance (Industrial Injuries) Act* also had this basis, *graduated benefits and contributions* being introduced by the *National Insurance Act 1961*, and *earnings-related unemployment and sickness benefits* by the *National Insurance Acts 1965* and *1966*. The 1966 Act also brought in *earnings-related supplement with injury benefit*.

flat rate pension, state. See *state flat rate pension*.

flat yield. As *current yield*.

Flexibel Arbetstid. Swedish term for the *flexible working hours* system.

flexible budget. *Budget* which takes account of a range of possible volumes. Sometimes referred to as a multi-volume budget. The range of possible outputs may be known as the relevant range. A flexible budget is necessary when a the actual volume of sales achieved may be at any point within a number of possible outputs; b a significant number of costs are variable. See also *flexing*.

flexible funding. See *controlled funding* (of pensions).

flexible time. Term used in an application of *flexible working hours (fwh)* for the periods during the day when each employee can choose his or her own working hours. The rest of the day is *core time* when all employees are expected to be present. See also *bandwidth*.

flexible working hours (fwh). System under which employees work a 'flexible working day' without fixed starting and finishing times. The day is divided between *flexible time* periods, when an employee chooses his own working time, and *core time* periods, when each employee is required to be present at work. Provided he or she works the *daily contracted hours* (or it may be weekly or even monthly contracted hours) each employee can start and finish work at any times between the earliest permitted starting time and the latest permitted finishing time, subject to being present during the core time periods. The core time is normally the middle part of the day, though it may be broken to allow a choice of lunch break. The period between the earliest permitted starting time and the latest permitted finishing time is known as the *bandwidth*. A flexible working hours scheme is likely to include arrangements for carrying forward credit or debit balances of hours worked from day to day or even week to week. One month is the most usual accounting period in which credits and debits have to be settled.

Fwh is known in French as *Horaire Dynamique*, in German as *Gleitzeit* (or 'gliding time'), in Italy as *Orario Flessibile*, and in Swedish as *Flexibel Arbetstid*. Fwh should not be confused with the *staggered working day*, under which daily starting and finishing times are arranged to avoid rush hour travel but without allowing individual choice.

flexing. In *budgetary control*, the process of adjusting the *budget* in relation to changes in volumes of production or sales. See also

Flextime *flexible budget.*

Flextime. Proprietary name for *flexible working hours.*

float. 1. In *critical path planning* and *network analysis,* the amount of leeway in the time allowed for a particular *activity* or, in network terms, arrow. If an activity uses up more than its float time the network has to be re-balanced. **2.** Cash kept in a till or petty cash system.

floating a company. See *'going public'.*

floating asset. As *current asset.*

floating charge. Property rights surrendered as *security* or *collateral* on a loan, though not restricting use of the property if the terms of the loan are met.

floating-charge debentures. See *debentures.*

floating exchange rate. Where a country ceases to have an official *exchange rate* for its currency with other currencies but allows its currency to float or find a natural exchange rate. This can in effect be a *devaluation.*

floating labo(u)r. Workers who change their jobs and/or job locations from time to time.

floor price. As *reserve price.*

floorwalker. Retail security guard or detective concerned with controlling shoplifting.

floppy disc. Mini external storage medium for a *computer* or *word processor.*

flow chart. Diagrammatic representation of inter-relationships between stages, activities, etc in a system, method of operation, etc.

flow charting. Method used by auditors to chart the internal control systems of a company.

flow diagram. Diagram used in *work study,* usually to scale, of locations of activities and of routes between them of men, materials, etc. Also known as *route diagram.* Alternatively, a flow diagram may simply indicate the order of activities, etc.

flow line production. Method of organizing work used mostly in *mass production* but also sometimes in *batch production.* Successive operations on a product are carried out in such a way that work flows in a single direction through the factory or workshop, the product being passed from operator to operator or from section to section for further work on it. An extreme form of flow line production is *assembly line production* in which workers carry out operations on products as they pass along on a conveyor belt. See also *cell(ular) organization.*

flow of income. See *circular flow of income.*

flow process chart. *Work study* chart showing the order of operations in an activity or process, usually with an indication of timings, transportations, distances, etc.

fluctuating price contract. One in which it is agreed that the price may be varied according to fluctuations in costs and/or other factors.

flyback timing. *Work measurement* term for timing a job with a stop watch which flies back to zero as each *element* is completed. See also *cumulative timing.*

flying pickets. Groups of individuals which can at short notice be sent to any location to picket a place of work. Normally used to reinforce local pickets so as to bring more pressure to bear on the management.

FME. *Foundation for Management Education.*

fob. *Free on board.*

focused interview. Somewhat misleading term, used particularly in *market research,* for an interview in which the interviewer seeks to obtain answers to particular questions without specifically asking them.

Follett, Mary Parker (1868-1933). US born social worker who helped pioneer community centres in early 1900's. Her interests included *vocational guidance* and leadership in industry. She was one of the early management thinkers and her special contribution was to focus attention on the importance of personal and group relationships at work. She also developed the concepts of *creative conflict* and the *Law of the Situation.*

Food and Agriculture Organization (FAO). *United Nations* agency charged with fighting poverty, hunger and malnutrition throughout the world.

Food, Drink and Tobacco Industry Training

Board. Established in UK in July 1968 under the *Industrial Training Act 1964*.

Food Hygiene Regulations 1970. UK regulations under the Food and Drugs Act 1965 covering the treatment and sale of milk, the handling of food, the sale of ice cream from stalls, the regulation of markets, the supervision of imported food, licensing of slaughter houses, and notification of cases of food poisoning. The Act is enforced by trading standards offices at county level and environmental health departments at district level.

Footwear, Leather and Fur Skin Industry Training Board. Established in UK in November 1968 under the *Industrial Training Act 1964*.

for. *Free on rail (or road)*.

forced choice approach. 1. In *performance appraisal* procedures, etc a method of rating staff by providing groups of descriptive phrases for a senior manager to select the phrase in each group most applicable to each individual. An early use of *multiple-choice questions*. The forced choice approach in performance appraisal carries the dangers of subjectivity since it has tended to be concerned with personal qualities rather than performance. Other performance appraisal techniques include *free report, controlled report, critical incident, task-based appraisal, ranking system, factor rating,* and forms of job evaluation. **2.** *Market research* survey in which *respondents* are asked whether or not a particular attribute is applicable to a particular brand. See also *product comparison, attribute comparisons* and *free choice of products*.

forced choice question. As *multiple choice question*.

Force Ouvrière. See *French trade unions*.

forecasting. Assessing the future normally using calculations and projections which take account of past performance, current trends and anticipated changes in the foreseeable period ahead. May include use of statistical and mathematical methods such as *moving averages, regression analysis* and *operational research*.

foreman. As *supervisor*.

forked (or bracket) tariff. Tariff or scale of charges with upper and lower limits set by reference to an average rate which would give a reasonable return to a well-managed firm. A forked tariff is used for road and rail transport under the *Common Transport Policy* for the *Common Market* or *European Economic Community*. See also the *reference tariff* used for inland waterways and bulk transport.

formation expenses. As *preliminary expenses*.

form relations test, NIIP. See *NIIP form relations test*.

formueskat til staten. Flat-rate net *wealth tax* in Denmark. See also *Danish income tax*.

Formula Translation. Source of the acronym, *'FORTRAN'*, a *high-level language*. See *computer language*.

FORTRAN. Acronym for Formula Translation. A *high-level language*. See *computer language*.

'Fortune'. US monthly business magazine.

forward contract. Contract in *futures* or in a *forward market*.

forward cover. Earmarking of cash, particularly foreign currency, to ensure that a *forward contract* can be hono(u)red.

forward integration. Where the manufacturer or main supplier of a product or service acquires or takes over certain customer or retail outlets in an endeavour to secure a further part of the market for the product or service. The opposite process, usually intended to give control over materials supplies, is *backward integration*.

forward market. Where there are dealings in promises to buy or sell commodities, foreign exchange or *securities* at a fixed price at a future date. Such a market is said to deal in *futures*. In contrast to a forward market, a *spot market* deals with prices for immediate delivery.

forward pass. *Network analysis/planning* term for an estimate of the earliest possible timing for an *activity* or *event*.

forward price. *Price* asked in a *forward market* or for *futures*.

forward rate. *Exchange rate* agreed for a *forward contract*.

foundation. 1. Endowment. **2.** Institution with perpetual funds or income.

Foundation for Management Education (FME). UK registered charity set up in 1960 to promote management education in the UK at university level. Has supported the establishment and expansion of management centres and schools at universities in conjunction with the University Grants Committee. Undertook the deployment of funds raised by appeal to British industry following the Franks and Normanbrook reports on behalf of the three sponsors, *British Institute of Management, Confederation of British Industry*, and the foundation itself.

founders' shares. Now relatively uncommon, *shares* or *stocks* issued to the original subscribers or founders of a public company and often entitled to special privileges.

Foundry Industry Training Committee (UK). Established September 1967 under the *Industrial Training Act 1964*. Technically a committee of the *Engineering Industry Training Board* but virtually an independent *industrial training board*.

fractional (or fragmented) bargaining. Form of *collective bargaining* on behalf of a minority of employees or to deal with a particular grievance. The term 'fragmented' tends to be used, rather than 'fractional', if the minority of employees carry out the negotiating for themselves, as in *autonomous bargaining*.

frame. 1. Information presented at one time in a *programmed text*, etc. 2. *Sampling frame*.

franc (Belgian). Basic unit of Belgian currency. Other currencies are listed in the Appendix: World Currencies.

franc (French). Basic unit of French currency. Other currencies are listed in the Appendix: World Currencies.

franchise. 1. Grant of a licence (license) to manufacture, market or distribute products or services. Often includes the use of *trade names*, know-how and finance in return for a continual stake in the profitability of the activities covered by the franchise. 2. Marine *insurance* clause disallowing minor claims unless the entire vessel is stranded or sunk.

Frankfurt Stock Exchange. Or Frankfurter Wertpapierbörse. One of the two principal stock exchanges in Federal Germany, the other being Düsseldorf.

Frankfurter Wertpapierbörse. *Frankfurt Stock Exchange.*

Franks Report (UK). Franks Committee produced 'British Business Schools' 1963 bringing about *Foundation for Management Education* and the London and Manchester *Business Schools*. (Not to be confused with another Franks Report, that of 1966 into running Oxford University).

F ratio. Formula used in *analysis of variance* to determine the statistical differences between two or more variances. Named F after the statistician Ronald Fisher. F = variance between groups (experimental effect)/variance between groups (chance error). From F a relationship between an independent variable and a dependent variable can be inferred.

free alongside ship (fas). Where the seller or supplier of goods is responsible for their delivery to the ship's side but the buyer is responsible for the cost of taking them on board ship.

free balance control. Storekeeping system similar to maximum/minimum control as a means of ensuring timely re-ordering of regular stocks, but also taking into account known forward commitments both inward and outward.

free choice of products. *Market research* survey in which *respondents* are asked to select which brand is applicable to any given attribute. See also *forced choice, attribute comparisons* and *product comparison*.

freedom of association. 1. Right of workers to organize themselves in a *trade union* or similar representative body. 2. Right of people generally to form themselves into organizations or groups.

Freedom of Association and Protection of the Right to Organize. See *Article 87 of the International Labor Organization*.

'freedom to manage'. Established for UK engineering employers from 1898 under terms of an agreement with the major trade unions in attempt at establishing *management prerogative* over production processes. See also *collective bargaining, joint consultation*, and *1922 Agreement in Engineering Industry*.

free economy. As *laissez-faire economy*.

free float. *Network analysis/planning* term for the extra time that can be taken over an *activity* without delaying the start of other activities.

free-market argument. Theory that the forces of *supply* and *demand* should be given free rein without any form of governmental intervention or direction as in a *laissez-faire economy*.

free movement of capital. Unrestricted movement of capital between countries without *exchange control* or any other form of government intervention.

free movement of capital (EEC). Articles 67-73 of the *Treaty of Rome 1957* set out, albeit rather loosely, the principles underlying the free movement of capital in the *Common Market* or *European Economic Community* in step with the *free movement of labo(u)r*, goods, services, etc.

In general terms, Article 67 calls on member states to abolish progressively restrictions on capital movements between each other and to abolish discrimination within the Community based on nationality or place of residence or where the capital has previously been invested. Article 68 calls on member states to be liberal in granting exchange authorizations, and Article 69 gives the *Council of Ministers* power to legislate to smooth such liberalization. Article 70 calls for co-ordination between member states in capital movements dealings with non-member states. Article 71 bans the introduction of new exchange regulations or restrictive modifications to existing regulations. Article 72 obliges member states to keep the *European Commission* informed of all known capital movements with non-member states. Article 73 provides member states with an escape clause in respect of capital movements that disturb their own domestic capital market.

free movement of labo(u)r. Where there is no restriction of movements of workers across national boundaries.

free movement of labour (EEC). Articles 48 and 49 of the *Treaty of Rome 1957* set out the principles of free movement of labo(u)r in the *European Economic Community* in line with the freedom of movement of goods, services and capital. Nationals of member states may enter other member states to take up or seek work on presentation of a passport or identity card and without a work permit. They are also entitled to equal treatment with nationals of the country they have entered in relation to remuneration, working conditions, etc and to residence permits for spouses and children of up to 21 years, these permits being for a minimum of five years if the worker's job is likely to last for at least one year. They may also, in certain circumstances, qualify for the right of permanent residence on retirement or on suffering permanent incapacity to work. Only nationals of member states are entitled to the right to move freely within the Community to work.

free on board (fob). Where the seller or supplier of goods is responsible for the cost of delivering them to the ship. See also *cif*.

free on rail (or road) (for). Where the seller or supplier of goods is responsible for the cost and administration of delivering them to the railway for transportation.

free port. 1. Port in which imported goods can be held or processed before re-export free of any customs duties. See *bonded warehouse*. 2. Harbo(u)r with port facilities open to all commercial vessels on equal terms.

free report. In *performance appraisal* procedures, etc a type of report in which a senior manager indicates the general strengths and weaknesses of a more junior executive. Other management appraisal techniques include *controlled report*, *task-based appraisal*, ranking system, *factor rating*, and *forced choice approach*.

free-rider. Employee who is not a *trade union* member but takes advantage of the fruits of a union's *collective bargaining* efforts by obtaining the same wages and terms and conditions of employment as union members.

free trade. Trade between nations free of *customs duties* or *tariff barriers*, as when two or more nations form a *customs union*.

free trade area. Trading area formed by two or more member states who have no *tariffs* on trade between them though, unlike a *customs union*, they do not have a *common external tariff* against non-member states.

freie Makler. Free brokers or dealers on the *Vienna Stock Exchange* or one of the *German (Federal) stock exchanges*. They operate alongside the officially appointed *Sensale* on the Vienna Stock Exchange or alongside the officially appointed *amtliche*

Kursmakler and the banking representatives on one of the German Stock Exchanges.

Freier Deutscher Gewerkschaftsbund. Confederation of Free German Trade Unions, the central *trade union* organization in the German Democratic Republic formed in 1945 and covering trade unions with some 6,500,000 members.

freight forwarder. See *shipping and forwarding agent*.

Freight Transport Association Ltd (UK). *Trade association* for own-account operators transporting their own goods, and one of the guaranteeing associations in the UK for the *TIR Carnet* system of customs clearance. See also the Road Freight Division of the *Department of the Environment* and the *Road Haulage Association*, a trade association for hire and reward transport operators.

French central bank. *Banque de France*.

French chambers of commerce. See *Chambre de Commerce de Paris*.

French companies. Forms of commercial company under French law include: a Partnership or *Société en Nom Collectif* in which all the partners are jointly and separately liable for the firm's debts to the full extent of their personal assets, and all partners are designated trader, or *commerçant*, unless the partnership's statutes state otherwise. The name of Société en Nom Collectif must include the name of at least one of the partners and be followed by the words 'en Companie', and shares may not be transferred without the agreement of all the partners; b Limited Partnership or *Société en Commandité Simple* in which some of the partners, *commandités*, are jointly and separately liable for the debts of the partnership while other partners, the *commanditaires*, are liable only to the extent of their participation; c Private Limited Company or *Société à Responsabilité Limitée (SARL)* with between two and 50 partners whose liability is limited to the extent of their contribution, but shares are not freely negotiable and can only be transferred to third parties with the agreement of partners representing at least 75 per cent of the capital; d Joint Stock Company or *Société Anonyme (SA)* in which shareholders are liable only to the extent of the capital subscribed (in much the same way as in the UK), a proviso being that the company must have at least seven shareholders and a share capital of at least 500,000 francs if subscribed to by the public or 100,000 francs if there is no public subscription; e Partnership Limited by shares or *Société en Commandité par Actions*, a form of company that has not been set up since 1966, official preference being given to the somewhat similar Société en Commandité Simple.

French Confederation of Christian Workers. Confédération Française des Travailleurs Chrétiens (CFTC). See *French trade unions*.

French Democratic Confederation of Labo(u)r. Confédération française democratique du Travail (CFDT). See *French trade unions*.

French income tax. Or *impôt sur le revenu*, the principal *income tax* in France. It is a *progressive tax* levied on all types of personal income including *capital gains*. There are also certain local taxes, including a land tax and a personal tax on occupiers of residential property.

French industrial training. Industrial training centres are run by *l'Association Nationale pour la Formation Professionnelle des Adultes*, a body controlled jointly by the Government, the employers' associations and the trade unions. The French Government scheme also uses private training facilities, the costs of training being shared with the employers of trainees.

French stock exchanges. Principal French stock exchange is the *Paris Stock Exchange* or *Paris Bourse*. There are also six provincial stock exchanges: a Bordeaux — Bourse de Bordeaux; b Lille — Bourse des Valeurs; c Lyon — Bourse des Valeurs; d Marseilles — Palais de la Bourse; e Nancy; f Nantes — Bourse de Commerce.

French trade unions. Four main federations of *trade unions* in France are: a Confédération Générale du Travail (CGT), formed in 1895 and covering trade unions with approximately 2,400,000 members. b Force Ouvrière, formed in 1948 in a breakaway from the CGT and covering trade unions with approximately one million members. c Confédération Française Démocratique du Travail (CFDT), formed in 1919 and covering trade unions with approximately one million members. Until 1964 the CFDT was known as the Confédération Française des Travailleurs Chrétiens (CFTC). d Confédération Générale des Syndicats Indépendants, formed in 1949 and covering trade unions having approximately 200,000 members.

frequency analysis (interviewing). Application of *time sampling* techniques to interviews or *dyad interactions*.

frequency distribution. Statistical term for method of condensing a large quantity of data by arranging it into various groups or classes which show the relative frequency with which members of the group have the various possible values of the variable quantity, eg:

Income	No of employees
Under £2000	50
£2000-£3000	40
Over £3000	15
Total	105

frictional overhead. Collective term for coordinators, expediters and other personal aides whose only role is to assist their superior in his work. *Drucker* identifies the growth of frictional overhead as one symptom of malorganization. See also *kitchen cabinet*.

frictional unemployment. Short term unemployment arising from breaks in production caused by such factors as seasonal fluctuations, random variations in sales or breakdown of supplies. See also *specific unemployment, structural unemployment*.

Friendly Societies Act 1896. Covers the UK *Registrar of Friendly Societies* with whom most trade unions chose to register or be certified under *Trade Unions Acts* 1871-1964 until this function was removed by the *Industrial Relations Act 1971* but re-established by the *Trade Union and Labour Relations Act 1974*.

friendly society. Association existing for the benefit of its members to provide them with assistance in sickness, bereavement, old age, etc. Traditionally, *trade unions* in the UK have had friendly society status under the *Friendly Societies Act 1897*.

fringe benefits. Or employee benefits. Rewards for employment in addition to remuneration or payment of wages or salaries. Fringe benefits may include the use of a car, pension arrangements, life insurance, subsidized meals, the provision of housing, special mortgage rates, and discounts on goods.

front-line supervisor. As *first-line supervisor*.

frozen pension. Or paid-up pension. A pension frozen at the point in time when an employee leaves the employment of a firm. Usually such a pension becomes payable at normal retirement age based on the period of employment. Most pensions are frozen for the employee when he leaves not of his own free will, such as when being made redundant, but some schemes grant the employee *vested rights* entitling him to a frozen pension even when he does leave of his own free will. See also *continuation option*.

FTC. Federal Trade Commission.

F test. See *F ratio*.

Fukuoka Stock Exchange. One of the main five *Japanese stock exchanges*.

full cost. *Cost* of manufacture including *direct cost* and *indirect cost* and arrived at by *absorption costing*.

full employment. Term used where there is not general unemployment but only *frictional unemployment* so that virtually all those who are unemployed have either temporarily stopped work or are in transit between jobs with a reasonable certainty of moving into a job for which they are suited. *Frictional unemployment* arises from breaks in production caused by such factors as seasonal fluctuations, random variations in sales or breakdown of supplies, etc while *specific unemployment* is that restricted to particular industries. More ominous and dangerous for the cause of full employment is *structural unemployment* which arises from profound changes in demand for products and/or skills.

Politicians and economists are generally chary of quantifying what is meant by full employment but Lord Beveridge (of the UK *Beveridge Report)* defined it in 1944 in his book, 'Full Employment in a Free Society', as a maximum level of three per cent unemployed.

Full Employment Action Council. US body drawing together labo(u)r, religious, civil rights and other organizations to urge legislation aimed at securing *full employment*.

full-line strategy. As *broad-line strategy*.

full negotiating rights. See *negotiating rights*.

Fulton Report on the Civil Service (UK). Made to the UK Government in 1968 by a Committee under Sir John Fulton. It gave a fresh impetus to the use of management techniques in central government, following the 1961 *Plowden Committee* Report. As long ago as 1937 there had been the *Brownlow Committee report* in the USA. The Fulton Report considered that the work of the Civil Service included four areas of management, namely, **a** formulation of policy under political direction, **b** creating the machinery for implementation of policy, **c** operation of the administrative machine, and **d** accountability to Parliament and the public. See also *Redcliffe-Maud Report on the Management of Local Government* (UK, 1967).

functional decentralization. One of two principles identified by *Drucker* as important in organization structure, the other being *federal decentralization*. Functional decentralization 'sets up integrated units with maximum responsibility for a major and distinct stage in the business process.'

function line structure. As in *line management*.

fundamental design method (FDM). Developed by E Matchett in the UK as a systematic approach to engineering design and similar creative work. The technique is based on *work study*, particularly *method study*, and involves self-interrogation by the designer at prescribed points.

funds flow analysis. Analysis of the flow of purchasing power into and out of an organization. Inward flows include *sales revenue*, sales of *fixed assets* and investments, and issues of *debentures*, loans and *shares*. Outward flows include purchases of fixed assets and investments, repayment of debt, payment of dividends and taxation on *profits*.

funds statement. Type of statement sometimes used in *financial accounting* procedures to provide details of a company's investment, and the sources of its funds for that investment, in a particular period. A funds statement provides an analysis of the flow of funds through an organization and of its *working capital*. Funds statements have become particularly common in the USA. They complement the information provided by the *balance sheet* and the *profit and loss account*. Sometimes known as a source and application of funds statement.

funnel interviewing technique. Type of *market research* interview that is not tightly structured but in which the interviewer guides the interviewee towards the subject of the market research.

Furniture and Timber Industry Training Board. Established in UK in December 1965 under the *Industrial Training Act 1964*.

further education. Post-school education, part-time and/or full-time, usually of a vocational kind leading to technical or professional qualifications but can be non-vocational.

futures. Promises to buy or sell commodities or *securities* at a fixed price at a future date. Futures are handled at *forward markets* (as opposed to *spot markets* which deal in *actuals* and in prices for immediate delivery).

fwh. *Flexible working hours.*

g

gain matrix. In *games theory* drawing up a table showing the gain that A will expect to make for every set of moves by two opponents or players (B & C).

gain-sharing. *Payment-by-results* plan of the *premium bonus scheme* type in which the worker receives a diminishing proportion of the value of the time saved as this time increases. See also *Bedaux* and *share-of-production plan*.

galloping inflation. Rapidly accelerating *inflation*, possibly leading to economic catastrophe.

games theory. Mathematical technique for solving problems through the use of model building. There are normally two or more contestants in a conflict situation and the aim of the game is to devise a strategy or plan which maximizes returns and minimizes losses.

gaming, scientific. Application of *business game* and other simulation and decision-making techniques, usually with *computer* assistance, in industry, commerce, government, public service, etc.

gang system. As *labo(u)r-only sub-contracting*.

Gantt chart. Widely used type of *bar chart* developed by *Henry Gantt* for planning and scheduling work and projects. Actual performance or output is plotted in bars against the quota or target performance over time. May also be used to plot actual and planned cumulative performance.

Gantt, Henry Lawrence (1861-1919). Worked closely with F W Taylor for some years and later as a management consultant. He focused attention on the use of correct methods and skills in performing work, and emphasized the importance of people and their motivation at work. Chiefly remembered for his work on payment systems, charting techniques and the social responsibility of business. See also *Gantt chart*.

Gantt chart

gap analysis. *Market research* term for statistical and other techniques used to identify gaps in market coverage.

GATB. *General Aptitude Test Battery.*

gate mechanism. Lupton and Gowler use 'type of accountability' as initial so-called gate mechanisms in drawing up a *situation profile* as a basis for establishing the *payment system* appropriate for a firm. 'Type of effort' may be skilled, professional, intensive, etc. The 'unit of accountability' may be the individual employee, the group, the plant, etc.

GATT. *General Agreement on Tariffs and Trade.*

gaussian curve. Symmetrical or bell-shaped curve which represents the normal frequency distribution when analyzing natural or industrial phenomena based on a large scale sample or population.

GAW. *Guaranteed annual wage.*

GCA. *Group capacity assessment.*

GDP. *Gross domestic product.*

geared incentive scheme. *Payment-by-results* scheme in which incentive payments go up in stages rather than directly in proportion to output. See also *measured daywork*.

gearing. Or, particularly in the USA, leverage. Extent to which the money capital of a company is divided between fixed interest or fixed dividend capital (eg *debentures, preference shares, loan capital*, etc) and *equity* or *ordinary shares* that are not entitled to a guaranteed return or minimum return. A company with a high proportion of fixed interest capital is said to be 'highly geared', while one with a high proportion of equity capital is 'low geared'. In good times, equity capital gets a better return for the shareholder in a highly geared company than in a low geared company, but in bad times or when interest rates are high the highly geared company may have difficulty in meeting even its fixed interest obligations. See also *trading on the equity* and *gearing ratio*.

gearing ratio. Or *leverage ratio* (US). Ratio of preference and outside loan capital to ordinary capital and reserves. See also *gearing*.

general agent. See *agent*.

General Agreement on Tariffs and Trade (GATT). International agreement to attempt to reduce the *tariffs* inhibiting trade between nations. Formed at Geneva in 1947 with the support of all the leading trading nations (between them they are responsible for some 80 per cent of world trade). GATT has often negotiated tariff reductions between individual countries and between 1964 and 1967 also negotiated the more general *Kennedy Round* of tariff reductions (particularly on cereals) and an anti-*dumping* code. In 1955 GATT set up the *Organization for Trade Cooperation* as its administrative body.

General and Municipal Workers Union. UK *trade union*, affiliated to the *Trades Union Congress* and having nearly one million members.

General Aptitude Test Battery (GATB) (US). Battery of 12 *aptitude tests*, presenting results in the form of a *profile* to be measured against standard profiles of 22 vocational groups. Used widely by occupational psychologists in *vocational guidance*.

General Certificate of Education (GCE). UK school examination taken by pupils in higher ability ranges, O (ordinary) levels at about 15 or 16 and A (advanced) levels at 17 or 18. O levels often important in determining immediate employment prospects and A levels in competing for university or *college* entrance.

general clerical test. Three-part *psychological test* developed in the USA and measuring verbal, numerical and clerical skills. The test takes about 30 minutes. See also *Short Employment Tests*.

General Confederation of Italian Industry. *Confederazione Generale dell'Industria Italiana* (or *Confindustria*), covering employers in the private sector.

General Confederation of Labo(u)r. Confédération Générale du Travail (CGT). See *French trade unions*.

General Confederation of Labo(u)r — Workforce. See *Confédération Générale du Travail — Force Ouvrière (CGT — FO)*.

General Index of Retail Prices (UK). Formal title of the *Retail Price Index*.

general learning ability test. Term used particularly in the USA in *psychological testing* for a wide-ranging *intelligence test* (rather than *achievement test*). It may be a combination of tests forming a *test battery*.

General Register. Must be kept by every employer or factory occupier in the UK in the form prescibed by the *Factories Act 1961*, etc. See *Factory Inspectorate (UK)*.

General Strike (1926). UK strike that lasted for nine days in May 1926, beginning with a strike by the coal miners against wage cuts. Through the *Trades Union Congress*, the miners were joined on strike by workers from other industries including transport, construction, printing and engineering. The miners themselves continued on strike for a further three months. The General Strike was followed by the Trade Disputes Act 1927 which made general strikes illegal and substituted *contracting-in* for *contracting-out* until its repeal in 1946.

general union. *Trade union* whose membership is drawn from all kinds of workers as opposed to the more specialized membership of, for example, a *craft union*.

Generalversammlung. General Meeting of the *Zürich Stock Exchange* or *Effektenbörsenverein Zürich*. Other governing bodies are the Board of Governors, or *Vorstand*, and the Auditors or *Rechnungrevisoren*.

Geneva Stock Exchange. Or *Chambre de la Bourse de Genève*. one of the principal stock exchanges of Switzerland. See *Swiss stock exchanges*.

Genoa Stock Exchange. *Borsa Valori di Genova*.

Genossenschaft. Cooperative under Austrian company law. See *Austrian companies*.

Genossenschaftliche Zentralbank Aktiengesellschaft. Cooperative *central bank* in Austria.

geographical mobility. See *labo(u)r mobility*.

Geregelter Freiverkehr. Or Regulated Free Market on the *Vienna Stock Exchange* for *securities* that are permitted on the trading floor but not on the Official List. The same term is used of the regulated free market or semi-official market in securities on *German Stock Exchanges*. Other markets on the latter are the official *Amtlicher Markt* and the unofficial *Telefonverkehr*.

German (Democratic Republic) Central Bank. *Staatsbank der Deutschen Demokratischen Republik*.

German (Democratic Republic) Chamber of Foreign Trade. *Kammer für Aussenhandel der Deutschen Demokratischen Republik*.

German (Democratic Republic) trade unions. *Freier Deutscher Gewerkschaftsbund*.

German (Federal) Central Bank. *Deutsche Bundesbank*.

German (Federal) Chambers of Industry and Commerce, Association of. *Deutscher Industrie-und Handelstag*.

German (Federal) companies. Forms of business partnership and company under the law of the Federal Republic of Germany include: **a** One-man Firm or *Einzelfirma;* **b** General Partnership or *Offene Handelsgesellschaft (OHG);* **c** Limited Partnership or *Kommanditgesellschaft (KG);* **d** Sleeping Partnership or *Stille Gesellschaft;* **e** Combined Limited Partnership and Limited Liability Company or *Gesellschaft mit beschränkter Haftung & Kommanditgesellschaft (GmbH & Co KG);* **f** Limited Partnership with Shares or *Kommanditgesellschaft auf Aktien (KG a A);* **g** Limited Liability Company or *Gesellschaft mit beschränkter Haftung (GmbH);* **h** Joint Stock Company or *Aktiengesellschaft (AG)*.

German (Federal) Employers' Associations, Confederation of. *Bundesvereinigung der Deutschen Arbeitgeberverbände*.

German (Federal) income tax. Or *Einkommensteuer*, divided between an assessed tax on total income: a progressive wage tax or *Lohnsteuer* deducted at source from salaries, wages, pensions, etc; a capital yields tax or *Kapitalertragsteuer;* and a flat-rate directors' tax or *Aufsichtsratsteuer* deducted at source from directors' fees receivable by non-resident supervisory directors. There are also a surcharge or *Ergänzungsabgabe* on income tax, and a net wealth tax.

German (Federal) Industries, Federation of. *Bundesverband der Deutschen Industrie*.

German (Federal) stock exchanges. In Federal Germany there are two principal stock exchanges — at Frankfurt am Main and

Geschäfttelle

Düsseldorf — and six other stock exchanges. The eight are as follows: **a** Frankfurt — *Frankfurter Wertpapierbörse;* **b** Düsseldorf (or Rhenish-Westphalian Exchange) *Rheinisch-Westfälische Börse zu Düsseldorf;* **c** Berlin — *Berliner Börse;* **d** Bremen — *Bremen Wertpapierbörse;* **e** Hamburg (or Hanseatic Stock Exchange) — *Hanseatische Wertpapierbörse (Hamburg Börse);* **f** Hannover (or Lower Saxony Exchange) — *Niederschische Börse zu Hannover;* **g** Münich — *Bayerische Börse in München;* **h** Stuttgart — *Wertpapierbörse in Stüttgart.* The Federation of German (Federal) Stock Exchanges *(Arbeitsgemeinschaft der Deutschen Wertpapierbörsen)* is situated in Dusseldorf. The oldest of the German Stock Exchanges is in Hamburg, founded in the sixteenth century, with most of the other seven following during the eighteenth century. Nowadays Frankfurt is the biggest Exchange followed by Dusseldorf, the two between them handling about three-quarters of all German Stock Exchange business. Each separate Exchange has its own Stock Exchange Regulations or *Börsenordnung,* its own Stock Exchange Board or *Börsenvorstand,* and its own Listing Committee or *Zulassungstelle.* Banks play a big part in the dealings of the German Stock Exchanges in addition to the stockbrokers or *Makler.* The latter have their own association, the *Maklerkammer.* There are two kinds of Makler, namely the *amtliche Kursmakler,* who are appointed by the government and have a role somewhat similar to the *stockjobber* on the London Stock Exchange; and the *freie Makler,* who are not governmentally appointed officials but are authorized to deal on the trading floor. There are three types of securities market in Germany, namely, the official market or *Amtlicher Markt;* the semi-official, regulated free market or *Geregelter Freiverkehr;* and the unofficial, unregulated market or *Telefonverkehr.*

Geschäftsstelle. Secretariat of the *Zurich Stock Exchange* or *Effektenbörsenverein Zürich.*

Gesellschaft mit beschränkter Haftung (GmbH). Limited liability company under Swiss, Austrian, and German company law. Also known in Switzerland as *Société à Responsabilité Limitée.* See *Austrian companies* and *German (Federal) companies.*

Gesellschaft mit beschrankter Haftung & Kommanditgesellschaft (GmbH & CoKG). Combined limited partnership and limited liability company under Federal German company law. See also *German (Federal) companies.*

Gesellschaftsteuer. Company capitalization tax on the initial acquisition of *shares* in Austrian companies. There is also a securities tax, or *Wertpapiersteuer,* on bonds when they are issued for the first time on the *Vienna Stock Exchange.* After the initial appearance of securities there is a stock exchange turnover tax on further dealings in them.

Gestalt psychology. Beginning as an academic school of thought in Germany early in the twentieth century, it is now often considered as having important practical applications in *personnel selection* and *psychological testing.* The basic thesis of Gestalt psychology is that a misleading and incomplete picture of mental and psychological processes is obtained if these processes are analyzed without taking into account the complete personality and the way the processes interrelate.

g factor. Concept developed by Charles Spearman that humans possess an underlying general intelligence or 'g' factor accompanied by a myriad of special abilities called 's' factors. See also *g test.*

Ghanaian central bank. *Bank of Ghana.*

Ghana National Chamber of Commerce. Established 1961.

Ghana Trades Union Congress. Established 1945.

Ghent Stock Exchange. (la) *Bourse de Fonds Publics de Ghent* (Fondsen en Wisselbours van Gent).

gifts tax. Or capital transfer tax. Tax paid by an individual, on all gifts to others above a certain value. One objective of this tax is to counter avoidance of *wealth tax.*

Gilbreth, Frank Bunker (1868-1924). In conjunction with his wife Dr Lillian Gilbreth developed *motion study* as a basic management technique. Also an early pioneer in *management succession* and *development.* Gave his name — in reverse — to *therblig.*

Gilbreth symbols. See *therbligs.*

Gildemeister classification. System of classifying components developed by a German machine tool company. Using a 10-digit code it uses the first four digits to classify components by geometric shape and the remaining six digits to code the main dimensions. See also *classification and coding systems*.

gilder. As *guilder*.

Giles-Archer lantern tests. Form of *colo(u)r vision test* in which the subject is presented with a number of lights of different colo(u)rs and different degrees of brightness. See also *Edridge-Green lantern tests*.

gilt-edged. Term used of *securities, shares, stocks*, etc, where there is very little risk that the investment will be lost or that the due interest will not be paid. The term is used particularly of *government securities* and local government stocks, government securities in the UK being *Consols*, which are irredeemable government consolidated stock the first issue of which was made with the launching of the *National Debt* in 1694. See also *blue chip investment*.

Girl Friday. Female version of *Man Friday*.

GIRO. Money transfer or postal cheque system operated by postal authorities in many European countries. UK Giro set up in 1968 by the Post Office providing current account banking and transfer facilities to individuals or companies.

Glacier project. Research project conducted by Elliott Jacques — associated with the Tavistock Institute of Human Relations in the early years — into the organization and management of the Glacier Metal Co Ltd. Covered reorganization, methods of payment, measurement of responsibility, joint consultation, etc.

glamo(u)r issues. *Stocks* and *shares* in fashionable industries such as electronics.

Gleitzeit. Term used in Germany for the *flexible working hours* system.

GmbH. *Gesellschaft mit beschränkter Haftung.* See *Austrian companies* and *German (Federal) companies*.

GmbH & CoK G. *Gesellschaft mit beschränkter Haftung & Kommanditgesellschaft.* See *German (Federal) companies*.

GMWU. *General and Municipal Workers Union.*

GNP. *Gross national product.*

goal obsession. Term used in *T-group train-*ing for too great concern with goals and too little concern with existing behavio(u)r patterns.

'going public'. Process by which a *private company* becomes a *public company*, offering shares for sale on a *stock exchange*, often with the advice of an *issuing house* or *merchant bank*.

gold and foreign exchange reserves. Gold and foreign currencies held in reserve by a country to enable it to settle debts that are called in and to cushion deficits in its *balance of payments*, both *current account* and *capital account*.

goldbricking. Term used particularly in the early days of *payment-by-results* schemes where workers find piece work rates tight and hold back their effort, giving up any hope of achieving more than *day rate*. Another problem can be *quota restriction*, where piece work rates are loose and workers restrict output for fear of *rate cutting*.

golden handshake. Colloquial term for *severance pay* given to a senior executive on termination of his *contract of employment* or cutting short of his *contract of service*. See also *redundancy*.

golden rule fallacy. Fallacious view in some *T-group training* that there is a right way for all people to interact in all situations.

good-faith bargaining. Where the parties to *collective bargaining* are genuinely trying to achieve agreement and have a system of communication that can be expected to forestall and/or solve disputes. It is a concept difficult to define and identify but pursued particularly keenly in the USA where criteria of good-faith bargaining are laid down by the *National Labor Relations Board* under the *Wagner Act* and the *Taft-Hartley Act*. The criteria cover such areas as dilatoriness in negotiations, refusal to make agreements in writing, and attempts at reducing the power and effectiveness of *trade unions*.

goods for process. UK importer may import free of *customs duty* — and relevant taxes such as *purchase tax* and *value added tax* — goods for process intended for re-export after a process or repair which will not change their form or character (eg textiles for bleaching or dyeing qualify, but not yarns for weaving into fabrics or fabrics for making up into clothes). *HM Customs and*

Excise issue Customs Notice 206 on goods for process in general and Customs Notice 207 on the import of British-made goods returned for repair or replacement. See also *drawback* and *bonded warehouse*.

goods-in-process. As *work-in-progress* or work-in-process.

goods on consignment. See *consignment account*.

goodwill. Vague and arguable excess value of a business or *asset* over its net worth. Normally goodwill — eg technical know-how, location, regular customers — is regarded as an intangible asset. Its value is difficult to judge but on the sale of a business or asset may take on 'real' value and enhance the price considerably.

goon squad. Term used particularly in the USA for hoodlums or strong-arm gangs used by either *trade unions* or management during *industrial action* to bring pressure to bear on the other side.

Gopertz curve. Curve which plots the actual or potential sales of a new product over time. Typically such curves show three stages — growth, plateau or constant sales, decay or decline. See also *product life cycle*.

Gordon personal inventory and profile. *Psychological inventories* developed in the USA for use in *temperament and personality testing*. The Profile is a relatively short test (15 to 20 minutes) producing scores for ascendancy, responsibility, emotional stability, sociability, and 'overall self-evaluation'. The Inventory measures cautiousness, original thinking, personal relations, vigour, and total score. See also *psychological testing*.

Gosbank USSR. State Bank or *central bank* of the USSR, originally established in 1921.

go-slow. Form of *industrial action* where, as in a *work-to-rule*, the workers do not *strike* or withdraw their labo(u)r but, instead, slow down and obstruct the progress of work, possibly by fastidious interpretation of their workplace rule books or customs. A go-slow is a form of *cut-price industrial action*. See also *overtime ban* and *sit-in*.

Government Broker. Officially appointed *stockbroker* who deals in *government securities* on the floor of the London *Stock Exchange*. The *Bank of England* deals through the Government Broker.

government securities. Issued by the Government when it raises loans, as with the *National Debt* in the UK. The Government is the biggest borrower on the *Stock Exchange* in the UK. See also *gilt-edged*.

Government Training Centres. Now known as Skill centres. Run in the UK by the *Training Opportunities Scheme* of the *Training Services Department* for the *Department of Employment*. Originally the GTCs offered mainly six-month courses in manual skills used in the engineering, construction and some other industries, but their courses are being expanded.

The GTCs have been noted for the development of certain training techniques, such as *accelerated vocational training*. One consequence of their work has been the *'dilutee'* problem some ex-trainees have encountered in gaining acceptance in industry and with trade unions. See also *Manpower Services Commission*.

gozinto chart. American term derived from 'goes into'. Lists all the items which are required to manufacture a product and indicates how all the items are assembled to produce it. Also known as assembly chart.

grabber. Employee who takes advantage of seniority or long service to obtain jobs with *loose rates* and therefore paying high bonuses under a *payment-by-results* scheme. Such loosely rated jobs are sometimes known as *gravy jobs* or *fat work*.

grade creep. Tendency to re-grade or re-classify employees as surreptitious method of allowing increases in pay. Grade creep can be an important contributor to *earnings drift*. It can be a major problem for an *incomes policy*, and is particularly common among *white collar* and executive employees. Sometimes known as grade drift.

graded hourly rates. Method of payment employed under some forms of *merit rating*.

graded measured daywork. Variation on conventional *measured daywork* in which there are different wage rates geared to different performance bands, instead of a single target rate of productivity rewarded by a single level of incentive payment. Graded measured daywork is sometimes known as *stepped daywork*.

graded schedule pension scheme. See *average salary pension scheme*.

grading. As *job grading* in *job evaluation*.

graduated benefits (or supplement) and contributions. Introduced in UK by the *National Insurance Act 1961* (in respect of retirement pensions) on top of the *flat-rate benefits and contributions* that were the basis of the original National Insurance Act and National Insurance (Industrial Injuries) Act. See also *earnings-related unemployment and sickness benefit*, introduced by the *National Insurance Acts 1965* and *1966*, and *earnings-related supplement with injury benefit* introduced by the 1966 Act.

graduated pension scheme, state. See *state graduated pension scheme*.

graveyard shift. Pejorative term for night shift.

gravy jobs. Easy *piece work* jobs or those with *loose rates*. May also be known as *fat work*. Jobs on which it is difficult to earn bonus may be known as *lean work* or *stinkers*.

Greek central bank. *Bank of Greece*.

Greek companies. Several forms of business partnership and company exist under Greek law but the only type of public company listed on the Athens Stock Exchange is the *Anonymos Etairia (AE)*, form of joint stock company.

Greek General Confederation of Labo(u)r. Central *trade union* organization in Greece formed in 1918 and covering trade unions which have approximately 400,000 members.

Greek stock exchange. See *Athens Stock Exchange*.

Greenwich Standard Time. Local time at Greenwich, in South-East England, on the zero meridian. It is often used as a world datum time for such purposes as international air travel and simultaneous meteorological reports. Standard time zones in the USA are *Eastern Standard Time* (EST or ET); *Central Standard Time* (CST or CT); *Mountain Standard Time* (MST or MT); *Pacific Standard Time* (PST or PT). See also *standard time* and Appendix: Time Zones.

grey (gray) area occupations. Term for types of work in which there is some ambiguity about whether the employee involved is a *blue collar worker* or a *white collar worker*. Grey (gray) area occupations tend to be critical points in the present-day moves in industry to extend *staff status* to blue collar and related workers. Typical grey (gray) area occupations are *works staff* appointments closely involved with production processes in a clerical, inspection or supervisory role.

grey (gray) market. Buying and selling of goods using business methods which, though generally frowned on, are still within the law.

grid theory. Management theory that the three universals interacting in any organization are **a** people; **b** production of goods or services (the theory is not limited to manufacturing organizations, and the services might be either those sold to a customer or those provided for other parts of the organization); and **c** the management hierarchy. A practical demonstration of grid theory is in the *managerial grid*.

grievance procedure. Procedure agreed between management and *trade unions* (or other employees' representatives) laying down the machinery to be used by workers or their representatives. Grievance procedures are usually written into *collective agreements* as part of the *agreed procedures*.

gross business product. That part of *gross national product* produced by business activity.

gross domestic product (GDP). As *gross national product* except that income from investments, property and earnings abroad is not included.

gross income. *Income tax* term for all of an individual's income from all sources before deduction of outgoings and allowances and calculation of *total income* and *taxable income*.

gross incremental capital-output ratio. See *incremental capital-output ratio (ICOR)*.

gross investment. Level of *investment*, or spending of current income on adding to stocks and to fixed capital, before deducting *depreciation* of equipment and stocks to give *net investment*.

gross national product (GNP). Expression in money terms of flow of goods and services produced by and made available to a nation

gross profit (or margin) during a particular period (usually one *fiscal year*). See also *real income* and *economic growth*.

gross profit (or margin). Amount by which sales revenue exceeds the factory cost of goods and services sold. *Net profit* is the gross profit minus the cost of the marketing, research and development, finance and administrative functions.

group appraisal. *Performance appraisal* of an employee by a group of his superiors.

group capacity assessment (GCA). Technique for the planning and control of indirect payroll costs based on the application of *clerical work measurement* to groups of office workers. Involving group rather than individual studies, the technique is not normally used as a basis for *payment-by-results* schemes.

group decision-making. As *group problem-solving*.

group dynamics. Study of behavio(u)r of groups and of interaction of behavio(u)r of individuals as members of a group. Also known as *group relations training*. See *sensitivity training, T-group training, interactive skills*.

Group Export Representation Scheme (DT). Run in UK by the *Special Export Services Branch* of the Export Services Division of the *Department of Trade*. The Branch assists exporters in the formation of groups of about four manufacturers of complementary products who agree to set up and share the cost of a representative overseas. If a market survey is required preparatory to forming a group, the Branch is prepared to pay up to one third of the costs.

group incentives. Incentive schemes, eg *Rucker* and Scanlon and *work study* schemes in which share of production plans are based on group and not individual worker performance.

group interview. Selection interview involving two or more candidates, sometimes as part of *group selection techniques*.

group life assurance policy. Where an employer takes out a life assurance (or *insurance*) policy on all or some of his employees so that widows or dependants receive a *lump sum death benefit* in the event of an employee's death in service. Such a scheme is usually non-contributory and pays a lump sum death benefit equivalent to a given number of years' salary. In the case of a *long service death benefit*, the lump sum benefit is increased according to length of service. It is most common for group life assurance premiums to be based on *term assurance*, that is, on the risk of death during the period of the premium only — but they may be based on higher cost *endowment assurance*. Where group schemes are contributory and linked with endowment assurance pension schemes, there is usually a full return of contributions at the same time as life assurance benefit, in the manner of many endowment assurance schemes, if an employee leaves the firm.

A *group personal accident policy* is sometimes arranged in conjunction with a group life assurance policy. See also *widows' and orphans' pension scheme*.

group personal accident policy. Arranged for a group of employees or people by an employer etc, sometimes in conjunction with a *group life assurance policy*, to provide a *lump sum death benefit* (usually equivalent to two or more years' salary) or a capital sum or income in the event of serious disablement. A group personal accident policy may be restricted to accidents at work but is more likely to apply to accidents elsewhere as well.

group problem-solving. Or group decision-making. Process in which a manager presents a problem to a group of subordinates in order to elicit a solution by discussion with and between them.

group processes. Interactions within groups of people. See *interactive skills*.

group production. As *group technology*.

group project training. *Project training* in which the projects are tackled by students in groups rather than individually.

group relations training. See *group dynamics*.

group selection techniques. Where, in *personnel selection*, a number of candidates for a vacancy are interviewed or assessed together, and judged partly on their relations with each other. It is usual for them to be given a problem or subject for discussion while the interviewers observe them.

group technology. Or group production.

Management technique in which the operations and plant involved in the manufacture of a product are brought together in related groups with the possibility of *job rotation* or movement of workers between jobs. In many situations, group technology has been found more economic and better for worker morale than the more conventional sharp division of labo(u)r and conveyor belt-orientation of *mass production* and even *batch production*. See also *cell(ular) organization*.

group training methods. Group rather than individual methods of training, including *brainstorming, critical incident technique, case histories, case studies, expert witness, instrumented laboratory training,* lectures, *T-group training,* etc.

group training scheme. Training arrangements common to a number of, usually, small or medium-sized firms that might otherwise not have the resources to provide training.

group working. Organizing of workers to increase the degree of autonomy and responsibility carried by the worker through the delegation of responsibilities to the work group.

growth stock. *Company* or *corporation shares* or *stock* deemed to have prospects for further growth in profits and share market price.

Grundsteuer, Or *impôt foncier.* A local tax in Luxembourg levied on the capital value of all real property, whether developed or not. See also *Luxembourg income tax*.

GST (or GT). *Greenwich Standard Time.*

GTC. *Government Training Centre* (UK).

g (test). *Non-verbal intelligence test* used in *personnel selection* and *vocational guidance.* Devised as part of the *engineering apprentice test-battery* of the National Institute of Industrial Psychology in the UK. See also *psychological testing, test battery,* and *g factor*.

guarantee company (UK). *Company* which has guarantors who have undertaken to meet its debts to a certain level in the event of *liquidation*.

guaranteed annual wage (GAW). Concept rather than a reality in *collective bargaining* aimed at achieving guaranteed *job security* at specific minimum wage.

guaranteed annuity option. Or *annuity option rate.* A provision in an *endowment assurance* scheme guaranteeing a minimum rate at which the endowment sum assured may be converted into an annuity on retirement.

guaranteed working week. An arrangement negotiated between employers and *trade unions* guaranteeing workers that they will be paid as for a full working week (usually exclusive of bonuses and other *premium payments*) even if there is insufficient work for a full week.

guest worker. Foreign national who is permitted to enter a country to work, but not settle there with his family. The term is used particularly in the *European Economic Community* for community workers from less developed non-EEC countries.

guide-chart profile method. Type of *job evaluation* technique developed in the UK and using three factors: *know-how,* problem-solving and *accountability* in the context of a particular salary scale.

guide price (EEC). Under the *Common Agricultural Policy* of the *Common Market* or *European Economic Community,* the *European Commission* sets for beef and veal a guide price which acts as a form of target price that producers are helped to achieve by, if necessary, import controls and intervention by the Commission on the home market. A form of guide price was also intended under the common fisheries policy. See also *intervention price, reserve (or fall-back) price, sluice-gate price, target price, threshold price,* and *export subsidy (or restitution)*.

Guild. As *Livery Company.* See also *guild socialism*.

guilder. Or gilder. Basic unit of the currency of the Netherlands.

guild-master. Member of one of the medieval UK *Guilds* or *Livery Companies* who was a master or employer of *apprentices* and *journeymen.* The term *master* lingered on after the guild-master/journeyman had been succeeded by industrialization.

guild socialism. Form of *syndicalism* that was advocated in the UK in the early twentieth century. Its aims were to bring back medieval guild ideas and to replace capitalism with nationalized industries run by *trade unions* and workers.

Guilford-Zimmerman temperament survey. *Temperament and personality test* of US origin. See *psychological testing* and *Guilford's inventories.*

Guilford's inventories. Range of *psychological inventories* developed in the USA at the University of Southern California for use in *temperament and personality testing*. There are three different inventories designed to measure 13 different components. The Inventory of Factors STDCR measures social introversion-extroversion; thinking introversion-extroversion; impulsiveness (rhaythmia); depression; and emotional stability (cycloid tendency). The Inventory of Factors GAMIN measures general activity; ascendance-submission; masculinity-femininity; inferiority of feelings; and nervousness. The third and most popular Guilford inventory is the personnel inventory 1 designed to measure objectivity; cooperativeness; and agreeableness. See also the *Thurstone temperament schedule* and *psychological testing.*

guillotine. Method of closing debate or discussion on a subject when the permitted time limit has been reached. The classic example of the use of the guillotine is in imposing time limits on debates in the House of Commons in the UK. See also *closure.*

Guttman scaling. See *scalogram.*

g(v)(test). *Verbal intelligence test* used in *personnel selection* and *vocational guidance.* Devised as part of the *engineering apprentice test-battery* of the National Institute of Industrial Psychology in the UK. See also *psychological testing* and *test battery.*

h

hall test. *Market research* and *sales promotion* technique involving bringing together a number of people or *informants* for the purposes of testing their reactions to products, packagings, advertising presentations, etc.

halo effect. Or horns effect. Result of an interviewer favouring a candidate on the basis of one favourable characteristic to the exclusion of all less favourable features.

Halsey Plan. (Also known as Towne-Halsey Plan). An early form of *payment-by-results* in which the worker is paid a bonus for exceeding target production but not in proportion to the amount by which he exceeded target, as happens with conventional *piece work*. Under the Halsey Plan the worker receives a bonus of between one third and one half of the difference between standard time and actual time instead of the total difference.

Hamburg Stock Exchange (or Hanseatic Stock Exchange). *Hanseatische Wertpapierbörse (Hamburg Börse).* One of eight German (Federal) stock exchanges.

hammered. Description of what happens to a stockbroker or stockjobber who becomes unable to meet his debts. Three strokes of a hammer echo through the *Stock Exchange.*

hand-over pay (or allowance). Payment made to *shift* workers with particular responsibilities for handing over to, or *coupling-up* with, workers on the next shift.

Hannover Stock Exchange (or Lower Saxony Exchange). *Niedersächsichse Börse zu Hannover.* One of eight German (Federal) stock exchanges.

Hanseatische Wertpapierbörse (Hamburg Börse). *Hamburg Stock Exchange.*

hard copy. Text or information in a form which can be read by the human eye, as opposed to *microcopy* or information stored on disc, tape or *visual display unit.*

hard core control. Small group of directors or senior executives who effectively lead and direct a company usually in long-term strategic issues.

hard core unemployed. People who because of lack of education, personal skills or discrimination on whatever grounds are unable to find long term employment and therefore remain out of work for long periods.

hard currency. Stable currency normally not subject to dramatic variations in the exchange rate.

hard sales promotion 1. *Sales promotion* directly concerned with increasing the consumption of a product or service, for example through reduced price offers or increased packet size. Hard sales promotion is usually higher cost but more effective than *soft sales promotion* such as competitions and *personality promotions.* **2.** Aggressive selling and marketing methods.

hardware. Physical apparatus of a *computer* system, as opposed to *programs*, codes, etc that form the *software.* The terms are sometimes used of other types of commercial and industrial equipment, too.

harmonization. *EEC* term for the *Treaty of Rome* requirements on harmonizing social and employment conditions among Common Market countries.

Harvard case method. Teaching of management subjects etc through the presentation of a succession of *case histories* and *case studies*, thus, in effect, providing concentrated practical experience in the classroom. Developed by the Harvard Business School (USA).

Hawthorne effect. Instinct of employees to

group together, formally or informally, and to improve performance or change behavio(u)r when conscious of being observed. Takes name from studies at Hawthorne Plant of Western Electric Company by Elton Mayo and other Harvard researchers in the 1920s and 1930s.

Hay clerical battery. Three-part *psychological test* developed in the USA and covering, in four minutes each, number perception, name finding, and series of numbers.

Hayes pegboard test. Short pegboard test of *psychomotor skills*, originating in the US. See also *psychological testing*.

Hazine Komiseri. Commissioner appointed by the Turkish Minister of Finance to manage the *Istanbul Stock Exchange*.

'head-hunter'. Or executive search consultant. *Selection consultant* who, acting for a client company or organization, seeks out suitable people in other firms etc rather than advertising for applicants in the conventional way. This technique is used particularly when filling vacancies for very senior appointments, partly because the kind of people suitable for such appointments tend to hesitate to reply to advertisements and thus make it known that they are interested in the possibility of moving jobs.

Health and Safety at Work Act 1974. UK legislation which provided for **a** a comprehensive and integrated system of law dealing with the health and safety of virtually all people at work; **b** the protection of members of the public where they may be affected by work activities; **c** the setting up of a health and safety commission and executive responsible to ministers for adminstering the legislation. The Act placed general duties on everybody concerned with health and safety at work, including employers, self-employed, employees, and manufacturers and suppliers of plant and machines used at work. The *Employment Medical Advisory Service* was also brought under the Act.

hedging. Decisions and activities which minimize potential problems or risks. Often applied to dealing in foreign currencies and commodities in anticipation of price rises or falls.

Helsingin Arvopaperipörssi. *Helsinki Stock Exchange.*

Helsinki Stock Exchange. Or *Helsingin Arvopaperipörssi*. The only stock exchange in Finland, it was founded in 1912 and is run by the Stock Exchange Council.

Her Majesty's Customs and Excise. UK Government agency coming under the *Department of Trade* having responsibilities embracing control of imports and exports, including commercial relationships with the *European Economic Community*, collection of *customs duty*, *excise duty* and *value added tax (VAT)*; and supervision of manufacture of dutiable goods.

Herzberg's theory. Findings of research by Frederick Herzberg in US in late 1950s and early 1960s on motivation at work. His findings lead to general theory that two sets of complementary factors can be distinguished. First, the 'motivators' or 'satisfiers' which create job interest and encourage the application of willing effort to job tasks. Second, the 'dissatisfiers' or 'hygiene' (also known as maintenance) factors associated with the environment in which the work is carried out. Although these hygiene factors do not create job interest, if they reach an acceptable level they prevent frustration and help individuals to justify their 'putting up' with work, eg good working conditions, status, job security, 'high' pay, etc. Both types of factors need to be satisfied ideally. The theory highlights the duality of motivation — people respond to their work content etc in one way and to their working environment in another way. Interesting work may motivate but needs to be associated with a satisfactory environment. Conversely, good conditions alone are not enough but need to be linked to the feeling that work done is interesting and worthwhile.

Various types of *job enrichment* schemes to improve *motivation* and *job satisfaction* have been developed as a result of this theory.

heuristic method. Training approach. See *discovery method*.

heuristic models. Use of mathematical modelling technique that takes into account the fruits of practical experience of actually getting the work etc in question done.

HEW. *US Department of Health, Education and Welfare.*

hidden assets. *Assets* not easily seen by examining the balance sheet. Particularly applied to under-valued property which may be shown at historical cost or at a revaluation figure which is no longer realistic in present times.

hierarchy of needs. See *Maslow's hierarchy*.

high credit. Highest aggregate amount of credit that has been allowed to a customer at one time. It covers the total indebtedness. See also *credit outstanding*.

high day rate. *Time-related payment scheme* which is not related directly to results as in *payment-by-results* but is fixed as a high level of *day rate* on the assumption that workers are highly skilled and familiar with the work. High day rate, which is in effect a high hourly rate of pay, should not be confused with *measured daywork*, which is the payment of a specified higher-than-day-rate level of pay in return for achievement of a specified daily production target.

Higher National Certificate. Taken in UK in technical or science subjects or in business studies after a two-year part-time advanced course by students entering at 18+ with, usually, an *Ordinary National Certificate/Diploma*, A levels or Scottish H grades.

Higher National Diploma. Taken in UK in technical or science subjects or in business studies after a two or three-year full-time or a three-year *sandwich course* by students entering at 18+ with, usually, *Ordinary National Certificate/Diploma*, A levels, or Scottish H grades and supporting O grades.

high-flier. As *ratebuster*.

high frequency work sampling. Variation on *work sampling* in which the time/output relationships for a group of workers are calculated on the basis of observations by *work study* officers and, particularly in the case of machine times, records kept by the workers themselves. See also *multi-minute measurement*.

Highlands and Islands Development Board. Provides loans and advice for firms in the seven crofting counties of Scotland. The remainder of Scotland is covered by the *Small Business Division of the Scottish Development Agency*. The comparable body for small firms in England is the *Council for Small Industries in Rural Areas*. The Welsh equivalent is the *Small Business Section of the Welsh Development Agency*. Ulster has the *Local Enterprise Development Unit*.

high-level language. Relatively sophisticated *computer language* capable of being used to write *programs* for a wide range of types of *computer* and for complex applications. An example of a high-level language used for commercial and industrial applications is *COBOL (Common Business Orientated Language)*. The most common for scientific and mathematical applications are *ALGOL (Algorithmic Language)* and *FORTRAN* (acronym for *Formula Translation*). A high-level language specially developed in an attempt at combining the features and qualities of both commercial and scientific languages is *PL/I (Programming Language I)*.

hire purchase. Or instalment purchase. Form of purchase where the purchaser pays an initial deposit followed by regular instalments that cover the rest of the purchase price plus interest. The purchaser does not become the legal owner of the goods purchased until the last instalment has been paid (one difference between hire purchase and *credit sale*). See also *lease (hire)*.

hiring rate. As *accessions rate (of labo(u)r)*.

Hiroshima Stock Exchange. One of the five major *Japanese stock exchanges*.

histogram. Method of representing graphically *frequency distributions* using the X axis for class intervals and the Y axis for frequencies. Also known as *column diagram* or *bar chart*.

historical costing. Recording and analysis of costs after they have been incurred.

HM Customs and Excise. See *Her Majesty's Customs and Excise*.

HM Factory Inspectorate. See *Factory Inspectorate (UK)*.

HM Inspectorate of Factories. Member of the *Factory Inspectorate (UK)*.

HNC. See *Higher National Certificate*.

HND. See *Higher National Diploma*.

Hobart Stock Exchange. One of six member stock exchanges of the *Australian Associated Stock Exchanges*.

hoeklieden. Stockjobbers on the *Amsterdam Stock Exchange*.

hold-back pay. Pay due to an employee but not yet paid because pay is calculated at specific intervals in arrears so that pay

holding company. Or parent company. Company which controls others (subsidiaries) by virtue of its owning a majority of the ordinary voting share capital.

holistic evaluation. Evaluation of a project or campaign as a whole.

Holmgren wools test. Form of *colo(u)r vision test* in which the subject has to match a variety of colo(u)red wools.

home audit. *Market research* for what is normally a combination of *dustbin check* and *pantry check* to obtain data on households' choice and volume of consumption of *consumer goods*.

home market. Term traditionally used for the market for a product within the country in which it is manufactured and therefore within the geographical area in which the product can be distributed without crossing a *tariff barrier* and without incurring *customs duties*. Where *customs unions* of two or more countries have been formed, and tariff barriers between them have been removed, they are sometimes jointly referred to as a home market.

homeostasis. In mathematical models or experimental situations the retention of an attribute or condition without change.

Hong Kong Stock Exchange. Also Far East Stock Exchange.

Horaire Dynamique. The French term for the *flexible working hours* system.

horizontal integration (or merger). Acquisition, amalgamation or reorganization of a number of formerly separate companies which extend activities in the same area, eg further production facilities in the case of manufacturing companies or additional shops in the case of retail organizations. See also *vertical integration*.

horizontal union. See *craft union*.

horns effect. As *halo effect*.

Hotel and Catering Industry Training Board. Established in UK in November 1966 under the *Industrial Training Act 1964*.

Hotel, Catering and Institutional Management Association. UK professional body formed in 1971 from a merger of the Institutional Management Association and the Hotel and Catering Institute. Concerned to give professional advice and promote professional standards in institutional catering.

hot money. Money attracted to a country by favo(u)rable interest rates/currency whose holders are trying to get it off their hands (in exchange for other currencies), usually because they see its official *exchange rate* as unrealistic or because they think it to be in danger of *devaluation* or *revaluation*. Sometimes the activities of *currency speculators* or holders can in themselves help to make a currency 'hot'.

hour-for-hour plan. *Payment-by-results* system in which pay is directly related to the achievement of *standard performance*.

'House'. 1. In-term for the London *Stock Exchange*. 2. House of Commons (UK).

house claim. Claim for more pay lodged on behalf of the employees of a single plant or company as the first move in *plant bargaining* or company bargaining. It is a term used particularly in the printing and publishing industries. A *national claim* is one made as the first move in *industry-wide bargaining*.

house journal (or magazine). Published by an industrial or commercial organization or company for the information of its own employees as part of personnel policy, and/or for the information of its customers as part of marketing policy.

house mark. *Brand* or *trade mark*.

house style. Graphic design and styling and associated standards adopted on a company-wide basis for letterheadings, packaging, sales literature, transport etc. See also *corporate image*.

house union. As *staff association*.

H-R-H pseudoisochromatic plates. Form of *colo(u)r vision test* developed and supplied by the British-American Optical Company Ltd.

human asset accounting. Measuring the value of the human factor in business and commerce in an attempt at identifying the economic and social impact of company policies on employees and, through them, on the company. The aim of this approach, which was developed jointly by the UK Institutes of Personnel Management and of

Cost and Management Accountants, is to ensure that manpower resources will be treated as assets rather than simply as costs so that the value of a company's manpower will be taken more fully into account when planning the use of resources and budgeting for personnel and training expenditure. See also *job enrichment* and *job satisfaction*.

human engineering. See *ergonomics*.

human relations department. As *employee relations department* or *personnel department*.

human relations school. Industrial sociology school of thought particularly active in the USA in the 1930s and 1940s and having its roots largely in the thinking of Elton Mayo. It saw good human relations between management and managed as the key to improving morale and productivity. It believed that management's key role was to provide *'supportive leadership'* in building up good social relations. The human relations school of thought remains influential in some parts of management education but also has its critics on the grounds that it has a manipulative approach to workers and disregards the traditional role of *trade unions*. A classic product of the human relations school of thought was the *Hawthorne effect*. See also *authoritarian management*, *shared values*, *structural-functionalist school*, *pluralistic theory*, *economic man theory*, and *integrated theory*.

human resources planning. Term commonly used in the USA for *manpower planning*.

Hungarian Chamber of Commerce. Formed in 1968.

Hungarian method. Operational research technique for calculating the optimal solution of transportation and similar type problems.

Hungarian Trade Unions, Central Council of. *Magyar Szakszervezetek Országos Tanácsa.*

Hungary, National Bank of. *Magyar Nemzeti Bank.*

hurdle rate. Minimum acceptable *rate of return* on a project or development.

hybrid computer. Computer system combining the features of an *analog(ue) computer* and a *digital computer*, with the two linked by a hybrid *interface* or with the analog(ue) computer operating as part of the digital computer's *central processing unit*. Hybrid computers can be particularly effective in scientific applications and in industrial process control, combining the digital computer's storage facilities and arithmetic speed with the analog(ue) computer's speed of integration.

hygiene factors. See *Herzberg's theory*.

hypermarket. Major mass merchandizing retail store typically selling a very wide range of food, clothing and household goods. Normally situated out of town within reach of a large conurbation. Provides car parking facilities and has more than 25 checkout points. See also *superstore*.

hypothecation, letter of. See *letter of hypothecation*.

i

IAEA. *International Atomic Energy Agency.*

IAM. *Institute of Administrative Management.*

IANEC. *Inter-American Nuclear Energy Commission.*

IATA. *International Air Transport Association.*

IBRD. *International Bank for Reconstruction and Development.*

ICA. *International Cooperative Alliance.*

ICAO. *International Civil Aviation Organization.*

ICATU. *International Confederation of Arab Trade Unions.*

ICC. 1. *International Chamber of Commerce.* **2.** *Interstate Commerce Commission.*

ICF. *International Confederation of Chemical and General Workers Unions.*

ICFC. *Industrial and Commercial Finance Corporation Ltd.*

ICFTU. *International Confederation of Free Trade Unions.*

ICMA. *Institute of Cost and Management Accountants.*

iconic models. Laboratory simulations of real-life situations, particularly in engineering.

ICOR. *Incremental capital-output ratio.*

ICSU. *International Council of Scientific Unions.*

ICTU. *Irish Congress of Trade Unions.*

IDA. *International Development Association.*

IDB. *Inter-American Development Bank.*

IDCs. *Industrial development certificates* (UK).

idle time. Period when available plant and/or labo(u)r is not being used productively. As *downtime* and *machine idle time*.

IDP. *Integrated data processing.*

IFC. *International Finance Corporation.*

IFF. *Institute for the Future.*

IIM. *Institution of Industrial Managers.*

illegal contracts. In general, certain types of contract cannot be regarded as legally binding under most legal codes. Such illegal contracts include the following: **a** Contracts in restraint of trade (hence, for example, *anti-trust legislation* in the USA or *monopolies* legislation in the UK and EEC). **b** Agreements against the national interest (for example, a contract with an enemy nation). **c** Agreements involving conflict between private interest and duty to an employer or under a prior contract (for example, an agreement by an employee to act against the interests of his employer). **d** Agreements to commit a criminal or civil wrong. **e** Agreements which hinder the administration of justice. **f** Agreements on wages and conditions of employment arrived at by collective bargaining have different legal standing in different countries. There are also differences in the extent to which *trade unions* can be held responsible for the consequences of *strikes* and other *industrial action*.

ILO. *International Labor Organization.*

image study. Study of consumer attitudes to a company and its products.

IMF. 1. *International Monetary Fund.*

2. *International Metalworkers Federation.*

IMI. *Irish Management Institute.*

immediate-access store. *Computer* store designed to give uniformly quick *access time* to all locations in the store.

immediate annuity rate. Going rate at which the endowment sum assured under a *'top hat' endowment pension scheme* may be converted into pension on maturity of the policy and retirement of the insured. However, an insurance policy under such a scheme may include an *annuity option rate* guaranteeing that it will in fact be converted into pension at the rate intended by the employer. See *'top hat' pension scheme.* See also *purchased life annuity* for individuals obtaining an annuity of their own accord.

impact day. Date of *public issue* of *shares.*

impact testing. Procedure for measuring the effect of an advertisement by discovering how much of it people recall.

Imperial System (or Units). See *British Imperial System.*

impingement pay (or money). Special payment to employees for working during what is normally holiday time. Originated in the printing industry.

import duty. As *tariff.*

imposed date. *Network analysis/planning* term for a time by which it is vital that a particular *activity* takes place.

imposta complementare progressiva sul reddito complessivo. Complementary tax or progressive *surtax* charged on an individual's total income from all sources in Italy. See *Italian income tax.*

imposta comunale sull'incremento di valore degli immobili. Italian municipal or communal tax charged on capital gains arising from the transfer of real property for a consideration or as a gift (but not on death) and also chargeable every ten years on capital appreciation of properties held by property companies. See *Italian income tax.*

imposta di ricchezza mobile sul reddito. Movable wealth tax charged as a proportional tax in Italy. See *Italian income tax.*

imposta sul reddito agrario. Italian agricultural income tax charged on income from agriculture and assessed on such bases as value of property, investment and number of employees. See *Italian income tax.*

imposta sul reddito dei Pabbricati. *Italian income tax* in the form of a buildings tax charged on annual rental value after the deduction of up to 25 per cent of maintenance costs.

imposta sul reddito dominicale dei terreni. *Italian income tax* in the form of a land tax charged on annual rental value.

imposto complementar. Complementary tax in Portugal charged as a progressive surtax on total income from all sources. See *Portuguese income tax.*

imposto de capitais. Tax on income from movable capital in Portugal. See *Portuguese income tax.*

imposto de mais-valias. Capital gains tax in Portugal. See *Portuguese income tax.*

imposto profissional. Professional tax on earned income in Portugal. See *Portuguese income tax.*

impôt à forfait. Or *Pauschalsteuer.* A graduated tax charged on incomes of certain foreigners in Switzerland instead of the national defence tax paid by nationals. See *Swiss income tax.*

impôt des personnes physiques. Or *personenbelasting.* In Belgian *income tax,* a *progressive tax* on total net income from real estate and personal property including capital and income from miscellaneous sources. There is also a *surcharge* on high incomes. There may also be additional local taxes — either **a** the *centimes additionelles* or *opcentiemen* or **b** the *taxe communale additionelle* or *aanvullende gemeentebelasting.* Under these local taxes, a municipality of residence may levy a surcharge of not more than six per cent on an individual's income tax.

impôt fédéral pour la défense nationale. Or *Eidgenössiche Wehrsteuer.* The federal national defence tax charged on total income from all sources in Switzerland. See *Swiss income tax.*

impôt foncier. Or *Grundsteuer.* A local tax in Luxembourg levied on the capital value of all real property, whether developed or not. See also *Luxembourg income tax.*

impôt sur la fortune. Or *Vermögensteuer*. A capital tax in Luxembourg on investments in agriculture, forestry, real property, industry, business, professions and other movable capital. See *Luxembourg income tax*.

impôt sur le revenu. Principal *income tax* in France and also in Luxembourg, a progressive tax levied on all types of personal income including capital gains. There are also certain local taxes, including a land tax and a personal tax on occupiers of residential property. In Luxembourg, impôt sur le revenu is also known by the German term, *Einkommensteuer*. See *French income tax* and *Luxembourg income tax*.

imprest. 1. Advance or loan. **2.** Method of keeping petty cash float. The initial advance or float is made up again at the end of each accounting period against vouchers for expenditure incurred.

improvement curve. 1. As *learning curve* and *experience curve*. **2.** Use of double logarithmic graph paper to plot the direct man-hours spent on a given unit of output as a function of the cumulative number of units produced. The relationship of cost to volume is typically a straight line sloping from left to right which reflects a steady rate of reduction given that the operators working on the job remain employed on the same work over a period of time. It merely illustrates that constant repetition of operations can lead to efficiency, declining costs and increased productivity.

impuesto general sobre la renta de las personas fisicas. General income tax in Spain, a progressive tax charged on total income. See *Spanish income tax*.

impuesto sobre actividades y beneficios commerciales e industriales. Industrial tax in Spain. See *Spanish income tax*.

impuesto sobre las rentas del capital. Tax on unearned income. See *Spanish income tax*.

impuesto sobre los rendimientos del trabajo personal. Tax on earned income from personal work. See *Spanish income tax*.

impulse goods. Consumer goods of a kind normally purchased as and when they catch the consumer's eye.

imputed costs. Those incurred, not in the trading transactions for which the company concerned was established, but as an inevitable concomitant of running a business. Interest payments are an example of imputed costs.

in-basket/tray method. See *in-tray exercise*.

incentive engineer. American term for a *work study* officer/engineer or *rate fixer* responsible for setting *payment-by-results* targets. See also *industrial engineer*.

incentive payment schemes. See *payment-by-results*.

incestuous share dealing. Buying and selling of each other's shares by associated companies with the object of securing overall tax or other financial advantages. Such dealings are often not public and in some cases are illegal. See also *warehousing* and *intermediary* or *nominee holdings* and *insider trading*.

incident process. Type of *case study* in which the participants have to obtain further information as the case study progresses.

income and expenditure. Similar to *profit and loss account*, it is used by non-profit making organizations which are concerned to show how income exceeds expenditure (or vice versa) rather than *profit* or *loss*.

income benefit insurance policy. Or safeguard benefit insurance policy. Provides income for dependants when the breadwinner dies before retirement age. May be arranged with a *whole life assurance policy* or an *endowment assurance policy*.

income bond. Company or corporation *bond* on which, though it is part of *debt capital* rather than *contributed capital*, interest is paid only if a *profit* is made.

income, circular flow of. See *circular flow of income*.

income elasticity of demand. Relationship between demand or sales volume and levels of income purchases. See also *price elasticity of demand*.

income fund. *Unit trust* or *mutual fund* whose prime investment objective is to obtain a high income yield rather than capital growth. Historically many so called have often also produced capital growth.

incomes policy. Where a government intervenes in the free negotiation of rates of pay, usually in an attempt at restricting pay increases with the object of holding down *inflation,* particularly *cost-push inflation.* See *prices and incomes policy.*

income statement. As *profit and loss account.*

income tax. Tax on the income of an individual. It may be a flat-rate tax or a *progressive tax* and, if the latter, on either a *slab scale* or a *slice scale.* Income tax may include such taxes as *capital gains tax* and *wealth tax.* The form income tax takes varies between countries. See under individual countries, as *Austrian income tax* etc.

in-company training. Training for the employees of a company held on the company's own premises. May be put on by outside bodies such as consultants. Also known as in-plant training, in-firm training or in-house training.

incorporator (US). Signatory to the *certificate of incorporation* at the start of a *corporation.*

incoterms. Terms for use in international trade contracts drawn up by the *International Chamber of Commerce.* Incoterms include *c and f, cif, ex-works, fas, fob* and *for.*

increasing returns. When output expands more than proportionately to the increase in the variable input. See also *diminishing return.*

incremental capital-output ratio (ICOR). Increase in *capital* stock divided by the increase in output of goods and services during a particular period. The ratio might be applied to an individual company, a complete industry or a national economy. When applied to the latter the ratio is usually known as the gross incremental capital-output ratio. See also *capital-output ratio.*

incremental costing. As *marginal costing.*

incremental payment system. Giving pay increments arising from increased merit, age or service in accordance with a predetermined scale.

incremental pricing. Use of a two-tier pricing system, one price covering *full cost* and the other being geared to the *marginal cost* of further production.

incremental profitability. Stepping up in profitability by such difficult-to-quantify measures as improving skills of workers or introducing more skilled workers. Attempt is made at establishing an incremental profit for each category of skilled employee.

indemnity fund. Used by an *employers' association,* particularly in the UK, to compensate member firms for losses incurred by adhering to association policy during *industrial action.* There is a strong similarity to the *employer strike insurance* system in the USA.

indenture. 1. Legal contract between an *apprentice* and his employer. **2.** (US) Legal contract between a *corporation* and its bondholders on the issue of *bonds.*

index linking. Systematic adjustment of the value of transactions in line with changing prices, particularly in times of *inflation.* An example of index linking is in *threshold agreements* for increasing pay in step with increases in prices.

index number. Statistical measure giving an overall indication of change over time particularly for such areas as prices, wage rates, cost of living, exports, imports, etc. Normally derived from detailed statistical data, an index number typically covers a base year which is assigned the value 100, and subsequent changes reflect deviations for each period measured.

India, Associated Chambers of Commerce and Industry of. Central organization for *chambers of commerce.*

Indian central bank. *Reserve Bank of India.*

Indian National Trade Union Congress (INTUC). Established 1947, it covers over 2,000 *trade unions* with approximately 2,250,000 members.

Indian stock exchanges. Major five *stock exchanges* in India are: **a** Ahmadabad Share and Stock Brokers' Association; **b** Bombay Stock Exchange; **c** Calcutta Stock Exchange Association Ltd; **d** Delhi Stock Exchange Association Ltd; **e** Madras Stock Exchange.

indicative planning. Planning by agreement and indication of desirable targets rather than by compulsion or decree. Also known as participative planning.

indirect cost. Cost not directly attributable to the production of a particular product as it is possible to attribute *direct cost,* but allotted to the product by a *cost absorption* accounting technique so that it takes its fair share of the total factory indirect cost or overhead. Direct cost added to manufacturing indirect cost gives *factory cost*. Also known as *overhead* or *burden*.

indirect demand. Or derived demand. Where *demand* for a product is for inclusion as a component part of another product (eg the components included in a car during manufacture) as opposed to *final demand* for a product for its end use (eg the motorist's demand for a car).

indirect labo(u)r. Workforce not engaged (like *direct labo(u)r*) directly in the manufacture of a product or the provision of a service but doing work without which the product could not be produced or the service provided effectively. Thus, in manufacturing production indirect labo(u)r might include maintenance workers and office staff. *Payment-by-results* schemes are more difficult to apply to indirect labo(u)r than to direct labo(u)r. Special management techniques such as *short interval scheduling* have been devised for indirect labo(u)r.

indirect labo(u)r cost. Or indirect wages. *Indirect cost* related to the pay of *indirect labo(u)r*.

indirect materials cost. *Indirect cost* of materials and components.

indirect review. Where management reviews the progress of work, not by direct monitoring or inspection *(direct review)* but indirectly through feedback in the form of complaints or *returned work*.

indirect tax. Taxes on goods or services, eg *sales tax, purchase tax, excise duty, import duties, value added tax*, etc.

indirect wages. As *indirect labo(u)r cost*.

indirect worker. Member of *indirect labo(u)r* force.

individual expectancy chart. Sometimes used following *psychological testing* in an attempt at predicting the degree of success a candidate or employee would have in a particular occupation. Another form of *expectancy chart* is the *institutional expectancy chart* on which the predicted levels of efficiency within a workforce are charted, note being made of such factors as the number of workers expected to be of above-average performance.

individual training methods. Individual as opposed to *group training methods*, including *programmed instruction* and personal job instruction.

indkomstskat til staten. State *income tax* in Denmark, a *progressive tax* charged on total income plus flat-rate dividend tax. There are also special, local, church and net *wealth taxes*. See *Danish income tax*.

induction training. Devised for school leaver entrants or other new employees in a firm to familiarize them with company practices (practises) and procedures.

indulgency pattern. Tolerant and lenient style of management. See also *management style*.

'Industria'. Swedish monthly publication on business, commerce and industry established in 1905;

industrial accident. Accident suffered at work. More specifically, under the UK *Factories Act* an accident causing death or more than three days' absence from work.

industrial action. Action taken by employees collectively to air either a grievance or a demand, usually on questions of pay and/or conditions of employment. Industrial action that goes as far as withdrawal of labo(u)r or refusal to work is a form of *strike* (see its various forms). Action to limit the effectiveness of work, rather than refusal to do it, includes *go-slow, overtime ban* and *work-to-rule*, and is sometimes categorized as *cut-price industrial action* (that is, 'cut-price' to those taking the action since it does not involve total loss of pay). Another form of industrial action, but by an employer or employers, is a *lock-out* which is intended to exclude workers from a factory during a dispute. A particularly modern form of industrial action is where workers stage a *sit-in* at a factory possibly operating and managing the factory themselves. See also *industrial dispute, trade dispute* and *grievance procedure*.

industrial action short of a strike, irregular. See *irregular industrial action short of a strike*, as introduced in the UK by the *Industrial Relations Act 1971*.

Industrial and Commercial Finance Corporation Ltd (UK). Provides for small and medium-sized firms long-term loan capital and share capital which is not obtainable through traditional banking facilities or a new issue. Other UK sources of finance other than traditional banking facilities include *Finance Corporation for Industry Ltd, Council for Small Industries in Rural Areas, Highlands and Islands Development Board,* and *Small Business Division of the Scottish Development Agency.*

Industrial and Commercial Policy Division (DT). Provides information for UK firms on *monopolies, restrictive practices (practises)* and consumer protection.

Industrial Arbitration Board (UK). Formerly the original *Industrial Court* set up under the *Industrial Courts Act 1919* to specialize for half a century in *voluntary arbitration* and since 1946 in arbitration under the *Fair Wages Resolution* before becoming the Industrial Arbitration Board under the *Industrial Relations Act 1971.*

See also, for earlier institutions, *Industrial Disputes Tribunal,* and, for other Industrial Relations Act 1971 Institutions, *Industrial Tribunals, Commission on Industrial Relations, Chief Registrar of Trade Unions and Employers' Associations.* (A source of possible confusion is that the National Industrial Relations Court set up under the Industrial Relations Act 1971 was sometimes known as the 'Industrial Court'.)

Industrial Association of Wales and Monmouthshire. Founder component, July 1965, of the *Confederation of British Industry.*

Industrial Bankers' Association (UK). Concerned with promoting high standards of industrial banking, tending to deal with smaller finance houses than those in membership of the *Finance Houses Association.*

industrial capital goods. Capital goods in the form of industrial buildings and/or equipment.

Industrial Courts Act 1919 (UK). Following *Whitley Committee* Report, provided for *voluntary arbitration* or *trade disputes* (see also *Conciliation Act 1896*) and created the Industrial Court for the purpose.

industrial democracy. General term for measures and policies intended to increase *workers' participation* and the voice workers have in management decision-making. Champions of industrial democracy usually argue that a company should regard its employees' interests as being at least as important as those of its *shareholders,* and some go further and advocate *workers' control.* A basic argument for industrial democracy is that the fruits of political democracy are inadequate without democracy in the working environment. See also *Industrial Democracy Bill* and *works councils.*

Industrial Democracy Bill. UK legislation drafted in 1974 with the intention of giving workers a bigger say in the running of their employing firms, partly by the appointment of directors elected by the workers. See also *workers' control* and *Trade Union and Labour Relations Act.*

industrial development certificates (IDCs). Issued to firms by the UK *Department of Industry* to accompany an application for planning permission to erect a building with industrial floor space greater than 15,000 sq ft (or 10,000 sq ft in the South East Economic Planning Region). However, IDCs are not required in *Special Development Areas* or *Development Areas,* and are in general available in the *Intermediate Areas.*

industrial disease. Disease attributable to exposure to harmful or poisonous substances and rays at work. These diseases include toxic conditions such as poisoning by lead, phosphorus, arsenic or mercury; fibrosis of the lungs caused by silica or asbestos; skin ailments such as dermatitis; and ulceration caused by chromic acid, pitch or tar.

industrial dispute. One between employers or their representatives and employees or their representatives (eg a *trade union* or unions) over pay, working conditions, etc. Such a dispute has sometimes been referred to as a *trade dispute,* particularly in legislation in the UK. An industrial dispute is sometimes regarded as including the confrontation between employers and employees that usually precedes (and sometimes forestalls) *industrial action* as well as the industrial action itself.

International Disputes Tribunal (UK). Succeeded the National Arbitration Tribunal in 1951 when Order 1376 succeeded Order 1305 (1940) (a legislative change which, incidentally, legalized strikes for the first time since the Second World War). The *Minister of Labour* could refer a dispute to *unilateral arbitration* by the Tribunal at the request of either party to the dispute. Such unilateral arbitration differed essentially from *voluntary arbitration* which could only be invoked with the agreement of both parties to a dispute. The Industrial Disputes

Tribunal was disbanded in 1959.

industrial distributor. *Distributor* dealing in *industrial goods*.

industrial engineer. Engineer skilled in *method study, production planning* and works management techniques, etc. See also *incentive engineer*.

industrial espionage. Planned attempts by a company or its agents at obtaining secret or confidential information from within or about a rival company. Industrial espionage takes a wide variety of forms, sometimes involving the use of sophisticated electronic equipment, bugging techniques and photography. On occasion, anti-espionage measures become equally sophisticated. The degree of illegality of industrial espionage varies from country to country.

industrial goods. Goods or components produced for sale to other manufacturers for inclusion in their products (as opposed to *consumer goods*). See also *capital goods*.

Industrial Health and Safety Centre (UK). Run by *Department of Employment* to give advice on health and safety in industry.

Industrial Injuries Advisory Committee (UK). Advises *Department of Health and Social Security* on matters concerned with *injury benefit, disablement benefit* and industrial diseases.

Industrial Injuries Fund. Set up in UK under the *National Insurance (Industrial Injuries) Acts 1946, 1965, 1966* and *1967*, as the fund from which payments are made under the state scheme to employees suffering industrial injuries. Like the *National Insurance Fund*, the Industrial Injuries Fund is sustained by contributions from employers, employees and general taxation. It comes under the *Department of Health and Social Security*.

Industrial Location Advisory Service (DI). Division of the *Department of Industry* (UK) responsible for advising industry on the most favo(u)rable conditions for regional development or expansion in the *Assisted Areas*, the collective term for *Special Development Areas, Development Areas* and *Intermediate Areas*.

industrial market. *Market* for *industrial goods*.

'Industrial Marketing'. US monthly publication established in 1916.

industrial market research. Branch of *market research* concerned particularly with establishing market potential for industrial goods — that is, with the selling of goods or services to industry. The other major branch of market research is in the consumer goods and services field.

industrial park (US). Industrial or real estate area zoned for industrial development.

industrial policy, common (EEC). See *common industrial policy (EEC)*.

industrial product. See *basic product*.

industrial property rights. As *patent* rights.

industrial relations. Factors affecting the relationship between employers and employees. See also *labo(u)r relations*.

Industrial Relations Act, 1971. UK Act most of which became law by stages between October 1971 and February 1972. Broadly, the Industrial Relations Act sought to make *collective bargaining* more constructive and enforceable, particularly through legally binding *collective agreements*, and to provide a new, legalistically defined system of industrial relations.

The Industrial Relations Act 1971 repealed or amended a wide range of earlier legislation and introduced or adapted the following institutions: the *National Industrial Relations Court*, the *Commission on Industrial Relations*, the *Industrial Tribunals*, the *Industrial Arbitration Board* and the *Chief Registrar of Trade Unions and Employers' Associations*.

The Industrial Relations Act 1971 was itself repealed in 1974 by the *Trade Union and Labour Relations Act*.

Industrial Safety Advisory Council. Advises the *Department of Employment* in the UK on aspects of industrial safety. The Council is composed mainly of people with experience of safety needs in industry.

Industrial Society. Founded in 1918 in UK as Industrial Welfare Society. An independent and self-financing body providing advice on personnel and welfare matters, organizing training courses and conferences as well as *'in-company'* training activities. With 8,000 corporate members, specializes in effective leadership, industrial relations, terms of employment and conditions of work, communication, development of young employees.

Industrial Technologies, Committee for. See *Committee for Industrial Technologies.*

industrial trade union. Where a single *trade union* represents all the workers in an industry (see *industrial unionism*) instead of the more common situation, known as *multi-unionism*, where unions represent particular skills or types of worker whatever the industries in which they are working. Many commentators have pointed to the multiplicity of trade unions in several industries as a root problem of British industrial relations. Countries such as Sweden have been said to benefit from having industrial trade unions.

Industrial Training Act 1964. Came on to the UK Statute Book in March 1964 with the following three main objectives: **a** to ensure an adequate supply of properly trained men and women at all levels in industry; **b** to secure an improvement in the quality and efficiency of industrial training; and **c** to share the cost of training more evenly between firms. The principal instruments of the Act were the *industrial training boards* set up with powers to levy all firms in their industries and to pay grants to firms deemed to be carrying out effective industrial training. The Industrial Training Act was modified by the *Employment and Training Act 1973.*

Industrial Training Act (Northern Ireland) 1964. Came into effect in Northern Ireland at much the same time and with much the same intent as the Industrial Training Act in England, Scotland and Wales. See also *industrial training boards.*

industrial training boards (ITBs). Statutory bodies set up in UK under *Industrial Training Act 1964* to cover range of industry specified by relevant Statutory Instrument. Under an 'independent' chairman, each contains equal numbers of employers and employees with smaller groups of educationists and Government Assessors. The *Employment and Training Act 1973* brought the ITBs under the *Training Services Division* (then Agency).

Industrial Training Service. Independent non-profit making UK organization sponsored by the *Department of Employment* and the *Training Services Division*. Its consulting services have been used by *industrial training boards* as well as by individual firms and employers' associations.

Industrial Tribunals. Set up in UK under the *Industrial Training Act 1964* to hear appeals against levy decisions (but not grant decisions) of the *industrial training boards*. The Industrial Tribunals have also been given jurisdiction to try cases under the *Contracts of Employment Act 1963*, the *Redundancy Payments Act 1965*, Section 51 of the *Docks and Harbours Act 1966*, the Selective Employments Act 1966, and the *Industrial Relations Act 1971*. The Tribunals also try cases under the *Equal Pay Act 1970*.

See also *National Arbitration Tribunal, Industrial Disputes Tribunal* and, for Industrial Relations Act institutions, *National Industrial Relations Court, Commission on Industrial Relations, Industrial Arbitration Board*, and *Chief Registrar of Trade Unions and Employers' Associations.*

industrial unionism. 1. Present-day movement for *industrial trade unions;* **2.** Movement early in this century for *syndicalism.*

Industry Act 1972. Provided for regional development in UK through special attention for the *Special Development Areas*, the *Development Areas*, the *Intermediate Areas*, Northern Ireland, etc.

industry-based student. College or university *sandwich course* student sponsored by an employer who arranges his/her industrial training periods. Cf *college-based student.*

'Industry Week'. US publication established in 1882.

industry-wide agreement. Or *national agreement. Collective agreement* or *bargain* between employers and *trade unions* on an industry-wide basis. At the other extreme is *workplace bargaining*. In between are *company agreements* and *factory agreements.*

industry-wide bargaining. Precursor of *industry-wide agreement.*

inelastic demand. Term used when the demand for a product or service changes only slightly (less than proportionately) in response to changes in price. A product or service for which a large (more than proportionate) change in demand occurs in response to a change in price is said to have *elastic demand.*

inertia selling

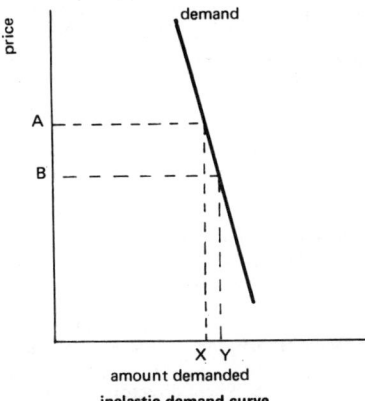

inelastic demand curve

inertia selling. Disreputable sales approach under which goods are delivered to possible purchasers without their consent, these purchasers then being pressed to pay up rather than go to the trouble of returning the goods.

in-firm training. As *in-company training*.

inflation. Economist's term for situation, sometimes occurring in conditions of *full employment*, where the *purchasing power* of the community has increased beyond the level at which it can affect *employment* or *real incomes* and has the principal effect of pushing up prices. In other words, the money income flow expands faster than the supply of goods and services. Inflation is generally distinguished from *reflation*, where the increase in purchasing power does stimulate employment and real incomes. Mild inflation is said by some economists to have a beneficial effect in giving an incentive to trade but runaway or *galloping inflation* leads to *boom* conditions and damage to the economy. See also *trade cycle*. A distinction is sometimes made between *cost-push inflation*, caused by increased costs, and *demand inflation* caused by increased demand.

inflation accounting. Financial accounting procedures that take cognizance of the likely effect of *inflation* on costs, revenues and profits, normally within an accounting period.

informant. Or *respondent*. A person providing views and/or information in a *market research* interview or survey.

information picture. Term sometimes used for *pictogram*.

Inland Revenue

information science. See *information storage and retrieval*.

information storage and retrieval. Science of storing large banks of information and of gaining access to particular items of information appropriate and needed at particular times. May entail computerization. Also known as information science.

information theory. Mathematically based and often computerized approach to communicating information effectively in terms of both quantity and quality.

infrastructure. Services such as roads, bridges, ports, airports, housing, hospitals, educational establishments, etc which are a vital underpinning of industry and the economy, largely in a way difficult to quantify, but do not have the direct effect on *economic growth* of, for example, industrial production. See also *capital-output ratio*.

in-house training. As *in-company training*.

injection. Injecting *purchasing power* into the *circular flow of income* in an economy, most commonly in the form of government expenditure or exports or industrial investment. The opposite is a withdrawal, normally through *savings*, taxation or imports. Government policy will tend to stress withdrawals at a time of *inflation*, but injections when the flow of income is not great enough to sustain *full employment*.

injury benefit. Under the UK *National Insurance (Industrial Injuries) Acts*, injury benefit may be payable to an employee for up to 156 days when he/she is unable to work following an injury or contraction of disease at the place of employment. Normally, benefit cannot be claimed for three 'waiting days'. A recipient of injury benefit cannot receive either *unemployment benefit* or *sickness benefit* but may also receive *earnings-related supplement with injury benefit*. *Disablement benefit* is also payable under the National Insurance (Industrial injuries) Acts. See also *Industrial Injuries Advisory Committee*.

ink blot test. See *Rorschach test*.

Inkomstenbelasting. *Netherlands income tax*, a *progressive tax* charged on net total income. There is also a flat-rate net *wealth tax* on property.

Inland Revenue. UK government agency

167

responsible for assessment and collection of income tax. See also the *Internal Revenue Service* (US).

inntektsskatt til kommunen. Local *income tax* in Norway charged on net total income. See *Norwegian income tax.*

inntektsskatt til statskassen. Norwegian state *income tax,* a graduated or *progressive tax* charged on a *slice scale* on total income from all sources. See *Norwegian income tax.*

in-plant training. As *in-company training.*

input(s). 1. Information and data fed into calculations as in *computers.* The results of the calculations are the *ouput(s).* **2.** *Value added tax* term for the tax on the value of goods and services at the beginning of a particular stage in their production or distribution. The tax on their value at the end of the stage is known as the *output.* The tax payable on that particular stage is the difference between the input and the output. **3.** The materials and resources fed into a process or department.

input buffer. To overcome the problem that the *input device* of a *computer* cannot operate as fast as its *central processing unit,* an input buffer makes it possible for more than one input device to be used so that the central processing unit is not delayed.

input device. Interpreter between human beings and a *computer,* designed to translate the language of people into a *machine code* and *computer language* comprehensible and acceptable to the *internal memory* of the computer's *central processing unit.* Tools of the input device's trade include *punched cards* and *paper tape* and, less commonly, *character recognition systems* and *light pens,* all designed for the purpose of supplying the internal memory with data and program instructions.

input-output analysis. *Market research* technique for setting out the purchases and sales between industries so that management can the more easily identify markets to be attacked. Input-output tables can present a very complex picture of multi-trading between industries enabling the market analyst to trace indirect demand for a product as well as the more straightforward direct demand. Comparison of input-output tables over a period of time can also give indications of changes in technology and consumer tastes.

INSEAD. *European Institute of Business Administration.*

insert. Loose and separately printed *advertisement,* enclosed with a journal or other publication.

insertion charge. Payment to be made to a newspaper, journal or other publication for carrying an advertisement or *insert.*

in-service training. Training undertaken during employment or service in order to develop capabilities relevant to that employment.

inside director. As *executive director.*

insider trading. Where directors, executives (or their close relatives or associates) take advantage of their inside knowledge of a company to make profit from dealing in the company's shares before such knowledge becomes available to the public. Such inside knowledge or information might involve impending *mergers,* new profit announcements, impending bankruptcies, etc. See also *nominee holdings, warehousing* and *incestuous share dealing.*

insolvency. Inability to pay debts as they become due.

instalment purchase. US term for *hire-purchase.*

Institute for the Future (IFF). American non-profit, tax exempt research organization established in 1968 in order to develop comprehensive computer oriented systems for forecasting and controlling the future.

Institute for Workers' Control. UK organization promoting the cause of workers' control in industry.

Institute of Administrative Management (IAM). UK professional body, formerly the Institute of Office Management.

Institute of Chartered Accountants in England and Wales. Major professional and qualifying body.

Institute of Chartered Accountants of Scotland. Major professional and qualifying body.

Institute of Chartered Secretaries and Administrators (UK). Professional and qualifying body for *company secretaries* and other administrators.

Institute of Cost and Management Accountants. UK professional body with membership of about 10,500 individual members. Concerned with developing *management accounting* practice (practise) and techniques.

Institute of Directors. UK organization with some 45,000 members who are all *company directors*.

Institute of Directors in Australia. See *Australia, Institute of Directors in.*

Institute of Export (UK). Provides overseas sales promotion service, and conducts professional examinations and specialized courses of value to exporters and potential exporters. See also *confirming house* and *export club.*

Institute of Freight Forwarders (UK). Professional body for, and source of advice on, *shipping and forwarding agents.*

Institute of Linguists. UK professional body established in 1910. Services include supplying names of translators able to deal with business correspondence and commercial literature. Translators may be members of the *Translators' Guild,* a branch of the Institute. See also *Centre for Information on Language Teaching.*

Institute of Management Consultants. UK professional body for individual management consultants (as distinct from the *Management Consultants Association,* which is a *trade association* for management consultant firms).

Institute of Management Services (UK) Professional and qualifying body in the fields of work study, organization and methods, etc.

Institute of Manpower Studies (IMS) (UK). Independent, national centre (center) of knowledge and practical experience in the fields of manpower management, labo(u)r market studies, issues of employment policy and manpower information. Located at Sussex University and London School of Economics.

Institute of Marine Engineers (UK). Member organization of the *Council of Engineering Institutions.*

Institute of Marketing. UK professional organization and examining body. The Institute also provides sales and marketing courses at its College of Marketing.

Institute of Personnel Management (IPM). UK professional personnel management organization offering a variety of services to companies and to individual managers concerned with the personnel and training functions. The IPM advises and is represented on a wide range of Government and other bodies. Services to members include an appointments service, an information and library service, the monthly publications, 'Personnel Management' and 'Digest'. Grades of membership are Member (MIPM) and Associate Member (AMIPM).

Institute of Public Relations. Professional body for *public relations officers (PROs)* in the UK.

Institute of Purchasing and Supply (InstPS). UK professional and examining body. Grades of membership are Member (MInstPS), Graduate and Student.

Institute of Scientific Business (UK). Professional institute for management studies graduates.

Institute of Supervisory Management (ISM). UK professional organization for foremen and supervisors. Provides information and training service for industry. See also *British Institute of Management.*

Institute of Trade Mark Agents (UK). Can provide a list of names and addresses of trade mark agents able to advise on trade marks and their registration with the Patent Office. These agents also advise on registration applications in overseas countries, particularly in countries that subscribe to the *International Convention for the Protection of Industrial Property.* See also *Chartered Institute of Patent Agents.*

institutional advertising. As *prestige advertising.*

institutional expectancy chart. Sometimes used following *psychological testing* in an attempt at predicting the levels of efficiency within a workforce, note being made of such factors as the number of workers expected to be of above-average performance. Another form of *expectancy chart* is the *individual expectancy chart* used in predicting the degree of success a candidate or employee would have in a particular occupation. Expectancy charts have been particularly highly developed in the USA. See also *personnel selection.*

Institution of Chemical Engineers (UK).

Member organization of the *Council of Engineering Institutions*.

Institution of Civil Engineers (UK). Member organization of the *Council of Engineering Institutions*. This institution is the most senior and longest standing of UK professional engineering institutions.

Institution of Electrical Engineers (UK). Member organization of the *Council of Engineering Institutions*.

Institution of Electronic and Radio Engineers (UK). Member organization of the *Council of Engineering Institutions*.

Institution of Gas Engineers (UK). Member organization of the *Council of Engineering Institutions*.

Institution of Industrial Managers (IIM). UK professional, qualifying and examining body for works managers etc.

Institution of Industrial Safety Officers. UK professional and examining body. Grades of membership are Fellows, Members, Graduate Members, Associates and Students.

Institution of Mechanical Engineers (UK). Member organization of the *Council of Engineering Institutions*.

Institution of Mining and Metallurgy (UK). Member organization of the *Council of Engineering Institutions*.

Insitution of Mining Engineers (UK). Member organization of the *Council of Engineering Institutions*.

Institution of Municipal Engineers (UK). Member organization of the *Council of Engineering Institutions*.

Institution of Production Engineers (UK). Member organization of the *Council of Engineering Institutions*.

Institution of Structural Engineers (UK). Member organization of the *Council of Engineering Institutions*.

Institution of Training Officers (ITO). UK professional association of practising training officers.

institutions. *Stock exchange* term for certain large organizations that have large shareholdings in various public companies and whose buying and selling of *shares* has a major influence on the stock market and, sometimes, the control of particular companies.

Inst M. *Institute of Marketing.*

Inst PS. *Institute of Purchasing and Supply.*

Instr (test). Ability to follow instructions test. See *test-battery*.

instructional objectives. Or behavio(u)ral objectives or performance objectives. Statements concerning the observable performance or behavio(u)r of which a trainee will be capable after a specific course of instruction.

instruction code (or set). As *machine code* (computer).

Instructor Training Colleges and Units. The UK *Training Services Division* provides one and two week instructional techniques courses at its two Instructor Training Colleges and at Units attached to the *Skillcentres*. Original ITCs started 1940.

instrumented laboratory training (IT). Form of *T-group training* with emphasis on systematic feedback, using *rating scales, check lists, rankings.*

insurance. Tends to be used interchangeably with *assurance* in practice (practise) but, technically, an insurance policy is taken out against what might happen while an assurance policy covers what is bound to happen (eg death and therefore payment of life cover) but at an unknown time.

Insurance and Companies Department (DT). Provides information for UK firms on company legislation, insurance other than export credit insurance, etc.

insurance broker. Arranges business between insurance companies and insured individuals, companies and organizations, acting for the insurance company.

insurance company. Company that enters into contracts with individuals or with companies, organizations, etc to pay compensation in specific circumstances in return for the regular payment of insurance premiums. Sometimes an insurance company does business with an insured person or organization through an *insurance broker*.

insurance underwriter. Member of a syndicate or a firm concerned with assessing and arranging *insurance* cover. See, for example, *Lloyds Corporation*.

insured employment. Economist's term for labo(u)r force requirements, that is, jobs available or, in times of scarcity, jobs taken.

intangible assets. Items which are considered to have a value and be worthy of inclusion in the *balance sheet* but are physically non-existent. They include *goodwill* and *patents*. See also *fictitious assets*.

integer programming. Mathematical programming technique that can be of more practical use than orthodox *linear programming* in some situations in that it works to nearest whole numbers and does not leave management with the problem of rounding off different quantities.

integral job evaluation. *Job evaluation* approach in which whole jobs are compared as a whole, as opposed to the approaches of *analytic job evaluation* or *dominant element job evaluation*. Integral job evaluation uses such techniques as *job grading* and *job ranking*. Sometimes known as whole-job evaluation.

integrated data processing (IDP). Term used of data processing, usually computerized, that brings together the different activities in running a company or organization. See also *electronic data processing*.

integrated learning system. Combined and planned use of a variety of methods of instruction and teaching aids (eg *audio-visual aids*) to achieve specified goals. See *integrated programmed instruction*.

integrated manager. One whose style of management is to be fully involved with individuals and groups. Characteristics include emphasis on group results, participation and involvement and frequent briefing meetings.

integrated programmed instruction. Including programmed instruction in an integrated learning system together with other educational aids, lectures, tutorials, practical work, etc. Cf *automated programmed instruction*.

integration. Special meaning is the process of levelling up the differences in terms and conditions of *blue collar* and *white collar* employment, and of the so-called *grey (gray) area occupations* in between. Where complete integration is achieved — that is where both blue and white collar workers have *staff status* — the employees are said to have *single status*. Integration in this sense is sometimes known as *mensualization* or *harmonization*, particularly in the *Common Market* countries.

intelligence quotient. See *IQ*.

intelligence tests. Form of *psychological testing* used for a wide range of applications but having a special usefulness for *personnel selection* purposes where those taking the test have no previous experience of the work in question so that it is necessary to identify which of them can be trained for the work. Other forms of psychological testing include *aptitude tests*, and *temperament and personality tests*. The term, 'intelligence testing', is sometimes used of *non-verbal intelligence tests* and *verbal intelligence tests* possibly as part of a *test-battery*.

interaction matrix. Design tool used in arranging plant layouts, activity relationships, etc particularly where physical positioning is a vital consideration. An example of an interaction matrix is illustrated overleaf. Another form of matrix is that used in the *morphological approach*.

interactive behavio(u)r. Behavio(u)r between members of a group. See *interactive skills*, *interface behavio(u)r*.

interactive skills. Skills in interacting with others in a group and in making a group work more effectively through the development of the social sensitivity of the individuals. Clashes of interest between the group members and their functions are said to raise questions of *territorial rights*. Interactive skills are involved in such group training methods as *group dynamics* and *T-group training*.

Inter-African Labo(u)r Institute. Set up in 1953 as an information and research centre on labo(u)r relations in Africa. It has members in some 30 countries.

Inter-American Commercial Arbitration Commission. Set up in 1934 to provide arbitration for the settlement of commercial disputes.

Inter-American Development Bank (IDB). Set up in 1959 to promote economic and social development, partly through the provision of technical assistance. Member

171

Inter-American Municipal Organization

countries include Argentina, Barbados, Bolivia, Brazil, Chile, Colombia, Costa Rica, Dominica, Ecuador, El Salvador, Guatemala, Haiti, Honduras, Jamaica, Mexico, Nicaragua, Panama, Paraguay, Peru, Trinidad and Tobago, the USA, Uruguay and Venezuela.

Inter-American Municipal Organization. Set up in 1938 to promote the study and development of municipal and urban administration. It has national organizations in some 20 countries.

Inter-American Nuclear Energy Commission (IANEC). Set up in 1959 as an agency of the *Organization of American States (OAS)*. It has the same member countries and the same address as the OAS.

Inter-American Regional Organization of Workers. Or Organizacion Regional Interamericana de Trabajadores (ORIT). Set up in 1951 to represent workers' interests, the Organization has members in some 40 countries.

interchangeability. Removal of demarcations between types of labo(u)r and jobs, having the advantage for employers of more economical use of labo(u)r and for employees of greater *job security*. See also *mobility of labo(u)r*.

intercompany comparison. As *interfirm comparison*.

interest. Money paid for the use of capital. Interest paid on shares is normally termed *dividend*. See also *yield*.

interest inventory. See *interest test or inventory*.

interest test or inventory. Used in *personnel selection*, career guidance, etc to obtain information on the personal and or leisure interests of candidates or employees. The theory is that such information can be an indication of abilities that might be put to use at work or can point to whether a person is likely to be happy in a particular working environment. Interest tests or inventories have been particularly highly developed in the USA, but they are also being used increasingly in the UK and other countries as well. Examples of interest inventories include the *APU occupational interests guide*, the *Connolly occupational interests questionnaire*, the *Kuder preference record*, the *Rothwell-Miller interest blank*, and the *Strong vocational interest blank*. See also *psychological testing*.

interface. 1. Equipment linking two parts of a *computer* system, particularly the *peripheral equipment* and the *central processing unit*. **2.** May also be used of the point of contact between people, jobs, systems, etc.

interface behavio(u)r. Behavio(u)r taking

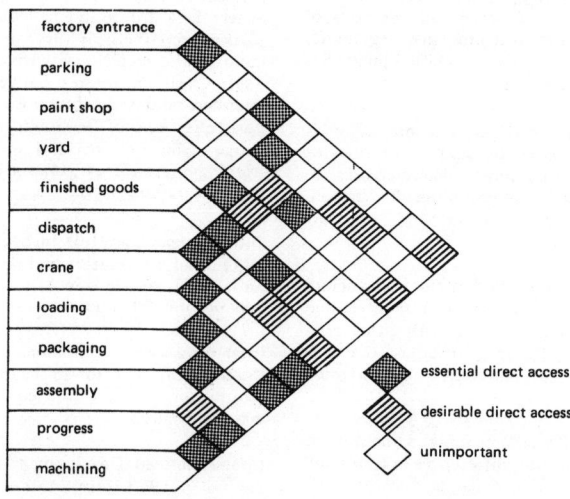

interaction matrix

place at the *interface* between jobs.

interference pay (or allowance). Payment made to an employee on a *payment-by-results* scheme where he has to interrupt his work to carry out other work the employer requires to be done. See also *fall-back pay*.

interfirm comparison. Method of checking company and management performance by comparing a wide range of data from firms with similar general characteristics in terms of production, sales, costs, etc. Such data for comparison might, for example, range across labo(u)r turnover, proportion of direct to indirect labo(u)r, stocks carried, variety of products, sales promotion, expenditure on research and development, etc. See also *intrafirm comparison* and *Centre for Interfirm Comparison*.

intermediary. 1. General term for a third party linking the main parties to negotiations or a business deal. **2.** Special meaning in the USA of a shareholder having *nominee holdings* or *intermediary holdings*.

intermediary holdings. As *nominee holdings*.

Intermediate Area. One of the forms of *Assisted Area* designated under the *Industry Act 1972* (UK) together with *Special Development Areas* and *Development Areas*. Employers in the Intermediate Areas can qualify for *Department of Industry regional development grants* for buildings and works but not for plant, machinery or mining works, though special tax allowances are available on buildings. They may also qualify for selective assistance in the form of a loan, for a DI *advance factory*, and for Department of Employment training assistance.

internal audit. Constant appraisal of the efficiency of management control systems etc in a company or organization by an internal audit executive or unit which reports directly to top management. To preserve his objectivity, an internal auditor does not normally check or audit any system that he might have been involved in setting up himself.

internal control questionnaire. Accounting/audit document designed to probe the effectiveness of procedures and the way in which they are being implemented. Analysis of the questionnaire leads to an *internal control report*.

internal control report. Accounting/*audit* term for a report based on the evidence of returns in an *internal control questionnaire*.

internal labo(u)r market. See *labo(u)r market*.

internal memory (or store). Part of the *central processing unit* of a *digital computer*. Produces information at the command of the *program control unit* for calculation by the *arithmetic unit*. The internal memory, consisting of a series of magnetic storage devices, stores data or program instructions in the form of 'words' or 'characters'. See also *computer*.

internal rate of return (IRR). Or *actuarial return*. The return on a project or enterprise as measured by *discounted cash flow* techniques. Also known as *investment rate*.

internal revenue. Income from taxation levied by a government within its country.

Internal Revenue Service. US government department responsible for the administration and collection of *income tax*, as is the *Inland Revenue* in the UK.

International Accountants' Society Inc. US professional accounting body.

International Advertising Association Inc (US). Set up in 1938 to promote advertising standards and the free market concept internationally. See also *European Association of Advertising Agencies*.

International Air Transport Association (IATA). Set up in 1945 to collaborate on international air transport and to promote safe and economical services. Some 90 international air lines are full members and some 20 domestic air lines are associate members. Based in Canada and Switzerland.

International Association for the Protection of Industrial Property. Set up in 1897 to promote the international protection of *patent* rights, the Association has members in more than 70 countries. Based in Switzerland. See also *International Patent Institute* and *International Union for the Protection of Industrial Property*.

International Association of Conference Interpreters. Professional body set up in 1953 and having approximately 1,000 members. Based in Switzerland.

International Association of Conference Translators. Professional body set up in 1962 and having more than 200 members in some 15 countries. Based in Switzerland.

International Association of Machinists and Aerospace Workers. *Trade union* in the USA and Canada, established in 1889 and having more than 900,000 members.

International Atomic Energy Agency. *United Nations* affiliated organization that seeks to promote the peaceful uses of atomic energy. Based in Austria.

International Bank for Reconstruction and Development. Or *World Bank.* Independent organization having a special relationship with the United Nations Organization which sponsored the Bank's beginnings, at the same time as the *International Monetary Fund*, at the *Brętton Woods Conference*, New Hampshire, USA in July 1944. The Bank helps to develop member countries by facilitating the use of its own or private capital for investment program(me)s. Its brief also includes the stimulation of international trade. The Bank is based in Washington, USA, and has 18 Executive Directors (who elect the President) together with a Board of Governors representing each of the Bank's 100-plus member states. In 1956 the Bank set up the *International Finance Corporation* to concentrate on underdeveloped countries, and in 1960 it established another affiliate, the *International Development Association.* Based in USA.

International Brotherhood of Teamsters, Chauffeurs, Warehousemen and Helpers of America. Usually abbreviated to the 'Teamsters'. The largest *trade union* in the USA and Canada, established in 1903 and having some two million members.

International Bureau of Fiscal Documentation. Set up in 1938, the Bureau provides advice on fiscal law and international taxation. Based in the Netherlands.

International Center for Settlement of Investment Disputes. Offshoot of the *World Bank,* the Center exists to advise in the settlement of disputes between nation states and overseas investors. Based in USA.

International Chamber of Commerce (ICC). Set up in 1919 as the international focal point for *chambers of commerce.* Based in France.

International Chemical Workers' Union (ICWU). Large *trade union* in the USA and Canada, established in 1940.

International Civil Aviation Organization (ICAO). *United Nations* agency charged with working for international cooperation on air transport and air navigation. Based in Canada.

international company. As *multi-national company.*

International Confederation of Arab Trade Unions (ICATU). Set up in 1956, the confederation has member *trade unions* in some 13 countries.

International Confederation of Chemical and General Workers Unions (ICF). Worldwide confederation of *trade unions* that keeps an increasingly close watch on the activities of international governmental organizations and *multinational companies.* A similar role is performed by the *International Metalworkers Federation (IMF).*

International Confederation of Free Trade Unions (ICFTU). Established in 1949 by a number of national trade union organizations, including the *Trades Union Congress* (UK), the *American Federation of Labor* and the *Congress of Industrial Organizations* (USA), as an alternative to the *World Federation of Trade Unions.* The latter organization was frowned upon by most ICFTU members on the grounds that its member trade union organizations from Communist countries were not democratic and independent.

International Convention for the Protection of Industrial Property. Agreement between major countries of the world under which an application for protection of a *patent, trade mark* or industrial property rights in the member countries of the Convention can bear the same date as the corresponding application in the applicant's home country. To qualify for the Convention's protection in the member countries, the application must be made within twelve months of the home country application in the case of patents or within six months in the case of designs or trade marks.

International Cooperative Alliance (ICA). Set up in 1895 as an international focal point for the cooperative movement. Based in UK.

International Council for Scientific Management (CIOS). Set up in 1924 to disseminate information on management techniques, etc. The Council's members are national organizations of some 40 countries. Based in Switzerland.

International Council of Scientific Unions (ICSU). Set up in 1931 with the object of promoting cooperation in the pure and applied sciences. Based in Rome.

International Court of Justice. Established at The Hague in April 1946 as the main judicial body of the *United Nations* and, in effect, an international arbitration tribunal between nations. See also *European Court of Justice.*

international credit clubs. Reciprocal agreements between leading European finance houses to arrange finance for the import and export of goods between their respective countries. See also *confirming house, export club, export house, export leasing,* and *shipping and forwarding agents.*

International Development Agency. See *Agency for International Development (AID).*

International Development Association. Affiliate of the *International Bank for Reconstruction and Development* (the *World Bank*), created in 1960 to concentrate particularly on using low-interest loans to stimulate economic growth in less developed countries. See also the World Bank's *International Finance Corporation.* Based in USA.

International Economic Association. Set up in 1949 to promote international collaboration particularly between individual economists, and to disseminate economic information. Based in France.

International Federation of Business and Professional Women. Set up in 1930 to promote the interests of women in business and the professions. The Federation has members in more than 50 countries. Based in UK.

International Federation of Stock Exchanges. Or Fédération Internationale des Bourses de Valeurs. Set up in 1961 to promote understanding among its member stock exchanges and to represent them internationally.

International Finance Corporation (IFC). Comes under the *United Nations* and is an affiliate of the *World Bank* and the *International Development Association.* The role of the IFC is to stimulate private investment and enterprise in the developing countries. Based in USA.

International Fiscal Association. Set up in 1938 to promote the international study of public finance, fiscal law and taxation. It has members in more than 60 countries. Based in the Netherlands.

International Industrial Relations Association. Set up in 1966 to disseminate knowledge and promote the study of industrial relations internationally. Based in Switzerland.

International Institute for Human Labo(u)r Problems. Set up in 1958, the Institute has members in some 30 countries. Based in Belgium.

International Labo(u)r Organization (ILO). Geneva-based body set up under the *United Nations.* See also *Article 98 of the ILO; Right to Organize and to Bargain Collectively,* and *Article 87; Freedom of Association and Protection of the Right to Organize.*

International Management Association, Inc. Set up in 1956 as an affiliate of the *American Management Association,* it has management centres in Argentina, Belgium, Brazil, Canada, Mexico, and Venezuela.

International Metalworkers Federation (IMF). World-wide confederation of *trade unions* that keeps an increasingly close watch on the activities of international governmental organizations and *multinational companies.* A similar role is performed by the International Confederation of Chemical and General Workers Unions (ICF). The IMF works closely with the *European Metalworkers Federation.*

International Monetary Fund (IMF). Independent organization having a special relationship with the *United Nations* which sponsored the Fund's beginnings, at the same time as the *International Bank of Reconstruction and Development* (the *World Bank*), at the *Bretton Woods Conference,* New Hampshire, USA, in July 1944. The Fund's brief is to promote international trade, employment and real income in its member countries, and stability of exchange rates, the latter being fixed in relation to the value of gold and the USA dollar. Member states pay into the Fund a specified quota, of which 25 per cent must be in gold (provided this is not equivalent to more than 10 per cent of the member state's official gold and dollar holdings; if it is, it pays the latter). The International Monetary Fund has a Managing Director, a Board of Executive Directors, and a Board of Governors representing each of its 100-plus member states.

International Organization for Standards (IOS). Established 1946 to bring about international agreement on industrial, technological and commercial standards. The national standards institutions of some 50 countries are members, including *American National Standards Inc* and the *British Standards Institution*. Based in Switzerland.

International Organization of Consumers' Unions (IOCU). Set up in 1960 to promote national consumers' unions and the comparative testing of products. The Organization has member organizations in some 35 countries. Based in the Netherlands.

International Organization of Employers (IOE). Set up in 1920 and concerned particularly with the *private sectors* of national industries. Based in Switzerland.

International Patent Institute. Set up in 1947 to advise individuals on the registering of *patents* in different countries and to undertake documentary research. The members of the Institute are the governments of Belgium, France, Luxembourg, Monaco, the Netherlands, Switzerland, Turkey and the UK. Based in the Netherlands. See also *International Association for the Protection of Industrial Property* and *Internation Union for the Protection of Industrial Property*.

International Public Relations Association. Set up in 1955 to promote *public relations* knowledge and practice (practise) internationally. Based in Switzerland.

International Savings Bank Institute. Set up in 1925, the Institute is an advice and intelligence centre (center) serving savings banks in more than 40 countries. Based in Switzerland.

International Secretariat for Volunteer Service (ISVS). Set up in 1962 to encourage and provide back-up services for national volunteer service organizations. There are more than 50 countries in membership. Based in Switzerland.

International Standard Classification of Occupations (ISCO). Developed by the *International Labo(u)r Organization (ILO)* as a basis for international comparison. See *occupational classification or group* and *socio-economic status*.

International Standard Industrial Classification. See *standard industrial classification*.

International System (SI). Or SI Units (Systeme International d'Unités). System of metric units of measurement that has gained widespread acceptance in more than 50 countries as a means of handling all forms of measurement. The *International Organization for Standards* (ISO) has developed a wide range of recommendations based on SI Units. Basic units of the SI system include the metre (length), the kilogramme (mass or weight force), the second (time), and the ampere (electric current). The International System is superseding the *US Customary System* in the USA for many purposes, particularly scientific and technical work. Similarly, it is superseding the *British Imperial System (BIS)* in the UK.

International Telecommunication Union (ITU). *United Nations* agency charged with encouraging international cooperation in the use and technical development of telecommunication. The ITU pre-dates the UN, having been set up in 1934 as the successor to the former International Telegraph Union. Based in Switzerland.

international trade federation. Organization of national *trade unions* with membership from particular industries or occupations. A dozen such federations are linked with the *World Confederation of Labo(u)r*. See also *international trade secretariat*.

International Trade Organization (ITO). Was to have been the administrative body of the abortive Havana Charter, 1947-48, on world trade and tariffs. Instead, the weaker *General Agreement on Tariffs and Trade (GATT)* was established with the *Organization for Trade Cooperation* as its administrative body.

international trade secretariat. Organization of national *trade unions* with membership from particular industries or occupations. Such secretariats are linked with the *International Confederation of Free Trade Unions*. See also *international trade federation*.

International Transport Workers' Federation (ITF). *Trade union* organization.

international union. *Trade union* with an international membership, particularly a US union with members in neighbo(u)ring countries.

International Union for the Protection of Industrial Property. Set up in 1883 to develop the international protection of *patent* rights. The Union's members are the governments of some 80 countries. Based in Switzerland. See also *International Association for the Protection of Industrial Property* and *International Patent Institute*.

International Union, United Automobile, Aerospace and Agricultural Implement Workers of America. *Trade union* in the USA and Canada, established in 1935 and having some 1,400,000 members.

interpersonal response trait. More or less stable and consistent disposition of an individual to respond to other persons in a characteristic way.

interrogation program. See *file interrogation program*.

Interstate Commerce Commission (ICC). US Government agency concerned with the regulation and supervision of commercial activities between states.

Interstate Conference of Employment Security Agencies Inc. US organization whose members represent state employment agencies as an information source on federal legislation in areas of job placement, *unemployment benefits* and manpower program(me)s.

intervening bank. Bank acting in a particular matter for an overseas bank or business.

intervention. In *organization development*, the action a third party or *change agent* takes in influencing the processes of the organization and the way in which it and the people within it respond to change.

intervention price (EEC). Under the *Common Agricultural Policy* of the *Common Market* or *European Economic Community*, the *European Commission* buys in surpluses of cereals at an intervention price to help producers in the member states achieve the official *target price*. See also *guide price, threshold price, sluice-gate price, reserve (or fall-back) price,* and *export subsidy (or restitution).*

interviewing procedures. General types of interview include the *connected conversation interview,* the *directive interview,* and the *non-directive interview*. Types of interview used particularly in *personnel section* include the *seven point plan,* the *five fold grading scheme,* the *panel interview,* and *group selection* interviews.

intracompany comparison. As *intrafirm comparison*.

intrafirm comparison. Systematic comparison of the levels of performance and profitability of the different departments within a company or organization. See also *interfirm comparison*.

in-tray exercise. Simulation of working situation by presenting trainee with an in-tray of memos, documents, letters, etc. The object is to deal with all the paperwork and make decisions within a given time. Also known as in-basket method.

intrinsic branching program(me). Form of *programmed instruction* where response of a trainee/student to the preceding *frame* determines frame to which he is directed or taken. Correct *responses* take trainee/student along main sequence of frames, sidetracking on to *remedial frames* or loops of frames as necessary. Student response to a frame usually measured by answer selected on *multiple choice* basis. See also *adaptive program(me), linear program(me), scrambled book/text,* and *skip program(me).*

intrinsic value. Term usually used to mean the intrinsic value of material before the added value of manufacture, etc.

introversion/extroversion. One of the spectra on which measurements are made in *temperament and personality testing*.

INTUC. *Indian National Trade Union Congress.*

inventory. Accounting term for the *cost of materials being processed in a firm at a given point in time, including *raw materials, work-in-progress* and *finished products*. Also applied to actual physical stock or the list of stock items.

inventory control. Or *stock control*. Use of various techniques to optimize levels of all types of stock, *raw materials, work-in-progress* and *finished goods*. Inventory control takes into account such factors as sales forecasts, economic batch quantities, *production planning and control,* etc.

inventory management. As *stock control*, but possibly taking into account plant, equipment, etc as well as stocks and products.

inventory turnover. Or *stock turnover*. Method of measuring aspects of business performance by comparing the inventory for an organization at different points in time or the inventories for similar organizations at the same point in time. See also *interfirm comparison* and *management ratios*.

Invercargill Stock Exchange. One of the *New Zealand stock exchanges*.

investment. Economist's term for spending current income on adding to *stocks* and to 'fixed' *capital*. In more everyday language investment is the making of an initial payment (as in the buying of *stocks* and *shares*) or a sacrifice in kind in the hope and expectation of receiving a return in the form of a regular *dividend* and/or a bigger repayment at a later date. One yardstick of company and/or management performance is *return on investment*. See also *consumption, depreciation, gross investment, industrial investment, net investment, social investment*.

investment appraisal. Analysis and evaluation of the return on investment of money etc. Also applicable to all management activity, including personnel, training, sales, etc even where it may not be possible to quantify the return precisely or where the investment is of executive time etc as well as (or instead of) money. Use of investment appraisal techniques in industry and commerce helps management avoid embarking on projects that would provide an inadequate *rate of return*. See also *discounted cash flow* and *pay-back*.

investment bank. Term used particularly in the USA for a bank that specializes in acquiring *new issues* and then selling them in smaller batches to investors, a role played in the UK by a *merchant bank* or an *issuing house*.

Investment Bankers Association of America. Established in 1912 as the central organization for investment bankers in the USA. The Association has some 630 members.

investment club. Group of people who invest jointly in an investment *portfolio* that can thus be larger and safer than any of the participants would be able to acquire on an individual basis.

investment rate. As *internal rate of return*.

investment trust (or company). Company that exists to invest its capital in other companies, usually in quoted *securities* but sometimes more riskily. An investment trust is said to have the advantage of giving small investors an opportunity to spread their investment widely and therefore safely. The difference between an investment trust and a *unit trust* is that investors are actually shareholders in the company in the case of the investment trust, while in the case of the unit trust the investors hold units which represent shares in the trust's investment *portfolio*.

invisible exports. Exports appearing in the *current account* of a country's *balance of payments* statement in the form of receipts for services such as banking, insurance, tourism, shipping, and profits and interest payments from overseas. Similarly, *invisible imports* appear under payments in the current account. There are also *visible exports* and *visible imports*.

invisible imports. Payments by a country for the kinds of services noted under *invisible exports*.

invoice. Document summarizing goods supplied, together with prices.

involuntary absenteeism. See *absenteeism*.

IOE. *International Organization of Employers*.

IOS. *International Organization for Standards*.

IPM. *Institute of Personnel Management (UK)*.

IQ. Or intelligence quotient. A measurement of intelligence expressed as a ratio of mental age to chronological age. Thus an IQ of 100 is the average for a particular age while an IQ of 140 is 40 per cent greater than average. The accuracy of IQ tests is sometimes challenged and so is their content, particularly on the grounds that they ignore certain important qualities such as creative abilities. See also *intelligence tests*.

Ireland, Central Bank of. Banc Ceannais na hÉireann, formed in 1942.

IRI. *Istituto per la Ricostruzione Industriale*, the Italian state company under which major parts of Italian industry have been nationalized.

Irish Association of Chambers of Commerce. Formed in 1923.

Irish Congress of Trade Unions. Formed 1959 and covering *trade unions* which have approximately 500,000 members, about 90 per cent of the organized workforce.

Irish Management Institute. Seeks to raise standards of management through courses, seminars, publications, etc.

Irish Stock Exchange. Modelled on, and in some ways an appendage of, the London *Stock Exchange*. It has been a member of the *Federation of Stock Exchanges in Great Britain and Ireland*, and in March 1973 became part of the *United Stock Exchange*. Activity on the Irish Exchange has been low, partly because investors' funds have been attracted by the greater activity of the London Stock Exchange. The two trading floors of the Irish Stock Exchange are in Dublin and Cork.

Iron and Steel Industry Trading Board (UK). Established July 1964 under the *Industrial Training Act 1964*.

ironclad contract. As *yellow-dog contract*.

iron law of oligarchy. Term of US origin meaning that real power in *trade unions* inevitably passes from the rank-and-file membership to its senior officers. The theory is of doubtful validity in the face of such developments as *autonomous bargaining* and *workplace bargaining*.

IRR. *Internal rate of return.*

irregular industrial action short of a strike. Term introduced by the *Industrial Relations Act 1971* (UK) and defined in section 33(4) of that Act as: 'Any concerted course of conduct (other than a strike) which, in contemplation or furtherance of an industrial dispute: **a** is carried on by a group of workers with the intention of preventing, reducing or otherwise interfering with the production of goods or the provision of services, and **b** in the case of some or all of them is carried on in breach of their contracts of employment or (where they are not employees) in breach of their terms and conditions of service.'

irrevocable documentary acceptance credit. Used in export trading. An overseas buyer opens a credit with a bank in the country of the exporter, the bank then issuing to the exporter a *letter of credit* in which it undertakes to accept a *bill of exchange* drawn on the bank against delivery of the relevant shipping documents.

irritation strike. Or *pearl strike* or *ca'canny*. Form of *industrial action* in which workers work badly and wastefully rather than directly going on strike. Sometimes a weapon of *syndicalism*.

IRS. *Internal Revenue Service* (US).

ISCO. *International Standard Classification of Occupations.*

Ishihara tests. Form of *colo(u)r vision test* supplied by the *National Foundation for Educational Research* (UK).

island. 1. *Display advertisement* surrounded by editorial material. **2.** Isolated *retail outlet* display.

ISM. *Institute of Supervisory Management.*

Israeli Stock Exchange. See *Tel Aviv Stock Exchange.*

issue by tender. Where tenders are invited for *shares* in a company and the shares are sold to the highest bidder(s).

issued capital (or share capital). *Nominal value* of all the *shares* or *securities* issued by a *company* or *corporation*. See also *paid-up capital.*

issuing house. Financial institution, often a *merchant bank*, which handles for client companies the raising of capital by new issues of *shares, securities,* etc. In some cases the client company will be *going public* — that is, converting from a *private company* to a *public company.*

Istanbul Menkul Kiymetler ve Kambiyo Borsasi. *Istanbul Stock Exchange.*

Istanbul Stock Exchange. Or Istanbul Menkul Kiymetler ve Kambiyo. A mid-nineteenth century foundation with a relatively low level of activity at the present time. The Stock Exchange is managed by a Commissioner, the *Hazine Komiseri*, appointed by the Minister of Finance.

Istituto per la Ricostruzione Industriale. Or *IRI*. Italian state company, a Government institution under which major parts of Italian industry have been nationalized.

ISVS. *International Secretariat for Volun-*

teer Service.

Italian central bank. *Banca d'Italia.*

Italian companies. Certain types of partnership are prescribed under Italian Civil Law, while other types of partnership conform to the Commercial Code. There are also companies under Italian law. The partnerships under Civil Law are; **a** Partnership in Fact or *Società di Fatto* where there is effectively a partnership though not a formal contract; **b** Irregular Partnership (or Company) or *Società Irregolari* where the proper legal formalities have not been completed; **c** Joint Venture or *Associazione in Partecipazione.* The forms of partnership under the Commercial Code are: **d** Partnership Limited by Shares or *Società in Accomandita per Azioni;* **e** Non Stock Company or *Società non Azionarie;* **f** Private Partnership or *Società Semplice;* **g** General Partnership or *Società in Nome Collettivo;* **h** Limited Partnership or *Società in Accomandita Semplice.* Corporations and companies under Italian law are: **i** Joint Stock Company or *Società per Azioni (SpA);* **j** Private Limited Liability Company or *Società a Responsabilita Limitata (Srl);* **k** Cooperative or *Società Cooperative.*

Italian Confederation of Autonomous Labo(u)r Unions. See *Confederazioni Italiana Sindicati Autonomi Lavoratori (CISAL).*

Italian Confederation of Labo(u)r Unions. See *Confederazione Italiana Sindicati Lavoratori (CISL).*

Italian Confederation of National Labo(u)r Unions. Confederazione Italiana Sindicati Nazionali Lavoratori (CISNAL).

Italian General Confederation of Labo(u)r. See *Confederazione Generale Italiana del Lavoro (CGIL).*

Italian income tax. Taxes on the different parts of an individual's income in Italy include: **a** land tax or *imposta sul reddito dominicale dei terreni* charged on annual rental value; **b** agricultural income tax or *imposta sul reddito agrario* charged on income from agriculture and assessed according to the value of property, investment, etc; **c** buildings tax or *imposta sul reddito dei Pabbricati* charged on annual rental value less up to 25 per cent of maintenance costs; and **d** a movable wealth tax or *imposta di ricchezza mobile sul reddito* charged on all income not subject to one of the earlier three taxes. There is also a progressive surtax or complementary tax known as the *imposta complementare progressiva sul reddito complessivo.* Italy also has a withholding tax charged on dividends and what is known as the family tax. The latter is a progressive municipal tax charged on the total income of each household. Another municipal tax is the communal tax on capital appreciation of real property known as the *imposta comunale sull' incremento di valore degli immobile.*

Italian Industry, General Confederation of. *Confederazione Generale dell'Industria Italiana (Confindustria).*

Italian Labo(u)r Union. See *Unione Italiana del Lavoro (UIL).*

Italian stock exchanges. Italy has a principal stock exchange at Milan and nine other stock exchanges. They are: **a** Milan – Borsa Valori di Milano; **b** Bologna – Agenti di Cambio; **c** Florence – Borsa Valori di Firenze. **d** Genoa – Borsa Valori di Genova; **e** Naples – Borsa Valori di Napoli. **f** Palermo – Borsa Valori di Palermo; **g** Rome – Borsa Valori di Roma; **h** Trieste – Borsa Valori di Trieste; **i** Turin – Borsa Valori di Torino; **j** Venice – Borsa Valori di Venezia. The Union of the Management Committees of the Italian Stock Exchanges (*Unione dei Comitati Derettivi delle Borsa Valori Italiane)* is based in Milan. Milan is the longest established of the Italian Exchanges (founded in 1808) and presently handles three-quarters of all Italy's stock exchange business. Members of the stock exchanges are stockbrokers, or *Agenti di Cambio,* who are public officials, together with non-bidding dealers, or *remisiers,* and observers from banks and credit institutions. See also *Italian companies.*

Italian trade unions. Twelve national federations of Italian *trade unions* are as follows: **a** Confederazione Artigiana Sindicati Autonomi (CASA), for artists' unions. **b** Confederazione Generale Italiana dell'Artigianato, formed in 1945 and covering some 150 unions. **c** Confederazione Generale Italiana de Professionisti e Artisti (CIPA), a white-collar organization covering some 20 trade unions. **d** Confederazione Generale Italiana del Lavoro (CGIL), a largely communist organization which covers 38 trade unions which have approximately 3,500,000 members. **e** Confederazione Italiana dei Dirigenti di Azienda (CIDA), an organization for management trade unions. **f** Confederazione Italiana Sindicati Autonomi Lavoratori (CISAL), the Italian

Confederation of Autonomous Labo(u)r Unions formed in 1957 and covering 57 trade unions which have approximately 300,000 members. **g** Confederazione Italiana Sindicati Lavoratori (CISL), the Italian Confederation of Labo(u)r Unions, a largely Christian Democrat organization formed in 1950 and covering 38 trade unions which have approximately 2,500,000 members. **h** Confederazione Italiana Sindicati Nazionali dei Lavoratori (CISNAL), a largely national syndicalist organization formed in 1950 and covering some 150 trade unions which have approximately 80,000 members. **i** Confederazione Nazionale del'Artigianoto (CNA), an organization of mainly provincial trade unions. **j** Federazione delle Associazione Nazionali dei Funzionari Direttivi della Amministrazione dello Stato (DIRSTAT), covering 36 trade unions. **k** Unione Italiana del Lavoro, a largely Social Democrat and Republican Federation formed in 1950 and covering some 50 trade unions which have approximately 500,000 members. **l** Unione Nazionale Sindacati Autonomi (UNSA), a federation covering some ten trade unions.

Italian Union of Chambers of Commerce. *Unione Italiana delle Camere di Commercio, Industria, Artigianato e Agricoltura.*

ITBs. *Industrial training boards.*

item analysis. Technique for selecting the items to be included in a *psychological test* so that they are relevant to both the purpose of the test and the people taking it.

iteration. Mathematical technique for performing a series of calculations repeatedly and making successive approximations, often using a digital computer. See *operational research.*

ITF. *International Transport Workers' Federation (ITF).*

ITO. 1. *International Trade Organization.* **2.** *Institution of Training Officers.*

ITU. *International Telecommunication Union.*

IVANOVO schedule. USSR shiftwork system which eliminates night work and allows employees two days off per week.

IWSP. *Institute of Work Study Practitioners* (UK).

j

Jamaica Stock Exchange Limited. One of two stock exchanges in the West Indies.

Japan Chamber of Commerce and Industry. *Nippon Shoko Kaigi-sho.*

Japan Federation of Employers' Associations. *Nihon Keieisha Dantai Renmei (NIKKEIREN).*

Japanese central bank. *Nippon Ginko.*

Japanese stock exchanges. Five major stock exchanges of Japan are: **a** Tokyo Stock Exchange; **b** Fukuoka Stock Exchange; **c** Hiroshima Stock Exchange; **d** Nagoya Stock Exchange; **e** Osaka Securities Exchange. There are also exchanges at Kobe, Sapporo, Nigata and Kyoto.

jerque note. Issued by a customs officer to certify that a ship's cargo is in order.

jet lag. Effect on a person of rapid air travel involving crossing a number of *time zones* and therefore having to adjust physically and mentally to a new diurnal rhythm or circle.

JIC. *Joint Industrial Council.*

JICNARS. *Joint Industry Committee for National Readership Surveys.*

jig and tool design. Design of new jigs, tools and equipment to meet the requirements of a new production run, or the design improvement of existing jigs and tools for use in existing or modified production runs.

job. Sum of the *tasks* carried out by an employee and, in a wider context, the social and physical environment in which he carries them out. Job is virtually synonymous with *role*.

job analysis. Examination of a job, its component parts and the circumstances in which it is performed. Purpose and slant of job analysis vary between *job evaluation, vocational guidance, personnel selection,* training, equipment, design, etc. Can be known as job study.

job-and-finish. System under which workers are free to leave work when they have completed an agreed amount of work rather than waiting until the normal *knocking-off time.* See also *flexible working hours* and *balancing time.*

jobber. See *stockjobber.*

jobber's turn. *Stockjobber's* profit margin between the buying and selling prices of *securities.*

jobbing production. As *job production.*

jobcentres. UK employment exchanges coming under the *Employment Service Division* and set up in various parts of the UK from mid-1973. Sited in town centres (centers), they offer three levels of service, namely **a** self-service section with details of available jobs, **b** an interviewing service for job-seekers needing advice, and **c** an *occupational guidance* service for job-seekers needing in-depth guidance. See also *Professional and Executive Recruitment* service.

job classification method. Non-analytical job evaluation technique involving the allocation of jobs into pre-determined job grades and/or levels. The characteristics of each grade will normally be defined in terms of level of responsibility or skill involved. Job classification schemes are often developed by means of *job ranking.* See also *job grading.*

job clinic. Technique used particularly in sales training where specific problems encountered by an individual are discussed with two or three colleagues and solutions suggested.

job cover plan. Usually drawn up following *manpower analysis* in *manpower planning* in the individual firm. Such a plan, often

183

presented in the form of a chart, carries a note of all the jobs and tasks in the firm or unit, both at present and in the predictable future, and of the extent to which each employee is capable of carrying out each of them. Special note is made of any problems of *undermanning* or *overmanning*, of individuals overworking in a manner damaging to their performance, of employees able to take on other jobs if necessary, of any impending technological change that will affect the demand for skills, of any marketing promotion that may affect demand for the firm's products, etc. The job cover plan provides an assessment of training needs on which a *training plan* can be based.

job description. Broad description of the purpose, scope, duties and responsibilities of a *job*. Also known as *position guide* or position statements.

job design. Designation of the activities and responsibilities of a *job* following *task analysis*, ie analysis of the tasks of which the job consists.

job engineering. Adapting responsibilities, methods, procedures and equipment of a *job* so changing its skill level. See also *de-skilling* and *ergonomics*.

job enlargement. Provision of *training* and practice (practise) in an increased range of skills in pursuit of *job enrichment* for the individual *employee* and/or a more flexible workforce for the *employer*.

job enrichment. Restructuring of job content and division of responsibility between jobs to increase the amount of responsibility in individual jobs and thus tend to an improvement in *job satisfaction*. A specialist involved in this process is the *occupational psychologist*.

job evaluation. Techniques used to establish the relative worth of jobs in a job hierarchy. The techniques may be **a** non-analytical, requiring the comparison of whole jobs and either placing them in rank order or assigning them to pre-determined grades (see *job classification, job grading, job ranking, integral job evaluation, non-analytic job evaluation* and *whole job ranking*); or **b** analytical, requiring the analysis and measurement of separately defined characteristics or factors such as responsibility, decisions or skill which are assumed to be common to all the jobs and will measure distances between them (see *analytic job evaluation, dominant element job evalu-* ation, *job factor comparison, points rating method,* and *profiling systems*); or **c** single factor, in which one factor is used as the basis for comparison (see *decision band method* and *time span analysis*). Also known as position evaluation (US).

job factor comparison. An analytical *job evaluation* technique used to define jobs and assess them in terms of certain common factors. Other job evaluation techniques include *decision band method, dominant element job evaluation, integral job evaluation, job grading, job ranking,* the *points rating method, profiling systems* and *time span analysis*. See also *factor comparison*.

job family. Group of *jobs* with basically similar content or skills. This term is used particularly in the USA in *psychological testing*.

job grading. Non-analytical *job evaluation* technique in which jobs with similar responsibilities, job content, etc are grouped into grades usually having similar rates of pay. Other job evaluation approaches include *decision band method, dominant element job evaluation, integral job evaluation, job classification method, job factor comparison, job grading, job ranking,* the *points rating method, profiling systems, factor comparison, points evaluation,* and *whole-job ranking*. See also *banding*.

job knowledge test. Or *trade test*. A term used particularly in the USA for an *achievement test* in a particular job or skill or range of skills. It is not, for example, concerned with testing an individual's potential after further training and/or experience.

job mobility. See *labo(u)r mobility*.

job number. In manufacturing, a numerical code assigned to each job or batch to aid identification etc throughout the process or journey through the works.

job preference survey, Purdue. See *Purdue job preference survey*.

job price contract. System of paying employees or contractors an agreed price for completing a specified job irrespective of how long it takes. See also *rate-fixing*.

job production. Manufacture of a single product to individual specifications. Differs from the quantity production of *batch production*, the standardized production of *mass production*, and the continuous production of *process production* or *assembly line* or *flow line production*.

job ranking. *Job evaluation* technique for determining the relative position of each job by comparison with all other jobs, though without indicating extent of difference between jobs at different levels. Other job evaluation techniques include *decision band method, dominant element job evaluation, integral job evaluation, job factor comparison, job grading,* the *points rating method, profiling systems* and *time span analysis.*

job requirements. Characteristics required of a worker to perform a particular job successfully. See *job specification.*

job restructuring. Modification of the job and responsibilities of the individual, by adding tasks of a similar level (horizontal restructuring) or tasks of a different level (vertical restructuring). See also *group working* and *organization structure.*

job rotation. Method, usually part of a *management development* plan, of moving managers or other employees between jobs to give them desired experience and know-how.

job sample test. Use of a *simulator* to test performance, actual or potential, in a job or range of jobs.

job satisfaction. Extent to which an employee is pleased or satisfied with the content and environment of his work or is displeased or frustrated by inadequate working conditions and tedious job content. The process of improving job satisfaction is often known as *job enrichment,* one of the special interests of the *occupational psychologist.*

job security. Extent to which an employee is assured that he will not lose his employment. This may be included in *collective agreements* under the head of *conditions of employment* or it may be written into individual *contracts of employment.* Job security or earnings security is also safeguarded to some extent by legislation such as the UK's *Redundancy Payments Act 1965.* See also *guaranteed working week.*

job shop. 1. In manufacturing, the organization of work by functions, such as drilling, assembly, machining, etc. **2.** Employment agency (US).

job specification. Based on *job analysis,* a detailed statement of the physical and mental activities demanded in a job. The term job specification is sometimes extended to include the qualifications, experience and personal qualities required to perform the job, although if this information is included the more appropriate term is *man specification.* See also *job requirements.*

job spoiler. Term used of a member of a *work group* who does not conform with that group's informally agreed *fiddle* or restricted output. The object of such restriction of output is usually to hide loose *piece work* rates or to smooth out piece work earnings. A member of a work group who conforms with a fiddle is known as a *conformer.* See also *rate-buster, high-flier* and *pacer.*

Jobs/Public Works Employment Act. US legislation of 1977 which sought to alleviate the impact of high *unemployment* in particular areas by instituting program(me)s of *public works.* The Act is administered by the *Economic Development Administration* of the *US Department of Commerce.*

job study. See *job analysis.*

job time. In *work measurement* the time for completing all the *elements* in a job.

Johannesburg Stock Exchange. One of two principal stock exchanges in South Africa.

joint consultation. Structure or procedure developed in the circumstances of a particular organization for promoting understanding and common purpose between management and employees. Traditionally, in joint consultation employees have *representational rights* to be consulted by management but not the much more comprehensive *negotiating* rights which are held under *collective bargaining* and which impinge more on *management prerogative.* See also *depth of trade union recognition.*

Joint Industrial Council. See *Whitley Committee on the Relations of Employers and Employed* and *Standing Joint Industrial Council.*

Joint Industry Committee for National Readership Surveys (UK). Committee of *advertising agents,* clients and publishers responsible for controlling newspaper and periodical readership surveys.

joint life and last survivor pension. Provides for an employee etc or for his wife if she survives him. A *single life pension,* on the other hand, provides only for the employee. See also *widows' and orphans' pension scheme*.

joint negotiating panel (of trade unions). Representatives of two or more organizations of workers or *trade unions* authorized by those organizations to engage in *collective bargaining* and enter into *collective agreements* on their behalf.

joint product. Two or more products requiring the same *raw materials* and processing in the early stages of production.

joint product offer. *Sales promotion* of two or more products at a reduced price, possibly in a *banded pack*.

joint regulation. Concept that managerial autonomy becomes modified in practice (practise) by a kind of balance of power between management and *trade unions*, imposing constraints that both sides come to accept. See also *pluralistic theory* and *countervailing power*.

joint shop stewards committee (JSSC). Official *multi-union* committee of which all *shop stewards* in a plant are members. JSSC normally elects a *convener* and an inner committee of senior shop stewards of the individual unions. See also *combine committee, industrial union* and *multi-union*.

joint stock bank. As *commercial bank*.

joint stock company. Original seventeenth century name for a company in which the liability of its members is limited to the nominal value of the shares taken up.

Joint Works Committee. See *Whitley Committee*.

journal. Or *day book*. Book of original entry in *double-entry bookkeeping* listing all transactions and indicating the specific accounts to which they belong.

journeyman. *Skilled man* who has completed an apprenticeship and is an employee, not an employer or a *self-employed* man. Originally a medieval term, when the journeyman was employed by a *guildmaster*. The terms artificer and artisan are virtually interchangeable with journeyman.

JSSC. See *joint shop stewards committee*.

Junta Sindical. Spanish Stock Exchange Committee. Composed of members of the exchange's Stockbrokers' Association or *Colegio de Agentes de Cambio y Bolsa*. See *Spanish stock exchanges*.

jurisdictional dispute (or issue). Question of which *trade union* should have the right to organize a particular group of workers. See also *multi-unionism, demarcation dispute, recognition dispute, Bridlington Principles, Croydon Procedure* (of the *TUC*).

k

(k). Coding for *spatial ability test* in the *engineering apprentice test-battery* of the National Institute of Industrial Psychology in the UK.

Kaiser Plan. Scheme adopted by the American Kaiser Steel Corporation and the Steelworkers Union to guarantee employees against possible loss of earnings or employment as a result of technological changes.

Kammer für Aussenhandel der Deutschen Demokratischen Republik. German Democratic Republic Chamber of Foreign Trade, established in 1952.

kangaroo court. Informal court with no legal standing, such as one conducted by workers to 'try' a colleague.

Kapitalertragsteuer. Capital yields tax on dividends and other distributions of company profits in Austria, Federal Germany and Luxembourg. Together with the wages tax *(Lohnsteuer)*, it forms the *income tax (Einkommensteuer)*. Austria also has the *Vermögensteuer*, a net wealth tax on the property of individuals; and the *Aufsichtratsabgabe*, a tax on fees paid to directors of Austrian companies. Germany has a flat-rate directors' tax, or *Aufsichtsratsteuer*, deducted at source from directors' fees paid to non-resident supervisory directors. Germany also charges a surcharge, or *Ergänzungsabgabe*, on *income tax*. In Luxembourg, Kapitalertragsteuer is also known by the French term, *retenue d'impôt sur les revenus de capitaux*.

Karachi Stock Exchange Limited. Pakistan's stock exchange, established in 1947.

Kartell. German for *cartel*. A form of international monopoly.

Kelly repertory grid. Technique sometimes used in *market research* interviews intended to establish *informants'* opinions on competing products and their *brand* images. The interviewer presents informants with the names of products in groups of three for them to select the product that is different from the other two and to describe how it is different. There is then a final sifting through all the products and brands in the test to check out the characteristics attributed to them. See also *triadic product test*.

Kennedy Round. Particularly significant agreement on general tariff reductions negotiated between member states of the *General Agreement on Tariffs and Trade (GATT)* between 1964 and 1967 on the initiative of the late US President John F Kennedy. The Kennedy Round also included a cereals agreement and the adoption of an *antidumping* code.

Kenya Stock Exchange. See *Nairobi Stock Exchange*.

key bargaining. As *pattern bargaining*.

keyed advertisement. One that is coded so that there can be an indication of the response to it. Thus the same advertisement appearing in several publications may be coded to show the pulling power of the different publications. See also *media analysis* and *split-run copy testing*.

key operation. Term used particularly in *work study* for the longest operation of two or more operations which take place at the same time and must all be completed before work can proceed to the next stage. See also *key task*.

key points/factors. Factors in *job analysis* vital to the performance of work and therefore of special note.

key punch. As *card punch*.

key results analysis. As *key task analysis*.

key task. One which conditions the time and/or quality of related *tasks* and the total *job* or operation which they form. See also *key operation*.

key task analysis. Or key results analysis. Analysis of key tasks to be performed, levels of performance required and methods of checking actual against desired performance. Used chiefly in management and supervisory training, though also in other training.

Key Workers Scheme (UK). Run by the *Department of Employment* to give assistance where an employer needs to transfer employees permanently or temporarily to a new plant in a *Special Development Area*, a *Development Area* or an *Intermediate Area*. For grant to be payable, the employees concerned must be key workers needed to install plant or machinery, to train local employees, or to form a nucleus around which a local labo(u)r force can be built. Another scheme run by the Department of Employment is the *Nucleus Labour Force Scheme*.

KG. *Kommanditgesellschaft,* or limited partnership under German company law. See also *Austrian companies* and *German (Federal) companies*.

KGaA. *Kommanditgesellschaft auf Aktien.* See also *German (Federal) companies*.

kibosh. Prohibition placed on a proposal or course of action. The term is most commonly expressed as 'to put the kibosh on . . .'

kick-back. Payment of money, usually a percentage payment, in confidence to someone able to influence or guide the agreeing of a business arrangement. Often the term is used to imply something corrupt or unsavo(u)ry about the payment. See also *rake-off*.

kicked upstairs. Term used of someone who is promoted in order to remove him from a position in which his inefficiency is creating problems. The term was first used of the elevation of people from the UK House of Commons to the House of Lords. See also *Peter Principle*.

kin(a)esthetics. Study of the use of body movements in conjunction with speech.

kirkeskat. Church tax, a form of *income tax* in Denmark in addition to national *income tax*, local tax and net *wealth tax*. See also *Danish income tax*.

kirkollisvero. Church *income tax* in Finland levied at a flat rate on members of the Orthodox and Evangelical Lutheran churches. This is in addition to state income tax, local income tax and net *wealth tax*. See also *Finnish income tax*.

kitchen cabinet. Group of personal aides gathered aroung a senior person in industry, politics, etc having responsibilities to that person rather than to the organization to which he belongs. See also *frictional overhead*.

kite. 1 Dud *cheque (check)*. 2 *Accommodation bill.*

Knights of Labor. Early US *trade union* which aimed at embracing all types of worker (see also *industrial union*). It originated in Philadelphia and between 1869 and 1886 developed a membership of about three-quarters of a million.

Knitting, Lace and Net Industry Training Board. Established March 1966 under the *Industrial Training Act 1964*.

knocked down. Of product, supplied in kit or sub-assembly form, usually to reduce bulk and hence freight costs etc.

knocking copy. *Advertising* which derides competitors' products or services.

knocking-off time. End of a working day or period.

know-how. Skill or ingenuity usually of a kind derived from practical experience.

Københavns Fondsbørs. *Copenhagen Stock Exchange.*

Kobe Stock Exchange. One of nine *Japanese stock exchanges*.

Kollektivgesellschaft. Or *Société en Nom Collectif*. A general partnership under Swiss company law. See also *Swiss companies*.

Kommanditaktiengesellschaft. Or *Société en Commandité par Actions*. A partnership limited by shares under Swiss company law. See also *Swiss companies*.

Kommanditgesellschaft. Limited partnership under Austrian, German or Swiss company law, being abbreviated to *KG* under German company law. An alternative name in Switzerland is Société en Comandité. See also *Austrian companies, German companies* and *Swiss companies*.

Kommanditgesellschaft auf Aktien. Abbr to

kommunal indkumstskat. KGaA. A limited partnership with shares under German company law. See *German (Federal) companies.*

kommunal indkumstskat. Local or county *income tax* in Denmark, as is *amtskommunal indkomstskat.* It is charged in addition to state income tax, special income tax, church tax and net *wealth tax.* See *Danish income tax.*

kommunal inkomstskatt. Flat-rate local *income tax* in Sweden. See *Swedish income tax.*

Konossement. German for *bill of lading.*

Korea Stock Exchange. See *Seoul Stock Exchange.*

KPRO. *Kuder Preference Record.*

krona. Basic unit of the currency of Sweden. Plural 'kronor'.

krone. Basic unit of the currencies of Denmark and Norway. Plural 'kroner'.

Kuala Lumpur Stock Exchange. Important stock exchange in Malaysia.

Kuder Preference Record. *Interest test* or *inventory* used in *personnel selection, careers guidance,* etc to build up a picture of the personal interests of a candidate or employee. The person being tested indicates his first and second choices in each of a number of groups of three activities. The items selected are scored according to the category to which they relate. See also *psychological testing.*

kunnallisvero. Local *income tax* in Finland charged in addition to state income tax, or *valtion tulovero,* and the church tax or *kirkollisvero.* See *Finnish income tax.*

kupongskatt. Or coupon tax, a flat-rate tax on dividends paid by Swedish companies to non-residents and certain residents. See *Swedish income tax.*

Kursmakler, amtliche. See *amtliche Kursmakler.*

Kyoto Stock Exchange. One of nine *Japanese stock exchanges.*

L

Labelling of Food Regulations 1970. UK legislation on the labelling of processed and packaged foods aimed at ensuring that the packets give an accurate and not misleading description of the contents. There are also requirements on the accuracy of lists of ingredients and of any pictorial representation. The regulations also require that the name and address of the manufacturer are given. Goods excluded from the regulations are biscuits, packaged cakes and margarine.

laboratory training. See *instrumented laboratory training*.

Labor Day (US). Or Labour Day (Canadian). First Monday in September, an official holiday in honour of the worker.

Labor Management Relations Act 1947 (US). Comprehensive legislation dealing with power of unions. Covers unfair union practices (practises), a federal mediation and conciliation service, strikes or lockouts in national emergencies. Also known as *Taft-Hartley Act*.

Labor-Management Reporting and Disclosure Act. Or *Landrum-Griffin Act*. US legislation of 1959 which requires public disclosure of certain information by labo(u)r unions and management. The Act is administered by the *Labor-Management Services Administration*. Labo(u)r unions are required to disclose information on their finances and membership, this information being available for inspection by the public.

Labor-Management Services Administration. *US Department of Labor* agency which has responsibility for administering and implementing the *Labor-Management Reporting and Disclosure Act* of 1959 (the *Landrum-Griffin Act*).

labor organization (US). As *trade union*.

labor union. As *trade union*.

labo(u)r. Workforce or the human physical and mental effort and skills involved in industry, commerce, etc. See also *labo(u)r-intensive* and *trade union*.

labo(u)r code. Used in some countries to regulate the relationship between employer and employee.

labo(u)r cost. Expenditure on *employee* pay and benefits.

labo(u)r cost ratio. Standard costing of direct labo(u)r divided by its actual cost.

labo(u)r exchange. As *employment office*.

labo(u)r, free movement of (EEC). See *free movement of labo(u)r (EEC)*. See also *common labo(u)r market (EEC)*.

labo(u)r hoarding. Where a firm employs more *labo(u)r* than immediately necessary (creating a concealed surplus) to guard against the possibility of being caught with insufficient labo(u)r later. A situation particularly likely to occur in (and magnify) conditions of *full employment, inflation* and/or *boom* when firms compete particularly keenly for labo(u)r resources. Inducements to labo(u)r to be hoarded may include workplace bargaining, special bonus payments and guaranteed overtime.

labo(u)r hour rate. Hourly payment.

labo(u)r-intensive (industry or firm). Where there is high use of *labo(u)r* with complementary low capital investment and mechanization. The opposite of *capital-intensive*.

labo(u)r law. Employment legislation dealing with relations between *employer* and *employee* and *industrial relations* in general.

labo(u)r market. Availability and demand for particular kinds of labo(u)r and skill, taking into account such factors as wage levels, terms and conditions of employment, activities and needs of competing

191

and neighbo(u)ring *employers*, outflows from educational institutions, *travel-to-work areas*, the national economy and local economic conditions. Labo(u)r markets exist nationally, locally and, as the 'internal labo(u)r market', within the individual employing organization.

Labo(u)r Market Board (Sweden). Public corporation financed from Government revenue, responsible for implementing the Swedish Government's manpower policy, including its industrial training program(me). The main provider of the training is the *Board of Education* which runs over 300 basic industrial training courses, from operator to technologist level, at the equivalent of the UK's *Government Training Centres*.

labo(u)r market, common (EEC). See *common labo(u)r market (EEC)*. See also *free movement of labo(u)r (EEC)*.

labo(u)r mobility. Or job mobility. Extent to which workers are prepared to change jobs geographically and/or in occupational terms, and the factors influencing their attitudes. 'Job mobility' tends to be used rather than 'labo(u)r mobility' of all levels of skill, including management.

labo(u)r-only subcontracting. Where a contractor, particularly in the construction industry, obtains labo(u)r, but not materials or components, from a sub-contractor who may be simply one man hiring out his own labo(u)r. Also known as *gang system*. See also *lump* and *butty system*.

labo(u)r relations. Tends to be used as synonymous with *industrial relations* though it is sometimes argued that a distinction between them is that industrial relations is concerned with union-management relations.

labo(u)r stability index. Ratio of number of *employees* who have been employed by a particular *employer* for at least a year to the number who were employed by him a year ago. See also *labo(u)r turnover*.

labo(u)r turnover. Flow of workers in and out of employment in an organization during a specified period. Normal measure is to express the number of leavers as a percentage of the average number of employees during the period in question. Also known as manpower turnover.

labo(u)r wastage. See *wastage*.

ladder activities. *Network analysis/pro-gramming* term for overlapping or interdependent *activities*.

LAFTA. *Latin American Free Trade Association*.

laggers. See *business indicators*.

Lagos Stock Exchange. Nigerian stock exchange established in 1960.

laissez-faire economy. Where economic forces operate freely without moderation or intervention from Government policy (a theoretical concept rather than a practical proposition in modern society). As *free economy*. See also *trade cycle*.

lame duck. Originally a term for a defaulter who is *hammered* and expelled from the *Stock Exchange*. More recently, has tended to be used of an ailing industrial enterprise particularly in the UK.

land bank. One that makes long-term loans on *real estate* in return for *mortgages*. See also *building society*.

Landesarbeitsgerichte. See *Arbeitsgerichte*.

Landeszentralbank. Central Regional Bank in Federal Germany.

land-grant. Made by the US Government under the Morrill Act of 1862 to state colleges that offer courses in agriculture and mechanical engineering.

land office. US term for a government office which records sales or transfers of public land.

Landrum-Griffin Act. US legislation of 1959. See the *Labor-Management Reporting and Disclosure Act*.

Landsorganisationen i Danmark (LO). *Danish Federation of Trade Unions*, consisting of 60 *trade unions* with about 900,000 members.

Landsorganisjonen i Norge (LO). Main *trade union* organization in Norway.

language laboratory. Purpose-built equipment in which students use twin or four-track tape recorders to compare their pronunciation, etc with those of a master tape.

Language Teaching, Centre for Information on. See *Centre for Information on Language Teaching*.

last-bag system. As *two-bin system*.

last-in, first-out. *LIFO*.

lateral integration. As *horizontal integration (or merger)*.

latest event time. Or latest allowable time. *Network analysis/programming* term for the latest time at which an *event* can be allowed to take place if it is not to delay the whole project.

Latin American Centre of Workers. Or Central Latinoamericana de Trabajadores (CLAT). Set up in 1954, its members are *trade unions* in some 35 countries.

Latin American Free Trade Association (LAFTA). Established at Montevideo in 1960 by a treaty to establish a *free trade* area within a *common external tariff* by stages over the following 12 years, though there have been some practical problems in implementing the treaty (largely because some of the countries involved are more industrialized than others). Founder member states were Argentina, Brazil, Colombia, Chile, Ecuador, Mexico, Paraguay, Peru, Uruguay and Venezuela, with Bolivia joining in 1967. See also *Central American Common Market* and *Alliance for Progress*, the latter being an example of cooperation between the USA and Latin America.

Latin square design. Term used particularly in *market research* for a survey or test designed to measure the effect on sales of a number of different factors. The different factors are plotted against each other. This technique makes for a considerably shorter overall survey or test than would be possible if separate tests were run for each factor. See also *factorial sample design*.

Lausanne Stock Exchange. *Bourse de Lausanne*. One of eight *Swiss stock exchanges*.

law merchant. Commercial and trade regulations based on merchants' customs in times past.

law of effect. Theory of learning and of *motivation*, originally formulated by E L Thorndike, which states that when several responses are made to the same situation, those which are accompanied or closely followed by satisfaction will, other things being equal, be more firmly connected with the situation so that, when it recurs, they will be more likely to recur. When, however, a response is accompanied by discomfort, it will have its connections with the situation weakened and is less likely to recur.

law of the situation. Concept developed by *Mary Parker Follett* that solutions in conflict situations should be dictated by the logic of facts and events and not by the superior power of either party involved in the conflict. It also means dealing with organizational or management problems in terms of the situational demands rather than in terms of any universal principles or laws. Another concept introduced by Mary Parker Follett is that of *creative conflict*.

Law Reform (Contributory Negligence) Act 1945. Laid down in UK that an *employee's contributory negligence* did not debar him from securing damages for injuries received in the course of his work, though the Act also provided that such damages 'be reduced to such extent as the court thinks just and equitable having regard to the claimant's share in the responsibility for the damage'. Such damages would also not be applicable where the employee had expressly made a *voluntary assumption of risk* according to the doctrine of *volenti non fit injuria*.

laws, approximation of (EEC). See *approximation of laws (EEC)*.

lay day. One on which a ship is allowed to stay in port without being charged fees.

lay-off. Where an employer is unable to continue employing workers, usually for lack of work, and suspends their employment. This may happen, for example, where a *strike* at a supplier's factory leads to a shortage of components. When employment is reduced to part-time, rather than being suspended completely, this is known as *short-time working*.

LC. *Library of Congress*.

L/C. *Letter of credit*.

Lda. Abbreviation for *Sociedade anonima de responsabilidade limitada*, a joint stock company under Portuguese law.

leader. As *loss leader*.

leaders. See *business indicators*.

lead/lag method. Technique used particularly in *marketing*. In preparing forecasts in a particular area, an analysis is made of trends or economic indicators that are known to be related to the data being forecast and tend to vary upwards or downwards in advance of

lead rate

this data. This can provide useful advance warning. See also *tied indicator*.

lead rate. Extra or *premium payment* made to an employee called upon to use exceptional skills or to take extra responsibility.

lead time. That which must be allowed for the completion of a job or operation. It may be either manufacturing time or the time to be allowed for orders for *bought-out* goods to be met.

lean work. Work on which it is difficult to earn high bonus under a *payment-by-results* scheme. Jobs of this kind may also be known as *stinkers*. Jobs with *loose rates* on which it is easier to earn bonus may be known as *fat work* or *gravy jobs*.

leap-frogging. Process by which a successful pay claim by one group of employees tends to encourage pay claims by further groups, often on the grounds that *pay differentials* should be maintained. The term is also used of the way in which increases in wages tend to push up *prices*, and vice versa, in terms of high *inflation*.

learnership. Formal training arrangement between employer and employee not involving indentured apprenticeship.

learning curve. Representation in graph form of rate of progress of trainee(s). Also known as skill acquisition curve. Rate of improvement is shown by plotting production against time or, if measurable, acquisition of skills against time. The target is normally *experienced worker standard/ level*.

learning plateau. Temporary flattening out in trainee/student's *learning curve* sometimes representing period of consolidation in acquisition of skills.

learning resource centre (center). Centre (center) providing variety of learning materials from which material can be selected by learner or teacher to provide the route to learning objectives most appropriate for an individual student or group of students.

learning time, real. See *real learning time*.

leaseback. Normally a long term lease of land or buildings which has been sold and then taken back under the terms of a new lease by the original seller.

lease (hire). Where the owner of buildings, land, factory equipment, office equipment, or transport, etc makes over its use to another individual or company for a particular period of time at a particular rent (the latter may be subject to review at specific intervals). The owner is known as the lessor and the other party as the lessee. Particularly in the case of machinery and equipment, the agreement may be that the goods become the property of the lessee at the end of the hire period. Lease hire has points of similarity with *hire purchase* but may be more attractive to the lessee in that there is not an initial deposit and there can also be tax advantages. See also *credit sale*.

leasing, export. See *export leasing*.

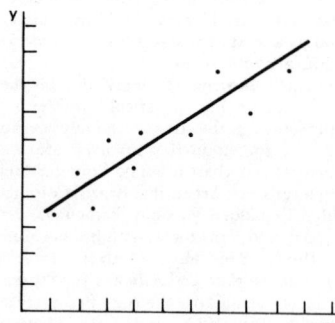

fitting of regression line to observed values of y

least-squares

least-squares. Method devised by the French mathematician Legendre for calculating the *regression* line which gives the best fit for a set of observed values so that the line may be used to predict the approximate value of one variable, given a known value of the other. The regression line which gives the best fit is that which, when drawn, is so placed between the points representing the observations that the sum of the squares of the separate distances between the line and each point is at a minimum value. This is shown in the illustration.

ledger account. Summary of all transactions with a particular firm. Goods supplied (debit notes), returns and allowances (credit notes) and payment and discount are all shown. By adding each of the two sides of the account and striking a balance, the amount outstanding is shown. Modern systems of accounting have tended to vary the actual amount of presentation, and accounts kept on *computers* must be programmed to print out the information that is required.

ledgerless accounting. As *slip system*.

Leeds Stock Exchange. UK provincial *stock exchange*.

legal holiday. Public holiday in the USA, etc. Cf *bank holiday* in the UK. Such holidays are common to most industries except for service industries such as catering.

legal reserve. Monies that a bank, *insurance company*, *building society*, etc, must keep in reserve as *security* in the conduct of its business. See, for example, *special deposits*.

legal tender. Amount of money of each denomination of a currency which a creditor must by law accept in payment of a debt.

lender of last resort. Function of a *central bank* where it lends money to the banking system of its country thereby influencing both *interest* rates and *money supply*.

letter-box company. *Company* or *corporation* nominally established with an address in a low-tax country though its real operation is in a higher tax country.

letter of credit. Issued by a bank or similar institution allowing a borrower to draw *bills of exchange* on it for specified purposes. In the case of international trade, an overseas buyer may arrange for a bank in the country of the vendor to issue the vendor with a letter of credit accepting a bill of exchange drawn on it against delivery of the relevant export shipping documents. Part of the latter procedure is normally that the overseas buyer opens an *irrevocable documentary acceptance credit* with the bank involved in the country of the vendor.

letter of hypothecation. Document held by a bank as evidence of its *lien* on goods which are the security or *collateral* against which it has granted a *loan* or *credit*.

letters of administration. Legal document entrusting the administration of the estate of a deceased person.

letter(s) of marque. 1. Documentation granted by a government to an individual authorizing the seizure of goods or citizens of another nation. **2.** Authorization to arm a ship to attack enemy ships. Also known as 'letter of marque and reprisal'.

letters patent. Documentation granting a *patent* to an inventor.

lettuce. Slang for 'paper money'.

leverage. US term for *gearing*.

leverage ratio. US term for *gearing ratio* designed to show the nature and sources of financing (particularly the relationship between *equity* and other sources of funds).

levy (training). Levy, usually a percentage of the payroll, made by a UK *Industrial Training Board* on the establishments or firms it covers.

liability. Any form of *debt* owed to others. *Current liabilities* are short-term debts which must be settled within twelve months or the financial year. *Secured liabilities* are claims that have specific assets pledged to ensure satisfaction in the event of default.

liability, vicarious. See *vicarious liability*.

liberal arts. Academic subjects in both the arts and sciences that are more concerned with cultural improvement of the individual than with practical or vocational training.

liberal studies. Studies introduced as a minor part of a course in order to broaden or liberalize the understanding and values of trainees/students. Usually taken to mean introducing social science or arts subjects for technology or science students, but liberalizing can also take the form of giving arts students an appreciation of technology.

Library of Congress (LC). US national library founded in Washington, DC, in 1830.

lickspittle. Obsequious and fawning subordinate.

Liège Stock Exchange. (la) *Bourse de Fonds Publics de Liège*. One of the provincial Belgian stock exchanges.

lien. Right to retain goods until the seller has been paid. When goods are sold on credit, normally no lien exists until the credit period has expired.

lieu days. Holidays taken in lieu of unpaid overtime.

lieu payment (or bonus). Paid to an employee as compensation for not being able to join a *payment-by-results* scheme, etc. See also *fall-back pay* and *make-up pay*.

life assurance policy. See *whole life insurance policy* and *group life assurance policy*.

LIFO. *Last-in, first-out.* **1.** Normally applied

to method of costing which assumes that whenever an item is sold it should be costed as though it was the last one purchased. See also *FIFO*. 2. In redundancy situations means the first employees to be made redundant are those most recently recruited. See also *first-in, last-out*.

light pen. *Input device* for passing data directly into the *internal memory or store* of a *computer* as drawings or graphs, without using a conventional *computer language*.

Lille Stock Exchange. *Bourse des Valeurs de Lille.*

Lima Stock Exchange. *Bolsa de Comercio de Lima.* Peru's stock exchange.

Limitation Acts. UK legislation (1939 and 1975) limiting the time lapse over which cases in contract or tort can be brought before the courts.

Limited Liability Act 1855. First legislation in the UK to limit the liability of a shareholder in a company to the amount of *capital* he has subscribed, in the event of the company's failure. This Act and another in 1862 stimulated the formation of *joint stock companies* and the operations of the *Stock Exchange*.

limited-line strategy. Production limited to a single product or as few product variations as possible.

linear program(me). Form of *programmed instruction* with strictly progressive sequence of *frames* or steps, all students following the same path. Each frame designed to present degree of difficulty and amount of information appropriate for average trainee/student in *target population*. Same principle applies to linear books and texts. See also *adaptive program(me), intrinsic branching program(me), skip program(me)* and *teaching machine*.

linear programming. Mathematical technique simulating real-life situations to solve allocation problems and maximize or minimize the linear function of variables. See *operational research*.

linear responsibility charting. Analysis of job functions on a large chart. Titles are listed across the page and all major job titles down the left-hand side of the sheet. A symbol is used to indicate which functions are covered by which jobs and the nature of this involvement (actual performance or supervision, etc of the work). The object is to provide a flexible type of *organization chart* which indicates functions and responsibilities, establishes overlapping duties, improves decision making and highlights training needs, etc.

linear trend. Statistical data represented as a straight line on a graph.

line authority. *Authority* belonging to *line management* or a member of it.

line management. Part of 'line and staff' concept (see illustration), derived in some respects from the military system which attempts to define the various functions and relationships within an organization. The three basic types of relationships are: Line management. Those concerned with managing the key activities for which the organization was set up. In a manufacturing company the line managers would therefore, for example, include the Works & Sales managers. In a retail store they would include the buyers and departmental managers. The line manager typically has control over a number of staff and responsibility for a major area. A key characteristic is that there is a clear relationship and *chain of command* both to top management and 'down the line' to subordinates. (Also known as 'direct' management). Staff management on the other hand are not concerned with the main activities of the organization but provide line management with specialist and advisory services. The staff specialists have responsibility for the service (and line authority over their own staff), but no authority over those who use it. 'Staff' management will of course have a line relationship with their own superiors but the relationship with other line managers is 'indirect'. They provide advice, information, specialist services but the line management can normally accept or reject it. Often the relationship of staff management to others is called 'functional'. The third type of relationship is variously known as the 'assistant to', 'staff officer' or 'personal assistant' type of appointment. Typically this is associated with a senior manager/ director who has a personal assistant to undertake various duties for him. The assistant has no responsibility or authority in his own right but acts as an extension of the boss he serves. In practice (practise) the theoretical distinctions between 'line', 'staff' and 'personal assistants' are often not clearly defined and many jobs may have an element of both line and staff functions. In many cases the authority of specific managers and their relationships to others may be modified — particularly in large

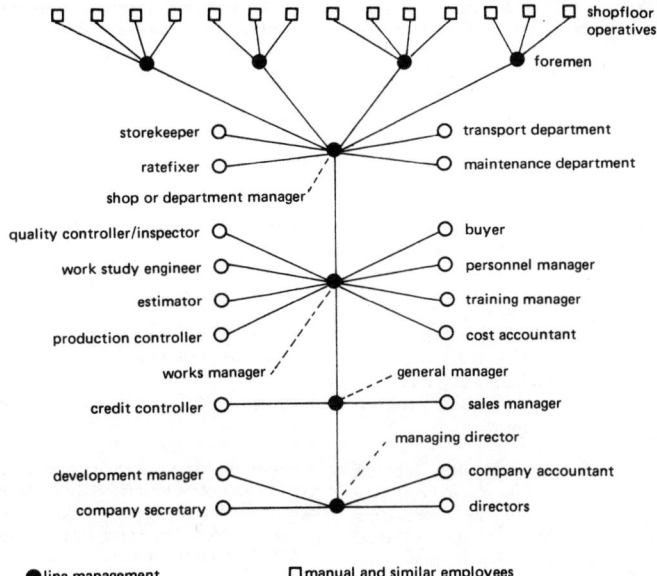

example of line-and-staff management

organizations which have geographically decentralized units — by various committee structures which may have specific control or influence over certain management functions. See also *staff management*.

line of balance technique. Method of scheduling and displaying the progress of manufacturing or project work, comparing planned and actual progress at particular points in time.

line of command. As *chain of command*.

line of credit. As *credit outstanding*.

line printer. See *output device* (computer).

Lipsey Equation. Devised by R G Lipsey in the UK in 1960. Like the *Phillips Curve*, the Lipsey Equation relates money wage rates to the level of unemployment but with the added refinement of taking into account changes in retail prices during the previous twelve months.

liquid assets. *Cash* or items that can be quickly converted into cash. They include cash at the bank and in hand; easily marketable securities; book debts; bills receivable.

liquidated damages. Those estimated to have been incurred by a breach of contract.

liquidation. Legal procedures which cause a company to be formally closed down and cease its existence.

liquidity. 1. Extent to which a company has access to *cash* or can realize some of its assets into cash without appreciable loss in value. **2.** Often also used to denote ability to meet financial obligations in cash or its equivalent.

liquidity ratio. As *cash ratio*.

liquid ratio. Involves identifying the value of stocks and separating this from other current *assets*. Liquid ratio is then the ratio of current assets minus stocks to current *liabilities*. This may be a safer yardstick for a company than *current ratio* (which is a straight ratio of current assets to current liabilities) because it does not involve reliance on stocks which, at least at the critical time, may not be readily saleable.

lira. Basic unit of Italian currency.

Lisbon Stock Exchange. Or *Bolsa de Lisboa*. See *Portuguese stock exchanges*.

list building. Or 'list selection' or 'list development'. *Direct mail selling* term for building up lists of names and addresses that can be expected to produce a good sales response for particular kinds of product or service. See also *list renting* and *sleepers*.

listed company. *Company* that has been granted a *quotation* (1).

list renting. Paying for the use of a list of names and addresses for *direct mail selling* purposes. Owners of such a list normally handle despatch of the *direct mail shot(s)* themselves rather than release the list and risk having it copied for other use by the hirer. To show that distrust is two-way, the hirer may insist on including in a mail shot so-called *sleepers*, which are control addresses known to the hirer.

literacy test of written English (comp). *Personnel selection* and *vocational guidance* test devised as part of the *engineering apprentice test-battery* of the National Institute of Industrial Psychology in the UK.

Liverpool Cotton Exchange. UK specialist *commodity exchange*.

Liverpool Stock Exchange. UK provincial *stock exchange*.

Livery Company. Or *Guild*. One of the present-day ceremonial but influential and usually well-heeled bodies in the City of London that were once the medieval custodians of the nation's craft skills and training. The Livery Companies or Guilds were in 1878 co-founders with the Corporation of London of the *City and Guilds of London Institute* examining body.

liveware. Personnel responsible for running *computers* and computer systems. See also *hardware* and *software*.

Lloyds, Corporation of. From modest but much romanticized beginnings in a *City of London* coffee house in the late seventeenth century, Lloyds has become a world-famous insurance centre (center), particularly for marine insurance but excluding life assurance. Business is operated through syndicates of Lloyds Brokers and Underwriters, with some 1,500 Lloyds agents and subagents operating around the world. Lloyds runs shipping intelligence services, a claims bureau, 'Lloyds Register of Shipping' (giving detailed information on vessels), and a daily newspaper called 'Lloyds List and Shipping Gazette'. Lloyds is often known simply as 'Lloyds of London'.

Lloyd's Register. Virtually comprehensive record of all ocean-going ships throughout the world, a record maintained in London by *Lloyds*.

LME. *London Metal Exchange.*

LMT. Local mean time.

LO. *Landsorganisationen i Danmark*, the Danish Federation of Trade Unions.

LO. *Landsorganisjonen i Norge*, the main *trade union* organization in Norway.

load chart. Visual display of workloading of plant or production equipment.

loading. 1. In cost accounting refers to adding *overhead* to prime costs. **2.** In *unit trusts* or *mutual funds* the additional amount to the market price of shares and stock to cover administrative costs, brokerage, management fees, etc. **3.** Generally of costs or prices the extra amount added to cover some contingency.

load levelling. 1. In freight ensuring that goods are evenly and safely stowed to spread the weight and avoid damage during transportation etc. **2.** In manufacturing scheduling jobs and tasks to spread the work evenly over a period of time.

loan capital. Or *debt capital*. Type of capital invested in a company, being entitled to a prescribed rate of interest no matter how the company fares. Loan capital is usually secured, perhaps by a *mortgage* on company property. See also *debentures* and *secured liability*.

loaned employee. Loaned or temporary employee who is owed the usual employer's duty of care by his temporary employer.

loan shark. Person or organization making loans at extortionately high interest rates.

lobster shift. Shift starting during the night.

local. (US) Common term for the local branch of a *trade union*.

Local Enterprise Development Unit (Northern Ireland). Provides technical and marketing advice for new and expanding firms employing fewer than 50 workers, being particularly concerned with firms having export potential. In England there is the *Council for Small Industries in Rural Areas* and in Scotland there are the *Highlands and Islands Development Board* and the *Small Business Division of the Scottish Development Agency*. The Welsh equivalent is the *Small Business Section of the Welsh Development Agency*.

Local Government Training Board (UK). Voluntary organization set up September 1967 in the style of an *industrial training board* though not formally under the *Industrial Training Act 1964*.

local option. Where local government or management has the right to decide an issue without reference to higher authority.

Local Science and Technology Centres (UK). Local link-ups between schools, industry and places of higher education with aim of increasing schools' awareness and appreciation of technology.

local union. Single-plant or single-company *trade union*, a basic unit into which most US trade unions, for example, are broken down.

location manager. See *project manager*.

locked in. Describes the position of an investor in stocks or shares who, for a variety of reasons, cannot readily sell his investments (eg if share dealings are suspended).

lock-out. Or shut-out. Situation in which employer brings pressure to bear on employees by refusing them access to the workplace; the reverse situation to the *strike*. See also *industrial action*.

logical tree. As *decision tree*.

Lohnsteuer. Wages tax in Austria and Federal Germany. Together with the capital yields tax *(Kapitalertragsteuer)*, it forms the *income tax (Einkommensteuer)*. Austria also has the *Vermögensteuer*, a net wealth tax on the property of individuals; and the *Aufsichtratsabgabe*, a tax on fees paid to directors of Austrian companies. West Germany has a flat-rate directors' tax, or *Aufsichtratsteuer*, deducted at source from directors' fees paid to non-resident supervisory directors. West Germany also charges a surcharge, or *Ergänzungsabgabe*, on income tax.

Lombard Street. Term sometimes used to mean the UK banking and financial world. Lombard Street is actually a street in the City of London named after the moneychangers and bankers who originally came from Lombardy to London in the eighteenth century.

London acceptance credit. See *acceptance credit*.

London Bankers' Clearing House. See *clearing banks*.

London Chamber of Commerce (UK). Activities include those of an examining body in commercial subjects. Cooperates with *Royal Society of Arts* in administering *Ordinary National Certificate* in Business Studies.

London Chamber of Commerce commercial services to business and industry include issuing *ATA Carnets* under the simplified customs procedure by which UK firms may temporarily export goods (without payment of customs duty) for use as sales samples or as exhibits at an international exhibition overseas. The London Chamber of Commerce is also responsible for the administration of certain *trade associations*.

London Court of Arbitration of the London Chamber of Commerce and Industry and the City Corporation. One of three tribunals in the UK that may be used for private arbitration where commercial disputes arise between suppliers and customers, including between UK exporters and overseas buyers. The other two tribunals of the same kind are the *Tribunal of Arbitration of the Manchester Chamber of Commerce and Industry* and the *Arbitration Committee of the Bradford Chamber of Commerce*.

London Fruit and Wool Exchange. Specialist UK *commodity exchange*.

London Metal Exchange. Specialist UK *commodity exchange* dealing in copper, tin, lead and zinc.

London Stock Exchange. See *Stock Exchange* (UK).

long. US term for ownership of securities.

long position. As *bull position*.

long-range corporate planning. As *corporate planning*.

Long Range Sharing Plan. See *cost-reduction plan*.

long service death benefit. Where a *group life assurance policy* provides for *lump sum death benefit* to be greater in relation to length of service. See also *insurance, pensions* and *superannuation*.

long-term liabilities. Those which will not have to be met within the next three years. See also *medium-term liabilities*.

Loop, The. Chicago's central business district.

loose insert. As *insert*.

loose rate. Where the *piece work* rate for completing a job, as established by a *rate fixer, work study officer*, etc is of a kind that enables a worker to earn *bonus earnings* relatively easily. Where rates are loose, a *work group* may informally hold back production under a *fiddle* or *quota restriction* for fear of *rate cutting*. The opposite of a loose rate is a *tight rate*.

loose rein. Open style of management which gives considerable freedom to managers to run their departments/functions as they see fit.

Lorenz curve. Statistical data depicted in chart form showing the distribution of wealth in an economy. Normally used to show the percentage of 'spending units' (often defined as families) and the percentage of income they receive.

Los Angeles Stock Exchange. See *Pacific Coast Stock Exchange*.

loss. Amount by which the *expenditure* for a project/enterprise exceeds its *revenue* or income. If *revenue* exceeds expenditure, there is a *profit* instead of a loss.

losses wedge. See *break-even chart*.

loss leader. Product or service offered at an uneconomically low price in order to attract customers for other products and/or services.

loss ratio. *Insurance* term for the ratio between the total of the premiums paid to an insurance company and the total value of the claims settled by the company.

lot tolerance percent defective (LTPD). In *statistical quality control* the decision on how many items should be inspected in a given batch or lot, in order to check on quality and determine rejection or acceptance of the total batch quantity.

low-level language. See *computer language*.

LS. On legal documents the 'place for the seal' (locus sigilli).

Ltda. Abbreviation for *Sociedade anonima de responsabilidade limitada*, a joint stock company under Portuguese law.

LTPD. See *lot tolerance percent defective*.

luddite. Luddites were groups of workers who violently opposed the introduction of machinery in factories in the early 19th century in the UK, particularly in the Nottingham hosiery industry. Loosely used in the 20th century to describe workers opposed to changes in technology and introduction of new working methods.

lulu. Slang term (US) for a flat payment made to members of a legislature instead of itemized payments.

lump labo(u)r. Type of labo(u)r met particularly in the construction industry, and sometimes known as *labo(u)r-only subcontracting*. Lump labo(u)r workers are self-employed and are paid a lump sum per day's work or per amount of completed work either by the contractor or by an agent or so-called labo(u)r master who in turn is paid by the contractor a lump sum for work done. Lump labo(u)rers in the UK have been notorious for avoiding *national insurance* contributions and *income tax*, sometimes by moving about the country and/or working under assumed names. The lump labour system has also been criticized as enabling employers to avoid accident and other insurance payments, and as encouraging unsafe working conditions.

lump sum death benefit. Payment to dependents etc of a lump sum in the event of an insured person's death as in *life assurance* (or *insurance*). See also *group life assurance policy*.

Lutine bell. Sounded at *Lloyds* to herald important announcements. It is rung twice for good news or once for bad. The bell was taken from the ship, the 'Lutine', which went down in the North Sea in 1799 with a bullion cargo.

Luxembourg companies. Forms of partnership and company under Luxembourg law, much the same as those under Belgian law, include: **a** Partnership or *Société en Nom Collectif*; **b** Limited Partnership or *Société en Commandité Simple*; **c** Partnership Limited by Shares or *Société en Commandité par Actions*; **d** Joint Stock Company or *Société Anonyme*; **e** Private Limited Company or *Société à Responsabilité Limitée*; **f** Cooperative or

Société Coopérative.

Luxembourg Declaration 1965. When, following President de Gaulle's boycott of *Common Market* affairs, the French foreign minister declared that France reserved the right to veto any Council of Ministers' decision that affected its vital interests. This was not a legally acceptable declaration, and it flew in the face of the provision of the *Treaty of Rome 1957* that decisions of the Council should be by majority voting, but the power of veto has continued informally.

Luxembourg General Confederation of Labo(u)r. *Confédération Générale du Travail de Luxembourg.*

Luxembourg income tax. Or *impôt sur le revenu* or *Einkommensteuer*. Component parts include: **a** a tax assessed on total income; **b** a graduated withholding tax on wages, salaries and pensions; **c** a flat-rate capital yields tax on dividends, etc known as *retenue d'impôt sur les revenus de capitaux* or Kapitalertragsteuer; and **d** a flat-rate tax deducted at source from specified income of non-residents. This latter tax is known as *retenue d'impôt sur les revenus échus à des contribuables non-residents* or *Steuerabzug von Einkünften bei beschrankten Steuerpflichtigen*. Also deducted at source from directors' fees is the directors' tax, known as *retenue d'impôt sur les tantièmes* or *Steuerabzug von Aufsichtsrats-Vergütungen*. Luxembourg also has a capital tax — the *impôt sur la fortune* or *Vermögensteuer* — and a local real property tax known as *impôt foncier* or *Grundsteuer*.

Luxembourg Stock Exchange. Or *Bourse de Luxembourg*. Founded in 1929 but gaining ground from the mid-1950s onwards, partly because Luxembourg offered more attractive tax and exchange control arrangements than some other countries and partly because of its central position in the *European Economic Community*. Luxembourg originated *European Units of Account* as an alternative to national currencies, and its stock market has become a centre for dealings in *Eurobonds*. Brokers may be either individuals or legal entities such as banks. See also *Luxembourg companies.*

Lyon Stock Exchange. *Bourse des Valeurs de Lyon.* See *French stock exchanges.*

m

(m). Coding for *mechanical comprehension tests* in the *engineering apprentice test-battery* of the National Institute of Industrial Psychology in the UK.

M1. See *money supply.*

M3. See *money supply.*

Maatschap. Civil partnership under Netherlands law. See also *Netherlands companies.*

Machiavellian. Disowning any moral or ethical standards and holding that the end justifies the use of any means, however ruthless. Machiavelli was an early sixteenth century Italian political theorist.

machine ancillary time. When plant is not being used for production so that setting up, cleaning, etc can take place. Machine ancillary time is thus production time lost for reasons necessary for continued efficient production, and in this respect it differs from *machine downtime.*

machine code. Or *computer code* or *instruction code (or set).* The coding system for a particular computer which activates its various mechanical operations.

machine downtime. When a machine is not being used for production work because of breakdowns, maintenance, etc.

machine hour rate. Rate at which the use of equipment is charged for estimating and costing purposes.

machine idle time. When a machine is available for production work but is kept out of action by lack of materials or labo(u)r or orders, etc.

machine loading and scheduling. *Production planning and control* term for planning the throughput of jobs and work on machines with the objectives of both keeping the machines continuously at work and processing jobs according to the timescales indicated on the works order documents.

machinery for consultation. Parts of *procedure agreements* providing for consultation on terms and *conditions of employment* and for settlement by negotiation or arbitration of points of contention between employers and employees.

MacQuarrie test for mechanical ability. *Psychological test* of US origin. It is chiefly a *mechanical comprehension test* but with elements of a *spatial ability test* and also a test of *psychomotor skills.* There are points of similiarity with the *revised Minnesota paper form board test.*

macro-aggregate manpower budgets (also plans). Broad budgets or plans not taking note of breakdowns between skills or between industries. See *manpower budgets.*

Madison Avenue. New York home of the US advertising business.

Madras Stock Exchange. One of seven major *Indian stock exchanges.*

Madrid Stock Exchange. Or *Bolsa de Madrid,* one of the principal stock exchanges of Spain. See *Spanish stock exchanges.*

magnetic ink character recognition (MICR). Type of *character recognition system* sometimes used in *input devices* to feed specific and prerecorded data into a *computer.* This system, used for example on bank cheques, employs lettering and numbering printed in ink impregnated with magnetized particles, the ink being magnetized before being presented to the input device so that the characters become recognizable to its read head. Another character recognition system is *optical character recognition.*

magnetic memory or store. *Computer* data storage device that operates electromagnetically. The most common forms are magnetic core storage, magnetic discs and *magnetic tape.*

magnetic tape. Medium for external *com-*

puter storage. An alternative medium is *disc* storage.

Magyar Nemzeti Bank. National Bank of Hungary, the *central bank* formed in 1924.

Magyar Szakszervezetek Országos Tanácsa. Central Council of Hungarian Trade Unions, formed in 1898 and covering *trade unions* which have approximately 3,500,000 members.

Maier's principle. If the facts do not conform with the theory then the facts are obviously in error.

mail order (MO). Supplying goods and/or services in response to orders received by post.

mail order house. Business organization concerned with *direct mail selling*.

mail order selling. Selling against orders received through the post directly from consumers/purchasers or agents. The order may be in response to advertisements of the *direct response promotion* or *coupon advertising* kind. Alternatively, the orders may be made from catalog(ue)s.

main frame. *Central processing unit*, particularly in a large *computer*.

main question. Where a *motion* and *amendments* to it are moved at a meeting or conference the main question is the resultant issue to be finally debated and voted on. If all amendments fail, the main question is the *original motion*. If amendments are carried, the amended motion or *substantive motion* becomes the main question and has to be put to the vote separately after the vote(s) on the amendment(s).

main street (or stem). Major street of a US town or city, similar to 'high street' in the UK. Sometimes used pejoratively to imply a small town, materialistic culture.

maintenance factors. As *hygiene factors* in *Herzberg's theory*.

maintenance shift. *Shift working* specifically for the purpose of maintaining and repairing plant and equipment at times that do not interfere with production work etc.

make or buy. Determining the differential costs arising from making a product or component or buying it from an outside supplier. Involves the use of *marginal costs*.

make-ready. Setting up a job on a machine, particularly in printing.

make-up pay. Extra payment made to a worker on *payment-by-results* who has not reached an agreed minimum level of payment irrespective of the amount of work achieved. See also *lieu payment*.

make-work. Or *busy-work*. Work done to keep employees occupied rather than to produce goods or services of marketable value.

make-work practices (practises). Form of *restrictive labo(u)r practices (practises)* to make work take longer.

Makler. Stockbrokers on a *German Stock Exchange*. They have their own association, the *Maklerkammer*. There are two kinds of Makler, namely, the *amtliche Kursmakler* appointed by the government and the *freie Makler* who are not governmentally appointed officials but are authorized to deal on the trading floor.

Maklerkammer. Association of Federal German *stockbrokers* or *Makler*.

malarkey. Slang term for exaggerated or nonsensical talk.

Malaysia Stock Exchange. See *Kuala Lumpur Stock Exchange*.

managed change technique (MCT). Approach developed by Westinghouse Electric Corporation (US) concerned with obtaining real involvement and commitment by managers and employees to implementing effective changes within an organization. Includes detailed analysis of business situations, explaining purpose and rationale of need for change and devising a means of achieving change through use of a change agent and coordinator.

managed costs. Those over which there is some degree of *management discretion* during the progress of a project/enterprise so that there is some scope for varying expenditure once the project/enterprise is under way (eg reducing costs to cut losses if things go badly). On the other hand, committed costs are those to which management is virtually irrevocably committed once the project/enterprise is launched. See also *break-even point*.

managed currency. Monetary system where the *money supply* and its buying power are regulated by the government or the *central bank*, instead of being on the gold standard.

managed expenditures. Items the levels of which are currently controllable by management, as opposed to items bequeathed by previous management or determined by external influences and factors.

managed fund (pensions). See *deposit administration fund.*

management. 1. Effective use and coordination of resources such as capital, plant, materials and labour to achieve defined objectives with maximum efficiency. **2.** People responsible for directing and running an organization.

management accounting. Branch of accounting geared to making the decision making of management better informed by providing detailed information, present and projected, on the costs of individual products, departments and activities. Management accounting is concerned with helping the manager optimize his performance rather than with the external reporting functions of *financial accounting.*

management appraisal. As *performance appraisal.*

management audit. Systematic assessment of standards and techniques of management. Can embrace use of personnel, career development, staff morale, effectiveness of planning, work standards, financial efficiency and performance, and use made of advisory services and consultants. A management audit may be carried out by an independent person or someone employed by the business itself. The object is to report on the use of resources and highlight where improvements in efficiency can be made. Sometimes management audit is also used to describe the critical appraisal of the management team itself and in this sense it is often synonymous with *performance appraisal* of senior executives.

Management Board (Vorstand). Part of the two-tier board structure in German industrial firms, being responsible for the day-to-day running of a firm. The Management Board is appointed by the *Supervisory Board (Aufsichtsrat)* which includes workers' representatives under the *co-determination* law. This two-tier board system has gained favour with the *European Commission* and has been introduced in other European countries.

management by crisis (or drive). *Management style* that concentrates on crash program(me)s intended to rectify apparent weaknesses as they arise. It tends to be unconstructive and to lose sight of the overall objectives of the organization.

management by exception. Method of operation by which subordinates keep their superiors informed on exceptional events likely to call for or influence management decision making but do not bother them with details that merely confirm that everything is going according to plan. Management by exception is related to the technique of *reporting by responsibility* and *Pareto's law.*

management by objectives (MBO). Technique of setting target or goal performances for executives at the various levels in an organization so that they and their superiors have a more quantifiable and objective measure than might otherwise be available of how effectively they are functioning. See also *performance appraisal systems.*

Management Consultants Association. *Trade association* representing the leading management consultant firms in the UK. See also *British Consultants Bureau* for the promotion of overseas work, and *Institute of Management Consultants.*

Management Consulting Services Information Bureau. Bureau established in 1965 by the *British Institute of Management* in collaboration with the *Confederation of British Industry* to provide information and advice on the services offered by over 1,000 management consultants. Assists in drawing up short lists of consultants suitable to undertake specific assignments.

management development. Planning the experience and further training of members of management to develop their potential and equip them for jobs further up the management ladder. See also *management succession, performance appraisal systems* and *assessment centres (centers).*

management discretion. Management's freedom of judgement and decision. See *time span of discretion.*

management education. Instruction in the principles and techniques of management and in subjects related to the duties of management and supervision. Can be *in-company* or at a college, university, business school, etc. Sometimes management education has only a thin dividing line with management training, and is often synonymous with *business studies*.

management game. As *business game*.

management information systems (MIS). Systems, often computerized, designed to provide the management of a particular company or organization with the key information needed for decision making.

management prerogative. Traditionally, exercising of complete authority by management, an authority that might become qualified during *collective bargaining* though not during *joint consultation*. See also *freedom to manage*.

management ratios. Means of keeping an eye on company and management performance by identifying relationships between quantifiable aspects of the company's activity and continuously recording these relationships, sometimes by plotting them on a graph. The relationships or ratios recorded in this way can cover a wide range but might include, for example, the ratio of *direct labour costs* to *indirect labour costs;* the ratio of maintenance costs to machine running time; the ratio of sales of one product size to another; the ratio of profit to sales; the ratio of sales to capital employed; the ratio of sales to fixed assets; the ratio of sales to stocks, etc. Management ratios can provide bases for financial control and a valuable early warning system complementary to the company's *costing system*, which is usually concerned more with operational and shorter term controls.

Two ratios commonly used for *credit rating* purposes and *current assets* to *current liabilities;* and *liquid assets* to *current liabilities*.

Management ratios may also be used to make comparisons between the performance of companies in *inter-firm comparisons*. In this context it is usual to define key ratios carefully and examine a hierarchy or pyramid of inter-related ratios which highlight strengths and weaknesses. Such ratios as growth in earnings per share; return on *equity;* and return on capital employed may then become significant. See *Centre for Interfirm Comparison* (UK), *accounting ratios, balance sheet ratios* and *manpower ratios*.

'Management Review'. US monthly publication published by the *American Management Association*. Established in 1923.

management science. Application of quantitative techniques to management problems and practice (practise).

management shares. As *deferred shares or capital*.

management style. Or managerial style. Approach adopted by management to exercising authority, encouraging participation in decision making, motivating staff, delegating authority, communicating information and maintaining control. Two extremes of management style are: **a** authoritarian, which is characterized by reliance on authority-obedience relationships to get work done, the rigid adherence to defined lines of command and centralized decision making; **b** democratic or participative, which is characterized by sharing of responsibility, reliance on the employees' own willingness to take whatever actions are required of them, and a high degree of employee participation in decision making. See also *theory X and Y*.

management succession. Process of assessing the management needs and hierarchy an organization will require in the future and of ensuring that there are junior managers able to succeed more senior management. Complementary to *management development* which is sometimes used as a term also embracing management succession.

management threshold. Stage in personal development which marks the transition period from specialist to a generalist concerned with managing the work of others. It is characterized by dramatic changes in the individual's outlook to work, its rewards, and social and family life.

'Management Today'. UK monthly publication of the *British Institute of Management*.

management trade union. Part of the general growth of *white collar trade unions*, such unions have deliberately set out to recruit a 'middle class' membership. See also *staff association*.

management training. Planned experience and training in the practices (practises) and techniques of management. Often *in-company* or even *on-the-job*. Can merge with *management education*.

manager. Executive who is responsible for *controlling* and *coordinating* the work of others.

manager development. See *management development*.

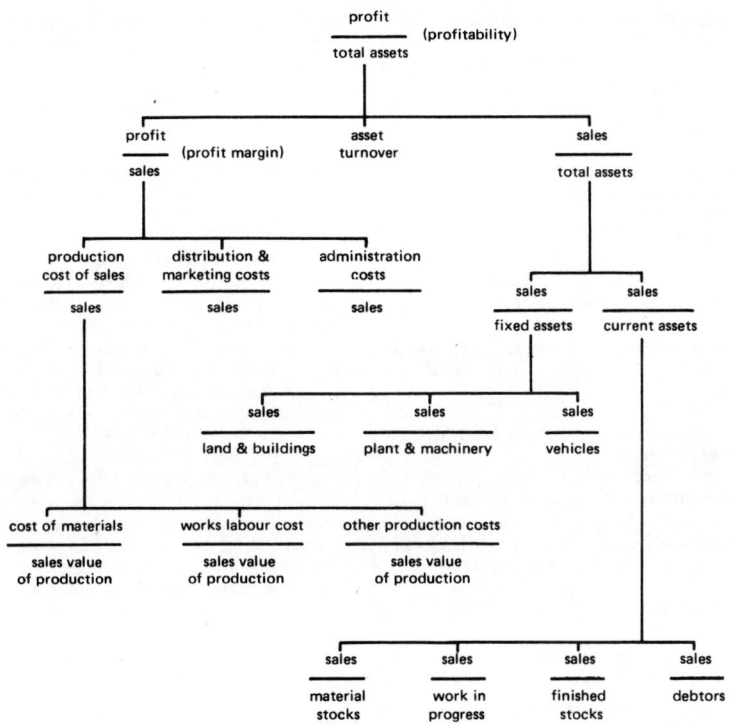

management ratios (relationships of various ratios)

Source: Graham Riay, Hardy Heating Co. Ltd. Management Accounting, Text and Cases, BBC Publications, London

managerial grid. Developed originally in the USA by Professors R R Blake and J S Mouton, the managerial grid is used particularly in *management development* program(me)s to plan the progress of individuals and organizations. As shown in the illustration, the horizontal axis has a nine-point scale representing 'concern for production', while the vertical axis has a nine-point scale representing 'concern for people'. The grid is used to plot the point where a manager's concern for people meets his concern for production, the position of this plot being said to indicate his 'managerial style'. For example, the average position is the 5.5 position while the 9.9 position represents the optimum integration of concern for people with that for production, an integration usually regarded as ideal for the good manager. The subject plotted on the grid can be an organization or department as well as an individual manager.

In all, of course, there are 81 different positions on the grid. The managerial grid is a demonstration of the *grid theory* that the three universals interacting in any organization are: **a** people, **b** production (of goods or services) and **c** the management hierarchy. The managerial grid is regarded in many companies as an important self-assessment tool for individual managers, usually after some training in its use at a course or seminar. It may also be used as a training tool, sometimes in a *T-group training* situation where members of the group examine their own and each other's styles of behavio(u)r.

managerial responsibility, span of. See *span of managerial responsibility*.

managerial style. As *management style*.

manager's letter. Used in some organizations as a statement of the manager or executive's responsibilities under *management by objectives*.

managing director. Normally the chief executive of a private or public company responsible for the day-to-day implementation of company policy and the coordination of the work of the other *company directors* and senior executives. Broadly equivalent to *president* in the USA.

Managua Stock Exchange (Camara de Comercio). Nicaragua's only *stock exchange*.

Manchester Stock Exchange. UK provincial *stock exchange*.

mandate. Instructions given by an organization to its delegate or representative on how he should vote on particular issues at a meeting or conference. See also *card vote*.

Man Friday. Close personal aide, à la Robinson Crusoe. Female version has become known as *Girl Friday*. See also *kitchen cabinet*.

Manila Stock Exchange. The important *stock exchange* in the Philippines.

Man-Made Fibres Producing Industry Training Board (UK). Established February 1966 under the *Industrial Training Act 1964*.

manpower analysis. First stage in *manpower planning* in the individual firm, it is an analysis of all the employees in the firm or unit by, for example, age, length of service, job title and wider occupational category. It may also be thought advisable to analyze the proportion of male to female workers, particularly where certain skills are traditionally associated with one of the sexes only. The ages of workers may also be analyzed as, for example, where there could be a problem of an ageing workforce. Manpower analysis may also involve an assessment of the effects of *labo(u)r turnover*, usually on the basis of the number of leavers in the previous year. After manpower analysis the next stage in manpower

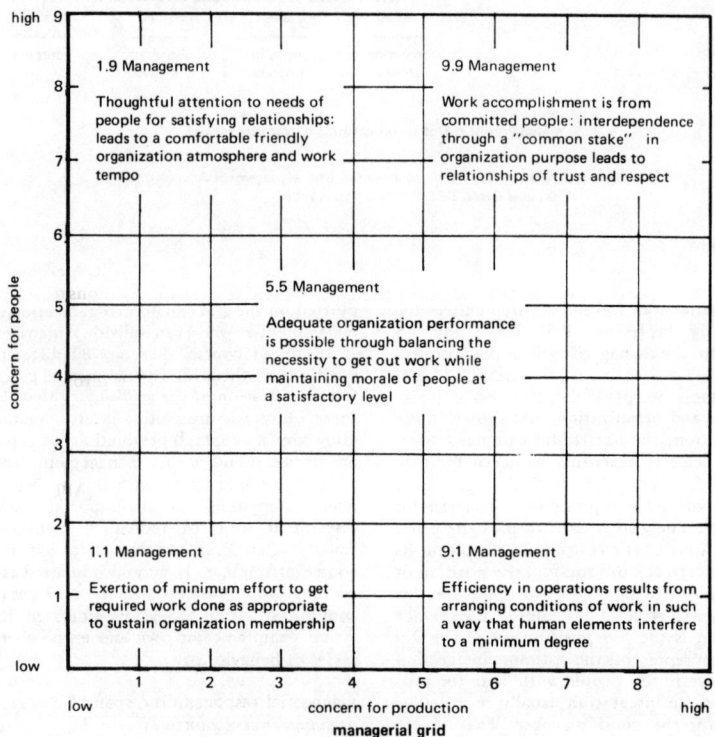

managerial grid

planning is usually drawing up a *job cover plan*.

Manpower and Automation Research. Register of sponsored projects published by the Office of Manpower, Automation and Training, *US Department of Labor*.

manpower budgeting. Balancing of future supply and demand for labo(u)r (see *manpower planning*).

manpower deficit. Excess of jobs available over manpower available. Opposite of *manpower surplus*.

manpower mobility. See *labo(u)r mobility*.

manpower planning. Analysis of present and projected future manpower requirements and the formulation of plans to meet forecast deficits or surpluses. Consists of manpower requirements and manpower supply planning. Manpower requirements planning uses *ratio-trend forecasting* for calculations based on existing manpower standards and *theoretical requirement forecasting* for calculations based on projections for future, new situations. See also *human resources planning*.

manpower ratios. *Management ratios* for monitoring employee costs and manpower utilization, including **a** total payroll costs as a percentage of sales revenue, **b** sales per employee, **c** *net profit* as a percentage of payroll costs, **d** *added value* per £100 of employee pay, and **e** the ratio of *direct* to *indirect labo(u)r*.

Manpower Services Commission (MSC). Set up in the UK in November 1972 by the *Secretary of State for Employment*, with the support of the *Confederation of British Industry* and the *Trades Union Congress*, to coordinate employment and training services in the UK. Introduced by the *Employment and Training Act 1973* as the statutory body responsible to the Secretary of State for arrangements to assist people to select, train for, obtain and retain employment, and to assist employers to obtain employees. The MSC has ten members, all appointed by the Secretary of State. In addition to the chairman, they are three employer representatives, three *trade union* representatives, two local authority representatives, and one representative of other education interests. The MSC has under it the *Employment Service Agency (ESA)* and the *Training Services Agency (TSA)*, both of which also became independent statutory bodies during 1974 under the Employment and Training Act 1973.

manpower surplus. Excess of manpower available over jobs available. Opposite of *manpower deficit*.

manpower turnover. As *labo(u)r turnover*.

man-profile (or specification). Objective statement of the qualities sought in the candidates for a vacant appointment. Usually drawn up following the devising of a *job specification* or *description*.

man-type flow process chart. *Flow process chart* which shows the activities of a worker or workers.

manual worker. Also known as a *blue collar worker*, is employed in manual work, whether skilled, semi-skilled or unskilled. Has been defined by the UK *Engineering Employers Federation* as an employee who 'is subject to the authority of the foreman and is not responsible for engagement or dismissal of other workers, and works with tools or uses instruments in the normal course of his work'.
Blue collar workers phase into the *grey (gray) area occupations* that are in an ambiguous middle ground between blue collar and *white collar* status. There is an increasing tendency for some form of *staff status* to be extended to blue collar workers.

manufactory. As *factory*.

MAP. *Master activity programming*.

map-graph. As *cartogram*.

MAPI method. Methods for evaluating machinery replacement decisions developed by the US Machinery & Allied Products Institute. There are two basic methods. One concentrates attention on comparisons for one year immediately ahead through the use of a relatively simple two page computing form. This gives the first year's after tax rate of return for a specific investment project. The results are similar to use of the *DCF* method. The second basic MAPI method puts emphasis on the return to be expected over the asset's full life.

marché hors-côté. Unofficial market for securities on the *Paris Stock Exchange* (or *Bourse*). It follows trading in Official List securities and is similarly supervised by the *Compagnie des Agents de Change* and the *Chambre Syndicale des Agents de Change*.

marginal accounts. Those relating to firms

marginal cost. *Cost* of producing one more item.

marginal costing. Technique of costing in which costs are segregated into *fixed costs* and the remaining costs, termed the marginal costs. For most practical purposes the marginal costs are the *variable costs*, ie those which tend to vary in total in relation to output. The marginal costing procedure is first to segregate fixed costs and then to apportion only the marginal costs to products or processes. The fixed costs are not charged to production but instead are written off to the profit and loss account in the year in which they are incurred. Deducting total management costs from sales revenue gives the *contribution* to fixed costs and profits. Marginal costing is used to obtain information on product profit contributions, *break-even points* and profit/volume decisions. It is distinguished from *absorption costing* which is the conventional accounting method of deducting all costs from sales revenue to arrive at the profit which has been earned, ie all costs are allocated or apportioned to products. The main problem in using marginal costing is that of distinguishing between variable and fixed costs. Marginal costing also assumes that fixed costs do not vary between products. In practice (practise), however, different cost centres (centers) may incur heavier or lighter totals of fixed costs. See also *stepped costs*.

marginal cost of capital. See *capital cut-off point*.

marginal pricing. Fixing the selling *price* of additional units with reference to the marginal cost of manufacturing the unit (see *marginal costing*). The theory of marginal pricing is that, after a company's total *fixed* and *variable costs* have been covered by the existing volume of production, the cost of producing an extra unit of production, ie marginal production, will only be the total variable cost of producing and selling that unit. In such circumstances, the selling prices of additional units could be reduced, if necessary, to match the total variable cost without any loss of profit to the company. Any amount by which the selling price exceeds the variable cost of marginal output could then be an extra or marginal contribution to the company's net profits or *cash flow*. Marginal pricing may be advantageous in the short term but, eventually, the company still has to ensure that total revenue exceeds total costs. Overdependence on marginal pricing can reduce total revenue below total costs in the longer

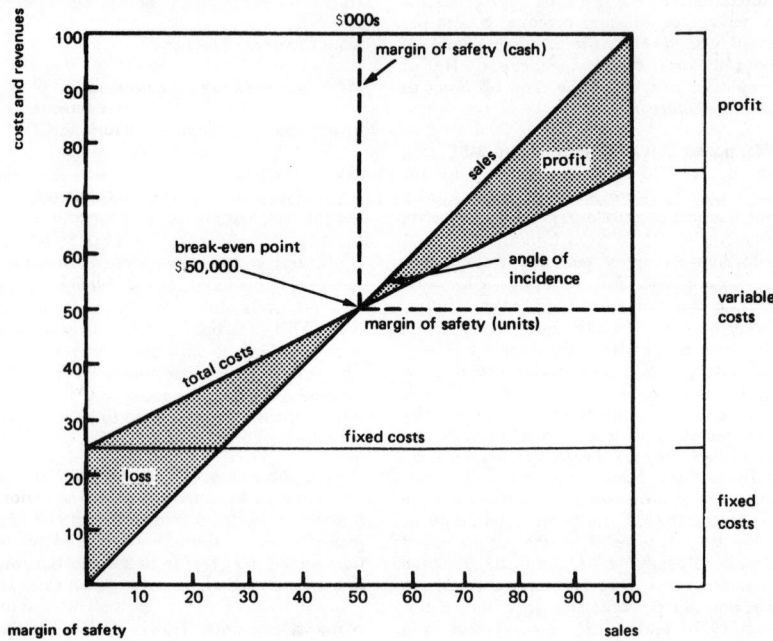

210

term because of its effects on competitors' pricing policies and on the buying behavio(u)r of the company's existing customers. See also *pricing methods* and *break-even chart*.

marginal propensity to consume. See *propensity to consume*.

marginal rate of tax. Ratio (expressed as a percentage) obtained by dividing the change in the income base on which it is levied i.e.

$$\frac{\text{change in total personal income tax}}{\text{change in total taxable income}}$$

marginal revenue. Increased income from selling one more item.

margin of safety. Extent to which sales volume or revenue exceeds the break-even point on a *break-even chart* (see illustration). The sales performance or target being checked is pinpointed on the sales revenue line above the break-even point. The margin of safety in financial terms is read off on the dotted vertical 'margin of safety (cash)' axis, or the margin of safety in terms of volume of product is read off on the dotted horizontal 'margin of safety (units)'. Management aims to achieve a reasonable margin of safety in order to be able to withstand any significant cut-back in sales and/or production. A related management aim is to achieve as large an *angle of incidence* as possible since this implies a high rate of profit once the break-even point has been reached.

Mark. See *Deutsche Mark* and *Ostmark*.

markdown. In retail business the amount of price reduction on the original selling price during clearance sales or special merchandising offers.

market. Number of customer or potential customer units which have in common one or more easily identifiable and recognizable characteristics, such as geographical location, income level, buying needs and habits, taste.

market and sales forecasting. Policies and techniques concerned with the potential and prospective sales volume or market trend for the individual product or company, and with setting a sales target for such product or company. Forecasting techniques used include *brick-by-brick, exponential smoothing, time series forecasting* and *serial correlation*.

market assessment. Identifying and evaluating all the relevant factors which affect a company's current or potential *market*. The process of market assessment involves: **a** identifying the market and the characteristics of buyers, users and distributors; **b** establishing the overall market structure and size; **c** identifying the external factors that could affect market size and the competitive situation, these factors including competitors' activities, national and international economic trends and government policies and legislation; **d** establishing the company's and its competitors' existing and potential shares of the market.

market capacity, overall. See *overall market capacity*.

Market Council. Colloquial term for the *Council of Ministers* of the *Common Market*.

market diversification. Planning to sell to different purchasers or in different *markets* by means of *product diversification*, establishing new markets, or exerting influence on buying habits and tastes.

market economy. An economy based on the production of goods and services for sale rather than for the personal consumption of the producer and his dependants.

market exploration. Assessment of the market for a product or a company's range of products.

market factor derivation. *Market and sales forecasting* based on identifying and isolating certain factors that can be expected to cause or increase the demand for a particular product or service.

market follower. New product introduced to compete with existing products, as distinct from a *pioneer product*, which is one of entirely new design and/or function, or a *brand leader* that is already in a dominant position in its field.

market identification. Process of **a** identifying existing or potential customers: **b** establishing the characteristics by which customers are grouped together in separate market segments; **c** establishing why and how the product or service is bought.

marketing. Creative management function which promotes business and employment by assessing needs of the end user of products or services, initiates research and development, and produces products and services which can be profitably provided to satisfy market requirements. It coordinates

211

the resources of production and distribution of goods and services, determines and directs the nature and scale of the total effort required to sell profitably the maximum production to the ultimate user.

marketing audits. Assessments of *marketing strategy*, services, functions and performance.

marketing channel. As *sales chain*.

marketing control. Process of **a** monitoring sales results and costs against targets and budgets and taking action when required to exploit opportunities or to overcome adverse results; **b** keeping informed of competitors' activities and changes in the marketing environment; **c** revising overall marketing plans where a review of results or a change in circumstances show that this is necessary.

marketing game. *Business game* with a strong marketing orientation.

marketing mix. Way in which the different parts and techniques of a company's marketing effort are combined and stressed. Component parts of the marketing mix include *marketing research* and *market intelligence; product strategy* and new product development; *market and sales forecasting; advertising* and *public relations; sales promotion, packaging* and *merchandising; direct selling; physical distribution;* and *marketing planning and control.* The emphasis in the marketing mix is different at different points in a *product life cycle*.

marketing model. Computerized model of the overall market for a company's products. Can be used to make projections to test the likely effect of a particular *marketing strategy*, such as the introduction of a new product or a new pricing policy, in relation to the total market competitors' activities, the standard of living, etc. Marketing models may be used in conjunction with *company models*, particularly in *corporate planning*.

marketing-oriented company. One that tends to manufacture what the consumer or customer needs rather than what best suits its production and technical facilities. A *production-oriented company*, on the other hand, tends to produce what it is technically convenient to make rather than what the consumer needs. Optimum business performance normally lies in compromise between marketing-orientation and production-orientation.

marketing planning. Process of: **a** deciding on the basis of *market assessments* the *markets* in which the company will operate; **b** deciding the products or services it will offer and the pricing policies it will adopt in order to achieve overall company profit and return on capital employed targets; **c** *market and sales forecasting*, including the broad marketing targets in terms of market share, sales turnover, profits and costs; **d** defining in outline the methods of promotion, selling, distribution and customer service; **e** assessing the manufacturing, financial and manpower resources required.

marketing planning and control. Wide range of techniques and activities covering such areas as identifying key tasks, setting objectives, acceptable performance levels, standards, goals, etc, developing programmes to achieve the desired objectives, measuring performance against these objectives, interpreting trends and results, and taking any necessary corrective action at the right time. See also *marketing mix*.

marketing research. Research to provide information for management to decide marketing policy, this information taking in *market research*, competitors' activities, the general economic climate, possible alternative goods or services, distribution methods, etc. Long-term marketing research tends to become an integral part of *corporate planning*.

marketing strategy. Overall plan for maximizing impact on the market in the short and long term. The strategy is based on *market research* and assessment and incorporates *product planning, sales promotion, sales planning* and *distribution planning*.

marketing, test. See *test marketing*.

market intelligence. Product of *market research* and *marketing research*. See also *marketing mix*.

Market Intelligence Library, DT Statistics and (UK). Operated by the *Department of Trade*. See *DT Statistics and Market Intelligence Library*.

market leader. Company which has the largest share in a market for particular goods or services.

market order. Instruction to buy or sell *shares, stocks* or *commodities* at the prevailing *market price*.

market penetration. Proportion, usually expressed as a percentage, of the *actual market volume* (that is, total sales by all suppliers) that is met by a particular company or its product. A further and related important indicator is *market saturation*, which is the proportion, also usually expressed as a percentage, that actual market volume is of *market potential* (that is, total possible sales).

market potential. Effective demand for a product or service at a given price within a specific market segment. See also *actual market volume, market prospective, market segment, capacity, market share*, and *overall market capacity*.

market price. *Price* of a product or service arrived at by the forces of *supply* and *demand*. Also known as 'market'.

market prospective. Quantity a company could sell in a particular *market segment* irrespective of any limitation in company resources. See also *actual market volume, market potential, market segment capacity, market share, overall market capacity*.

market research. Process of identifying and assessing the markets for existing or proposed products and/or services including the *buying behaviour* and life style of customers. Statistical techniques are often used, and the purpose is to assess not only the size of the markets, but such factors as the *value* prospective purchasers put on the product or service and, therefore, the *price* that can be asked for it. Market research has tended to divide into two specialisms, namely, *industrial market research*, concerned with selling to industry, and *consumer research* concerned with markets for consumer goods. Compare *marketing research*.

market research agency. Organization which is in business to give *market research* advice to client firms and to carry out surveys, etc for them using such techniques as *random sampling*. In addition to services tailored to the needs of a particular client, a market research agency may offer *syndicated market research* and/or participation in *omnibus surveys* to a number of clients.

Market Research Society. UK professional and advisory body.

market-ripe. Description of produce not yet ripe but expected to be so at the time that it goes to market.

market saturation. Proportion, usually expressed as a percentage, showing the relationship of *actual market volume* (that is, sales actually made) to *market potential* (that is, sales that could be made). A further and related important indicator is *market penetration*, which is the proportion, also usually expressed as a percentage, of the actual market volume for a product that is met by a particular company or its product.

market segmentation. Analysis of the purchasers in a *market* by reference to such characteristics as *buying behavio(u)r*, need patterns, *socio-economic status* or age in order to divide the market into sectors or segments in each of which the customers are of a similar nature and are influenced by similar buying motives. Marketing effort can then be directed more specifically to defined segments. See also *buying behavio(u)r, organismic theory* and *test marketing*.

market segment capacity. Amount of a product or service that could be absorbed in the future by a specialized segment of a market irrespective of *price* considerations. See also *actual market volume, market potential, market prospective, market share, overall market capacity*.

market share. Sales of a product in a particular *market segment* as a proportion of the total sales or *actual market volume* in that segment. See also *market potential, market prospective, market segment capacity, overall market capacity*.

market sharing agreement. One made between two or more companies or organizations producing and/or *marketing* similar products. They agree that each shall deal only with a particular part of the available market rather than competing with each other in the market as a whole. In many countries such agreements are illegal on the grounds that they limit *consumer* choice and are an unwarranted restraint of trade. See also *price fixing*.

market stability. Product qualities such as durability (for example, how much in danger of obsolescence is the product?), breadth of use (is it used locally, nationally or internationally?), whether it has a captive market, and the security of any *patents*. See also *product life cycle*.

market visit. As *field inspection*.

market volume, actual. See *actual market*

volume.

mark-up. 1. Difference between wholesale price and retail price. **2.** The difference between prices at various stages in between the prime producer and the final supplier to the end user. **3.** An increase in price of a product or service.

mark-up pricing. Application of a constant *mark-up* (1).

Marseille Stock Exchange. *Palais de la Bourse, Marseille.* One of six provincial French stock exchanges.

Maslow's hierarchy of needs. Five levels of human needs for satisfaction developed by A H Maslow in 1943. **1.** Basic physiological (survival) needs, eg food, shelter. **2.** Safety and security. **3.** Belongingness. **4.** Self-esteem and status. **5.** Self-actualization, self-realization and sense of achievement. Maslow's basic concept was that man is a 'wanting animal'. As one need is satisfied the next higher need emerges as more important until the highest self-actualization or self-fulfilment needs are reached, which can never be completely satisfied. Once a need is satisfied, however, it can no longer be a motivator. Maslow argues that these levels are interdependent and overlapping so that each higher level comes into prominence before the lower levels have been completely satisfied.

mass picketing. US term where large number of pickets is involved, as opposed to *pink-tea picketing.* See also *peaceful picketing.*

mass production. Manufacture of a product on a large scale and to standard specifications both in product design and in the method of production. The latter may involve the individual worker in continuous repetition of relatively simple *tasks,* possibly to a pace dictated by the other workers or even an impersonal conveyor belt, as in *assembly line* or *flow line production.* Differs from the one-off production of *job production,* the relatively small quantity production of *batch production,* and the continuous but less *labo(u)r-intensive* production of *process production.*

Mass production is one of the three major *systems of production* identified and described by Drucker, the others being *process production* and *unique-product production.* Drucker defines mass production as 'the assembly of varied products — in large numbers or small — out of uniform and standardized parts', but distinguishes between 'old style' mass production of uniform products and 'new style' mass production of uniform parts for assembly into diversified products. He sees the complexitites of the 'new style' as having been made manageable by modern management techniques like *operations* (or *operational*) *research,* making possible continuous production in combination with an output of diversified production.

mass unemployment. Symptom and one of the evils of *slump* conditions which can usually be allayed by some form of *reflation* of the community's purchasing power. See *trade cycle* and *full employment.*

master. 1. Term for employer that originated with the *guild-master* of medieval Guilds but continued to be used after the industrial revolution. **2.** Also used in context of 'master and servant' common law in UK to describe wide range of duties and remedies in cases of industrial dispute.

master activity programming (MAP). Approach to simplification of office systems and methods based on setting standards for control purposes which are developed from random observations during the course of the investigation.

master budget. Overall or final control budget of a company or organization, coordinating the various sectional budgets.

master clerical data (MCD). Proprietary form of clerical work measurement based on MTM developed by Serge Birn Co (US). Covers detailed true values for twelve major types of clerical operations (eg calculating, machine operating, reading, writing).

master record index. As *build schedule.*

master sample. Statistical sample used frequently. It may be kept by a *market research* agency and used as required to meet clients' needs.

master standard data (MSD). Form of *predetermined motion time system* of US origin.

master unit. Part of a system which controls the performance or activity of other parts, or *slave units,* in the same system.

matched samples. Two samples of items or people having identical characteristics statistically so that they should produce virtually the same results in a survey or study. One may be used to check results produced with the other. Or the two samples may be used on two different subjects to give a comparison between the subjects. See also *random sample*.

matching item. Test question requiring the testee to match individual works, statements or figures from one list with others from a second list.

materials handling. Application of analytical methods and equipment design considerations to the problems of storing, packaging and moving products and materials in any form in the prescribed sequence and to the locations required. The aim is to specify the safest and most economical methods, equipment, containers, handling devices, etc.

materials-type flow process chart. *Flow process chart* which shows the progressive use and development of materials during production.

Maternity rights (UK). A pregnant woman who has been in the continuous employ of one company for two years or more, and who works until 11 weeks or less before confinement, is protected under the Employment Protection Act of 1975. She is entitled to a leave of absence of 40 weeks and to return to her original job after that period without loss of seniority. In that period she will receive remuneration at nine-tenths her normal salary (less National Insurance maternity allowance). This is recoverable by her employer. It is possible, however, that changes to these regulations may be made in subsequent legislation.

mathematical models. Mathematical or symbolic representation of real and theoretical business and other situations. Their purpose is normally to seek ways of optimizing the use of resources or improving performance.

matrices, Raven's progressive. See *Raven's progressive matrices*.

matrix organization. One such as a research laboratory or management consultancy in which there are a number of functions or disciplines, the members of which may be assigned to special project teams. Individuals may be accountable to two superiors, one (the functional head) on a continuing basis for overall performance in a particular function or discipline, and the other (the project leader) for performance on a particular project. See illustration opposite and also *interaction matrix*.

mature student. One who enters further or higher education after a period in employment, rather than straight from school.

maturity. Full development or completion of contract, such as an insurance policy.

maturity curves. System of *salary progression curves*.

maturity stage (or period). Term used by some economists for the final stage of *economic growth* in which the community attains a state of high mass *consumption*.

Maud Report on the Management of Local Government (UK). See *Redcliffe-Maud Report*.

maximum distribution. *Retail audit* term for the proportion of shops in a survey that have stocked the product being surveyed since the previous audit. *Net effective distribution* is the term for the proportion of shops actually stocking the product at the audit.

maximum/minimum control. Storekeeping system under which regularly used components and materials are re-ordered up to the prescribed 'maximum' levels whenever stocks drop to the prescribed 'minimum' levels. A further refinement, known as fine balance control, takes into account forward commitments of both supply and demand.

maximum working area. Space over which a seated or standing worker has to make full length arm movements (ie from the shoulder) in order to reach and use tools, materials and equipment. See *workplace layout, normal working area, motion study*.

May Day. Time of socialist and labo(u)r celebration in many parts of the world. See also *Labor Day* in the USA.

MBA. Master of Business Adminstration.

MBO. *Management by objectives.*

MCD. *Master clerical data.*

McGregor's theories. See *Theory X* and *Theory Y*.

MCT. *Managed change technique.*

MDW. *Measured daywork.*

mean. See *arithmetic average*.

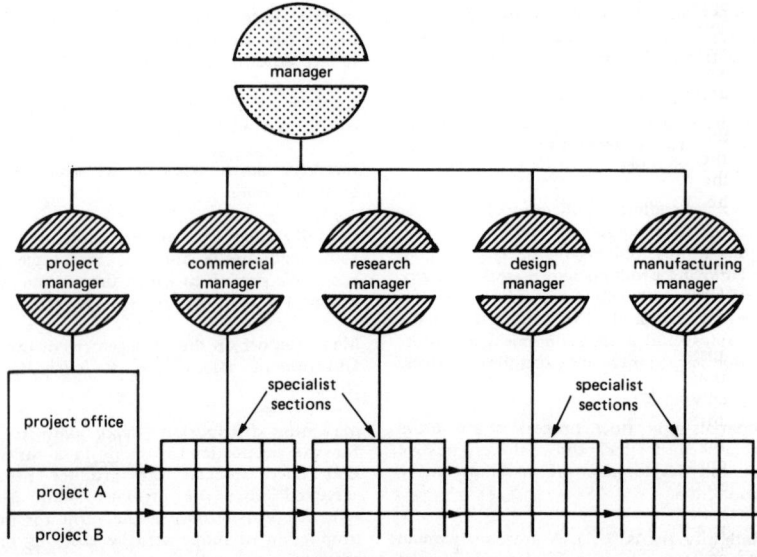

matrix organization

mean audit date. *Retail audit* term for the date on which the average shop in a sample is audited. This date is necessary because in most audits it is not physically possible for all the shops to be covered on the same day. The spread of audit dates either side of the mean audit date can also be significant.

means-ends analysis. Analytical approach to questioning decision making. The purpose is to establish connections between desired ends and the practical action required to achieve the results.

measured daywork (MDW). Management technique which involves defining a target daily rate of productivity but then, instead of employing conventional direct *payment-by-results*, establishes a regular wage level to be paid for each day that the operative or production unit concerned reaches target. Targets set under measured daywork are often established using *work measurement* and, when this is so, the technique may be called *controlled daywork*. A further refinement is stepped daywork or *graded measured day work (GMDW)* in which there are different wage rates geared to different performance bands (see also *banding*).

Measured daywork has the attraction for workers of providing uniformly high pay and for management the attraction of high, controlled output.

measurement systems. See the principal systems of measurement, namely, the *British Imperial System* (BIS), the *International System (SI)* of metric units, and the *US Customary System*.

measures of central tendency. Way of indicating the place on a distribution curve where the largest number of items is concentrated. See *mode*, *median* and *average*.

mechanical aptitude tests. Used in *personnel selection* etc to test ability to understand how movement can be transmitted mechanically. See also *psychological testing* and *aptitude tests*. Examples of mechanical aptitude tests include the *mechanical comprehension tests*, the *Morrisby mechanical ability test*, and the *Vincent mechanical diagrams test*.

mechanical comprehension tests. *Mechanical aptitude tests*, particularly those devised by Bennett. See also *psychological testing* and *aptitude tests*. The mechanical comprehension tests are used for *personnel selection* and *vocational guidance* as part of the *engineering apprentice test-battery* of the National Institute of Industrial Psychology in the UK. In this latter battery they are coded (m). Bennett's mechanical comprehension tests also have a much wider use internationally, particularly in the USA where they are held in high regard as predictors of success in tests for machine tool operatives, maintenance mechanics, engineering apprentices, technician and professional engineers, and women entering engineering. Different combinations of tests are used for these different categories of employee or prospective employee. See also the *O'Rourke mechanical aptitude test*, the *Purdue mechanical adaptibility test*, the *SRA mechanical aptitudes test*, and the *MacQuarrie test for mechanical ability*.

mechanical principles test, knowledge of. As *mechanical comprehension test*. A term used particularly in the USA.

mechanistic organization. Term used by T Burns and G M Stalker to describe what is essentially a *bureaucratic organization*. The mechanistic type organization has the following characteristics: **a** emphasis on functional specialization; **b** people tend to work on their specialist tasks without much regard for the overall task of the organization; **c** duties, powers and methods associated with each job are precisely defined; **d** communication takes place along the line of command. The mechanistic organization is contrasted with the more loosely structured *organic organizations*. A mechanistic type of organization is sometimes referred to as a 'closed' or 'formal' organization.

mechanization. Replacement and/or extension of muscle function by machine.

media analysis. Assessment of the value of publicity media for advertising particular goods and services or for reaching particular audiences. Media analysis may include the use of *keyed advertisements* and *split-run copy testing*.

median. *Measure of central tendency* obtained by arranging items in order of magnitude from the lowest to the highest, the mid point item in such an array being the median. Where n = number in array the median = $\frac{n+1}{2}$. See *average* and *mode*.

media research. Analysis of newspaper readership, radio listeners, television viewers, cinema goers, etc in terms of attitudes, advertising potential, etc. See also *Audit Bureau of Circulations*.

media testing. Testing the response from the different types of advertising media.

mediation. See *conciliation*.

Medicare. Medical aid program(me) for the aged run by the US Social Security Administration.

medium-term liabilities. Those which must be met within about three years but are not so imminent as to be classed as current. See also *long-term liabilities*.

meetings procedure. See *committee procedure*.

Mehrwertsteuer. (Federal) German for *value added tax*.

MEL. *Minimum earnings level.*

Melbourne Stock Exchange. One of six *Australian stock exchanges*.

member bank. Term in the USA for what is known in the UK as a *commercial bank* or a *clearing bank*, or in Western Europe as a *credit bank*.

membership groups. Type of *reference group* brought together for the purpose of examining *consumer* buying motives. Members of a membership group are people who belong naturally to it and are recognized as doing so by the others, so that there tends to be a natural identification with the group's ideals, values, tastes and behaviour. A *family group* is one form of membership group. Other forms of reference group are *dissociative groups, aspirational groups* and *face-to-face groups*.

memo-motion study. *Work study* technique involving the cine-filming of statistically selected samples of work followed by analysis of the film. See also *motion study* and *work measurement*.

memorandum of association. Sets out the purpose for which the company concerned has been formed and the amount and different classes of share capital. The memorandum is drawn up on the formation of a company (in the UK) together with the *articles of association* which represent a contract between the company and its shareholders and set out the powers of the directors and the legal framework of the company.

memory, magnetic. See *magnetic memory or store* (computer).

MEMP. Maximize expected maximum profit. Term used for operational research technique to describe method of determinging profit optimization.

mensualization. Term of French origin for extending to *blue collar* or manual workers terms and conditions of employment associated with *staff status*. Strictly speaking, the term means switching to monthly payment though this is not necessarily a condition of staff status. The process of levelling up the terms and conditions of blue collar and white collar employment is also known as *integration* or *harmonization*. Where staff status applies to both blue and white collar workers they are said to have *single status*.

mental ability test. As *intelligence test*.

MEPT staff. Abbreviation sometimes used for 'Managerial, Executive, Professional and Technical Staff'.

mercado a plazo. Forward settlement market on *Spanish stock exchanges*.

mercado de contado. Cash or spot market on *Spanish stock exchanges*.

mercantile agent. Or commercial agent. A person who has authority, in the ordinary course of his business, to buy, sell or consign for the purpose of sale any goods entrusted to him by his principal. Mercantile agents are sometimes appointed by overseas customers.

mercantile credit. Or commercial credit. Term used to indicate the allowable limits of a transaction. Strictly speaking, it covers business between manufacturer or wholesaler and other levels of the trade before it reaches the *consumer*. In practice (practise), mercantile credit is also a term used of transactions prior to manufacturing, such as when materials and components are supplied to the manufacturer.

merchandise. 1. As *consumer goods*. 2. Goods bought for resale.

merchandise balance. As national *balance of payments* but excluding *invisible exports* and *invisible imports* such as financial and insurance services.

merchandise planning. Defined by *Drucker* as 'the systematic design of quality goods for mass distribution, the systematic development of mass producers for them.'

merchandising. Term used in marketing **a** where a manufacturing or wholesaling company acts directly to encourage *sales promotion* by the retail outlets it serves, **b** where psychological persuasion is used on consumers at the point of purchase without the use of personal salesmanship, **c** where a retailing company is planning the range of products to be sold and promoted. See also *marketing mix*.

merchant. Type of *wholesaler*, and sometimes retailer, who is not committed to handling goods from a particular supplier or selling to particular outlets. See also *del credere agent, distributor, stocking agent, stockist, wholesaler*.

merchant bank. UK bank providing long-term venture capital or *risk capital* rather than the short-term loans handled by *commercial banks* or *clearing banks*. Merchant banks also advise on *mergers* and *take-overs* and deal in specialist services such as those of *accepting houses, issuing houses* and *investment trusts*, in *portfolio management*, in gold and foreign currency, in insurance and related activities, in *hire purchase*, etc.

merger. Where two companies agree to merge or fuse as distinct from a *take-over* where one company effects the *acquisition* of another. See also *horizontal merger* and *vertical merger*.

Merger Treaty 1967. Treaty which formally united the *European Economic Community (EEC)*, the *European Atomic Energy Community (Euratom)* and the *European Coal and Steel Community (ECSC)* under the *Council of Ministers* and the *European Commision*.

merimiesvero. Seamen's tax in Finland. See also *Finnish Income Tax*.

merit pay. Extra pay or salary awarded to an employee, executive, etc in recognition of particular qualities of value to the employer. See also *merit rating, bonus schemes* and *payment-by-results* and *graded hourly rates*.

merit rating. Technique for rating individual operators. Recognizes that different people doing the same job can have different values to their firm and therefore merit different pay. Merit rating factors can include *absenteeism*, punctuality, length of service, adaptability, health and safety records, attitude to management, etc. See also *job evaluation* and *card-stacking method*.

merit system. Where promotion is by examination or other objective demonstration of ability. Different, for example, from *spoils system*.

Metal Exchange, London. See *London Metal Exchange*.

meta system. General term for a macro or overall view of a system, or system which takes all factors into account.

Meteorological Office. UK Government agency responsible for weather forecasting and data collection.

methods engineer. Engineer skilled in method study and possibly *production planning* techniques. His work often overlaps or is synonymous with that of the *industrial engineer* and the *work study officer* (or engineer).

methods time measurement (MTM). System of synthetic standard times for standard human movements sometimes used in *motion study*. Other such systems include *predetermined motion time systems (PMTS)* and *work factor*.

method study. Part of work study concerned with the systematic recording and critical examination of existing and proposed ways of doing work, as a means of developing and applying easier and more effective methods and reducing cost. Precedes *work measurement* in the application of *work study*.

metrication. Process of transferring from a non-metric measurement system, such as the *US Customary System* or the *British Imperial System*, to a metric system, particularly the *International System (SI)*.

Metrication Board (UK). Quasi-governmental body responsible for sign-posting the way to metrication in the UK.

metric ton. Or tonne. 1,000 kilograms (18 kilograms lighter than an Imperial ton).

metropolitan shift system. *Shift working* arrangement under which workers change shifts every few days.

MG. *Managerial grid*.

MICR. *Magnetic ink character recognition*.

micro-computer. Relatively small and low-cost *computer* designed for specific applications. See also *mini-computer*.

microchip. As *chip*; see *micro processor*.

microcopy. Text in a form too small to be read by the human eye without the assistance of such equipment as *microfiche* readers.

micro electronics. Generic term for a variety of miniature electronic components and circuits.

microfiche. Small sheet of *microfilm* carrying the equivalent of several pages of text of a book. The text can be read using a microfiche reader. Microfiche is important as a space saving tool of *information storage and retrieval*.

microfilm. Film carrying reduced-size photographs of documents etc.

micro processor. Miniature integrated circuits on microchips which can interpret and execute instructions. Applications include *data processing* and *information storage and retrieval*, process control, etc.

middleman. *Wholesaler*, agent or other businessman coming between the producer or the manufacturer and retailer in the *sales chain*. His basic role in the distribution of goods is to buy from the producer and sell to the retailer. The term 'middleman' is often used in a pejorative sense implying that the *profit* made by the 'middleman' increases the *end price* to the consumer. This is not strictly fair if the middleman is playing an efficient role but it is the case, on analysis, that a surprisingly large number of middlemen are involved with some products. In modern times, on the other hand, the *marketing* of proprietary *consumer goods* has increasingly 'cut out the middleman' in favour of direct transactions between producer and retailer. Indeed, when techniques such as *direct mail selling* are used, the retailer is cut out as well though, in cost terms, this may only be substituting one type of *selling cost* for another. See also *distributive industry*.

Midlands & Western Stock Exchange. UK provincial stock exchange in Birmingham.

Midwest Stock Exchange. One of the major *US stock exchanges*, based in Chicago.

migrant worker. As *guest worker*.

migration (of labo(u)r). Movement of labo(u)r into and out of a particular area.

Milan Stock Exchange. Or *Borsa Valori di Milano*. The principal stock exchange of Italy.

Milletydings Act 1937. See *antitrust*

219

legislation (US).

mini-computer. Relatively small and low-cost *computer* for general purpose use. See also *micro-computer*.

minimum earnings level (MEL). Nationally agreed minimum wage applicable in industries where wage levels are largely determined by local agreements.

minimum entitlement. Minimum pay an employee can receive under a particular *payment system*, including a *payment-by-results* scheme.

minimum lending rate (MLR). In mid-1972 succeeded *bank rate* as the rate at which the Bank of England was prepared to lend to UK banks. Tends to influence bank interest rates generally, but not as directly and dramatically as did bank rate. The minimum lending rate is tied automatically to the weekly rate for *Treasury Bills*.

minimum manufacturing quantity (MMQ). *Production planning and control* term for the minimum production run economically acceptable for a product. The optimum run is the *economic manufacturing quantity (EMQ)*.

minimum movements. Movements which, while natural, are the minimum necessary for the job. See *motion study*.

minimum piece work standard (MPS). Level of earnings formerly agreed in the UK engineering industry as that which should be obtained by the worker of average ability on *payment-by-results* schemes.

minimum stock. As *buffer stock*.

minimum time rate (MTR). The lowest rate of pay payable to a particular type of employee.

Ministers (EEC). See *Council of Ministers*.

Ministry of Labour (UK). First created in 1916. Government Department responsible for legislation on industrial relations, industrial training, etc in the UK until being renamed in April 1968 the Department of Employment and Productivity. Name changed again to *Department of Employment* in July 1970.

Minnesota clerical test. Two-part *psychological test* developed in the USA and covering number comparison and name comparison.

Minnesota engineering analogies test (MEAT). *Psychologial test* of US origin devised specifically for professional engineers or prospective engineering students. It has elements of both an *achievement test* and an *intelligence test*.

Minnesota paper form board, revised. See *revised Minnesota paper form board*.

Minnesota rate of manipulation test. Test of *psychomotor skills* of US origin. Concerned particularly with measuring the speed and accuracy of finger, hand and arm movements. See also *Stromberg dexterity test* and *psychological testing*.

MIS. *Management information systems.*

misfeasance. Improper and unlawful execution of an act that in itself is lawful. Someone perpetrating a misfeasance is a 'misfeasor'. See also *nonfeasance*.

mixed benefits scheme (pensions). Where the total retirement benefits of a *pension* scheme are a combination of pension and *lump sum cash benefits*, together being the *total retirement benefits*. See also *average salary pension* and *final salary pension*.

mixed cost. One composed of a combination of *fixed cost* and *variable cost*. A telephone bill, for example, is a combination of a fixed rent and a variable charge according to actual usage. See also *semi-variable cost* and *stepped cost*.

mixed economy. Economic system combining private enterprise and a free market with state run enterprises and some central government control of the economy.

MLR. *Minimum lending rate.*

MMQ. *Minimum manufacturing quantity.*

MO (or mo). 1. *Mail order.* **2.** *Money order.*

mobility of labo(u)r. As *labo(u)r mobility*.

mode. Statistical measure of central tendency which reflects the most frequent item in a range of data. Eg if the majority of customers ordered goods six times a year the mode would be 6. See also *median* and *average*.

models. Two or three dimensional representation of an object or objects, usually less than actual size. A *mathematical model* provides an abstract representation of a situation as in *cybernetics, operational research* or *systems analysis*. See also *accounting models, analog(ue) models, heuristic models*, and *symbolic models*.

modem. *Interface* device between a *computer terminal* and the communications line.

module training. Method of training developed particularly by the UK *Engineering Industry Training Board*. Based on concept of building up skills and knowledge in units as needed by individual trainee/student. Each training module includes a training element, an experience element and a further education element. See *multi-skill (progressive) training*.

modus operandi. Methods and manner by which an organization etc operates. See also *management style*.

modus vivendi. Manner and style of living, particularly one arrived at by a compromise between clashing interests.

monadic product test. *Market research* term for a test of a single product. See also *diadic product test* (two products) and *triadic product test* (three products).

monetary measures. Government action to counteract *deflation* or *inflation* by controlling the amount of spending power available through banks, *hire purchase* companies, etc and the cost of borrowing by changes in *bank rate, minimum lending rate*, etc. See also *fiscal measures*.

monetary union. Where two or more countries share a common currency and common financial institutions and policies. See also *economic and monetary union (EEC)*.

money at call. Debt or loan which must be repaid on demand.

money broker. Financial institution that specializes in dealing in the money market in short-term *securities* and loans and in gold and foreign currencies. Other types of institution dealing in the money market include *acceptance houses, commercial banks* and *discount houses*. See also *hot money*.

money manager. Manager of investments and related financial matters.

money purchase pension scheme. Like the *average salary pension scheme*, the money purchase scheme is based on an accumulating of pension according to the salary received throughout the years of membership of the scheme (unlike the *final salary pension scheme*). The special characteristic of the money purchase scheme is that the contributions of both employees and employers are fixed, with the amount of pension produced depending on the insurance contract obtained. As a scheme based on salary and contributions throughout working life, the money purchase scheme can suffer from inflation in the same way as the average salary pension scheme.

money shop. Offers banking and consumer-finance services including instalment credit and *hire purchase*. Money shops are usually run by fringe banks. They are normally sited in shopping centres and are open for conventional retail shopping hours rather than conventional banking hours.

money supply. Broadly speaking, the amount of money which is circulating in a national or other economy. Two of the current definitions or measures of money supply are the M1 and the M3. M1 is a measure of notes and coins in circulation with the public, plus current accounts but less an allowance for items in transit. M3 covers the ground covered by M1 but also includes money in deposit accounts, deposits of overseas currencies, money with discount houses, etc and money deposited with banks by the *public sector of the economy*.

Monopolies (and Mergers) Commission (UK). Monopolies Commission was established under the Monopolies and Mergers Acts 1948 and 1965. It also discharges responsibilities under the *Restrictive Trade Practices Act 1956* and the *Fair Trading Act 1973*. Under the latter Act it was renamed the Monopolies and Mergers Commission. Reporting to and appointed by the *Department of Trade*, the Monopolies Commission may be called upon to investigate an apparent *monopoly* in the production or supply of goods and services; a prospective merger that might produce a monopoly situation; or an unregistered restrictive trade practice (practise). The Department of Trade can nullify agreements on the strength of Monopolies Commission reports, and the Commission was strengthened, as well as re-named, by the Fair Trading Act 1973.

monopoly. Situation where at least one-third of a local or national market is controlled by one company, corporation or group of people. In the US, monopolies have been curbed since the late nineteenth century by *antitrust legislation*. Legislation in the UK has included the Monopolies and Mergers Acts 1948 and 1965 and the *Fair Trading Act 1973*. Monopolies and mergers are also among the *restrictive trade practices (practises)* covered by the *rules of competition* of the *Common Market*.

monopsony. Where one purchaser has sole control of a market for products, services or labo(u)r even though there may be several sellers.

Monte Carlo techniques. Simulation, sometimes using a computer, of a work situation that is complicated by random elements.

Montevideo Stock Exchange. (Rincone Missiones). The important stock exchange in Uruguay.

Montreal Stock Exchange. One of six major *Canadian stock exchanges*.

moonlighting. Doing a second job, usually in the evenings, in addition to one's normal daytime job. See also *twilight shift* and *double employment*.

morale survey. As *attitude survey* (1).

morphological approach. Design tool developed by Professor Zwicky in the USA. It uses sets of matrices with which the designer checks the effectiveness of his creative work. See also *interaction matrix*.

morphological research. Marketing man's term for an exploratory approach to *technological forecasting* through a detailed analysis of the various parameters of a product's design, materials and function. Other techniques of technological forecasting include *brainstorming*, the *Delphi approach*, *exploratory forecasting techniques*, *normative forecasting techniques*, the *scenario writing approach*, and *technological trend extrapolation*.

Morrisby compound series test. *Non-verbal intelligence test*, involving problems with bead patterns and matrices. The test takes 20 or 30 minutes and has special norms for the general population, for schools and for graduates. See also *psychological testing* and *aptitude tests*.

Morrisby GAT-N test. *Numerical aptitude test* that takes a total of about 35 minutes and is in three parts covering simple computation, number series and matrices. See also *psychological testing* and *aptitude tests*.

Morrisby GAT-V test. *Verbal intelligence test* divided into three parts, each taking about 20 minutes. The test has norms for the general population, for schools and for graduates. See also *psychological testing* and *aptitude tests*.

Morrisby mechanical ability test. *Mechanical aptitude test* that uses practical examples of a wide range of mechanical principles. See also *psychological testing* and *aptitude tests*.

Morrisby shapes tests. *Spatial ability* or *aptitude test* (takes about 15 minutes). See also *psychological testing* and *aptitude tests*.

Morrisby speed test 1. *Clerical aptitude test* in which pairs of numbers and names are checked against each other within a time limit. The test takes 10 to 15 minutes. See also *psychological testing* and *aptitude tests*.

mortgage. 1. Where a finanical organization such as a *building society* or an *insurance company*, makes a loan of part or all of a house purchase price to a mortgagor, either an individual or a company, the mortgagee retaining qualified ownership of the property as security for the loan. See also *lease (hire)*. **2.** Temporary and conditional pledge of property to a *creditor* as security against a *debt*.

mortgage bonds (US). As *mortgage debentures*.

mortgage debentures. See *debentures*.

mortmain. Or 'dead hand'. Non-transferrable and perpetual ownership of *real estate* or property by institutions such as churches.

motion. Proposal put to, or moved at, a meeting or conference by one of those present, who is known as the *mover*. If the motion has a *seconder* it is then debated and voted on by those present unless, for example, the organization holding the meeting has a rule that all motions or certain types of motion must be referred without discussion to a sub-committee for consideration and report before being debated and voted on by the full committee or meeting.

It is important that the *standing orders* and rules of debate on a motion give all those present the maximum possible opportunity to consider and give their views on what is being proposed, but it is also important to have firm rules of procedure so that the meeting does not descend into anarchy and a clear decision can be reached. An organization or committee will normally have a rule that certain *notice of motion* must be given so that there is time for individual members to brief themselves on the proposal and, usually, for the motion to be written into the agenda for the meeting. Once the meeting is convened, it is a fundamental rule that all contributions be addressed to the chairman. It is also common practice for the mover of a motion to have a right of reply at the end of the discussion and before the vote is taken. It is often a sound general rule for each person present to be allowed to speak once only on a motion. Exceptions to the practice of permitting individuals to speak once only on a motion is where they are allowed to put to the chairman a *point of order*, a *point of information* or a *point of personal explanation*. In some cases, the rules of a committee or organization allow a seconder to reserve the right to speak later in the debate instead of immediately after the mover.

In the form in which it is moved initially, a motion is known as an *original motion*. However, various types of *amendment* or amendments to the original motion may be moved during a debate. If such an amendment or amendments should be passed by the meeting, and therefore incorporated in the original motion, the resulting motion is known as a *substantive motion* and is discussed and voted on after the amendments have been dealt with.

The most common majority required for a motion to be passed is a simple majority, in which a majority of one vote is sufficient and the chairman may use his *casting vote* in the event of a tie. In some cases, however, such as matters affecting the constitution of an organization, there may be a rule or standing order requiring a more emphatic majority, perhaps a two-thirds or even a three-quarters majority. Sometimes there is a more complex formula such as 'a simple majority of the votes cast'. Once a motion has been passed, it becomes a *resolution*. A useful safeguard at both formal and informal meetings is to ensure that the responsibility for action on any resolution is clearly laid down. See also *addendum, adjournment, card vote, casting vote, committee procedure, closure, composite motion, direct negative, main question, mandate, next business, omnibus motion, previous question, putting the question, quorum, reference back, roll call vote, standing committee, standing order.*

motion study. Study of repetitive worker movements broken down into very small elements, virtually as micro-scale *method study*. Aim is to eliminate unnecessary movements and identify most efficient and least tiring combination of movements. *Work measurement* can then follow, possibly using synthetic times and values derived from *predetermined motion time systems (PMTS), work factor,* or *methods time measurement (MTM).* Movements analyzed in motion study include *minimum movements, simultaneous movements, rhythmical movements, continuous movements.*

motivate. To ensure that people carry out effectively and willingly the tasks assigned to them by providing them with reasons for behaving in certain ways. The reasons may include rewards, incentives or other forms of encouragement which act as positive motivation by demonstrating that given behavio(u)rs will satisfy the individual's *needs*. The threat or use of punishment can be seen as a form of negative motivation.

motivation. Processes or factors that cause people to act or behave in certain ways. To *motivate* is to induce someone to take action. The process of motivation consists of: **a** identification or appreciation of an unsatisfied *need;* **b** the establishment of a goal which will satisfy the need; and **c** determination of the action required to satisfy the need. Best known theories of motivation are those propounded by *F Herzberg*, A H Maslow and *V Vroom.* See also *law of effect* and *needs.*

motivation(al) research. Term used in marketing for investigating the reasons or *motivation* consumers have for buying one product rather than another.

motivation-hygiene theory. See *Herzberg's theory.*

motivation study. *Market research* technique for identifying the *motivations* responsible for the behavio(u)r pattern of a *market*.

motivators. See *Herzberg's theory.*

motor activity. Execution of a pattern of muscular activity to manipulate an object or respond to a situation. See also *sensory-motor activity.*

223

motor skills. Those connected with the *motor activity* of muscles.

Motor Spd Acc (test). Coding for *motor speed and accuracy mechanical test* in the *engineering apprentice test-battery* of the National Institute of Industrial Psychology in the UK.

motor speed and accuracy mechanical test (Motor Spd Acc). *Personnel selection* and *vocational guidance* test devised as part of the *engineering apprentice test-battery* of the National Institute of Industrial Psychology in the UK. See also *psychological testing* and *test battery*.

Mountain Standard Time (MST or MT). Local time at a point in the USA at the 105th meridian. See *standard time* and Appendix: Time Zones.

movements. See *motion study*.

mover. Someone moving a *motion* at a meeting or conference.

moving average. Simple arithmetic technique for updating the accuracy of short-term forecasting which is based on extrapolating from past performance. For example, the forecast of demand for a product may be based on the average sales in, say, the previous four weeks. Thus for Week 5 the forecast would be the average of sales in Weeks 1 to 4 but for Week 6, using a moving average, the average would move forward one week and be based on sales in Weeks 2 to 5. A more sophisticated mathematical technique for weighting short-term forecasting is *exponential smoothing*.

moving-parity (exchange rate). Concept that offers a compromise between fixed parity and *floating exchange rates* by automatically adjusting the par rate for a currency according to a *moving average* of the rates of previous months. Another compromise is the *sliding-parity* or crawling peg concept.

MPA. Master of Public Administration or Master of Public Accounting, degrees awarded particularly by US universities and colleges.

MPS. *Minimum piece work standard.*

MRA. *Multiple regression analysis.*

MSC. *Manpower Services Commission.*

MSD. *Master standard data.*

MSL (or msl). Mean sea level.

MST (or MT). *Mountain Standard Time.*

MTM. *Methods time measurement.*

MTR. *Minimum time rate.*

muckraker. Person who seeks to unearth corruption in the business and/or political worlds, possibly himself using unscrupulous methods.

multi-employer bargaining. Or association bargaining. Form of *collective bargaining* in which a number of employers participate, as in *industry-wide* bargaining, sometimes through an *employers' association*. Collective bargaining for which two or more *trade unions* join forces is sometimes known as *coalition bargaining*.

multi-grade salary structure. Salary structure with a relatively large number of grades. A structure with a small number of grades is a *broad-banded salary structure*. See also *banding*.

multi-level distributorship. As *pyramid selling*.

multi-minute measurement. *Work sampling* technique for taking measurements at few-minute intervals over a long enough period of time to arrive at an acceptable value. See also *high frequency work sampling*.

multi-national company. Commercial organization with whole or majority ownership of interests or subsidiaries in a variety of countries, the commercial strategy of the organization tending to be international in its approach.

multi-plant bargaining. *Collective bargaining* in a *multi-plant company*.

multi-plant company. Company operating more than one *plant* or *factory*.

multiple. *Retail outlets* under one ownership selling similar products.

multiple-activity chart. Visual display of the inter-relationship between two or more activities.

multiple bar chart. Or, sometimes, compound bar chart. A *bar chart*, as in the

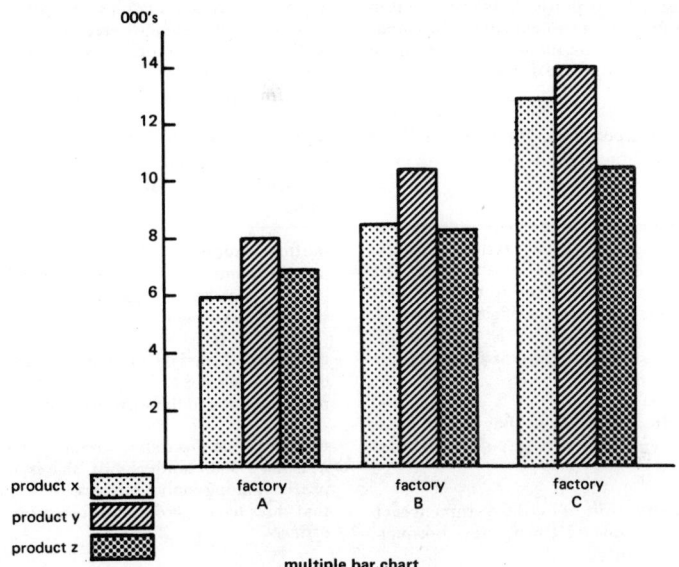

multiple bar chart

illustration, which includes groups of bars to facilitate different types of comparisons. See also *component bar chart*.

multiple branding. *Marketing* of virtually the same product under different *brand* names.

multiple choice question. Where the trainee/student chooses the answer to a question or problem from a choice of answers presented to him. Used particularly in *programmed learning*. Also used in market and attitude research and surveys.

multiple-cutoff approach. Where, in *psychological testing*, a candidate is given a number of tests (eg a *test battery*), but it is necessary to ensure that a weakness in one test score is not compensated for and obscured by high scores in other tests. A minimum cutoff score is established for each test and a candidate falling below such a score is picked out whatever his/her total score for all tests.

multiple exchange rates. Operation of a variety of *exchange rates* for different purposes or transactions.

multiple management. Form of *participation* involving employee committees and a so-called junior board at middle management level.

multiple offer. Offer for sale of several products as a single purchase, a type of offer particularly common in *direct mail selling* in order to reduce *selling costs*. An offer of an individual product or service for sale is a *solus offer*. An *add-on sale* is one made to a customer satisfied on earlier occasions.

multiple regression analysis. Statistical technique for investigating the relationships between a number of independent and dependent variables and obtaining a *regression* equation for predicting the latter in terms of the former. Multiple regression analysis is sometimes used in a *job evaluation* exercise in order to determine the weighting to be attached to different factors.

multiple role plays. See *role play*.

multiple-task role. *Job* or *role* that is concerned with a variety of *tasks* and may involve decisions on priorities between the tasks and *borrowing time*. A role concerned primarily with one task only is known as a *single-task role*.

multiprocessing. Operating two or more *computers* under a single control.

multiprogramming. Techniques enabling two or more independent *programs* to be handled at the same time by parts of a *computer*. This is particularly important in overcoming the problem that the *input device* and the *peripheral equipment* in general cannot operate as fast as the *central processing unit*.

multi-skill (progressive) training. Building a series of additional skills on common basic training.

multi-unionism. Where *trade unions* represent particular skills or types of worker whatever the industries in which they are working, a situation often leading to there being several unions in a single industry, or even a single firm. This is the opposite situation to *industrial unionism* with *industrial trade unions*.

Munich Stock Exchange. (Bayerische Börse in Munchen). One of eight *German stock exchanges*.

municipality. Unit of local government such as a parish, village, town, city, borough, district or county.

Murphy's Law. Theory that if it is humanly possible for an item of equipment to be assembled, fitted or repaired incorrectly then someone, somewhere, at some time, will do it. Sometimes expressed as 'if anything can go wrong, it will'. Hence the need for equipment to be foolproof.

mutual fund. Or *open-end investment company*. Portfolio of securities held and managed on behalf of joint owners. Eg *unit trusts*.

mutual insurance. Where the insured pay into a common fund from which any indemnifications are made. There are no shareholders as such.

mutuality. Principle in industrial relations that *piece work* rates are negotiable between management and the workers involved.

mutual office. *Insurance company* that does not have shareholders but shares out all profits among policyholders. A company that does have shareholders is a *proprietary office*.

mutual strike aid. As *employer strike insurance*. See also *indemnity fund*.

n

Naamloze Vennootschap (NV). A *joint stock company* under Netherlands law. Only a small proportion of such companies are quoted on the *Amsterdam Stock Exchange*, largely because many of them remain in private or family ownership. See also *Netherlands companies*.

NACED. *National Advisory Council on the Employment of the Disabled.*

NAF. Norsk Arbeidsgiverforening, the *Norwegian Employers' Confederation*.

Nagoya Stock Exchange. One of the five major *Japanese stock exchanges*.

Nairobi Stock Exchange. The stock exchange of Kenya.

naked debenture. Or simple debenture. *Debenture* issued against an unsecured loan.

NAM. *National Association of Manufacturers.*

named vote. Vote taken at a meeting by recording by name the way in which each voter votes. This procedure is usually reserved only for critically important issues. See also *card vote* and *roll call vote*.

name screening. *Market research* technique for checking that the prospective name of a product or service conveys the intended image, does not imply unfortunate associations, and avoids confusion with other brand names.

Naples Stock Exchange (Borsa Valori di Napoli). One of ten *Italian stock exchanges*.

Narodna Banka Jugoslavije. National Bank of Yugoslavia, *central bank* established originally in 1883.

Narodowy Bank Polski. National Bank of Poland, *central bank* established in 1945.

NASA. *National Aeronautics and Space Administration.*

National Advisory Council for Education for Industry and Commerce (UK). Advises Secretary of State for Education and Science on facilities for technical and commercial education at all levels including management.

National Advisory Council on the Employment of the Disabled (NACED). Set up in the UK under *Disabled Persons (Employment) Acts 1944 and 1958*. Responsible to the *Secretary of State for Employment*.

National Aeronautics and Space Administration (NASA). US Government agency responsible for research and development in aerospace flight and exploration. Also responsible for US space flights.

national agreement. As *industry-wide agreement* on wages, conditions of employment, etc usually made between the appropriate *employers' association* and *trade union(s)*. See also *national procedure agreement*.

National Association of Accountants (US). Established 1919, a professional body with some 65,000 members in the USA and various chapters overseas.

National Association of British Manufacturers. Now defunct founder component of the *Confederation of British Industry* in 1965.

National Association of Manufacturers (US). Major US *employers' association* established in 1895.

National Association of Personnel Consultants. US association of private *employment agencies*.

National Association of Purchasing Management (US). Established in 1915, a professional body having a membership of approximately 20,000.

national bank. 1. As *central bank*. **2.** In the US, one of the privately owned banks which by law must be an investing member of its district *Federal Reserve Bank*, which in turn is a member of the *Federal Reserve System*. Such a national bank must be insured by the *Federal Deposit Insurance Corporation*.

national bargaining. As *industry-wide bargaining*.

National Board for Prices and Incomes. Set up in UK under the *Prices and Incomes Act 1966* to consider proposed price and wages increases referred to it by the then Minister of Labour under the early warning system, Its general directive from the Minister was to keep within a 3½ per cent norm, except for certain *productivity bargaining*. Board dissolved in 1970.

National Chamber of Trade (UK). Established in 1897 and covering local *chambers of trade* and *trade associations*. See also *Association of British Chambers of Commerce* and *London Chamber of Commerce*.

national claim. Claim for more pay or improved conditions, etc lodged by *trade unions* as the first move in *industry-wide bargaining*. See also *house claim*.

National Colleges. Provide advanced courses in UK related specifically to particular industries or technological fields. Receive grants direct from *Department of Education and Science*. National Colleges include College of Air Training, Cranfield Institute of Technology, Further Education Staff College, National College of Agricultural Engineering, National College for Heating, Ventilating, Refrigeration and Fan Engineering, National College of Food Technology, National College of Rubber Technology, National Foundry College, National Leathersellers College, Royal College of Art.

National Commission on Employment and Unemployment Statistics. US commission appointed by the President to appraise the collection and analysis of national labo(u)r force statistics.

National Council on Employment Policy. US nonprofit research organization which works on *employment*, training and manpower issues, financed by grants from the *Employment and Training Administration* of the *US Department of Labor* and the Ford Foundation.

national debt. Debt owed by a national government, usually in the form of a combination of short-term and long-term loans. The UK's National Debt was established in 1694. See also *Government securities* and *consols*.

National Economic Development Council (NEDC). UK independent body normally meeting monthly and including representatives of both sides of industry — represented by senior people from both the *Confederation of British Industry* and the *Trades Union Congress* — and also Government Ministers. NEDC and its members make pronouncements on the national economic position and advise the Government, particularly in the light of investigations by the *National Economic Development Office (NEDO)*. NEDC was set up in 1965, originally with a large number of committees — 'Little Neddies' — for individual industries. Some of the Little Neddies were later disbanded.

National Economic Development Office (NEDO). UK Government-financed unit that makes independent assessments of the nation's economic position and prospects, normally reporting to the *National Economic Development Council* and often publishing reports on its findings. NEDO was established in 1965. NEDO and/or NEDC are sometimes referred to colloquially as 'Neddy'.

National Examinations Board in Supervisory Studies (UK). Set up by *Secretary of State for Education and Science* shortly after the *Industrial Training Act 1964*. Administered by the *City and Guilds of London Institute*, with a Board representing industry, commerce, education and the professions. NEBSS awards the Certificate in Supervisory Studies.

National Federation of Construction Unions. Federation of *trade unions* in the construction industry in the UK, covering a wide area of activity.

National Foundation for Educational Research. UK research organization concerned with promoting new techniques in learning and teaching. Also produces a wide range of publications and *psychological tests*.

National Grange (US). Farmers' *employers' association* in the USA established in 1867. See also *Farmers Educational Cooperative Union of America*.

National Health Service (UK). Created by Act of Parliament in 1946 to provide for UK residents a free general medical service for the treatment and prevention of illness. *Occupational health* in the UK is the concern of the *Employment Medical Advisory Service* and the *Factory Inspectorate*, both of which are responsible to the *Secretary of State for Employment*.

national income. Income in money terms earned by the people of a nation for the use of their *labo(u)r* or *capital* in the production of goods and services. In effect, is another way of expressing *net national product*. See also *real income*.

National Industrial Relations Court (NIRC). Operated under *Industrial Relations Act 1971* (UK) to adjudicate on complaints concerning organizations rather than individuals (the latter being more the concern of the *Industrial Tribunals*). The NIRC had High Court status until 1974.

National Institute of Public Management. US nonprofit centre (center) undertaking research and analysis of current and future *employment* issues.

national insurance. State operated insurance scheme against unemployment and/or sickness.

National Insurance Act 1961 (UK). Added to the *flat rate benefits and contributions* of the earlier National Insurance Acts a graduated part of the national insurance retirement pension linked to *graduated contributions*.

National Insurance Act 1965 (UK). Consolidated earlier legislation, dividing the adult population into Class 1, *employed persons;* Class 2, *self-employed persons;* and Class 3, *non-employed persons*. The Act also divided benefits and allowances between a *flat rate benefits*, and b *graduated supplement* to retirement pension and *earnings-related unemployment and sickness benefit.* See also *National Insurance (Industrial Injuries) Act 1965.*

National Insurance Act 1966 (UK). Added to the *flat-rate benefits* of earlier National Insurance Acts *earnings-related* supplements to *unemployment and sickness benefit* and a supplement to the widow's allowance. The extra cost to the *National Insurance Fund* was to be met by additional graduated contributions. The 1966 Act has also widened the industrial injuries scheme of the *National Insurance (Industrial Injuries) Acts*, by introducing *earnings-related supplement with injury benefit* and a new constant attendance allowance in cases of exceptionally severe disablement. Decisions under the 1965 Act are normally made and administered through the processes of the *Department of Health and Social Security*.

National Insurance Act 1967 (UK). Consolidated and updated the earlier National Insurance Acts.

National Insurance Fund. Set up in the UK under the *National Insurance Acts* as the fund from which the National Health Service, family allowances, unemployment and sickness benefit, and other social security payments are made. Like the *Industrial Injuries Fund*, the National Insurance Fund is financed from employer and employee contributions and general taxation.

National Insurance (Industrial Injuries) Act 1946 (UK). Replaced the workmen's compensation system of the Workmen's Compensation Act 1897 by a system of state responsibility for insuring employees against industrial injuries, the new system being financed by contributions from employers, employees and general taxation. The *Industrial Injuries Fund* was set up under the Act for the purpose. The 1946 Act was modified by the *National Insurance (Industrial Injuries) Acts 1965*, and the *National Insurance Acts 1966* and *1967*.

National Insurance (Industrial Injuries) Act 1965 (UK). Extended the 1946 Act, for example where section 8 of the 1965 Act brought time travelling to work within the definition of working time in certain circumstances. Section 9 also widened the definition of 'in the course of employment'. Under the 1965 Act either *injury benefit* or *disablement benefit* may be adjudged payable, qualification for the latter not necessarily requiring the employee to have had time off work. Unlike the old Workmen's Compensation Act system, adjudication on industrial injuries is through the processes of the *Department of Health and Social Security*, not the Courts.

nationalization. State ownership of industry.

National Joint Apprenticeship Councils. Bodies in the UK that traditionally establish length of apprenticeship, wage and career structures, age of entry to apprenticeship, and distinctions between occupations.

National Labor Relations Act 1935 (US). Legislation which requires the employer to recognize *collective bargaining* and provides for the election of a representative with exclusive bargaining rights for all workers in the appropriate *bargaining unit.*

National Labor Relations Board (NLRB) (US). Independent agency in the USA advising on *industrial relations* generally. See also *Federal Mediation and Conciliation Service.*

National Manpower Institute. US nonprofit research and development organization which works with educational institutions and business to forecast manpower needs and training of the future workforce. The Institute is funded by a combination of government contracts and grants from foundations and corporations.

national procedure agreement. Made between the *employers' association(s)* and the *trade union(s)* in a particular industry to lay down the procedure to be followed in the event of *industrial disputes,* etc. See also *national agreement* and *association bargaining.*

national product, gross. See *gross national product.*

National Productivity Council (US). Body appointed by the President to coordinate federal program(me)s aimed at improving *productivity* in the *private* and *public sectors of the economy.* The Council liaises with the private sector and state and local governments.

National Reference Library of Science and Inventions (UK). British Library's London Division, formerly known as the Patent Office Library, is the major UK reference library for the physical sciences, engineering and technology, its public reference collection containing some 450,000 volumes, two thirds of them from overseas. The Library also subscribes to over 24,000 journals annually. It comes under the *Department of Trade.*

National Research Development Corporation (NRDC). Autonomous body in the UK responsible to the *Secretary of State for Industry* for developing inventions and research findings to the point where they have industrial or other applications. The NRDC sometimes provides financial help for firms developing new technology and inventions which are in the national interest.

National Technical Information Service. *US Department of Commerce* agency which sells reports and other technical analyses prepared by federal agencies, their contractors, or grantees. The Service offers more than one million titles, a *computer*-generated bibliographic search service, and a *microfiche* service.

National Union of Mineworkers. UK *trade union* affiliated to the *Trades Union Congress* and having about 250,000 members.

National Union of Railwaymen. UK *trade union* affiliated to the *Trades Union Congress* and having about 200,000 members. The NUR was formed in 1913 by a merger between the Amalgamated Society of Railwaymen, the General Railway Workers Union and the United Pointsmen and Signalmen's Society.

NATO. *North Atlantic Treaty Organization.*

NATO codification system. An overall commodity classification and coding system based on the American Federal Supply classification and adopted by members of NATO to establish unique stores numbers and titles for items used, stored and issued by the Forces. It is used internationally to facilitate the interchange of equipment and stores between NATO forces and in procurement orders. Consists of 13 digits indicating country of origin, identification number, type of equipment. See also *classification and coding systems.*

natural wastage. Process of reducing number of people employed in a firm or organization by not taking on new employees to replace those leaving of their own accord. Often preferred to making employees redundant after decision has been taken to cut numbers particularly if this decision is a result of the introduction of new management systems treated with suspicion by employees.

NCW. *Nederlands Christelijk Werkgeversverbond,* one of the Dutch confederations of *employers' associations.*

NDP. *Net domestic product.*

near money. US term for assets which, though not as liquid as cash, can be converted into cash relatively easily, eg deposits, Treasury bills, 'cash in' value of life assurance policies, etc. See also *liquid assets.*

NEDC. *National Economic Development Council* (UK).

Neddy. Colloquialism in the UK for the

National Economic Development Council (NEDC) and/or the National Economic Development Office (NEDO). The term 'Little Neddy' is also used of the NEDC's committees for individual industries.

Nederlandsche Bank NV. Central bank of the Netherlands, formed in 1814.

Nederlands Christelijk Werkgeversverbond (NCW). *Netherlands Christian Employers' Federation*, one of the Dutch confederations of *employers' associations*, the other being *VNO*.

Nederlands Katholiek Vakverbond (NKV). See *Netherlands trade unions*.

Nederlands Verbond van Vakverenigingen (NVV). See *Netherlands trade unions*.

NEDO. *National Economic Development Office* (UK).

needs. Or, sometimes, *wants*. The positive driving forces which impel a person towards certain objectives or conditions. In many *motivation* theories both positive and negative forces are subsumed in the single term, need, want or motive. See also *Maslow's hierarchy* of needs.

needs analysis. Term used in training management for analysis to establish the instructional program(me) required by a particular trainee to bring him/her to the standard laid down in the relevant *job description*.

negative cash flow. Where less cash is flowing into a project or enterprise than out of it. Where the larger flow is into the project/enterprise there is said to be *positive cash flow*. See also *cash flow* and *discounted cash flow*. The initial period of negative cash flow before *break-even point* is reached is known as the *pay-out period*.

negative income tax. *Income tax* system which not only collects tax from individuals according to the levels of their incomes but also provides for payments to be made to individuals whose income falls below certain levels. See also *taxable income* and *tax-credit system*.

negative motion. One moved at a meeting or conference with entirely negative intent. It should not be accepted by the chairman because it makes no more contribution to the work of the meeting than if it has been left unsaid. See also *motion* and *direct negative*.

negative self-selection. *Personnel selection* term for the situation where a candidate decides to withdraw his application for a job.

negative strike. *Industrial action* to fight against a worsening of wages and/or conditions.

negative transfer. Interference by new learning, usually on a *simulator*, with an action or operation learned previously.

negotiable instrument. Document representing freely assignable rights in a contract. Examples of negotiable instruments are *bearer bonds, bills of exchange, promissory notes*, and bank notes (on which the promise or contract to pay a certain amount of cash is made to the bearer).

(joint) negotiating panel. See *joint negotiating panel of trade unions*.

negotiating rights. Or *full negotiating rights.* Traditionally, where a trade union has the established right to enter into full negotiations and *collective bargaining* with employer. Thus negotiating rights extend beyond *representational rights*, and have more impact on *management prerogative*. See also *trade union recognition*.

Nellie, sitting or learning with. Mythical lady of great renown. Term refers to practice (practise) of having new employees pick up tasks haphazardly by watching supposedly experienced production workers instead of being given planned training to develop skills.

neo-human relations school. See *human relations school* (of management and *behavio(u)ral scientists*) and *participative management*.

net. Term used to indicate that the full amount of the invoice is payable. Deduction of any form of discount would be contrary to the terms of the contract. Also *nett*.

net asset value. For *investment trusts* the market value of all shares and stock owned divided by the number of trust shares. Historically the net asset value exceeds the price of trusts' shares.

net book amount (or value). Value of a *fixed asset* after allowing for the amount written off for *depreciation* and shown in the accounts of a company. Net book amount is virtually synonymous with *written down* value. also the *Rotterdam Stock Exchange.*

net current assets. *Current assets* less *current liabilities.* Also known as net working capital.

net domestic product (NDP). Figures arrived at by deducting an estimate of the *depreciation* of a country's *capital goods* from *gross domestic product.*

net effective distribution. *Retail audit* term for the proportion of shops in a survey that actually have the product being surveyed in stock at the time of an audit. *Maximum distribution* is the term for the proportion of shops that have stocked the product at some time since the last audit.

Netherlands Bank. *Nederlandsche Bank NV.*

Netherlands Catholic Federation of Trade Unions. See *Nederlands Katholiek Vakverbond (NKV).*

Netherlands Christian Employers' Federation. See *Nederlands Christeljik Werkgeversverbond (NCW).*

Netherlands companies. Forms of commercial partnership or company, etc under Netherlands law include: **a** Proprietorship or *Eenmanszaak;* **b** General Partnership or *Vennootschap onder Firma,* a form of association found particularly among medium size and family firms; **c** Limited Partnership or *Commanditaire Vennootschap;* **d** Civil Partnership or *Maatschap;* **e** Limited Partnership with Shares or *Commanditaire Vennootschap op ·Aandelen;* **f** Cooperative or *Cooperatie;* **g** Joint Stock Company or *Naamloze Vennootschap (NV);* **h** Private or Closed Limited Company or *Besloten Vennootschap (BV).* See also *Amsterdam Stock Exchange.*

Netherlands Federation of Trade Unions. *Nederlands Verbond van Vakverenigingen (NVV).* See *Netherlands trade unions.*

Netherlands income tax. Or *Inkomstenbelasting.* A *progressive tax* charged on net total income. There is also a flat-rate net wealth tax on property.

Netherlands Industry, Federation of. *Verbond van Nederlandsche Ondernemingen.*

Netherlands stock exchange. See *Amsterdam Stock Exchange,* the principal stock exchange in the Netherlands. There is also the *Rotterdam Stock Exchange.*

Netherlands trade unions. Three central federations of *trade unions* in the Netherlands are as follows: **a** *Nederlands Verbond van Vakverenigingen (NVV),* the Netherlands Federation of Trade Unions formed in 1906 and covering 14 trade unions which have approximately 500,000 members. **b** *Nederlands Katholiek Vakverbond (NKV),* the Netherlands Catholic Trade Union Federation formed in 1909 and covering 19 trade unions which have approximately 400,000 members. **c** *Christelijk Nationaal Vakverbond in Nederland (CNV),* the Christian National Federation of Trade Unions in the Netherlands formed in 1909 and covering 20 trade unions which have approximately 200,000 trade unionists in membership.

net investment. Level of investment after *depreciation* of equipment and stocks has been deducted from *gross investment* in adding to stocks and to fixed capital. Broadly, net investment is a better indication than gross investment of the provision made for future *economic growth.*

net margin. As *net profit.*

net national product (NNP). Figure arrived at by deducting *depreciation* of a country's *capital goods* from *gross national product.*

net present value method (NPV). Yardstick for the assessment of a project or enterprise based on *discounted cash flow* techniques. A zero NPV indicates that the project repays the *capital* invested plus the minimum acceptable return. A positive NPV indicates a better return, while a negative NPV indicates a worse return.

net profit. Or net revenue. *Gross profit* minus the cost of the marketing, finance and administrative functions. In a *marginal costing* system, net profit is sales revenue minus marginal costs (equals contribution) minus fixed costs (fixed factory overheads, marketing costs, research and development costs, financial and administration costs).

net revenue. As *net profit.*

net terminal value. *Terminal value* less cash outflows.

net wealth tax. *Wealth tax* applied to wealth in excess of a stipulated level.

network analysis/planning. Range of *critical*

path planning techniques for planning and controlling complex projects by recording their component parts and representing them diagrammatically as a network of inter-related activities. *Events* are represented by circles, *activities* by arrows, and the lengths of activities by the lengths of the arrows. There are also dotted arrows for *dummy activities* between events that have a time rather than activity relationship. Optimizing networks often involves the use of computers. Network analysis techniques include *Program(me) Evaluation and Review Technique (PERT)* and *Critical Path Method (CPM)*. See also *branching network*.

net working capital. As *net current assets*.

net worth. Total *assets* less *current liabilities*. Also known as net total assets.

new issue. New long-term capital in the form of *shares* and *securities*, usually sought on the new issue market through *issuing houses*, *merchant banks* or similar financial institutions helped by an issuing broker. Borrowers in the new issue market may be *private companies* in the process of *'going public'* or they may be established *public companies* seeking capital for new investment.

New Orleans Stock Exchange. One of about 20 *US stock exchanges*.

New Town. Term used in the UK of towns built under the New Towns Acts 1946-66. Such developments have been financed by the central government and each developed as a self-sufficient and balanced community by a specially appointed *Development Corporation*. An important aspect of the desired balance in the community is that industrial and housing development should be complementary at all stages. Eventually the Development Corporation is phased out and its work transferred to the national New Towns Commission. Similarly, there is a transfer of local powers to the democratically elected local government authority.

New York Clearing House Association. Central clearing house for US *commercial banks*. Established in 1853. See also *Federal Reserve Bank* and *Federal Reserve System*.

New York Stock Exchange. See *Wall Street* and *US stock exchanges*.

'New York Times'. Daily newspaper with particularly influential coverage of finance and business.

New Zealand, Associated Chambers of Commerce of. Members are local *chambers of commerce* in some 50 towns.

New Zealand central bank. *Reserve Bank of New Zealand.*

New Zealand Employers' Federation (NZEF). Established in 1902, the central organization for *employers' associations*.

New Zealand Federation of Labour (NZFL). Central *trade union* organization, established 1937.

New Zealand stock exchanges. Four major New Zealand *stock exchanges* are: **a** Auckland Stock Exchange; **b** Christchurch Stock Exchange; **c** Dunedin Stock Ex-

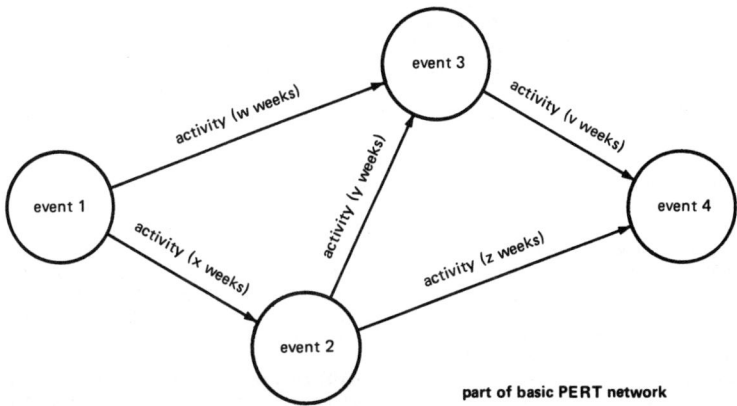

part of basic PERT network

change; **d** Wellington Stock Exchange. There is also an exchange at Invercargill.

next business. *Motion* moved from the floor of a meeting or conference with the object of ending discussion on the item of business in hand. If the motion is seconded and then carried, the meeting abandons the item in hand and moves immediately to the next item on the agenda. The chairman has discretion to reject a motion for next business but if he accepts it, it must be put to the vote immediately, usually without discussion. A motion for next business has much in common with a *previous question* motion. See also *closure.*

Nicaragua Stock Exchange. See *Managua Stock Exchange.*

Nicosia Stock Exchange. The *stock exchange* in Cyprus.

Niedersachsische Börse zu Hannover. *Hannover (or Lower Saxony) Stock Exchange.*

Nigate Stock Exchange. One of Japan's *stock exchanges.*

Nigeria, Central Bank of. Established 1958.

Nigerian Association of Chambers of Commerce. Members are the *chambers of commerce* of the major towns.

Nigerian Employers' Consultative Association. Established 1961 as a central organization for *employers' associations.*

Nigerian Stock Exchange. Established 1960 in Lagos.

Nigerian trade unions. Principal four federations of *trade unions* are as follows: **a** Labour Unity Front (established 1963); **b** Nigerian Trade Union Congress (NTUC); **c** Nigerian Workers' Council (established 1962); **d** United Labour Congress of Nigeria.

Nihon Keieisha Dantai Renmei (NIKKEIREN). Japan Federation of Employers' Associations, established in 1948 and having approximately one hundred member organizations.

NIIP. National Institute of Industrial Psychology (UK). Merged in 1973 with the *National Foundation for Educational Research.*

NIIP form relations test. Spatial ability or aptitude test. Similar to the *NIIP group tests 80A, 81 and 82.* See also *psychological testing* and *aptitude tests.*

NIIP group test 20. *Clerical aptitude test* in which pairs of numbers and names are checked against each other within a time limit. The test takes 10 to 15 minutes. See also *NIIP group test 61, psychological testing* and *aptitude tests.*

NIIP group test 61. *Clerical aptitude test* in three parts covering or simulating alphabetical filing, classification under particular headings, and checking of addresses and invoices. The test takes about 35 minutes. See also *NIIP group test 20, psychological testing* and *aptitude tests.*

NIIP group test 66. *Numerical aptitude test* that takes a total of about 15 minutes and covers simple computation and some commercial arithmetic. See also *psychological testing* and *aptitude tests.*

NIIP group tests 70 and 70B. *Non-verbal intelligence tests* for medium and higher ability people, each taking about 30 minutes. The tests have norms for apprentices, school pupils and graduates. See also *psychological testing* and *aptitude tests.*

NIIP group tests 72 and 73. *Non-verbal intelligence tests* for lower ability levels, each test taking about 20 minutes. The tests are in domino form. See also *psychological testing* and *aptitude tests.*

NIIP group tests 80A, 81 and 82. *Spatial ability or aptitude tests,* each of them taking about 25 minutes and dealing with various shapes. The *NIIP form relations test* has a similar use. See also *psychological testing* and *aptitude tests.*

NIIP group tests 90A and 90B. *Verbal intelligence tests,* each taking about 30 minutes and having four parts with about 40 questions in each. The tests have norms for apprentices, for school leavers and for graduates. See also *psychological testing* and *aptitude tests.*

NIIP test EA2. Part of the *engineering apprentice test-battery,* a *numerical aptitude test* that takes about 20 minutes and includes simple computations and practical arithmetic problems. See also *psychological testing* and *aptitude tests.*

NIIP Vincent mechanical diagrams test. See *Vincent mechanical diagrams test.* Also *psychological testing* and *aptitude tests.*

Niitmash system. Russian classification and coding system for components. See also *classification and coding systems.*

NIKKEIREN. *Nihon Keieisha Dantai Renmei,* the Japanese Federation of Employers' Associations.

1922 Agreement in Engineering Industry (UK). Began from premise that the employers have the right to manage their establishments and the *trade unions* have the right to exercise their functions (see *'freedom to manage'*). The 1922 Agreement, arrived at after a national *lock-out* in the engineering industry, established the industry's *disputes procedure* based on *works conferences, local conferences* and national conferences at York, the whole procedure often taking as long as three months. The *engineering procedure* established by the Agreement was ended in 1971.

Nippon Ginko. Bank of Japan, *central bank* established in 1882.

Nippon Shoko Kaigi-sho. Japan Chamber of Commerce and Industry, established in 1922 and covering more than 450 local *chambers of commerce.*

NKV. *Nederlands Katholiek Vakverbond.* See *Netherlands trade unions.*

NLRB. *National Labor Relations Board (US).*

NNP. *Net national product.*

nominal capital. Or share capital. Total of the *nominal value* of the shares in a company.

nominal value. Or *par value* of a share. The value of a share when it was issued, as stated on its share certificate and in the company's *memorandum of association,* and not its market value (which may be above, at or below *par*). Also known as *face value.*

nominee holdings. Or *intermediary holdings* (particularly in the USA). Shares held in a company through a nominee, not disclosing the owner's identity. Where such anonymous holdings are built up in preparation for a *takeover* battle this process is known as *warehousing.* See also *insider trading.*

non-analytic job evaluation. Methods used to establish the relative worth of jobs by comparing whole jobs and either placing them in rank order or assigning them to pre-determined grades. See *analytic job evaluation, job evaluation.*

non-contributory pension scheme. Where employees do not themselves contribute to their *superannuation* or *pension scheme,* only the employer making contributions.

non-directive interview. Where, particularly in *attitude surveys,* the interviewer encourages a free exchange of views instead of working to the detailed and tighter structure of a *directive interview.* The non-directive interview has points of similarity with the *connected conversation interview* sometimes used in *personnel selection.*

non-employed person. One who is neither in employment nor seeking it. A term used, for example, for *national insurance* purposes in the UK, other categories being *employed person, self-employed person* and *unemployed person.*

non-executive director. Or outside director. *Director* who is not a full-time *employee* of the *company* or *corporation* concerned and is not therefore an *executive director.*

nonfeasance. Failure to perform a legal requirement or official duty. See also *misfeasance.*

Non-Participation, Certificate of (UK). See *Certificate of Non-Participation* (in the *state graduated pension scheme*).

non-profit endowment assurance. Or *without-profits endowment assurance.* A policy with a fixed sum assured instead of having a share of the insurance company's profits added to it as in the case of *with-profits endowment assurance.* A higher premium is payable for the latter type of assurance. See also *endowment assurance policy.*

non-qualified stock option (US). Option which is not eligible for capital gains tax.

non-recourse finance. Finance raised in a manner that does not leave the applicant for it responsible for any failure to repay. An *export finance house,* for example, may help an exporter by giving credit directly to the overseas buyer without recourse to the exporter.

non-stock corporation. US *corporation* which has no issued share capital. Includes mutual savings banks, credit unions and charitable bodies.

non-verbal intelligence test (g). *Personnel selection* and *vocational guidance* test devised as part of the *engineering apprentice test-battery* of the National Institute of Industrial Psychology in the UK. See also *psychological testing* and *test battery*.

no par value shares. Shares which do not have a *nominal value*. They are illegal in the UK but common in North America.

no-poaching agreement. Or no-raiding agreement. One made between *trade unions* not to try to recruit each other's members. See also *Bridlington Principles Procedure* and *Croydon Principles* in the UK and *demarcation dispute, jurisdictional dispute* and *rival unionism*.

no-raiding agreement. As *no-poaching agreement*.

Nordic Council. Advisory body on economic and social matters, etc serving Denmark, Iceland, Finland, Norway and Sweden.

Nordic Federation of Factory Workers' Unions. Promotes collaboration between *trade unions* in Denmark, Finland, Norway and Sweden.

Norges Bank. Bank of Norway. *Central bank* established in 1816.

Norges Industriforbund. Federation of Norwegian Industries, established in 1919 as the central organization for *employers' associations*.

norm. 1. Normal or average. **2.** Scale used in *psychological testing* to translate a *raw test score* to a common base for a particular type of candidate or a particular type of occupation. Thus the same test, but different norms, might be used for school leavers and graduates for example. It is also possible to use the same tests for jobs demanding different levels of ability by applying different norms to the results. **3.** Behavio(u)r expected of and by members of a social group.

normal curve. See *Gaussian Curve*.

normal working area. Space within which a seated or standing person can reach and use tools, materials and equipment. See *workplace layout, maximum working area, motion study*.

normative forecasting techniques. Types of technique used, for example, in *technological forecasting*, which begin with a consideration of the likely future structure and needs of society, and then consider the developments necessary to create that structure and meet those needs. On the other hand, *exploratory forecasting techniques* make projections based on present knowledge of a technology or product without trying to take into account the likely overall future picture. Particular techniques of technological forecasting include *brainstorming*, the *Delphi approach, morphological research*, the *scenario writing approach*, and *technological trend extrapolation*.

Norris-La Guardia Act (US). Employment legislation banning *yellow dog contracts* and limiting the use of legal intervention during *industrial action*.

Norsk Arbeidsgiverforening (NAF). *Norwegian Employers' Confederation*.

North Atlantic Treaty Organization (NATO). Established in 1949 by a defence (defense) agreement between Belgium, Canada, Denmark, France, Iceland, Italy, Luxembourg, the Netherlands, Norway, Portugal, the USA and the UK. Further states that have since joined NATO include West Germany, Greece and Turkey. NATO headquarters were in Paris until March 1966 when they were moved to Brussels after a contretemps with France.

Northern Ireland Local Enterprise Development Unit. See *Local Enterprise Development Unit (Northern Ireland)*.

Northern Stock Exchange. UK organization based on the Manchester Stock Exchange and also covering the Leeds, Liverpool and York Stock Exchanges. See also *Stock Exchange* (UK).

Norwegian central bank. *Norges Bank.*

Norwegian chambers of commerce. Some 12 towns in Norway have *chambers of commerce*.

Norwegian companies. Forms of business association under Norwegian law include limited partnership; general partnership; individual ownership; and *joint stock company* or *aksjeselskap (A/S)*.

Norwegian Employers' Confederation. See *Norsk Arbeidsgiverforening*.

Norwegian income tax. Forms of Norwegian income tax include: a State income tax, or *inntektsskatt til statskassen,* a graduated tax charged on a *slice scale* on total income from all sources; **b** Local income tax, or *inntektsskatt til kommunen,* charged on net total income; **c** Mutual tax, or *fellesskatt,* levied on taxable income as computed for local income tax; **d** Seamen's tax, or *sjømannsskatt,* charged on the wages of seamen in place of other forms of income tax; **e** Tax on foreign artists' fees, or *argift på honorarer til utenlandske kunstnere,* levied at a flat-rate on gross fees instead of normal taxes; **f** Special development tax, or *soerskatt til utviklingshjelp,* used to finance Norwegian aid to developing countries and paid on income chargeable to local income tax; **g** Flat-rate state *net wealth tax;* **h** Flat-rate local net wealth tax; and **i** State capital gains tax on profits from the sale of shares.

Norwegian Industries, Federation of. *Norges Industriforbund.*

Norwegian stock exchange. See *Oslo Stock Exchange.*

Norwegian trade unions. See *Landsorganisasjonen i Norge (LO).*

note of hand. As *promissory note.*

notice of motion. Requirement often applying to formal meetings and conferences that someone seeking to move a *motion* on a matter of significance must give a minimum specified notice of the motion so that it can be put on the agenda and those attending the meeting have an opportunity to consider the matter in advance. Latter point is particularly important if a delegate needs to get a *mandate* from the organization he represents at a *delegate meeting.*

NPV. *Net present value method.*

NRA. *National Recovery Administration* (US).

NRDC. *National Research Development Corporation* (UK).

NTUC. Nigerian Trade Union Congress. See *Nigerian trade unions.*

Nucleus Labour Force Scheme. Run by the UK *Department of Employment* to give assistance where an employer setting up or expanding in a *Special Development Area,* a *Development Area* or an *Intermediate Area* needs to transfer employees temporarily to a parent factory for training. See also *Key Workers Scheme.* Information is available from local *employment offices.*

NUM. *National Union of Mineworkers* (UK).

NUMAS. National Union of Manufacturers' Advisory Service. Now part of *Industrial and Commercial Finance Corporation Ltd* management advisory service.

number completion test. Sometimes used in *psychological testing.* The subject has to complete or continue a series of numbers related according to a definite principle or principles.

numerical aptitude tests. Used in *personnel selection* etc to test facility in the use of numbers (which is not necessarily the same as mathematical attainment). See also *psychological testing* and *aptitude tests.* Examples of numerical aptitude tests include the *Morrisby GAT-N test,* the *NIIP group test 66,* the *NIIP test EA2,* and the *Vernon graded arithmetic-mathematics test.*

NUR. *National Union of Railwaymen.*

nursed account. Supplier whose account with a particular customer has always been paid on time so that he can be relied upon for a good *trade reference* in spite of the fact that the customer has a reputation as a bad payer among other suppliers.

nursery finance. Loans by *institutions* or *stockjobbers* to profitable private companies which expect to become public companies within three years or so.

NV. Or *Naamloze Vennootschap,* a *joint stock company* under Netherlands law. See also *Netherlands companies.*

NVV. *Nederlands Verbond van Vakverenigingen.* See *Netherlands trade unions.*

NYSE. New York Stock Exchange. See *US stock exchanges.*

NZEF. *New Zealand Employers' Federation.*

NZFL. *New Zealand Federation of Labour.*

O

O & M. See *organization and methods*.

OAPEC. *Organization of Arab Petroleum Exporting Countries.*

OAS. *Organization of American States.*

objectives. 1. Specific aims of an organization. In a commercial enterprise these may be set out under the headings suggested by *Drucker:* market standing, profitability and growth, innovation, productivity, resources, personnel, community relations. Objectives may be set out in the form of performance *targets* for a particular function or position and may be analyzed into an objectives hierarchy or objectives tree which shows interdependent objectives and their contributory sub-objectives. 2. See *instructional objectives* or *behavio(u)ral objectives* or performance objectives.

objective test. In market research or education a test or test item which can be scored unambiguously by any marker. Such tests are more correctly termed 'objectively scored tests'. They include *true-false questions, multiple-choice questions*, and some forms of *completion item* or *matching item*. Because it minimizes the judgement of the marker, a carefully constructed objective test may be better than a *subjective test*.

objects clause (UK). Statement of *company* objects in its *memorandum of association*.

observation ratio study. As *activity sampling* or *work sampling*.

o/c. Overcharge.

OCAM. *Organisation Commune Africaine, Malgache et Mauricienne.*

occupation. 1. Group of *jobs* with a significant number of *tasks* in common. 2. A person's trade, vocation or principal means of earning a living.

occupational analysis. Identifying those *jobs* which have sufficient main *tasks* in common to be grouped under a common occupation-name. Can lead to an *occupational description*.

occupational classification or group. Classification of *jobs* or *occupations*. Typically, occupation groups might include: **a** professional; **b** employers, managers and administrators; **c** scientists, engineers and technologists; **d** clerical workers; **e** foremen, inspectors and supervisors; **f** skilled manual workers; **g** semi-skilled manual workers; **h** unskilled manual workers. Official classifications are the *International Standard Classification of Occupations (ISCO)* and the *Classification of Occupations and Directory of Occupational Titles (CODOT)*.

occupational description. Statement of the characteristics of the jobs grouped in an occupation. See *occupational analysis*.

occupational guidance. Advising individuals on the types of occupation for which they are suited, often on the evidence of *psychological testing*. Occupational guidance is similar to careers guidance though more concerned with identifying suitable immediate employment.

Occupational Guidance Scheme. Set up in the UK by the *Department of Employment* and further developed by the *Employment Service Agency*, the scheme is designed to assist people in need of advice on choosing a career or making career changes.

occupational health. Prevention and treatment of illness or injury suffered by employees during or as a result of their work.

occupational mobility. *Labo(u)r mobility* between jobs and types of work, rather than geographically.

occupational pension scheme. Pension scheme for which an employee is eligible by reason of his/her employment. It may be either *contributory* or *non-contributory*. Some occupational pension schemes in the UK are *contracted-out* from the *state graduated pension scheme* (though not, of course, from the *state flat-rate pension scheme*).

occupational profile. Analysis of breakdown of skills or *occupation(s)*, for example within a firm, expressed as ratios or proportions. Sometimes qualified as 'ideal' (the profile a firm requires) or 'real' (the profile it actually has).

occupational psychologist. Type of psychologist whose industrial interests include *ergonomics, job enrichment* and *job satisfaction, programmed instruction,* training methods, *vocational guidance* and, perhaps most obviously of all, *personnel selection* and *psychological testing* techniques. Types of selection test used by the occupational psychologist include *intelligence tests, aptitude tests* and *temperament and personality tests*. See also *test battery*. Other kinds of psychologist are the clinical psychologist and the educational psychologist.

occupational structure. Pattern of *occupations*, usually meant nationally but might be used of an industry or even of an individual firm.

occupational union. *Trade union* for people working in a particular occupation(s). See also *industrial union*.

O'Connor finger dexterity test. Pegboard test of *psychomotor skills*, originating in the USA. The test involves sorting out small brass pins and placing them in groups of three in holes. See also *psychological testing*.

OCR. *Optical character recognition.*

ODECA. *Organization of Central American States.*

OECD. *Organization for Economic Co-operation and Development.*

OEEC. *Organization for European Economic Cooperation.*

Offene Handelsgesellschaft. OHG. General partnership under both Austrian and Federal German company law. See *Austrian companies* and *German companies*.

offer for sale. Where an *issuing house* buys the *shares* of a company and offers them for resale.

Office and Professional Employees International Union (US). *White collar trade union* in the USA and Canada. It has some 90,000 members.

Office of Consumer Affairs (US). Government agency.

Office of Economic Opportunity (US). Government agency responsible for administering Federal program(me)s for the alleviation of poverty.

Office of Management and Budget (US). Agency for the Federal budget and for advising on the management of Federal program(me)s.

Office of Manpower Economics (OME). Independent UK non-statutory body established in 1970 to advise Government Ministers on remuneration, pay structures, etc.

office planning, panoramic. See *panoramic office planning (POP)*.

Offices, Shops and Railway Premises Act 1963 (UK). Modelled on, and has invariably been interpreted by the norms of, the *Factories Act 1961*. Points covered by the 1963 Act include cleanliness; overcrowding; temperature; ventilation; lighting; sanitary conveniences; washing facilities; supply of drinking water; accommodation for clothing; seating facilities; eating facilities in shops; condition of floors, passages and stairs; safety, including fencing machinery; health; noise and vibrations; magistrates' powers to prohibit the use of dangerous premises, plant or processes; the prohibition of heavy work; first-aid facilities; fire precautions.

The 1963 Act is generally enforced by local authorities, except that the *Factory Inspectorate* are responsible for railway premises, and some other places; that mines and quarries inspectors are responsible for offices and shops forming part of a mine or quarry; and that fire authorities check fire precautions.

'Official Journal of the Communities'. Provides regular reports on the *secondary legislation* and other progress of the *Common Market* or *European Economic Community*. The Journal is published in Dutch, English, French, German and Italian.

Official Receiver (UK). Official called in

by the *Department of Trade* to smooth the *liquidation* of *companies*.

official strike. Traditionally a withdrawal of labo(u)r or *strike* by workers with formal *trade union* approval and support. See also *unconstitutional strike* and *unofficial strike*.

off-line. Description of a part of a *computer* system or activity that is not directly under the control of the *central processing unit*, as opposed to *on-line* which does imply being under such control. Off-line processing, for example, includes the handling of information by a computer's *input device*.

offshore company. *Company* registered in a country where there is little government control over its financial dealings and where there are usually low tax rates.

Offshore Supplies Interest Relief Grants (UK). Introduced by the UK Government in 1973 to assist and encourage the offshore oil and natural gas industries by reducing the cost of *credit* obtained by a firm, whether as *supplier credit* or as *buyer credit*. The system was introduced specifically to finance the supply of UK goods and services to companies developing oil and gas resources on the UK Continental Shelf, particularly in the North Sea and the Celtic Sea.

off the books payments. Payment for labo(u)r, services or goods which are not recorded in the business' accounting books. Usually illegal payments since they avoid taxation and other statutory charges etc.

off-the-job training. Training organized in *training centres* etc away from work/ production, usually in conjunction with complementary *on-the-job training* and *further education*.

OHG. *Offene Handelsgesellschaft*. See *Austrian companies* and *German (Federal) companies*.

oligopoly. Where the number of sellers of a product is so small that each seller must consider his competitors' reactions to pricing and other marketing activities in relation to his own. Between them, this small number of sellers can dominate the market. See also *monopoly*.

oligopsony. *Market* with a very limited number of buyers.

OM. *Ostmark*.

OME. *Office of Manpower Economics* (UK).

omnibus motion. *Motion* put to a meeting or conference, each clause covering a different topic or subject. It differs from a *composite motion*, which is a combining of a number of different motions on the same subject.

omnibus survey. Type of survey made regularly by some *market research agencies* in which they seek information on a wide range of topics on behalf of a number of clients. See also *syndicated market research*.

OMPAs. *One man pension arrangements*.

OMS. *Output per manshift*.

ONC. *Ordinary National Certificate* (UK).

on cost. As *indirect cost*.

OND. *Ordinary National Diploma* (UK).

Ondernemingsrad. *Works council* which is a legal requirement in the Netherlands in firms with more than 100 employees.

one man pension arrangements (OMPAs). Discretionary endowment pension scheme designed to arrange a pension for an individual employee. See *top hat pension scheme*.

'1-2-3 bank'. One that carries higher status and prestige than a moneylender but does not have the standing and proved resources of a *commercial bank* or *clearing bank* or *member bank*. 1-2-3 banks are part of the *secondary banking sector*, as are finance houses or *fringe banks*. See also *issuing house* and *merchant bank*.

on-line. Description of a part of a *computer* system that is directly under the control of the *central processing unit*, as opposed to *off-line* activities which take place in the computer system but not under the control of the central processing unit. For example, 'on-line data reduction' means the processing of data by the central processing unit as soon as it reaches the computer system rather than being handled by an *input device* or an *off-line storage device*.

on-line storage. Where a *computer* data store is directly controlled by the *central processing unit* of a *computer*. See *input device*.

on-site training. See *on-the-job training*.

on stream. Descriptive term for an integral

241

and/or continuous part of a process or activity.

on-the-job training. Training at the place of work, possibly while at work, as opposed to *off-the-job training*. See also *Nellie, sitting next to*.

opcentiemen. Additional local tax. See *Belgian income tax*.

OPEC. *Organization of Petroleum Exporting Countries*.

Open Account Scheme. Scheme operated in the UK under which the *Export Credits Guarantee Department* guarantees to an exporting firm's UK bank the financing of short-term transactions made on *open account terms*. The Open Account Scheme is, in effect, an extension of the ECGD's *Bills Scheme* operated in respect of *bills of exchange* and *promissory notes*.

open account terms. Sometimes used in export trading, where an overseas buyer is instructed to make payment to the exporter's bank's overseas correspondent. The exporter's bank may then be prepared to make immediate advances in anticipation of future payments. See also *export club* and *shipping and forwarding agent*.

open-circuit television (OCTV). Broadcast transmission of television signals to an unrestricted audience, as opposed to closed circuit television (CCTV) by cable.

open cover (or policy). Where goods are insured for a general or provisional sum, for example in a marine insurance policy, because their precise value is not known.

open door policy. 1. Where *trade union* officials and/or *shop stewards* have a right of immediate access to senior management. **2.** Where any employee has a right of access to senior management in order to air grievances, etc.

open-ended. Approach to learning etc that leaves trainee/student free to work between a variety of solutions or paths rather than having to produce a single, definitive answer. See *group project training* and *project training*.

open-end investment company. As *mutual fund*.

open house. As *open shop*.

opening balance. Balance on an account at the start of an *accounting period*.

open market operations. Buying and selling of *securities* in the open market by a *central bank* such as the *Bank of England*. Central banks use such operations, as well as directives to banks, to regulate the *money supply*.

open office planning. Design and layout of large open office areas. Purpose is to provide a good working environment, improved communications and scope for flexibility to meet changing conditions. Usually involves use of acoustic ceilings, carpeted flooring, screens, plants, etc. Also known as *panoramic office planning*, *office landscaping* and *Bürolandschaft*.

open position. As *bear position*.

operation process chart. Or outline process chart. *Work study* or *method study* chart setting out the operations of a process in the order in which they are undertaken, or are to be undertaken, but without the detail or timescale of a *flow process chart*.

open prospectus. *Prospectus* which seeks support or investment without spelling out clearly the purposes for which the support is to be used.

open shop. Factory or workshop where employment is not restricted to *trade union* members or to members of a particular trade union. See also *closed shop* and *union shop*, and *yellow dog contracts*.

open union. *Trade union* which virtually any type of worker is qualified to join. See also *industrial union*, *craft union* and *occupational union*.

Open University. Set up in the UK to provide courses consisting of correspondence packages, television and radio program(me)s, summer and weekend schools, and regionally organized tutorial and counselling systems. No formal academic qualifications are required for registration as a student and Open University students are normally at least 21; the majority of them are in full-time employment. Program(me)s of study are designed to embrace a wide range of disciplines, covering both arts and science subjects. The six main lines of study at undergraduate level are arts, educational studies, mathematics, science, social sciences and technology. The Uni-

operational research (OR). Or *operations research*. Use of scientific methods of analysis, including *mathematical models*, to process complex information and arrive at decisions achieving an optimum balance of probabilities as well as identifiable facts. Developed during Second World War and now firmly established. OR style techniques include *queuing theory, simulation, linear programming, forecasting, extrapolation, iteration, allocation, critical path method.*

Operational Research Society. Professional association concerned with promoting *operational research* studies and standards.

operational stocks. As *work-in-progress stocks* or *buffer stocks.*

operations research. US term for *operational research.*

operator/operative. Manual worker with, usually, a narrower range of skills and adaptability than the *craftsman.*

Opinions (EEC) of the *Council of Ministers* and/or the *European Commission* of the *Common Market* or *European Economic Community.* See *Recommendations (EEC).*

Opitz classification. A German classification and coding system for tools and components based on shape characteristics and significant features using a 5-digit primary code. A 4-digit supplementary code provides information on dimensions, material, form and accuracy. See also *classification and coding systems.*

Oporto Stock Exchange. Or *Bolsa de Porto.* See *Portuguese stock exchanges.*

opportunity costs. The cost in terms of lost income or profit of the foregone alternative investment or course of action. Where management fails to make a decision or take an opportunity that would have produced a better net return than the decision it does in fact make (including where its decision is to do nothing or simply to carry on as before, or even to avoid making a decision), the lost revenue is an opportunity cost. (Perhaps it would be more appropriate if it were called a 'lost opportunity cost'). More positively, opportunity costs may be deliberately calculated when evaluating alternative investment or other marginal decisions. See also *avoidable costs.* In the computer world, opportunity costs are sometimes known as *shadow prices.*

optical character recognition (OCR). Type of *character recognition system* sometimes used in *input devices* to feed specific and prerecorded data into a *computer.* This system is used, for example, in handling electricity, gas, telephone and similar bills and is based on recognition by the input device of the shape of particular numbers and letters by measuring their optical reflectivity. Another character recognition system is *magnetic ink character recognition.*

optimization. Balancing the parameters and variables (for example, the different management activities) in a total business or other situation to produce the most effective or optimum performance from the whole.

option dealing. *Stock exchange* practice (practise) under which a person can make an agreement to buy or sell *shares* at their present price at or within a specified future time. When arranging such an option a speculator pays 'option money' which he loses if he does not take up the option. Options to sell are known as deals for the 'put', while options to buy are deals for the 'call'. A speculator might make a deal for the 'call' in particular shares that he believes are about to increase in price so that he will be able to make a profit by buying at present prices and selling at future prices almost simultaneously. A *company director* is barred by law from option dealings in the shares of his or associated companies.

OR. *Operations research* (US) or *operational research* (UK).

Orario Flessibile. Italian term for *flexible working hours.*

order-call ratio. Relationship between number or value of orders placed and number of calls made by salesmen or representatives necessary to obtain them over a specified period of time.

ordinary shares. Constitute the *equity capital* of a company and take precedence after *debentures* and *preference shares* in entitlement to the company's distributed profits. In some cases, ordinary shares may have a right to a share of any profits but not voting rights.

organic organization. Term used by T Burns

and G M Stalker to describe an organization with the following characteristics; a *jobs* are loosely defined and are constantly redefined; b *tasks* are likely to be performed in the light of a knowledge of the firm's overall objectives; c people communicate with each other across the organization as much as within the formal *chain of command;* d where people from different levels communicate with each other the process is more like consultation than command. The organic organization is sometimes referred to as an 'open' or 'informal' organization. It is contrasted with the more formal *mechanistic organization.*

Organisation des États Centraméricains. Abbr *ODECA.*

Organisation Commune Africaine, Malgache et Mauricienne (OCAM). Set up in 1965 to promote political and economic cooperation between Cameroon, the Central African Republic, Chad, Congo, Dahomey, Gabon, Ivory Coast, Madagascar, Mauritius, Niger, Rwanda, Senegal, Togo, Upper Volta and Zaïre.

organismic theory. Theory developed by Andras Angyal that there is a continuous interaction between the organism (the customer) and the environment and that because of the continuity of this interaction it is impossible to differentiate one from the other. The theory is used as a means of analyzing *buying behavio(u)r* by directing attention to the likelihood that customers in a given *market segment* are influenced by similar forces to similar degrees.

organization. Sub-division and delegation of the overall management task by allocating responsibility and authority to carry out defined work and by defining the relationships that should exist between different functions and positions.

organization and methods (O & M). Disciplined examination of the methods of operation of a company or other form of organization, covering any or all aspects of organization from clerical procedures to management structure. In practice (practise). O & M is often an application of *method study* and sometimes work measurement techniques to office procedures but in recent years has also phased into *systems analysis* and *operational research.* See also *clerical work evaluation (CWE), clerical work improvement program (CWIP), group capacity assessment (GCA), variable factor programming (VFP), short interval sched-*uling, and *questioning approach.*

organization chart. Or *organization tree.* Schematic or pictorial representation of the formal relationship between functions and people in an organization. The chief executive is normally placed at the top of the chart with others, according to rank and status below him, though some organizations seek to avoid such an authoritarian presentation by placing the chief executive on the left and designing the chart from left to right. Organization charts may also be inverted, with the chief executive at the bottom and the most junior functionaries in the top line. Line or executive responsibility is usually indicated in an organization chart by linking functions with continuous lines, while staff or advisory relationships are usually indicated by dotted lines.

organization climate. Atmosphere created in an organization by the prevalent *management style* and the way in which managers and staff work together. The climate can be described in terms of: a the amount and quality of team-work and cooperation within the organization; b the degree of commitment among the members of the organization; c the effectiveness of communications; d the extent to which planning and creativity are encouraged; e the way in which conflicts or differences of opinion are resolved; f the extent to which employees participate in decision making; g the extent to which the organization relies upon mutual confidence and trust between managers and subordinates rather than relying on authority-obedience relationships.

organization costs. As *preliminary expenses.*

organization design (or structuring). Determination and specification of appropriate operational and functional roles and the resulting relationships. The aim of organization design is to provide for an effective organization structure which enables the best use to be made of the minds, judgments and energies of the members of the organization. See also *socio-technical system* and *organization planning.*

organization development (OD). Process of improving the way in which an organization functions and is managed, especially in response to change. The aims of organization development are: a to ensure that the organization and the people within it can adapt themselves appropriately to changes in objectives, technologies and the environment; b to help management to improve the way in which it manages the organization; **c** to improve teamwork based on mutual confidence, interdependence and share of responsibility; **d** to increase the commitment of the members of the organization; **e** to develop improved communications; **f** to ensure that the best use is made of the members of the organization; **g** generally to improve the effectiveness of people and the climate in which they work. Organization development operates through planned *interventions* by a *change agent* in the organization's *processes*. It is managed from the top, associated with the organization's overall objects and uses behavio(u)ral knowledge and skill. Organization development often involves teambuilding activities. See also *managerial grid*.

Organization for Economic Cooperation and Development (OECD). Established in 1961 in succession to the *Organization for European Economic Cooperation (OEEC)* to promote economic cooperation and development and world trade. Founder member states were Austria, Belgium, Canada, Denmark, France, Federal Germany, Greece, Iceland, Ireland, Italy, Luxembourg, the Netherlands, Norway, Portugal, Spain, Sweden, Switzerland, Turkey, the UK and the USA. Finland and Japan joined later.

Organization for European Economic Cooperation (OOEC). Operated from 1948 until being succeeded by the *Organization for Economic Cooperation and Development* in 1961. The OEEC was set up under the *Marshall Plan* or *European Recovery Program(me)*.

Organization for Trade Cooperation. See *General Agreement on Tariffs and Trade (GATT)*.

Organization of American States (OAS). Set up in 1948 to promote cooperation, including economic cooperation, between the member states. These include Argentina, Barbados, Bolivia, Brazil, Chile, Colombia, Costa Rica, Dominica, Ecuador, El Salvador, Guatemala, Haiti, Honduras, Jamaica, Mexico, Nicaragua, Panama, Paraguay, Peru, Trinidad and Tobago, the USA, Uruguay and Venezuela. Canada is an observer.

Organization of Arab Petroleum Exporting Countries (OAPEC). Set up in 1968 to promote the joint interests of its member states, namely, Abu Dhabi, Algeria, Bahrain, Dubai, Egypt, Kuwait, Libya, Qatar, Saudi Arabia and Syria.

Organization of Central American States (ODECA). Promotes cooperation and development, including economic, between its member states, namely Costa Rica, El Salvador, Guatemala, Honduras and Nicaragua.

Organization of the Petroleum Exporting Countries (OPEC). Set up in 1960 to coordinate policies and promote the joint interests of the member states, namely, Abu Dhabi, Algeria, Indonesia, Iran, Iraq, Kuwait, Libya, Nigeria, Qatar, Saudi Arabia and Venezuela. See also the *Organization of Arab Petroleum Exporting Countries (OAPEC)*.

organization planning. Process of analyzing the way in which an enterprise or other body functions and is structured and staffed in order to design and to develop a more effective organization and ensure that the staff resources required will be available.

organization structure. Arrangement of the work of the organization into units and management positions between which there are defined relationships involving the exercise of authority and the communication of instructions and information. For organization structuring see *organization design*.

organization tree. As *organization chart*.

orientation program(me). As *induction training*.

original motion. *Motion* in the form in which it is initially moved at a meeting or conference before any amendment to it is moved. If an amendment is moved and carried, the amended motion is known as a *substantive motion*. See also *main question*.

ORIT. See *Inter-American Regional Organization of Workers*.

O'Rourke mechanical aptitude test. Early *psychological test* of the *mechanical comprehension* kind. Of US origin, it is basically an *achievement* test but has also been used as an *aptitude test*.

Ortho-Rater. Binocular testing instrument used in vision testing, particularly in the USA.

Osaka Securities Exchange. One of the major *Japanese stock exchanges*.

Osgood scales. System of *multiple-choice questions* or *pre-coded questions* developed

245

in the USA by Osgood for use in *market research* interviews. The *informant* chooses his answer to each interview question from a list of prepared answers presented or suggested to him in the manner of *multiple-choice questions*. See also *semantic differential*.

Oslo Bourse. See *Oslo Stock Market*.

Oslo Stock Market. Oslo Bourse was founded initially under legislation of 1818. The Oslo Stock Exchange is run by a government-appointed committee consisting of four businessmen and a Bourse commissioner who is responsible for day-to-day administration.

Österreichische Nationalbank. Austrian National Bank or *central bank*.

Österreichischer Gewerkschaftsbund. Austrian Federation of Trade Unions. Established in 1945, it covers 16 *trade unions* which have some 1,527,000 members.

ostmark. Basic unit of the currency of the German Democratic Republic.

other revenue. In accounting and financial reports income from minor sources or from activities which do not form part of the normal business activities, eg dividends from minor trade investments, profits from disposal of assets, etc.

Otis self-administering tests of mental ability. *Intelligence test* used particularly in the USA. Developed originally for work in schools, the test has been adopted in industry and business. See also *Wonderlic personnel test* and *psychological testing*.

outline process chart. As *operation process chart*.

output(s). 1. Information and data produced as the result of calculations by, for example, a *computer*. **2.** *Value added tax* term for the tax on the total value of goods and services at the end of a particular stage in their production or distribution. The tax on their value at the beginning of the stage is known as the *input*. The tax payable on that particular stage is the difference between the input and the output. **3.** The product produced by a particular process or department.

output budgeting. As *program(me) budgeting* or *planning, programming, budgeting system*.

output device. Translates the information produced by the *central processing unit* of a *computer* in the form of electrical impulses into a form comprehensible to human beings. The most usual form of output device is either electro-mechanical *line printer*, or a xerographic *page printer*, or *punched cards* produced by a *card punch* or *paper tape punch* linked to the central processing unit. Other forms of output device include *console typewriters* and *visual display units*.

output per manshift (OMS). Production or other output of an industrial unit averaged out per employee per working shift. The term is used particularly in coalmining, where the output from a particular coalface may be expressed as 'face OMS' or 'face output per manshift'.

out-turn. *Output*, particularly in the petroleum and certain other processing industries.

outward trade mission. Term in the UK for a group of British businessmen going overseas to sell UK goods and services with financial support from the *Fairs and Promotions Branch* of the *Department of Trade* and with the sponsorship of a *trade association*, *chamber of commerce* or similar non-trading organization.

outwork. Work carried out for a company outside its own premises, particularly by people working in their own homes. Sometimes known, particularly in the USA, as the 'putting-out' system.

overall impression method of selection. Sometimes used where there are many applications for a single vacancy, a procedure in which applications are divided on initial reading into 'unsuitable', 'possible' and 'probable' categories. Cf *analytic method*.

overall market capacity. Amount of a product or service that could be absorbed in an overall market without taking into account price or *market segmentation* considerations. Thus, the future overall market capacity for cars would include consumers who would like to own a car but are not able or willing to pay the existing price, as well as those who are. See also *actual market volume, market potential, market prospective, market segment capacity, market share*.

overcapitalize. 1. To give too high an estimate of the value of property, etc. **2.** To place an unreasonably or even unlawfully high value on the nominal *capital* of a company, *corporation*, etc. **3.** To provide an enterprise with more capital than it needs.

overdue. Any item that remains unpaid after the due date for payment.

overevaluating. Term used in *psychological testing* where too much reliance is placed on test results.

overhead. As *indirect cost*.

overhead absorption. Allocation of *indirect costs* to products, *cost centres (centers)*, etc. See *absorption costing*.

overhead projector. Projects transparencies or the silhouettes of three-dimensional objects on to a screen behind the operator/lecturer who is well placed to speak to pupils/trainees because he has both them and the transparencies in front of him. See also *audiovisual aid*.

overmanning. Manning of plant by more employees than are required to operate efficiently. Opposite of *undermanning*.

overseas countries and territories, association of, (EEC). See *association of overseas countries and territories (EEC)*.

Overseas, Diplomatic Service Commercial Officers. See *Diplomatic Service Commercial Officers Overseas*.

Overseas Finance and Projects Division (DT). Overseas Projects Group of this Division of the *Department of Trade* acts in UK as a focal point to which consultants, contractors, manufacturers and bankers can look for assistance, including coordination of official support, when pursuing contract work on important capital projects overseas. The Group also has an experimental fund to help UK consultants, contractors or manufacturers to offer potential customers abroad studies up to the feasibility stage of projects which might pave the way for substantial exports of UK capital goods and related services. See also *British Consultants Bureau*.

Overseas Projects and Technology Division (DT). Provides information for UK firms on overseas capital projects and consultancy.

overstaffing. As *overmanning*, though possibly with an emphasis on *white collar workers*.

over-the-counter-market. Dealing in *securities* not normally listed by an official *stock exchange*. Particularly used in the USA by smaller companies or companies with a limited number of shareholders.

overtime. Time worked over and above the agreed normal hours of work, and usually rewarded at agreed overtime rates of pay.

overtime ban. Refusal to work *overtime*. Can be very effective form of *industrial action* where a 24 hours-a-day or shift system can only be maintained if gaps between shifts are filled by individuals working overtime. An overtime ban is not normally in breach of a *contract of employment* unless, exceptionally, the contract provides for compulsory overtime. An overtime ban is a form of *cut-price industrial action*. See also *strike*.

overtrading. Where a company expands in such a way and at such a rate that, even if it is highly profitable, it cannot pay its own way for lack of *working capital* and thus has *liquidity* problems.

overturn. As *turnover*.

over-training. Training and/or education to a higher level than is necessary for the performance of the work of the trainee. One consequence can be that the person trained experiences the frustrations of *under-employment*. Thus the effects of over-training may have significance for *job satisfaction* and *job enrichment*.

own brand, or label. Selling of goods — usually by a *retail outlet* — under their own *brand* name. Also known as private brand.

Oxbridge. Contraction for the Universities of Oxford and Cambridge in the UK.

p

PABLA system. Acronym for 'problem analysis by logical approach', developed originally by the UK Atomic Energy Authority as a method of improving the effectiveness of design and research and development work. The system involves the use of cards requiring information from the designer at prescribed points.

pacers. Or speeders or bell-horses. Fast workers used by management to set the pace in a factory or even to establish *piece work* rates (though the latter practice (practise), in particular, is often resisted by *trade unions*). See also *ratebuster*.

Pacific Coast Stock Exchange. One of the major *US stock exchanges* based in Los Angeles.

Pacific Standard Time (PST or PT). Local time at a point in the USA at the 120th meridian. See *standard time* and the Appendix: Time Zones.

pacing. Describes the rigidity (or otherwise) of time allowed in assembly or flow line work for completing certain operations or jobs.

package, computer. See *computer package*.

package courses. Prepared teaching/instructional materials often involving use of variety of educational and communications aids, eg combination of books, slides, film strips or films, etc. See also *integrated learning system*.

package deal. Agreement which covers a number of issues and points, providing a comprehensive package in which the different parties make concessions on particular aspects in order to achieve a total agreement considered to be of overall advantage to all concerned. Trade agreements are often a form of package deal, and so is *productivity bargaining*.

package-deal system. Comprehensive arrangement usually involving not only the supply of materials, but also provision of specialized services, know-how, etc. Used particularly in civil engineering where a single firm acts as both contractor and designer or consulting engineer.

package store. US term for a store that sells sealed bottles of alcoholic drinks for consumption away from the premises. Similar to 'off-licence' in the UK.

package tour. Holiday tour for which a single fee is paid to cover travel, accommodation, excursions, etc arranged by the package tour operator.

packaging. Protecting products and containing them in prescribed quantities. In recent years has also developed a *sales promotion* role as a vehicle for promoting product and/or company image. Developments in packaging have also contributed to improvements in product life, particularly in the storage of *consumer disposables*, such as food. See also *marketing mix*.

packing list. As *consignment note*.

pack test. *Market research* technique for checking the effectiveness of a product's pack, functionally, aesthetically and in establishing the product's identity and image.

page printer. See *output device* (computer).

paid-in capital. As *contributed capital*.

paid-in surplus. Money received by a *company* or *corporation* for the issue of its *shares* over and above their *nominal value*. See also *share premium*.

paid-up capital. Or share capital. As *issued capital* but specifically on which all monies due have been paid. See also *called up capital*.

paid-up pension. As *frozen pension*. See also *superannuation*.

paired comparisons. See *whole-job ranking.*

Pakistan, State Bank of. *Central bank* established in 1948.

Pakistan Stock Exchange. Established 1947 in Karachi.

Palais de la Bourse, Marseille. *Marseille Stock Exchange.* See also *French stock exchanges.*

Palermo Stock Exchange (Borsa Valori di Palermo). One of ten *Italian stock exchanges.*

palletization. Warehousing and distribution of goods on wooden frames or pallets designed for easy transportation and stacking by fork-lift trucks. In effect, an elementary form of *containerization.*

Pan-African Workers Congress (PAWC). Formed in 1959 by an amalgamation of existing *trade union* confederations. See also *African Trade Union Confederation (ATUC)* and *All African Trade Union Federation (AATUF).*

panel interview. In *personnel selection,* interviewing a candidate by an interviewing panel rather than by an individual interviewer. A panel interview may be used, for example, where the appointment to be filled has a bearing on the work of several departments and it is therefore reasonable that the candidate be seen and assessed by people from those departments. A panel interview is usually regarded as complementary to other parts of a selection procedure such as individual interviews, *psychological testing,* etc.

panel methods. Or audit methods. *Market research* term where product testing panels of consumers or users are used to obtain views on products and *product acceptance.* See also *reference groups.*

Panel on Takeovers and Mergers. *City of London* body which considers the propriety of *take-over bids* involving publicly quoted companies.

panoramic office planning (POP). As *open office planning,* also known as *Bürolandschaft.*

pantry check. *Market research* term for a check of households to discover how many of them have a certain product or products available for use or *consumption.* A pantry check and a *dustbin check* may be known jointly as a *home audit.* See also *retail audit.*

Paper and Paper Products Industry Training Board. Established in UK in 1968 under the *Industrial Training Act 1964.*

Paper form board test. See *Revised Minnesota paper form board test.*

paper tape. Alternative to *punched cards* for feeding information into the *input device* of a *computer.* Usually computers use a tape with an eight-track code. The tape is normally an inch wide and stored in 1,000 ft reels.

paper tape punch. Used in the preparation of *paper tape.*

PAR. *Program(me) analysis and review.*

parallel pricing. Aligning price increases with the price increases of competitors.

parent company. As *holding company.*

Pareto's law. In most business activities a small fraction of the total produces the major problems, costs, profits or some other measure of significance. Has been called 'the law of the trivial many and the critical few'. It has universal application, eg in sales 80 per cent of the volume is accounted for by 20 per cent of the customers, or in stock control, for example, about 15 per cent of the inventory accounts for say 75 per cent of the total stock value. The corollary of Pareto's law is that management should concentrate on the efficiency and performance of the crucial 20 per cent and not on the insignificant items. Also known as eighty-twenty rule, *concentration analysis* and *ABC method.*

Paris Bourse. See *Paris Stock Exchange.*

Paris Stock Exchange. Or *Paris Bourse.* The largest in the original *European Economic Community* but it is much smaller than either the *London Stock Exchange* or New York's *Wall Street.* There are also six provincial stock exchanges in France (see *French stock exchanges).* The Paris Stock Exchange is run by the *Commission des Opérations de Bourse,* with the Professional Association of Brokers, or *Chambre Syndicale des Agents de Change,* responsible for implementing the Stock Exchange rules and for drawing up and publishing the Official List of securities. There is also the *Société Interprofessionnelle pour la Com-*

pensation des Valeurs Mobilières (SICOVAM) which acts as a central clearing house for the settlement of Stock Exchange operations. Stockbrokers, or *Agents de Change,* are Government nominees and are members of the *Compagnie des Agents de Change* (who elect the Chambre Syndicale des Agents de Change). These latter bodies supervise the unofficial market, or le *marché hors-côté,* as well as the Official List. For address see Appendix: World Stock Exchanges.

Paris Treaty. Common term for the *Treaty of Paris 1951* which established the *European Coal and Steel Community (ECSC).*

Parkinson's Law. 'Work expands to fill the time available', the law pronounced by Professor Northcote Parkinson of the UK.

participation. Generic term for a variety of ways of increasing the involvement and commitment of employees to their own jobs and to corporate goals. Originally participation implied that the system of ownership needed changing as in guild socialism. Currently participation normally implies some form of *profit-sharing* or *co-partnership* scheme and involvement in decision making through *joint consultation, project groups,* etc. See also *workers' participation.*

participative management (or supervision). Style of management that lays stress on the importance of good human relations and of *workers' participation* in management decision making (though such participation can vary in practice (practise) from being a hoped for safety valve for employee discontent to involving genuine consultation and even decision making). Participative management involves a blurring of the traditional demarcation lines between management and workers and a diminution of *management prerogative.* Some acceptance of the values of participative management is implicit in such modern thinking on the nature of management as that in the *managerial grid* and *Theory Y,* or in the rise of *joint consultation* and *works councils.* However, the basis of participative management owes much to the *human relations school* of management and behavio(u)ral science that originated in the USA in the 1920s and 1930s. Indeed, modern advocates of participative management are sometimes referred to as being of the neo-human relations school. See also *industrial democracy* and *management style.*

part method or part-progressive method. Where an operation to be learnt is divided into parts which are learnt and practised separately before being brought together and practised as a whole. Cf *cumulative-part method, whole method.*

partnership. Form of business association or company in which the partners are fully responsible for the partnership's liabilities.

Partnership Act 1890 (UK). Made the members of a partnership liable for the wrongful acts or omissions of any partner acting in the ordinary course of the business or with the authority of his partners. They also shared responsibility for the actions of their employees.

parts list. *Production planning and control* term for a list of the components and materials required for particular work, giving for each item such information as part numbers and descriptions, date of issue, any modifications, etc.

partsman. A storekeeper or salesman who handles orders for spare parts, particularly in the motor vehicle business.

party plan. Method of selling in which prospective purchasers are brought together in a social situation at the home of one of them. A representative of the company marketing the product then endeavours to secure from each of the 'guests' both an order for goods and an undertaking to give their own party. The host for a party is paid a commission, normally in the form of a present of the company's goods, the value of this commission being related both to sales at the party and to the number of guests undertaking to give their own parties. See also *pyramid selling.*

par value. Of shares. As *nominal value.*

pass-book. 1. Bank book. 2. Book for recording *credit sales.*

password. *Computer* term for the set of characters that identify a user in order to enable him to log-on to and use the system.

PA system. Public address system.

patent. It is granted to the 'first and true inventor' of an article or process. Grants the sole right to make, use or sell the invention which, once it is patented, becomes known as an industrial property. *Letters patent* may be granted to either a person or a company or corporation. In order for letters patent to be granted, an invention must be genuinely novel, not already known to the public, and neither illegal nor immoral. In the UK, for example, a patent remains in force for 16 years provided it is properly registered at the Patent Office — usually with the professional guidance of a Chartered Patent Agent — and the renewal fee paid annually. It may be possible for a patent to be renewed further after the initial 16-year period. The protection of a patent must be sought separately in each country where the invention is to be sold or made under licence (license) but most industrialized countries subscribe to the *International Convention for the Protection of Industrial Property* which gives help in arranging protection in overseas countries. See also *copyright* and *trade mark*.

Patent Office and Industrial Property and Copyright Department (DT). Handles and registers *patents, trade marks* and *industrial property rights* in the UK. The former Patent Office Library, a source of information on existing patents and trade marks registered in other countries, is now known as the *National Reference Library of Science and Invention* (Holborn Division).

Patent and Trademark Office. *US Department of Commerce* agency which grants *patents*, registers *trade marks*, and maintains a scientific library and search file of US and foreign patents for public use.

Patents Act 1949 (UK). Section 56(2) allowed for the benefit of an invention to be apportioned between employer and employee. In most cases, however, the employee's *contract of employment* will prohibit him from exploiting inventions made in the course of his employment. In any event, the general legal position is that it is the employer who has the right to exploit inventions arising out of the employee's work (even when they are not directly related to the employer's business) unless there is an agreement under the Patents Act 1949 to share the benefit of inventions.

Patents Act 1977 (UK). This simplified patent procedures, redefined patentable inventions and what constitutes an 'inventive step', extended the patent term from 16 to 20 years, established a Patents Court and strengthened the position of employee inventors.

paternalism. *Management style* which is a blend of authoritarianism and the provision of extensive welfare facilities.

Paterson method. Method of *job evaluation* devised by Professor T T Paterson of Strathclyde University (Scotland). Method assumes that all jobs can be analyzed by the degree of decision making involved in a job, eg policy making, interpretative decisions, etc.

patrial. Term used in the UK under the Immigration Act 1971 for a Commonwealth or colonial citizen at least one of whose parents was born in the UK. Patrials were not made subject to immigration control under the Act.

pattern bargaining. As whipsawing or key bargaining. Where *trade unions* in negotiation or conflict with an employer use as levers the examples of favo(u)rable *collective agreements* made with other, similar employers. See also *leapfrogging* and *bumper strike*.

Pauschalsteuer. Or *impôt à forfait*. Graduated tax charged on incomes of certain foreigners in Switzerland instead of the national defence (defense) tax. See *Swiss income tax*.

PAV. Potential acquisition valuation method.

PAWC. *Pan-African Workers Congress.*

pawn-broker. Small-time moneylender who normally holds borrowers' personal goods as *collateral.*

pay-as-you-earn (PAYE). Deduction of income tax etc at source as the income is paid. See also *withholding tax*.

pay-as-you-go. Where retirement pensions are paid out of contributions currently being paid into the scheme by present contributors, as distinct from being related directly to the premiums paid in the past by the individual pensioner.

payback. 1. As *rate of return*. 2. Techniques for forecasting when a project/enterprise will reach its *break-even point*. More sophisticated than ordinary payback techniques is *discounted payback* which allows for the need to secure a return on the *investment*, not merely to recover the investment.

Pay Board. Set up in UK under the Counter-Inflation Act 1973 as an independent agency charged with monitoring implementation of the UK Government's policy on pay, the monitoring of prices being a responsibility of the *Price Com-*

mission. Provision was made for firms failing to comply with an Order or Notice of the Pay Board to be prosecuted, subject to explicit permission being given by the Attorney-General. The Pay Board ceased operating in 1974.

pay differential. Variance in pay of different types of employee.

PAYE. *Pay-as-you-earn.*

payee. Recipient of payment under a *bill of exchange*, etc, from the *drawee*, often a bank, on the instructions of the *drawer*.

payment-by-results (PBR). Or *performance-linked pay*. Systems of wage payment geared to worker output, often based on *work study*. See also *measured day work, share of production plan, piece work*, and *rate fixing*. A *payment system* based on time worked rather than units or results produced is a *time-related payment scheme*.

Payment in Lieu (PIL). Made by an employer to the *Department of Health and Social Security* in UK in respect of an employee leaving an *occupational pension scheme* that is contracted-out of the *state graduated pension scheme*. This payment is then to be incorporated in the employee's state pension. The amount of pension earned under the occupational scheme must be at least equal — the *Equivalent Pension Benefit* — to the maximum the employee could have earned during the same period under the state scheme. Also used when an employee is paid a lump sum on dismissal which is equivalent to what he would have earned had he served his full notice. See also the *Certificate of Assurance* arrangement.

Payment of Wages Act 1960 (UK). Allows an employer to pay an employee by *cheque (check)* if the latter makes a request in writing, such an arrangement being subject to cancellation by either side at four weeks' notice in writing. This Act also provides for an employer to pay absent workers by postal or money order, subject to certain restrictions.

payment pause. Temporary freezing of pay by government order or decree.

pay plan. As *payment system.*

payment system. Procedure relating employees' pay to their effort or work and, preferably, establishing administrative, negotiating and disputes handling machinery. The two basic methods of payment are *time-related payment* (eg 'so much per hour') and *payment-by-results*. These two methods are often combined in a payment system. A *situation profile* may be used in deciding upon a payment system.

pay-out period. Early period of *negative cash flow* in a project or enterprise before *start-up costs* and cumulative *running costs* have been recovered and *break-even point* has been achieved.

pay package. As *total remuneration.*

pay pause. As *payment pause.*

payroll deductions. As *check-off.*

PBR. *Payment-by-results.*

PCT. *Wesman personnel classification test.*

PDG (Fr). Président Directeur Général. Chief Executive of French limited liability public company *(SA).*

PDM. *Physical distribution management.*

peaceful picketing. Peaceful, non-violent persuasion by *strikers* seeking to dissuade a *black-leg* labour from replacing them, and/or **b** their employer's customers from dealing with him. See also *mass picketing, pink-tea picketing* and *sympathy strike.*

peak absences. Points in a working or demand cycle where the work load or demand is relatively light. Opposite of *peak loads.*

peak loads. Points in a working or demand cycle where the work load or demand is at its heaviest. Converse of *peak absences.*

pearl strike. As *irritation strike.*

peer goal-setting. Joint setting of goals by people of similar standing.

peer rating. Method of student assessment used in some business schools, particularly in the USA. Certain broad yardsticks are established for the levels of attainment and understanding expected of students at particular points in a course. Qualitative assessments are then made of whether each student measures up to these levels. Sometimes a paired comparisons type of assessment is used.

peg. *Exchange rate* normally acceptable to the *central bank* of the country concerned.

pegging. Fixing or holding prices or currency exchange rates for a period of time.

pegboard test. Manual dexterity or manual coordination test in which the person being tested has to fit pegs into specially designed boards in test conditions and within certain time limits. It is thus a test of *psychomotor skills* that calls for coordination between mind and muscle in the individual. Types of pegboard test, mainly of US origin, include the *Crawford small parts dexterity test*, the *Hayes pegboard test*, the *O'Connor finger dexterity test*, and the *Purdue pegboard test*. See also *psychological testing*.

penetration pricing. Launching a new product at a low price in order quickly to capture as large a share of the market as possible. The opposite policy, *skimming*, is to put the product on sale at a high price and then reduce the price by stages to saturate the market from the top downwards.

pension. Regular payment made to a person who has reached retirement age (when the pension may be known as *superannuation*) or who has suffered a disability, or to dependants of a person dying before or after retirement. Types of retirement pension scheme in the UK include *average salary pension schemes*, discretionary endowment pension schemes, *excepted provident fund* (or *'cloth cap pension scheme'*), *final salary pension schemes*, *money purchase pension schemes*, *one man pension arrangements*, *purchased life annuities*, *staff assurance schemes*, *state flat rate pensions*, *state graduated pensions*, *statutory pension schemes*, and *'top hat' pension schemes*. Occupational pension schemes may be either *contributory* or *non-contributory* and may be based on either *with-profits* or *non-profit endowment assurance*. The disabled receive disability pensions under occupational and/or state schemes. Typical pension schemes for dependants include the *five-year guarantee scheme, group life assurance policies, joint life and last survivor pensions, income benefit insurance policies, widows' allowances, widows' and orphans' pension schemes,* and *widow's pension options*. Several larger US firms have pension plans or retirement plans, either contributory or noncontributory, the latter form being that most sought by labo(u)r unions in their contracts. A vested pension plan is one under which a pension can be transferred to new employment when an employee moves to new employment. Usually, the US Internal Revenue Code will only allow a pension fund as a business expense if it is funded.

pensionable salary (or earnings). That part of a person's salary or earnings taken into account in calculating entitlement to pension. This may be total earnings or it may exclude such items as bonuses, commission, *overtime* and *premium payments* generally. In the case of an *average salary pension scheme*, pensionable salary may be known as *average salary*.

pensionable service. Years of employment taken into account for the purposes of calculating the level of pension due. See also *final salary pension scheme*.

Pension Benefit Guaranty Corporation. US independent nonprofit corporation wholly owned by the US government. It guarantees payments under insured benefit plans and gives advice on tax-qualified individual retirement accounts and other individual retirement program(me)s.

Pension Rights Center. US nonprofit organization funded by foundations, organizations and individuals to expand pension rights, especially for women, to provide information on pension benefits and plans, to give technical assistance in the analysis of pension problems and issues, to work for change in the retirement income system, and to publish 'Pension Facts'.

Pentagon, the. Headquarters of the US Department of Defense and armed forces at Arlington, Virginia, near Washington DC. The name is derived from the five-sided shape of the building.

PER. *Professional and Executive Recruitment* service in the UK of the *Department of Employment*. Known until 1973 as the Professional and Executive Register. Came under the independent statutory body, the *Employment Service Agency*, during 1974.

PERA system. Classification code for components covering material, initial form (eg casting), length, diameter and batch size. Developed by the Production Engineering Research Association in the UK. See also *classification and coding system*.

P/E ratio. Price earnings ratio.

perceptual distortion. *Market research* term for the extent to which an interviewee's assessment of a product etc is distorted by his own interests and values.

perceptual skills. Ability to put things, events, information, etc in perspective in the context of a particular situation or job.

performance appraisal. Systematic assessment of an individual's performance in order to assess training needs, potential for promotion, eligibility for a merit increment as part of a pay or *salary review* or for *management succession* planning. Methods of appraisal include the *controlled report, factor rating, forced choice approach, ranking system* and *task-based appraisal.* See also *management by objectives.*

performance index. Technique for measuring management performance according to certain agreed indices. Such indices might be measures of personal performance or of the performance of units, eg returns on capital invested. Performance index may be linked to *management by objectives* schemes.

performance-linked pay. As *payment-by-results.*

performance objectives. As *behavio(u)ral objectives.*

performance review. Form of *performance appraisal* of managers by their immediate superiors under *management by objectives.*

performance tolerance. Error or inefficiency which can be tolerated in an operator's performance.

period of grace. Period of time allowed to a party to a contract to meet the obligations laid upon him under the contract. Such a contract may be voluntary (eg an undertaking to repay a loan) or one imposed statutorily or by custom (eg an automobile licence (license) or payment for services such as electricity supply).

peripheral equipment or unit (or peripherals). *Input devices, output devices* and *external storage devices* linked to the *central processing unit* of a *computer.*

period bill. As *time bill.*

perishable dispute. *Strike* over issues which the management would win by default if the workers did not act immediately and before being overtaken by events.

perks. Or perquisites. *Fringe benefits,* often of an informal kind.

permanent sickness and accident policy. As *disability pension.*

perms. Permanent employees as distinct from those who may be hired on a casual or temporary basis.

perpetual inventory. *Stock control* system involving constant checks on stock levels.

personal accident policy. An insurance policy that pays a *lump sum death benefit* on the death by accident of the insured and/or a capital sum or income in the event of serious disablement. See also *group personal accident policy, endowment assurance,* and *whole life assurance policy.*

Personal Injury, Royal Commission on Civil Liability and Compensation for. See *Royal Commission on Civil Liability and Compensation for Personal Injury.*

personality promotion. *Soft sales promotion* technique where publicity is given to the fact that a personality is at large in a neighbo(u)rhood to give prizes to users of the product they are promoting. They may, for example, give cash prizes to housewives who can produce a product and recite a much publicized jingle about it.

personality tests. See *temperament and personality tests.*

Personalized System of Instruction (PSI). See *Keller Plan.*

personal property. Movable or temporary property as opposed to *real property* or *real estate.*

personal records system. Personal records or *profiles* of an organization or company's employees assembled in a system designed for ease of information, identification and retrieval.

personal selling. Selling conducted by direct contact with the *prospect.* Defined by *marketing* men as creating a desire for what you have to sell so that the *prospect* wants it more than the scarce resources of money and time.

personenbelasting. See *impôt des personnes physiques,* the Belgian *income tax.*

personnel agency (US). As *employment agency.*

personnel department. Or *employee relations department.* Responsible in an industrial, commercial or other organization for advising on, devising and implementing the organization's personnel policies and

personnel placement. practices (practises). Such policies and practices (practises) may range across recruitment and selection; training; *pay and salary structures* and reviews; *fringe benefits; job evaluation; performance appraisal; industrial relations*, including disciplinary, *redundancy* and *joint consultation* procedures; safety, health and welfare; *manpower planning; management development;* and personnel records and statistics. A personnel department may be headed by a personnel officer, manager or director. It may also be known as a human relations department.

personnel placement. Process of fitting available personnel as effectively as possible into the available jobs. The converse of *personnel selection*, it is most likely to occur in conditions of *full employment*.

personnel selection. Process of selecting the most suitable from a group of applicants for a job, involving both classification of current performance and prediction of future performance. Cf *personnel placement*. In personnel selection, written applications may be first screened by the *analytic method of selection* or by the more cursory *overall impression method of selection*. The next stage may be to subject candidates to *psychological testing* devised by *occupational psychologists*. Typical selection interview procedures are the *seven point plan* and the *five fold grading scheme*. Other general types of interview are the *connected conversation interview*, the *directive interview* and the *non-directive interview*. Two other types of interview sometimes used in personnel selection are the *panel interview*, when a single interviewee is confronted by a panel of interviewers, and the *group selection* interview when several candidates are seen together.

personnel specification. Description of the kind of person needed for a job — in terms of qualifications, experience and other characteristics — in the light of the *job specification*.

personnel testing. See *personnel selection* and *psychological testing*.

PERT. *Program(me) Evaluation and Review Technique.*

Perth Stock Exchange. One of six *Australian Associated Stock Exchanges*.

Peru Stock Exchange. See *Lima Stock Exchange*.

peseta. Basic unit of the currency of Spain.

Peter Principle. 'In a hierarchy every employee tends to rise to his level of incompetence', the principle enunciated by Dr Lawrence J Peter, of the University of Southern California.

Petroleum Industry Training Board. Established in UK in May 1967 under the *Industrial Training Act 1964*.

phantom stocks. Form of bonus plan in which participants receive partial or complete financial benefit of stock or share ownership without actually owning any stock.

Phase 2 and 3. See *Counter-Inflation Act 1973*.

Philadelphia-Baltimore-Washington Stock Exchange. One of about 20 *US stock exchanges*.

Philadelphia, Declaration of. See *Declaration of Philadelphia*.

Philadelphia lawyer. One skilled in discovering legal loopholes.

Philadelphia Stock Exchange. See *Philadelphia - Baltimore - Washington Stock Exchange*.

Phillipines Stock Exchange. See *Manila Stock Exchange*.

Phillips Curve. Devised by A W Phillips in the UK in 1958 to relate changes in money wage rates to the percentage of the labo(u)r force which is unemployed. A further refinement two years later was the *Lipsey Equation*.

phototelegram service. Operated by the *Post Office* in the UK, provides at home or overseas facsimile representations of plans, products for sale, etc.

physical distribution management (PDM). Study, control and management of all the factors involved in the distribution of materials and finished goods. Involves an integrated approach to materials handling, protective packaging, freight transport, warehousing, inventory control, location of depots. Underlying the PDM concept is the high cost of distribution as a percentage of total costs and the need to coordinate all the areas which go to make up the movement and storage of stock. See also *distribution* *planning.*

PI. *Programmed instruction.*

physical inventory. As *stocktaking.*

picketing. See *peaceful picketing, mass picketing, pink-tea picketing, secondary picketing.*

picking. Selecting and withdrawing components or goods from stores to meet requisitions or customers' orders.

pictogram. Diagram in which items or objects are drawn in different sizes or quantities to represent actual sizes or quantities. For example, the different outputs of two factories might be represented by products of proportional sizes.

piece work. Form of *payment-by-results* or *performance-related pay* in which the worker is paid at a particular rate per product or component produced. In the UK engineering industry, for example, about half of the one million workers are paid predominantly at piece work rates. Traditionally, these rates are arranged by subjective *rate fixing* rather than by more objective techniques such as *work study.* The term is also used generally, on occasion, of *payment-by-results* schemes. Where piece work rates are of a kind that make it difficult for a worker to earn bonus, they are said to be *tight rates.* If bonus can be earned relatively easily, the rates are said to be *loose rates.* See also *effort bargain* and *premium payment.*

pieceworkers' guarantee. As *fall-back payment.*

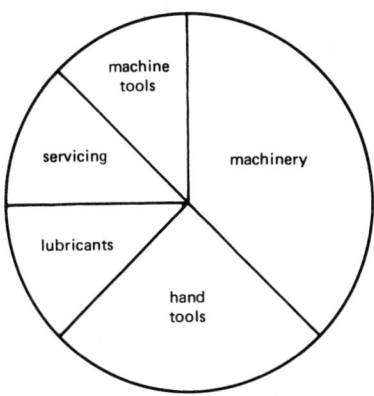

annual sales by product type
pie chart

pie chart (or diagram). Or circle chart. Diagram consisting of a circle with radii dividing it into sectors proportional in angle and therefore area to the relative sizes of the quantities represented.

piggybacking. 1. Handling of further products related to one's normal product lines in order to expand or optimize one's business effort. 2. In direct mail or marketing promoting a second product or service at minimal extra cost at the same time as the first.

PIL. *Payment in lieu* (pensions).

pilotage. 1. Fee paid to a nautical pilot. 2. Techniques used by a pilot, navigator, etc.

pilot interview. Or *throw away interview.* Designed to test an interviewing technique before undertaking a full-scale survey.

pilot production. Initial production of a product in shop floor conditions, partly to establish the best production methods and system. Often introduced in conjunction with the *test marketing* of a new product.

pink-tea picketing. American term for picketing involving only a small number of pickets behaving discreetly. See also *mass picketing, peaceful picketing, secondary picketing.*

pioneer product. Product of entirely new design and/or function. Differs from a *market follower,* which is a product introduced to compete with existing products, and from a *brand leader* that is already in a dominant position in its field.

pipage. 1. Transmission of liquids and other materials by pipeline. 2. Charge made for such transmission.

pitch. Any sales presentation by a salesman to a buyer. Also used in advertising to describe an agency presentation to a prospective client.

Pittler classification. Method of classifying and coding components. Uses a 9-digit code to summarize a wide range of information about components. See also *classification and coding systems.*

PL. *Programmed learning.*

placement test, product. See *product placement test.*

placings. Or placements. Issuing of *shares* at a fixed or negotiated price, rather than by public issue.

plain time rate. Term sometimes used for time rate or *time related payment* to emphasize that it does not include *bonus* or *premium payment*.

PLAN. Acronym for Programming Language Nineteenhundred, a low-level but complex *computer language* developed particularly for the ICL 1900 series of *digital computers*.

planned funding. See *controlled funding* (of *pensions*).

planned learning experience. Where an employee or trainee is directed to undertake work that is selected for the particular employee/trainee as being especially relevant to complementary training he is undertaking or to his career development. Planned learning experience may involve *job rotation* between different types of work. It may be planned as part of a company's *management development* policy.

planned maintenance. As *preventive maintenance*.

planned obsolescence. See *built-in obsolescence*.

planning blight. Where an urban area falls into decay and in part into disuse once it is known that development is planned for the future and people lose interest in maintaining the old buildings. See also *twilight area*.

planning, programming, budgeting system (PPBS). Or output budgeting. Wide-ranging management technique introduced into the USA in the mid-1960s, not always with ready cooperation from the administrators, and based on the industrial management technique of *program(me) budgeting*. Subsequently, the technique has been introduced into other countries, including the UK where it is often called output budgeting. PPBS is in effect an integrating of a number of techniques in a planning and budgeting process for identifying, costing and assigning a complexity of resources, for establishing priorities and strategies in a major program(me), and for forecasting costs, expenditure and achievements within the immediate financial year or over a longer period.

plans. Statements of the things to be done and the sequence and timing in which they should be done in order to achieve a given end. Planning involves deciding on aims and objectives, selecting the correct strategies and program(me)s to achieve the aims, determining and allocating the resources required and ensuring that plans are communicated to all concerned.

plant bargaining. Wage or *collective bargaining* conducted at the level of the individual factory or plant, rather than company bargaining which may cover several factories owned by the same company or national bargaining covering all the factories in a particular industry.

plateau. See *learning plateau*.

PL/1. Or *Programming Language 1*. A *high-level language* specially developed to combine the qualities of commercial and scientific languages. See *computer language*.

Plowden Committee on the Control of Public Expenditure (UK). Committee which reported to the *Chancellor of the Exchequer* in 1961, making recommendations that led to a number of management reforms in public expenditure, planning and control. The Plowden Committee stressed the importance of management techniques and efficiency, in a way comparable with the 1937 report of the *Brownlow Committee* to President Roosevelt in the USA. The 1967 *Redcliffe-Maud Report on the Management of Local Government* in the UK dealt with the use of management techniques in local government. The 1968 *Fulton Report on the Civil Service* also stressed the role of management in UK public administration.

plug. Promote an organization, product or service, usually at little or no cost.

plural executive. Collective exercise of management authority by a group of executives.

pluralistic theory. Theory, often subscribed to in industrial relations/industrial psychology, that there are inevitably divergent interests in industry, particularly between employers and employees, but that there is also ultimately a framework of common interests. For example, management should recognize the right of workers to organize collectively but should further see that such recognition makes it easier to effect an acceptable compromise in the interests of both parties when a dispute does arise. In other words, acceptance that there are differences in outlook can ultimately be for the greater good of all. See also *joint* *regulation.* Cf *human relations school* and *structural-functionalist school.*

PMAT. *Purdue mechanical adaptability test.*

PMTS. *Pre-determined motion time study.*

P/N (or pn). *Promissory note.*

poaching. Practice (practise) indulged in by less scrupulous firms of poaching trained workers from elsewhere rather than investing in training themselves.

point of information. Put to a meeting or conference through its chairman, a point of information is either a short, factual statement to clarify a point under discussion or a question seeking such clarification. See also *motion.*

point of order. Query put to the chairman of a meeting or conference by a participant who believes that the business of the meeting is not being conducted according to its rules of debate or *standing orders.* See also *motion.*

point of personal explanation. Where an individual seeks leave of a meeting or conference to explain his personal position on an issue on which he believes he has either been misunderstood or is in danger of being misunderstood. See also *motion.*

point of sale material. Display material designed and arranged to stimulate retail sales, etc.

point of sale, or purchase. Place, such as a *retail outlet,* where goods are shown and sold to customers.

points rating method (or evaluation). *Job evaluation* method of evaluating jobs numerically by analyzing component job factors in detail and giving them points values from within a defined range. Other job evaluation techniques include *analytic job evaluation, dominant element job evaluation, integral job evaluation, job factor comparison, job grading, job ranking* and *profiling systems.*

policies. Statements of aims, purposes, principles or intentions which serve as continuing guidelines for management in accomplishing objectives.

Polish central bank. *Narodowy Bank Polski.*

Polish Central Council of Trade Unions. *Centralna Rada Zwaizkow Zawodowych (CRZZ).*

Polish Chamber of Foreign Trade. *Polska Izba Handlu Zagranicznego.*

political fund. That part of a UK *trade union's* funds which, since the *Trade Union Act 1913,* has been applicable to political objects. The political fund of a union is financed from the *political levy* part of trade union dues with individual union members having a *contracting-out* right (from 1927 until 1946 *contracting-in* was employed instead).

political levy. Part of a UK *trade union* member's *trade union dues* that goes into the union's *political fund* and can be used for the political objects first outlined in the *Trade Union Act 1913.*

political union. Uniting of two or more countries or territories under a common government. The *European Economic Community,* for example, was conceived by its original advocates after the Second World War as a basis for political union that would prevent further wars in Europe, though it was set up under the *Treaty of Rome 1957* as a *Common Market* that could lead to political union, if the member states wished. An area in which the member states can be said to have made moves towards political union has been their work on a *common foreign policy.* Progress towards political union in the EEC raises questions of the relationship with the USA and other *North Atlantic Treaty Organization* countries and with the Communist Countries. The status of the *European Parliament* or *Assembly* also becomes crucial. See also *economic union* and *monetary union.*

Polska Izba Handlu Zagranicznego. Polish Chamber of Foreign Trade, established in 1949.

polytechnics (UK). **a** Thirty new polytechnics formed mainly from groupings of existing colleges and designated by the Secretary of State for Science and Education as major centres of higher education within the maintained sector following the White Paper, 'A Plan for Polytechnics and Other Colleges' (Cmnd 3006), of May 1966. Virtually the comprehensives of tertiary education. **b** The old polytechnics, a small number of colleges of further education in the Greater London area (some of which have in fact been assimilated into new polytechnics).

POP. *Panoramic office planning.*

population. The total number of people or items represented by the findings of a survey in *statistical quality control, market research,* etc.

portfolio investment. *Investment* in a range or 'portfolio' of *shares* or *securities,* usually in order to spread the risk.

portfolio management. Management and tactical operation, by a *stockbroker* or financial institution, of an assortment of *securities* owned by an investor client.

portfolio selection. Use of mathematical techniques of the *decision theory* and *risk analysis* kind to select new areas of business or companies for *acquisition.*

Portuguese central bank. *Banco de Portugal.*

Portuguese chambers of commerce. *Associacão Comercial de Lisboa – Camera de Comércio.*

Portuguese companies. Forms of business partnership and company under Portuguese law include: **a** Incorporated Partnership or *Sociedade em nome colectivo;* **b** General Partnership or *Sociedade em comandita simple;* **c** Partnership Limited by Shares or *Sociedade em comandita por accoes;* **d** Co-operative or *Sociedade Cooperativa;* **e** Joint Stock Company or *Sociedade anonima a Responsabilidade Limitada (Lda, Ltd, Ltda);* **f** Limited Liability Company or *Sociedade per cotas.* See also *Portuguese stock exchanges.*

Portuguese income tax. Forms of income tax in Portugal include: **a** property tax, or *contribuição predial;* **b** industrial tax, or *contribuição industrial,* on business income; **c** professional tax, or *imposto profissional,* on earned income; **d** a tax on income from movable capital, the *imposto de capitais;* **e** a complementary tax, or *imposto complementar,* charged as a progressive surtax on total income from all sources; **f** a defence tax on certain profits; **g** capital gains tax, or *imposto de mais-valias,* on certain types of capital gains.

Portuguese stock exchanges. Portugal has two stock exchanges, the *Lisbon Stock Exchange,* or *Bolsa de Lisboa,* and the *Oporto Stock Exchange* or *Bolsa de Porto,* the latter dating back to the late fourteenth century. At the present time, both stock exchanges have a limited range of dealing by international standards. Each stock exchange is run by a Commission of its Chambers of Brokers. Members of the Stock Exchanges are stockbrokers or *corretores* who are public officials.

POSDCORB. Planning, organizing, staffing, directing, coordinating, reporting and budgeting.

position audit. Assessment of the position of an organization in the context of its environment.

position evaluation. US term for *job evaluation.*

position guide. US term for document outlining the responsibilities, duties and authority of specific jobs. Normally synonymous with *job description.*

position statement. 1. As *balance sheet.* **2.** As *job description.*

positive cash flow. Where more cash is flowing into a project or enterprise than out of it. Where the larger flow is out of the project/enterprise there is said to be *negative cash flow.* See also *cash flow* and *discounted cash flow.*

positive transfer. See *training transfer.*

postdoctoral. Academic work, particularly research, beyond the level of a doctorate.

post-entry closed shop. Factory or workshop where the employees are required to join a *trade union* (usually a particular one) after taking up employment if they are not already members. See also *closed shop, open shop, pre-entry closed shop, preferential shop* and *union shop.*

Post Office (UK). Responsible to the Postmaster General for postal and telecommunications services in and from the UK. Services of particular interest to industry and commerce include *Datapost, Datel, phototelegram* and *telex.* The Post Office publishes the 'Post Office Guide' on an annual basis.

post-test. 1. *Market research* and *sales promotion* test to check how effective a sales or advertising campaign has been. **2.** Test at the end of a training programme to check the effectiveness of the programme and/or the performance of trainees. The post-test is normally compared with a *pre-test.* See also *criterion test.*

postural discrimination. Type of *psychomotor skill*. An individual's ability to respond to postural or physical cues, as distinct from visual cues, in adjusting working position. See also *motion study*.

potential acquisition valuation method (PAV). Systematic approach, involving ten stages, to evaluate investment proposals. Analyzes costs involved and expected return on investment ie annual net income. See also *rate of return*.

potential assessment. Formal review of employees' career potential and prospects.

potential demand. Likely future demand for a product or service. The size of the potential demand for a product is governed by the number of people who have needs which will be satisfied by the product, the amount of the product that will satisfy those needs and the number of people with the financial resources required to buy the product.

potential review. As *potential assessment*.

pound sterling. Basic unit of UK currency.

poverty trap. Where a country has a system of *social security* benefits payable to the lowest paid, the poverty trap is the level of wage payment at which an increase in wage will not in practice (practise) benefit the recipient because it is cancelled out by a loss of *social security* benefits. See also *statutory minimum wage* and *sweated labour*.

power of attorney. Legal document authorizing a person to act for another.

power test. Type of *intelligence test* or other *psychological test* in which some questions or items are pitched deliberately high so that they will be too difficult for some testees to complete. An alternative form of test is a *speed test* in which the number of items completed is more critical than the difficulty of particular items.

PPB. As *program(me) budgeting*.

PPB(S). *Planning, programming, budgeting system*. As *program(me) budgeting*.

PPE. *Pre-publication evaluation of advertising*.

PR. *Public relations*.

precedence diagram. See *activity on node*.

preceding year basis. Where *income tax* or any other form of tax is calculated on the profits etc of the previous tax year instead of figures for the current year. This basis may be necessary, for example, in taxing irregular incomes.

pre-coded question. *Multiple-choice question* for which an answer is chosen from a number of prepared alternatives, usually by ticking one of them. Pre-coded questions are often used in surveys and questionnaires so that the answers can be processed relatively easily. See also *ranking, Osgood scales* and *semantic differential*.

predetermined motion time systems (PMTS). System of synthetic *standard times* for standard human movements sometimes used in *motion study*. Other such systems include *work factor* and *methods time measurement (MTM)*. Synthetic times have the advantage of having been measured extremely accurately, but the disadvantage of not being able to take into account all the circumstances of each application.

predictive bargaining. Approach to wage bargaining that attempts to anticipate and even structure change rather than simply working from the past and trying to catch up with the present.

pre-entry closed shop. Factory or workshop where prospective employees will not be considered for employment unless they are already members of a *trade union*. See also *closed shop, open shop, post-entry closed shop, preferential shop* and *union shop*.

preference inventory. As *interest inventory* (in *psychological testing*).

preference shares. Take precedence over *ordinary shares* of a company but take their turn after *debentures* both in the payment of dividends and in the settlement of claims if a company goes into *liquidation*. In some cases the right of a holder of a preference share to a specified rate of dividend may be cumulative, so that if the company does not have a good enough year to pay the specified dividend, the unpaid dividend remains a liability on the company's future profits until it is paid.

preferential creditor. One who is owed money by a company or individual and takes preference over *unsecured* creditors in recovering the money. A preferential creditor may be assured of the return of his loan by having a *debenture* on *assets* of the *debtor* company.

preferential hiring. Term used particularly in the USA for an agreement under which an employer agrees to give first choice of jobs as vacancies occur to members of a particular *trade union*.

preferential shop. Factory where it has been agreed that members of a particular *trade union* shall have first choice of jobs, as in *preferential hiring*, and promotional and other advantages over non-union members. See also *closed shop, open shop, post-entry closed shop, pre-entry closed shop* and *union shop*.

preferential trade agreement (EEC). Or *association agreement*. The *Common Market* or *European Economic Community*, represented by the *European Commission*, may negotiate preferential trade agreements with associated states. An example of such an agreement is that negotiated with Spain in October 1970, following earlier agreements with Greece, Israel, Malta, Morocco, Tunisia and Turkey. Countries having such agreements with the EEC are known as *associated states*. See also the *Arusha Agreement* with three Commonwealth countries and the *Yaoundé Convention* with 18 developing countries.

preferred stock (US). *Stocks* (2) which carry preferential rights over common stock, rather in the manner of *preference shares*.

preliminary expenses. Or formation expenses or organization costs. Professional and other expenses involved in setting up a *company* or *corporation*.

premie makelaars. Options specialist on the *Amsterdam Stock Exchange*.

premium. 1. *Stock exchange* term for the amount by which *stocks* or *shares* are sold above their issue price. See also *stag*. **2.** Rate to be paid for insurance/assurance cover. **3.** See also *premium payment* and *time-related payment* or *premium plan*.

premium bonus scheme. Or time-saved bonus scheme. *Payment-by-results* scheme in which the bonus payment is calculated on the basis of time saved compared with *standard time*.

premium offer. Offer of selected merchandise at very competitive prices to purchasers of specific products in return for a number of labels, coupons, vouchers, etc.

premium payment. Wage payment over and above basic time rate, especially in engineering.

premium pay plan. Type of *measured daywork* developed by Philips Industries and using the *predetermined motion time system* to establish standards.

premium plan. Early form of *payment-by-results* under which workers were paid a *premium* for each day that they exceeded the target production figure. At least superficially has some points in common with present day *measured day work*.

premium pricing. As *prestige pricing*.

prepaid expense. *Expenditure* from which there has not yet been any benefit.

Pre-publication evaluation of advertising (PPE). Tests of the effectiveness in communication terms of a projected advertisement. The results of such a test or evaluation may lead to modifications in the advertising copy or presentation.

present value. Term in *discounted cash flow* for the current value attributed to expected incoming cash, this current or present value being at a discount to allow for the fact that cash presently available is worth more, and is more certain, than anticipated cash.

president. Normally the chief executive of a US company. Broadly equivalent to *managing director* in the UK.

président directeur général. See *PDG*.

President of the Council of Ministers (EEC). Presidency or chairmanship of the *Council of Ministers* of the *Common Market* is normally held in turn for periods of six months by the foreign ministers of the member states.

President's Commission on Pension Policy. US body appointed by the President to develop national policies for retirement, survivor and disability program(me)s.

press relations. Systematic development of effective communication with newspapers, radio, television and the media generally through such techniques as press releases and other contacts.

Prestel. Proprietary name for Viewdata system pioneered and marketed by UK Post Office in 1979.

prestige advertising. Or institutional advertising. *Advertising* aimed at promoting the public esteem or *corporate image* of a *company*, *corporation* or other organization rather than particular products.

prestige pricing. Or premium pricing. Charging a high *price* for a product where it is judged that this in itself will give it prestige and make it more sought after.

pre-take-off stage (or period). Term used by some economists for the stage of national *economic growth* in which, following the *traditional society* stage, there are distinct trends towards the higher standards of living of industrialized societies. See also later stages or periods of growth, namely, *take-off*, *drive to maturity*, and *maturity*.

pre-test. 1. *Market research* and *sales promotion* term for a test of a product, packaging, advertising presentation, etc before being launched more widely. **2.** Test given to a trainee/student before taking a training program(me) to test his/her suitability for the program(me) and, by comparison with a *post-test*, to gauge the program(me)'s effectiveness.

preventive maintenance. Or planned maintenance. Plant, equipment or building maintenance program(me)s planned to ensure that they operate or remain trouble-free for a predetermined period.

previous question. Moving 'that the previous question now be put' at a meeting or conference is a tactic similar to a motion for *next business*. If accepted by the chairman, then seconded and carried by the meeting, the effect of such a motion is broadly to have the business in hand put to the vote immediately. See also *closure* and *motion*.

price. Sum of money or equivalent asked for a product or service at a particular time in a particular market. To be distinguished from the *cost* to the producer of producing the product or service, and from the *value* of the product or service to the purchaser. The three concepts of cost, price and value are related in the technique of *product analysis pricing*. See also *price mechanism*, *market price* and *pricing policy*.

Price Commission. Set up in UK under the Counter-Inflation Act 1973 as an independent agency to monitor implementation of the then UK Government's policy on prices, the monitoring of pay being the responsibility of the *Pay Board*.

price discretion. Where a salesman has the authority to vary the price of a product in order to make a sale.

price earnings ratio. Or *P/E ratio*. Market price per *ordinary share* divided by earnings per ordinary share after tax. Expressed as the multiple of the latest reported earnings that the market is willing to pay for the ordinary shares. The P/E ratio expresses the market value placed on the expectation of future earnings; ie the number of years required to earn the price paid for the shares out of profits at the current rate. See *earnings yield*.

price elasticity. Drop in sales when the *price* of a product is increased. See also *demand elasticity*.

price elasticity of demand. Way in which demand varies with changes in price of a product or service. Demand is 'elastic' if a small change in price produces a large change in demand (that is, the product or service is *price sensitive*), or 'inelastic' if demand does not vary significantly with changes in price. See also *income elasticity of demand* and *pricing policy*.

price fixing. Where companies in competition with each other agree to charge the same price for a product or service, a practice (practise) that is now generally illegal in the UK, under the *Restrictive Trades Practices Act 1956*, etc. As price ring.

price leadership. Where competing companies operate similar *pricing policies*, charge similar prices and make price increases in step with each other as a result of one of the companies giving a lead to the others. The process of price leadership does not include the active cooperation and collusion between competing companies that constitute *price fixing* or a *restrictive trade practice (practise)*.

price-lining. Policy of charging a standard price for a number of products though their production costs may be very different.

price mechanism. 1. Process in a *free economy* or *laissez-faire economy* by which prices are said to be determined by the resultant of the buyer's need and preparedness to pay and the supplier's ability and desire to supply. **2.** Under the *Common Agricultural Policy* of the *Common Market* or *European Economic Community*, see *export subsidy (or restitution)*, *guide price*, *intervention price*, *reserve (or fall-back)* *price, sluice-gate price, target price* and *threshold price*, all aimed broadly at maintaining levels of market prices for producers in the member states. Price mechanisms under the Community's *common transport policy* include the *forked (or bracket) tariff* or scale of charges (prescribing maximum and minimum prices) for road and rail transport and the *reference tariff* or scale of charges (by which any prices outside recommended maximum and minimum prices must be published as such) for inland waterways and bulk transport.

price plateau. Price level or band which is accepted by customers as being reasonable for a particular product which is part of a range of products sold at different qualities and prices. The assumed existence of a price plateau may lead a manufacturer to restrict price increases until evidence is obtained of the acceptability to customers of a higher price for the product.

price ring. Agreement (usually a secret one) between manufacturers or suppliers to charge the same price for a product or service rather than compete on price. Price rings are now illegal in many countries.

prices and incomes policy. Where a government intervenes in the economy to restrain prices and incomes with the object of holding down *inflation.* See also *incomes policy.*

price sensitive. Used of a product or service for which demand is likely to fall off quickly if the price is increased. See also *demand elasticity.*

pricing methods. Two basic methods are: **a** cost plus an addition for profit, a traditional approach relying on the concepts of a standard *mark-up* over total costs and a conventional cost level of profits; **b** market demand pricing in which the product quality and price appropriate for each *market segment* is assessed and a product is then developed with controlled costs to give a satisfactory profit. *Marginal pricing* is a special type of market demand pricing as is follow-the-market pricing in which the company adopts the passive approach of following the pricing policies of competitors. See also *cost-plus pricing, penetration pricing, product analysis pricing, skimming, unit pricing.*

pricing policies. They express a company's view of the relationship that should exist between its prices and those of its competitors. The basic choices are between adopting: **a** a high pricing policy to give a new product prestige or glamour (supported by heavy *sales promotion* financed by the additional profits) or to take advantage of a short-term strong market position for a unique product; **b** a low pricing policy to obtain a high market share or a high degree of *market penetration;* or **c** policy of matching the prices of leading competitors and allocating whatever margin is left between sales turnover and basic costs to cover marketing cost and to provide a profit. See also *pricing methods.*

primary boycott. Term used particularly in the USA but also in the UK where pressure is applied to the employer by those directly in dispute with him through *industrial action,* such as a *strike.* See also *secondary boycott* and *sympathy* (or *sympathetic*) *strike.*

primary legislation (EEC). Of the *Common Market* or *European Economic Community,* are the Treaties that created the Common Market. These were the *Treaty of Rome 1957* that established the European Economic Community (EEC) itself; the *Euratom Treaty 1957* that established the *European Atomic Energy Community (Euratom);* and the *Treaty of Paris 1951* that established the *European Coal and Steel Community (ECSC).* The *secondary legislation* of the EEC is that produced by the institutions — the *Council of Ministers,* the *European Commission,* the *European Parliament,* etc — created by the primary legislation. Secondary legislation takes such forms as *Regulations, Directives, Decisions, Recommendations* and *Opinions.*

primary products. Products of agriculture, forestry, fishing, mining or quarrying.

primary standard data (PSD). Form of *predetermined motion time system* related to *methods-time measurement.*

prime cost. As *direct cost.*

Princeton Admission Test for Graduate Study in Business. *Psychological test* used in the selection of applicants for places on postgraduate business studies courses. This test enjoys a high reputation among business schools internationally.

principles of management. The so-called principles of management are guidelines on *organization structure* developed by management theorists such as *F W Taylor, H Fayol,* L F Urwick and J D Mooney. The most widely recognized principles are: **a** *span of control* — there is an optimum number of subordinates an executive can control; **b** levels of management — too many levels of management reduce the effectiveness of communication and control; **c** unity of command — each man should report to only one manager or supervisor; **d** delegation — work must be delegated to subordinates who should be given sufficient authority to enable them to discharge their responsibilites, though bearing in mind that responsibility can be delegated but not relinquished in that the executive who delegates a task remains accountable for its achievement; **e** rational assignment — people should be assigned to tasks rationally and economically so as to ensure full utilization of manpower; **f** action decisions — matters requiring a decision should be dealt with as near to the point of action as possible; **g** line and staff — it is desirable to separate the control of operations as a management function from the provision of services or advice to operational units.

Many commentators, especially behavio(u)ral scientists who have emerged in recent years, question the universal validity of these principles and suggest that paying too much attention to them increases the rigidity of organizations and hence reduces their effectiveness, particularly in rapidly changing conditions.

printer's devil. Printing trade apprentice.

Printing and Publishing Industry Training Board (UK). Established May 1968 under the *Industrial Training Act 1964*.

printout. Printed data produced by a *computer* printer.

private brand or label. As *own brand*.

prior charge. Loan which is a first claim on the *assets* of a *company* in the event of liquidation or *winding-up*.

private company. UK limited liability company which has a relatively small number of shareholders and is not permitted to offer its shares to the public. A private company may become a *public company* by 'going public', usually with the advice of an *issuing house* or *merchant bank*. See also *close company*.

private sector of the economy. Part of a nation's economy that is not controlled either by the Government or by *nationalized* or publicly owned undertakings. See also *public sector of the economy*.

privileged subscription. As *rights issue*.

PRO. *Public relations officer.*

proactive inhibition. Where a person's attitude of mind as a result of previous work, learning or experience makes it difficult for him to learn and retain new skills or information. This may happen, for example, where a method of doing a job is changed but it is difficult for employees to learn the new method because it has become instinctive to use the old method.

probability theory. Mathematical techniques for establishing the likelihood of particular events taking place. Probability of an event ranges from 0 to 1 (0 = event will certainly not occur, 1 = event is certain).

procedural (or procedure) agreement. Either a separate agreement or a part of a *collective agreement* outlining the procedures to be followed by the relevant *trade union* or management in the event of their having a grievance or being in dispute. See also *grievance procedure*. A *substantive agreement* is the part of a collective agreement dealing with matters of substance such as wages.

proceduralize. To introduce a procedure or method of action for.

procedure statement. Formal presentation in logical sequence of the steps and operations in a procedure drawn up by *organization and methods (O & M)* or *work study*.

process. In *organization development*, the way in which people in groups behave and interact when they are setting objectives, solving problems or introducing change.

process audit. *Social audit* approach developed by Bauer and Fenn of the Harvard Business School.

process chart. Charts which represent the sequence of work and the nature of events in a process. Provides a basis for visualizing, examining and possibly improving the way the work is carried out in conjunction with *work study* techniques.

process mix. Balance between manufactured components and *bought-out* components in the production of goods.

process planning. Determining how the product or part should be manufactured by referring to the component and assembly drawings and: **a** drafting an operation sequence for each component; **b** deciding the machines or hand-tools to be used; **c** drawing up the manufacturing layout for each component and sub-assembly, showing the sequence of operations, the departments and type of labo(u)r to perform the operations and specifying the tools, fixtures and gauges to be used.

process production. More or less continuous and *capital-intensive* manufacture of a product using plant designed to fit the technological requirements of the process (as in production of chemicals, for example) rather than needing to accommodate a large number of successive worker operations. The latter condition is more commonly a major characteristic of *mass production,* perhaps in the form of *assembly line* or *flow line production.* Process production differs too, from the one-off production of *job production* and the relatively small quanity production of *batch production.*

Process production was one of the three major *systems of production* identified and described by *Drucker,* the others being *mass production* and *unique-product production.* He sees it as being able to produce only the products for which it has been designed (for example, coal mining, transportation, oil refining).

procurement. As *purchasing.*

produced goods. Raw materials, *capital goods* and tools expended to produce *consumer goods.*

producer goods. As *industrial goods.*

product acceptance. *Marketing* term for extent to which a product gains acceptance in its intended market.

product analysis pricing. Technique which attempts to calculate the price to be asked for a product or service by balancing the concepts and, as far as possible, the realities of *cost, price* and *value.* Product analysis pricing is the antithesis of *cost-plus pricing,* in which cost is mainly considered.

product comparison. *Market research* survey in which *respondents* are asked to state which particular brand each of a number of different attributes is most appli̇dable. See also *attribute comparisons, forced choice* and *free choice of products.*

product-determined (or process-determined) industry. One whose activities are very much determined by the nature of its product and do not allow great freedom to diversify or diverge from the central purpose of the industry into wider markets. Typical such industries are coal and copper and other mining and other basic industries, such as steel production and rail transport. See also *process production.*

product development. Creating and investigating ideas for new or improved products to be added to or to replace existing products and implementing the program(me) of research and development required to produce the new or improved products.

product differentiation. Influencing the customer to buy the marketer's product and not a competing brand by pointing out the salient features of the product that are not possessed by competing products. See also *product features.*

product diversification. Development, manufacture and marketing of alternative or different products.

product drawing list. Record of drafting and design office work necessary to undertake and complete a particular job or project. May be used as the basis of a *build schedule.*

product features. Those presented to a customer when promoting the product. Functional features are the quantitative or qualitative aspects of a product that either are non-existent in competing products or exist to a lesser extent. Tangential features are those that do not directly relate to the product's performance but that in some way distinguish a product from equally performing competing products.

production control. Planning the manufacture of components and the assembly of finished products to meet sales requirements and ensuring that the planned program(me) of production is achieved. Production control functions include: **a** translating sales requirements into a production plan; **b** estimating future factory load and determining resource requirements of equipment, labo(u)r, raw materials, components and *bought-out* parts; **c** preparing detailed manufacturing timetables; **d** scheduling work on to the manufacturing shops or machines; **e** controlling works order documents; **f** monitoring performance against the plan; and **g** expediting late work or re-planning program(me) arrears. See also *production planning.*

production engineering. Specification and planning of the most suitable manufacturing processes. It embraces: **a** specification of the productive materials required during manufacture; **b** specification of manufacturing methods; **c** determining the sequence of operations; **d** determining the work content of each operation; **e** planning the overall time cycles within which all manufacturing activities are carried out; **f** specifying the lead times which occur before the manufacturing activities take place; **g** specifying the resources required in the form of labo(u)r, plant, tools and fixtures, raw materials and *bought-in (or out)* parts; **h** scheduling work to manufacturing departments; and **i** monitoring and controlling production against the plan. Production engineering activities and functions include *jig and tool design, materials handling, method study, process planning, production control, production planning* and *value analysis engineering.*

production flow analysis. In *group technology*, establishing families of components and processes so that plant and machinery can be regrouped within a factory to improve efficiency.

production line. See *flow line production.*

production-oriented company. One that tends to manufacture what it is technically convenient to make rather than what the consumer needs. A *marketing-oriented company*, on the other hand, produces what the consumer or customer needs rather than what best suits its production and technical capacity.

production planning. Aspect of *production control* particularly concerned with analyzing sales demands and developing production program(me)s and timetables to satisfy the demands.

production, systems of. *Drucker* has distinguished between three systems of production, namely, *process production, mass production* and *unique-product production*, further sub-dividing mass production between 'old style' production of uniform products and 'new style' mass production of uniform parts for assembly into diversified products.

production transfer. Employee mobility within an organization following changes in product, production method and/or technology.

productivity. Relationship between *input* and *output* of an industrial unit etc, input being measured in men, machines, materials and money, and output in products and services. Reliable methods of productivity measurement are elusive but various ad hoc yardsticks have been produced.

productivity agreement. Product of *productivity bargaining.*

productivity bargaining. System of establishing pay levels for a particular company or plant with productivity agreements that incorporate methods of increasing productivity and changes in work arrangements together with, possibly, a wide range of terms and conditions in a *package deal*. Like *workplace bargaining*, productivity bargaining has gained ground at the expense of *national agreements*, particularly in the engineering industry in the UK. See also *effort bargain* and *Fawley Blue Book.*

productivity differential. Difference in *productivity* at two specified points in time.

productivity increase. Extra pay or salary awarded to an employee, executive, etc in recognition of improved *productivity.*

productivity restriction. As *quota restriction,* etc.

productivity, spread of. Range of performance or *productivity* among workers.

productivity training. See *booster training.*

product life cycle. Complete life of a product ranging through early planning and preparatory investment, design, production, sales build-up, maximum sales, declining sales, withdrawal of the product. The stages of a normal product life cycle are sometimes summarized as the research and development stage; the introductory stage; the market development stage; the exploitation stage; the maturation stage; the saturation stage; and finally the decline stage. See also *marketing mix, top-out* and *Gopertz curve.*

product manager. *Marketing* executive responsible for effective sales and marketing of a specific product or product range. See also *brand manager.*

product mix (range). Combination of products and product ranges produced by a company. An object of company policy will normally be to produce the optimum product mix in terms of profitability, bearing in mind both the *market potential* and the company's own production and technical resources. See also *marketing-oriented company* and *production-oriented company.*

267

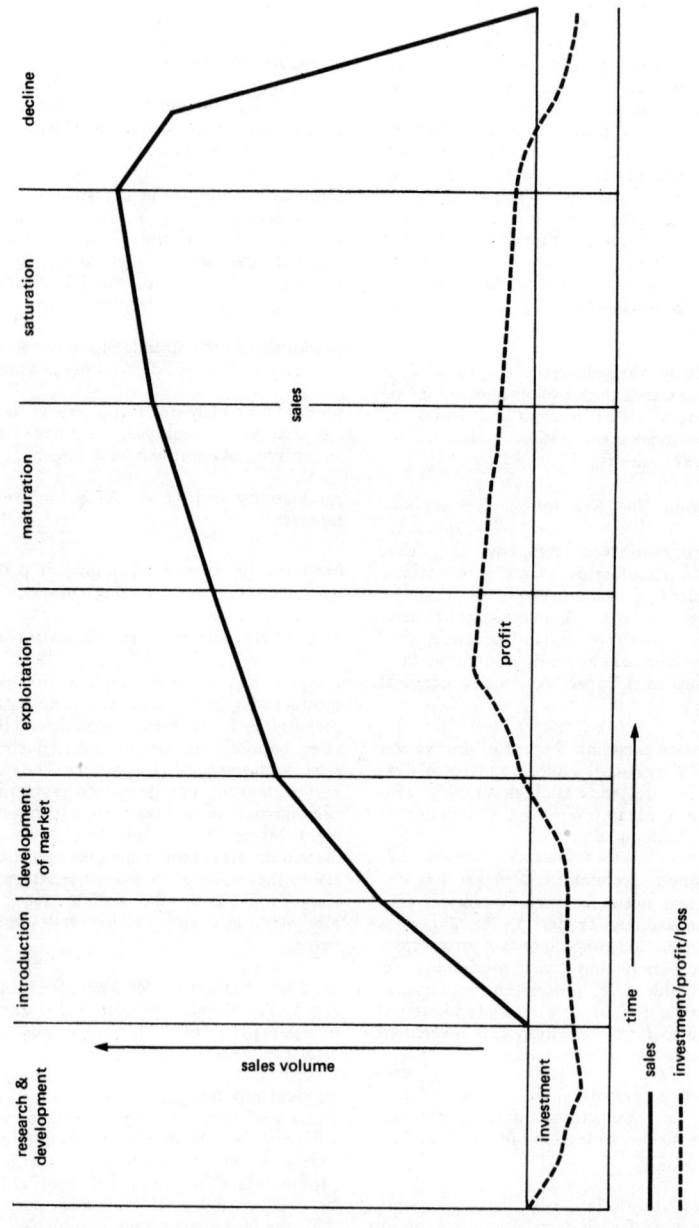

product placement test. *Market research* term for a test in which a product is left with a potential user — perhaps a householder or an industrial user — for him to form an impression of its usefulness and value. See also *home audit.*

product planning. Determining in the light of *market research* and assessment the products to be produced, the particular design features of the products, the quantities to be produced and the prices at which they are sold. See also *product strategy.*

product-plus. *Marketing* term for the selling point that gives a product the edge over its competitors and can be built upon by advertising and *sales promotion.* See also *value satisfactions, product differentiation* and *product features.*

product strategy. Company's new product development policy, covering the revitalization and development of existing products, the development of new products for both existing and new markets, and the withdrawal of products that are no longer profitable. See also *marketing mix* and *product planning.*

product test. Test of consumer's reactions to sample products. See, for example, *hall test* and *product placement test.*

product weighted distribution. *Retail audit* term for weighting the distribution of products between retail outlets so as to allow for the fact that some shops have a more significant trade in them.

Professional and Executive Recruitment Service (PER). Established in UK in 1973 as a renaming and restyling of the former Professional and Executive Register of the *Department of Employment.* Later became a responsibility of the *Employment Service Division* of the *Manpower Services Commission.*

proficiency test. Test of ability to perform a task or skill. Cf *attainment test.*

profile. Set of measures of different characteristics of an individual or group which have been standardized in order to facilitate comparison. Profiles are frequently graphic representations of *test batteries.*

profile of a firm. Used in establishing the *payment system* appropriate to the firm. See *situation profile.*

profile (personnel). Information on an employee recorded in a company's personnel records system. This information normally includes details of education, experience, current working record and assessment of the employee's potential.

profiling systems. Used in *job evaluation* to grade jobs by analyzing the basic or benchmark jobs and then weighting other jobs in relation to them. Other job evaluation approaches include *analytic job evaluation, decision band method, dominant element job evaluation, integral job evaluation, job factor comparison, job grading, job ranking* and the *points rating method.*

profit. Amount by which *revenue* or income for a project/enterprise exceeds *expenditure.* May be expressed as before or after tax and/or interest. If, in fact, expenditure exceeds revenue, there is a *loss* instead of a profit. Trading profit is trading revenue minus trade expenses. Profit before tax is trading profit plus net non-trading revenue. Gross profit is determined by deducting from sales the ex-works cost of goods (or services) sold and net profit is the gross profit minus the expenditure incurred in the marketing, finance and administration functions. See also *stock profits.*

profit and loss account. Or income statement. A statement showing company performance over a given period of time, particularly the *financial year.* The complementary tool of *financial accounting* is the *balance sheet* showing a company's financial position at a particular point in time.

profit centre (center). Typically a department, unit or geographical location which for costing/budgetary control purposes is treated as a distinct entity enabling expenses and revenue to be ascertained, allocated and apportioned so that profitability and performance can be measured and controlled. See *cost centre (center).*

profit planning. Planning the direction and control of a company or organization's future operations towards its profit goals. The term is usually used of long-term planning beyond the immediate *financial year.*

profit-sharing scheme. Methods by which some of the profits of a business are distributed to some or all employees in the form of cash or shares. Typically the schemes provide for such distributions to be made annually to employees fulfilling cer-

profit/volume (P/V) ratio． Sales revenue minus variable costs divided by sales revenue. Involves the calculation of *break-even points*, marginal costing, etc to plot profit against volume of sales of a product. Profit-volume analysis is concerned with the difference between total sales revenue and variable cost that is available for meeting fixed costs and profits. Can help management decisions on which products can be expanded most profitably to achieve the desirable *product mix*.

profit wedge. See *break-even chart*.

pro forma. Term applied to the submission of an *invoice* before delivery of the goods.

program control unit (or controller). Part of the *central processing unit* of a *computer* that examines and interprets the instructions given by the *program*, selecting data and information from the *internal memory* and bringing the *arithmetic unit* into action.

program(me). 1. *Computer program*. **2.** Logical arrangement and presentation of information as in programmed instruction. See, for example, *adaptive program(me)* and *linear program(me)*.

program(me) analysis and review (PAR). Management technique and approach used in government departments and other public administration for analyzing and assessing whether resources are in fact being used effectively in a project or program(me). It is often part of a wider ranging *planning, programming, budgeting system (PPBS)*. PAR is basically a check on the performance of a planning and budgeting system without actually changing the system or becoming one itself. *Zero base review* can be regarded as a form of PAR.

program(me) budgeting. Or *PPB* or output budgeting. Management technique for measuring the benefit produced by each activity or department in a company or organization. It is the basis of *planning, programming, budgeting system*. May be used as a tool in *cost-benefit analysis* or in *resource allocation*.

programmed instruction/learning. Use of *programmed tests*, sometimes in conjunction with a form of *teaching machine*. See *adaptive program(me)*, *intrinsic branching program(me)*, *linear program(me)*.

programmed text. Teaching material presented or programmed step by step in a manner that can be adapted to the needs of the individual student or trainee. Sometimes presented on a form of teaching machine. See *adaptive program(me)*, *intrinsic branching program(me)*, *linear program(me)*, *scrambled book/test*, *skip program(me)*.

Program(me) Evaluation and Review Technique (PERT). One of the *critical path planning or network analysis* techniques. The technique was adopted by industry after development in the Polaris system defence program(me).

Programming Language Nineteenhundred. Computer language. See *PLAN*.

Programming Language 1. *PL/1*. See also *computer language*.

progress billing (US). Charging for work under contract at various stages as the work progresses. Also known as stage payments.

progress chart. Horizontal *bar chart* of the *component bar chart* type with the variously shaded or colo(u)red component parts representing the completion of successive stages.

progress chart. Horizontal *bar chart* of the *component bar chart* type with the variously shaded or coloured component parts representing the completion of successive stages.

progress chasing (and control). Ensuring that manufacturing work is completed according to plan. May involve speeding up or re-scheduling work; urging delivery of raw materials, sub-assemblies or *bought-out (or in)* parts; expediting the transfer of components and sub-assemblies between different parts of the factory and, in general, tracing the causes of delays in order to indicate the corrective action required.

progressive consumer. *Marketing* term for a *consumer* who would be receptive to an offer of a better product or service at a slightly higher price. The opposite, the *retrogressive consumer*, is one keen to economize on an existing product or service.

progressive-part method. Where an operation to be learned or a course to be taken is divided into parts which are learned separately but as each is completed it is integrated with what has already been learned. The sequence may be represented as A, B, A + B, C, A + B + C, D, A + B + C + D. Cf *cumulative-part method, whole method, part method*.

progressive tax. *Income tax* which levies an increasing proportion of an income as the income rises. The increases may be on either a *slab scale* or a *slice scale*.

progress payments. Made on completion of agreed stages in the progress of a contract. A particularly common arrangement in large construction projects.

project group. Ad hoc committee, typically for a limited duration, set up to examine, tackle and solve specific problem areas, eg metrication, moving to a new site, etc.

projection. Psychologist's term for the process of ascribing to other persons one's own unacceptable wants and faults.

projective techniques or tests. Term used in *psychological testing* for *personality tests* that are not of the direct, questionnaire type but set tasks through which the person being tested projects or displays his or her underlying attitudes, beliefs and behavio(u)r patterns. Analysis of responses to such a test is undertaken by a professional *occupational psychologist*. Typical tests of the projective techniques kind are the *Rohrschach test* (the 'ink blot' test) and the *thematic apperception test*.

projectized organization. One based on a number of project teams with a pool of specialists (or *staff management*) available to be called on by the *project managers* for particular projects. See also *matrix organization*.

project ledger. Comprehensive documentation on the estimates, budgets, modifications and progress of a project.

project management. Or program(me) management. Arrangement of management and management techniques designed to coordinate resources and specialisms as effectively as possible in preparing, running and completing a project. It does not have the preoccupation with single line function tasks of, for example, *line management*, usually having a less rigid and less permanent hierarchy and being concerned with lateral coordination as well as vertical and line communication. May be used in a wide range of industrial situations, particularly in engineering and construction. Project management involves optimizing resources (including manpower), timescales, communications, inspection, quality and reliability, operation conditions, costs, etc in pursuit of the overall objectives of the project. It often involves the use of sophisticated techniques such as *critical path planning* and *network analysis*, and may be organized by two or more companies jointly as a *consortium project*. See also *corporate management, matrix organization* and *projectized organization*.

project manager. Concerned with optimizing and coordinating resources in *project management*. The authority of a project manager can vary from executive responsibility in a *line management* sense to that of a coordinator by persuasion. His *span of control* over personnel, budgets, etc also varies from project to project. Responsibility may also be divided up geographically between location managers.

project milestones. Points at which the performance and costs of a major project are checked.

project purchasing. Policy of purchasing at one time all the materials and components required for a particular project or contract, as distinct from *stock purchasing* of items to be drawn from stores as and when required.

project training. Training technique in which trainees/students extend their experience and know-how through tackling carefully planned but usually open-ended and problem-solving projects. See also *group project training*.

promissory note. Defined legally as an 'unconditional promise in writing made by one person to another, signed by the maker, agreeing to pay, on demand or at a fixed or determinable future time, a sum certain in money to, or to the order of, a specified person, or to bearer'. Thus, a promissory note is an IOU with a time clause. See also *bill of exchange* (which is the reverse of a promissory note in that it is a requirement to be paid, not a promise to pay) and the *Bills Scheme* operated in the UK by the *Exports Credits Guarantee Department*.

promotional mix. Mix or combination of techniques and media used by an organization to project its image and/or promote its products or services.

prompt note. Reminder to a purchaser or

creditor of money due and of the date on which it becomes (or has become) due.

proof of delivery. Signed receipt showing the date of delivery to the consignee. The signature may be that of an *agent*. If the goods are part of a *consolidation* arrangement delivery to the consolidator is usually sufficient.

propensity to consume. Economist's term for the proportion of all income in an economy which is passed on in the *circular flow of income* through the purchase of home market-produced *consumer goods* instead of being leaked from the circular flow through *withdrawals*. Where there is any change in the proportion passed on, this is known as the marginal propensity to consume.

proprietary office. *Insurance company* that has shareholders. A company that does not have shareholders but shares out all profits among policy holders is a *mutual office*.

prospect. Potential purchaser who is the target of a sales interview or campaign.

prospecting. 1. *Marketing* term for quest for new sales openings and opportunities. **2.** Exploration for mineral deposits.

prospectus. Statement of a company's or organization's present strength and future prospects, published as part of a quest for support or investment, normally when a company goes public, ie offers its shares for sale. Drawn up with the aid of an *issuing house*, lawyers and reporting accountants.

prospectus, public issue by. See *public issue by prospectus* (shares).

pro-tanto increase (or settlement). As *tapered increase*.

protection. Economist's term for protecting a home industry or industries from foreign competition in the home market by *tariffs*, *quota systems* or *subsidies*.

Protection of Employment Bill. UK legislation drafted in 1974 with the intention of strengthening the rights of employed persons. See also *Trade Union and Labour Relations Act* and *Industrial Democracy Bill*.

protective industrial legislation. Governmental enactments to protect the interests, safety, health, etc of employees.

protective output norm. Where a *work group* informally holds down production levels as under productivity restriction, *quota restriction*, a *fiddle*, or a *work group output norm*.

protective practice (practise). Term used by trade unionists where they insist, in what they see as the interests of *job security* and *security of tenure*, on restricting the way in which production and other techniques are operated. See also *restrictive practice (practise), closed shop*, etc.

provident benefit. Term used generally of *sickness benefit* but in particular of payments made from a *trade union* provident fund to provide sickness benefit, etc for its members in times of need. Such a fund is financed out of *trade union dues* paid by members and out of the return on investments made by the trade union concerned.

provident fund. Source of finance for a *pension scheme*, sickness insurance scheme, etc.

Provincial Brokers Stock Exchange. UK organization based on the York Stock Exchange. See also *Stock Exchange* (UK).

provisioning. *Production control* term for the buying and control of materials.

PSD. *Primary standard data.*

pseudoisochromatic plates H-R-H. See *H-R-H pseudoisochromatic plates*.

PSG. *Psycho-galvanometer.*

PSI. *Personalized system of instruction.*

psycho-galvanometer (PSG). Equipment sometimes used in *market research* that measures the *basal skin resistance (BSR)* or electromagnetic change in the skin of a subject on meeting a product, sales promotion, situation, etc. The equipment is able to measure certain changes in human skin — for example, in sweat gland secretion — and can be a useful tool of psychological research. But its practical value in market research etc is limited by the difficulty in identifying precisely the emotion or feeling responsible for a particular change in basal skin resistance. The psycho-galvanometer is sometimes called a 'lie detector' in more general use.

psychological inventory. Often confused with *psychological test*, but in fact there is a distinction to be made between them. An inventory reflects what the person being tested says he/she feels, while a test measures what he/she knows or can do. Examples of psychological inventory, mainly originating in the USA, include the *Bernreuter personality inventory*, the *activity vector analysis*, the *California psychological inventory*, the *Gordon personal inventory and profile*, *Guilford's inventories* and the *Thurstone temperament schedule*.

psychological price. Or charm price. A price which by tradition, custom or gentle advertising persuasion tends to be readily acceptable to customers. It is not necessarily a low price.

psychological test(ing). Tests devised by *occupational psychologists* for *personnel selection*, *personnel placement*, *vocational guidance*, etc. Basic types of psychological tests include *intelligence tests*, *aptitude tests*, and *temperament and personality tests*. Sources of psychological tests in the UK include the National Institute of Industrial Psychology and the *National Foundation for Educational Research*, while those in the USA include the *United States Employment Service*. Adaptations of the basic tests developed chiefly in the USA include *achievement tests* (devised to test present performance in particular skills, etc), *adaptability tests*, creative ability tests, *general learning ability tests*, *job knowledge tests* (or *trade tests*), *mechanical comprehension tests*, and *spatial ability tests*. A group of tests taken at one time to measure a number of complementary abilities is known as a *test battery*. Examples of such test batteries are the *engineering apprentice test battery* developed in the UK by the National Institute of Industrial Psychology and the *USES general aptitude test battery* developed in the USA. See also *expectancy charts*, *interest inventory*, *psychological inventory*, *norm* and *raw test score*.

psychometric test. *Psychological test* which seeks to measure particular factors, producing quantified results.

psychomotor skills. Those requiring co-operation between mind and muscle in an individual. They are tested by various forms of *psychological testing*, largely developed in the USA. Psychomotor skills are usually a combination of skill in selecting the correct response to a situation followed by skill in making that response. Examples of psychomotor skills include *fine control sensitivity*; *response orientation*; *postural discrimination*; *aiming*; and *wrist-finger speed*. See also *motion study*. Types of test of psychomotor skills include the *Minnesota rate of manipulation test*, the *Stromberg dexterity test*, the *MacQuarrie test for mechanical ability*.

Pty. Abbr for proprietary. Australian equivalent to *company* or *corporation*.

public company. Company whose shares are quoted and dealt with on a stock exchange. A *private company* may become a public company by *'going public'* usually with the advice of an *issuing house* or *merchant bank*. See also *close company*.

public issue (offer) by prospectus. Offer of shares to the general public normally by a company which is coming to the market for the first time. See also *prospectus*, and *public company*.

public relations (PR). Planned and sustained effort to establish and maintain mutual understanding between an organization and its publics. While PR is concerned with influencing points of view, including editorial points of view, a distinction between it and advertising is that the latter is largely concerned with propagating its message through paid-for advertisements. A company using public relations expertise may employ its own *public relations officer (PRO)* or it may have a contractual arrangement with public relations consultants.

public relations officer (PRO). Practitioner in public relations. See also *Institute of Public Relations* (UK) and *Public Relations Society of America*.

Public Relations Society of America Inc. US national professional organization for public relations officers and consultants.

public sector of the economy. Part of the economy concerned with provision of basic civil, public and welfare services and with operation of nationalized or publicly owned industries. See also *private sector of the economy*.

public service corporation. Form of *public utility*.

public utility. Organization that provides the public with such services as water, energy, transport, telecommunications, etc. It will be subject to governmental regulation although it is possible that it may be privately owned.

public works. Construction projects, such as highways, for governmental agencies for the use of the general public.

Public Works Loans Board. Organization in the UK through which local government authorities may raise or negotiate loans.

public corporation. Body set up by governmental statute or decree to administer some form of public service. See also *public utility*.

PUD. Pick-up and delivery (service offered by a freight carrier).

punched cards. Cards carrying data and information represented by punched holes. The cards can be processed in various ways — from extraction by a hand-held needle to being interpreted by the *input device* of a *computer* — in order to perform such operations as adding, subtracting, comparing, collating, etc. Numbers and letters are indicated according to the code used by their position on the punched card. When fed into a computer, a card reader may be used.

punt. *Stock exchange* term for an investment in *shares* that have only an outside chance of proving to be profitable.

purchased life annuity. Term used where an employee purchases an annuity with the lump sum cash benefit available to him/her under the conditions of a firm's *pension scheme*. See also *annuity option rate*.

purchase engineering. Application of techniques designed to improve buying performance.

purchase tax. Type of sales tax formerly levied in UK on certain consumer goods on the wholesale price. Replaced by *value added tax*.

purchasing. All activities concerned with the acquisition of goods and services including ordering, commercial negotiations and delivery chasing. Also known as buying or procurement.

purchasing power. Availability of income in an economy to purchase goods and services. See *circular flow of income*.

Purdue clerical adaptability test. Six-part *psychological test* developed in the USA and covering spelling; computation; checking; word meaning; copying; and arithmetic reasoning.

Purdue creativity test. *Psychological test* of US origin devised particularly for engineers and engineering workers. See also *AC test of creative ability*.

Purdue hand precision test. US test of *psychomotor skills*. See also *psychological testing*.

Purdue industrial mathematics test. *Psychological test* for industrial workers and tradesmen.

Purdue industrial training classification test. *Psychological test* that is basically an *achievement test* measuring ability to apply arithmetic in practical situations.

Purdue job preference survey. *Preference or interest inventory* developed at Purdue University in the USA for *personnel selection* of unskilled and semi-skilled workers. Personnel taking the inventory or test (see *psychological inventory*) express preferences between the following antagonistic pairs of job activity types: routine/varied; indoor/outdoor; repetitive/varied; responsible/non-responsible; hazardous/non-hazardous; sedentary/bodily active; isolative/gregarious; precise/approximate. See also *psychological testing*.

Purdue mechanical adaptability test (PMAT). *Psychological test* of the *mechanical comprehension* kind that is an inventory, rather than a test, of an individual's practical knowledge in the fields of mechanical and electrical engineering. It is basically an *achievement test* but may also be used as an *aptitude test*.

Purdue pegboard test. *Pegboard test* of *psychomotor skills*, originating in the USA. The test measures finger, hand and arm coordination in single-handed or double-handed operations. See also *psychological testing*.

Purdue personnel tests. Range of *psychological tests*, particularly in the fields of welding, carpentry and machine shops.

Purdue test for machinists and machine operators. *Psychological test* dealing with machine shop practices (practises).

pure endowment assurance policy. Does not include any element of *life assurance*. See *endowment assurance policy*.

pure risk. *Insurance* world's term for the risk inherent in such factors as accident, fire, health, weather, etc as distinct from the *speculative risk* inherent in the element of business speculation in a project or enterprise.

put and calls. Options to sell (put) or buy (call) fixed quantities of specific *securities* at specified prices within a given period of time.

putting-out system. Arrangement, probably most common in the garment and clothing industry, under which *outwork* is carried out by people working in their own homes.

putting the question. Taking the vote on an issue or *motion* at a meeting or conference. A method of ending discussion on an item on an agenda can be by a motion from the floor 'that the question now be put'. See also *closure*.

P/V ratio. *Profit/volume ratio.*

pyramid ratios. Concept that *management* and *financial ratios* are best analyzed in a hierarchical sequence starting with profits related to capital, eg *operating profits*, operating assets, etc. The key ratios form the apex of a pyramid of ratios and can be sub-analyzed as operating profits/sales and sales/operating assets. This approach was developed by *Centre for Interfirm Comparison*.

pyramid selling. System of selling in which purchasers buy the right to sell a product and, often, contract to handle a minimum quantity of it. The right to sell the product may carry with it a title such as 'agent', 'sales supervisor'. 'area manager' or something even more exalted. Success depends on selling to further people the right to sell the product. Thus the business of the company is not so much in selling its products as in selling the right to sell. The system is clearly open to abuse and, indeed, has been made illegal in some countries including the UK. Also known as multi-level distributorship.

q

QSEs. *Manpower planning* shorthand for qualified scientists and engineers.

quadratic programming. *Operations* or *operational research* technique used for problems having non-linear relationships.

qualified accounts. Auditor's report drawing attention to doubts, limitations or disagreements over any item in the accounts. It may, for example, express an opinion about the accuracy of certain figures, comment on incomplete data or indicate doubts about stock valuations.

qualified circulation journal. As *controlled circulation journal.*

qualified report. As *qualified accounts.*

quality control and reliability. Techniques for ensuring that during design, production, servicing, etc both work and materials are within limits that will produce the desired product performance and reliability. Quality control can mean avoiding too high quality (if *planned obsolescence* is built into a design, for example) as well as the more obvious avoidance of too low quality.

quality market. Market in which quality matters more than price.

quality of working life (QWL). Approach to job and *organization design* seeking to improve the working environment and employer-employee relations.

quality protection. Measures introduced as part of a *quality control* program(me) (or, sometimes, in lieu of comprehensive quality control) to guard against below-standard components or products.

quantitative restriction. Import restriction, not in the form of a financial disincentive such as a *customs duty*, but eg as a limitation on the physical quantity of a product that may be imported during a given period.

quantity discount. Allowance given for an order for a large quantity of goods.

quartering. *Clocking-in* system under which an employee loses a full 15 minutes pay if he is a few minutes late.

quartile. Statistical measure of dispersion in a frequency distribution. There are three quartiles, lower Q_1 ($\frac{N}{4}$), Q_2 (synonymous with median) and Q_3 ($\frac{3N}{4}$).

Queen's Award to Industry. Established in the UK in 1965 to recognize outstanding achievements by industrial firms or organizations in increasing exports or in technological innovation or both. Exporters of services such as banking, insurance, contracting, transport, tourism and the professions have also been eligible for the Award since 1970. Award winners are entitled, for the following five years, to display its emblem.

questioning approach. What? How? When? Where? Who? Key questions which are valid in analyzing methods, systems, *work study, O & M.*, etc. See illustration below.

question, putting the. See *putting the question* committee procedure, etc).

queueing theory. Mathematical techniques, including *probability theory*, used in *operations* or *operational research* to identify, illustrate and, it is hoped, influence the characteristics of queues, whether of people, materials, work-in-progress, etc. The object is to find the best way of planning the sequence of events so that bottlenecks can be avoided.

quick ratio. As *acid test ratio.*

quit claim. Transfer or renouncement of a title, right or claim.

(to) quit on the job. To cease putting any effort into work.

Quito Stock Exchange. The stock exchange in Ecuador.

quit rate. *Labo(u)r turnover* other than

	CURRENT FACTS	REASONS	POSSIBLE ALTERNATIVES	REVIEW PURPOSE
WHAT?	what is done now?	why is it done?	what *else* could be done?	what *should* be done?
HOW?	how is it done?	why in that way?	how *else* could it be done?	how *should* it be done?
WHEN?	when is it done?	why at that time?	when *else* could it be done?	when *should* it be done?
WHERE?	where is it done?	why in that place?	where *else* could it be done?	where *should* it be done?
WHO?	who does it?	why that person(s)?	who *else* could do it?	who *should* do it?

questioning approach

dismissals or redundancies created by the policy and decisions of management.

quorum. Minimum number of people who must be present at a meeting before it can proceed to conduct business. The quorum level is normally laid down in the rules and regulations or *standing orders* of the organization concerned. When there is a quorum, a meeting is said to be 'quorate'. See also *motion*.

quota restriction. 1. Where goods or services supplied to an organization or person are restricted to a specified limit or quota for a given period of time. This may happen, for example, when they are in short supply and a modified form of rationing becomes necessary. **2.** Where, under *payment-by-results* or *performance-related pay* schemes, a work group working to loose *piece work* rates hold down output so as not to draw attention to the looseness of the rates. Another problem can be *goldbricking*, where piece work rates are tight. Workers who do not join their colleagues in quota restriction have been known, particularly in the USA, as *ratebusters*. The unofficial target of a work group in conditions of quota restriction is its *bogey*. Quota restriction is sometimes known as productivity restriction, *protective output norm, work group output norm,* or a *fiddle*.

quota sampling. Poor man's version of *random sampling* used particularly in *market research,* as when interviewers are given a quota of interviewees or *informants* broken down by required classification — such as *socio-economic status,* age, sex, etc — but without the further refinement of the choice of interviewees within groups being made on a proper random sampling basis.

quota system. Use of physical controls, rather than *tariff* duties, to restrict imports or exports of particular or all goods. Also known as *quantitative restriction*. The term is also used more widely of any situation in which a limited number of items is permitted.

quotation. 1. Must be granted to the *shares* of a *public company* by the Stock Exchange Council before they can be dealt in on a *Stock Exchange*. **2.** An offer to carry out specified work, or to provide a specified service, for payment. See also *fixed-price contract*.

QWL. *Quality of working life.*

r

rabble hypothesis. Theory that always pursue only their own self-interest, a view rejected by the *human relations school* of management.

Race Relations Act 1968. UK legislation making discrimination on grounds of race illegal in industry as elsewhere. Established the *Race Relations Board* and the *Community Relations Commission.* See also *Civil Rights Act 1964* (US).

Race Relations Act 1976. Unlike the 1968 Act the 1976 Act applied to contract workers as well as direct employees. It also applied to partnerships of more than six people, to *trade unions*, to employers' and professional organizations, to vocational training bodies, to qualifying bodies and to employment agencies.

Race Relations Board. Set up in the UK under the *Race Relations Act 1968* to institute conciliation procedures and, where necessary, take legal action.

Race Relations Employment Advisory Service (RREAS) (UK). Operated by the Department of Employment under the *Race Relations Act 1968* to advise employers, trade unions, etc, on the promotion of harmonious relations in a multi-racial workforce and on any related problems.

rack jobber. *Wholesaler* (often specializing in non-food products) who regularly maintains and merchandises racks and displays of goods in retail shops. The retailer may purchase the goods outright or on a 'sale or return' basis.

rack rent. Full commercial rent obtainable.

rain check. Delay in accepting an offer. Thus, 'to take a rain check' is to delay making a decision, usually while checking the facts of the matter.

rake-off. Slang term for a share of the profit from a deal or enterprise, particularly one paid corruptly. See also *kick-back*.

RAM. Acronym for random access memory, a *computer store* which can be accessed in any order. See *random access storage*.

R & D. *Research and development.*

random access storage. Or *direct access storage.* A flexible form of *computer* storage which affords virtually instant access to any of its files or locations, however randomly information is required by the user and without the need to process the files in any particular order.

random sampling. Picking out of individual items or people on a basis that gives every individual item or person in the group an equal chance of being selected. The basic techniques of random sampling have a wide range of industrial and commercial applications, from *production control* and shop floor inspection (see *work sampling*) to the selection of interview samples in *market research*. A number of short-cut techniques have also been evolved in industry and business using the basic concepts of random sampling. Such a short-cut technique, used particularly in market research, is *quota sampling*. See also *probability theory, cluster sampling, differential sampling, master sample, matched samples, quota sampling, sampling, stratification.*

random walk (or route). *Market research* technique in which interviewers walk along prescribed routes calling on houses selected on *random sampling* principles in order to interview the householders.

ranking. 1. In *performance appraisal* procedures etc a system by which a senior manager lists his subordinate executives in order of merit, perhaps using a *paired comparison* technique. Alternatively, the executives might be divided in a forced distribution between, say, top 5 per cent, 'very good'; next 20 per cent, 'good'; middle 50 per cent, 'average'; next 20 per cent, 'fair'; bottom 5 per cent, 'poor'. Carries dangers of being subjective. Other performance appraisal techniques include *free report*, *controlled report*, *task-based appraisal*, *factor rating* and the *forced choice approach*. **2.** *Market research* term for the use of *pre-coded questions* of the multiple-choice kind that ask *informants* to rank products, packagings, advertising presentations, etc in order of preference or in order of certain attributes. See also *Osgood scales* and *semantic differential*. **3.** Used in the *instrumented laboratory training* method of *group training* to compare aspects of personal behaviour. See also *job ranking* used in *job evaluation*.

ratebuster. Or *cowboy* or *high-flier*. US term for *piece work* worker who takes advantage of *loose rates* to earn high bonus payments instead of joining his fellow workers in *quota restriction* or holding back production to the level of the *bogey* agreed unofficially by the *work group*. Ratebusters are unpopular with fellow workers who fear management will react by tightening rates, or *rate cutting*. A ratebuster may also be known, particularly in the UK, as a *job spoiler*. See also *pacers*.

rate changing. Amending of *payment-by-results* or *performance-linked pay* standards or rates that have been found in practice (practise) to be too tight or too loose. Making such changes is usually an awkward problem for management as workers understandably fear *rate cutting*. Identifying rates that need changing on grounds of looseness can also be difficult where *work groups* tend to hide them by informally setting their own *bogey* and indulging in *quota restriction*.

rate cutting. Cutting of *piece work* rates by management when such rates are found to be *loose rates*. Where members of a *work group* endeavour to hide such looseness by holding back production effort, they are said to be indulging in *quota restriction*, a term originating in the USA, or a *protective output norm*, etc. Workers who refuse to join their colleagues in quota restriction are known as *ratebusters* or *job spoilers*.

rate fixing. Shop floor practice (practise) particularly common in the engineering industry by which *piece work* rates for the production of particular components are fixed by rate fixers on the basis of their experience of similar work, and subject to challenge and bargaining by shop floor *trade union* leaders. Rate fixing is more subjective than techniques such as *work study* but can be faster, and has often become a traditional part of *workplace* bargaining. See also *payment-by-results* and *rate-setting*.

Where rates are of a kind that make it difficult for a worker to earn bonus, they are said to be *tight rates*. If bonus can be earned relatively easily, the rates are said to be *loose rates*.

rate of exchange. As *exchange rate*.

rate of return. Income derived from an investment or the average annual *profit* expressed as a percentage of the original capital outlay. See also *discounted cash flow*.

rate-setting. Term used particularly in the USA for establishing *payment-by-results* or *performance-linked pay* rates, usually following some form of *work measurement* though rate-setting is sometimes virtually synonymous with *rate-fixing*.

rating. 1. Insurance term for measuring risk to determine premium rates. **2.** In television and radio estimating the number of viewers/listeners for specific program(me)s or at specific times. Usually based on *random sampling* or viewer/listener panels. **3.** In finance determining credit worthiness of customers and potential customers using trade references and credit agencies. **4.** See *rating scale*.

rating scale. 1. *Work study* term for the scale on which work is rated in *work measurement*. Such scales include '60-80', '75-100' and '100-133', where the lower of the two figures on each scale is the performance of an average worker. **2.** *Market research* etc term for the use of *pre-coded questions* that ask *informants* to choose or tick off their answer to each question from a prepared scale of answers. For example, an informant may be asked to indicate whether he uses a particular product 'always', 'frequently', 'rarely', or 'never'. See also *Osgood scales*. **3.** Method of group training to measure such factors as group structure; mutual support and trust among members; levelling; group accomplishments; group development and group cohesion. See also *merit rating*.

ratio analysis. See *management ratios*.

ratio-delay study. *Work sampling* technique to determine frequency of occurrence of unavoidable delays in order to build these into *standard times*.

rationalization. Reorganization into a more effective structure.

rational working hours. System of German origin under which hours of work are varied according to the work load. See also *flexible working hours*.

ratios, management. See *management ratios*.

ratio-trend forecasting. Mathematical technique used particularly in *manpower planning* to calculate forecasts of needs based on existing relationships between activity levels and the numbers of staff required (these may be expressed as manpower standards).

Raven's progressive matrices. *Non-verbal intelligence test* that has often been very effective but needs to be used with care and, preferably, the advice of a professional *occupational psychologist*. See also *psychological testing* and *aptitude tests*.

raw materials stocks. *Stocks* of materials purchased by a manufacturer as the ingredients to be used in making his own products. Other forms of stocks include *bought-out goods, work-in-progress* and *finished goods*. See also *stock control*.

raw test score. Basic score produced by an employee or candidate in *psychological testing*. This score has then to be adapted by the appropriate *norm* to give a common base according to type of candidate and/or job.

rcpt. Receipt.

RE. *Real estate*.

reader reply form or card. Form usually incorporated in an advertisement for the reader to complete and send to the advertiser either placing an order for the goods/services advertised or requesting further information. Use of a reader reply form is sometimes known as *coupon advertising*. A reader reply card may have a similar function, being either loosely inserted or stitched into the publication carrying the advertisement, or it may be for reply to the publisher for him to pass on enquiries to an advertiser or advertisers. A reader reply card may also be used in *direct mail selling* and it may be reply paid (that is, postage is paid by the advertiser, not by the reader). See also *direct response promotion* and *advertising*.

real estate (RE). Landed property including its natural resources and man-made additions such as permanent buildings. To be distinguished from *personal property*.

real income. Flow of goods and services available and therefore determining the *standard of living* of an individual or community. Calculated using such criteria as the *BLS Consumer Price Index* or the *Retail Price Index* to allow for variations in the value of money. See also *economic growth, gross national product, national income, real income per head per annum*.

real income per head per annum. Average *real income* of each member of a nation or community in one year. May be better than money income as a guide to standard of living of a nation.

real investment. Expansion of the community's stock of buildings, plant, roads, transport, the economic *infrastructure*, etc.

real learning time. Time taken for a trainee to become capable of working at the speed and quality of the average experienced worker.

real property. As *real estate*.

real time. Facility enabling a *computer* to give an immediate response on receipt of a message, as with an airline booking system that can operate efficiently only if an immediate answer can be given to a request for a particular booking.

rears. Advertising spaces on the backs of buses etc.

recession. Severe decline in business activity accompanied by high unemployment etc. See *slump*.

Rechnungsrevisoren. Auditors of the *Zürich Stock Exchange* or *Effektenbörsenverein Zürich*. Other governing bodies of this exchange are the General Meeting, or *Generalversammlung*, and the Board of Governors or *Vorstand*.

reciprocal trading. When a supplier of goods or services gives an undertaking to a customer to buy certain other goods and/or services in return.

recognition dispute. Dispute over which *trade union* has the right to negotiate with management in a particular industry, firm or plant. A recognition dispute can be between management and trade union(s) or it can be between two or more trade unions. In the latter event in the UK the dispute might come before the Disputes Committee of the *Trades Union Congress* under the *Bridlington Principles* of 1939 and the *Croydon*

Procedure of 1969.

See also *trade union recognition, representational rights, jurisdictional dispute,* and *negotiating rights.*

Recommendations (EEC). And *Opinions* of the *Council of Ministers* and/or *European Commission* of the *Common Market* or *European Economic Community.* Such Recommendations and Opinions do not have binding force.

Regulations of the Council and/or Commission are binding in their entirety and apply directly in all member states. *Decisions* are also binding, but only on those towards whom they are specifically directed. *Directives* are binding on all member states, but the form and method of their implementation are at the discretion of the individual member states.

RecomPension. Recognized Company Pension.

recruitment and selection consultant. See *selection consultant.*

Redcliffe-Maud Report on the Management of Local Government (UK). Made to the UK Government in 1967 by a Committee under the chairmanship of Lord Redcliffe-Maud (then Sir John Maud). The Committee's terms of reference were 'to review in the light of modern conditions, how local government might best continue to attract and retain people (both elected representatives and principal officers) of the calibre necessary to ensure its maximum effectiveness'. The Report gave an impetus to the use of management techniques in local government, and recommended the setting up of new, larger 'unitary' local authorities responsible for all local government services. In fact, the Local Government Act 1972 was to introduce a system of two-tier authorities (Metropolitan County and District Councils or, in other parts of the country, Non-Metropolitan Counties and Districts) with local government responsibilities divided between them. Major influences on the development of management techniques in central government have been the *Brownlow Committee* Report of 1937 in the USA and the *Plowden Committee* Report of 1961 in the UK.

redeemable bond, share, stock, etc. One that the issuer has the right to buy back.

redeployment. Re-allocation and *retraining* of labour as changes in technology and business situation call for *labo(u)r mobility* between skills (and perhaps raise danger of structural unemployment).

reducing balance method. Method of spreading the cost of a *fixed asset* over its estimated useful life. The amount of depreciation charged each year decreases over the life of the asset. The percentage rate chosen is applied every year to the balance remaining from the previous year. Eg

	£/$
Initial Cost	1,200.00
Depreciation 1st year 20%	240.00
	Balance 960.00
Year 2 20%	192.00
	Balance 768.00
Year 3 20%	153.60 etc

Also known as diminishing balance or declining balance method. See also *straight-line depreciation.*

redundancy. Dismissal of an employee when his job ceases to exist, usually as a result of technological or economic change.

Redundancy Fund. Set up in the UK under the *Redundancy Payments Act 1965* to part-finance the rebates stipulated under the Act where employers make redundancy payments to former employees. The Fund is financed from employer contributions to *National Insurance* stamps.

Redundancy Payments Act 1965. UK Act which laid down that an employee may claim a redundancy payment from his employer when dismissed as redundant provided he has served a minimum period of 104 weeks continuous employment, the payment being geared to age, the length of employment, and the level of earnings, up to certain maxima. Redundancy has been defined broadly as occurring when the work on which the worker was employed has disappeared, but in practice (practise) there have been various differences of opinion over whether a dismissal has been actually for that reason or whether an employer has offered reasonable alternative employment.

The Act provides in section 15 that persons on a *fixed-term contract* or *contract of service* for two years or more may claim a redundancy payment if the contract is not renewed, unless the employee has agreed to waive his right before the contract expires. Employees with fixed-term contracts of less than two years may link successive contracts for calculation of continuity of employment under the Redundancy Payments Act 1965. Section 2 of the Act excludes redundancy payments where the employee refuses a renewal of contract on the old terms or an offer of suitable alternative employment.

When an employer makes a redundancy payment he claims a rebate from the *Redundancy Fund* which is financed from employer contributions to *National Insurance* stamps.

reference back. Where a principal committee does not accept a report from one of its sub-committees but refers it back to the sub-committee for reconsideration. This is the conventional way of opposing such a report. See also *motion*.

reference groups. *Marketing* term for specially structured groups of people brought together for the purpose of examining *consumer* buying motives. Such reference groups include *membership groups, dissociative groups, aspirational groups, face-to-face groups,* and *family groups.* See also *panel (or audit) methods.*

reference tariff (EEC). Tariff or scale of charges which is not restricted to the upper and lower limits of a *forked (or bracket) tariff* but any charges or rates outside the reference fork must be published as such. Such a reference tariff is used for inland waterways and bulk transport under the *common transport policy* of the *Common Market* or *European Economic Community*. Scales of charges for road and rail transport are normally restricted to a forked tariff.

reflation. Economist's term for situation where the general *purchasing power* of the community is increasing with a beneficial, stimulating effect on *employment* and *real incomes*. Further increases in purchasing power beyond the level at which it can affect employment and real incomes is harmful to an economy and is known as *inflation.* See also *trade cycle*.

refresher training. Training to revise and underline existing skills and knowledge. Cf *booster training, conversion training, retraining, updating training, upgraded training.*

regional development grants. Special government grants to stimulate economic activity and therefore employment opportunities in regions that are becoming economically and industrially run down. Regional development grants take such forms as assistance with *capital expenditure* on industrial buildings and/or equipment and with the training and retraining of inhabitants of the region. The UK, for example, has *Assisted Areas* — the *Special Development Areas, Development Areas* and *Intermediate Areas* — mainly in the North of England and Scotland and Wales. See also *common regional policy (EEC).*

Regional Employment Premium. Payable in the UK to industrial employers in the *Special Development Areas* and the *Development Areas,* though not usually in *Intermediate Areas*. The Regional Employment Premium was intended as a contribution to labo(u)r costs and an extra incentive to employers in *labo(u)r-intensive* firms. It applied to both full-time and part-time employees.

Regional Industrial Development Division. UK Department of Trade Division which provides information for UK firms on industrial aspects of regional development policy.

regional policy, common (EEC). See *common regional policy (EEC)* and *European Social Fund.*

registered company (UK). Company or corporation registered with the *Registrar of Companies* with whom it has deposited its *articles of association, memorandum of association,* annual accounts, etc, as required by the *Companies Act.*

registered trade union. From UK Trade Union Act 1871, *trade unions* have the option of registering as such with the *Registrar of Friendly Societies.* A more recent arrangement is that of certification as an independent trade union by the Certification Officer under the *Trade Union and Labour Relations Act 1974.*

Registrar of Business Names. Has register of business names indicating names of owners.

Register of Companies (UK). Official responsible to the Secretary of State for Trade for checking and approving applications to set up a *registered company.* He also makes the legally required information on companies available to the public at *Companies House.*

Registrar of Friendly Societies. Has register of trade unions under Trade Union Acts 1871-1964 and *Friendly Societies Act 1896.*

Registrar of Restrictive Trading Agreements. Registers UK exempted trading agreements under the *Restrictive Trade Practices Act 1956* and the *Resale Prices*

Act 1964. The *Fair Trading Act 1973* has replaced the Registrar with the *Director-General of Fair Trading*.

regression. 1. In statistics, method for investigating relationships between variables by expressing an approximate functional relationship between them. Regression lines are often calculated by using the *least-squares* method. 2. In psychology, a manifestation of earlier and less mature behavio(u)r, after having learned more mature form, as a result of frustration.

regression analysis. Technique, particularly common in *market research*, which uses trends in one type of activity as a guide to the likely future level of another, related activity. Thus, a general rise in standards of living may be used as evidence for a forecast of increased sales of cars, refrigerators, deep freezers, etc. In the same way, an increase in the number of married women going out to work could be linked to demand for ready-prepared meals. See also *multiple regression analysis* and *business indicators*.

regressive tax. Tax that takes a larger proportion of income from the low income earner than from the higher paid, ie a tax whose percentage rate decreases as the tax base increases. See also *progressive* tax.

Regulations (EEC). Of the *Council of Ministers* and/or the *European Commission* of the *Common Market* or *European Economic Community*. Such Regulations are binding in their entirety and apply directly in all member states.
Decisions of the Council or the Commission are also binding, but only on those towards whom they are specifically directed. *Directives* are binding on all member states, but the form and method of their implementation are at the discretion of the individual member states. *Recommendations* and *Opinions* of the Council and/or Commission do not have any binding force.
Regulations, Decisions, Directives, Recommendations and Opinions form the *secondary legislation* of the Common Market.

reinsurance. 'Insurance of insurance', particularly of large scale risks, with several insurers or brokers agreeing to share the risks involved.

relations analysis. One of three techniques identified by *Drucker* to be used in deciding the *organization structure* appropriate for a company, the other techniques being *activi-ties analysis* and *decision analysis*. Relations analysis is used to pick out the relationships between managers and between management levels in the company, including lateral relationships.

relaxation allowance. As *compensating rest*.

relevance analysis. Techniques, originally developed for military program(me)s, used to attempt to assess how relevant particular research and development (R & D) programmes are, or would be, to company needs. Relevance analysis uses so-called *relevance trees* and other schematic aids to match R & D to company objectives.

relevance trees. Identification and evaluation of various *inputs* in order of importance in order to achieve a specific goal or objective.

reliability. See *quality control and reliability*.

remedial frames. Frames in an *intrinsic branching programme* to which a trainee/student is referred in order to correct a wrong answer or to make up for a lack of understanding revealed by an answer or answers.

remisiers. Non-bidding dealers allowed to buy and sell *securities* at *Italian stock exchanges*, but not through trading floor bidding. The latter activity is the prerogative of the stockbrokers, or *Agenti di Cambio*.

remuneration. Earnings and financial benefits received from employment, including basic salary or pay and additional direct or indirect financial benefits such as *bonus* schemes, *profit sharing schemes*, share ownership schemes, *pensions*, *life assurance*, company cars, low interest loans, accommodation benefits, medical benefits, subsidized meals, etc. See also *total remuneration concept* and *fringe benefits*.

rent. Price paid per unit of time for the use of accommodation or equipment. See also *rack rent*.

re-opener clause. As *threshold agreement*, though usually prescribing that pay negotiations be re-opened when the *cost of living* reaches a particular point rather than having a scale of pay directly related to the cost of living.

reorder level, or point. Or reordering level. *Stock control* term for the stock level at which an item must be reordered.

repeat demand. *Marketing* term for demand concerned with meeting requirements for frequently purchased *consumer goods*. Other types of demand are *replacement demand* associated with *consumer durables* and *industrial capital goods*, and *expansion demand* which is concerned with completely new consumers or users entering the market for a particular type of product.

replacement analysis. Technique used to establish the optimum times to replace plant and machinery, allowing for *depreciation*, effectiveness of existing equipment and potential of available new equipment.

replacement chart. Chart showing the back-up or replacement for each key member of management.

replacement cost. *Prices* which have to be paid **a** to replace plant or **b** to replace goods for sale or stock, or components, materials, etc used in manufacture, distribution, etc. See also *stock profits*.

replacement demand. *Marketing* term for demand associated with consumers or users scrapping and replacing *consumer durables* or *industrial capital goods*. Other types of demand are *repeat demand* concerned with frequently purchased *consumer goods*, and *expansion demand* which is related to completely new consumers or users.

replacement method. Method of *depreciation* which reflects the anticipated *replacement cost* of *assets* and not simply their original cost.

replacement theory. Accounting techniques related to *discounted cash flow* and used to identify the optimum points in time at which to replace equipment and plant. Takes into account such factors as second hand value of existing plant, price of new plant, relative maintenance costs, tax considerations, etc.

Report of the Committee of Inquiry on Small Firms (Cmnd 4811). See *Bolton Report on Small Firms (UK)*.

reporting by responsibility. Ensuring that managers receive the information they need to do their jobs but are not encumbered with unnecessary information. Reporting by responsibility is related to *management by exception*.

reporting pay. As *attendance bonus (or money)*.

representational rights. Traditionally, where a *trade union* has an established right to *joint consultation* with management and to process the grievances of individual members, but not the fuller *negotiating rights* of traditional *collective bargaining*.

reprographics. Technology of reproduction of printed material including photocopying, small offset printing and kindred activities.

resale price maintenance. Fixing by the manufacturer or supplier of the price at which goods or services are to be retailed to the consumer with penalties imposed on retailers who do not observe the fixed price. In the UK resale price maintenance has been largely abolished by the combined effect of the *Restrictive Trade Practices Act 1956*, the *Resale Prices Act 1964* and the *Fair Trading Act 1973*. The *fair trade laws* are the relevant legislation in the USA.

Resale Prices Act 1964. UK legislation abolishing resale price maintenance for a wide range of goods and services by laying down that manufacturers and suppliers should not dictate to retailers the prices at which goods are sold to the consumer. Manufacturers are allowed under the Act to state 'recommended prices' but they are not allowed to withhold supplies from retailers selling below these recommended prices unless the goods are being used as *loss leaders*.

Resale price maintenance is allowed under the Resale Prices Act 1964 only if **a** there would otherwise be a decline in the quality of the goods or in the number of places at which they would be available; **b** there would otherwise be a tendency for prices to increase; **c** the goods would be sold in a way dangerous to health; or **d** vital ancillary services would no longer be available to the consumer.

Goods exempted for one of the above reasons have had to be approved as exempted goods by the *Restrictive Practices Court* and registered with the *Registrar of Restrictive Trading Agreements*.

Research and Development (R & D). Technical and applied scientific activity concerned with the development of new products and manufacturing processes. Initial stage of *product life cycle*.

reseller. As *middleman*.

reserve. As *retained earnings*.

Reserve Bank of Australia. Australian central bank, established in 1911 as the Commonwealth Bank of Australia and renamed and reconstituted in 1959.

Reserve Bank of India. Indian *central bank*, established in 1935 and nationalized in 1949.

Reserve Bank of New Zealand. New Zealand *central bank*, established in 1934 and nationalized in 1936.

reserve price. One below which the vendor is not prepared to sell at an auction or sale. May also be known as a floor price or *upset price*.

reserve (or fall-back) price (EEC). Under the *Common Agricultural Policy* of the *Common Market* or *European Economic Community*, producers of fruit and vegetables may fix a reserve or fall-back price for each commodity and, if necessary, call upon the assistance of Community funds to ensure that the produce fetches its reserve price. See also *guide price, intervention price, sluice-gate price, target price, threshold price,* and *export subsidy (or restitution)*.

reserves. See *gold and foreign exchange reserves*.

reserve stock. As *buffer stock*.

Resettlement Transfer Scheme (UK). Provides financial help for people moving to a new job in another area sometimes, but not necessarily, after training under the *Training Opportunities Scheme*.

residual income method. Method of measuring and controlling divisional performance which attempts to align divisional goals with those of the company as a whole by measuring return on investment allowing for capital charges at various rates, intracompany trading at open market prices and valuing assets at net book value.

resolution. *Motion* that has been passed or carried at a meeting or conference.

resource allocation (or scheduling). Techniques, often associated with *critical path* planning, for allocating resources to the different sections of an organization or project at the right time.

resource appraisal. Management technique developed to keep the resources of a company under review and make available to top management the kinds of information necessary for decisions on *acquisitions* or *diversification, variety reduction,* or for defence against *take-over bids*. Appraisal of resources may range across all departments, financial and physical resources and expertise, etc.

respondent. As *informant*.

response. 1. Reaction of trainee/student to *stimulus* provided by instructor/teacher. 2. *Market research* term for the reaction of *respondents* or *informants* to a survey's approach or *stimulus*.

response budgeting. Type of two-tier budget in which two figures are given for key control areas — the object is to strive to achieve higher input results and lower expenditure.

response orientation. Type of *psychomotor skill*. An individual's ability to select and make the correct response from several alternatives in a work etc situation.

restraint of trade, convenants in. See *convenants in restraint of trade*.

restricter. Employee who performs at below the optimum, at a level considered as the norm by fellow workers. See also *ratebuster*.

restriction of output. As *quota restriction*.

restrictive labo(u)r practice (practise). Term often used by management for *trade union* insistence on restricting the way in which production and other techniques are operated, usually in what the unions see as the interest of *job security* or *security of tenure*. Other side of coin from *protective practice (practise)*.

restrictive practice (practise). See *restrictive labo(u)r practice (practise)* and *restrictive trade practice (practise)*.

Restrictive Practices Court. Set up in the UK to investigate complaints and trading agreements under the *Restrictive Trade Practices Act 1956* and the *Resale Prices Act 1964*, and to prohibit agreements found to be against the public interest. The work of the Court was expanded by the *Fair Trading Act 1973* which replaced the *Registrar of Restrictive Trading Agreements* with the *Director-General of Fair Trading*.

restrictive trade practice (practise). Broadly, in modern times, a trading practice (practise) or agreement that is not in the public interest, particularly, in the UK, as defined in the *Restrictive Trade Practices Act 1956*, the *Resale Prices Act 1964* and the *Fair Trading Act 1973*. Restrictive trade practices (practises) also offend the *rules of competition* of the *Common Market* as outlined in Articles 85-94 of the *Treaty of Rome 1957*.

Restrictive Trade Practices Act 1956. UK law which laid down that *trade associations* etc, might not impose restrictions such as price agreements against the public interest. The Act established the *Registrar of Restrictive Trading Agreements*, an official who also operated under the *Resale Prices Act 1964* but was abolished under the *Fair Trading Act 1973*.

resume. As *curriculum vitae*.

retail audit. Or shop audit. *Market research* technique involving studying retail outlets to obtain information on sales, stocks, advertising, presentations, point-of-sales displays, physical distribution, etc.

retail gravitation. Study of situations in which the public use particular kinds of *retail outlet*, or can be attracted to them.

retail outlet. Shop selling directly to the *consumer*.

Retail Price Index. Official UK measure of changes in the value of money produced monthly by the *Department of Employment*. See also *Wholesale Price Index* and *BLS Consumer Price Index (US)*.

retained earnings. Profits not distributed by way of *dividend* payments, but retained within the organization as part of a company's capital reserves. See also *revenue reserves*.

retention money. Part of the agreed price for a building or other contract which is retained by the purchaser to allow for sufficient time to inspect the quality of the contractor's work and to check that it has been carried out to the agreed specification.

retenue d'impôt sur les revenus de capitaux. Or *Kapitalerstragsteuer*. A capital yields tax which is part of the *Luxembourg income tax*. The capital yields tax is a flat-rate tax deducted at source on dividends, interest, etc but with a lower rate for certain incomes.

retenue d'impôt sur les revenus échus à des contribuables non-residents. Or *Steuerabzug von Einkünften bei beschränkt Steuerpflichtigen*. A form of *Luxembourg income tax* consisting of a flat-rate tax deducted at source from specified income of non-residents.

retenue d'impôt sur les tantièmes. Or *Steuerabzug von Aufsichtsrats-Vergütungen*. A flat-rate directors' tax deducted at source from directors' fees in Luxembourg. See *Luxembourg income tax*.

retirement benefit scheme. As *excepted provident fund (EPF)*.

retraining. Training for a new occupation or job.

retroactive association. Association of ideas and know-how between one point in a program(me) or series and an earlier point.

retrogressive consumer. *Marketing* term for a *consumer* who is keen to economize on an existing product or service. The opposite, the *progressive consumer*, is one who would be receptive to an offer of a better product or service at a slightly higher price.

retrospective payment. Payment of wages etc, as a result of an agreement to back date a new system or level of pay. Differs from *back pay*, which is payment due under the system of payment in force at the time that the work was done.

returned work. Products returned by customers as sub-standard. The *indirect review* method of inspection depends partly on feedback from complaints and returned work. See also *re-work*.

return on assets managed (ROAM). Yardstick of company and/or management performance which expresses sales minus the cost of goods sold as a percentage of assets managed minus liabilities. In this computation assets managed are normally treated as the sum of all fixed assets at current replacement cost; plus all inventories, *stocks*, debtors and prepayments, cash in hand and in back accounts, bills receivable, *patents*, selling rights, *goodwill*, and unquoted *investments*, all at *net book amount (or value)*; plus quoted investments at market value. Thus, in short, assets managed are those which management can influence in order to affect the return to the company. ROAM is often regarded as a more effective yardstick than *return on investment (ROI)* because of the problem, in practice (practise), that the figure for investments tends to have a

289

variety of interpretations. See also *balance sheet ratios* and *return on capital*.

return on capital (ROC). Where an average expected *profit* is estimated on several years of a proposed project or enterprise, this then being expressed as a percentage of the *capital employed*. See also *balance sheet ratios, payback, return on assets managed,* and *return on investment*.

return on investment (ROI). Yardstick, sometimes expressed as *rate of return*, of company and/or management performance, though *return on assets managed (ROAM)*. tends to be regarded as a better yardstick because investment may be interpreted in a variety of ways in practice (practise). See also *balance sheet ratios* and *return on capital*.

revaluation. 1. Writing up the value of an asset to its current market value. **2.** Change made by a country in the official rate at which its currency is exchanged for other currencies. The term is usually used of upward changes in a currency's exchange rate, *devaluation* being the term normally used of reductions in exchange rate.

revenue. Result of turning real *assets* into cash by a company or organization. The opposite process, *expenditure*, is the result of turning cash into real assets, and the difference between revenue and expenditure for a project/enterprise is its *profit* or *loss*.

revenue account. Record of a company's income and of the expenditure chargeable against it. It does not include items in the *capital account*.

revenue duty. As *tariff* or *excise duty*.

revenue reserves. *Retained earnings* forming part of the total *equity* or net worth of a business.

reverse take-over bid. *Take-over bid* where the company making the bid has the object of having the management of the company taken over run the resulting combined company. This might happen, for example, where a long established company with a moderate growth record in recent years seeks to take over a smaller and younger company with a record of aggressively rapid growth.

Revised Minnesota paper form board. Highly regarded *spatial ability* or *aptitude test* that takes about 20 minutes. See also *psychological testing* and *aptitude tests*.

revolving credit. As *continuous credit* or *revolving loan*.

revolving loan. Banking or finance house term for an arrangement under which a customer or borrower takes out and then repays a loan but is able to borrow the same sum again when it is needed for a further transaction. *Continuous credit* has a similar meaning except that it is normally used only of personal or individual facilities.

reward system. Methods used by an organization to provide rewards and incentive to its employees. The system used will depend on the *management style* and values of the organization and in particular on the importance attached to money as a motivator as distinct from the other rewards available, such as promotion, responsibility, recognition for achievement, status.

reward-value (or valence). See *expectancy theory*.

re-work. To repeat or revise work, usually because it was done inadequately the first time. See also *returned work*.

Rheinisch-Westfälische Börse zu Düsseldorf. *Düsseldorf Stock Exchange* or Rhenish-Westphalian Stock Exchange. See also *German (Federal) stock exchanges*.

Rhodesian stock exchanges. There are two stock exchanges in Rhodesia, situated in Bulawayo and in Salisbury.

rhythmical movements. Sequence of movements which induce a natural rhythm when repeated. See *motion study*.

right of recourse. Right to reclaim or recover a bad debt such as a dishono(u)red *bill of exchange*.

right of reply. See *motion*.

right of search. Or 'right of visit and search'. Internationally recognized right of a nation at war to stop neutral vessels on the high seas and search for contraband.

right of way. Right to pass over property owned by another, or the right of a person, vessel or vehicle to pass in front of another.

rights issue. New issue of *shares* in a company offered to shareholders in proportion to their existing holdings and on advantageous terms. The individual shareholder may accept the offer himself or he may renounce all or part of his rights in favour of others. A company will make a rights issue when it is seeking to raise new capital. When it has reserves which it wishes to capitalize it will issue *bonus shares* to its shareholders.

Right to Organize and to Bargain Collectively. See *Article 98 of the International Labor Organization.*

right to the job. As *right to work.*

right to work. Has been a conviction of the *trade union* movement since its beginnings, particularly when opposed by *free-market argument* or when coming up against employers' *lock-outs,* and has been prominent through the modern *sit-in* movement.

right-to-work laws. State laws in some parts of the USA that ban discrimination against job applicants or holders because they are not *trade union* members.

Riksbank. Sweden's *central bank.*

ring-fenced. Where action has been taken to ensure that a particular item in the accounts of a company or organization is treated separately and is not, for example, offset against other items or activities for tax purposes.

Rio de Janeiro Stock Exchange (Bolsa Official de Valores de Rio de Janeiro). One of two Brazilian stock exchanges. The other is in São Paulo.

risk analysis. One of the decision theory group of mathematical techniques, risk analysis is a complex study of probabilities used, sometimes as part of *operations* or *operational research.* The purpose is to evaluate risks and to analyze how far forecasts might go wrong and at what cost. Other decision theory techniques include *games theory, sensitivity tests* and *utility theory.*

risk capital. Or venture capital or, sometimes, equity capital. Long-term loans or capital invested in situations or businesses with a high degree of risk. Sources of risk capital in the UK include *merchant banks* and special institutions such as the *Industrial and Commercial Finance Corporation* and the *National Research Development Corporation.*

risk economist. Specialist in measuring the element of risk in *insurance* terms in a project or enterprise. The risk economist operates over a wider range and with less precise techniques than does the *actuary* who works in the field of life assurance or insurance.

risk manager. Insurance specialist who diagnoses the risks to which a project or enterprise is subject and prescribes appropriate action.

rival unionism. Where two or more *trade unions* are competing for members and recognition in the same industry or company. Rival unionism differs from *dual unionism* in that there is competition rather than acceptance of co-existence between the unions. See also *recognition dispute.*

Road Haulage Association. *Trade association* in UK for hire and reward transport operators, concerned with direct road services to Europe as well as throughout the UK. The Road Haulage Association is one of the guaranteeing associations in the UK for the *TIR Carnet* system of customs clearance. See also the Road Freight Division of the *Department of the Environment* and the *Freight Transport Association Ltd,* a trade association for own-account operators transporting their own goods.

Road Transport Industry Training Board. Established in UK in September 1966 under the *Industrial Training Act 1964.*

ROAM. *Return on assets managed.*

Robinson Patman Act 1936. See *antitrust legislation* (US).

ROC. *Return on capital.*

ROGBY. Personality assessment technique devised by William Isbister (UK). Based on hypothesis that each individual is a 'confused mass of colours' which can be analyzed and broken down into basic colo(u)rs red, orange, green, blue, yellow, etc. The technique involves collection of biographical information and the 'judgement phase'. It is claimed to provide a reliable means of personality assessment and lays stress on reliable prediction of future behavio(u)r provided past behavio(u)r is accurately recorded and analyzed.

rogue product. One that malfunctions or breaks down with alarming and inexplicable frequency.

Rohrschach Test. Or *ink blot test.* A *personality test* of the *projective technique* kind in which a person is presented with ten standard ink blots and asked to say what he or she reads into them. The responses are interpreted by an *occupational psychologist*. Cf the *Thematic Apperception Test*. See also *psychological testing*.

ROI. *Return on investment.*

role. In management terms, function undertaken and/or position held by an employee etc within an organization. Role is virtually synonymous with *job* but is used more of executive than, for example, shop-floor jobs.

role conflict. Situation in which an individual is expected to play two roles that are competing or antagonistic.

role perception. How a person sees his or other people's roles in particular situations.

role play. *Role playing* situation, most commonly a 'single role play' with, say, two or three people playing out roles in front of the other participants. 'Multiple role plays' are where all the learners or participants break up into groups for everyone to role play, each group then reporting back to a plenary discussion. See also *role reversal, role rotation, spontaneous role plays, skit-completion role plays*.

role playing. Group learning/teaching techniques in which students resolve a problem situation by acting out the roles of the protagonists in the situation.

role reversal. *Role playing* where two protagonists exchange roles in order to heighten their understanding of both sides. Thus, participants role-playing a *managing director* and a *convenor* might change places at an appropriate point in the *role play*.

role rotation. *Role-playing* in which the participants take it in turns to play the different roles in order to widen their perceptions of the problem or situation.

roll-back. Cutting of prices or wages to an earlier, lower level. The term is used mostly of government action to this effect.

roll call vote. Where a vote is taken at a meeting or conference by calling out the names of those entitled to vote and formally recording how they vote. See also *card vote* and *named vote*.

rolling plan. Long-term plan that is revised regularly and at each revision is projected forward again for the same period as the original plan. Thus a three-year rolling plan might be revised each year, so that at the end of year one the plan is revised and fresh projections made to the end of year four.

rollover. Borrower's option to renew loan, usually for a short period.

rollover bonus. Bonus paid partially during the period in which it was earned, with the balance paid later.

ROM. Acronym for read only memory, a random access *computer store* which cannot be overwritten.

Romanian central bank. *Banca Nationalà a Republicii Socialiste Romania.*

Romanian Chamber of Commerce. Established 1949.

Romanian General Trade Union Confederation. Established in 1906, it covers *trade unions* which have approximately five million members.

Rome Stock Exchange. (Borsa Valori di Roma). One of ten *Italian stock exchanges*. The others are at Bologna, Florence, Genoa, Milan, Naples, Palermo, Trieste, Turin and Venice.

Rome Treaty. Common term for the *Treaty of Rome 1957* which established the *European Economic Community (EEC)*.

Rookes v Barnard (1964) (UK). Rookes was a draughtsman employed by British Overseas Airways Corporation and a member of the Association of Engineering and Shipbuilding Draughtsmen (AESD) until resigning from that *trade union* in November 1955. Barnard and two other respondents were members or officials of the AESD, which had a *closed shop* agreement with BOAC who, under threat of a strike by the AESD, dismissed Rookes in January 1960. On appeal to the House of Lords in 1964, Rookes was awarded £7,500 damages in a judgment which upset the view hitherto that the *Trade Disputes Act 1906* had given trade unions complete legal immunity from the consequences of *industrial action*. Following Rookes v Barnard, this complete legal immunity was quickly restored by the *Trade Disputes Act 1965*.

rotating shift. As *alternating shift*.

Rothwell-Miller interest blank. *Interest test*

or *inventory* used in *personnel selection*, careers guidance, etc, to build up a picture of the personal interests of a candidate or employee. The blank consists of nine sets of 12 job titles, the candidate having to rank each set in order of preference.

Rotterdam Stock Exchange. Or *Vereeniging van Effectenhandelaren*. Very much overshadowed by, and subsidiary to, the *Amsterdam Stock Exchange*.

round-trippers loan. As *revolving loan*.

roustabout. 1. Drilling rig and production labo(u)rer in the petroleum industry. **2.** Deck or wharf labo(u)rer.

route card (or sheet). Card outlining the operations to be carried out on a product during manufacture or processing.

route diagram. As *flow diagram*.

Royal Aeronautical Society (UK). Member organization of the *Council of Engineering Institutions*.

Royal Commission on Civil Liability and Compensation for Personal Injury. Set up in UK early in March 1973 under Lord Pearson 'to consider to what extent, in what circumstances and by what means compensation should be payable in respect of death or personal injury (including ante-natal injury) suffered by any person, **a** in the course of employment; **b** through the use of a motor vehicle or other means of transport; **c** through the manufacture, supply or use of goods or services **d** on premises belonging to or occupied by another; or **e** otherwise through the act or omission of another where compensation under the present law is recoverable only on proof of fault or under the rules of strict liability, having regard to the cost and other implications of the arrangements for the recovery of compensation, whether by way of compulsory insurance or otherwise'. See also *Employers' Liability (Compulsory Insurance) Act 1969* (UK).

Royal Commissions on Trade Unions (UK). First, in 1867 under Sir William Earle leading to the Criminal Law Amendment Act 1871 and the Trade Union Act 1871. Second, in 1872 under Chief Justice Cockburn leading to the Conspiracy and Protection of Property Act 1875 and the Employers and Workmen Act 1875. Third, in 1891 under the Duke of Devonshire leading to the *Conciliation Act 1896*. Fourth, in 1903 under Lord Dunedin leading to the *Trade Disputes Act 1906*. Fifth, in 1965-8 under Lord Donovan. See also *Whitley Committee Report*.

Royal Society of Arts (UK). Activities include those of an examining body in commercial subjects. Cooperated with *London Chamber of Commerce* in administering *Ordinary National Certificate* in Business Studies.

royalty. 1. Payment made for the use of a *patent* or work process. **2.** Percentage of book sales revenue paid to an author.

RREAS. *Race Relations Employment Advisory Service* (UK).

Rubber and Plastics Processing Industry Training Board. Established in UK in August 1967 under the *Industrial Training Act 1964*.

Rubber Exchange. Specialist *commodity exchange* in UK dealing in both cash and futures.

Rucker plan. Cash incentive scheme for employees based on a formula relating payroll costs to sales value added by manufacture. See *Scanlon Plan* and *share of production plan*.

ruled-bin system. Stock control system in which the reordering levels for components are marked on their containers.

rules of competition (EEC). In the *Common Market*. Article 85 of the Treaty of Rome prohibits restrictive practices (practises) that distort competition in trade between the member states. Such *restrictive trade practices (practises)* include *price fixing*, *market sharing*, restriction of production or technical developments, and discriminatory supply markets. This provision in the Treaty of Rome covers agreements between firms and member states of the Common Market and it also covers agreements between firms in the Common Market and firms in non-member states. This had led to the introduction of several Community rules and *regulations*, and the *European Commission* has gathered know-how and precedents to guide it in identifying agreements which are incompatible with the objectives of the Treaty of Rome as outlined, on this point, in Articles 85-94. These Articles also cover monopolies and *mergers*, *dumping* by one member state against another, and state aid for industry.

The Common Market is also working towards a *common technological policy* and a *common industrial policy* involving harmonization of technical standards (this being important to fair competition which can be seriously inhibited by variations in acceptability of standards between nations).

rules of debate/procedure. See *committee procedure, motion* and *standing orders*.

running costs. Costs directly or indirectly related to keeping equipment or an enterprise operational. Such costs might include wages, rents, interest payments, taxes, day-to-day services, consumable equipment, replacement of goods sold, etc. Running costs are distinguished from *capital* costs and *start-up costs*. See also *break-even point* and *payback* period.

running down clause. Marine *insurance* term for a type of collision clause.

running yield. As *current yield*.

rupee. Basic unit of Indian currency.

'Russian'. See entries under *USSR*.

S

SA. *Société Anonyme.* See also *Belgian companies* and *French companies.*

SACL. *South African Confederation of Labour.*

saerlig indkomstskat. Special flat-rate *income tax* in Denmark charged on certain capital gains and lump-sum payments in lieu of the ordinary progressive state income tax, or *indkomstkat til staten.* There are also local, church and *net wealth taxes.* See *Danish income tax.*

SAF. *Svenska Arbetsgivareföreningen,* the Swedish Employers' Confederation.

safeguard benefit insurance policy. As *income benefit insurance policy.*

safety stock. As *buffer stock.*

safe working conditions. UK employer has a common law duty to use reasonable care to ensure that his employees enjoy safe working conditions. See also *employee's contributory negligence, employee's indemnity against liabilities and losses, voluntary assumption of risk,* the *Factories Act 1961, Health and Safety at Work Act 1974.*

SAK. *Suomen Ammattiliittojen Keskusjärjeste* (Confederation of Finnish Trade Unions).

salary classes. Salary brackets used in calculating entitlements and contributions under certain *pension schemes.* See, for example, *average salary pension scheme* and also *banding.*

salary club. Informal association of employers for the purpose of surveying or comparing salary levels, *fringe benefits,* etc.

salary increment. Regular increase in salary, usually annual, written into pay scales and individual *contracts of employment.* Particularly common in government and other public service.

salary progression curve. Graph relating salary to age or experience. Often used for research or technical staff or recently engaged graduates where a precise form of *job grading* is not feasible. Used by some firms in making *salary reviews.*

salary review. Re-examination of employees' salaries with regard to performance and/or inflation. Often an established — usually annual — part of company policy and/or individual *contracts of employment.* May involve the use of *job evaluation* techniques and annual *appraisal interviews,* and call upon the findings of *performance appraisal systems.* See also *salary increment.*

salary sacrifice. Insurer's term where an employee relinquishes part of his salary so that his employer can pay the equivalent amount on an *endowment assurance policy* for the employee for use in increasing pension on retirement.

salary structure. Use of a system of *job evaluation* or grading, and possibly *salary progression curves.* Salary maxima and minima are often fixed for each grade following job evaluation. Sometimes a formal *ranking* system is established. Graded salary structures with only a small number of grades are known as *broad-banded salary structures* while those with a large number of grades are *multi-grade salary structures.* A salary structure may provide for specific *salary increments* or it may provide for annual (or other) *salary reviews,* possibly involving annual *appraisal interviews* and *performance appraisal systems.* A salary structure may also allow for *merit pay* and *productivity increases.*

sales audit. Analysis of sales by product, size of product, geographical distribution, etc.

sales chain. Process or chain along which a product passes from the producer to the *consumer* or end user. The classic sales chain is that from manufacturer to *wholesaler* to retailer to consumer, though there are now many variations on this pattern, either shortening or extending the sales chain. Where *direct mail selling* techniques are used, for example, the retailer is cut out, and possibly the wholesaler too. In other situations the sales chain may be lengthened and the number of middlemen increased, as when an extra wholesaler or an agent becomes involved or when a manufacturer also factors the products of other manufacturers in order to extend the range of goods he can offer to wholesalers.

sales costs. As *selling costs*.

sales coverage. Ratio between the number of potential customers in an area and the number which can be effectively serviced by a salesman.

sales depth test. Accounting/*audit* term for a detailed examination of the processing of sales orders, from the initial receipt of orders to the despatch of goods and the mailing of invoices. Such a test can show up unnecessary time-lags.

sales forecasting. See *market and sales forecasting*.

sales ledger. Day to day record of sales made.

sales manual. Booklet or other form of document laying down a company's selling policy and the techniques and selling methods to be used by its salesmen, etc.

sales operations planning and control. Integrated management information system which focuses attention on the current results of a company in the areas of marketing, production, stocks and distribution.

sales order processing. Administrative work involved in checking customers' orders, including the credit-worthiness of the customer, and raising the necessary documents for despatch or production. These documents include the invoice, despatch note, packing note and delivery note, and these are often produced in one process as a multi-document set.

sales or market analysis. Alternative term for *market intelligence*.

sales planning. Determining detailed *sales targets* for all *sales territories* and customer categories and planning the deployment of all relevant marketing resources, including the sales force, over a stated period of time. In particular, the sales plan coordinates the timing of sales promotion and selling effort for sales campaigns. Sales planning is thus a detailed extension of the marketing plan.

sales promotion. Activities and techniques not involved in *direct selling* but used with the intention of bringing a company's potential customers into contact with its products and services. Sales promotion activities include advertising, public relations, merchandising, selling aids, exhibitions, demonstrations, dealer and consumer education, competitions, deals, offers, samples, etc. See also *marketing mix, consumer promotions, trade promotions, hard sales promotion* and *soft sales promotion*.

sales promotion planning. Determining the scale and program(me) of *sales promotion* activities required to achieve marketing targets.

sales revenue. Cash receivable for goods or services supplied during a particular period of time.

sales revenue line. See *break-even chart*.

sales target. Pre-determined volume or value of sales that should be obtained for a product, a market or a sales force.

sales tax. One levied on the retail price and collected by the retailer.

sales team, commando. See *commando sales team*.

sales territory. Geographical area into which existing and potential customers are grouped and for which a salesman or sales team is responsible.

Salisbury Stock Exchange. One of two *Zimbabwean stock exchanges*.

Salt Lake City Stock Exchange. One of the *US stock exchanges*.

sample survey. *Market research* or other kind of survey based on an examination of a representative part of the *total population*. A survey of the total population or prospective market is a *census survey*.

sampling. Statistical technique which involves collection of attitudes, facts, etc from a representative number of people or items in the total population which is appropriate to the survey. See also *differential sampling*, *quota sampling*, and *random sampling*.

sampling error. Where a sample assembled for a survey or study is not an accurate microcosm of the whole or *population* it is intended to represent. See also *standard error*.

sampling frame. Information on a *population* or *universe* that is used in defining and assembling a sample for survey purposes. See also *random sampling*.

sampling orders. Trial orders for a product by a prospective buyer who may place large orders if the samples meet his requirements for price, quality, etc.

sampling point. *Market research* term for a point at or around which *informants* are gathered or located for a survey or study. Thus the place used for a *hall test* is a sampling point, and so is a geographical area used in *cluster sampling*.

sandwich course. Course, usually at undergraduate level, in which periods of study in university or college are alternated with periods of training and experience in industry, the professions or commerce.

São Paulo Stock Exchange. (Bolsa Official de Valores de Sao Paulo). One of two *Brazilian stock exchanges*. The other is at *Rio de Janeiro*.

San Francisco Stock Exchange (Pacific Coast Stock Exchange). One of the *US stock exchanges*.

Santiago Stock Exchange. (La Bolsa de Commercio). One of two *Chilean stock exchanges*.

Sapporo Stock Exchange. One of nine *Japanese stock exchanges*.

sarkild sjomansskatt. *Seamen's tax* levied on the income of seamen in Sweden. See *Swedish income tax*.

SARL. *Société à Responsabilité Limitée.*

satisfiers. See *Herzberg's theory*.

Save As You Earn (SAYE). UK national scheme enabling employees to have savings deducted from pay on a regular basis.

saving. Economist's term for *income* that is not spent on *consumption*.

savings account. Or *deposit account*. Bank account from which withdrawals can only be made after giving required notice but *interest* is paid on money deposited in the account. Savings account is a US term while deposit account is a UK term. See also *checking account* or *current account*.

savings bank. One that pays interest on deposits which it in turn re-invests.

savings bond. Nontransferable registered bond issued by the US Government.

SAYE. *Save As You Earn.*

SCA. *Société en Commandité par Actions.* See also *Belgian companies*.

scab. As *black-leg*. Worker who continues working during a *strike* or who takes a striker's place.

scatter diagram. Chart or diagram showing the relationship between two or more variables. Shows how data varies in a *frequency distribution*.

scalar principle. Concept that subordinates should communicate with their senior colleagues only through the intermediate superiors following the *chain of command*.

scalogram. Planning and analysis board sometimes used in *market research* to pick out underlying patterns from a complexity of data, rather in the manner of *factor analysis*. Where the data is very complex, it is likely to be processed by *computer*. The use of a scalogram is sometimes known as Guttman scaling after its inventor, Louis Guttman.

Scandinavian Institute for Administrative Research. Centre of management and business research in Stockholm.

Scanlon Plan. Cash incentive scheme for employees based on sharing any reduction in labo(u)r cost norms. The plan was developed in the 1930s and 1940s by Joseph Scanlon of Massachusetts Institute of Technology and implemented with the cooperation of the United Steelworkers' Union and incorporates an employees' *suggestion scheme*. Cf *Rucker plan*. See *share of production plan*.

scenario. *Corporate planning* term used to describe a broad assessment of the long range position of the organization in relation to estimates of the various economic, technological, market, political and social forces that will affect its future development.

scenario writing approach. In *technological forecasting* or *advertising*. An intuitive approach beginning with the story of the development to date of a particular technology or product followed by systematic projections of likely future trends, problems and developments. Other techniques of technological forecasting include *brainstorming*, the *Delphi approach*, *exploratory forecasting techniques*, *morphological research*, *normative forecasting techniques*, and *technological trend extrapolation*.

Schweizerischer Gewerkschaftsbund. Swiss Federation of Trade Unions, the central organization for *trade unions* in Switzerland. Established in 1880, it covers trade unions which have approximately 450,000 members.

Science Research Council (SRC). UK organization responsible to the *Department of Education and Science* for promoting research and development in science and technology. Awards made by the SRC for postgraduate education and research include Research Studentships; Advance Course Studentships; Science and Industry Awards (taken up by graduates after one to five years in industry); Industrial Studentships; Industrial Fellowships; and Research Fellowships.

scientific gaming. See *gaming, scientific*.

SCORE. Acronym for Service Corps of Retired Executives. US group sponsored by the *Small Business Administration* providing free advisory and consultative services to smaller firms.

SCOTBEC. *Scottish Business Education Council.*

Scottish Business Education Council (SCOTBEC). Professional and examining body.

Scottish Education Department. UK Government Department which has responsibility for public education in Scotland.

Scottish Electrical Training Scheme Ltd (SETS). *Group training scheme* devised particularly for graduate apprentices in electrical engineering.

Scottish Export Committee. Stimulates, directs and coordinates Scottish export efforts through *trade missions*, etc. The Committee's sponsors include the *Confederation of British Industry*, and the *Scottish Trade Union Congress*.

Scottish Stock Exchange. UK provincial *stock exchange* based in Glasgow.

Scottish Tourist Board. Advises on tourism in Scotland.

Scottish Trades Union Congress. Central *trade union* organization in Scotland though many of its member unions are also members of the London-based *Trades Union Congress*.

scrambled book/text. Programmed instruction book using *intrinsic branching program(me)*.

scrambled merchandising. Offer for sale by a *retail outlet* of goods other than its normal wares.

screening. 1. In personnel, making a preliminary assessment of job applications or candidates and deciding that some are unsuitable. **2.** Generally assessing ideas, suggestions, etc methodically and rejecting those which do not meet essential criteria.

scrip issue. Bonus (free) issue or allotment of *shares* to shareholders normally related to the number of shares held. Also known as capitalization issue or *bonus shares*.

SCS. *Société en Commandité Simple.* See also *Belgian companies* and *French companies*.

SDRs. *Special drawing rights.*

SE. *Societas Europea.* See the *European Company.*

seamen's tax. Special form of *income tax* on the remuneration of seamen. See, for example, *Danish income tax*, *Finnish income tax*, *Norwegian income tax*, *Swedish income tax*.

SEC. *Securities and Exchange Commission (US).*

secondary banking sector. Financial institutions such as *'1-2-3 banks'* and *fringe banks* that carry out a wide range of banking activities but do not have the standing and proven resources of a *clearing bank, credit bank, member bank* or recognized *commercial bank*.

secondary boycott. Term used particularly in the USA but also in the UK where pressure is applied to the employer by persons other than those actually in dispute with him. The *sympathy* (or *sympathetic*) *strike* is one of the most common forms of secondary boycott. See also *primary boycott, industrial action*, etc.

secondary legislation (EEC). Of the *Common Market* or *European Economic Community* in the form of *Regulations, Directives, Decisions, Recommendations* and *Opinions* emanating from the *Council of Ministers* and the *European Commission*, often after consultation with the *European Parliament* and other institutions of the Common Market. This secondary legislation is secondary to, or derived from, the Common Market's *primary legislation*, namely, the *Treaty of Rome 1957* that established the *European Economic Community (EEC);* the *Euratom Treaty 1957* that established the *European Atomic Energy Community (Euratom)* and the *Treaty of Paris 1951* that established the *European Coal and Steel Community (ECSC)*.

secondary picketing. *Picketing* in furtherance of a trade dispute by individuals or groups not directly party to the main dispute.

seconder. Someone seconding a *motion* at a meeting or conference.

second-injury laws (US). Legislation providing that if an injury suffered by a worker aggravates an earlier injury suffered with a previous *employer*, both employers have a responsibility to compensate the worker. In some states employers contribute to 'second-injury funds' from which such compensation is paid.

second penetration product. Applied particularly to high technology products (eg aeroplanes, electronic equipment, etc) which evolve and develop within a few years of the original product.

Secretary of State for Education and Science. Senior UK Minister (with Cabinet Minister rank) in the *Department of Education and Science*.

Secretary of State for Employment. Senior UK Minister (with Cabinet Minister rank) in the *Department of Employment*. Responsible for introducing and executing legislation dealing with industrial relations, industrial training, safety, health and welfare, etc.

secured liability. *Debt* incurred against the pledging of specific *assets* by the borrower so that the lender can be certain of recovering the value of the debt if the debt itself is not repaid.

Securities and Exchange Commission (SEC) (US). Federal government agency responsible for implementing and administering Federal law on securities etc, supervising the exchange of *securities* with the object of protecting investors against malpractice (malpractise).

security. Technically has the meaning of a guarantee given by the borrower as a safeguard for a loan but the term is used more loosely to mean *debentures, shares* or any other negotiable documents with a cash value. Portfolios of securities held and managed on behalf of joint owners are *mutual funds*. See also *open-end investment companies*.

Security Council. Permanent council of the *United Nations* concerned particularly with peace keeping. It has five permanent members and ten elected members.

security export controls. Export of goods with so-called 'strategic uses', such as materials usable in sophisticated military equipment, is subject to licensing control, particularly if destined for markets in the Soviet bloc or China.

security of tenure. Strength of a tenant's right to continue to hold his tenancy or of an employee's right to continue to hold his job (see *job security*).

segmentation analysis. See *market segmentation*.

segregated trust. As *split-level investment trust*.

selection consultant. One specializing in the recruitment and selection of middle and senior executives on behalf of client companies. These consultants are normally expert in selection techniques, including *psychological testing* and interviewing and assessment procedures. They usually handle recruitment advertising as an integral part of their recruitment and selection service. Often, they act as a kind of broker between applicant and prospective employer, sometimes undertaking not to divulge the applicant's name and identity to the prospective employer until and unless the applicant gives permission. In the case of vacancies for very senior appointments, a selection consultant may act as a so-called *head-hunter* or *executive search* consultant, seeking out suitable people in other firms rather than advertising for applicants in the conventional way. Selection consultants are usually independent organizations or individuals, or they may be Government sponsored bodies such as the *Professional and Executive Recruitment* service (PER) in the UK. A distinction should normally be made between selection consultants and *employment agencies*, these latter organizations being largely concerned with introducing office staff and unskilled or semi-skilled manual staff to prospective employers. See also *temporary staff contracting service*.

selection tests. See *test battery* and *psychological testing*.

self-administered fund. Of an employer's pension scheme. *Controlled funding* techniques are used to forecast the future salaries and pensions of employees and to express as a percentage of pensionable payroll the contribution which the fund will need to pay the promised benefits. A fund will usually provide pensions by the purchase of *annuities* for employees as they reach retirement age so that the fund does not itself bear a mortality risk on an employee's life after retirement age. A self-administered fund is different from a *deposit administration fund* in that the latter is managed and its deposits invested by an insurance company.

self-assessment questions. Term used for questions posed to a student during a course to help him judge for himself how well he is faring and comprehending the course content. See also *computer marked assessment*.

self-completion questionnaire. *Market research* term for one that is completed by the *informant*, not the interviewer, eg a postal questionnaire. See also *sentence completion*.

self-employed person. One working on his own, or in business on his own account.

Other categories for *National Insurance* purposes in the UK are *employed persons* working for an employer and *non-employed persons*.

self-financing. See *auto financing*.

self-fulfilling prophecy. Where a forecast or 'prophecy' is made the more realizable because management effort is applied to achieving it. Thus this may happen in *personnel selection* where people selected as of high calibre are given exceptional opportunities to prove it while others have much more restricted scope. It may also happen in *marketing*, for example, where a decision that a particular product or market is the most promising prospect is followed by concentration of management effort in that direction.

self-instructional course. Material, such as *programmed texts*, which trainee/student can use without constant supervision of instructor/teacher.

self-insurance. Setting aside reserves (rather than taking out an insurance policy) so that in the event of a loss all or part can be covered by internally held funds.

self-selection store. Like a *self-service store* in that the customer selects from the goods on display, but normally with the added facility that staff are on hand to pack the goods and deal with queries as well as collect payment.

self-service store. One where the customers select from the goods on display, paying for those they have collected at a check point before leaving the store. See also *self-selection store*.

sell and leaseback. Arrangement by which owner sells land or property to an investor (eg bank, insurance company, etc) and then agrees to continue occupying the property on a long term lease.

selling, benefit method of. See *benefit method of selling*.

selling costs. Costs which can be directly attributed to sales activities.

selling platform. Central theme of a marketing or *advertising* campaign.

selling-price sliding scale. Wage agreement under which pay varies with the selling price of the product. Cf *threshold agreement*.

selling, systems. See *systems selling*.

sell short. To sell for future delivery what one does not yet possess.

semantic differential. Market research term for the use of *pre-coded questions* to discover where *informants'* attitudes to a product etc lie on a given scale. See also *Osgood scales* and *ranking*.

semi-fixed cost. See *break-even chart* and *stepped cost*.

semimanufactures. Goods processed to the state of *raw materials* for further manufacture.

seminar. Short course or conference with high degree of participation and discussion between delegates/students. Can be a kind of group tutorial.

semi-skilled worker. Generally taken to mean reasonably highly skilled *operator/operative* though not as highly skilled as a *craftsman* who has served an apprenticeship.

semi-variable cost. One that varies indirectly with changes in the level of business activity but not as directly as a so-called *variable cost* (which may be, in effect, a constant cost per unit of production). An example of a semi-variable cost may be power which usually increases with an increase in a factory's production but not to a directly proportional extent. See also *fixed cost*, *stepped cost* and *mixed cost*.

seniority wage system. Payment of higher wages to longer serving employees.

Sensale. Official brokers on the *Vienna Stock Exchange*. They are public officials who have to pass official examinations and be nominated by the members of the Stock Exchange. The Sensale are sworn into office by government officers and, as well as dealing with *securities*, have authority to deal in *bills of exchange*, coins, precious metals, foreign currencies, etc. Other brokers on the floor of the Vienna Stock Exchange are the *Freie Makler* or free brokers.

sensitivity tests (or analysis). *Decision theory* technique that is a simplified version of *risk analysis* involving a reworking and re-evaluation of the calculations on which a management decision is based to arrive at the most likely fit and an idea of the consequences of any use of wrong assumptions. Other decision theory techniques include risk analysis, *games theory* and *utility theory*.

sensitivity training. Group training method to develop social skills and ability to see how others see one. See *T-group training, group dynamics, interactive skills, Coverdale training*.

sensory. Refers to structures and phenomena on the receptor and afferent side of the psycho-organic system, the stimuli affecting the receptors or sense organs and the nerves and nerve centres.

sensory-motor activity. *Responses* following sensory stimulation.

sentence completion. Form of question sometimes used in *market research* questionnaires (particularly *self-completion questionnaires*), in *attitude surveys*, and in *sales promotion* back-up. For example, *informants* might be asked to complete such a sentence as, 'I give the children Wiz-wam because . . .'

Seoul Stock Exchange. (The Korea Stock Exchange). Korea's only stock exchange.

separable programming. *Operations* or *operational research* technique akin to *linear programming* but usable in some problem situations where some of the relationships are not completely linear. See also *quadratic programming*.

separated manager. Characterized by overzealous regard for rules and procedures and concern that work is carried out 'by the book'. Tends to judge others by whether they deviate from company plans, policies and methods, and tends also to be a poor communicator, relying on written rather than verbal contact with others.

separation rate. As *wastage rate*.

sequential storage. *Computer* storage in which records are stored in a required order and are normally processed in that order, though access to individual files may also be possible. An example of the use of sequential storage is in the handling of a payroll. Other forms of computer storage include *random access storage* and *serial storage*.

serial correlation. Forecasting techniques, used particularly in *market and sales forecasting*, for making projections into the future based on past experience. It is a crude

301

version of *time series forecasting*, being based on less extensive data.

serial storage. *Computer* storage in which information is stored in the order in which it happens to arrive and can only be processed in that order thereafter. Other forms of computer storage include *random access storage* and *sequential storage*.

service increments. Increases in pay due after completion of an agreed length of employment.

service mark. Design, device or *trade mark* used to establish the identity of a service offered to the public. See also *corporate image*.

servomechanism control. Management information and control system which includes the *feedback concept*.

session synopsis. Synopsis of topics to be covered in a training session.

set. 1. Psychologist's term for state of expectancy or predisposition to behave in a certain way. Cf *attitude* and *behavio(u)r*. 2. In statistics grouping together items sharing a common feature or having a relationship to each other, eg all data relating to teenagers.

set up. Product completely assembled and ready to use; the opposite of *knocked down* product.

set up time. Time it takes to change a machine or method from producing one product, component or process to another.

seven point plan. Formula for assessing employment potential of individuals under the seven headings of attainments, general intelligence, special aptitudes, health, interests, disposition and circumstances. Used in *personnel selection* etc. Plan developed by Alec Rodger for the *National Institute of Industrial Psychology*. See also *five fold grading scheme*.

severance pay. Payment made to an employee when a *contract of employment* is terminated or to a person on contract when a *contract of service* is cut short. See also *fixed term contract*, *golden handshake*, *contracts of employment*, *Contracts of Employment Act 1963*, *Redundancy Payments Act 1965*.

Sex Discrimination Act 1975. UK legislation which sought to eliminate discrimination between sexes, particularly that against women, in virtually all areas of society including *employment*. It became fully operational on the same day as the *Equal Pay Act 1970*. See also *Equal Opportunities Commission* and *maternity rights*.

's-Gravenhage Stock Exchange (Bond Voor den Greld-en Effectenhandel in de Provincie Te's-Gravenhage). One of three *Dutch stock exchanges*.

shadow price. Computer world's term for *opportunity cost*.

shake-out. Process of making employees redundant.

share capital. As *contributed capital* or *paid up capital*.

shared values. Traditional, orthodox view of industrial sociologists, particularly those of the *structural-functionalist school* in the USA, that stability and equilibrium are normal in society and are sustained by the fact that people from all strata of society — and therefore all levels of industry — have certain 'shared values'. This view has sometimes been challenged in modern times by the view that there are also cultural gaps between the different strata of society — eg between management and shop floor workers — gaps that create an inevitable division between values and views on what is a reasonable course of action. The holding of 'shared values' may also be hindered by the sub-culture of a particular industry or a particular region. See also *community integration*, *human relations school* and *sub-culture*.

shareholder. Owner of *shares* or *stocks* in a *company* or limited partnership.

Share Incentive Scheme. Introduced in the UK by the Finance Act 1973. Under the Scheme, full-time employees are able to contribute regularly to Save As You Earn, the proceeds being used to buy shares in the employing company at a price below normal market value without incurring tax on a benefit.

share index. Index of the prices of a group or parcel of *shares* selected as being representative of shares in general and therefore a guide to overall fluctuations in the stock market. Well known share indices include the *Financial Times Index* in the UK and the *Dow Jones Index* and *Standard and Poor's* 500 Index in the USA.

share of production plan. Incentive or *payment-by-results* scheme in which payment is dependent on company or organization performance, not individual worker performance. Types of share of production plan include *Rucker plan* and *Scanlon plan*. See also *group incentives*.

share option scheme. Arrangement granting a specific right to acquire particular *shares*, possibly at a specific price. May be used as a form of *profit sharing scheme* for employees. See also *Share Incentive Scheme*.

share premium. As *paid-in surplus*.

shares. Or company shares. A part of the *equity* capital or ownership of a company, particular types of shares including *preference shares, ordinary shares* and *deferred shares*. In the UK a *private company* has at least two shareholders and a *public company* at least seven (see also *close company*). When *going public*, a company must obtain a quotation from the Council of the *Stock Exchange* after which its shares may be sold and bought there. Methods of selling shares to the public include *issue by tender, offer for sale, placings, public issue by prospectus*, and *rights issues*. A public company may also create new shares by issuing *bonus shares* to its existing shareholders.

shell company. 1. Company which exists on paper but does not apparently trade or operate, possibly being used as a cover for illegal or unethical activities. **2.** Company registered for the purpose of its name and registration being sold subsequently to someone needing a ready-made company.

Sherman Act 1890. See *antitrust legislation* (US).

shift. 1. Period of time in *shift working*. **2.** The workforce employed during that period of time.

shift premium. Extra payment made to shift workers, over and above day rate, to compensate for the social inconvenience of *shift working*. As a general and broad rule, the shift premium for three-shift, round-the-clock shift working is about ten per cent of daywork pay.

shift working. Arrangement by which a group of workers at the end of a working day of normal length is succeeded by another group which carries on with the same work. Such an arrangement may be vital in a continuous process plant or in certain public services that have to be provided at all times. Shift working may also be desirable in other types of industry to utilize equipment economically and/or to satisfy demand for a product or service. In a continuous process plant the 24 hours of the day may be covered by three shifts each with an eight hour working day. A common arrangement where continuous working is not inherently necessary is to have two shifts a day — for example, from 6 am to 2 pm and from 2 pm to 10 pm — with maintenance and repair work taking place during the remainder of the 24-hour day. There may be special *maintenance shifts* for the latter purpose, including at weekends. A special kind of shift working found particularly in light industrial work done by women is the *twilight shift* from, say, 6 pm to 10 pm, to extend the utilization of a factory beyond that of an ordinary working day but not to the extent of full shift working. See also *flexible working hours, staggered working day, balancing time, twilight shift* and *unsocial hours*.

Shindica method. Analytical approach for investigating and isolating potential problem areas in the management of complex projects. The object is to be prepared for difficulties and take corrective action instead of responding to a crisis as in *management by crisis*.

Shipbuilding Industry Training Board (UK). Established November 1964 under the *Industrial Training Act 1964*.

shipping and forwarding agent. Or 'freight forwarder'. Services provided include arranging efficient through-transport from the exporter's factory to the overseas buyer's premises; arranging import of materials, including customs clearance; advising on appropriate routes and methods of transport; expediting export documentation; and organizing packing facilities and warehousing, including container services where appropriate.

shipping note. Type of *consignment note*.

shop. 1. Building where goods are sold or offered for sale to the public on cash or credit terms. **2.** Department or section of a factory (eg 'paint shop' etc).

shop audit. As *retail audit*.

shop control. *Production control* term for the actual physical control of production on the *shop floor* or factory floor.

shop floor. Production or other factory working area.

shop steward. Elected workplace representative of a *trade union* who can sometimes have a difficult dual allegiance to his union's policy and to the immediate needs of his constituents on the shop floor. The shop steward, who first emerged in the First World War, has become much more powerful in post World War years through such factors as the shortage of industrial skills, the increasing expectations of trade union members, the inflexibilities of industry-wide and traditional *collective bargaining* procedures, the growth of *plant bargaining* and *productivity bargaining*, and the rapid growth of *workplace bargaining* and the securing of piecemeal concessions through *bargaining creep*.

The nature of a shop steward's duties is likely to vary with type of technology or production process, with the character of management and of the trade union, with type of payment system, with the effectiveness of industry-wide collective agreements, with the nature of any *multi-unionism*, and with local traditions. There are more than 300,000 shop stewards in British industry. See also *convenor, joint shop stewards committee (JSSC), unofficial shop stewards committee*, and *industrial trade union*.

In certain industries, such as printing and publishing, the shop steward may be known as the *father of the chapel*.

shop stewards committee, joint. See *joint shop stewards committee (JSSC)*.

shop stewards committee, unofficial. See *unofficial shop stewards committee*.

shop-talk. Gossip or talk about professional, business or work matters. The most common use of the term is in the expression, 'talking shop'.

short account. 1. Account of someone dealing in *short sales*. **2.** Total short sales of a particular *commodity, security* or *share* on the open market.

Short Employment Tests. Group of three *psychological tests* for clerical workers developed in the USA and measuring verbal, numerical and clerical skills. The verbal and numerical tests are sometimes combined to be used as an *intelligence test*.

short interval scheduling. Assigning tasks and a planned quantity of work to specific employees to be completed within a given period of time. The basic concept is that performance can be improved and controlled if work is assigned and monitored over short periods of time.

short position. As *bear position*.

short sale. Sale of *commodities, securities* and *shares* not yet in the possession of the seller but which are expected to be before the contract is completed.

short-time working. State where shortage of work leads an employer to reduce hours of work to a part-time basis, hopefully temporarily. The most usual reason for introducing short-time working is a breakdown in supplies of components. If it becomes necessary for the employer to suspend employment entirely, this is known as a *lay-off*.

shut-down. Temporary closing of a factory or plant.

shrinkage. 1. Losses as a result of stock deterioration, scrap or waste. **2.** Goods shoplifted by customers or stolen by employees.

shut-out. As *lock-out*.

shyster. Unscrupulous and usually unethical business or professional man, especially a lawyer or politician. The term is used particularly in the USA.

SI (Units). See *International System (SI)* of metric units.

SIAR. Scandinavian Institute for Administrative Research.

SIC. Standard Industrial Classification.

sickness and accident policy. Insurance policy providing income temporarily, in many cases up to a maximum of one year, in the event of sickness or accident. There are also *permanent sickness and accident policies* or disability pensions.

sickness benefit. Payment made to an individual to provide income to compensate for loss of earnings during absence from work as a result of illness.

sick pay. As *sickness benefit*.

SICOVAM. *Société Interprofessionnelle pour la Compensation des Valeurs Mo-*

bilieres, the clearing house for the settlement of operations on the *Paris Stock Exchange* (or *Bourse*).

sight bill. *Bill of exchange* to be paid immediately on presentation.

Sight Screener. Binocular testing instrument used in vision testing, particularly in the USA.

silicon chip. See *chip*.

silicosis. Progressive and potentially lethal disease of lungs resulting from breathing in silica in coal mining, quarrying, pottery, iron and steel, refractory products and other industries. See *asbestosis* and *byssinosis*.

simo chart. Or simultaneous motion cycle chart. Chart used to record the movements and timings of the limbs of workers.

simple debenture. As *naked debenture*.

simulated training. Training in specially created conditions simulating real working conditions and giving opportunity for formal instruction. See *simulator*.

simulation. Construction of mathematical models to represent the operation of real-life processes or situations. The object is to explore the effect of different policies on the model to deduce what might happen in practice (practise) without going to the expense or risk of trial and error in the real environment.

simulation-game. *Group training* activity combining the competitive characteristics of a *game* with the real-life substitutes of a *simulation*.

simulator. Represents certain parts of a real working situation, reproducing operational conditions and giving the trainee/student specific experience and training in a way not usually possible on the job itself. Developed from flight simulator concept.

simultaneous movements. Movements in which different limbs are working at the same time. See *motion study*.

Singapore Employers' Federation. Central organization for *employers' associations*, established in 1948.

Singapore International Chamber of Commerce. Established 1837.

Singapore National Trades Union Congress. Covers some 140 *trade unions* with about 120,000 members.

Singapore Stock Exchange. (Stock Exchange of Malaysia and Singapore.) One of two *Malaysian stock exchanges*.

single-entry. Book-keeping system (now largely obsolete) using only a single account for monies due and monies owed. See also *double entry*.

single-industry union. As *industrial trade union*.

single life pension. *Pension* scheme providing for an employee only, not for his wife if she survives him. However, such a pension can in some cases be converted to a *joint life and last survivor pension* through a *widow's pension option*.

single line store. Retail shop carrying only a selection of related merchandise, eg all sports goods, kitchen furniture, garden accessories, etc.

single premium costing (pensions). Where, in a pension scheme such as an *average salary pension scheme* or a *works pension scheme*, the pension earned in a particular year is paid for in the premium for that year. Such a costing is only applicable where the pension earned in a particular year can be calculated at the time (thus it would not be applicable to a *final salary pension scheme*). An alternative to single premium costing is *annual premium costing* where the cost of the total pension is expressed as a level annual premium payable each year.

single status. When both the *blue collar* and *white collar* workers in a firm have *staff status*. The process of levelling up the differences in terms and conditions of blue collar and white collar employment is known as *integration* or *mensualization* or, particularly in Common Market circles, as *harmonization*.

single-task role. *Job* or *role* that is concerned primarily with one *task* only. A role concerned with a variety of tasks is known as a *multiple-task role*.

sinking fund. Investment made by an organization in order to build up sufficient resources to finance future projects or activity.

SIS. *Short interval scheduling.*

sit-down strike. Type of *strike* or *industrial action* in which workers refuse to work but also refuse to leave the workplace until an agreement has been reached. See also *downer*.

sit-in. Form of *industrial action* that hit headlines in UK with Upper Clyde Shipbuilders' troubles from mid-1971 and those at the Lip Factory in France in 1973. Instead of a *strike* or withdrawal of labo(u)r, workers pursue the *right to work* and occupy their *factory* on a 24 hours-a-day basis to forestall the possibility of a *lock-out*. See also *go-slow, overtime ban, work-to-rule, cut-price industrial action*.

situation profile. Or *firm's profile*. Used in establishing the *payment system* for a firm, a department, a section or an individual. Lupton and Gowler have identified the following 21 profile dimensions, the first nine being technological dimensions, the next three being labo(u)r market dimensions, the next two being concerned with disputes and dispute procedures, and the final seven being structural dimensions. **a** Length of the job cycle; **b** Number of job modifications per job; **c** Degree of automation; **d** Rate of product change; **e** Recorded job stoppages; **f** Average length of job stoppages; **g** Percentage of job elements specified by management for operator; **h** Percentage of material scrapped; **i** Percentage of defective products; **j** Time required to fill vacancy, including training time; **k** Labo(u)r stability index; **l** Annual labo(u)r turnover; **m** Number of stoppages due to pay disputes; **n** Average length of such stoppages; **o** Percentage of total pay settled outside firm; **p** Number of unions negotiating separately in the firm; **q** Numbers of job grades, or work units and of shifts; **r** Recorded absence as proportion of normal time; **s** Average age of work force; **t** Percentage of labo(u)r cost in total cost; **u** Percentage of males in work force.

Lupton and Gowler also take into account initially under technological dimensions two so-called *gate mechanisms* (namely, 'type of effort' and 'unit of accountability') that guide the way in which the profile dimensions are built up.

16 personality factor questionnaire (16PF). Type of *personality test* based on the theory of personality structure of R B Cattell of the USA. Its purpose is to measure 16 'primary' personality factors plus a number of 'secondary' and 'tertiary' factors. These factors are then matched with a number of occupational group profiles. This test is sometimes used in *personnel selection* with guidance from an *occupational psychologist*. See also *psychological testing*.

size-effect. Theory that *industrial relations* problems increase with increases in size of industrial organizations.

sjømannsskatt. *Seamen's tax* in Norway charged on the wages of seamen in place of other income taxes.

skewness. Statistical term sometimes used of a *sample* that is biased in some way or of a distribution curve that is asymmetrical rather than representing a normal distribution (see *Gaussian Curve*).

skill acquisition curve. As *learning curve*.

skill-composition. Breakdown between type of *job* in a labo(u)r force.

skill dissipation. Loss of skill over a period of time.

skilled man (or worker). *Craftsman* in a particular occupation, trade or craft who is able to apply a wide range of skills and know-how to basically non-repetitive work with a minimum of direction and supervision. Historically, a *craftsman* or *journeyman* has served an *apprenticeship*. See also *semi-skilled worker*.

skills analysis training. Identification and recording of the psycho-physiological characteristics of skilled performance, and the determination of the effector, receptor and decision making functions involved. Usually followed by process of designing *simulators* to develop the skills of the different elements of the job in question and then building up worker performance first on individual elements and then on combinations of elements. Involves use of *learning curves*. Technique originated in *operator/operative* training.

skill testing. Testing for level of attainment in a particular skill, either to assess training required or to assess level attained after training. See *criterion behavio(u)r*.

skimming. Type of pricing policy designed to maximize profit margins by putting a product on sale at a high price and then reducing the price by stages to saturate the market. The opposite approach, *penetration pricing*, is to sieze as large a share of the market as possible as early as possible by putting the product on sale at a low price.

skip program(me). *Programmed text* where

a trainee/student making a correct response to a frame by-passes some of the following frames. A hybrid kind of program(me) sometimes divided between skip-linear and skip-branching. See *adaptive program(me), intrinsic branching program(me), linear program(me).*

skip question. As *filter question.*

slab scale. Income tax term for a scale where progressive rates apply to the whole of the taxable income. Thus, if an income is below 100, tax is x per cent on the whole of the income, but if an income is 100 or over then tax becomes y per cent on the whole income. Cf *slice scale,* where different rates are charged for the different 'slices' of an income. See also *progressive tax.*

slave unit. Part of a system whose performance or activity is controlled by a *master unit* in the system, the slave unit possibly operating in exact imitation of the master unit.

sleeper. 1. Manager (or organization) which is defensive, negative and does not exploit situations and opportunities. Cf *thruster.* **2.** Control address included in a *direct mail shot* to provide a check on whether mail is reaching its target.

slice scale. Income tax term for a scale where slices of income are charged at progressive rates. Thus, the first 100 slice may be at x per cent, and the next 100 slice at y per cent, etc. Cf *slab scale.* See also *progressive tax.*

sliding-parity (exchange rates). Or *crawling-peg.* Concept that offers a compromise between fixed parity and *floating exchange rates* by spreading any currency devaluation or revaluation over several months. Another compromise is the *moving-parity* concept.

slip chart. Used in particular to record and check the progress of research and development (R & D) program(me)s or of construction projects. A slip chart records scheduled times for stages in a project on a vertical axis and real or actual times on a horizontal axis, using the same scale on each axis so that a line at 45 degrees will represent the ideal path of events. Scheduled times of stages in the project are marked off on the vertical axis and the real times are then plotted horizontally from those points. Any deviation from the schedule is indicated by a bending of the line from the 45 degrees ideal: flattening out if there is *slippage,* getting steeper if there is gain.

slippage. Time lost during a project, etc.

slip system. Accounting method using original documents for posting items to ledger accounts. In a slip sales or purchase ledger the copies of *invoices* are retained in an unpaid file until actual payment is received. Also known as ledgerless accounting, bookless accounting and file posting.

slowdown. Form of *industrial action* in which workers reduce their pace of work but do not actually withdraw their labo(u)r. Has similar effect to *go-slow* or *work-to-rule.*

sluice-gate price (EEC). Under the *Common Agricultural Policy* of the *Common Market* or *European Economic Community,* so-called sluice-gate prices are fixed each quarter by the *European Commission* as the minimum prices for the import into the Community from non-member states of pigmeat, eggs, chickens and other poultry meat. If goods enter at less than sluice-gate price, levies are paid according to the country of origin. Variable levies are imposed above the sluice-gate prices as necessary to ensure preference for non-member states. See also *guide price, intervention price, reserve (or fall-back) price, target price, threshold price,* and *export subsidy (or restitution),*

slump. Where economic and industrial activity is at its lowest, in the depths of *deflation* and with *mass unemployment.* See also *trade cycle.*

slumpflation. Harsh economic conditions created by a combination of simultaneous *recession* and growing *unemployment* as well as rapid price *inflation.* See also *trade cycle.*

slush fund. 1. Fund raised by a group of employees to finance an outing or other form of entertainment. **2.** Fund raised for political bribery or corruption. **3.** (Original meaning) Proceeds from the sale of a warship's garbage used for the crew's benefit and entertainment.

Small Business Administration. US Federal Government agency established in 1953 to advise, assist and protect small businesses. The four major areas of assistance are financial, government contracts, procurement management and technical assistance.

Small Business Division of the Scottish Development Agency. Scottish equivalent of the English *Council for Small Industries* *in Rural Areas.* Provides loans and technical and management advice for firms employing fewer than 20 skilled workers.

Small Business Section of the Welsh Development Agency. Welsh equivalent of the English *Council for Small Industries in Rural Areas.*

Small Firms, Bolton Report on. See *Bolton Report on Small Firms.* (UK).

Small Industries Council for the Rural Areas of Scotland. Operates throughout Scotland except for the seven crofting counties, which are covered by the *Highlands and Islands Development Board.* The Small Industries Council provides loans and technical and management advice for firms employing fewer than 20 skilled workers. The equivalent body in England and Wales is the *Council for Small Industries in Rural Areas.*

smoothing, exponential. See *exponential smoothing.*

snake. Or 'snake in a tunnel'. Internal currency system of the *European Economic Community* introduced under the first phase of the Community's plans for progress towards full *monetary union.* Under the 'snake' system the currencies of the member countries are fixed in relation to each other but float as a group in relation to external currencies. Initially at least, however, Ireland, Italy and the UK did not join the snake, preferring to leave their currencies floating separately.

snap reading method. See *work sampling.*

snap time. When a meal or meal break is taken, a term particularly common in traditional industries and manual work. The meal itself may be referred to as 'snap'.

SNC. *Société en Nom Collectif.* See also *Belgian companies.*

Snellen chart. Standard chart used in vision testing, including for *personnel placement* purposes.

social accounting. Economic evaluation of projects assessing and taking into account *social costs.* See *cost benefit analysis.*

social audit. Study of the social impact of company or national policies, including how far they are realising and being affected by social expectations. Such a study may range across the employment of disabled workers, pollution control, utilisation of resources, accident prevention, safety, time lost through *industrial action,* equality of opportunity, employment conditions, and the social effects of investment policies, *mergers, acquisitions, asset stripping,* etc.

social costs. Costs, often difficult to quantify, in terms of effects on social amenities, the lives and happiness of people and such environmental factors as pollution. Taking into account social costs involves *social accounting.*

social drives. *Affiliation needs, ego-identity,* self-esteem, etc.

social investment. Investment in parts of an economy's *infrastructure* that are concerned with social needs such as schools, hospitals and housing.

socialism. Various forms of state or community ownership of means of production, distribution, etc.

social policy, common (EEC). See *common social policy (EEC).*

Social Science Research Council (SSRC). UK organization responsible to the Department of Education and Science for promoting research in the social sciences.

social security. Government measures to give financial assistance to disadvantaged members of the community such as the unemployed, the disabled and the elderly.

Social Security Act 1973. Provided for the introduction for all employees in the UK of the *State Reserve Pension Scheme* by April 1975, except where a Recognized Company Pension (or *RecomPension*) is in operation. The basic purpose of the Act was to provide everyone with a second pension.

Sociedad anonima. Joint stock company under Spanish law. See *Spanish companies* and *Sociedad en comandita.*

Sociedad de responsabilidad limitada. Spanish limited liability company.

Sociedade anonima de responsabilidade limitada. Abbreviated to Lda, Ltd or Ltda. A joint stock company under Portuguese law, formed by either private or public subscription. See *Portuguese companies.*

Sociedade cooperativa. Cooperative, a form of business association under Portuguese law. See *Portuguese companies.*

Sociedade em comandita por accoes. Partnership limited by shares under Portuguese law. See *Portuguese companies*.

Sociedade em comandita simple. General Partnership under Portuguese law. See *Portuguese companies*.

Sociedade em nome colectivo. Incorporated partnership under Portuguese law. See *Portuguese companies*.

Sociedad en comandita. Limited partnership under Spanish Law. See *Spanish companies*.

Sociedade per cotas. Limited liability company under Portuguese law. Such a company must include the word 'limitada' in its name. See also *Portuguese companies*.

Società a Responsabilita Limitata (Srl). A Private Limited Liability Company under Italian Law. See also *Italian companies*.

Società Cooperative. Cooperative under Italian law. See also *Italian companies*.

Società di Fatto. 'Partnership in fact' under Italian Civil Law. It is effectively a partnership though not one bound by a formal contract. See also *Italian companies*.

Società in Accomandita per Azioni. Partnership Limited by Shares under the Italian Commercial Code. See also *Italian companies*.

Società in Accomandita Semplice. Limited Partnership under the Italian Commercial Code. See *Italian companies*.

Società in Nome Collettivo. General Partnership under the Italian Commercial Code. See *Italian companies*.

Società irregolarà. Irregular partnership or Company under Italian Civil Law. It is one where the proper legal formalities have not been completed. See also *Italian companies*.

Società non Azionarie. Non-stock company under the Italian Commercial Code. See also *Italian companies*.

Società per Azioni (SpA). A joint stock company under Italian Law. See also *Italian companies*.

Società Semplice. Private partnership under the Italian Commercial Code. See *Italian companies*.

Societas Europea (SE). See the *European Company* concept.

Société Anonyme (SA). A French, Belgian, Luxembourg or Swiss *joint stock company* in which *shareholders* are liable only to the extent of the capital subscribed (in much the same way as in the UK). In Switzerland an alternative term for Societe Anonyme is *Aktiengesellschaft*. See also *Belgian companies*, *French companies*, *Luxembourg companies*, *Swiss companies*.

Société à Responsabilité Limitée (SARL). A French or Luxembourg private limited company with between two and 50 partners whose liability is limited to the extent of their contribution. Shares are not freely negotiable, being transferrable to third parties only with the agreement of partners representing at least 75 per cent of the capital. See also *French companies*, *Luxembourg companies* and *Swiss companies*. Also known in Switzerland as *Gesellschaft mit Beschränkter Haftung*.

Société Cooperative. Cooperative; a form of business organization under both Belgian law and Luxembourg law. See also *Belgian companies* and *Luxembourg companies*.

Société de Personnes à Responsabilité Limitée (SPRL). A Belgian private limited company in which shares are not negotiable and only individuals may hold shares. See also *Belgian companies*.

Société en Commandité. Or *Kommanditgesellschaft*. A limited partnership under Swiss law. See also *Swiss companies*.

Société en Commandité par Actions (SCA). A Belgian or French or Luxembourg partnership limited by shares, certain partners (the commandités) being liable for the partnership debts while others (the commanditaires) are liable only up to the extent of their participation. No further companies of this kind have been set up in France since 1966, the *Société en Commandité Simple* being officially preferred. See also *Belgian companies*, *French companies* and *Luxembourg companies*.

Société en Commandité par Actions. Or *Kommanditaktiengesellschaft*. A partnership limited by shares under Swiss company law. See also *Swiss companies*.

Société en Commandité Simple (SCS). A Belgian or French or Luxembourg limited partnership. In the French case, some of the partners, the *commandités*, are jointly and separately liable for the debts of the partnership while other partners, the *commanditaires*, are liable only to the extent of their participation. See also *Belgian companies, French companies,* and *Luxembourg companies.*

Société en Nom Collectif (SNC). A Belgian or French, Luxembourg or Swiss partnership where all the partners are jointly and separately liable for the partnership liabilities. In the case of a partnership under French law, partners are liable to the full extent of their personal assets and all partners are formally designated traders or commercants unless the partnership's statutes state otherwise. French law also lays down that the name of the firm be followed by the words 'en Compagnie' and that shares are not negotiable without the agreement of all the partners. An alternative name in Switzerland is *Kollektivgesellschaft.* See also *Belgian companies, French companies, Luxembourg companies* and *Swiss companies.*

Société Interprofessionnelle pour la Compensation des Valeurs Mobilières. Or *SICOVAM;* the clearing house for the settlement of operations on the *Paris Stock Exchange* (or *Bourse*).

Société Simple. Or *Einfache Gesellschaft.* A simple partnership under Swiss company law. See also *Swiss companies.*

socio-economic accounting. Taking social consequences of decisions into account in financial management information and accounting procedures. See *cost benefit analysis* and *social costs.*

socio-economic status. Social grades into which heads of UK households are usually divided (A, B, C1, C2, D and E). The social status implied by these grades, together with the kinds of occupation they cover and the percentage of UK households each represents, are as follows: Social Grade A — Upper middle class, consisting of higher managerial, administrative or professional people, and forming three per cent of UK households. Social Grade B — Middle class, consisting of intermediate managerial, administrative or professional people, and forming nine per cent of UK households. Social Grade C1 — Lower middle class, consisting of supervisory or clerical, and junior managerial, administrative or professional people, and forming 22 per cent of UK households. Social Grade C2 — Skilled working class, consisting of skilled manual workers, and forming 31 per cent of UK households. Social Grade D — Working class, consisting of semi and unskilled manual workers, and forming 26 per cent of UK households. Social Grade E — Lowest levels of subsistence, consisting of state pensioners, widows, and casual and lowest-grade workers, and forming nine per cent of UK households. See also *market segmentation.*

socio-technical system. Approach to *organization development* by the UK *Tavistock Institute* in which the aim is to 'jointly optimize' the conditions for task performance and for the satisfaction of human needs.

soerskatt til utviklingshjelp. Special development tax levied on incomes in Norway to finance aid to developing countries. See *Norwegian income tax.*

soft currency. Currency which is unstable because of *balance of payments* deficits or international speculative dealing and therefore vulnerable to *devaluation.* See also *floating exchange rate.*

soft goods. As *dry goods.*

soft loan. 1. Long term loan, particularly to developing countries at no or low interest rates. **2.** Loan in international trading to be repaid only in the borrower's currency. As this is often impractical such loans are often effectively gifts, particularly in foreign aid program(me)s.

soft sales promotion. *Sales promotion* of a kind that is not concerned with actually making the product itself more attractive — as in the reduced price offers and increased quantities of *hard sales promotion* — but with drawing attention to the product in peripheral ways. The latter might include competitions or *personality promotions* that do not intrinsically have anything to do with the quality or quantity of the product or service. Soft sales promotion is usually a relatively low-cost form of promotion but one that is correspondingly of limited effect.

software. Or *computer package.* The *programs,* codes, etc through which a *computer* is given its instructions, as opposed to the physical apparatus that forms the *hardware* of the computer system. The terms are sometimes used similarly of other types of equipment.

soldiering. Time wasting or *restrictive labo(u)r practices (practises).*

sole trader. Individual trading on his own,

not as a *company, corporation* or *partnership.*

solicitor. UK lawyer and member of the Law Society. See *barrister* and *attorney.*

solus position. Advertisement position in a newspaper or journal that is amongst editorial material and apart from other advertisements. Higher rates are usually charged for a solus position.

solus offer. Offer for sale of a single product or service. Where several products are included in a single offer for sale this is known as a *multiple offer.* An *add-on sale* is one made to a customer satisfied on earlier occasions.

somandsskat. Special *seamen's income tax* in Denmark. It is deducted at source from the wages of seamen employed on Danish ships in lieu of national *income tax,* local taxes, church tax and national pensions contributions. See also *Danish income tax.*

SOP. Standard operating procedure.

SOPC. *Sales operations planning and control.*

South African Association of Chambers of Commerce. Established 1892, has some 120 local *chambers of commerce* affiliated to it.

South African Confederation of Labour (SACL). Central organization for white workers' *trade unions.*

South African Reserve Bank. *Central bank* established in 1920.

South African stock exchanges. Principal two stock exchanges are: **a** Johannesburg Stock Exchange; **b** Cape Town Stock Exchange.

SpA. *Società per Azioni* or joint stock company under Italian law. See also *Italian companies.*

space relations test. As *spatial ability test.*

space selling. Selling space for advertisements in publications.

spacial ability or aptitude test. See *spatial ability (or aptitude) test.*

Spanish central bank. *Banco de España.*

Spanish chambers of commerce. See *Consejo Superior de las Cámaras Oficiales de Comercio, Industria y Navegación de España.*

Spanish companies. Forms of business partnership and company under Spanish law include: **a** Partnership or *Compania colectiva;* **b** Limited partnership or *Sociedad en comandita;* **c** Limited liability company or *Sociedad de responsabilidad limitada;* **d** Joint stock company or *Sociedad anonima.* See also *Spanish stock exchanges.*

Spanish Employers' Federation. *Confederación Patronal Española.*

Spanish income tax. Forms of *income tax* in Spain include: **a** general income tax, or *impuesto general sobre la renta de las personas físicas,* a progressive tax charged on total income from all sources; **b** urban land tax, or *contribución territorial urbana;* **c** agricultural land tax, or *contribución territorial rustica y pecuaria;* **d** industrial tax, or *impuesto sobre actividades y beneficios commerciales e industriales;* **e** tax on earned income from personal work, or *impuesto sobre los rendimientos del trabajo personal;* **f** tax on income from capital, or *impuesto sobre las rentas del capital.*

Spanish stock exchanges. In Spain there are two principal stock exchanges — at Madrid and Barcelona — and two others. The four are **a** *Madrid Stock Exchange* or *Bolsa de Madrid;* **b** *Barcelona Stock Exchange* or *Bolsa de Barcelona;* **c** Bilbao Stock Exchange or Bolsa de Bilbao; **d** Valencia Stock Exchange or Bolsa de Valencia. The Ministry of Finance is responsible for the regulation of the stock exchanges. Each exchange has a Stock Exchange Committee, or *Junta Sindical,* composed of members of its Stockbrokers' Association or *Colegio de Agentes de Cambio y Bolsa.* The official market consists of a cash or *spot market,* or *mercado de contado,* with provision for a forward settlement market or *mercado a plazo.* See also *Spanish companies.*

span of control. Theory of management, derived in part from military experience, that an executive or supervisor cannot operate efficiently if he has more than a limited number of subordinates directly responsible to him. The limit to the number of subordinates varies with the type and level of work. By and large, the higher the level of work, the smaller the number of direct subordinates. The span of control for a *managing director,* for example, may be six subordinates while that for a shop floor supervisor might extend to three figures.

span of managerial responsibility. Treated by *Drucker* as 'the extent to which assistance and teaching are needed' by subordinates. It covers a considerably greater number of subordinates than does *span of control*.

spatial ability (or aptitude) test. Test, used in *personnel selection* etc, of ability to judge and manipulate shapes and sizes, an ability that is an element of general intelligence as well as having a special significance in freehand drawing and technical drawing. Examples of spatial ability or aptitude tests include the *Morrisby Shapes Test*, the *NIIP Group Tests 80A, 81* and *82*, the *NIIP Form Relations Test*, and the *Revised Minnesota Paper Form Board*. See also *psychological testing* and *aptitude tests*.

spatial reasoning (or relations) test. As *spatial ability test*. 'Spatial reasoning test' is a particularly common term in the USA.

special agent. *Agent* appointed to act for his principal in a particular matter. This may be a restrictive appointment, authorizing him to act only within the terms specified or it may be the conferring of special powers which would not apply to a general agent. An agent acting regularly for a principal may be known as a 'general agent'.

special deposits. Monies which UK *clearing banks* are required to deposit with the *Bank of England* with the object of limiting their lending by holding down their *cash ratio* or *liquidity ratio*. See also *legal reserve*.

Special Development Area. Category of Development Area receiving special attention under the regional development policies of the UK. Special Development Areas, *Development Areas* and *Intermediate Areas* are collectively known as *Assisted Areas*. A Special Development Area has more acute employment problems than a Development Area but employers in it are eligible for a similar pattern of *regional development grants*, selective assistance, and training assistance. Special tax allowances are also available together with the *Regional Employment Premium* and the *Contracts Preference Schemes*. The Special Development Areas are concentrated around Glasgow, Newcastle upon Tyne, Cockermouth and north of Cardiff.

special drawing rights (SDRs). Fund drawing rights enjoyed by member countries of the *International Monetary Fund*.

Special Export Services Branch (UK). Part of the *Export Services Division* of the *Department of Trade*, the Branch runs the *Group Export Representation Scheme*.

specialization of labo(u)r. As *division of labo(u)r*.

specific unemployment. Unemployment in particular industries. See also *frictional unemployment*, *full employment* and *structural unemployment*.

speculative risk. Risk inherent in the element of business speculation in a project or enterprise, as distinct from the *pure risk* of such factors as accident, fire, health, weather, etc.

speeders. As *pacers*.

speed test. Type of intelligence test or other *psychological test* in which the sheer number of items or questions answered is a critical factor. See also *power test*.

speed-up. US term for *management* action to force workers to produce goods more quickly.

spin off. Secondary or incidental effects of major technological or social projects. Usually applied particularly to the effects of advanced technological developments, eg aerospace program(me)s, on suppliers and sub-contractors.

split inventory method. As *ABC method*.

split-level investment trust. Or dual purpose trust or segregated trust. *Investment trust* having two kinds of *shares*, income shares paying a *dividend* and capital shares carrying rights to the trust's *assets*.

split-run copy testing. *Advertising* technique for comparing the effects an advertisement has in different media. It is part of *media analysis* and often uses *keyed advertisements*.

split shift. *Shift* divided into two or more periods of work on the same day, an arrangement sometimes operated in, for example, catering.

spoilage. Materials wasted or spoiled during production etc.

spoils system. Where winning candidates in

spontaneous strike

elections reward their supporters with appointments to public office.

spontaneous strike. As *demonstration strike*.

spot market. Where goods or *securities* are dealt in at prices for immediate delivery. In contrast, a *forward market* deals in *futures*, or promises to buy or sell at a future date.

Springer-arbeiter. German term for a worker who is trained in several skills so that he can man any position in an assembly line in the event of other employees being absent. Such an arrangement is invaluable, for example, in an application of *flexible working hours*.

SPRL. *Societe de Personnes a Responsabilite Limitee*. See also *Belgian companies*.

SRA clerical test. Three-part *psychological test* developed in the USA and covering vocabulary; arithmetic; and checking.

SRA mechanical aptitude tests. *Psychological tests* of the *mechanical comprehension* kind originally used with US services personnel during the Second World War. Particular tests in this battery include 'Mechanical Knowledge', 'Space Relations' and 'Shop Arithmetic'.

SRA non-verbal test. *General learning ability test* or intelligence test developed in the USA for use in *psychological testing*.

SRC. *Science Research Council* (UK).

Srl. *Società a Responsabilita Limitata* or Private Limited Liability Company under Italian law. See also *Italian companies*.

SSRC. *Social Science Research Council* (UK).

Staatsbank der Deutschen Demokratischen Republik. *Central bank* of the German Democratic Republic (East Germany), established as such in 1968.

stability/neurosis (spectrum). One of the three spectra on which people are measured in *temperament and personality tests*, the other two spectra being the *convergent/divergent* and the *introversion/extroversion*. In general, individuals at the neurotic end of the stability/neurosis spectrum may present problems. For example, the neurotic introvert is likely to be anxious and obsessional while the neurotic extrovert is likely to be given to aggression and hysteria. Research has shown that an individual's position on

staff status (or conditions)

these spectra can be indicators of degree of accident proneness.

staff appraisal. Use of techniques designed to assess the abilities and potential of employees and how far these measure up to the company's or organization's needs. Used in *manpower planning*, etc. particularly for *white-collar workers*. See also *assessment centre*.

staff association. Form of, usually, *white collar trade union* peculiar to a particular firm and often dominated by it. Also known as staff committee or company union or house union.

staff assurance scheme. *Discretionary endowment pension scheme* designed to provide pensions for assorted small groups of employees in small firms. See *'top hat' pension scheme*.

Staff Central Conference. Final stage in the UK engineering industry's former *disputes procedure* involving *white collar workers*. See *engineering procedure*.

staff committee. See *staff association*.

staff management. Part of 'line and staff' concept derived in some respects from military system. Staff management, broadly, is concerned with the provision of support and professional services (eg accounting, transportation, etc, whilst line management describes those responsible for managing the key operating departments such as manufacturing, quality control, etc. See *line management* and *chain of command*.

staff status (or conditions). Terms and conditions of employment and *fringe benefits* (such as pension and sickness benefit schemes) traditionally associated with executive and, often, *white collar* status. Where both white and *blue collar* workers in a firm enjoy staff status they are said to have *single status*. A characteristic of staff status is sometimes the receipt of a monthly salary, rather than a weekly wage on hourly rates and sometimes at least partly on *payment-by-results*. Clocking-in may also be abolished with staff status, or may be extended to all employees.

In Europe in recent years, changes in legislation, collective agreements and company policies have strengthened the trend towards *single status*. This movement has been greatest of all in the Netherlands.

In general, British and European experience suggests that extending all the benefits

313

of staff status to blue collar workers has the effect of increasing labour costs by about 10 per cent. Managements have sometimes objected to such an extension of staff status on the grounds that it can bring increased *absenteeism* (as a consequence of sick pay schemes) and the loss of the direct incentive of payment-by-results or *performance-linked pay* schemes. On the other hand, of course, in other firms and industries the passing of payments-by-results is not regretted by either management or unions.

Broadly, 15 variables in a staff conditions scheme are: hours per week; method of wage regulation; method of wage payment; interval between wage payment; overtime arrangements; shift work arrangements; holiday arrangements; period of notice; clocking in arrangements; dismissals and redundancy practice; sick pay schemes; pension schemes; ad hoc leave of absence; welfare facilities, discipline, etc.

stag. *Stock exchange* term for a speculator who subscribes to a new issue of *shares* with the intention, not of holding any shares allotted to him, but of selling them immediately at a profit — that is, at a *premium* over the issue price he pays to the company.

stage payments. See *progress billing*.

stagflation. Where *inflation* exists at the same time as limited economic growth or economic stagnation.

staggered working day. Where working hours are arranged to be different from the hours traditionally worked by other firms in the area, usually with the object of allowing employees to avoid rush hour travel. The staggered working day system normally calls for all the employees in a company or workforce or work group to work the same hours. This differs from the *flexible working hours (fwh)* system.

stamina building. Process of building up the performance of trainee operators/operatives to the speed and sustained effort required in the production situation. See *skills anaylsis training*.

stamp trading. Where a retailer gives a small *discount*, not in cash but in the form of trading stamps which the customer redeems for goods supplied by the trading stamp company when sufficient stamps have been collected. Stamp trading began in the 1920s but really got under way in the 1960s.

Standard and Poor. US corporation providing financial and stock exchange data. Publishers of Standard and Poor 500 Index. See also *share index*.

standard costing. Techniques used mainly in *mass production* or *batch production* as a tool of management control. Costs for standard parts of processes are established by *work study* or (less satisfactorily) past experience, actual costs then being checked constantly against the standard costs. Standard costs of *direct labo(u)r* normally involve the fixing of standard times by work study. Overheads or *indirect costs* are normally divided between *variable* and *fixed costs* in relation to volume of production, a point that becomes of particular significance with *marginal costing*. Standard costing gives management the opportunity to control costs, not only by comparing standard costs with actual costs at any particular time, but by using *variance analysis* techniques to monitor variations in costs from one period of time to another. The division of overheads between variable and fixed can be important in variance analysis. See also *budgetary control, contribution* and *break-even chart*.

standard deviation. Statistical term for the most widely used measure of the extent to which figures are spread around the *average*. It is a measure of the variability of a distribution.

standard error. Statistical term for describing the accuracy of survey findings etc using two dimensions for this description. These dimensions are confidence level and confidence limit. For example, the standard error in a particular set of findings may be expressed as, say, 'accurate to within a confidence limit of two per cent at the 90 per cent confidence level'. Statisticians mean by this that they are 90 per cent certain that the true answer lies within two per cent of the survey findings. If a higher confidence level is required it is likely that a higher confidence limit will have to be accepted probably at a higher cost. See also *design factor* and *error*.

Standard Industrial Classifications. Classification by industry, not occupation, used in UK Government Departments and elsewhere for statistical purposes. Phases in with the International Standard Industrial Classification.

standard metropolitan area. *US Bureau of Census* definition of a county or group of counties including a city with a population of 50,000 or more.

standard of living. Individuals' expectations and attitudes about their personal and family quality of life and level of economic prosperity.

standard performance. *Work study* term for the rate of output qualified workers will naturally achieve without over-exertion, as an average over the working day or shift, provided they know and adhere to the specified method and are motivated to apply themselves to their work. See also *work measurement* and *rating scale*.

standard profit. Net amount earned per unit of production in a *standard costing* system.

standard rating. *Work study* term for average rate at which qualified workers will naturally work at a job, provided they know and adhere to the specified method and are motivated to apply themselves to their work. If standard rating is maintained, taking into account *compensating rest* and other allowances, a worker will achieve *standard performance* over the working day or shift.

standards, common (EEC). See *common industrial policy (EEC)*.

standard time. 1. *Work study* term for the total time in which a job should be completed at *standard performance*, allowing for relaxation allowances or *compensating rest*, contingency allowances and, where applicable, unoccupied time and interference allowances. **2.** Local time in any one of the 24 time zones in the world, the time in each being generally one hour different from the next. The mean solar time in a zone is at its central meridian. The standard time at the zero meridian is *Greenwich Standard Time* recorded in the UK. Four standard time zones in the USA are *Eastern Standard Time* (EST or ET) based on the 75th meridian; *Central Standard Time* (CST or CT) based on the 90th meridian; *Mountain Standard Time* (MST or MT) based on the 105th meridian; and *Pacific Standard Time* (PST or PT) based on the 120th meridian. See also Appendix: World Time Zones.

Standard Weights and Measures Division (DI). Provides information for UK firms on weights and measures and on the *Common Market* programme for harmonizing national legislation on technical design and *quality control*.

standby pay. Payment made to a worker for making himself available or on call for work irrespective of whether, in the event, it is necessary to perform the work.

standing committee. Sub-committee of an executive committee or council. It may have defined executive powers delegated to it.

standing cost. As *fixed cost*.

Standing Joint Industrial Council. Or Joint Organization of Employers and Employees. A joint employer/*trade union* body in the UK that is concerned with the negotiation of wages and working conditions and the setting up of procedures for the settling of disputes.

standing orders. Code drawn up by an organization for the conduct of its meetings. Standing orders usually cover such matters as the size of a *quorum*, the order of business, the *rules of debate*, the procedure for moving motions and amendments, methods of closure, any time limits on speeches, voting procedures, and any guidance or rules on the length of meetings. See also *committee procedure*.

Other forms of standing orders include those drawn up for local and national government contracts.

start-up costs. Costs involved in launching a project or enterprise, over and above the normal *running costs* once the project/enterprise is operational. Achieving *break-even point* entails recovering both start-up costs and cumulative running costs.

state flat rate pension. Basic state pension due on retirement to all people making contributions in the UK under the *National Insurance Acts*. Additionally, all people contributing as *employed persons* qualify for either the *state graduated pension* or a pension under an *occupational pension scheme* that is contracted-out from the state *graduated pension scheme*.

state graduated pension scheme. Payable to *employed persons* in the UK in addition to the basic *state flat-rate pension* unless they have joined an *occupational pension scheme* that is contracted-out from the state graduated scheme. In the latter event they receive only the flat-rate pension from the state.

statements (of account). Documents sent to customers, listing all items of account outstanding. They are often treated as the official request for payment.

State Reserve Pension Scheme. Planned for introduction in the UK in April 1975 under the *Social Security Act 1973* except in the case of those firms with a recognized Company Pension scheme (RecomPension), but not implemented following a change of government. See also *pension.*

state university. US university that is part of a state's public educational system.

statistical quality control. See *quality control and reliability.* Statistical techniques, often highly mathematical, are used to obtain the optimum balance between the cost of eliminating faults in a product and the value that has to be placed on a fault-free performance. Normally involves setting standards of inspection based on *random sampling.* Thus, the average family car could be made more reliable but at a production cost that would price it out of its market.

statistical stock control. See *stock control.*

Statistics and Market Intelligence Library. See *DT Statistics and Market Intelligence Library.*

statlig formogenhetsskat. *Net wealth tax* levied by the state in Sweden at a progressive rate on the capital value of individual assets at the end of the year, less the capital value of liabilities on the same date. See *Swedish income tax.*

statlig inkomstskatt. Progressive state income tax in Sweden. See *Swedish income tax.*

Statni banka ceskoslovenska. Czechoslovak State Bank, or *central bank.* Established 1950.

status agreement. *Collective agreement* granting *staff status* to manual workers.

status inquiry. As *credit rating.*

status symbol. 1. Normally prestigious product or services obtained more for the image they create than for their usefulness. 2. Particularly applied to executive offices and *perks*, any items (eg size of office, type of car, etc) which are intended to indicate the seniority or level of an employee.

statutory company, or corporation. *Company* or *corporation* established by government decision to provide a public service. See also *public utility.*

statutory minimum wage. Minimum wage an employer must pay an employee by law. A number of countries have such a law to protect the lower paid and prevent any unscrupulous employer using *sweated labo(u)r* instead of paying a fair wage. See also *poverty trap.*

statutory monopoly. See *monopoly.*

statutory pension schemes. Schemes set up statutorily in the UK for civil servants, employees of the nationalized industries and public services, servicemen, etc.

statutory undertaking. As *public utility.*

stepped cost. *Fixed cost* that remains such until a particular new level of business activity is reached and then changes to a new fixed cost. This might happen, for example, if production is increased to the point where more factory space has to be rented. See also *variable cost, semi-variable cost, mixed cost,* and *break-even chart.*

stepped daywork. As *graded measured daywork.*

stepped increase. Where a *collective agreement* makes different pay awards to different types of worker. See also *tapered increase.*

sterling area. Arrangement which ceased to exist with the floating of the pound in July 1972, whereby a group of countries — the so-called scheduled territories — forming the sterling area were subject to the UK's *exchange control* with other currencies. The sterling area was established in 1931.

Steuerabzug von Aufsichsrats-Vergütungen. Or *retenue d'impôt sur les tantièmes.* A flat-rate directors' tax deducted at source from directors' fees in Luxembourg. See *Luxembourg income tax.*

Steuerabzug von Einkünften bei beschrankten Steuerpflichtigen. Or *retenue d'impôt sur les revenus échus à des contribuables non-residents.* A form of *Luxembourg income tax* consisting of a flat-rate tax deducted at source from specified income of non-residents.

stewardship accounting. General and orderly recording and monitoring of the business transactions of a company or organization, but to a less detailed and sophisticated extent than *financial accounting* or *management accounting.*

sticker. Worker who does not want promotion. Cf *sleeper*.

Stille Gesellschaft. Sleeping partnership under Austrian or Federal German company law. See also *Austrian companies* and *German (Federal) companies*.

Stilling Tests. Form of colo(u)r *vision test*. Like the *Ishihara Tests*, the Stilling Tests are confusion tests in which the person being tested tries to identify letters, numbers or forms printed in colo(u)rs that become confused with the background if his or her vision has a colo(u)r defect.

stimulus. Environmental factor that provokes a *response*.

stinkers. Difficult *piece work* jobs or those with *tight rates*. May also be known as *lean work*. Jobs with *loose rates* on which bonus is earned relatively easily are known as *gravy jobs* or *fat work*.

Stirling Stock Exchange. Provincial UK *stock exchange in Scotland*.

stock appreciation profit. As *stock profit*.

stockbroker. Member of the *Stock Exchange* who acts as an agent for members of the public who pay him a fixed commission for dealing in *stocks* and *shares* on their behalf. Other members of the London Stock Exchange are *stockjobbers* who are wholesalers in particular types of stocks and shares and may not be approached by the public directly, but only through stockbrokers. A transaction between a stockbroker and a stockjobber is a *bargain*.

stock control. Or *inventory management*. Use of management techniques designed to determine and implement the holding of optimum levels of stocks, whether *raw materials stocks*, *bought-out goods*, *work-in-progress* or *finished goods*. Stock control takes into account such factors as the ordering time required by suppliers, the cost of placing an order, the available discounts for bulk purchases, the amount of money and space tied up in stocks, the needs of production departments, type and availability of transport, and *marketing* strategy. Where statistical techniques are used to devise and implement stock control, often with *computer* assistance, this is known as statistical stock control.

stock cover. Length of time present stocks will last if sales continue at the same rate as in the immediate past.

stock exchange. Centre for trading in the shares of public companies. For the stock exchanges of a particular country see under the name of that country.

Stock Exchange (UK). Set up in 1733, before which time the *stockbrokers* and *stockjobbers* of the City of London had done their business in coffee houses (hence the term *waiters* still used of the uniformed attendants of the present-day Stock Exchange). An Act of 1697 had regulated the activities of the London stockbrokers. By the time of the setting up of the London Stock Exchange, Amsterdam, Bruges and Antwerp had all achieved fame as international financial centres. London achieved pre-eminence in this field by the second half of the nineteenth century.

The business of the *London Stock Exchange*, like that of other major stock exchanges, is to provide facilities for the buying and selling of *stock, shares, securities*, etc, the London exchange being noted for its market in *Government securities* through the *Bank of England* and the *Government Broker*. The London Stock Exchange is known to the initiated as the *House*. It publishes a daily official list of share prices, and its Council lays down the conditions to be met to float a company or seek a *quotation* on the Stock Exchange. The London Stock Exchange operates in 20 fortnightly and four three-weekly *account periods* a year, people buying and selling shares being expected to settle their accounts at the end of each period unless they have *contango* or similar facilities. An exception to the account period arrangement is in the buying and selling of *gilt-edged* securities, transactions in these being settled daily.

From 1965 the London Stock Exchange was linked with the Irish stock exchanges and the UK provincial exchanges through the *Federation of Stock Exchanges in Great Britain and Ireland*. From 1973 these exchanges have been linked more strongly as the *United Stock Exchange*. The provincial

From 1965 the London Stock Exchange was linked with the Irish stock exchanges and the UK provincial exchanges through the *Federation of Stock Exchanges in Great Britain and Ireland*. From 1973 these exchanges have been linked more strongly as the *United Stock Exchange*. The provincial stock exchanges in the UK are: **a** Belfast Stock Exchange; **b** Midlands and Western Stock Exchange, Birmingham; **c** Manchester Stock Exchange (administrative centre of the *Northern Stock Exchange*); **d** Leeds Stock Exchange; **e** Liverpool Stock Exchange; **f** York Stock Exchange *(Provincial*

Brokers Stock Exchange); **g** Scottish Stock Exchange, Glasgow; **h** Aberdeen Stock Exchange; **i** Dundee Stock Exchange; **j** Edinburgh Stock Exchange; **k** Stirling Stock Exchange. The *Council of Associated Stock Exchanges* is administered from the Liverpool Stock Exchange.

Stock Exchanges, International Federation of. See *International Federation of Stock Exchanges.*

stockholding cost. *Cost* of holding *stocks* (1), including warehousing, interest payments, etc.

Stockholm Fondbörs. *Stockholm Stock Exchange,* the only one in Sweden.

Stockholm Stock Exchange. Originally founded in 1863 but only really getting under way when the banks were admitted as members in 1907, the Stockholm Stock Exchange or *Stockholm Fondbörs* is the only one in Sweden and the major one in Scandinavia. The Exchange is run by the Stock Exchange Council and purchases and sales may only be made by members of the Stock Exchange or by members' agents, or *börsombud,* approved by the Council. In addition to Stock Exchange dealings there is a similar volume of dealing in securities outside the Exchange, such dealings being subject to the scrutiny of the Riksbank, the State Bank.

stocking agent. Type of *middleman* who provides *warehousing* facilities and handles stocks for which he is often paid a fixed sum retainer. He does not purchase the goods he is selling but receives commission on sales. See also *del credere agent, distributor, merchant, stockist, wholesaler.*

stock-in-trade. 1. Amount of stock held. 2. Type of business normally conducted by an organization, or type of goods or services normally handled.

stockist. Trader who receives trade *discount* and buying terms, and probably *credit* terms, from a manufacturer in return for an undertaking to hold specific levels of stocks of a range of products. See also *del credere agent, distributor, merchant, stocking agent, wholesaler.*

stockjobber. Member of the London *Stock Exchange* who is a specialist and wholesaler in particular types of *stocks* and *shares* who may not deal with the public directly, but only through a *stockbroker.* The latter, also a member of the Stock Exchange, acts as an agent for members of the public who pay him a fixed commission. Unlike the stockbroker, the stockjobber does not receive a commission but makes his living by the profit he makes from buying and selling shares. A transaction between a stockbroker and a stockjobber is traditionally known as a *bargain.* A stockjobber who becomes unable to meet his debts is *hammered.*

stock losses. Decreases in the *value* of *stocks* compared with the price or cost at which they were originally obtained. See also *stock profits.*

stock market chartist. Professional analyst of trends and likely future developments in the market for *stocks* and *shares.*

stockout. 1. No stock available. 2. Cost to a company of not having an item in stock. The costs may be tangible, eg lack of raw materials causes production delay; or intangible eg inability to satisfy customers' orders causes dissatisfaction and lost sales. Stockout costs can be calculated by taking into account stock turnover probabilities and average monthly investment associated with existing stock levels. The object is to strike a balance between these costs and the costs of carrying a larger inventory.

stockpile. Store of materials etc for future use.

stock profits. *Profits* accruing from increases in the value of goods or *stocks* (components, materials, etc) compared with the *prices* for which they were originally obtained. Stock profits are likely to increase rapidly at times of inflation, but so are replacement costs. Stock profits are also known as 'stock appreciation profits'.

stock purchasing. *Purchasing* of components and materials to sustain general stock levels (for example, under *maximum/minimum control*), as distinct from *project purchasing* for particular purposes. See also *stock control* (or inventory management).

stocks. 1. Components and part-finished goods kept in a firm's stores to be used in manufacture at some future date. Stocks include *raw materials, work-in-progress, bought-out goods, finished goods,* etc. 2. Holdings in a company that differ from *shares* only in that they are not normally divided up into units of a prescribed size, though stocks may sometimes be divided up into 'stock units' of a common size.

stocktaking. Checking and listing of all

items held in stock.

stock turnover. 1. Ratio of sales to *stock-in-trade*. 2. Ratio of cost of sales to stock-in trade.

stoppage. Where production or other processes are stopped temporarily as a result of one of the forms of *strike* action. See also *go-slow*, *work-to-rule*, *industrial dispute*, *trade dispute*, *industrial action* and *cut-price industrial action*.

straight-line depreciation. Simple linear method of spreading the cost of a *fixed asset* over its estimated useful life. Consists of dividing the cost, less estimated scrap value, of an asset by its estimated economic life. If, for example, a machine costs £1,200 and has an expected scrap value of £200 after 10 years then the annual straight line depreciation would be:

$$\frac{£1,200-£200}{10} = \frac{£1,000}{10} = £100$$

per annum for ten years. See also *reducing balance method*.

straight yield. As *current yield*.

stranger group. People previously unknown to each other brought together in *group training methods*.

stratification. *Market research* term for the process by which a *population* or *universe* may be divided up (by age groups, for example, or regionally) in devising *samples* for a survey.

(on) stream. In a state of full production, a term used particularly in the petroleum and other processing industries.

(the) Street. Colloquialism for a *Wall Street* in New York; b Fleet Street in London (the centre of the UK press).

street-name stocks. US term for *negotiable bonds* drawn on brokers' houses rather than individuals.

stress interview. *Interview* conducted in a deliberately discordant or hostile manner.

stretch out. Process of getting workers to take on more output or wider responsibilities as operations are mechanized or automated.

strike. Organized and concerted temporary withdrawal of labo(u)r or refusal to work by employees seeking remedy of what they see as a grievance or seeking to enforce a demand. May be an *official strike* with *trade union* backing, an *unofficial strike* without formal trade union backing, or an *unconstitutional strike* which, with or without trade union backing, is in breach of the *agreed procedure* or the *procedure agreement*. The effect of strikes is usually measured in *striker-days* or *working days lost*. See also *cut-price industrial action*, *demonstration strike*, *doomsday strike*, *downer*, *go-slow*, *industrial dispute*, *lock-out*, *negative strike*, *overtime ban*, *perishable dispute*, *primary boycott*, *secondary boycott*, *stoppage*, *sympathy (or sympathetic) strike*, *trade dispute*, *wildcat strike*, *work-to-rule*.

strike-breaker. As *black-leg* or *scab*, but may also mean someone who supplies black-leg labo(u)r during a *strike*.

strike pay. Or *dispute benefit*. Paid by a *trade union* to its members to compensate for loss of income during a strike or other industrial *action*.

striker. Employee taking part in a *strike*.

striker-days. Units sometimes used in measuring the size of a *strike* or strikes, the number of people on strike being multiplied by the number of days the strike lasts. 'Striker-days' is often a more meaningful term than the more common official term *working days lost* (see latter term for reasons).

string diagram. *Method study* diagram representing a workplace layout on which the routes taken by workers and/or materials are represented by string, often of different colo(u)rs.

strip question. As *filter question*.

Stromberg dexterity test. Test of *psychomotor skills* of US origin. It is concerned with both speed and accuracy in making simple judgments and speed of finger, hand and arm movements. See also *psychological testing*.

Strong vocational interest blank. *Interest test or inventory* that has been used in *personnel selection* and careers guidance for some fifty years since first being developed in the USA. The test is used to build up a picture of the interests of a candidate or employee who answers 'like', 'indifferent', or 'dislike' against some 400 activities or topics. The responses given are compared with keys for different occupational groups. See also *psychological testing*.

structural determinants of behavio(u)r. Conditions and environmental factors which shape the attitudes of people and working groups.

structural-functionalist school. Industrial psychology school of thought, particularly strong in the USA, which believes that stability and equilibrium are the norm in society and in industry, and that people from all levels have certain *shared values*. See also *human relations school* and *pluralistic theory*.

structural unemployment. Unemployment arising from long-term, perhaps permanent, changes in demand for products and/or skills. See also *frictional unemployment, full employment, specific unemployment, mobility of labo(u)r*.

student assessment (of staff and courses). Practice (practise) particularly highly developed at US Business Schools of conducting regular surveys of students' assessments, the findings being taken into account for such purposes as staff promotion and course design. Harvard, for example, has developed a six-part assessment scheme for evaluating staff and several other Business Schools have developed and adopted such surveys of students' opinions.

study of values. *Preference* or *interest inventory* developed in the USA in the early 1950s as a *psychological test* of whether a person's personal interests are conducive to high performance in a particular type of work. It seeks to measure six main areas of interest, namely, theoretical; economic; aesthetic; social; political; and religious.

Stuttgart Stock Exchange (Die Wertpapierbörse in Stuttgart). One of eight *German (Federal) stock exchanges*.

subchapter s corporation. As *tax-option corporation*.

sub-culture. Sociologist's term for the values and way of life of a particular group of people (the workers in a particular industry, for example), leading them to have views and attitudes different in some respects from those of the general culture of the country or society in which they live. The existence of such a sub-culture is often particularly marked in industries such as mining where the workers and their families tend to live together in isolated communi-

ties. See also *shared value* and *community integration*.

subject population. As *target population*.

subjective test. Test scored on the basis of the examiner's own judgment of the value of the answers given rather than the less ambiguous marking of an *objective test*.

subliminal advertising. Presentation of advertisements on television, flashing signs, etc at such a rapid speed (measured in microseconds rather than seconds) that they make an impact on the subconscious mind of the viewer without being seen consciously. Subliminal advertising is illegal in many countries because it is in effect a brainwashing technique taking advantage of viewers.

sub-network. Used in *network analysis/planning* to show part of the network for a project in detail. A *summary network* may be used for a general view of the overall network.

subrogation. Where an insurer who has paid a claim for loss or damage to goods takes over the rights of the insured for the purposes of taking legal action against the parties causing the loss or damage.

subsidy. Grant paid to a supplier of goods or services, often by government, so that the goods or services are made available at less than the *market price*.

substantive agreement. Product of *collective bargaining* between management and *trade union* representatives on substantive reforms such as a wage payment system, a disciplinary code, etc. A *procedural agreement* or *procedure agreement*, deals with such matters as *machinery for consultation, negotiating rights*, and certain rights of individual workers.

substantive motion. *Motion* in its amended form following the moving and carrying of an *amendment* or amendments. Before any such amendment the motion is known as an *original motion*. See also *main question*.

successive approximations. Succession of approximately but not exactly correct results or statements that get progressively closer to an exact or definitive result as they are re-calculated. A feature of the mathematical technique of *iteration*.

suggestion scheme (or system). Provision of

a formal channel through which employees at all levels in a company may make suggestions for increasing *productivity* without going through the normal hierarchy. Suggestions are usually posted in boxes in canteens, etc, for consideration by committees consisting of represenatives of both management and workers. Awards are usually made to employees whose suggestions are accepted and implemented.

suite (of programs). *Computer* term for a group of programs.

summary network. Used in *network analysis/planning* to show in general the overall network for a project etc. *Subnetworks* may then be used for the details of the different parts of the project and network.

sunk capital. As *fixed capital.*

sunk costs. US term for costs already incurred or committed to a policy or project which cannot readily be recovered in the event of a decision to cancel.

sunlighting. Taking on a job after retirement.

Suomen Ammattiliittojen Keskusjarjesto (SAK). Confederation of Finnish Trade Unions, established in 1907. It covers some 30 *trade unions* which have approximately 700,000 members.

Suomen Keskuskauppakamari. Central Chamber of Commerce of Finland, established in 1918 and now linked with some 20 local *chambers of commerce.* See also *Finnish Foreign Trade Association.*

Suomen Pankki. Bank of Finland, the country's *central bank*, established in 1811.

Suomen Puunjalostusteollisuuden Keskusliitto. Central Association of Finnish Woodworking Industries, established in 1918. The employers' associations of other Finnish industries come under the *Suomen Teollisuusliitto.*

Suomen Teollisuusliitto. Federation of Finnish Industries, established in 1921. There is a separate *employers' association* for the woodworking industries, the *Suomen Puunjalostusteollisuuden Keskusliitto.*

superannuation. Retirement *pension*, particularly that payable under an *occupational pension scheme.*

superintendent. Usually a manager of a factory, department or division. Seniority varies and in some organizations and countries may be akin to *supervisor,* general foreman or works manager.

supermarket. Retail outlet of more than 2,000 square feet operated on a self-service basis with at least three *check out* points. See also *hypermarket* and *superstore.*

supernumerary. Someone surplus to the requirements of a job or activity, as in *overmanning.*

superstore. Large retail store — but smaller than a *hypermarket* — situated normally on the outskirts of a town. Offers wide range of merchandise including food and household goods mainly on a self-service basis plus car parking facilities and normally has less than 25 check out points. See also *hypermarket, self-selection store* and *self-service store.*

supervisor. Foreman, first line of *management* with responsibility for the work of others. See also *line management* and *staff management.*

Supervisory Board (Aufsichtsrat). Upper part of the two-tier board structure in German industrial firms, being responsible for appointing the lower tier *Management Board (Vorstand).* Workers have a right to representation on the Supervisory Board under the *co-determination law.*

Supervisory Board (Netherlands). From July 1973 workers have had a right to have members on the Supervisory Boards of companies which have a capital of 10 million florins and have more than 100 employees.

Supervisory Studies, Certificate in. See *National Examinations Board in Supervisory Studies.*

supervisory training. Courses and planned experience for supervisors/foremen. See *National Examinations Board in Supervisory Studies, Training Within Industry.*

Supplementary Benefits Commission. Set up in the UK under the Ministry of Social Security Act 1966 to be responsible for payment of non-contributory pensions and benefits. Operates through the *Department of Health and Social Security.*

supplementary training. See *upgraded training.*

supplier credit. *Credit* allowed by a bank etc, to enable an individual or company to invest in the manufacture and/or factoring of goods and services until they are sold. Another form of credit is *buyer credit*.

supply. Availability of goods or services. See also *demand*.

Supply of Goods (Implied Terms) Act 1973. UK legislation making it illegal to include exclusion of common law responsibility clauses in 'consumer' sale contracts. An 'unfair and unreasonable' clause in a business contract may similarly be declared void by a Court under the Act, though the Act is not applicable to the sale of services (as opposed to goods) to the public.

support activities. Term sometimes used of the activities of *indirect labo(u)r* and services that serve, but are not central to, the manufacture of a product etc. See also *staff management*.

support buying. Buying of currencies or commodities by a governmental agency, such as a *central bank*, in order to support or maintain their market position.

supportive leadership. Management emphasis on the building up of good social relations within an organization, a feature of the *human relations school* of thought.

surcharge. 1. *Income tax* term for a percentage addition to a tax. 2. An additional amount added to the usual cost or price. 3 An overcharge, sometimes an illegal one.

surety. 1. Guarantee that loss, damage or default will be made good. 2. Person who makes himself responsible for the activities and/or liabilities of another.

surface chart. Graph on which the area beneath the line drawn through the coordinate points is shaded or colo(u)red, as in the illustration. Such a graph may usefully convey an impression of the scale and movement of the items being plotted. A further refinement where a graph has two or more lines plotted on it is the *band curve chart* or *cumulative band chart* with different types of shading or colo(u)rs between the lines plotted and under the lowest.

surrender value. Cashable value of an *insurance* policy etc.

surtax. Additional tax on income, usually levied in addition to *income tax*, on personal

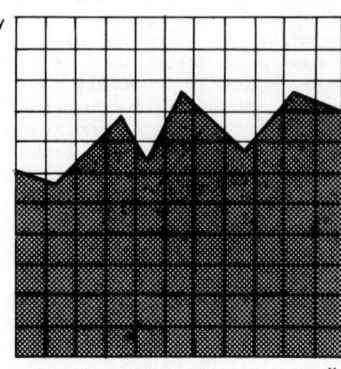
surface chart

incomes above a certain level.

survivorship. Right of a surviving partner or joint owner to the joint ownership of what was previously jointly owned.

suspense account. One in which credits and debits or charges are entered temporarily until they can be allocated to the correct permanent account.

Svenska Arbetsgivareforeningen (SAF). Swedish Employers' Confederation, the central organization for *employers' associations* established in 1902. See also *Sveriges Industriforbund*, the Federation of Swedish Industries.

Sveriges Industriforbund. Federation of Swedish Industries, established in 1910. See also *Svenska Arbetsgivareforeningen (SAF)*, the Swedish Employers' Confederation.

Sveriges Riksbank. Bank of Sweden, *central bank* founded in 1668 based in Stockholm.

svgs. Savings.

SVIB. *Strong Vocational Interest Blank* (as in *psychological testing*).

sweated labo(u)r. Workers who are paid low wages and/or work in poor conditions for unscrupulous employers. Such wages may be in contravention of the law of the land, especially where there is a *statutory minimum wage*. Such working conditions are also likely to contravene health, safety and factories legislation, etc. See also *poverty trap*.

Swedish central bank. *Sveriges Riksbank.*

Swedish chambers of commerce. There are some 12 *chambers of commerce* in Sweden.

Swedish companies. Trading partnerships, limited partnerships and cooperatives are among the forms of business association under Swedish law, but the *joint stock company* is the only permitted form of company based on *shares*.

Swedish Employers' Confederation. *Svenska Arbetsgivareföreningen (SAF).*

Swedish income tax. Forms of *income tax* in Sweden include: **a** progressive state income tax, or *statlig inkomstskatt;* **b** a flat-rate local income tax, or *kommunal inkomstskatt;* **c** a progressive net wealth tax, or *statlig formogenhetsskat;* **d** a flat-rate coupon tax, or *kupongskatt*, on dividends paid by Swedish companies to non-residents and certain residents; **e** a seamen's tax, or *särkild sjömansskatt*, on the pay of seamen; **f** a flat-rate tax on public entertainers; and **g** a tax on distribution of company assets, a tax known as *utskiftningskatt*.

Swedish Industries, Federation of. *Sveriges Industriförbund.*

Swedish stock exchange. See *Stockholm Stock Exchange.*

Swedish Trade Union Confederation. See *Landsorganizationen i Sverige.*

sweetheart contract. Term originating from a US Supreme Court judgment and used of agreements between management and *trade unions* that are of mutual advantage to the signatories but are not in the best and true interests of the workers involved.

swing shift. *Shift* prepared to work variable shift hours to maintain continuity of operation in a factory.

Swiss central bank. *Banque Nationale Suisse.*

Swiss companies. Forms of commercial company and commercial partnership under Swiss law include: **a** Simple Partnership or *Einfache Gesellschaft* or *Société Simple* in which individuals associate for temporary joint ventures other than manufacturing operations; **b** General Partnership or *Kollektivgesellschaft* or *Société en Nom Collectif;* **c** Limited Partnership or *Kommanditgesellschaft* or *Société en Commandité;* **d** Limited Liability Company or *Gesellschaft mit Beschränkter Haftung* or *Société à Responsabilité Limitée;* **e** Partnership Limited by Shares or *Kommanditaktiengesellschaft* or *Société en Commandité par Actions;* **f** Joint Stock Company or *Aktiengesellschaft (AG)* or *Société Anonyme (SA);* **g** Cooperatives. See also *Swiss stock exchanges.*

Swiss income tax. Forms of *income tax* in Switzerland include the following: **a** the federal national defence tax on total income from all sources, a tax known as *impôt fédéral pour la défense nationale* or *Eidgenössiche Wehrsteuer;* **b** cantonal income taxes; **c** communal income taxes mainly charged as a multiple of the cantonal taxes; **d** a graduated tax — the *impôt à forfait* or *Pauschalsteuer* — charged on certain foreigners instead of the national defence tax; **e** a proportional anticipatory tax — the *taxe anticipé* or *Verrechnungssteuer* — deducted at source from dividends, interest, etc. Each of the 25 Swiss Cantons has its own system of tax on income and capital, so have many communes.

Swiss stock exchanges. In Switzerland there are three principal stock exchanges — at Zurich, Basel and Geneva — and five other stock exchanges. The eight are: **a** Zurich — *Effektenborsenverein Zurich;* **b** Basel — *Borsenkammer des Basel-Stadt;* **c** Geneva — *Chambre de la Bourse de Geneve;* **d** Bern — Berner Borsenverein; **e** Lausanne — Bourse de Lausanne; **f** Neuchatel — Bourse de Neuchatel; **g** Coire, where there is a stock exchange of minor significance. The different Swiss stock exchanges come under the control of the governments of the cantons in which they are sited, the canton of Zürich, for example, exercising its control of the *Zürich Stock* governments of the cantons in which they are sited, the canton of Zurich, for example, exercising its control of the *Zurich Stock Exchange* through a *Borsenkommissariat* and a *Borsenkommissar* while the regulations of the Geneva Stock Exchange have to be approved by the Conseil d'Etat of Geneva. The governing bodies of the Zurich Stock Exchange are the General Meeting or *Generalversammlung,* the Board of Governors or *Vorstand,* the Auditors or *Rechnungsrevisoren,* and the Secretariat or *Geschaftsstelle.* A stockbroker is an *agent de change* and a trader on the Zurich Stock Exchange is known as a Borsenagent. See also *Swiss companies.*

Swiss trade unions. See *Schweizerischer Gewerkschaftsbund.*

switch selling. Attracting a prospective customer with an apparent bargain offer but then trying to sell him a dearer product.

SWOT analysis. Analyzing an organization's strengths, weaknesses, opportunities and threats. May be undertaken by group discussion, project teams, *brainstorming* or using the *Delphi approach*.

Sydney Stock Exchange (The Stock Exchange). One of six *Australian Associated Stock Exchanges*.

syllabus. Main heads and topics to be covered by a course of study or instruction.

syllogism. In *decision theory* the logical deduction that where 'a implies b' and 'b implies c' then 'a implies c'. Also called chaining.

symbolic information. Information leading to action in accordance with conventions or arbitrary rules rather than sensory information received by person concerned. Happens, for example, in *computer* programming. Information that is used intellectually rather than intuitively.

symbolic models. Simulation of business or other situations in symbolic or mathematical form (hence *mathematical models*), often with the use of *computers*.

sympathy (or sympathetic) action or strike. Form of *secondary boycott* or *strike* in which workers apply pressure to an employer in sympathy with other workers who are in dispute with that employer. Sometimes, particularly in modern times, sympathetic action may also be taken to bring pressure to bear on an industry or a government.

The right to stage a sympathy strike has generally been regarded as an integral part of the right to strike.

symposium. Meeting to hear and discuss a range of lectures and papers on a particular subject.

syndicalism. Movement, particularly strong between 1900 and 1920, that advocated workers' ownership of industry — and eventually control of the State — and the securing of this by *industrial action*. A prominent movement in France, Spain and the USA (where the very militant Industrial Workers of the World were active) and one that gained considerable working class support in the UK immediately before the First World War and lingered on up to the time of the *General Strike* of 1926. In 1910 the Industrial Syndicalist Education League was formed in the UK, partly as a result of working class disenchantment with the rate of progress in Parliament, though the *Trades Union Congress* rejected syndicalism in 1912.

Syndicalism was sometimes known as *industrial unionism*. See also *guild socialism*.

syndicate. 1. Association of businesses for a specific purpose such as a joint project. **2.** Small group of course students or delegates separated out from the rest of the course in order to undertake a specific project or investigation.

syndicated market research. Where the costs of the research are shared by a number of firms, each of which has access to the results. Syndicated market research is normally organized by a *market research agency*. See also *omnibus survey*.

synergy. Where combining two or more courses of action is more effective than pursuing them individually. In *marketing*, implies that the *marketing mix* will make for overall effectiveness.

synthetic standards (or values). *Work study* term for *standard times* derived from synthetic data such as the *pre-determined motion time system (PMTS)* and *methods time measurement (MTM)*.

synthetic training device. As *simulator*.

Système International d'Unités. See *International System (SI)*.

systems analysis. Analysis of methods required by an organization or system and, usually, use of *computer* in creating and designing solutions. See also *organization and methods* and *systems engineering*.

systems engineering. Design and organization of a complex of resources and devices to perform specified strategies and functions in an optimal manner. See also *systems analysis*.

systems of production. By *Drucker*. See *production systems*.

systems selling. Where a group of products that perform related functions is sold as a package rather than as single and separate products.

t

tachistoscope. Or variometer. Device used in *advertising, sales promotion, market research*, etc in working out the optimum time for displaying an advertisement and/or slogan on television, flashing signs, etc. Subjects or *informants* look into an aperture in the device for the image to be flashed at them for varying times, tests then being made to see which length of time was most effective in getting the message across. See also *subliminal advertising*.

tactics. Detailed plans and approaches to the implementation of decisions and the best way of achieving results.

tactual. Or tactile. Involving sense of touch.

Taft-Hartley Act 1947. US labo(u)r-management relations act concerned with unfair labo(u)r practices (practises), union shops, emergency disputes and cooling-off periods.

tainted goods. Or blacked goods. Products or supplies that have been blacked by a *trade union*. See also *boycott, fair list* and *union label*.

take-home pay. Pay actually received by an employee after adding on *bonus earnings*, etc, and subtracting tax, insurance and other deductions.

take-offs. Effects, good and bad, of using sales agents in export markets.

take-off stage (or period). Term used by some economists for the stage of national *economic growth* following the *traditional society* and *pre-take-off stages*. In the take-off stage the trends towards industrialized society standards of the pre-take-off stage accelerate to a rapid rate of change. See also *drive to maturity*, a later stage.

take-over bid. Where one company attempts to effect the *acquisition* of another by an offer of either *cash* or *equity*. In the case of *public companies*, this involves a public — and occasionally much publicized — offer to the *shareholders*. See also *reverse take-over bid, intermediary holdings, nominee holdings* and *warehousing*.

talking shop. Chatting about one's own business or working activities.

tallyman. 1. Record-keeper. **2.** Tradesman who collects regular, usually weekly, payments from customers without invoicing them or giving receipts on each occasion. The amount paid is usually recorded in a notebook or tallybook.

tangential features. See *product features*.

tangible assets. *Assets* that are real but are not intended for resale. They include land and buildings; plant and machinery; fixtures and fittings; motor vehicles; investments.

tapered increase. Or *pro-tanto increase*. Where a *collective agreement* gives greater increases in pay to the lower paid than to the higher paid, thus tapering the pay difference or *differential* between them.

tap issue. See *Treasury Bills*.

tare. 1. Weight of packing cases or materials. **2.** In freight, the weight of an empty truck or goods wagon.

target. Quantified aim or result to be achieved or bettered within a stated period of time.

target population. 1. Or subject population. Statistician's term for the *total population*, or total number of people or things involved, as defined for the specific purposes of a particular survey etc. **2.** Training Officer's term for the type of student for whom instructional material is devised.

target price (EEC). Under the *Common Agricultural Policy* of the *Common Market* or *European Economic Community*, the *European Commission* sets a target price for cereals which is intended as an average price and is not a guaranteed price. The Commission assists producers to achieve the target price by setting a *threshold price* as a minimum for imports from non-member states and an *intervention price* at which cereal surpluses are bought-in by the Community. See also *guide price, reserve (or fall-back) price, sluice-gate price,* and *export subsidy (or restitution).*

tariff. 1. Or customs duty. Tax imposed on a commodity when it is imported into a country or *customs union.* **2.** Price list or scale of charges.

tariff barrier. Point — eg a national or *customs union* boundary — where a tariff becomes payable.

Tariff Division (DT). Provides information for UK firms on anti-*dumping* and *countervailing duties* and on import licensing.

task. Major element or combination of elements of a *job.* Also see *occupation.* A task may be a continuing element in a job or *role* or it may be a specific responsibility or item of work with a discrete completion point in time. Where a job or role is concerned virtually with one task only it is a *single-task role.* If more than one task is involved, it is a *multiple-task role.*

task analysis. Analysis of a *task* to identify areas of difficulty in carrying it out and to identify the training techniques and learning aids called for.

task-based appraisal. In *performance appraisal* procedures, etc a type of report in which a senior manager comments on a more junior executive's performance in the particular areas of work allocated to him, often by reference to results achieved compared with previously agreed objectives, targets or standards. Other performance appraisal techniques include *free report, controlled report, ranking* systems, *factor rating, forced choice* report.

task-based participation. Forms of *workers' participation* concerned more with organizing methods than participation in management decision-making or policy making. *Autonomous work groups,* for example, are a type of task-based participation. Task-based participation can be said to cover a wide range of activity. There is an element of it implied in *participative management* and supervision, in the work of some *works councils,* in the application of some modern management techniques, and in positive

efforts at making work more interesting through *job enrichment,* etc.

task bonus system. *Payment-by-results* scheme in which bonuses are made on the basis of savings effected.

task description. Statement of activities involved in carrying out a particular task in terms of perceptions, discriminations, decisions, techniques and procedures.

task method of budgeting. *Marketing* term for making budgeting as realistic as possible by basing it on a detailed assessment of the task to be performed.

task orientation. Of management behaviо(u)r or style, the extent to which a manager or group concentrates its attention and efforts towards completing a task.

TAT. *Thematic apperception test* (in *psychological testing*).

Tavistock Institute of Human Relations. UK research and advisory organization concerned with human relations, at work and in the family.

taxable income. *Income tax* term for that part of an individual's income remaining after deduction of outgoings, expenditure and allowances. See also *total income.*

taxation policy, common (EEC). See *common taxation policy (EEC).*

tax avoidance. Or tax planning. Reducing an *income tax* bill by legal means such as ensuring that all expenses, outgoings and allowances are claimed. Attempts at reducing a tax bill by illegal means is *tax evasion.*

tax-credit system. *Income tax* system incorporating *social security* considerations for the lower paid by giving actual cash credits instead of allowances (which are useless to those not earning enough to pay income tax). Under UK *PAYE* an employer collects tax from employees with tax bills bigger than their tax credits but pays the net tax credit to those with bigger tax credits than tax bills.

taxe à la valeur ajoutée (TVA). French *value added tax.*

taxe anticipé. Or *Verrechnungssteuer* or anticipatory tax. A proportional tax de-

taxe communale additionelle

ducted at source in Switzerland from dividends, interest, etc. See *Swiss income tax*.

taxe communale additionelle. Additional local tax. See *Belgian income tax*.

tax evasion. Attempts, successful or unsuccessful, at reducing an *income tax* bill by illegal means such as concealing income or inventing expenses.

tax ferret. US term for government agent employed to track down tax evaders.

tax haven. Country which offers low tax rates and other special advantages to foreign companies. Also known as tax shelter.

tax holiday. Tax relief or exemption granted temporarily. May be used, for example, to encourage industrial development.

taxiplane. Aircraft available for hire for short charter flights.

tax-option corporation. US *corporation* which pays no *income tax* – corporate earnings are taxed instead as partnership income to the shareholders. To exercise the option corporations must have, inter alia, no more than ten shareholders (none of whom can be corporations) and no more than 20 per cent of corporate income deriving from investments.

tax planning. As *tax avoidance*.

tax schedules. Categories of income for *income tax* purposes. For example, in the UK the tax schedules include: Schedule A, income from rents; Schedules C and F, concerned with company and public authority taxes; Schedule D, income from self-employed work, from investments and annuities and from overseas; and Schedule E, income from employment. Schedule B is for certain income from running woodland as a business.

tax shelter. As *tax haven*.

Tax System, Unified. See *Unified Tax System*.

tax year. Normally as *fiscal year*.

Taylor, Frederick Winslow (1856–1915). One of the first to apply scientific methods to solving factory and production problems. He is chiefly remembered for his papers, 'Shop Management' (1903), 'Principles of Scientific Management' (1911) and as father of *work study* and *payment-by-results*.

technological forecasting

TCD. Management technique of *total cost approach to distribution*.

Tea Auctions. UK specialist *commodity exchange*.

teaching machine. *Hardware* of varying degrees of sophistication sometimes used in the presentation of programmed texts.

teamster. Truck or lorry driver, originally the driver of a horse-drawn wagon.

Teamsters. *International Brotherhood of Teamsters, Chauffeurs, Warehousemen and Helpers of America.*

team training. Group training taken to the firm or organization and to work groups already in existence.

Technical Help to Exporters (BSI). In addition to its testing and approvals services, the *British Standards Institution* houses the 'Technical Help to Exporters' service which provides information and advice on meeting overseas statutory and other technical requirements. The Service advises on problems affecting the technical specification of any product for export. It also provides information on overseas national and provincial regulations, on countries where approval systems are operated, and on ways of obtaining approval or certification and at what cost.

technician. Person employed to use his or her skills within a laid down framework, eg dental technician. Traditionally between *craftsman* and technologist in workplace hierarchy.

Technician Education Council. Set up in the UK in March 1973 by the *Secretary of State for Education and Science* with the cooperation of the City and Guilds of London Institute. As proposed in the 1969 Haselgrave Report, the central task of the Council is to plan, administer and keep under review the development of a unified national system of courses for all levels of technicians in industry and elsewhere.

technological change. Process of change in methods and requirements of industry (including labo(u)r and training requirements) as new technologies succeed each other. Interlinked with economic change and *labo(u)r mobility* questions. See also *structural unemployment* and *technological forecasting*.

technological forecasting. Forecasting that

327

attempts to anticipate changes in technology and their likely implications for particular firms and products. Probably the most difficult component in *manpower planning*. Techniques of technological forecasting include *brainstorming*, the *Delphi approach*, *exploratory forecasting techniques*, *morphological research*, *normative forecasting techniques*, the *scenario writing approach*, and *technological trend extrapolation*.

technological policy, common (EEC). See *common technological policy (EEC)*.

technological trend extrapolation. Technique of *technological forecasting* in which projections are made into the future on the basis of historic and present data on a technology or a product.

technological unemployment. Unemployment resulting from the introduction of improved production methods or the displacement of employees by machinery.

technological universities. In the UK the former *colleges of advanced technology* which were granted university status in 1966 on the recommendation of the 1963 Robbins Report. Particularly noted for engineering and technological teaching and research and for *sandwich courses*.

technologist. University (or equivalent) graduate and/or *chartered engineer* engaged on work in technical or applied science fields. See *technician*.

Tel-Aviv Stock Exchange. Israel's only stock exchange.

telebinocular tester. Binocular testing instrument used in vision testing particularly in the USA.

Telefonverkehr. Unregulated and unofficial market for trading in *securities*, on *German (Federal) stock exchanges*. The term arises from the fact that most of such trading is done by telephone. Other markets are the official Amtlicher Markt and the semi-official *Geregelter Freiverkehr*.

teleprocessing. Using *computers* via terminals in various locations for data *input* and *output*.

teleselling. Selling by telephone.

Telex. Telegraph service giving instant printed communications between subscribers.

temp. Temporary employee hired through a *temporary staff contracting service*. One working as a 'temp' is said to be 'temping'.

temperament and personality tests. Usually questionnaire-type *psychological testing*. Can be particularly useful for predicting adjustment to contact-with-people jobs such as management and sales, and for building up a stable workforce. Three spectra on which temperament and personality are measured are the *convergent/divergent*, the *introversion/extroversion* and the *stable/neurotic* spectra. In using temperament and personality tests, an *occupational psychologist* attempts to assess the person being tested according to a combination of the findings on the different spectra. Other forms of psychological testing include *intelligence tests*, *aptitude tests* and manual dexterity tests. See also *test battery*.

temporary exports. Arrangements to send or take goods abroad temporarily without paying *customs duty* for such purposes as showing them as sales samples or exhibiting them at an international exhibition overseas.

temporary staff contracting service. Organization, often part of an *employment agency*, which hires out temporary staff or, as they are commonly known, *temps*. Such temporary staff normally remain employees of the agency itself. Employers often find it necessary to take on staff temporarily to fill gaps made by holiday arrangements or to handle rush jobs. Where a 'temp' hired through a temporary staff contracting service proves so satisfactory that he/she is offered and accepts permanent employment, the employer usually becomes liable to pay the service or agency a fee.

tender, issue by. See *issue by tender* (shares).

tender offer (US). *Take-over bid* in the form of a public invitation to *shareholders* and *stockholders* to tender a price for their *stocks* and *shares*.

Tennessee Valley Authority (TVA). US Government corporation set up in 1933 to build and operate the dams, hydroelectric plants and flood-control installations of the Tennessee Valley.

term assurance. Usual method of paying for *life assurance* etc, the premium being based only on the risk of death during the period covered by the premium. Thus such a premium is lower than that for *endowment assurance* where provision has to be made

term bill

for a capital sum to be available on maturity of the policy. A *convertible term assurance policy* is one that can be converted from term assurance to endowment assurance.

term bill. As *time bill*.

terminal. See *computer terminal*.

terminal arbitration. *Arbitration* agreed to by both parties to a collective agreement as being the final stage in settling a grievance or dispute.

terminal behavio(u)r. Actual behavio(u)r of trainee/student after training. Effectiveness of a training program(me) can be measured by difference between *criterion behavio(u)r* and terminal behavio(u)r.

terminal market. As *forward market*.

terminal qualifications. Qualifications regarded particularly for grant-awarding purposes as terminating education and training required by individual — eg a first degree.

terminal value. Value of a sum of money or *cash flow* at a specified future time allowing for appreciation at compound interest. The difference between present and terminal value is the *accumulation factor*.

term loan (US). Bank loan to be repaid by a particular point in term, often by instalments.

terms and conditions of employment. See *conditions of employment*.

Terms and Conditions of Employment Act 1959. Section 8 provided for compulsory or *unilateral arbitration* based on terms and conditions comparable with those arrived at by *collective bargaining* or the *Fair Wages Resolution*. The Industrial Court could find against an individual employer on the action of a trade union. The Act applied to public and local authorities, as well as to industry, but not to Government Departments.

term shares. Those which cannot be sold for a specified period of time. These shares enable organizations such as *building societies* and *land banks* to operate more confidently and without fear of a sudden outflow of capital. In return, investors are normally paid a higher-than-usual rate of *interest*.

terms of trade. Measure of international trade performance expressed as a ratio derived by dividing a price index for exports by a price index for imports, and multiplying by 100. The ratio is 'favo(u)rable' if it exceeds 100 — ie if export prices have risen relatively more than import prices or alternatively fallen relatively less — and 'unfavo(u)rable' if below 100.

terotechnology. Technology of installation, commissioning, maintenance, replacement and removal of plant, machinery and equipment, using feedback of information. The object is to reduce long term costs and maintenance.

territorial rights. Interests and standpoints of the different kinds of function — for example, personnel, finance, marketing, factory line management, etc — represented by the participants in an *interactive skills* situation.

test battery. Range of complementary *psychological tests* combined to test a wide range of abilities for the purposes of *personnel selection, vocational guidance*, etc. Typical well known test batteries include the *engineering apprentice test battery* developed in the UK by the National Institute of Industrial Psychology and the *USES General Aptitude Test Battery* developed in the USA by the *United States Employment Service*.

test in depth. Accounting/audit term for a detailed check on an aspect of the accounts of a company or organization. A test in depth may take the form of a detailed examination of a particular transaction and its documentation through all its stages. See also *block check, management ratios* and *volume checking*.

test marketing. Launching of a new product in a limited area and in a manner designed to minimize the financial risk of a full-scale marketing operation. The new product may also require *pilot production* arrangements.

test town. Marketing term for a place chosen for *test marketing*.

T-group training. Method of training in human relations using informal roles and climate in a group structured to direct participants' attention to inter-personal events and relations. Participants learn by extending their awareness of their actual and possible behavio(u)r within the group. Other *group training methods* include *group*

SYMBOL	NAME	COLOUR CODING
⌒	search	black
⊙	find	grey
→	select	light grey
∩	grasp	red
⊓	hold	gold ochre
⌣	transport load	green
9	position	blue
#	assemble	violet
U	use	purple
⧣	disassemble	light violet
0	inspect	burnt ochre
⚇	pre-position	pale blue
⌢	release load	carmine red
⌣	transport empty	olive green
ℛ	rest for over-coming fatigue	orange
△	unavoidable delay	yellow
⌐	avoidable delay	lemon yellow
℘	plan	brown

therblig symbols

dynamics, *sensitivity training*, the development of *interactive skills*, and *instrumented laboratory training*. See also *D-group* and *Coverdale training*.

TGWU. *Transport and General Workers Union.*

Thematic apperception test. Personality test of the *projective technique* kind in which the person being tested is presented with a set of approximately 20 pictures that can be interpreted in a variety of ways. The person then has to make up a story based on the pictures. This story is used as the basis for analysis of the person's personality by an *occupational psychologist*. See also *psychological testing*.

theoretical requirement forecasting. Calculations based on projections for future, new situations. Used in *manpower planning* etc. Cf *ratio-trend forecasting*.

theory of concentration. Tenet of Marxism that the larger capitalists gradually take over the smaller capitalists and concentrate power in their own hands.

theory of games. See *games theory*.

Theory X and Theory Y. Produced by Professor Douglas MacGregor in 'The Human Side of Enterprise'. In broad terms Theory X sees the average person as naturally disliking work, lacking ambition and needing authoritarian management, while Theory Y sees man as having a potential for work and responsibility that only fails to be realized through management's failure to harness it. See also *management style*.

therblig. Anagram of *Gilbreth*, its inventor. There are 18 therbligs which are symbols describing types of movements, eg select, grasp, transport, assemble, inspect, use, etc. They are used in *work study* and *motion study* as a simple shorthand for recording complex work operations as in the illustration.

threshold agreement. Agreement between employer and employees whereby increases in pay are awarded automatically whenever the *cost of living index* rises by a predetermined amount.

threshold price (EEC). Under the *Common Agricultural Policy* of the *Common Market* or *European Economic Community*, the *European Commission* sets a threshold price for the import of cereals from non-member states in order to help producers in member states achieve the official target price. See also *guide price, intervention price, sluice-gate price, reserve (or fall-back) price*, and *export subsidy (or restitution)*.

threshold worker. *Employee* beginning his/her first employment.

throw away interview. As *pilot interview*.

thruster. Manager (or organization) which acts aggressively, is dynamic, positive and exploits opportunities. Cf *sleeper, sticker*.

Thurstone temperament schedule. *Psychological inventory* developed in the USA for use in *termperament and personality testing*. It is designed to measure seven different components, namely, vigour (abbreviated to V); impulsiveness (I); activity (A); dominance (D); stability (B); sociability (S); and reflectiveness (R). See also *Guilford's inventories* and *psychological testing*.

tied indicator. Marketing term for a product whose sales performance may be related to the likely future performance of other products. See also *lead/lag method*.

tight rate. Where the *piece work* rate for completing a job, as established by a rate fixer, *work study officer*, etc is of a kind that makes it difficult for a worker to earn *bonus earnings*. In this situation there is a danger that the workers will not even try to earn bonus and will fall back on *day work* level of earnings, to the detriment of production output. This reaction from workers is known, particularly in the USA, as *goldbricking*

time and motion study. See *time study*.

time bill. *Bill of exchange* payable at a specified future time.

time borrowing. See *borrowing time*.

timecard. Card or form on which an employee's arrival ('clocking-on') and departure ('clocking-off') times are recorded, possibly in a manner suited for wages computation. Entries on a timecard are usually recorded by a *time clock* though in other systems entries may be made by the employee himself or by his superior.

time clock. Records or indicates employees' arrival ('clocking-on') and departure ('clocking-off') times, usually by stamping them on *timecards* inserted into a special aperture in the clock.

time loan. One that has to be repaid within a certain period of time.

time note. *Promissory note* or similar document which specifies a date or dates of repayment.

time preference. Economist's term for the relative value to an individual or company of present *consumption* as against future consumption. In broad terms, this is a question of balancing the attractions of the rate of interest to be expected if income is invested against the so-called 'rate of time preference' (in other words, how badly it is needed for present consumption). The resultant of these two forces gives *saving*, or income not spent on consumption.

time rate (payment scheme). As *time-related payment scheme*.

time-related payment scheme. Where pay is related to units of time (eg hours) worked rather than to units of production or other form of output as, for example, in *payment-by-results schemes*. The basic time-related payment scheme is *day-rate*.

time sampling (T-group). Where the instructor/teacher notes at regular intervals of a few seconds which trainee is speaking during *T-group training*.

time-saved bonus scheme. As *premium bonus scheme*.

time series forecasting. Techniques that take into account seasonal ups-and-downs and other fluctuations experienced in the past, and project these findings into the future. A cruder version of time series forecasting is *serial correlation*.

time served worker. Skilled craftsman or worker who has completed a formal apprenticeship.

time-sharing. Where equipment is used for two or more operations concurrently, particularly in relation to a *computer*. This is particularly important in overcoming the problem that the *input device* and the *peripheral equipment* in general cannot operate as fast as the *central processing unit*.

Times 1000. Annual UK publication giving financial and other information on the leading 1000 British companies with appendices on leading companies in major countries.

time span of discretion. Length of time a member of management can be left to get on with his job without needing management decisions from superiors. Technically, time during which marginally sub-standard discretion could be exercised in a *role* before information about the accumulating sub-standard work would become available to the manager in charge of the role (Elliott Jaques). Sometimes taken into account in *job evaluation* and *salary reviews*.

time standard. As *standard time* (1).

time study. Archaic and inaccurate term for *work measurement*, just as time and motion study is for *work study*.

time up the cuff. Where employees on *piece work* record more time than the actual time taken in order to have leeway to be able to book less than the actual time taken on any later job that proves to have *tight rates*. Arranging time up the cuff is a form of *cross booking*.

timework. Work for which wages or salary are paid at *day rate* or *time rate*, rather than on a *payment-by-results* or *performance-related* scheme.

timework rate. As *time rate*.

timework stroke. Level of work or effort expected of worker on *day rate* or *time rate*.

time zones. With *Greenwich Mean Time (GMT)*. as the mean solar time based on the longitude of $0°$ at Greenwich, England, each $15°$ zone east and west represents one hour of time in theory. See Appendix on 'Time Zones'.

TIR Carnet. Transport International Routier Carnet. Using the TIR Carnet system for road transportation, the container or vehicle is sealed by the Customs before export and can then be carried to any customs office destination abroad with a minimum of customs examination and documentation in the countries passed through en route, the intermediate countries waiving the payment or deposit of duties. To qualify for the TIR Carnet system, the goods must be carried in vehicles or containers which have been approved as meeting the TIR Convention's construction and equipment requirements, and which are covered by an approved guaranteeing association. Information on technical requirements of the TIR Convention and on certificate of approval procedures is available in the UK from local traffic area offices of the *Department of the Environment*. The guaranteeing associations in the UK to whom applications for TIR Carnets should be made are the *Freight Transport Association Ltd* or the *Road Haulage Association.*

Tjänstemännens Centralorganisation (TCO). Central Organization of Salaried Employees in Sweden, a *white-collar trade union* independent of the Swedish Trade Union Congress, the *Landsorganisationen i Sverige.* The TCO has some 700,000 members.

tommy shop. Formerly employer owned shop providing goods for employees in place of cash wages. See *Truck Acts.*

Toyko Stock Exchange. One of 9 *Japanese stock exchanges.*

top hat pension scheme. Or *discretionary endowment pension scheme.* Provides especially attractive pension arrangements for senior executives in addition to a company's normal pension scheme. A 'top hat' scheme may be organized as either an *average salary pension scheme*, a *final salary pension scheme* or a *money purchase pension scheme.*

top-out. High point in a *product life cycle* before demand for it begins to diminish.

Toronto Stock Exchange (The Stock Exchange). One of six *Canadian stock exchanges.*

tort. Legal term for a wrongful act against another person which may lead to court proceedings.

total cost approach to distribution (TCD). Management technique, emanating from the USA, used to identify and aggregate the more obscure distribution-related costs as well as the more obvious and commonly recognized distribution costs. Used to arrive at far-reaching cost-cutting, particularly in large and complex organizations.

total cost line. See *break-even chart.*

total float. *Network analysis/planning* term for how far the time for an *activity* may be varied without affecting the total project time.

total income. *Income tax* term for an individual's income after outgoings or expenditure have been deducted from the *gross income* from all sources. Allowances have then to be deducted from the total income to arrive at the *taxable income.*

total loss control. Training and security program(me) designed to reduce and, if possible, eliminate all factors which cause loss, eg through accident and fire prevention, industrial health and hygiene, security precautions, pollution control, etc.

total population. Statistician's term for all the people measuring up to the same specification, such as a common age or educational attainment, as those considered as a *target population* for the purposes of a particular survey, etc. See also *census survey.*

total remuneration concept. Building up the different types of *remuneration* (salary/pay and other benefits) so that the mix of benefits provides a total package which gives the maximum reward and satisfaction to the individuals concerned. Regarded as particularly important for higher paid staff as a means of allowing more choice of benefits and of mitigating the effect of progressive taxation. See also *cafeteria system.*

total retirement benefits. *Pension* and/or lump sum cash benefit payable on retirement under a pension scheme. Where both pension and lump sum benefit are paid the scheme is a *mixed benefits scheme.*

total task/total reward schemes. *Payment-by-results* type schemes in which payment is not directly proportional to output but, broadly, offers a particular level of pay for a particular level of output. For example, *measured daywork.*

Towne-Halsey Plan. As *Halsey Plan,* an early *payment-by-results* scheme.

track record. US term for 'past performance'. Used in *personnel selection,* for example, when talking of an employee's or applicant's working record.

track sheet. US term for *production control* documentation giving instructions on the use and flow of materials in a production line.

trade. 1. A craftsman's *occupation.* Hence 'learn a trade'. **2.** Commercial transactions.

'Trade and Industry'. UK publication providing weekly information on the procedures and progress of the *Common Market* or *European Economic Community.*

trade association. Voluntary association for employers that is concerned with commercial and kindred matters (including industrial training in some cases) rather than with questions of employment and industrial relations. The latter questions are usually the concern of *employers' associations*.

trade barrier. *Customs tariff* or *import duty*.

Trade Bill. US legislation of 1974 aimed at producing 'a more open and equitable' economic order with its trading partners.

trade boards. Established under the Trade Boards Act 1909 as forerunners of the *Wages Councils* in the UK.

trade cycle. Economic pattern, rather than an exactly repeating cycle, that is said broadly, at least in a *laissez-faire* or free economy, to begin with recovery from economic depression or *slump* through *reflation* of the community's *purchasing power* until, with *full employment*, there comes an *inflation* phase in which purchasing power increases beyond the level where it can affect employment and *real incomes* until a boom condition is reached; the downward phases in the so-called trade cycle are then *disinflation*, when price increases tend to be checked, followed by *deflation* and the evils of *mass unemployment* and return to slump conditions.

Trade Descriptions Act 1968. Sets out to ban in the UK 'misdescriptions of goods, services, accommodation and facilities provided in the course of trade' and also misleading information on price. Penalties under the Act include fines of up to £400 and imprisonment of up to two years.

trade discount. Allowance that is deducted from the selling price by a manufacturer or wholesaler for another trader. By this means, bulk dealers can be given a large discount and resell the goods at a lower discount.

trade dispute. Term used particularly in the UK for *industrial dispute*.

Trade Disputes Act 1906. In UK defined *trade dispute* and in effect gave *trade unions* and their officers and members immunity in *tort* from the consequences of *strikes* and other industrial action. The Act made *peaceful picketing* by one or more strikers lawful. See *Rookes v. Barnard (1964)* and *Trade Disputes Act 1965*.

Trade Disputes Act 1965. Introduced in UK to plug the gap in the *Trade Disputes Act 1906* uncovered by *Rookes v Barnard*

(1964), in which case it had been held that *trade unions* did not have immunity in *tort* and could be legally responsible for the consequences of *industrial action*. The 1965 Act restored immunity in tort to trade unions.

Trade Disputes and Trade Union Act 1927. Introduced in UK, in the wake of the *General Strike 1926*, the system of *contracting-in* whereby a trade unionist's *trade union dues* included a *political levy* component only if he contracted positively and in writing to make such a payment. This was the opposite of *contracting-out* introduced by the *Trade Union Act 1913* and later reinstated by the *Trade Disputes and Trade Union Act 1946*. The 1927 Act also made illegal *sympathy strikes* of a scale deemed to be a threat to the Government and the nation.

Trade Disputes and Trade Union Act 1946. Reinstated in UK the system of *contracting-out* first introduced by the *Trade Union Act 1913*, under which a trade unionist could opt out from paying a *political levy* as part of his *trade union dues*. This reversed the system of *contracting-in* introduced by the *Trade Disputes and Trade Union Act 1927*.

trade drive. Sustained program(me) of *trade fairs* and other promotional activity aimed at promoting goods and services usually in an overseas market.

Trade Expansion Act (US). American legislation which protected its own industries by tariff barriers. The expiry of the Act in June 1967 helped to make possible the international *Kennedy Round* of tariff reductions.

trade fair (or exhibition). Event organized to give manufacturers and distributors an opportunity to display and promote their wares.

trade magazine. Periodical dealing with news and developments in a particular trade or industry.

trade mark. Motif and/or wording registered by a manufacturer and used by him to make his products immediately recognizable. A trade mark normally has to be registered separately in each country where it is used. Registration is usually at the same registry as for *patents*. See also *copyright*, *industrial property* and *service mark*.

trade mission. See *outward trade mission*. A trade mission may also be from overseas to

trade name. Name under which a company trades or a product is sold. May be part of a *trade mark*. Cf *business name*.

trade-off. Weighing up the use of alternative approaches to achieve an objective — the purpose is to select the optimum alternative, conceding some points in exchange for other advantages. See *opportunity cost*.

trade promotions. *Sales promotion* aimed at retailers and other distributors by giving them incentives in such forms as bulk discounts and dealer competitions. Promotions aimed at the consumer or ultimate customer are known as *consumer promotions*.

trade reference. Reference provided by a supplier who has traded with a *company/corporation* or person commenting on its/his *credit worthiness*. But see *nursed account*.

trades council. Local council of representatives of the *trade unions* in the locality. Trades councils have direct representation on the *Trades Union Congress* in the UK.

trade society. Early name for *trade union* perpetuated in names of some present-day trade unions.

Trades Union Congress (TUC). Central UK organization of *trade unions* founded in 1868 — at a time when there was still little trade union activity in other countries — to seek legal protection of union funds and amendment of the laws on conspiracy, intimidation, coercion and picketing. At the present time, the TUC covers some 140 trade unions with a combined membership of 11 million. In recent years, an increasing proportion of these trade unionists have been *white collar* workers. TUC activities include applying the *Bridlington Principles* and the *Croydon Procedure* in disputes between unions. There is also the *Scottish Trades Union Congress*.

trade test. As *job knowledge test*.

trade union. Organization that exists to represent workpeople and employees collectively in matters of pay and terms and conditions of employment. It may be a *craft union* or represent workers throughout an industry *(industrial union)*.

Trade Union Act 1913. Principal purpose of this UK Act was to reverse the finding in *Amalgamated Society of Railway Servants v Osborne (1910)* that a *trade union* should not take part in political activities. Section 3 of the Act laid down that the funds of a trade union could be applied to particular political purposes provided there was a separate *political fund* with a *contracting-out* provision available to individual trade unionists not wishing to pay a *political levy*. See also *contracting-in*.

Trade Union (Amalgamations) Act 1964. Eased the way for mergers of trade unions in UK.

Trade Union and Labour Relations Act 1974. UK legislation repealing the *Industrial Relations Act 1971*, including the latter Act's requirements on the registration of *trade unions* and *employers' associations*. The Trade Union and Labour Relations Act restored legal immunities for trade unions and individuals acting in comtemplation or furtherance of a *trade dispute*. It also abolished the National Industrial Relations Court which had been set up by the 1971 Act.

trade union dues. Membership fees for a *trade union*, usually payable or due weekly or sometimes monthly. May include a *political levy* where the trade union member does not go through *contracting-out* procedure.

trade union federations. Formal groupings of trade unions for the purposes of negotiation with employers, *collective bargaining*, etc. Long established trade union federations in the UK include the *Confederation of Shipbuilding and Engineering Unions*, the *National Federation of Construction Unions* and the Printing and Kindred Trades Federation. See also *dual unionism* and *multi-unionism*.

trade union recognition. Traditionally, the extent to which a union is recognized by management, extending to the *representational rights* of *joint consultation* or, going much further, to the *negotiating rights* of *collective bargaining*.

trading down. Policy to achieve high turnover and attract high volume of customers by concentrating on cheaper/lower quality products. May also imply provision of minimum of customer services, eg no credit or delivery facilities. See also *trading up*.

trading on the equity. Borrowing funds to

augment the invested capital of a company in the anticipation of earning higher returns within the business than the interest charges. See *gearing*.

trading post system. Stock exchange term for the practice (practise) at some exchanges – for example, *Wall Street*, Sydney and Melbourne – of transactions in a certain type of security being conducted at a particular meeting point on the floor of the exchange. See also *call over*.

trading profit. Trading revenue minus trading expenses. Profit before tax is calculated by deducting net non-trading revenue from trading revenue. See also *stock profits*.

trading stamps. See *stamp trading*.

trading up. Policy to sell to the 'top end' of the market by concentrating on high quality and high price merchandise supported by high level of services. See also *trading down*.

traditional society stage (or period). Term used by some economists for the first stage of national economic growth, a stage in which growth is limited to the simple advances of basic husbandry and industrial crafts. See also later stages or periods of growth, namely *pre-take-off*, *take-off*, *drive to maturity*, and *maturity stage*.

trainability test. One designed to test a person's potential for learning new skills. Usually such a test is designed to test ability to learn a particular skill (perhaps in the form of a *work sample test*) but it may be designed to test a more general trainability. Has been found particularly useful in selecting older workers for *retraining*. See also *psychological testing*, *aptitude tests* and *personnel selection*.

trainee turnover. Index of training effectiveness and other basic information for designing company training plans.

training adviser. Term sometimes used, for example by some UK *Industrial Training Boards*, for *training officer*, to stress advisory rather than executive role.

training audit. Identification and assessment of the training needs of a firm or organization.

training bay. Area within a factory reserved for training purposes. A sort of halfway house to a training centre. See also *off-the-job training*.

training benefit. See *training transfer*.

Training Centres, Government. See *Government Training Centres*.

training design. Design or policy drawn up by a *training officer* in attempt at getting optimum mix of variables he can control or regulate. Takes into account *cost effectiveness*, etc.

training development officer/adviser. *Training officer* who is competent to give advice, not only at company level, but at regional or even national level.

training device/mock up. Used to enable trainee/student to gain experience of a task or situation without quite simulating real conditions. Cf *simulator*.

training function. Four main steps are normally taken to be: the identification of training needs in terms of jobs and people; the formulation of a training policy for management's consideration; the implementation of the training process using most appropriate methods and aids; and the *assessment of training effectiveness*.

training loop. Process of: identifying training needs; determining training objectives; devising training program(me)s; implementing program(me)s and assessing results of training. With built-in *feedback* at all intermediate stages and final stage.

training module. See *module training*.

training officer. Takes central advisory and executive responsibility for implementing the *training function*.

Training Opportunities Scheme. Took over from the former *Vocational Training Scheme* in the UK. The *Employment and Training Act 1973* brought the Training Opportunities Scheme under the *Training Services Division*.

training plan. Program(me) of training necessary to equip the employees of a firm or unit with the further skills needed to sustain the present and predicted operations of the firm. A training plan may be arrived at following *manpower analysis* and the drawing up of a *job cover plan*. The training plan should incorporate information on the availability of both trainees and instructors at the required times to fit in with the plan, and it should cover costings including trainees' *employment costs* (wages or salaries, insurance, etc), subsistence and travel allowances to trainees, course fees (for external courses) or instructor's time (for in-company training), and costs of materials, facilities and space used for training. From these costs may be deducted the value of any useful production output during training. See also *learning curve*.

training recommendation. Training prescribed by an *Industrial Training Board* in the UK in respect of a particular *occupation* or group of occupations as qualifying for payment of grant.

Training Services Division (TSD). Introduced in the UK by the *Employment and Training Act 1973* as a statutory body coming under the *Manpower Services Commission* and working alongside the *Employment Service Division*. Responsibilities of the TSD include the *Training Opportunities Scheme, Training Within Industry (TWI)*, and coordination of the *Industrial Training Boards*.

training specification. Training requirement indicated by comparison between a trainee's present level of competence and the *job specification*.

training time. Time taken for a trainee to reach the standard of an experienced worker.

training transfer. Extent to which effectiveness of training on a simulator or in training situation transfers to effectiveness on the job. Also known as positive transfer, transfer of training or training benefit.

Training Within Industry (TWI). Mostly two-week full-time or correspondingly longer part-time courses introduced into the UK from the USA at the end of the last war. Now provided by *Department of Employment* Training Officers in-plant or on DE premises. Courses include 'Job Instruction and Communication,' 'Job Relations', 'Job Safety', 'Job Methods', '30-hour Course for Office Supervisors', '30-hour Course for Retail Supervisors', '30-hour Course for Hospital Supervisors', 'Union Job Relations for Shop Stewards', 'Export Office Procedure', etc.

train spot (UK). *Advertisement* displayed in a railway carriage.

transfer of training. See *training transfer*.

transfer pricing. Allocation of costs to divisions, departments or *cost* and *profit centres*. The purpose is to charge out the internal transfer of goods and services in an attempt to cost more accurately movements within an organization and decentralize decision making. The basis of transfer costs is controversial and may be based on actual costs incurred, market prices, *cost plus*, etc.

transhipment. Process of arranging for goods to be handled by more than one carrier. Basically an export term but also used of road hauliers, for example.

Translators' Guild. Branch of the *Institute of Linguists* (UK) consisting of experienced translators and interpreters.

trans-national company (or group). As *multi-national company* (or group).

Transport Act 1968. Extensive UK legislation covering such topics as **a** a new form of carriers' licensing known as operators' licensing; **b** the abolition of carriers' licensing for light goods vehicles; **c** revised hours of work and a new system of recording hours of work. See also *Common Transport Policy (EEC)*.

Transport and General Workers' Union. Major UK *trade union* affiliated to the Trades Union Congress and having more than one million members.

Transport Experts, Consultative Committee of (EEC). See *Consultative Committee of Transport Experts (EEC)*.

transport international routier. See *TIR Carnet*.

transport policy, common (EEC). See *common transport policy (EEC)*.

Treasury. 1. UK government department responsible to the *Chancellor of the Exchequer* for coordinating national economic policy and overseeing public expenditure. **2.** US Department of the Treasury headed by Secretary who is responsible to the President and deals with all Federal fiscal matters.

Treasury Bills. *Promissory notes* used by the UK and US Governments to raise short-term loans either at a fixed price to government departments *(tap issues)* or by tenders invited each week from *discount houses* and *money brokers*, who use the Bills as security in dealing in the money market.

Treaty of Accession 1972. Amended the *Treaty of Rome 1957* to provide for

Denmark, the Irish Republic and the UK to join the *European Economic Community (EEC)* or *Common Market* from 1 January 1973. All trade barriers between the founder states and the newly joined states were to be removed by 1975. The Treaty of Accession also provided for the new member states to join the *European Atomic Energy Community (Euratom)* (originally established by the *Euratom Treaty 1957*) and the *European Coal and Steel Community (ECSC)* (originally established by the *Treaty of Paris 1951*).

Treaty of Paris 1951. Established the *European Coal and Steel Community (ECSC)* among the founder members of the *Common Market*, namely, France, West Germany, Italy, the Netherlands, Belgium and Luxembourg. The Treaty of Paris was signed in April 1951 and became operational in August 1952, the prototype Common Market. The *Treaty of Rome 1957* was to establish the *European Economic Community (EEC)*, and the *Euratom Treaty 1957* the *European Atomic Energy Community (Euratom)*. The three communities were joined by the *Merger Treaty 1967*. The Treaty of Paris, the Treaty of Rome and the Euratom Treaty are the *primary legislation* of the Common Market.

Treaty of Rome 1957. Created the *European Economic Community (EEC)* or *Common Market* with, as founder members, France, West Germany, Italy, the Netherlands, Belgium and Luxembourg. The Treaty of Rome was signed on 25 March 1957, came into force on 1 January 1958 with a period of adjustment leading to complete implementation of the Treaty customs provisions in 1968. The *Treaty of Accession 1972* was to include Denmark, the Irish Republic and the UK in the Common Market from 1 January 1973.

The *Euratom Treaty*, also signed in Rome in 1957, established the *European Atomic Energy Community (Euratom)*. The *Treaty of Paris 1951* had already established the *European Coal and Steel Community (ECSC)*. The three communities were joined by the *Merger Treaty 1967* and were all covered by the *Treaty of Accession 1972* by which Denmark, the Irish Republic and the UK joined the Common Market.

Articles 2 and 3 of the Treaty of Rome state the following objectives: Article 2 — The Community shall have as its task, by establishing a common market and progressively approximating the economic policies of member states, to promote throughout the Community a harmonious development of economic activities, a continuous and balanced expansion, an increase in stability, an accelerated raising of the standard of living and closer relations between the states belonging to it.

Article 3 — For the purposes set out in Article 2, the activities of the Community shall include, as provided in this Treaty and in accordance with the timetables set out therein: **a** the elimination, as between member states, of *customs duties* and of quantitative restrictions on the import and export of goods, and of all other measures having equivalent effect; **b** the establishment of a *common customs tariff* and of a *common commercial policy* towards other countries; **c** the abolition, as between member states, of obstacles to freedom of movement for persons, services and capital; **d** the adoption of a common policy in the sphere of agriculture; **e** the adoption of a common policy in the sphere of transport; **f** the institution of a system ensuring that competition in the common market is not distorted; **g** the application of procedures by which the economic policies of member states can be coordinated and disequilibria in their balances of payment remedied; **h** the approximation of the laws of member states to the extent required for the proper functioning of the common market; **i** the creation of a *European Social Fund* in order to improve employment opportunities for workers and to contribute to the raising of their standard of living; **j** the establishment of a *European Investment Bank* to facilitate the economic expansion of the Community by opening up fresh resources; **k** the association of the overseas countries and territories in order to increase trade and to promote jointly economic and social development.

The Treaty of Rome 1957, the Euratom Treaty 1957 and the Treaty of Paris 1951 are known as the *primary legislation* of the Common Market.

trend. Prevailing tendency such as a sustained upward movement in price levels.

trend bucker. US term for *corporation* whose earnings remain high at times of economic recession when many other businesses are performing badly.

triadic product test. *Market research* term for a *product test* in which *informants* are each presented with three unmarked products, two of which are identical, and asked to pick out the one which is different. With a large enough sample, it is possible statistically to eliminate the guesses made by some informants and to ascertain whether the different product really is different to the *consumer*. See also *diadic product test, discrimination test, Kelly repertory grid.*

trial balance. Book-keeping term for checking whether all the *debit* and *credit* items in a double-entry ledger are in balance.

triangular test. As *triadic product test.*

tribology. Science and technology of the interaction of surfaces by rubbing, sliding, rolling, etc. Tribology includes the design of bearings, the application of lubricants and the environment in which surfaces interact.

Tribunal of Arbitration of the Manchester Chamber of Commerce and Industry. One of three tribunals in the UK that may be used for private arbitration where commercial disputes arise between suppliers and customers, including between UK exporters and overseas buyers. The other two tribunals of the same kind are the *London Court of Arbitration of the London Chamber of Commerce and Industry* and the *City Corporation* and the *Arbitration Committee of the Bradford Chamber of Commerce.*

Trieste Stock Exchange. See *Italian stock exchanges.*

trigger price mechanism. 1. A price level at which certain action is taken. **2.** In the USA a minimum price specified by Government for certain imported goods. If price falls below level set then the US Treasury investigates to ascertain whether *dumping* is involved.

Trinidad Stock Exchange. (West Indies Stock Exchange Ltd). One of two *West Indian stock exchanges.*

Truck Acts 1831-1940. Passed in UK in 1831, 1870, 1896 and 1940, lay down that payment of wages to a workman or artificer must be in current coin of the realm and cannot be subjected to the *tommy shop* system, or have deductions imposed by the employer for damage to goods or materials or for debt to a third person. Certain deductions such as rent can be written into contracts. See also *Payment of Wages Act 1960*, permitting an employer to pay an employee by cheque at the latter's written request. Related legislation covering particular industries has included the *Factories Act 1961*, where it requires particulars of rates of wages to be given to textile employees, and where it prohibits deductions by an employer in respect of anything to be done in pursuance of the Act.

truck farm. US term for farm producing vegetables for market.

truck system. Payment of wages in goods or in kind, rather than in cash.

trustbuster. Government officer concerned with probing and dissolving illegal business organizations or associations.

trust company. 1. *Corporation*, usually a bank, which manages trusts. **2.** An investment trust corporation which invests in a portfolio of other company shares.

trustee. Person entrusted to administer on behalf of others.

trust fund. Cash, *securities*, etc held in trust.

truth in lending law. US statute officially known as *Consumer Credit Protection Act.*

TSD. *Training Services Division.*

TUC. *Trades Union Congress.*

Turin Stock Exchange. (Borsa Valori di Torino). One of nine *Italian stock exchanges.*

Turkish central bank. *Turkiye Cumhuriyet Merkez Bankasi.*

Turkish chambers of commerce. There are *chambers of commerce* and industry in most towns. Their central organization is the Union of Chambers of Commerce, Industry and Commodity Exchange of Turkey.

Turkish stock exchange. See *Istanbul Stock Exchange.*

Turkish Trade Union Confederation. *Türkiye Isci Sendikalari Konfederasyonu-Türk Is.*

Türkiye Cumhuriyet Merkez Bankasi. *Central bank* of the Republic of Turkey, eatablished in 1931.

Turkiye Isci Sendikalari Konfederasyonu-Turk Is. Turkish Trade Union Confederation, established in 1929 and covering some 35 *trade unions* which have approximately one million members.

turnkey. *Computer* term for a *password* which constitutes a security device.

turnkey contracts. Contracts for the provision, control and management of a wide range of services supplied as an integrated 'package' by one organization.

turnover. Or overturn. **1.** The amount of business transacted during a given period of time. **2.** The number of times a particular good or stock of goods is sold during a given period of time. **3.** Total sales income plus any other income from other sources.

turnover tax. Or cascade tax. One levied on the price of a product or service at each stage in the *sales chain* or distribution chain. This differs from *value added tax (VAT)* which is a tax on the value added at each stage (the difference between *inputs* and *outputs*).

tutorial system. Method of instruction in which one trainee/student or a small group of them receive personal instruction and guidance from a tutor or instructor. See also *Keller Plan*.

TVA (Fr). Taxe à la valeur ajoutée — *value added tax*.

twilight area. Urban area in a state of some decay though not to the extent of slum conditions. See also *planning blight*.

twilight shift. Evening shift, usually of 3 or 4 hours, particularly common in light industries. Twilight shift workers are often married women. Sometimes they are people doing a second job in addition to their normal daytime work (such people are sometimes said to be *moonlighting*).

two-bin system. Or last-bag system. *Stock control* system in which there is a reserve bin for each component, withdrawals from this bin being the signal for reordering.

two-tier board. System of West German origin devised to extend employee *participation* in the running of *companies*. A *management board* is responsible for day-to-day senior management but is responsible to a *supervisory board* which includes employee or *trade union* representatives.

two-tier monetary system. Where a country operates two separate *exchange control* sets of rules as part of its strategy to protect its currency and its *balance of payments* selectively. See also *monetary union*.

U

UAW. 1. *United Automobile, Aerospace and Agricultural Implement Workers of America.* **2.** *United Automobile Workers of America.*

UCATT. *Union of Construction, Allied Trades and Technicians.*

UCCA. *Universities Central Council on Admissions.*

UDC. *Universal Decimal Classification.*

UGTAN. *Union Générale des Travailleurs d'Afrique Noire.*

UIL. *Unione Italiana del Lavoro,* one of the Italian confederations of *trade unions.*

UK central bank. *Bank of England.*

UK chambers of commerce. See *Association of British Chambers of Commerce* and *National Chamber of Trade.*

UK employers' associations. See *Confederation of British Industry.*

UK trade unions. See *Trades Union Congress.*

ultra vires. Legal term for 'beyond the powers'. Applied to any action by a company which exceeds its statutory objectives and is not authorized by its *memorandum of association.*

UMWA. United Mine Workers of America.

UN. *United Nations.*

unabsorbed cost. Where *overhead* expenses are allocated to an anticipated or budgeted total volume of production per unit of output (often on a percentage basis) but the expected volume is not achieved so that some overhead costs remain unallocated and under-recovered.

uncalled capital. That part of the *capital* of a company which is authorized but which shareholders have not yet been asked to subscribe.

unconstitutional strike. *Strike* called, with or without official *trade union* backing, in breach of an *agreed procedure* or *procedural agreement.* An agreed procedure, or disputes procedure, usually specifies a system, such as the *engineering procedure* in the UK, through which a grievance should be processed before a strike can be called constitutionally. See also *unofficial strike* (one called without official trade union backing). An unconstitutional strike or an unofficial strike is sometimes known as a *wildcat strike,* particularly if called at short notice.

uncontrollable costs. Those affecting a manager or management's budget and area of activity but outside his or its *discretion* and ability to affect. Thus the management of an individual company may have costs such as group services, *rents,* etc, laid down by the management of the group by which it is owned. Changes in government policies may also introduce uncontrollable costs for management. See also *committed costs* and *managed costs.*

uncovered. Opposite of *covered* in dealings, particularly on forward markets.

UNCTAD. *United Nations Conference on Trade and Development.*

under-employment. Where a person or persons are employed on work of a lower level than that for which they are equipped by ability and/or training. Thus their skills are not fully utilized and they may experience frustration. See also *over-training* and *job satisfaction.*

undermanning. Where a plant is manned or a job performed by too few employees for it to operate at a high level of efficiency. Opposite of *overmanning.*

underwriter. 1. As *insurance underwriter.* **2.** Person or firm that guarantees irrespective of the result of the offer for sale the purchase of the full issue of *stocks*, shares, etc. See also *merchant bank*.

UNDP. *United Nations Development Program(me).*

unearned income. *Income tax* term for income derived from dividends, investments, etc, as distinct from *earned income* derived from employment.

unearned increment. Increase in property value which does not result from any effort or action by the owner. This may happen, for example, where land formerly used for farming is needed by the community as building land.

unemployed person. One who is out of work but seeking employment and likely to be in receipt of *unemployment benefit*. Exact definitions of unemployed person vary from country to country, but in broad terms the essential point is that the person would be working if the work were available. Methods of measuring the number of unemployed persons also vary from country to country. The UK, for example, assumes this number to be simply the number of unemployed registered at *employment offices* while other countries, such as the USA, make estimates of the numbers of people who would be working if possible irrespective of whether they are formally registered as unemployed. The latter approach obviously produces a higher number, particularly of certain types of employee, such as married women, that might not qualify for unemployment benefit by registering as seeking work. In addition to unemployed person, categories recognized for *national insurance* purposes in the UK include *employed person* working for an employer; *self-employed person* working on his own account; and *non-employed person* neither in employment nor seeking it.

unemployment. See *frictional unemployment, full employment, specific unemployment,* and *structural unemployment.*

unemployment benefit. Payment made to a person available for employment to compensate for the fact that he is unable to obtain work and a regular income. See also *unemployed person.*

UNESCO. *United Nations Educational, Scientific and Cultural Organization.*

UNEUROP. *European Economic Association.*

unfair dismissal. Dismissal of an employee in a manner or for reasons deemed unfair and/or illegal.

unfair house (or shop). Where wages and/or working conditions are inferior to those in the industry or locality generally. A term originating in the printing industry.

unfair industrial practices (practises). Practices (practises) such as infringing an employee's right to join a *trade union* and take part in its activities, *unfair dismissal,* conducting or threatening a *lockout,* failure to uphold an agreement, etc.

unfair labor practises. Adjudicated in the USA by the *National Labor Relations Board* under the *Wagner Act 1935* and the *Taft-Hartley Act 1947.*

UNICE. Central employers' organization in the *European Economic Community (EEC).*

UNIDO. *United Nations Industrial Development Organization.*

uniform accounting. Accounting systems tailored to the needs of specific industries or trades and widely adopted by businesses particularly by trade association members.

Uniform Commercial Code. US legal code which many states have adopted for commercial transactions to simplify trade between states having different laws.

unilateral arbitration. Where reference can be made to the relevant tribunal on the application, or with the agreement, of either party (not necessarily both parties) to an industrial dispute. Unilateral arbitration existed in the UK from 1940 until 1959.

Unione dei Comitati Derettivi delle Borse Valori Italiane. Union of the Management Committees of the Italian Stock Exchanges. See *Italian stock exchanges.*

Unione Italiana del Lavoro (UIL). *Italian Labo(u)r Union,* covering *trade unions* with combined membership of just under one million. Other Italian confederations of trade unions are the *CGIL,* the *CISL,* the *CISNAL,* and the *CISAL.*

Unione Italiana delle Camere di Commercio, Industria, Artizianato e Agricoltura. Italian Union of Chambers of Commerce, Industry, Crafts and Agriculture.

Union Générale des Travailleurs d'Afrique

Noire (UGTAN). Body set up in 1956 as a confederation of *trade unions*, mostly in West African countries that were formerly French colonies.

union label. 1. Mark attached to a product to identify it as having been produced by members of a particular *trade union*. **2.** Form of *boycott* by trade unions, particularly common in the USA, is one in which preference is given to goods made by trade union labo(u)r. See also *fair list*.

Union of Construction, Allied Trades and Technicians. Major UK *trade union* affiliated to the *Trades Union Congress*, and formed in 1972 from a merger of the Amalgamated Society of Woodworkers and Painters, the Amalgamated Union of Building Trade Workers and the Association of Building Technicians. See also *National Federation of Construction Unions*.

Union of Shop, Distributive and Allied Workers. Major UK *trade union* affiliated to the *Trades Union Congress*.

union reference. Where a *trade union* or its representatives seek to use a *disputes procedure* or a *grievance procedure*. Such a step by an employer is known as an *employer reference*.

union security clauses. Written into *collective agreements*, particularly in Canada and the USA, to protect the *trade union* concerned from incursions on its authority by either the employer or other unions.

union shop. Form of *post-entry closed shop*.

unique-product production. One of the three major *systems of production* identified and described by *Drucker*, the others being *mass production* and *process production*. He defines the basic principle of unique-product production as 'organization into homogeneous stages' which are self-sufficient entities in themselves and designed to produce a particular product.

unique selling point (USP). Selling feature peculiar to a particular product or service and therefore stressed in *advertising* and sales presentations. A USP should give particular and distinct advantage(s) over competitors' products.

unitary system. Management or other system in which authority is concentrated at a single point. See also *autocratic control* and *Caesar management*.

unit cost. Cost per individual item or unit of production. May be expressed as cost per kilo, per machine hour, per hourly labo(u)r rate, etc.

United Automobile Workers of America (UAW). US labo(u)r union renamed the *Allied Industrial Workers of America: international union (AIW)* in 1956.

United Brotherhood of Carpenters and Joiners of America. US *trade union* established in 1881 and having about 850,000 members.

United Engineering Center (US). Facilities shared by the American Institute of Consulting Engineers, the American Institute of Mining, Metallurgical and Petroleum Engineers, the American Society of Civil Engineers, the *American Society of Mechanical Engineers*, The Engineering Foundation, etc.

United Mine Workers of America (UMWA). Washington-based labo(u)r union with some 277,000 members in more than 1,000 *local unions*. John L Lewis was its president from 1920 to 1960.

United Nations. Officially created on 24 October 1945 with 51 founder member nations, a figure that has now increased to more than 130. The principal objectives of the UN are: **a** to maintain international peace and security; **b** to develop friendly relations among nations; **c** to cooperate internationally in solving international economic, social, cultural and humanitarian problems and in promoting respect for human rights and fundamental freedoms; and **d** to be a centre (center) for harmonizing the actions of nations in attaining these common ends. The UN has such agencies as the *International Development Association (IDA)*, the *International Finance Corporation (IFC)*, the *International Monetary Fund (IMF)*, the *Food and Agriculture Organization (FAO)*, the *General Agreement on Tariffs and Trade (GATT)*, the Inter-Governmental Maritime Consultative Organization (IMCO), the *International Civil Aviation Organization (ICAO)*, the *International Labo(u)r Organization (ILO)*, the *International Telecommunication Union (ITU)*, the *Universal Postal Union (UPU)*, the *World Bank*, the *World Health Organization (WHO)*, and the *World Meteorological Organization (WMO)*. Other UN agencies and bodies have 'United Nations' in their name — eg *United Nations Educational, Scientific and Cultural Organ-*

ization *(UNESCO)*. The UN's *Economic Commission for Europe (ECE)* is situated in Geneva. Other Regional Economic Commissions of the UN are: the *Economic Commission for Asia and the Far East (ECAFE)*; the *Economic Commission for Latin America (ECLA)*; and the *Economic Commission for Africa (ECA)*.

United Nations Capital Development Fund. Established in 1966 to provide grants-in-aid and low-interest capital for developing countries. Associated with the *United Nations Development Program(me)*.

United Nations Conference on Trade and Development (UNCTAD). Established in 1964 to try to counter the problems of the widening gap between the standard of living in developing countries and that in developed countries. UNCTAD held major international meetings in 1964, 1968 and 1972, and has cooperated with the *General Agreement on Tariffs and Trade*, the *International Bank for Reconstruction and Development*, and the *International Monetary Fund*. A major UNCTAD success came in 1971 when, for a ten-year period with annual reviews, the *European Economic Community*, the *European Free Trade Area* and the United States all agreed to give preferences in certain manufactured goods to the developing countries. See also *associated states of the Common Market*.

United Nations Development Program(me) (UNDP). United Nations agency set up in 1965 to assist in the development of developing countries through economic and social projects. See also *United Nations Industrial Development Organization*.

United Nations Educational, Scientific and Cultural Organization (UNESCO). Established in November 1946 with a General Conference of United Nations member states, an Executive Board, and a Director-General and Secretariat based in Paris. UNESCO has developed a wide range of activities in discharging its responsibility to work 'for peace and security by promoting collaboration among the nations through education, science and culture in order to further universal respect for justice, for the rule of law, and for the human rights and fundamental freedoms which are affirmed ... by the Charter of the United Nations.'

United Nations Industrial Development Organization (UNIDO). *United Nations* agency set up in 1967 to mobilize national and international resources for the promotion of industrial development, particularly manufacturing industry in the developing countries.

United States Employment Service (USES). Provides industry in the USA with a national consultancy and publications service on employment, training, selection and related topics. Products of the USES include the *USES General Aptitude Test Battery* used in *psychological testing*.

United Steelworkers of America. Large US trade union.

United Stock Exchange. Formed in 1973 in the UK from a uniting of the trading floors of the London *Stock Exchange*, the provincial exchanges of the UK and the *Irish Stock Exchange*. These exchanges had been coordinated since 1965 by the *Federation of Stock Exchanges in Great Britain and Ireland*.

unit pricing. Policy, often advocated by consumers' organizations, of all competing products carrying a price per common unit (normally either weight or volume; eg x (p) per lb or kilo, or y (p) per pint or litre) so that the purchaser is not confused by the differences in packaging and presentation of competing products.

unit trust. Trust or organization that invests, over a wide portfolio of investments, funds subscribed by the public, in return for which they receive units which represent equal shares in the investment portfolio. The trust undertakes to buy back units from investors when requested. Unit trusts have the attraction of enabling small investors to spread their investment and risk widely. A unit trust subscriber receives his income from his share of the return on the portfolio investment. Unit trusts are run by professional managers who are paid on a percentage basis, the trustees who hold the trust's securities usually being banks or insurance companies. Trusts' activities are regulated in the UK by the *Department of Trade*. Also known as *mutual funds* (US).

unity of command. General management principle that one man can have only one boss.

unity of direction. Concept that one head and one plan for a group of activities having the same objective is essential to effective management.

Universal Decimal Classification (UDC). System of classifying total field of knowledge, derived from the *Dewey Decimal*

Classification (DC), into ten main branches and thence by further subdivisions by ten with increasing specialization. Used by librarians and information services for classifying books and other literature and to a lesser extent for information retrieval systems. See *Classification of Training Information*. See also *information storage and retrieval*.

Universal Postal Union (UPU). *United Nations* agency charged with promoting international cooperation on the development of international postal services. The UPU pre-dates the UN, having been set up in 1924 as the General Postal Union.

Universal Time. As *Greenwich Mean Time (GMT)* or, in Germany, *Weltzeit (World Time)*. See Appendix on Time Zones.

universe. As *total population*.

Universities Central Council on Admissions (UCCA). Central 'clearing house' through which applications for places in all UK universities are processed. Sixth formers state their choice of university courses on an *UCCA* form to begin the selection process.

university-based student. As *college-based student*.

unlimited accounts. Businesses that are eligible for any amount of credit. Large stores and companies with a world-wide reputation often come into this category.

unloading. Slang term for selling goods (usually a large number and often in export markets) at a relatively low price. Usually synonymous with *dumping*.

unofficial shop stewards committee. Type of committee that has come into existence in many firms fortuitously as much as by intent as *shop steward* power has grown at the expense of official *trade union* control, and as *workplace bargaining* has become stronger locally and *industry-wide agreements* have become remote and ineffectual.

unofficial strike (or action). *Strike* not authorized by the *trade union* of the strikers, though possibly organized by *shop stewards* or *unofficial shop stewards committee*. See also *stoppage, unconstitutional strike, go-slow, work-to-rule*. An unofficial strike or an unconstitutional strike is sometimes referred to as a *wildcat strike*, particularly if called at short or no notice.

unpaid dividend. 1. An unclaimed dividend. **2.** A declared dividend not yet paid. **3.** A passed dividend on cumulative shares.

unproductive time. Time spent in manufacturing and other processes in which no effective contribution is made to the end product or service.

unregistered trade union. Under the Trade Union Acts 1871-1964 an unregistered UK union was one not registered with the *Registrar of Friendly Societies*. With the *Industrial Relations Act 1971* the term took on the meaning of trade union not registered with the *Chief Registrar of Trade Unions and Employers' Associations* until the *Trade Union and Labour Relations Act 1974*. See also *registered trade union*.

unsecured creditor. One who is owed money by a company or individual but does not have a guarantee that the money will be recovered. Unsecured creditors can only claim recovery of losses after *preferential creditors* have been paid.

unsocial hours. Term used particularly in UK *prices and incomes policy* for hours of work that do not coincide with the hours worked by most other people and must to some extent interfere with social and family life. *Shift working*, for example, may involve working some unsocial hours. So may employment, whether on a shift basis or not, in certain industries such as hotel and catering, newspaper printing and journalism, public entertainment, etc.

Unsolicited Goods and Services Act 1971. Made it illegal in the UK to send goods or invoices for goods or services where they had not been ordered by the recipient. The Act was intended to protect both industrial firms and consumers against this particular kind of high pressure salesmanship and to alter the earlier legal position, namely, that the onus was on the recipient to return goods received unsolicited or pay for them. See also *Fair Trading Act 1973* and *Director General of Fair Trading*.

updating training. Training to bring skills and knowledge up to date with new processes and materials. Cf *booster training, conversion training, refresher training, retraining, upgraded training*.

upgraded training. Training to give supplementary skills and knowledge to increase versatility and mobility of labo(u)r. Sometimes known as supplementary training. Cf booster training, conversion training, refresher training, retraining, updating training.

upset price. Or *reserve price* or *floor price*. The price below which an item is withdrawn from sale at an auction or public sale.

upstanding wage. As *guaranteed working week*.

UPU. *Universal Postal Union.*

URA. Urban Renewal Administration (USA).

urban plant. US term for the stock of physical assets such as streets, sewers, buildings, etc, which serve the community.

Uruguay Stock Exchange. See *Montevideo Stock Exchange*.

US. See also *'American'*.

usage-value classification. As *ABC method or analysis*.

US Bureau of Labor Statistics. US Government agency responsible for the compilation of employment information and statistics.

US central bank. See *Federal Reserve System*.

US, Chamber of Commerce of the. Established 1912, the Chamber has more than 3,750 member *chambers of commerce*, etc. See also *US Junior Chamber of Commerce* (Jay Cees) and *British-American Chamber of Commerce*.

US Customary System. System of units of measurement derived from the *British Imperial System* though varying from it at some points (for example, in liquid measures). The US Customary System, like the British Imperial System, has the foot and the pound weight as basic units. Both these systems are being superseded in some areas by the *International System (SI)*.

USDAW. *Union of Shop, Distributive and Allied Workers.*

US Department of Commerce. US federal government department concerned with trade and business matters and maintaining field offices throughout the USA. Responsible for a variety of specialist divisions, eg *Bureau of the Census*, Office of Business Economics, etc.

US Department of Defense. US government department which includes the Air Force Department, the Army Department, and the Navy Department, all housed at the *Pentagon* in Washington. Interests of the Defense Department include advanced research projects, atomic and nuclear energy, intelligence, communication, and national and international security.

US Department of Energy. US government department with wide responsibilities in the fields of energy conservation and application. Its agencies include the Economic Regulatory Commission, the Energy Information Administration, and the *Federal Energy Regulatory Commission*.

US Department of Health, Education and Welfare (HEW). Federal department of government.

US Department of Labor. Government department responsible for promoting the welfare of wage earners, administering federal labo(u)r laws, and advising the President on the implementation of policies relating to wage earners, working conditions and employment opportunities. The Department's constituent parts include the *Bureau of Labor Statistics*.

US employers' associations. See, for example, *American Mining Congress* and *National Association of Manufacturers*.

user value. As *existing use value*.

USES. *United States Employment Service.*

USES general aptitude test battery. Battery of *psychological tests* developed by the Worker Analysis Section of the *United States Employment Service*. The battery has 12 tests to measure performance of the following nine types: intelligence; verbal aptitude; numerical aptitude; spatial aptitude; form perception; clerical perception; motor coordination; finger dexterity; and manual dexterity. See also *test battery*.

USGPO. United States Government Printing Office.

US Junior Chamber of Commerce. 'United States Jay Cees', established 1920, and having more than 250,000 individual members. See also *US Chamber of Commerce* and *British-American Chamber of Commerce*.

USP. *Unique selling point.*

USPO. United States Post Office.

USSR central bank. *Gosbank USSR.*

USSR Chamber of Commerce. Established 1832.

USSR trade unions. Central body for USSR *trade unions* is the All-Union Central Council of Trade Unions. It covers some 90 million trade union members.

US stock exchanges. 20 or so major US *stock exchanges* are as follows: **a** American Stock Exchange, New York; **b** New York Stock Exchange (the famous *Wall Street*); **c** Baltimore Stock Exchange; **d** Boston Stock Exchange; **e** Cincinatti Stock Exchange; **f** Colorado Springs Stock Exchange; **g** Detroit Stock Exchange; **h** Honolulu Stock Exchange; **i** Midwest Stock Exchange, Cleveland; **j** Minneapolis St Paul Stock Exchange; **k** National Stock Exchange, New York; **l** New Orleans Stock Exchange; **m** Pacific Coast Stock Exchange, San Francisco and Los Angeles Division; **n** Philadelphia — Baltimore — Washington Stock Exchange, Philadelphia; **o** Pittsburgh Stock Exchange; **p** Richmond Stock Exchange; **q** Salt Lake Stock Exchange; **r** San Francisco Mining Exchange; **s** Spokane Stock Exchange; **t** Honolulu Stock Exchange.

Ustredni rada revolucniho odboroveho hnuti (ROH). Central Council of the Czechoslovak Revolutionary Trade Union Movement, established in 1945. It covers some 24 *trade unions* which have approximately 5,500,000 members.

utility theory. One of the decision theory techniques for calculating acceptable risk-taking in business and project planning. Other decision theory techniques include *games theory, risk analysis* and *sensitivity tests.*

utskiftningskatt. Tax on distribution of company assets in Sweden. See *Swedish income tax.*

V

valence. See *expectancy theory*.

validation (of training). Tests of whether a training programme has succeeded in teaching what it set out to teach (internal validation) and whether this was a realistic training need (external validation). Techniques include written tests, oral tests, observation interviews, subjective reports, and post-training assessment.

Valparaiso Stock Exchange. One of two *Chilean stock exchanges*.

valtion tulovero. State *income tax* in Finland charged on total income from all sources. There are also local, church and net *wealth taxes* and a *seamen's tax*. See also *Finnish income tax*.

value. Sum of money or equivalent a purchaser or user is prepared to pay for a product or service. To be distinguished from the *price* asked for the product or service and from the *cost* to the producer of producing the product or service.

value added. As *added value*.

Value Added Tax (VAT). Tax on consumption levied at each point where goods or services are exchanged in the course of production and distribution until they reach the ultimate consumer. At each stage the tax is levied on the difference between the cost of the *inputs* — that is, the goods or services bought in at the beginning of the stage — and the sale of the *outputs* sold at the exchange point at the end of the stage. Thus, for example, a retailer is taxed on the difference between the wholesale price which is the cost to him and the retail price at which he sells to the consumer. VAT is now the principal *indirect tax* in many countries, including the *European Economic Community*, and in April 1973 was introduced in the UK where it replaced *purchase tax* and selective employment tax. VAT can be either flat-rate and charged at a single standard rate (with certain goods and services possibly exempted) or it may be charged at a variety of rates. Also known as added value tax.

value analysis/engineering. Technique for analyzing design, production and marketing of existing products to ensure that operation at each stage is as economic as possible. Overall aim of technique is to enhance the product's value and/or reduce its cost. Value engineering often more specifically refers to the use of value analysis at the engineering and design and development stage of new products.

value satisfactions *Marketing* term for the satisfactions or reasons that lead a consumer to purchase a particular product or service. These satisfactions include logical benefits, such as product performance; psychological benefits, such as prestige, snob appeal and aesthetic appeal; apparent benefits, such as price/value relationships; and the satisfaction of dealing with a particular company or even a particular salesman.

Vancouver Stock Exchange. (The Stock Exchange). One of six *Canadian stock exchanges*.

variable cost. One that varies virtually directly with the level of business activity and may, for example, be constant per unit of production. A cost that varies only indirectly with changes in the level of activity is known as a *semi-variable cost* (power is likely to be in this category, for example). The opposite of a variable cost is a *fixed cost* that remains constant whatever the level of business activity (this is likely to be the case with rent, for example). A cost that remains fixed until a particular new level of activity is reached and then changes to a new constant level is known as a *stepped cost* (for example, if production is increased to the point where more factory space has to be rented). A cost that has both fixed and variable elements is known as a *mixed cost* (for example, the telephone bill composed of a combination of fixed cost rent and variable cost charge according to usage). See also *break-even point*.

variable expenses. Those that vary with output. Expenses which remain constant regardless of the level of business activity are *fixed expenses.*

variable factor programming (VFP). Management technique involving the use of *work study* to step up the productivity of clerical workers. Provides means of determining the time required to do a given volume of work and then controlling daily work loads. See also *estimate analysis.*

variable working hours. Virtually as *flexible working hours* although sometimes used to describe a less formal system which allows employees even greater freedom of choice in working hours.

variance. 1. Statistical measure of dispersion of a *frequency distribution,* the summation of the squares of the differences between each item and the *arithmetic average* of the distribution and then dividing by the number of items. **2.** In accounting, the difference between budget or *standard costs* and actual costs. **3.** In law, discrepancy between charge or allegation and what is offered or proved as evidence.

variance analysis. Mathematically based technique for analyzing the effect, influence and importance of different parameters in a complex business situation.

variety reduction. Techniques for simplification and cost reduction in design, production, warehousing, etc. Normally implies standardization and rationalization of product range, raw materials and stocks of parts. Variety reduction is usually undertaken periodically by a special project team who study the problem, report on their findings and help to implement the proposals.

variometer. As *tachistoscope.*

VAT. *Value Added Tax.*

VDU. *Visual display unit.*

Vebleu effect. When high level of consumption or affluence leads to increased demand for higher priced products or services.

Veće Saveza sindikata Jugoslavije. Council of the Confederation of Trade Unions of Yugoslavia, covering six *trade unions* which have approximately 3,250,000 members.

vendor rating. Ranking suppliers' performance and reliability in meeting delivery promises, quality standards, etc. See also *weighted-points plan.*

Venezuela Stock Exchange. See *Bolsa de Comercio de Caracas.*

Venice Stock Exchange. Borsa Valori di Venezia. One of nine *Italian stock exchanges.*

Vennootschap onder Firma. General partnership under Netherlands law, a form of business association particularly common among medium size and family firms. See also *Netherlands companies.*

verbal aptitude or intelligence tests. Used in *personnel selection* etc to test facility in the use of words in oral and written communication. See also *psychological testing* and *aptitude tests.*

verbal intelligence test (g(v)). *Personnel selection* and *vocational guidance* test devised as part of the *engineering apprentice test-battery* of the National Institute of Industrial Psychology in the UK. See also *psychological testing* and *test battery.*

Verband Osterreichischer Banken und Bankiers. Association of Austrian Banks and Bankers.

Verbond van Nederlandse Ondernemingen (VNO). *Federation of Netherlands Industry,* one of the two Dutch confederations of employers' associations, the other being the *NCW.*

Vereeniging van Effectenhandelaren (Rotterdam). *Rotterdam Stock Exchange.*

Vereeniging voor den Effectenhandel (Amsterdam). *Amsterdam Stock Exchange.*

Vermögensteuer. Net *wealth tax* on the property of individuals in Austria and in Luxembourg. See also *Einkommensteuer,* the Austrian income tax; and *Aufsichtratsabgabe,* a tax on fees paid to directors of Austrian Companies. In Luxembourg, Vermögensteuer is also known by the French term, *impôt sur la fortune.* See also *Luxembourg income tax.*

Vernon graded arithmetic-mathematics test. Test of mathematical attainment also used as a *numerical aptitude test* in the *engineering apprentice test-battery* of the NIIP. The test is also widely used in the

USA and has sets of problems designed for different age groups, expressing scores in arithmetic-mathematics ages for the general population. See also *psychological testing* and *aptitude tests*.

Verrechnungssteuer. Or *taxe anticipé* or anticipatory tax. A proportional tax deducted at source in Switzerland from dividends, interest etc. See *Swiss income tax*.

vertical integration (or merger). Acquisition, amalgamation, or reorganization of a number of formerly separate companies which extend activities 'back' towards the supply of raw materials, components, etc, and/or 'forward' to various elements in the production, marketing and distribution chain. See *horizontal integration, backward integration* and *forward integration*.

vested rights. Provision in a firm's *pension scheme* that if an employee leaves the firm, even of his own free will, he may retain his pension rights in the form of a *frozen* or *paid-up pension*. See also *continuation option*.

VFP. *Variable factor programming.*

vicarious liability. Where an employer is liable for wrongful acts of his employee which are committed within the scope of his employment.

Vienna Stock Exchange. Or *Wiener Börse*. Originally founded in 1771 as an instrument of government, and becoming an autonomous institution in 1875, the Vienna Stock Exchange was the pre-eminent stock exchange of south eastern Europe at the commencement of the Second World War. All Austrian trading in securities does not have to take place through the Vienna Stock Exchange but the *Winkelbörsen*, or corner exchanges, which have come into being are illegal. The Council of the Vienna Stock Exchange is the *Wiener Börsekammer* and its Councillors are the *Börseräte*. The members of the Stock Exchange do not have to deal with each other through the two types of broker. There are official brokers, or *Sensale*, and free brokers, or *Freie Makler*, who are not appointed officially. The two principal types of market on the Vienna Stock Exchange are the Official Market listed on the Official list and the Regulated Free Market, or *Geregelter Freiverkehr*, for securities permitted on the trading floor but not on the Official List.

Viewdata. Generic term for information systems which call up *computer* held data (normally a page at a time) using the telephone network and a video or television screen.

vigilance men. *Trade union* members responsible for reporting to their unions the emergence of any grievances or potential grievances at the workplace.

Vincent mechanical diagrams test. Mechanical *aptitude test* developed and promoted in the UK with the cooperation of the National Institute of Industrial Psychology. See also *psychological testing* and *aptitude test*.

visible exports. Exports of physically visible goods appearing as receipts in the *current account* of a country's *balance of payments* statement.

visible imports. Imports of physically visible goods appearing as payments in the *current account* of a country's *balance of payments* statement. See also *invisible imports*.

'Vision'. French monthly business magazine published in four languages. Established in 1970.

VISTA. Acronym of Volunteers in Service to America. Sponsored by the US Office of Economic Opportunity, the members of VISTA set out to provide education and training in useful skills for the poor and underprivileged.

visual abilities test. Type of *personnel selection* test designed to test such visual abilities as acuity or sharpness of vision at various distances and the ability to perceive depth.

visual display unit. Part of the *output device* of a *computer* or *word processor* that uses a cathode ray tube to display, in the form of characters or graphs, data from the *central processing unit*.

vital statistics. Statistics relating to births, marriages, divorce and death usually for the whole population of a country.

VNO. *Verbond van Nederlandse Ondernemingen*, one of the Dutch confederations of *employers' associations*.

Voc(test). *NIIP* English vocabulary level test. See *test battery*.

vocabulary test. Sometimes used in *psycho-*

logical testing to discover a person's store of understood words. Such a test often consists of a standard list of words which the subject is asked to define.

vocational guidance. Assessment of an individual's abilities and aptitudes followed by advice on how these may be matched effectively with appropriate education, training and/or occupations. A specialist involved in vocational guidance is the *occupational psychologist*.

Vocational Interest Blank, Strong. See *Strong Vocational Interest Blank*.

vocational orientation. Training to give a realistic appreciation of the nature of various occupations.

vocational training. Training designed to equip the trainee with the skills and knowledge to undertake a particular kind of work.

Vocational Training Scheme. UK Government scheme involving the *Government Training Centres* and a relatively small number of training places in further education and industry. In February 1972, the VTS was changed to the *Training Opportunities Scheme* being brought under the *Training Services Agency* in 1974.

'volenti non fit injuria'. See *voluntary assumption of risk*.

volume checking. Accounting and *audit* term for examining all the accounts of a company or organization in detail. Modern auditing is more likely to be a matter of examining the accounting systems and controls, making a detailed check of only part of the accounts as in *auditing by rotation*. See also *block check* and *test in depth*.

voluntarism. Term used in *industrial relations* of the concept of government non-intervention in relations between employers and *trade unions*.

voluntary arbitration. Where reference can be made to the relevant tribunal only with the agreement of both parties to an industrial dispute.

voluntary assumption of risk. For it to be held that an employee took a risk at work completely voluntarily it must be shown that he expressly admitted that the employer should not be liable in case of accident. In lawyers' language, the doctrine of *'volenti non fit injuria'*. See also *employee's contributory negligence, safe working conditions*, and the *Law Reform (Contributory Negligence) Act 1945*.

Volunteers in Service to America. See *VISTA*.

Vorstand. 1. Board of Governors of the Zürich Stock Exchange or *Effektenborsenverein Zürich*. Other governing bodies of this exchange are the General Meeting, or *Generalversammlung*, and the Auditors or *Rechnungsrevisoren*. **2.** Management board in German companies. See *Aufsichtsrat* and *supervisory board*.

voting right. The right of a shareholder or stockholder to vote in the affairs of a company or corporation. A voting share or stock is that carrying such a right in a particular situation.

VPC (Fr). La vente par correspondance, ie mail order.

Vroom, V. H. Writer on *motivation* who used the concept of *valence* to describe the state in which people express preferences between outcomes. An outcome is positively valent when the person prefers attaining it to not attaining it, has a valence of zero when the person is indifferent to attaining or not attaining it, and is negatively valent when he prefers not attaining it to attaining it. Vroom also studied the role of motivation in work performance and formulated what has been termed Vroom's Law which states that the effects of ability and motivation on performance are not additive but interactive. The relationship is expressed by the formula, Performance = f (Ability x Motivation). Vroom uses this analysis to emphasize the importance of ability concurrently with motivation.

Vuoso classification. Czech system for analyzing and classifying components and equipment and provision of statistics for optimizing machine tool design. Uses a 4 digit code. See also *classification and coding system*.

W

W-2 form. Statutory US form given each year to all employees, showing earnings, social deductions, tax deductions, tax payments, etc. Similar to UK form P60.

wage audit. See *annual wage audit*.

wage drift. Tendency for actual pay to rise above nationally agreed levels. See also *earnings drift*.

wage freeze. Prohibition on increases in wages usually introduced by a government to combat *inflation* as part of an *incomes policy* or *prices and incomes policy*.

wage-price spiral. Vicious circle created by changes in wages and prices which in turn induce further chain reactions of increased wages and higher prices.

wages. Remuneration of hourly paid workers.

wage scale. Levels of wages paid for different types of levels of job within a factory, company or industry. See also *banding* and *job evaluation*.

wages councils. Succeeded *trade boards* in 1945 as bodies reponsible for fixing minimum wages and holiday arrangements in industries where workers had not been able to establish reasonable wages by *collective bargaining*.

Wages Councils Act 1959 (UK). Consolidated earlier *wages council* legislation.

wages drift. See *wage drift*.

wages regulation order. Made in the UK by the *Secretary of State for Employment* by way of statutory instrument after acceptance of a *wages regulation proposal* by a *wages council*. Such an order stipulating a minimum remuneration for some or all of the workers in the industry covered by the council carries both civil and criminal law sanctions against an erring employer.

wages regulation proposal. Made by a *Wages Council* to the *Secretary of State for Employment* (UK) in respect of the minimum remuneration of all or some of the workers in the industry covered by the council. In normal times, the Secretary of State either accepts the proposal and introduces a *wages regulation* order or he refers it back to the council, but if the council sends it back unchanged, the Secretary of State must translate it into a wages regulation order. A wages regulation proposal cannot cover *conditions of employment*. A wages regulation proposed may be overridden in times of *incomes policy*.

Wages Stabilization Board (US). US Government agency charged with monitoring movements in levels of wage payment.

wage structure. Interrelationship of the levels of pay of the different kinds and types of employee in an organization or industry.

wage-work bargaining. *Collective bargaining* that takes working performance into account, as with *effort bargaining*.

wageworker. Employee receiving wages rather than salary. More likely to be a *blue collar worker* than a *white collar worker*.

Wagner Act 1935 (US). Basic US labo(u)r legislation that advocated recognition of trade unions and *collective bargaining*. Indeed, it was based on the thesis that the denial of such recognition provoked bad industrial relations. See also *Taft-Hartley Act* (US).

'waiters'. Name given to the uniformed attendants at the London *Stock Exchange*. Origin of the name dates back to the days when *stockbrokers* and *stockjobbers* used to meet in coffee houses before their Stock Exchange was opened in 1773. The present stock exchange was opened 200 years later.

waiting-line theory. As *queueing theory*.

waiting time. When a worker is available but prevented from working by such events as machinery breakdown and *machine idle time*.

Wales Tourist Board. Based in Cardiff. See also *English Tourist Board* and *Scottish Tourist Board*.

walking delegate. Term used particularly in the USA for a *trade union* officer appointed to deal with *local unions* or to represent the union in dealing with employers.

Wall Street. Term sometimes used to mean the New York banking and financial world, particularly New York *Stock Exchange*. Wall Street is the main street of New York's financial district.

want. Economist's term for what would be a *demand* for a product or service but for the fact that the possessor of the want lacks the purchasing power to translate it into a real demand.

warehousing. 1. Physical storage of goods in a *warehouse* etc. **2.** Where nominee holdings in a company's shares are built up anonymously, perhaps in preparation for a takeover battle. See also *insider dealing*.

WASP. 1. *Workshop Analysis and Scheduling Programming.* **2.** White Anglo-Saxon Protestant (US).

wastage. Proportion of employees, actual or predicted, leaving an employing organization or type or category of employment. See also *natural wastage*.

wastage rate. Percentages of particular kinds of employee leaving an employing organization during a particular period, usually a year. Effective analysis and understanding of wastage rates are necessary to develop policies on recruitment, promotion, deployment, training and career progression within organizations.

Water Supply Industry Training Board. Established in the UK in June 1965 under the *Industrial Training Act 1964*.

waybill (WB). Statement of the goods in a shipment together with shipping instructions.

WB (or wb). 1. *Waybill.* **2.** *Weather Bureau* (US).

WCL. *World Confederation of Labo(u)r.*

wealth tax. Tax in many countries on the wealth held by an individual in the form of property, investments, cash, etc. It is usually expressed as a 'net wealth tax', that is a tax on the wealth held above a certain figure allowable before tax. See also *income tax* and *capital transfer tax*.

Weather Bureau (WB). Part of the *US Department of Commerce* responsible for assembling meteorological data.

Weber's Law. For a salary structure to have uniform incentive value the salary levels should increase in geometric proportions.

Wechsel (Ger). *Bill of exchange.*

weighted application blank. Form containing scales specially devised to assist in making preliminary assessments of written applications for a vacant appointment. A *personnel selection* tool developed in the USA and weighted or keyed on the evidence of the performance of applicants employed previously in similar appointments.

weighted average. Measure of the arithmetic mean in which the relative importance of each item is taken into account. Each item is multiplied by a number to give due weight to its importance — the sum of the products is divided by the sum of the 'weights'.

weighted-points plan. Method of evaluating suppliers by rating service, quality, price, etc and weighting this according to their relative importance to the buyer. See also *vendor rating*.

weighted sample. *Market research* etc term for a sample with a specific bias, rather than *random sampling*.

Weights and Measures Act 1963. UK legislation laying down that the weights of all pre-packed and packaged goods must be declared.

Weights and Measures Division, Standard (DI). See *Standard Weights and Measures Division (DI)*.

welch. As *welsh*.

Wellington Stock Exchange. One of five *New Zealand stock exchanges*.

welsh (or welch). To fail to meet a debt or obligation.

Weltzeit (World Time). German equivalent

of *Greenwich Mean Time (GMT)* or *Universal Time*. See Appendix: Time Zones.

Wertpapiersteuer. Securities tax on bonds when they are issued for the first time on the *Vienna Stock Exchange*. There is also a company capitalization tax, or *Gesellschaftsteuer*, on the initial acquisition of *shares* in Austrian companies. After the initial appearance of securities there is a Stock Exchange Turnover Tax on further dealings in them.

Wesman personnel classification test. *Mental ability* or *intelligence test* developed in the USA and including both analog(ue)-type questions (eg 'x' is to water as eat is to 'y', the testee having to fill in 'x' or 'y' from lists of alternatives) and arithmetical computations. See also *psychological testing*.

Western European Union (WEU). Established in May 1955, taking over from the *Brussels Treaty Organization*. Member states are Belgium, France, West Germany, Italy, Luxembourg, the Netherlands, and the UK. The WEU has a council of Foreign Ministers, an Armaments Control Agency and a joint Standing Armaments Committee with the *North Atlantic Treaty Organization*. The WEU also participates in the Consultative Assembly of the Council of Europe.

West Indian stock exchanges. There are two stock exchanges: **a** Jamaica; **b** Trinidad.

wet money. Special additional pay allowance for working in wet conditions.

WEU. *Western European Union.*

WFTU. *World Federation of Trade Unions.*

wheeler-dealing. Colloquialism for the practice (practise) of driving bargains according to commercial opportunity and without regard for ethical or moral considerations. A person who acts in this way is a wheeler-dealer.

whips. Fast workers introduced by management to set a hot pace for other workers. See also *pacers*.

white collar trade union. *Trade union* representing non-manual workers, often with staff status, or even members of management. An increasingly common form of trade union as white collar workers find themselves with less *job security* and as they form an increasingly large proportion of the total workforce in many countries. Some manual worker or *blue collar trade unions* have developed white collar offshoots.

white collar workers. Non-manual employees, normally excluding those in managerial grades though members of management and white collar workers are coming closer together in some ways through the development of *management trade unions*. Manual workers are sometimes known as *blue collar workers*, particularly in the USA. White collar workers usually enjoy *staff status* of some kind and in many firms this is gradually being extended to blue collar workers. There are also the so-called *grey area occupations* in an often ambiguous position between blue collar and white collar status.

'white' land. Building development and planning term in the UK for land not included in current development plans or planning permission.

Whitley Committee on the Relations of Employers and Employed 1916-17. Set up in the UK in 1916 under J H Whitley, Speaker of the House of Commons, the Committee reported in 1917. Led to the setting up of *Joint Industrial Councils (Whitley Councils)* and of *Joint Works Committees (Whitley Committees)*. It was believed that the setting up of such Councils and Committees would allay demands for *syndicalism* and *workers' control*. It was intended that these Councils and Committees of employers and employees would be concerned with wages, conditions of employment, industrial efficiency and management. In the event, Whitley Councils became established only in Government employment, for example in the Post Office, the Civil Service and the Royal Dockyards, where they gave an impetus to *collective bargaining*.

Whitley recommendations that there should be a permanent court of arbitration and that the Minister of Labour should have greater powers to enquire into *trade disputes* led to the *Industrial Courts Act 1919*. Whitley also recommended the statutory regulation of wages in industries where there was no collective bargaining (see also *wages councils*).

Whitley Councils. See *Whitley Committee on the Relations of Employers and Employed*.

WHO. *World Health Organization.*

whole-job ranking. *Job grading* technique which consists of making a series of paired comparisons, comparing each job with each of the other jobs to be graded until a rank order is built up right across the range of jobs. The pairs are compared by such yardsticks as which has the greater responsibilities, which has the greater impact on the company, etc.

whole life assurance policy. Where the sum assured is payable on death only. Differs from an *endowment assurance policy*, the essence of which is that the sum assured is payable at the end of a fixed period if the insured is still alive. An employer may take out a *group life assurance policy* on a number of employees.

whole method. Where an operation or a course is not divided into parts for training purposes but is learned as a whole. Cf. *cumulative* and *progressive part method*.

Wholesale Price Index. 1. Published in the UK by the *Department of Trade*. See also *Retail Price Index* (UK) and *BLS Consumer Price Index* (US). **2.** US monthly index computed and published by the *US Bureau of Labor Statistics*.

wholesaler. *Middleman* buying, stocking and re-selling goods without having a special relationship with particular suppliers. The wholesaler normally provides the facilities of a forward warehouse and information and advice to retailers, breaks bulk quantities, and offers a delivery service. See also *del credere agent, distributor, merchant, stocking agent, stockist*.

Widow's Allowance(s) (UK). Payable under the *National Insurance Acts* for the first 26 weeks after the husband's death, if the widow is under 60 at the time and the husband has not already retired. She may also receive a Widow's Supplementary Allowance if her husband has been paying National Insurance contributions as an employed person. After the six-month period she may then qualify for the Widow's Pension, for the Widowed Mothers' Allowance, and/or for the Widowed Mother's Personal Allowance. Further allowances may also be available from the *Supplementary Benefits Commission*. Up-to-date information on all allowances is available from offices of the *Department of Health and Social Security*.

widows and dependants' lump sum death benefits. See *group life assurance policy*.

widows' and orphans' pension scheme. Provides pensions for widows and dependants of employees who die before retirement. It may be based on a pension of about one quarter of salary or a proportion of the employee's expected pension, this being particularly common where the employee was on a flat-rate *works pension scheme*. Sometimes a widows' and orphans' pension scheme also provides for payment of a *lump sum death benefit*. Where there is no formal widows' and orphans' pension scheme there may be a guarantee arrangement under which in the event of a retired employee's death during the first few years of retirement his pension or a lump sum equivalent continues to be payable to his widow for the rest of, say, a five-year period. Or the employee may adapt his own pension provision with a *widow's pension option*, which usually means exchanging his *single life pension* for a smaller *joint life and last survivor pension* calculated by actuaries to be of equivalent value.

widow's pension option. Step taken by an employee in a *superannuation* or *pension* scheme to provide a pension for his wife after his own death, usually by exchanging his *single life pension* for a smaller *joint life and last survivor pension* calculated by actuaries to be of equivalent value.

Wiener Börse. *Vienna Stock Exchange*.

Wiener Börsekammer. Council of the *Vienna Stock Exchange*.

wife's earnings election. UK *income tax* term for a husband and wife choosing to have their incomes taxed separately.

wildcat strike. *Unconstitutional strike* and/or *unofficial strike* called at short or no notice without going through the *agreed procedure* for settling grievances.

winding up. Process, either voluntary or compulsory, leading up to the *liquidation* of a company.

Winkelbörsen. Corner exchanges dealing illegally in *securities* in Austria. See also *Vienna Stock Exchange*.

Winnipeg Stock Exchange (The Stock Exchange). One of six *Canadian stock exchanges*.

withdrawal. 1. Response to frustration in which a person removes himself from the frustrating obstacle and obtains *want satis-*

faction in ways such as daydreaming, sleeping, drug addiction or escape into work.
2. Economist's term for withdrawing *purchasing power* from the *circular flow of income* in an economy, usually in the form of *savings*, taxation or imports. The opposite is an *injection*, usually in the form of government expenditure, exports or industrial *investment*. Government policy will tend to stress withdrawals at a time of *inflation*, but injections when the flow of income is not great enough to sustain *full employment*.

withdrawal of labo(u)r. See *strike*.

withholding tax. Part of an employee's wages or salary withheld by his employer as part or whole payment of *income tax*. See also *pay-as-you-earn (PAYE)*.

without-profits endowment assurance. Or *non-profit endowment assurance*. A policy with a fixed sum assured instead of having a share of the insurance company's profits added to it as in the case of a *with-profits endowment assurance*. A higher premium is payable for the latter type of assurance. See also *endowment assurance policy*.

with-profits endowment assurance. Where the insured person pays a higher premium than for a *non-profit* (or *without-profits*) *endowment assurance*, and in return a share of any profit made by the insurance company during the term of the policy is added to the sum assured. A variation on the with-profit policy applied to an employers' pension scheme is where pensions are guaranteed but any profits are returned to the employer in the form of a rebate of future premiums. See also *endowment assurance policy*.

WMCW. *World Movement of Christian Workers.*

Wonderlic personnel test. *General learning ability test* that is particularly widely used by industry and business in the USA. Developed in the 1960s, it is derived partly from the *Otis self-administering test of mental ability*. See also *psychological testing* and *personnel selection*.

Wool Auctions. Specialist *commodity exchange*. Auctions are held at the *London Fruit and Wool Exchange*, while wool *futures* are dealt in at the London Commodity Exchange.

Wool, Jute and Flax Industry Training Board. Established in the UK in June 1964 under the *Industrial Training Act 1964*.

woolly backs. Employees who have a complacent and non-militant approach in industrial relations. They have been given the name by other more militant employees who see the woolly backs as behaving like sheep in their relations with employers. The expression is used particularly among miners in the UK coal mining industry.

word processor. Keyboard machine with *visual display unit* capable of rapid production and printing of text, of producing individualized variations on text stored on *floppy discs*, and of information storage, sorting and retrieval.

work cycle. Sequence of *elements* involved in a *job*.

worker participation (in management). See *workers' participation*.

workers' control. School of thought — and sometimes action — rooted partly in the *workers' participation* arguments but also in opposition to the capitalist system of industrial ownership and control. Movements for workers' control can be traced back at least to Robert Owen's attempts at setting up cooperative communes in the UK and the USA in the first half of the nineteenth century and to the *syndicalist movement* of the early twentieth century that sought to secure ownership of industry by the workers in Europe and the USA. In general, *nationalization* has not satisfied demands for workers' control. Modern champions include the *Institute for Workers' Control* in the UK. Forms of workers' control that have been implemented in some places include coownership and *cooperatives*, the latter being a form of company with special recognition in some European countries. See also *industrial democracy* and *guild socialism*.

workers' directors. Workers' representatives on the *board of directors* of a company or organization. They are sometimes regarded as one of the ultimates of *industrial democracy* and *workers' participation*, though experience of appointing workers to policy-making boards has not always had the effect of creating either true representation or true participation, where, as in early experience of *nationalization* in the UK, they have neither represented workers' views nor provided feedback to the workers. Workers' directors have often played a positive and participatory role in forms of *co-ownership* and the *co-operative* movement in general has advocated them. The move towards workers' directors has also been encouraged by the *co-determination laws* of West Germany and the extension of their two-tier board system (an upper *supervisory board*, including workers' representatives, and a lower *management board*) to other member states of the *European Economic Community*.

workers' participation. General term for a wide spectrum of activities intended to increase the influence employees have in management decision making, particularly in matters that have traditionally been part of *management prerogative*. The strongest pressure in the growing movement towards greater workers' participation has come from the desire and demands of employees themselves, often through the *trade unions*, but such a pressure has also come from some employers who have seen this as important in improving employee motivation (see also *human relations school* of social scientists and managements) or, in rare cases, have seen it as morally right that employees should have such an influence. Government legislation in some countries has also encouraged, or even enforced, increased workers' participation.

Aspects or facets of the growth in practice (practise) of worker's participation have included recognition of trade unions, agreement on *restrictive practices (practises)* or *protective practices (practises)*, collective bargaining, joint consultation, increased *plant bargaining* or *workplace bargaining*, suggestion schemes, *share of production plans*, the development of *works councils*, and the emergence of coownership, *cooperatives* and *profit-sharing schemes*. Modern management techniques, to be effective, often depend on employee cooperation (eg *work study* can only be effective if the workers agree to be studied), and workers' participation is complementary to the *participative management* styles often sought by modern management (see, for example, *managerial grid* and *Theory Y*). The modern quest for *job satisfaction* and *job enrichment* also tends to strengthen workers' participation, at least where the search is genuine, and allied to this has been the setting up in some factories of *autonomous work groups* responsible for organizing their own work and working environment. The latter type of participation directly geared to method of work is known as *task-based participation*. One form of this is *work structuring* developed in Holland by the Philips organization to suit job content to the capacities and ambitions of the individual employee.

Another distinctive form of workers' participation has been the form of works council developed in the UK by the Glacier Metal Company, where the works council representing all types of employee is the supreme legislative body within whose sanction management operates and manages. The ultimate in workers' participation is probably *workers' control*, a concept rooted not only in a quest for participation but in opposition to the capitalist system of ownership and control. See also *industrial democracy* and *guild socialism*.

work factor. Proprietary system of synthetic standard times for standard human movements sometimes used in *motion study*. Other such systems include *predetermined motion time systems (PMTS)* and *methods time measurement (MTM)*.

work group. Employees engaged on similar or related work and tending to be linked by social as well as working ties. The term is used particularly if the employees are on the same *payment-by-results* scheme (whether this is a group or an individual incentive scheme).

work group output norm. Where a *work group* informally holds down production levels as under *quota restriction, productivity restriction, protective output norm,* or a *fiddle*.

working area. See *workplace layout*.

working assets. Stocks of all kinds (raw materials, work in progress and finished goods), cash in hand and amounts due from debtors.

working capital. Or *circulating capital*. That part of a company's capital which is circulating or in use rather than tied up in fixed *assets* etc. A general yardstick for identifying working capital is to subtract current *liabilities* from current assets (and hope the answer is not a minus figure). The relationship of current assets to current liabilities is sometimes known as the *current ratio*.

working capital cycle. Process by which cash is continually being expended as expenditure on raw materials, operating, selling and administrative costs and, hopefully, is continually being received from debtors as *revenue*. See also *cash flow* and *funds statement*.

working capital ratio. As *current ratio*.

working days lost. Units commonly used in measuring the size of a *strike* or strikes, the number of people on strike being multiplied by the number of days the strike lasts. However, it is sometimes objected that 'working days lost' is a misleading term because it implies that time spent in striking can never be made up afterwards (sometimes at least part of it can be, in certain industrial situations) while also ignoring the fact that true working days lost may extend to industrial establishments where there is no strike but where working time is lost through the non-arrival of components as a result of a strike elsewhere. For these reasons, the term *'striker-days'* is often preferred to 'working days lost'. International comparisons of working days lost are difficult and sometimes misleading. For example, in certain countries where strikes can be illegal there is often a tendency to ignore officially that a strike has taken place in order to avoid the time, trouble and disturbance of legal action. Different countries also use different formulae in compiling their statistics, one of the conventions in the UK, for example, being that the *Department of Employment* statistics do not include strikes involving less than 100 workers or lasting less than one day unless the time lost totals at least 100 working days.

working day/week. Basic daily or weekly hours of work beyond which overtime rates of wages normally become payable.

Working Together Campaign. UK independent body composed of industrialists and academics. Objects of the campaign are to improve communications in industry and to 'create a sense of awareness by management and workers of their mutual interests'.

working-to-rule. As *work-to-rule.*

working week, guaranteed. See *guaranteed working week.*

work in process. As *work in progress.*

work in progress. Products or materials and components passing through the production process but not yet completed or finally inspected as finished products.

work measurement. Application of techniques such as *time study* and *work sampling* to establish the time for a qualified worker to carry out a specified job at a defined level of performance. Follows *method study* in the application of *work study.* See also *rate fixing,* particularly in the engineering industry, and *rating scale.*

workmen's compensation. US system of compensation for injuries received at work paid for by employer insurance contributions and administered by state commissions.

workplace bargaining. *Collective bargaining* or *plant bargaining* over local rates of pay and conditions of work in part of a plant or factory, conducted between *shop stewards* and local management, sometimes with disregard to both *trade unions* and employers' organizations, and gaining increasing power vis-a-vis *industry-wide agreements,* sometimes through *bargaining creep.*

workplace layout. Space, facilities and conditions provided for a worker in the performance of a specified job. See *maximum working area* and *normal working area.*

work sample test. *Presonnel selection* etc test designed to assess a person's ability to learn a particular skill or job of work, the test taking the form of a short instructional lesson in an aspect of the work followed by a test. A work sample is often the form used for a *trainability test.* See also *psychological testing.*

work sampling. Technique of *work study* and *work measurement* in which a series of measurements of the time/output relationship or of observations of the work activity are made at random intervals of time. At its most general the technique can be a broad guide to manning requirements. At its most particular, work sampling can produce statistically correct *standard times.* See also *high frequency work sampling* and *multiminute measurement.*

Works Conference. Preceded *Local Conference* and *Central Conference* in the UK engineering procedure.

works councils. Bodies which are among the instruments of *joint consultation* between management and workers. Works councils usually include representatives from all levels in the company and are often chaired jointly or in turn by a member of management and a workers' representative. At worst, a works council may be little more than a talking shop or a safety valve for worker discontent, but at best it may have a positive influence on management decision making. Some UK firms have had works councils for many years on a voluntary and widely varying basis. Other countries, notably in the *European Economic Community*, have a legal requirement for works councils with specific rights and responsibilities. For example, Belgian firms with more than 150 employees have a *conseil d'entreprise;* French firms with more than 50 employees have a *comité d'entreprise;* German firms have a *Betriebsrat* under the *co-determination law;* Italian firms with more than 40 employees have a *commissione interna;* and Netherlands firms with more than 100 employees have an *ondernemingsrad.*

worksharing. Methods of sharing the available work between a greater number of workers through such policies as reduced working hours, elimination of *overtime*, adoption of more labo(u)r-intensive working practices (practises), etc.

workshop analysis and scheduling programming (WASP). System of comprehensive, computer-aided *production control.* WASP is particularly suitable for the engineering jobbing shop making one-off items or small batches, but it can also be applied in any other manufacturing industry having the type of job which requires the use of a number of facilities operating on components in a varying sequence together with an assembly function.

workshop bargaining. As *workplace bargaining.*

work simplification. Part of *work study* and *O & M* approach. Concerned with simple techniques of analyzing any aspects of work or systems with the object of cutting out all unnecessary effort. May involve eliminating, combining, rearranging or simplifying work.

works pension scheme. Flat-rate pension scheme used particularly for hourly paid manual workers. Such a scheme is usually non-contributory but employees are sometimes called upon to make a small weekly contribution. The most usual type of work pension scheme provides for a flat-rate pension related to length of service. Another version of the scheme gives a very small flat-rate pension irrespective of length of service. A works pension scheme usually provides only a subsistence level pension, though the term is sometimes used of more generous schemes that are really *average salary pension schemes.*

works staff. Office, supervisory or other *white collar* workers whose occupations are closely involved with the manufacturing or production processes in a factory. Works staff sometimes have *staff status.* Often they hold a middle ground in terms of status between *blue collar* manual workers and office staff in general, and as such tend to be grouped among the so-called *grey (gray) area occupations.*

work structuring. Concept developed in Holland by the Philips company for organizing work and working conditions in a way that encourages *workers' participation* within working groups and stimulates *job enrichment* by suiting job content as far as possible to the capacities and ambitions of the individual employee.

work study. Embraces techniques such as *method study* and *work measurement* to examine all aspects of a particular area of work to make it more efficient and economic. See also *rate fixing*, particularly in the engineering industry.

work study officer. Engineer or executive responsible for applying *work study* techniques, both *method study* and *work measurement.*

work-to-rule. Form of *industrial action* where workers do not withdraw their labo(u)r or go on *strike* but, instead, remain at work to slow operations down by a pedantic adherence to the rules of the workplace. This process may constitute a *go-slow.* The wider a worker's area of *discretion* or sanction, the greater can be his disruptive influence during a work-to-rule. This latter factor accounts for the apparent anomaly that working to rule can slow a job down. See also *go-slow, sit-in* and *overtime ban.*

World Bank. See *International Bank for Reconstruction and Development.*

World Confederation of Labo(u)r (WCL). Founded in 1920 as the International Foundation of Christian Trade Unions (IFCTU), changing to its present name in 1968. It has member *trade unions* in some 80 countries. Based in Belgium.

World Federation of Scientific Workers. Set up in 1946 to promote the interests of science and scientists. The Federation has members in some 30 countries. Based in UK.

World Federation of Trade Unions (WFTU). Established in 1945 by *trade union* organizations from more than 50 countries. The *American Federation of Labor* cold-shouldered the WFTU on the grounds that the trade unions involved from Communist countries were not democratic and independent. In 1949, the *Trades Union Congress* (UK), the *Congress of Industrial Organizations* (USA) and the national bodies of certain other states withdrew from WFTU to form the *International Confederation of Free Trade Unions (ICFTU)*. Based in Czechoslovakia.

World Health Organization (WHO). Established in April 1948 as a special agency of the United Nations Organization, WHO has some 25 member states. It has a Geneva-based Director-General, Secretariat and Executive Board, and is responsible to the World Health Assembly. It advises countries on public health administration, operates public health teams to combat and prevent disease, provides health training, and produces and publishes standards and statistics.

World Meteorological Organization (WMO). *United Nations* agency charged with promoting international cooperation on the provision of compatible meteorological services. Based in Switzerland.

World Movement of Christian Workers (WMCW). Set up in 1961, the movement has affiliates in more than 30 countries. Based in Belgium.

World Time. See *Weltzeit*.

worry factor. *Insurance* world's term for the stress or worry created by inadequate insurance of a business project.

wrist-finger speed. Type of *psychomotor skill*. A measure of an individual's ability to make rotary and other wrist movements. See also *motion study*.

write-down. Reduction of the value of an asset in a company's accounts by deducting depreciation. Partial *write-off*.

write-off. 1. To reduce periodically the value of an *asset*. **2.** To *write down* bad debts.

write up. 1. To overstate the value of *assets* in accounts. See also *overcapitalize*. **2.** To write a report or descriptive piece, possibly for publication.

writing-down allowance. Sum that may be deducted from taxable trading profits for *depreciation*.

written down value. Value of an *asset* after *depreciation* has been taken into account. Written down value is virtually synonymous with *net book amount*.

wrongful dismissal. As *unfair dismissal*.

XYZ

X-axis. On a graph, the horizontal axis. See also *Y-axis*.

Yaoundé Convention. Agreement made first in 1964 then again in July 1969, and subsequently updated, between the member-states of the *Common Market* and ten African states to provide collective aid for certain developing countries, and to set up the *European Development Fund* for the purpose. The developing countries concerned also have reciprocal trade arrangements with the Common Market. A new European Development Fund is in prospect. Developing countries in the British Commonwealth are expected to benefit from the Yaoundé Conventions which extend the *Treaty of Rome* provisions for *association of overseas countries and territories*. Indeed, three Commonwealth countries, Kenya, Tanzania and Uganda made the *Arusha Agreement* with the Common Market in advance of British entry.

Y-axis. On a graph, the vertical axis. See also *X-axis*.

year's purchase. Value of a business, land or property where the price is related to the anticipated future average annual profits or income from rent expressed in years. For example, if purchase price of a business is £50,000 and average annual profits are estimated at £10,000, then the price is five times the 'year's purchase'.

'yellow-dog' contract. Term originating in the USA for a contract in which an employee gives his employer an undertaking not to join a *trade union*. Yellow-dog contracts are illegal in both the USA and the UK and their banning has been advocated by the *International Labo(u)r Organization*.

yellow journalism. Sensationalized and exaggerated journalism.

yen. Basic unit of Japanese currency.

yield. 1. Return or profit earned on an investment in particular *stocks* or *shares*, being expressed as a percentage of the money invested or the current market value of the stocks or shares. See also *dividend yield, earnings yield, price earnings ratio*. **2.** Amount produced or extracted from raw materials after processing.

yield rate. As *internal rate of return*.

yield variance. In *standard costing*, and particularly in process industries, the calculation of the actual amounts produced compared with norms or standards and expressing this variance as a percentage.

York, Central Conference at. See *Central Conference*, part of the *engineering procedure*.

York Memorandum. See *engineering procedure*.

York Stock Exchange. *Provincial Brokers Stock Exchange*. See also *Stock Exchange*. For address see Appendix: World Stock Exchanges.

Yugoslav central bank. *Narodna Banka Jugoslavije*.

Yugoslav chamber of commerce. Federal Chamber of Economy.

Yugoslav trade unions. See *Vece Saveza sindikata Jugoslavije*, the Council of the Confederation of Trade Unions of Yugoslavia.

Zafo classification. Complex three-part classification and coding system developed in Germany. It is used to classify shape, tolerances, surface finish, material, size of components. See also *classification and coding system*.

zatacode. Data processing code for indexing individual records by descriptors.

ZBR. *Zero Base Review.*

Z chart. Graph, as in the illustration,

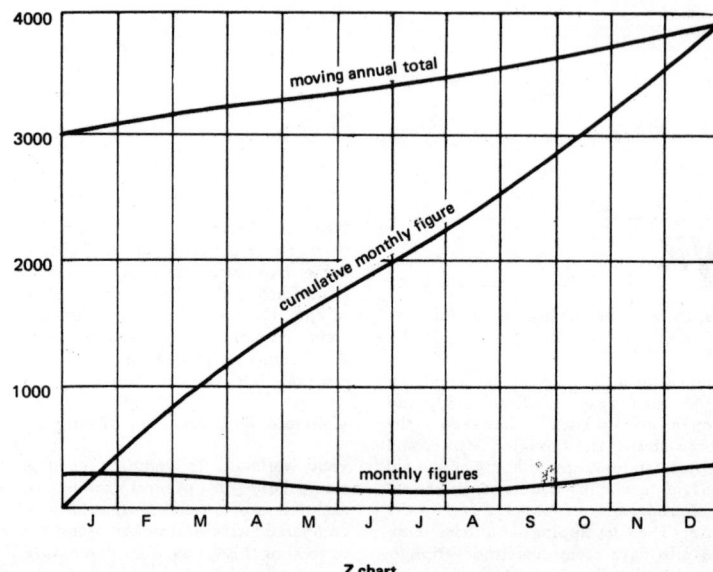

Z chart showing three aspects of production or sales volume — totals for the period (weekly or monthly), cumulative totals and moving annual total.

Zero Base Review (ZBR). Management technique or approach developed in public administration in the USA. It is a planning and budgeting process which deliberately refuses to accept that past and present practice (practise) is necessarily a good thing and assumes that no resources will be allocated to a project or program(me) in future unless it can be demonstrated that there is not a more effective alternative use for these resources. Zero Base Review has points of similarity with *program(me) analysis and review (PAR)*.

zero defects. System of rewarding workers who make no mistakes and waste no materials over a given and specified period of time.

zero-sum game. *Game* in which players can only win at the expense of other players.

Zimbabwean stock exchanges. There are two stock exchanges in Zimbabwe, situated in Bulawayo and in Salisbury.

Zip Code. Postal code system in the USA designed to speed up delivery of mail in conjunction with automatic sorting procedures. Each delivery area has a five-digit number which is written at the end of the address on an envelope. The first three digits indicate the district and the last two the local zone.

zone curve chart. Graph carrying not single plots but maxima and minima for each reading, these maxima and minima being linked with vertical lines to give a broad curve. The resulting shading is known as a zone curve and may be used, for example, to show the spread of earnings, prices, etc. See also *band curve chart*.

zone-time. *Standard time* within a particular *time zone*.

Zulassungsstelle. Listing Committee of a *German Stock Exchange*.

Zürich Stock Exchange. Or *Effektenbörsenverein Zürich*. One of the principal stock exchanges of Switzerland. See *Swiss stock exchanges*.

Appendices

A. Time Zones
B. The World's Currencies

Appendix A

Time Zones

Universal Time or Greenwich Mean Time (GMT) (or, in Germany, Weltzeit or World Time) is based on the mean solar time using the longitude of Greenwich, south of London in England, as its reference meridian. With Greenwich as 0° longitude, each 15° zone east and west of it represents one hour of time on a strict interpretation of the division of the world into 24 time zones as the world rotates about its axis at a rate of one revolution per day. To the west of Greenwich, time is behind GMT by one hour per 15°, while to the east time is ahead of GMT by one hour per 15°. Local time measured strictly on this basis is known as 'apparent time'.

180° from Greenwich in both directions is the International Date Line where places on different sides of it, yet only a few miles apart, are a whole day apart. To cross the International Date Line from east to west means jumping forward 24 hours while crossing it in the other direction has the opposite effect. In practice, travellers miss out a day when crossing from east to west, but give two consecutive days the same name when crossing from west to east.

The International Date Line would obviously be very confusing for local inhabitants but such confusion is relatively limited because the Line runs down the Pacific Ocean touching land only in north-east Siberia and at various islands.

Though there is general agreement on the International Date Line, interpretation of local time varies from 'apparent time' in some countries, largely for political and economic reasons. An outline of the way in which the time zones of the world operate in practice is illustrated here. Some countries refine the process further than most by using half-hour time intervals, based on 7' 30° of longitude, rather than one-hour intervals. At the other extreme, China stretches into four separate time zones in theory but uses only a single time in practice, based on the 120th meridian at her eastern seaboard.

Within the USA, too, the time zones have been adapted in practice, largely to fit in with the needs of the different States, in a manner drawn up and administered by the Department of Transportation under the Uniform Time Act 1966. It was the advent of transcontinental railroad travel in the USA in the nineteenth century that brought to a head the need for governmental recognition of time zones.

The practical effect of the Uniform Time Act in the USA on Pacific Standard Time, Mountain Standard Time, Central Standard Time and Eastern Standard Time is also illustrated here. In all, the USA has eight official time zones from Atlantic Time (60°W) for Puerto Rico and the Virgin Islands to Bering Time (165°W) for western Alaska and the Aleutian Islands.

Appendix A

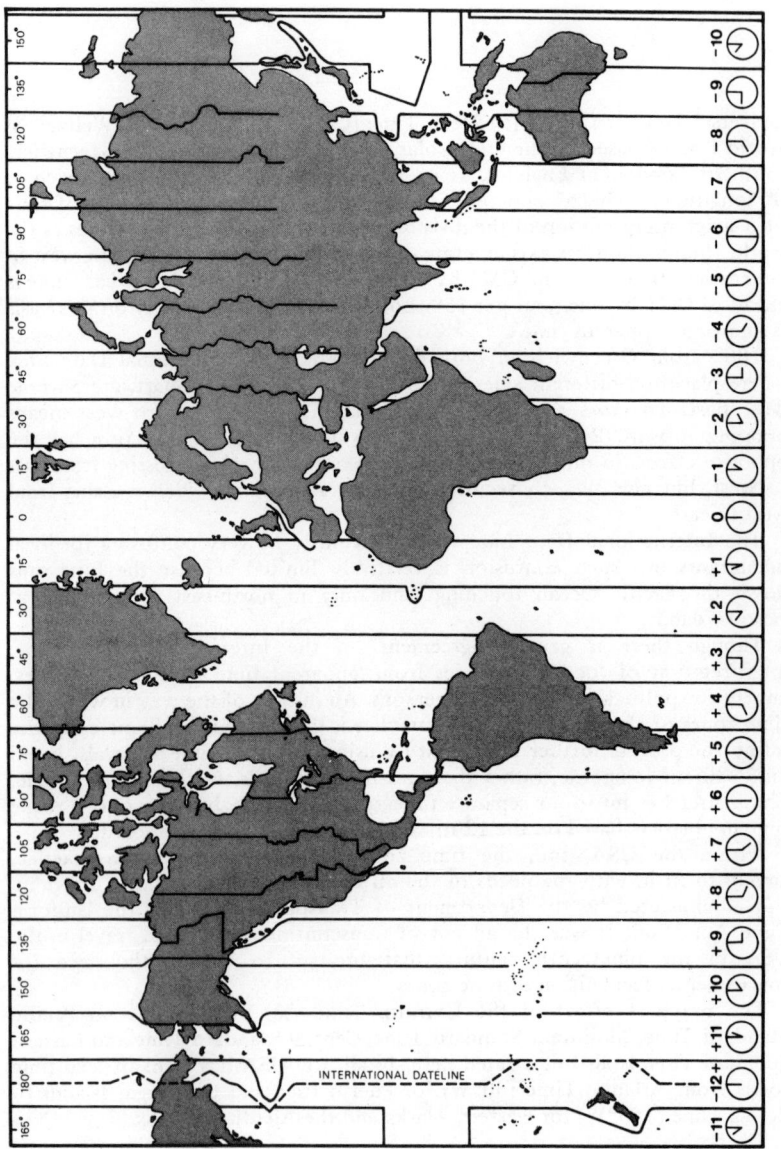

The World's Time Zones

Appendix A

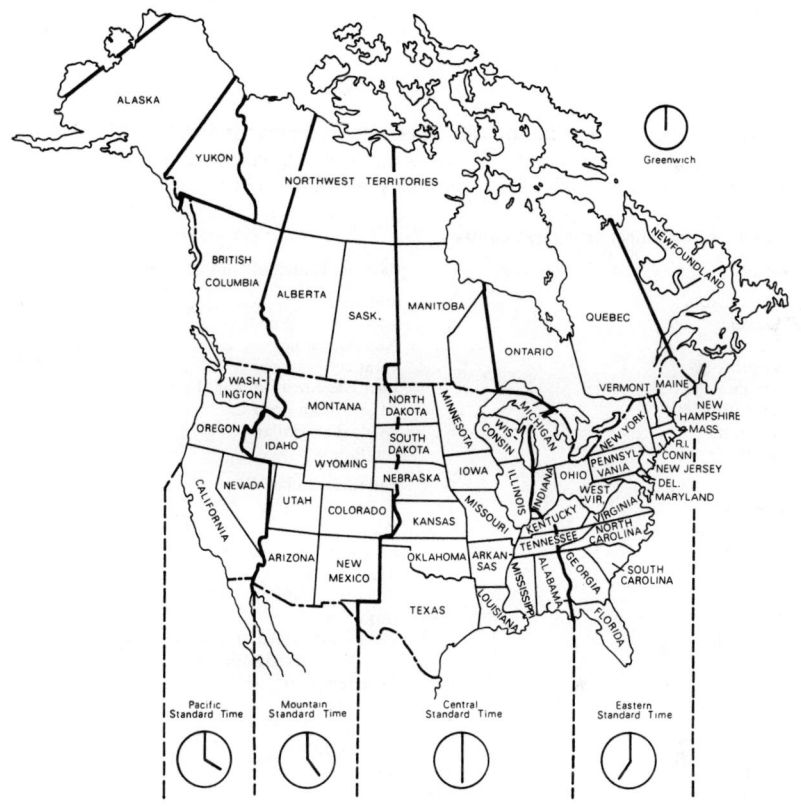

North American Time Zones

Appendix B

The World's Currencies

Against each country in the alphabetical list below is indicated its basic or principal unit of currency. There is then an alphabetical list of currencies with a note against each of the countries where it is in use.

Part 1. Alphabetical listing by country

Country	Basic or Principal Unit of Currency
Afghanistan	afghani
Albania	lekë
Algeria	Algerian dinar
Angola	kwanze
Antigua	East Caribbean dollar (EC$)
Argentina	Argentinian peso
Australia	Australian dollar
Austria	schilling
Bahamas, The	Bahamas dollar (B$)
Bahrain	Bahrain dinar
Bangladesh	taka
Barbados	East Caribbean dollar (EC$)
Belgium	Belgian franc
Belize	Belizean dollar
Benin	franc
Bermuda	Bermudan dollar (Canadian, UK and US currencies also in use)
Bolivia	Bolivian peso
Botswana	pula
Brazil	cruzeiro
Brunei	Brunei dollar
Bulgaria	lev
Burma	kyat
Burundi	Burundi franc
Cameroon	Franc de la Communauté Financière Africaine (CFA) (or franc CFA)
Canada	Canadian dollar
Central African Republic	Franc de la Communauté Financière Africaine (CFA) (or franc CFA)
Cape Verde Islands	escudo
Cayman Islands	dollar
Central American Common Market	Central American peso (CA$)
Chad	Franc de la Communauté Financière Africaine (CFA) (or franc CFA)
Chile	new peso
China, People's Republic of	yuan or renminbi
Colombia	Colombian peso
Congo (Brazzaville)	Franc de la Communauté Financière Africaine (CFA) (or franc CFA)
Costa Rica	Costa Rican colon
Cuba	Cuban peso
Cyprus	Cyprus pound
Czechoslovakia	koruna

Appendix B

Dahomey	Franc de la Communauté Financière Africaine (CFA) (or franc CFA)
Denmark	Danish krone
Dominica	East Caribbean dollar (EC$)
Dominican Republic	Dominican Republic peso (DR$)
East Caribbean Territory	East Caribbean Dollar (EC$)
Ecuador	sucre
Egypt	Egyptian pound (£E)
El Salvador	El Salvador colon
Equatorial Guinea	ekuele
Ethiopia	Ethiopian dollar
Falkland Islands	pound
Faroe Islands	krone
Fiji	Fijian dollar ($F)
Finland	markka or Finnmark
Formosa	new Taiwan dollar
France	French franc
French Community	franc CFA
Gabon	Franc de la Communauté Financière Africaine (CFA) (or franc CFA)
Gambia	dalasi
German Democratic Republic	Ostmark or DDR-Mark
Germany, Federal Republic	Deutsche Mark (DM)
Ghana	cedi
Gibraltar	Gibraltar pound
Greece	drachma
Grenada	East Caribbean dollar (EC$)
Guadeloupe	French franc
Guatemala	quetzal
Guinea	Guinean franc
Guinea-Bissau	escudo
Guinea, Equatorial	ekuele
Guyana	Guyanese dollar ($G)
Haiti	gourde
Honduras	lempira (L)
Hong Kong	Hong Kong dollar (HK$)
Hungary	forint
Iceland	Icelandic krona
India	Indian rupee
Indonesia	rupiah (Rp)
Iran	Iranian rial
Iraq	Iraqi dinar
Ireland	Irish pound
Israel	Israeli pound (I£)
Italy	Italian lira
Ivory Coast	Franc de la Communauté Financière Africaine (CFA) (or franc CFA)
Jamaica	Jamaican dollar (J$)
Japan	yen
Jordan	Jordanian dinar (JD)
Kenya	Kenya shilling (Ks)
Korea, Democratic People's Republic of (North Korea)	won
Korea, Republic of (South Korea)	won
Kuwait	Kuwait dinar (KD)
Laos	kip
Lebanon	Lebanese pound (£L)
Lesotho	South African rand
Liberia	Liberian dollar (also US dollar)

Appendix B

Libya	Libyan dinar (LD)
Liechtenstein	franken or Swiss franc
Luxembourg	Luxembourg franc
Macau	pataca
Malagasy Republic	franc Malgache (FMG)
Malawi	kwacha (K)
Malaysia	Malaysian dollar (M$)
Maldive Islands	rupee
Mali	Mali franc
Malta	Maltese pound
Mauritania	ouguiya
Mauritius	Mauritiun rupee
Mexico	Mexican peso
Monaco	French franc
Mongolia	tugrik
Montserrat	East Caribbean dollar (EC$)
Morocco	dirham
Mozambique	conto
Namibia (South West Africa)	South African rand
Nepal	Nepali rupee (NR)
Netherlands	Netherlands gulden or guilder or florin
Netherlands Antilles	Netherlands Antilles florin (NAFI) or guilder
New Zealand	New Zealand dollar ($NZ)
Nicaragua	cordoba
Niger	Franc de la Communauté Financière Africaine (CFA) (or franc CFA)
Nigeria	naira
Norway	Norwegian krone
Oman	Omani ryal
Pakistan	Pakistan rupee
Panama	balboa
Papua New Guinea	kina
Paraguay	guarani
Peru	sol
Philippines	Philippine peso
Pitcairn Islands	East Caribbean dollar (EC$)
Poland	zloty
Portugal	Portuguese escudo
Portuguese Timor	escudo
Puerto Rico	US dollar ($)
Qatar	Qatar ryal
Réunion	franc (CFA)
Romania	leu
Rwanda	Rwanda franc
St Kitts	East Caribbean dollar (EC$)
St Lucia	East Caribbean dollar (EC$)
St Vincent	East Caribbean dollar (EC$)
Samoa (Western)	tala
St Tomé and Principé	escudo
Saudi Arabia	Saudi Arabian riyal
Senegal	Franc de la Communauté Financière Africaine (CFA) (or franc CFA)
Seychelles	rupee
Sierra Leone	leone
Sikkim	Indian rupee
Singapore	Singapore dollar (S$)
Solomon Islands	Solomon Islands dollar
Somalia	Somali shilling

Appendix B

South Africa, Republic of	rand (R)
South West Africa (Namibia)	South African rand
Spain	Spanish peseta
Sri Lanka	Sri Lanka rupee
Sudan	Sudanese pound
Surinam	Surinam guilder (also Netherlands currency)
Swaziland	lilangeni
Sweden	Swedish krona
Switzerland	franken or Swiss franc
Syria	Syrian pound (£S)
Taiwan	New Taiwan dollar
Tanzania	Tanzanian shilling
Thailand	baht
Togo	Franc de la Communauté Financière Africaine (CFA) (or franc CFA)
Tonga	paanga ($T)
Trinidad and Tobago	Trinidad and Tobago dollar
Tunisia	Tunisian dinar
Turkey	Turkish lira (TL)
Uganda	Ugandan shilling
United Arab Emirates	dirham
United Kingdom (UK)	pound sterling (£)
United States of America (USA)	US dollar ($)
Upper Volta	Franc de la Communauté Financière Africaine (CFA) (or franc CFA)
Uruguay	Uruguayan new peso
USSR	rouble
Venezuela	bolivar
Vietnam	dong
Western Samoa	tala (WS$)
West Indies Associated States	East Caribbean dollar (EC$)
Yemen Arab Republic	Yemeni riyal
Yemen, People's Democratic Republic of	Southern Yemen dinar
Yugoslavia	Yugoslav dinar
Zaire	zaire
Zambia	kwacha (K)
Zimbabwe	dollar

Part 2. Alphabetical listing by unit of currency

Basic Unit of Currency	Where Used
afghani	Afghanistan
baht	Thailand
balboa	Panama
bolivar	Venezuela
cedi	Ghana
colon, Costa Rican	Costa Rica
colon, El Salvador	El Salvador
conto	Mozambique
cordoba	Nicaragua
cruzeiro	Brazil
dalasi	Gambia
DDR-Mark (or Ostmark)	German Democratic Republic
Deutsche Mark (DM)	Germany, Federal Republic
dinar, Algerian	Algeria
dinar, Bahrain	Bahrain

Appendix B

dinar, Iraqi	Iraq
dinar, Jordanian (JD)	Jordan
dinar, Kuwait (KD)	Kuwait
dinar, Libyan (LD)	Libya
dinar, Southern Yemen	People's Democratic Republic of Yemen
dinar, Tunisian	Tunisia
dinar, Yugoslav	Yugoslavia
dirham	Morocco, United Arab Emirates
dollar, Australian	Australia
dollar, Bahamas (B$)	The Bahamas
dollar, Belizean	Belize
dollar, Bermudan	Bermuda
dollar, Brunei	Brunei
dollar, Canadian	Canada
dollar, East Caribbean (EC$)	Barbados, Montserrat, Pitcairn Islands, West Indies Associated States (Antigua, Dominica, Grenada, St Kitts, etc)
dollar, Ethiopian	Ethiopia
dollar, Fijian ($F)	Fiji
dollar, Guyanese ($G)	Guyana
dollar, Hong Kong (HK$)	Hong Kong
dollar, Jamaican (J$)	Jamaica
dollar, Liberian	Liberia
dollar, Malaysian (M$)	Malaysia
dollar, New Taiwan	Taiwan/Formosa
dollar, New Zealand ($NZ)	New Zealand
dollar, Solomon Islands	Solomon Islands
dollar, Trinidad and Tobago	Trinidad and Tobago
dollar, US	United States of America (USA), Puerto Rico
dollar, Zimbabwean	Zimbabwe
dong	Vietnam
drachma	Greece
ekuele	Equatorial Guinea
escudo, Portuguese	Portugal, Guinea-Bissau, Portuguese Timor
escudo	St Tomé and Principé
Finnmark (or markka)	Finland
florin (or Netherlands gulden or guilder)	Netherlands
florin or guilder, Netherlands Antilles	Netherlands Antilles
forint	Hungary
franc, Belgian	Belgium
franc, Benin	Benin
franc Burundi	Burundi
Franc de la Communauté Financière Africaine (CFA) or franc CFA	Cameroon, Central African Republic, Chad, Congo (Brazzaville), Dahomey, Gabon, Ivory Coast, Niger, Senegal, Togo, Upper Volta
franc, French	France, French Guinea, Guadeloupe, Martinique, Monaco, Réunion
franc, Guinean	Guinea
franc, Luxembourg	Luxembourg
franc, Malgache (FMG)	Malagasy Republic
franc, Mali	Mali
franc, Rwanda	Rwanda
franc, Swiss or franken	Switzerland, Liechtenstein
gourde	Haiti
guarani	Paraguay
guilder or Netherlands gulden or florin	Netherlands
guilder, Surinam	Surinam
gulden, Netherlands	Netherlands

Appendix B

kina	Papua New Guinea
kip	Laos
koruna	Czechoslovakia
krona, Icelandic	Iceland
krona, Swedish	Sweden
krone, Danish	Denmark
krone, Faroe Islands	Faroe Islands
krone, Norwegian	Norway
kwacha (K), Malawian	Malawi
kwacha (K), Zambian	Zambia
kwanze	Angola
kyat	Burma
lekë	Albania
lempira (L)	Honduras
leone	Sierra Leone
leu	Romania
lev	Bulgaria
lilangeni	Swaziland
lira, Italian	Italy
lira, Turkish (TL)	Turkey
markka or Finnmark	Finland
naira	Nigeria
Ostmark or DDR-Mark	German Democratic Republic
ouguiya	Mauritania
paanga ($T)	Tonga
pataca	Macau
peseta	Spain
peso, Argentinian	Argentina
peso, Bolivian	Bolivia
peso, Central American (CA$)	Central American Common Market
peso, Chilean	Chile
peso, Colombian	Colombia
peso, Cuban	Cuba
peso, Dominican Republic (DR$)	Dominican Republic
peso, Mexican	Mexico
peso, Philippine	The Philippines
peso, Uruguayan	Uruguay
pound, Cyprus	Cyprus
pound, Egyptian (£E)	Egypt
pound, Falkland Islands	Falkland Islands
pound, Gibraltar	Gibraltar
pound, Irish	Ireland
pound, Israeli (I£)	Israel
pound, Lebanese (£L)	Lebanon
pound, Maltese	Malta
pound sterling (£)	United Kingdom (UK)
pound, Sudanese	Sudan
pound, Syrian (£S)	Syria
quetzal	Guatemala
rand	Republic of South Africa, Lesotho, South West Africa (Namibia)
renminbi	China
rial, Iranian	Iran
riyal, Saudi Arabian	Saudi Arabia
riyal, Yemeni	Yemeni Arab Republic
rouble	USSR
rupee, Indian	India
rupee, Maldive Islands	Maldive Islands
rupee, Mauritiun	Mauritius

Appendix B

rupee, Nepali (NR)	Nepal
rupee, Pakistan	Pakistan
rupee, Seychelles	Seychelles
rupee, Sri Lanka	Sri Lanka
rupiah (Rp)	Indonesia
ryal Omani	Oman
ryal, Qatar	Qatar
schilling	Austria
schilling, Kenya (Ks)	Kenya
shilling, Somali	Somalia
shilling, Tanzanian	Tanzania
shilling, Uganda	Uganda
sol	Peru
sucre	Ecuador
taka	Bangladesh
tala (WS$)	Western Samoa
tugrik	Mongolia
won	Democratic People's Republic of Korea, Republic of Korea
yen	Japan
yuan	China
zaire	Zaire
zloty	Poland